PUBLICATIONS OF THE NEW CHAUCER SOCIETY

THE NEW CHAUCER SOCIETY

Studies in the Age of Chaucer, the yearbook of The New Chaucer Society, is published annually. Each issue contains substantial articles on all aspects of Chaucer and his age, book reviews, and an annotated Chaucer bibliography. Manuscripts should follow the *Chicago Manual of Style*, 16th edition. Unsolicited reviews are not accepted. All correspondence regarding manuscript submissions should be directed to the Editors, Michelle Karnes and Sebastian Sobecki, studiesintheageofchaucer@gmail.com. Subscriptions to The New Chaucer Society and information about the Society's activities should be directed to Tom Goodmann, chaucer@miami.edu. Back issues of the journal may be ordered from University of Notre Dame Press, c/o Longleaf Services, Inc., 116 S. Boundary St., Chapel Hill, N.C. 27514-3808; email: orders@longleafservices.org; phone: 800-848-6224; fax: 800-272-6817; from outside the United States, phone: 919-966-7449; fax: 919-962-2704.

Studies in the Age of Chaucer

Studies in the Age of Chaucer

Volume 41
2019

EDITORS

MICHELLE KARNES AND SEBASTIAN SOBECKI

PUBLISHED ANNUALLY BY THE NEW CHAUCER SOCIETY
UNIVERSITY OF MIAMI IN CORAL GABLES, FLORIDA

Copyright © 2019 by The New Chaucer Society, University of Miami. First edition. Published by University of Notre Dame Press for The New Chaucer Society.

ISBN-10 0-933784-43-0
ISBN-13 978-0-933784-43-7
ISSN 0190-2407

CONTENTS

CONTENTS

REVIEWS

CONTENTS

Studies in the Age of Chaucer

THE PRESIDENTIAL ADDRESS
The New Chaucer Society
Twenty-First International Congress
July 10–15, 2018
Victoria University, Toronto, Canada

The Presidential Address

The Dream of Language: Chaucer "en son Latin"

Ardis Butterfield
Yale University

Abstract

Taking its cue from the efforts to revive the Ojibwe language in the aftermath of residential schools' closure in Canada, this lecture draws on Giorgio Agamben's essay "The Dream of Language" to make a fresh exploration of the medieval history of language change. Reviewing Agamben's argument that the bilingual Latin–Italian *Hypnerotomachia Polyphili* (1499) marks the moment when Latin starts being viewed as a dead language, it traces the complex earlier perspectives on Latin and vernacular through a reverse chronology from Villon to Chaucer via Guillaume de Machaut and Dante's writings on language. The case is made that it is misleading to view the relation between Latin and vernacular in the Middle Ages as clear-cut and oppositional. Once we understand medieval writers to be working in a plurilingual and hence only semigrammatical environment it becomes possible to see how notions of vernacularity and Latin were much more subtly entangled than it is usually assumed. Medieval writers, even in ostensibly monolingual texts, do not deal with a hard-edged distinction between Latin and vernacular, but instead work creatively with the often painful recognition that the power relations between languages involve loss and extinction. The figure of the dream, and also of a female dream-body, central to the playful multilingualism of the love between Polia and Polifilo in the *Hypnerotomachia*, is shown to be an earlier preoccupation of Chaucer through his creation of Criseyde. Drawing on Machaut's use of dreams to figure linguistic boundaries, Chaucer presents Criseyde as a prototype of Polia, the name and love of language, a figure of linguistic loss and death, yet also of hope and aspiration.

This lecture is dedicated to my mother, Ruth Butterfield-Felix, September 16, 1928–October 3, 2018. For many kinds of help, during a difficult period, my warm thanks to Nancy Regalado, Emma Cayley, Chris Cannon, Julia King, Ruth Evans, Alastair Minnis, Adrian Butterfield, Gaby Felix, Penelope Gardner-Chloros, and Andrew Kraebel.

Studies in the Age of Chaucer 41 (2019): 3–29

Keywords

Latin; vernacular; *Troilus and Criseyde*; Machaut; Dante; multilingualism; Agamben; language death; Villon; dream poetry

I T IS A GREAT HONOR to stand here in Canada, here in Toronto, here at the university, and participate in two experiences that are completely new for the New Chaucer Society: smudging, and the recital of Carter Revard's poetry. It is no exaggeration to say I have been looking forward to this for two years. I want to learn from both and have been thinking for some time about what it means for us as medievalists, and students of Chaucer and his age, to find ourselves here. In part this is always true of our congresses as they begin. We wonder where we are, what the grand themes of the congress are and will turn out to be; we feel the excitement of being on the cusp of so many new ideas, information, and emphases; we feel that rhythm of the biennial meeting where we gather up collectively the topics we are really passionate about thinking about. We ask ourselves, and one another, where are we now? And (to paraphrase Primo Levi and of course our own Carolyn Dinshaw) we then ask when is now?[1]

Let me ask this question of the languages of the peoples whose land we are on. The University of Toronto sits on the traditional land of the Huron-Wendat, the Seneca, and most recently the Mississaugas of the Credit River. The Mississaugas are part of the Anishinaabe people, and their language group is also called Anishinaabe (plural, Anishinaabeg). This language group is known too as Ojibwe, which has many different dialects. I understand that for a very painful period, aboriginal languages were actively and even violently suppressed through the residential schools that operated from the 1880s into the closing decades of the twentieth century. More recently, the tide has turned and (to quote from a documentary broadcast on Canadian TV):

A new generation of Ojibwe scholars and educators are racing against time to save the language. Working with the remaining fluent-speaking Ojibwe elders,

---

[1] Primo Levi, *Se non ora, quando?* [*If Not Now, When?*] (Turin: Einaudi, 1982); Carolyn Dinshaw, *How Soon Is Now? Medieval Texts, Amateur Readers, and the Queerness of Time* (Durham, N.C.: Duke University Press, 2012).

they hope to pass the language on to the next generation. But can this language be saved? Told by Ojibwe elders, scholars, writers, historians and teachers, this tpt original production is filled with hope for the future.[2]

Here, and in many similar situations in other parts of the world, languages are being revived: attempts to reverse their extinction being led by new emphases in education.[3]

I think what strikes me most in my efforts to learn a little about what is for me an unfamiliar culture is the profound pain of change and assimilation. How does one keep respect for the past when conditions make earlier patterns of "unique ways and daily conversation" difficult or even impossible to maintain?[4] Marriages outside a community happen and make a difference. New economic conditions create new kinds of aspiration. The loss of language is a terrible loss, akin to the loss of a species, but it is a poignant and terribly difficult truth that education is often a means toward that loss. Was change negotiated better in previous centuries? Maybe it is also true that change really has happened faster in the past century than we have been able to deal with. It's as if our cultural responses to change, learned and honed over many generations in our many social, linguistic, and historical contexts, are now struggling to move at a different pace. And in that struggle are resisting, collapsing, or just showing confusion. Do we resurrect dead languages? Or do we let them go? Do we recreate nations? Or do we look for alternatives? The European Union (EU), given its commitment to a Europe without borders, is a confusing witness to new nation state creation: it has grown since 1951 from six to twenty-eight members, and of those several are newly formed or re-formed, such the Czech Republic (1993) Slovakia, and Estonia (1991).[5] There are twenty-four official languages for these member countries, and over sixty indigenous regional

---

[2] https://www.tpt.org/first-speakers-restoring-the-ojibwe-language/ (accessed May 29, 2019). The abbreviation tpt stands for Twin Cities PBS.

[3] On this topic in relation to Welsh, see briefly Ardis Butterfield, "Chaucerian Vernaculars," *SAC* 31 (2009), 25–51 (28 and n. 10).

[4] I quote from the mission statement of the Language Department of the Osage Nation website: "Our mission is to revitalize the Osage Language to its purest form, and to teach our people to speak Osage within the realm of our unique ways and in daily conversation"; https://www.osagenation-nsn.gov/who-we-are/language-department (accessed May 29, 2019).

[5] I write this as Britain's government struggles with schismatic chaos in relation to the close referendum result of 2016 on whether Britain should remain a member of the European Union or leave it.

or minority languages (such as Basque, Catalan, Frisian, Saami, Welsh, and Yiddish). It depends on the study, but many languages, even official ones such as Latvian, are felt to be at risk of extinction. It is the younger age group (15–24) that are the most active learners of new languages and also most fluent in English.[6] Fun fact: one of the EU's multilingualism goals is for every European to speak two languages in addition to their mother tongue.[7]

Outside Europe, the picture is in some ways more complexly multilingual, including, but not of course exclusively, areas that were colonized by western cultures such as Singapore, Hong Kong, Indonesia, India, and South America. Here language change is rapid and rife.

With so much evidence of uncontrollable as well as controlled change, what should our response as educators be?[8] Do we work actively for new and much more fluid and multiple senses of linguistic identity, or do we try to protect those who feel threatened and devalued by those new senses? In a nutshell: *Whom* do we seek to protect? And *why*?

The *Hypnerotomachia Polyphili* and Language Death

This lecture takes its starting-point from a strange but compelling work from the fifteenth century: the *Hypnerotomachia Polyphili* by Francesco Colonna. A publishing sensation in its time (though it was exceptionally rare and expensive to produce) it is very hard to describe: at once a text exquisitely produced by the master printed-book craftsman Aldus Manutius, and a set of fantastically conceived architectural engravings, it is an overblown, sensuous, erotic dream-narrative about the lovers Polifili and Polia built on a scaffolding of older texts—mostly Latin and Italian love visions from the great triumvirate Dante, Petrarch, and Boccaccio, and the Latin texts they knew intimately. The work starts, *Commedia*-like, with Polifili lost in a forest. He finds a river, and stops to drink. Here the lovers first catch sight of each other.[9]

---

[6] Directorate-General for Communication, "Special Eurobarometer 386: Europeans and Their Languages" (http://data.europa.eu/euodp/data/dataset/S1049_77_1_EBS386 [accessed May 29, 2019]): a survey conducted in February–March 2012.

[7] https://europa.eu/european-union/topics/multilingualism_en (accessed May 29, 2019).

[8] In asking this question, I gladly acknowledge an earlier version of it in a previous Presidential Address: Mary Carruthers, " 'Micrological Aggregates': Is the New Chaucer Society Speaking in Tongues?," *SAC* 21 (1991): 3–26.

[9] I have consulted the British Library copy of the Aldine 1499 edition, *Hypnerotomachia Poliphili, ubi humana omnia non nisi somnium esse docet, atque obiter plurima scitu sane*

The weirdest feature of the *Hypnerotomachia* is the language, a corus-catingly hyper-rich super-language of Tuscan mixed up with Latin and Greek, with occasional inscriptions of what he calls variously Attic, Ionic, Doric, hieroglyphs, Arabic, and Hebrew. Colonna (the name is part of an acrostic and its author has not been securely identified) creates an invented language in which a vernacular syntax is so heavily studded with Latinized lexis, and a Latinized lexis so thickly moulded into ver-nacular syntactical structures, that it is hard to tell whether either lan-guage remains intact or distinct. As Giorgio Agamben (whose essay title I have borrowed) puts it: "the effect of estrangement that its language produces so disorients the reader that he literally does not know what language he is reading, whether it is Latin, the vernacular, or a third idiom . . . the *lingua poliphylesca*."[10] The author delights in creating neol-ogisms, grafting prefixes and suffixes onto vernacular words that create possible but never-before-known formations of meaning. A carefully timed example occurs just as Polifilo is about to meet Polia for the first time:

Et sopra tutto lalta sperancia che io firmamente teniua secondo le regie & fatale promissione di ritrouare la mia Isotrichechrysa Polia. "Heu me, Polia" so-spirante diceva.[11]

[Above all, I held on firmly to the high hopes confirmed by the royal and fateful promise that I would find my golden-haired Polia. "Alas, Polia!," I sighed to myself.][12]

Here it is the word "Isotrichechrysa" that stands out. As Pozzi explains in his note, it is a hybrid Greek word meaning "hair equal to gold," yet

---

quam digna commemorat (Venice: Aldus Manutius, 1499); and the British Library's copy of the French translation by Jean Martin, *Hypnerotomachie; ou, Discours du songe de Poli-phile, deduisant comme Amour le combat a l'occasion de Polia* . . . [By Francesco Colonna.] *Nouuellement traduict de langage Italien en Francois* (Paris: printed for I. Keruer by L. Cyancus, 1546).

[10] Giorgio Agamben, *The End of the Poem: Essays in Poetics* (Stanford: Stanford University Press, 1999), 44.

[11] Citations from the *Hypnerotomachia Poliphili* are all taken from the Aldine 1499 edition; for the standard modern edition, see Francesco Colonna, *Hypnerotomachia Poli-phili*, ed. Giovanni Pozzi and Lucia A. Ciapponi, 2 vols. (Padua: Antenore, 1980), 1.134.

[12] Francesco Colonna, *Hypnerotomachia Poliphili: The Strife of Love in a Dream*, trans. Joscelyn Godwin (New York: Thames & Hudson, 1999), 141.

three-part compounds are most uncharacteristic of Greek.[13] The linguistic extravagance draws visual attention to her golden hair in a way that is inseparable from its own visual and aural overstatement. Another more intricate example is the Latin phrase *Amor vincit omnia*. Commonplace enough to have been set into the Prioress's gold brooch,[14] in the *Hypnerotomachia* it acts more unusually as a translation of three hieroglyphs. The two lovers have set sail on Cupid's boat, at the mast of which flies a blue silk banner with an elaborate, bejeweled design on which are displayed the three images: "an antique vase, in whose open mouth a flame burned; then the world; and a little branch linking the two together." These, says Colonna:

> . . . Lo interpreto degli
> quali cusi io el
> feci.
> Amor uincit omnia.

["I interpreted" as "Love conquers all."][15]

Vincit has three overlapping meanings that cross between Latin and Italian: conquer, bind, and (only in Italian) a plant that binds. From the image we see this osier plant being used to show the flame of love binding the world. Latin serves here as a way of translating not only a picture language but Latin's own vernacular, in a playful inversion of the expected direction of translation from the learned to the more accessible by moving from image to language.[16]

Agamben's brilliant—though sometimes enigmatic—argument sees the *Hypnerotomachia* as a work that celebrates language death. To understand this Agamben directs us to go back to Dante's *De vulgari eloquentia* and *Convivio* from the cusp of the fourteenth century (c. 1304–7). Dante seeks here to promote his own treasured vernacular, Tuscan.[17] He gives the vernacular extravagant praise: it is a mother tongue, and it is

[13] As Pozzi notes: "isotrichechrysa, coi capelli di oro uguale; formazione de Col[onna] su ἴσος, uguale, θρίξ, capello, χρυσός, oro" (in Colonna, *Hypnerotomachia Poliphili*, ed. Pozzi and Ciapponi, 2.129).

[14] *GP*, I.162.

[15] Colonna, *Hypnerotomachia Poliphili*, trans. Godwin, 284–85 (lit. "I interpreted it as this which I have made").

[16] I take this interesting example from Ian White, "Multiple Words, Multiple Meanings, in the *Hypnerotomachia*," *Word & Image* 31, no. 2 (2005): 74–80.

[17] Although it is important to point out that Dante's view of Italian vernaculars is complex and even contradictory: he pours scorn on Tuscan later in the *De vulgari* (I.xiii).

"noble," more noble than a language one learns through grammar (for which read Latin).

vulgarem locutionem appellamus eam quam infantes assuefiunt ab assistentibus cum primitus distinguere voces incipiunt . . . Est et inde alia locutio secundaria nobis, quam Romani gramaticam vocaverunt. . . . Harum quoque duarum nobilior est vulgaris.

[I call "vernacular language" that which infants acquire from those around them when they first begin to distinguish sounds; . . . There also exists another kind of language, at one remove from us, which the Romans called *gramatica*. . . . Of these two kinds of language, the more noble is the vernacular.][18]

Now, before turning more directly to Agamben's argument, some clarifications are necessary. He uses Dante partly as a foil for the *Hypnerotomachia* and partly as an explanation for it. It might seem at first as if Agamben is claiming that Dante prefigures the *Hypnerotomachia* in celebrating the death of Latin, but this would be misleading. In my own gloss (on Dante and on Agamben), although Dante uses the word "noble" he is not promoting vernacular over Latin in any simple way, and not through saying that Latin is defunct (he is, of course, choosing to make these remarks about the vernacular in Latin). It is tempting to think Dante is saying something similar to the way that people may think now of endangered languages that are under threat of permanent loss. For a language to be "living" seems good and a desired state: a language that is dead demands our pity; it is undesired and an undesirable state of affairs. In fact, Dante is saying the opposite. The vernacular is wonderful, he says, but not because it is "alive." Vernaculars constantly die; it is the volatile vernacular, not Latin, that is perishable:

lo latino è perpetuo e non corruttibile, e lo volgare è non stabile e corruttibile. Onde vedemo ne le scritture antiche de le comedie a tragedie latine, che non si possono transmutare, quello medisimo che oggi avemo; che non avviene del volgare, lo quale a piacimento artificiato si transmuta.

[Latin is perpetual and not corruptible, while the vernacular is both unstable and corruptible. Thus we perceive that the language of ancient writings, both

---

[18]Dante Alighieri, *De vulgari eloquentia*, ed. and trans. Steven Botterill (Cambridge: Cambridge University Press, 2005), 2–3.

comedies and tragedies, is the same Latin we have today: no writer can modify it on his own. This is indeed true of the vernacular, which can be modified at will by every writer who uses it.]

que quidem gramatica nichil aliud est quam quedam inalterabilis locutionis idemptitas diversis temporibus atque locis.

[for indeed grammar is nothing other than a certain unalterable identity of speech through diverse times and places.][19]

That vernaculars die is part of what makes them desirable, as well as vulnerable, and we are wrong to mourn them or accuse Latin of over-powering them. The vernacular lives and thrives through a genealogy of instruction, example, method—through grammar, in short. Dante wants the vernacular to gain the stability of Latin; but for him this is a subtle negotiation between transience and stability in the relationship between the two languages, not between one language dying and another taking life. Latin is a means for the vernacular to gain ground, not its agonistic opponent. Dante could not have imagined the death of Latin, let alone have wanted to celebrate it.

There's a puzzling contradiction: Dante wants vernacularity to tri-umph, but through saying that it perishes. How is one to connect this with the complex language games of the *Hypnerotomachia*? Agamben deals with this contradiction between Dante and the *Hypnerotomachia* by saying that the *idea* of a dead language changes between his time and that of the late fifteenth century. Between 1302 and 1499 the language that is described as dead has become Latin, the new living language the vernacular. But all is still not quite what it seems. In a crucial twist, it turns out that in celebrating death, the *Hypnerotomachia* is really promot-ing the living. Language death is really about life, and language birth is really about death. We find that ceding life to the vernacular has resulted in a strange new life for Latin. This new life for Latin consists in its new living role as a dead language. "Polia" means "the grey woman, the old woman" and "Polifilo" means "the lover of Polia." When we read the *Hypnerotomachia* more closely we find that Polia is not just old but already dead: she is a desiccated flower that Polifilo tries

[19] Dante, *Il convivio*, I.v. Cited in Rita Copeland, *Rhetoric, Hermeneutics, and Translation in the Middle Ages* (Cambridge: Cambridge University Press, 1991), 104–5.

in vain to animate through the process of a dream.[20] In short, she is the old, dead language of Latin, and Polifilo—the new thrusting vernacular—is her lover. But this does not finish her off. The tomb-like printed book both inters her (it finishes with an epitaph) and gives her new life.[21] Even more—and the underlying Christian frame of reference is clear[22]—it is only through death that she can live.

There is more to say (and I will) on what Agamben is trying to tease out here in relation to Latin and vernacular. But let me pause a little first over this notion of language death. Do languages die? There is a school of thought that death and birth are not in fact good metaphors for understanding language in history. Some argue that languages do not die, they change.[23] But my interest (and competence) is not really in whether empirically they die or change, but rather (as a literary scholar) in the moments and contexts in which change is *remarked*. It is crucial to understand the *De vulgari* as a text *about* language change, to whatever extent we wish to use it as an index *of* language change. What Agamben raises is this double chronology: the moment at which change occurs (deeply obscure) and the moment when change is perceived. The *De vulgari* was not well known in the fourteenth century (there are just three manuscripts, none in Dante's hand);[24] it was only with its sixteenth-century printing that his arguments started to have an impact on discourses *about* language. Agamben wants to have it both ways, I think. Agamben uses the *De vulgari* as a signal of a decisive difference between the medieval and the humanistic, but also seeks to demonstrate that it is the *De vulgari* itself that is partly causing Italian humanistic discourse to change.[25]

My effort in this lecture is to go back over this time period in a reverse chronology, from 1499 to 1302, testing to see what happens when we

---

[20] Colonna, *Hypnerotomachia Poliphili*, trans. Godwin, 49.

[21] Agamben, *The End of the Poem*, 49.

[22] This last point is my addition.

[23] This case is made by Daniel Heller-Roazen, *Echolalias: On the Forgetting of Language* (New York: Zone, 2005), Ch. 7, 53–65. It's a position that could be modified for example with reference to languages that have died without issue, such as Palaic, an extinct Indo-European language. I am grateful to Joshua Katz for his comments on this issue.

[24] Wendy Pfeffer, "A Note on Dante, "De vulgari", and the Manuscript Tradition," *Romance Notes* 46 (2005): 69–76.

[25] Nonetheless, Dante's thinking on language did not of course occur in a vacuum. On the very large topic of language theory in Italian medieval and Renaissance Italy, see Angelo Mazzocco, *Linguistic Theories in Dante and the Humanists: Studies of Language and Intellectual History in Late Medieval and Early Renaissance Italy* (Leiden: Brill, 1993).

take this modern Italian's argument about a medieval Italian author's influence upon a humanist multilingual *jeu d'esprit* back through France and toward England, and eventually Chaucer . . .

Is Latin a Vernacular?

Let me pause again but over a different question. Agamben's argument about language status, although subtle, still treats Latin and vernacular as dichotomous. But are Latin and vernacular really so distinct? In the past decade scholars of medieval English literature have started to pay dramatically increased attention to the substantial field of French, and Anglo-French, with great dividends (in fact scholars in French departments are now working on a much wider linguistic and geographical frame for French than ever before, and are traveling [in terms of their reading] into the Mediterranean and the Middle East); such attention is also beginning to happen freshly in the field of England's third (or is it first?) language of Latin.[26] But it is still early days, and the Toronto Anglo-Latinist A. G. Rigg's 1992 description of the landscape of post-Conquest Anglo-Latin as empty of literary explorers remains unfortunately more intact than one would wish.[27] Chaucerians all know how important Latin is, just as we all know how important French is, but we don't necessarily do the reading.[28] Toronto of all places is where we

[26] Pioneering work includes: on English, continental, and insular French, Ardis Butterfield, *The Familiar Enemy: Chaucer, Language, and Nation in the Hundred Years War* (Oxford: Oxford University Press, 2009); on English and insular French, Jocelyn Wogan-Browne, ed., *Language and Culture in Medieval Britain: The French of England c. 1100–c. 1500* (Woodbridge: York Medieval, 2009); and on topics in multilingualism, Judith Jefferson, Ad Putter, and Amanda Hopkins, eds., *Multilingualism in Medieval Britain (c. 1066–1520): Sources and Analysis* (Turnhout: Brepols, 2013). On French, see also Sharon Kinoshita, *Medieval Boundaries: Rethinking Difference in Old French Literature* (Philadelphia: University of Pennsylvania Press, 2006), and Simon Gaunt, *Marco Polo's "Le devisement du monde": Narrative Voice, Language and Diversity* (Cambridge: D. S. Brewer, 2013); on Italian, Alison Cornish, *Vernacular Translation in Dante's Italy: Illiterate Literature* (New York: Cambridge University Press, 2011); on Latin, Ralph J. Hexter and David Townsend, eds., *Oxford Handbook of Medieval Latin Literature* (New York: Oxford University Press, 2012); on the emerging field of Mediterranean studies, Peregrine Horden and Sharon Kinoshita, *A Companion to Mediterranean History* (Chichester: Wiley Blackwell, 2014). For a literary history, see David Wallace, ed., *Europe: A Literary History, 1348–1418*, 2 vols. (Oxford: Oxford University Press, 2016).

[27] A. G. Rigg, *A History of Anglo-Latin Literature, 1066–1422* (Cambridge: Cambridge University Press, 1992), 1.

[28] I hope it goes without saying that of course I do not mean to slight the extensive and very distinguished history of scholarship on Chaucer and Latin authors; the emphasis here is on Latin as a medium for writing (and speaking) and thinking about language,

should feel inspired to do so! Conscious of my temerity in this distinguished center for Latin studies, but precisely because of our location here for this congress, I want to sketch briefly some of the new insights that are emerging, from classicists working on bilingualism and so-called late Latin, from romance scholars on late Latin, from musicologists and liturgists, and of course from medieval Latinists themselves, about the status and character of Latin.

There is not time to mention more than a few salient points. First of all, if we go back early enough then of course Latin is a mother tongue too. But the notion of mother tongue, as I have argued in relation to Anglo-French, is complex.[29] It is often confused with the term "vernacular."[30] And it is often sentimentalized by modern monolinguals. I take an example from the 2011 Official Census of Aboriginal Languages in Canada: "In 2011, almost 213,400 people reported speaking an Aboriginal language at home. While 82.2% of them reported that same Aboriginal language as their mother tongue, the other 17.8% reported a different language, such as English or French, as mother tongue."[31] So

---

a topic that it seems fair to say is currently more prominent in Langland studies and vernacular religious writings than in Chaucer studies. See, for just two instances, Fiona Somerset and Nicholas Watson, eds, *The Vulgar Tongue: Medieval and Postmedieval Vernacularity* (University Park: Pennsylvania State University Press, 2003); and Fiona Somerset, "'Al þe commonys with o voys atonys': Multilingual Latin and Vernacular Voice," in *YLS* 19 (2005): 107–36.

[29] Butterfield, *Familiar Enemy*, Ch. 9.

[30] In brief, debates about the status of insular French for an older generation of scholars were polarized around its status as a "true vernacular" (See Johan Vising, *Anglo-Norman Language and Literature* [London: Oxford University Press, 1923], 18; and William Rothwell, "The Role of French in Thirteenth-Century England," *Bulletin of the John Rylands Library* 58, no. 2 [1976]: 445–66), for which a simplified notion of mother tongue was often substituted. Christopher Cannon, "Class Distinction and the French of England," in *Traditions and Innovations in the Study of Medieval English Literature: The Influence of Derek Brewer*, ed. Charlotte Brewer and Barry Windeatt (Cambridge: D. S. Brewer, 2013), 48–59, relying on such scholarship, makes the same confusion. But as much recent work in many fields has shown, this is a misleading dichotomy: linguistic competence takes a wide variety of forms, and the varying status of French (or Latin) in any multilingual community cannot be assessed unless this is understood. See, for example, Serge Lusignan, *Parler vulgairement: Les intellectuels et la langue française aux XIIIe et XIVe siècles* (Paris: Vrin; Montreal: Presses de l'Université de Montréal, 1986), and Serge Lusignan, *La langue des rois au Moyen Age: Le français en France et en Angleterre* (Paris: Presses universitaires de France, 2004); Butterfield, *Familiar Enemy*, passim; and the many important articles (whose implications await proper exploration) by the late David Trotter on the prior need to calibrate language distinctions, identities, oralities, and literacies very carefully in the period.

[31] https://www12.statcan.gc.ca/census-recensement/2011/as-sa/98–314-x/98–314-x2011003_3-eng.cfm (accessed May 29, 2019).

one can have a mother tongue that one does not speak at home; and a mother tongue that is different from one's parents' mother tongues.

Now, as then, people have learned languages in many ways, with more or less fluency and education. Monolingual assumptions about what a "mother tongue" is are often far off the mark about multilingual competencies and practices. In the case of Latin, it becomes a fascinating and moot point as to when and to what degree it continues to be spoken as a living language. It does not come as a surprise that Latin was a spoken language in the seventh century, but perhaps it is more unexpected to hear Roger Bacon describe it as a mother tongue in the thirteenth century.[32] The point, though, is not how one defines mother tongue, but rather, as David Townsend puts it, that we should see "Latinity and Vernacularity as a Continuum of Linguistic Register."[33] The old days of thinking there to be a sharp distinction between Latin and vernacular need to be put behind us.[34]

One reason that particularly interested me in *Familiar Enemy*—and I revive it here—concerns perception, again. People carried on thinking that what they were speaking was Latin long after a modern linguist would describe what they were speaking as vernacular. We can see some of this in the references to "en son Latin" in Occitan and French texts that often mean "vernacular" or "jargon" (there's a famous example in Guillaume de Poitou's so-called Red Cat song, "Farai un vers"),[35] although they can mean "Latin" too.[36] The groundbreaking work by Roger Wright in the early 1990s on the transition from Latin to romance languages, being discussed freshly in recent work on early and

---

[32] Ryan Szpiech, "Latin as a Language of Authoritative Tradition," in Hexter and Townsend, *Oxford Handbook of Medieval Latin Literature*, 63–84 (71).

[33] David Townsend, "The Current Questions and Future Prospects of Medieval Latin Studies," in Hexter and Townsend, *Oxford Handbook of Medieval Latin Literature*, 3–24 (15).

[34] See also the important arguments by Alastair Minnis, *Translations of Authority in Medieval English Literature: Valuing the Vernacular* (Cambridge: Cambridge University Press, 2009), 102–3.

[35] One of the ladies says to the poet-narrator: "La una·m diz en son Latin" (one of them says to me in her high-class speech). For further discussion of this song see Ardis Butterfield, "Medieval Lyric: A Translatable or Untranslatable Zone?" in *World Poetics, Comparative Poetics*, ed. Jonathan Hart and Ming Xie, special issue of *UTQ* 88 (2019): 142–59.

[36] The Arabic term for "foreign language" (*lugha ʿāmmiyya*) was translated as "Latin" in a twelfth-century Latin translation of the Qurʾān; see Szpiech, "Latin as a Language of Authoritative Tradition," 74.

late Latin, raises fundamental questions about how languages are under-stood.[37] Can people be bilingual without realizing that they are? One response is that languages can only properly be regarded as different from one another if their actual speakers think they are different languages. Another response is languages come to be recognized as different from one another (as opposed to being part of a single, complex language) only after they start to be written down. Or again, if there is a perception within a community that its speakers are monolingual, then this will override any sense of difference between them—but once that perception changes then the differences start to matter and be recognized as such. One of Wright's central arguments is that writing is the key, but if you like, slow, factor in a sense of change. For users of Latin in these earlier periods the gap between what they spoke and what was written was not of interest: it was all Latin. In short, if any confusion arises for us it is because the use of a term like "Latin" in a vernacular text tends to mean spoken use.[38]

A third element in the continuum between Latin and vernacular relates to their manifold variety of linguistic forms. Latin is a vernacular because it, too, is plural and unstable. This was obvious to Augustine in the fourth and fifth centuries, to Isidore of Seville and Virgilius Maro Grammaticus in the seventh, and to Bacon in the thirteenth. Taking a historical perspective, Isidore distinguished four kinds:

Latinas autem linguas quattuor esse quidam dixerunt, id est Priscam, Latinam, Romanam, Mixtam. Prisca est, quam vetustissimi Italiae sub Iano et Saturno sunt usi . . . Latina, quam sub Latino et regibus Tusci et ceteri in Latio sunt locuti . . . Romana, quae post reges exactos a populo Romano coepta est . . . Mixta, quae post imperium latius promotum simul cum moribus et hominibus in Romanam civitatem inrupit, integritatem verbi per soloecismos et barbarismos corrumpens.

[Some say that there are four kinds of Latin, that is the Ancient, the Latin, the Roman, and the Mixed. The Ancient is that which the very earliest inhabitants

[37] Roger Wright, ed., *Latin and the Romance Languages in the Early Middle Ages* (London: Routledge, 1991); and Roger Wright, *A Sociophilological Study of Late Latin* (Turnhout: Brepols, 2003); for reassessments of Wright, see James Adams and Nigel Vincent, eds., *Early and Late Latin: Continuity or Change?* (Cambridge: Cambridge University Press, 2016).

[38] Carin Ruff, "Latin as an Acquired Language," in Hexter and Townsend, *Oxford Handbook of Medieval Latin Literature*, 47–60.

of Italy used . . . The Latin is that which the Tuscans and others in Latium used under Latinus and the kings . . . The Roman is that which was begun after the kings were driven out by the Roman people . . . The Mixed is that which, after the expansion of the empire, entered the Roman state along with customs and peoples, corrupting the integrity of the language with solecisms and barbarisms.][39]

Virgilius Maro speaks more broadly and synchronically:

[T]am multa sit et copiosa latinitatis totius regio et ut ita dicam pelagus inmensum, ut discerni omnino diuersitates ipsius et nouae adinuentiones et incognitae, ut putantur, a nemine ad liquidum possint.

[{T}he realm of all of Latinity is so vast and abundant and, so to speak, an immense ocean, that no one would be able, as they might think, to discern clearly all its varieties and new and unheard-of innovations.][40]

For Augustine, it was obvious as soon as one considered Bible translation (and Augustine was always considering Bible translation). First of all, Latin was only one of the three main languages of the Bible, and the least authoritative. Hebrew and Greek were far superior. One could not begin to understand the Bible without knowing Hebrew and Greek, he says (although in fact, unlike Jerome, he did not know Hebrew) because the very multiplicity of Latin translations made it necessary to check back at every turn.

Et latinae quidem linguae homines, quos nunc instruendos suscepimus, duabus aliis ad scripturarum divinarum cognitionem opus habent, hebraea scilicet et graeca, ut ad exemplaria praecedentia recurratur si quam dubitationem attulerit latinorum interpretum infinita varietas.

[Users of the Latin language—and it is these that I have now undertaken to instruct—need two others, Hebrew and Greek, for an understanding of the

---

[39] Isidore of Seville, *The Etymologies of Isidore of Seville*, ed. and trans. Stephen A. Barney (Cambridge: Cambridge University Press, 2006), IX.i.6–7. On the possible connections between this passage of Isidore and Chaucer's description of Custance's language as "a maner Latyn corrupt" in the *Man of Law's Tale* (512–20), see J. A. Burrow, "A maner Latyn corrupt," *MÆ*, 30, no. 1 (1961): 33–37.

[40] Virgilius Maro Grammaticus, *Epistulae*, 2.119–22, cited and translated in part in Vivien Law, *Wisdom, Authority and Grammar in the Seventh Century: Decoding Virgilius Maro Grammaticus* (Cambridge: Cambridge University Press, 1995), 53.

divine scriptures, so that recourse may be had to the original versions if any uncertainty arises from the infinite variety of Latin translators.][41]

It was because of such variety, such instability, such feckless proliferation, so it has recently been argued, that the massive effort of Latin exegesis and writing in succeeding centuries came about. If Latin came to be regarded as authoritative in the Middle Ages then it was only as a result of an acute sense of its inadequacy in the face not only of Hebrew and Greek, but also of Arabic.[42] Ryan Szpiech and Thomas Burman have even suggested that no sooner did it achieve such status than it had to work all the harder in relation to the rising vernaculars. Far from Latin's having an overpowering authority, a picture of it is being painted by these modern commentators as a language end-stopped by competition and managing only a temporary dominance. One may think there to be an element of exaggeration in such claims, but it is good to be asked to hold this thought experiment—at least for a moment or two—of a struggling and insecure Latin, rather than a complacently overweening one.[43]

For my part, it may be just as valuable to cast the situation slightly differently, and see it as about not so much an overmastering authority as a condition of incipient authority working semi-submerged in the midst of an uncontrollable linguistic energy that sprang from all kinds of local situation. For example, the question of whether Latin was a vernacular in the period looks entirely different depending on whether one is thinking about (or in) Italian, French, or English contexts. Agamben's argument about Latin and vernacular is grounded on an Italian view of Latin; this of course is very different from French or English or German views of Latin. And even these labels are very misleading: Dante's argument is not about Italian but Tuscan, and the swirl of languages in which he places his claim that Tuscan should come top contains at least fourteen Italian vernaculars (several of which he starts to subdivide).

[41] Augustine, *De doctrina Christiana*, ed. and trans. R. P. H. Green, Oxford Early Christian Texts (Oxford: Clarendon Press, 1995), XI.xvi.34, pp. 72–73.

[42] Szpiech, "Latin as a Language of Authoritative Tradition," 72.

[43] This new emphasis differs in important ways (that cannot be addressed here but await further discussion) from older arguments about "the confrontation between Latinity and vernacularity" (Copeland, *Rhetoric, Hermeneutics, and Translation*, 223) that are also at the basis, for example, of Mark Amsler, "Creole Grammar and Multilingual Poetics," in *Medieval Multilingualism: The Francophone World and Its Neighbours*, ed. Christopher Kleinhenz and Keith Busby (Turnhout: Brepols, 2010), 15–42.

Et dextri regiones sunt Apulia, sed non tota, Roma, Ducatus, Tuscia et Ianuensis Marchia; sinistri autem pars Apulie, Marchia Anconitana, Romandiola, Lombardia, Marchia, Trivisiana cum Venetiis. Forum Iulii vero et Ystria non nisi leve Ytalie esse possunt; nee insule Tyrene maris, videlicet Sicilia et Sardinia, non nisi dextre Ytalie sunt, vel ad dextram Ytaliam sociande. In utroque quidem duorum laterum, et hiis que secuntur ad ea, lingue hominum variantur: ut lingua Siculorum cum Apulis, Apulorum cum Romanis, Romanorum cum Spoletanis, horum cum Tuscis, Tuscorum cum Ianuensibus, Ianuensium cum Sardis; nee non Calabrorum cum Anconitanis, horum cum Romandiolis, Romandiolorum cum Lombardis, Lombardorum cum Trivisianis et Venetis, horum cum Aquilegiensibus, et istorum cum Ystrianis. De quo Latinorum neminem nobiscum dissentire putamus. Quare adminus xiiii vulgaribus sola videtur Ytalia variari. Que adhuc omnia vulgaria in sese variantur, ut puta in Tuscia Senenses et Aretini, in Lombardia Ferrarenses et Placentini; nee non in eadem civitate aliqualem variationem perpendimus, ut superius in capitulo inmediato posuimus.

Quapropter, si primas et secundarias et subsecundarias vulgaris Ytalie variationes calculare velimus, et in hoc minimo mundi angulo non solum ad millenam loquele variationem venire contigerit, sed etiam ad magis ultra.

Apulia (though not all of it), Rome, the Duchy, Tuscany, and the Genoese Marches; those on the left, however, are the other part of Apulia, the Marches of Ancona, Romagna, Lombardy, the Marches of Treviso, and Venice. As for Friuli and Istria, they can only belong to the left-hand side of Italy, while the islands in the Tyrrhenian—Sicily and Sardinia—clearly belong to the right-hand side, or at least are to be associated with it. On each of the two sides, as well as in the areas associated with them, the language of the inhabitants varies. Thus the language of the Sicilians is different from that of the Apulians, that of the Apulians from that of the Romans, that of the Romans from that of the people of Spoleto, theirs from that of the Tuscans, that of the Tuscans from that of the Genoese, and that of the Genoese from that of the Sardinians; and, likewise, the language of the Calabrians is different from that of the people of Ancona, theirs from that of the people of Romagna, that of the people of Romagna from that of the Lombards, that of the Lombards from that of the people of Treviso and the Venetians, theirs from that of the people of Aquileia, and theirs from that of the Istrians. And I think that no Italian will disagree with me about this.

So we see that Italy alone presents a range of at least fourteen different vernaculars. All these vernaculars also vary internally, so that the Tuscan of Siena is distinguished from that of Arezzo, or the Lombard of Ferrara from that of Piacenza; moreover, we can detect some variation even within a single city, as was suggested above, in the preceding chapter. For this reason, if we wished to calculate the number of primary, and secondary, and still further subordinate varieties of the Italian vernacular, we would find that, even in this tiny corner of the world, the count would take us not only to a thousand different types of speech, but well beyond that figure.[44]

In this playful display of the dizzying variety and fluidity of "Italian" vernacular classification Dante demonstrates that the term "vernacular," and hence its relation to "Latin," is deeply unstable.

The Name and Love of Grammar

Polia does not only mean "the old woman." She means "the name and love of language," as Agamben (or rather his translator, Daniel Heller-Roazen) puts it. Consider the depiction of Grammar in Martianus Capella's *De nuptiis Philologiae et Mercurii* (*Marriage of Philology and Mercury*) as "an old woman indeed but of great charm."[45] Casting Latin and vernacular as mutually in love seems to me a stroke of genius on the part of the *Hypnerotomachia* author. The relationship between Latin and vernacular is intimate. And it is about grammar. Again, I must be brief, especially in relation to such a vast topic.[46] By starting to talk about writing we start to talk about grammar. This is the crucial differential between the two lovers. But however true this is, a sharp dichotomy must be avoided. Just because grammar was always used to teach writing, it does not mean either that Latin is written and the vernacular is spoken, or that teachers did not teach Latin through a variety of oral means, both Latin and vernacular. Various consequences follow: for instance, there is no monolithic process happening linguistically throughout the Middle Ages; the dominance that Latin does achieve takes place in and through the love of, the sly prior yielding of, the vernacular. And by the time we

---

[44] Dante, *De vulgari eloquentia*, 24–25.

[45] William Harris Stahl and Richard Johnson, trans., *Martianus Capella and the Seven Liberal Arts* (New York: Columbia University Press, 1971), 64. (The larger context is: "unam priore loco Mercorialium ministrarum aetate quidem longaeuam, sed comitate blandissimam"; *Martianus Capella*, ed. Adolf Dick [Leipzig: B. G. Teubner, 1925], 82.)

[46] This not the place for a full bibliography on medieval grammar. I mention here only the useful material assembled concisely in Amsler, "Creole Grammar and Multilingual Poetics," 30–36; and Lusignan, *Parler vulgairement*, 67, 98.

get to Jean de Meun, Dante, Boccaccio, Petrarch, Machaut, and Chaucer we find all kinds of balancing acts, tensions, and imaginative inventions that play with that "intimate discord" that "language has . . . with itself."[47]

The latter part of this lecture will now—as promised—work east: through France and back toward England, and eventually Chaucer.

"Le temps jadis"

Let me now frame our sense of that "intimate discord" that "language has . . . with itself" by means of a poet who wrote just two decades or so prior to Colonna's *Hypnerotomachia*, in French. This is the great François Villon. Villon's extraordinarily insistent sense of personal presence throughout his poetry (always brilliantly and artfully crafted) has dominated not just modern interpretation of him, but the modern French notion of the Middle Ages. (Until the work of Daniel Poirion in the mid-1960s, medieval French literature was the *Chanson de Roland* and Villon, with nothing much in between.)[48] But in this lecture I want to draw attention to an aspect of his writing that has been little studied in detail since the 1940s: his interest in historicizing French as a language.[49] It is the third of his celebrated *balades* "du temps jadis," given the title by Clément Marot of "ballade en vieil langage françois."[50] So to recall: the first "des dames du temps jadis" gives a roll-call of dead women, from the ancient past (Flora and Echo) to his close contemporary Jeanne d'Arc, with the famous refrain "Mais ou sont les neiges d'anten?" (immortalized in English poetic literary history by Dante Gabriel Rossetti as "but where are the snows of yesteryear?").[51] The second, also on the *ubi sunt* topos, turns to "les seigneurs du temps jadis." The third changes the focus to language. Villon evokes further images of the dead, this time more generalized (from the apostles, the pope, and the emperor, to the dauphin and unnamed heralds and trumpeters) and marked by his choice of an archaicizing Old French.

---

[47] Agamben, *The End of the Poem*, 59.

[48] Daniel Poirion, *Le poète et le prince: L'évolution du lyrisme courtois de Guillaume de Machaut à Charles d'Orléans* (Paris: Presses universitaires de France, 1965).

[49] See Jean Damourette, "Archaïsmes et pastiches," *Le français moderne*, 9 (1941): 181–206.

[50] Marot gave titles to the *balades* in his 1533 edition of Villon's poetry; there are none in the manuscripts of the poems.

[51] Dante Gabriel Rossetti, *Poems* (London: F. S. Ellis, 1870), 177–78.

What is intriguing about this French is its liminality. There are questions that need more research and discussion about whether the French is "genuine" Old French, a not wholly successful attempt to create a genuine Old French, or a pastiche invented by Villon designed to create an image of archaicism.[52] The archaisms include the use of "ly" instead of the article "le," "cy," and "cilz"; the "s"s used in the singular subject cases and their modifying adjectives; and such lexical choices as "aorez" instead of "adorez," or "ceinct" for "ceint."

> Car ou soit ly sains appostolles,
> D'aubes vestuz, d'amys coeffez,
> Qui ne seint fors saintes estolles
> Dont par le col prent ly mauffez
> De mal talent tous eschauffez,
> Aussi bien meurt que cilz servans,
> De ceste vie cy buffet:
> Autant en emporte ly vens![53]

Kathleen Loysen makes the interesting case that the refrain "Autant en emporte ly vens" is also archaicizing—it is a widely attested proverb whose earliest known instance occurs in the *Roman de la Rose* (line 15040).[54] I can't help also wondering whether there is an allusion to Arnaut Daniel's envoy in his song "En cest sonet": "Ieu sui Arnautz

[52] With the pioneering exception (as far as I can tell, confirming Loysen: see below) of Damourette, earlier commentators saw these features as mistakes. See François Villon, *Œuvres*, ed. Louis Thuasne (Paris: A. Picard, 1923); *Le testament Villon*, ed. Jean Rychner and Albert Henry, 2 vols., Textes littéraires français 207–8 (Geneva: Droz, 1974), 2.59 ("la façon fantaisiste dont ces traits sont distribués montre que, s'ils évoquaient encore une époque, leur valeur linguistique n'était plus perçue"); Italo Siciliano, *François Villon et les thèmes poétiques du Moyen Age* (1967; repr., Paris: A.-G. Nizet, 1992), 275. However, more recent work on Villon's intertexuality and strategic use of misquotation has suggested that there are more subtle factors at play in Villon's depiction of "vieux français"; see Nancy Freeman Regalado, "Villon's Legacy from *Le Testament of Jean de Meun*: Misquotation, Memory, and the Wisdom of Fools," in *Villon at Oxford: The Drama of the Text; Proceedings of the Conference Held at St. Hilda's College Oxford, March 1996*, ed. Mike Freeman and Jane H. M. Taylor (Amsterdam: Rodopi, 1999), 282–311; Nancy Freeman Regalado, *L'art poétique de François Villon: Effet de réel* (Orléans: Paradigme, 2018), 47. I am indebted to Nancy Regalado for her advice on this point and for references, and also especially to an important unpublished paper by Kathleen A. Loysen, "L'effet de passé: Les procédés de la nostalgie chez Villon." I hope to return to this topic in Villon in a subsequent publication. For more comment on the notion of linguistic "mistakes," see Butterfield, "Medieval Lyric."
[53] *Le testament Villon*, Vol. 1, lines 385–92.
[54] Probably undergirded, one might add, by Psalm 103.

qu'amàs l'aura" (I am Arnaud who hoards/embraces/loves the wind), who may also be alluding to the same Psalm; but even without this, the possibility that Villon is making allusions to past texts as well as to a past period of the language suggests that he wants his readers to understand language as itself making a complicated allusion to the past.

For our current purposes, I want to link this with two other observations. Kenneth Varty, in a classic essay, points out that Villon's three *balades* owe a great deal to the *danse macabre* tradition. He suggests that the Old French in this third *balade* is a *"danse macabre* mirror to the living language he uses in his poetry."[55] Villon, like Colonna, makes powerful use of ekphrasis as a way of debating time's hold over life and language. It is like an exploration in miniature of how a single image, or tradition of image-making, can be condensed into a much broader perception of what language death and linguistic transience might mean chronologically. Villon's poetry reminds us how differently Latin signifies for him as opposed to Colonna (or Agamben): this third *balade* is a moment in microcosm in which *French* gains the kind of linguistic past that (with obviously far greater expansiveness) Colonna explores in relation to Tuscan and Latin. Where Tuscan looked back in its history to Latin, Villon, remarkably, and precociously, gives French its own ancestor— Old French—and plays up the distance between the two to create a subtle argument about now and then—*maintenant* and *jadis*.

The Dream of the Fountain

In talking of "the dream of language," Agamben points us back to the strange non-language, or what he calls the "pure self-referentiality" of the language of the *Hypnerotomachia Polyphili*.[56] Any attempt to understand language through dream before the late fifteenth century must ultimately reckon with the *Roman de la Rose*: but here I want to meditate on the references to dreaming and fountains in Chaucer's great mentor, and the *Rose*'s great interpreter, Guillaume de Machaut. The legacy by way of Villon is clear: a member of the court of Charles d'Orléans in

[55] Kenneth Varty, "Villon's Three *Ballades du Temps Jadis* and the *Danse Macabre*," in *Littera et sensus: Essays on Form and Meaning in Old French Literature Presented to John Fox*, ed. D. A. Trotter (Exeter: University of Exeter, 1989), 73–93 (91).
[56] Agamben, *The End of the Poem*, 60.

Blois, Villon was part of the charmed circle that wrote a seemingly endless series of *balades* on the line "Je meurs de soif auprès de la fontaine."[57] The *locus classicus* of this motif of the fountain was again of course the *Rose*,[58] but I want to spend time briefly instead on Machaut's focused retake, *La fonteine amoureuse*. The extraordinary visual detail of the *Hypnerotomachia*'s fountains and a myriad other monuments recalls the carved details on the Hesdin park fountain, and the enameled bodies painted and chiseled on its surface.[59] Chaucerians usually spend most time on the sections of this poem that Chaucer re-visioned in *The Book of the Duchess*, namely the Ceyx and Alcyone story. Let me isolate one detail from this and then turn to the fountain.

Machaut begins this Ovidian retelling through a picture of the sleeping god in the cave of dreams. In Machaut's scene he is not alone but surrounded by a thousand sons and daughters all shape-changing in the work of dreams. As Miranda Griffin beautifully remarks, "To enter, in a *dit amoureux*, a house full of ever-shifting dream-bodies is to visualize the process of metaphor, the process of *translatio* whereby one thing is expressed in terms of another."[60] Not only do they change form, Machaut describes them as able to speak languages and "murmures" from all countries.

> Les mille fieus qui entour lui estoient,
> Et les filles aussi, se transmuoient
> A leur voloir, car les fourmes prenoient
> Des creatures
> Si qu'en dormant, par songes, se moustroient
> Diversement; pour ce les gens songeoient
> Et en songant meintes choses veöient,
> Douces ou sures.
> Les unes sons pongnans, les autres dures;

---

[57] Philippe Ménard, "Je meurs de soif auprès de la fontaine: D'un mythe antique à une image lyrique," *Romania* 87 (1966), 394–400; R. A. Dwyer, "Je meurs de soif auprès de la fontaine," *MÆ* 23 (1969), 225–28.

[58] Though there are Latin antecedents, notably Alain de Lille's *De planctu naturae* (met. 3).

[59] See the story of Narcissus, and the rhymes "entaillie"/"esmaillie"/"vis"/"vis,"; Guillaume de Machaut, *Le livre de la fontaine amoureuse*, ed. and trans. Jacqueline Cerquiglini-Toulet (Paris: Stock, 1993), lines 1308–12.

[60] Miranda Griffin, *Transforming Tales: Rewriting Metamorphosis in Medieval French Literature* (Oxford: Oxford University Press, 2015), 217–18.

L'une est clere, les autres sont obscures;
De tous païs, langages et murmures
Parler savoient;
D'iaue, de feu, de toutes aventures,
De fer, de fust, prenoient les figures.
Autre mestier n'avoient, n'autres cures.
Par tout aloient.

(*Fontaine*, 635–50)

[The thousand sons and daughters who surrounded him transformed them-selves at will, for they took the forms of creatures, so that, during sleep, they manifested themselves in diverse ways: this is why people dream, and, while they are dreaming, see many sweet or bitter things. Some are spiky, others harsh, one is bright, the others dark. They know how to speak the language and murmurs of all countries. They take the shape of water, of fire, of iron, of wood, of all eventualities. They have no other occupation, no other care. They go everywhere.][61]

Machaut seems to understand dreamwork as also a more "literal" form of *translatio*, a place of many languages in translation, rather like the Translation Centre for the Bodies of the EU.

When we get to the fountain, however, the mobile, plural, shifting world of dream reduces sharply down to one: a single dream that lord and poet share. This has always seemed to me one of the most intriguing and mysterious structural decisions of the poem. Pondering it in the context of language-shifts makes me wonder whether, by this simple yet bold device, Machaut is exploring an old philosophical conundrum: the question of what kind of language can possibly be expressed in or through dreams. Dreams are the ultimate invented and incommunicable language: by sharing the same dream, poet and lord are able to share in an unshareable experience. Can we go further and wonder whether Machaut sees dream as a means of translating uncommunicable emo-tions and fears from bodies to words?

In the final, somewhat gnomic, paragraphs of his essay, Agamben talks of the "essential and irreducible bilingualism" that characterizes dream language.[62] For me, the issue can be broken down into several different components: the kind of language one speaks (or hears) in a

---

[61] Machaut, *La fontaine amoureuse*, ed. Cerquiglini-Toulet, lines 635–50; cited (with English translation) in Griffin, *Transforming Tales*, 216.
[62] Agamben, *The End of the Poem*, 50.

dream; the process of translation into the language in which one retells it; and the means by which the experience of dreaming can itself be shared, through words. Machaut explores all three with great creativity: through rhyme; through inset lyric (2206); and through the dream-crossing materiality of a ruby ring, exchanged for a diamond one between the lover and his lady in the dream, and visible on his finger when he and the poet wake up. The extra element, lightly but sensitively articulated by Machaut, is the emotional function of the dream to turn the love-patron from desperate pain to joy, from a refusal to be consoled to shocked delight at the translation of a symbol of love into a dazzling, tangible object on his finger. We might say, for Machaut, the dream is a translation machine that verbalizes and, in the form of poetry, even materializes, emotion.

Troilus and the Dream of Language

My final port of call in this reverse chronology back from the *Hypnerotomachia Poliphili* to Chaucer is *Troilus and Criseyde*. I want to revisit the two dreams: the one in Book II, line 918, straight after Antigone's song; and Troilus's dream of the boar in Book V, line 1233. Both dreams involve pain. Strictly speaking, the replacing of Criseyde's heart by an eagle with long claws is allegedly *not* painful ("of which she nought agroos ne nothing smerte" [II.930]).[63] But as many readers have remarked, the action is painfully described ("out hire herte he rente" [II.928]), and leaves anxiety about the future littering the text. The second dream in Book V is much more explicitly embedded in the now almost completely unfolded tragedy: Troilus has waited "bitwixen hope and drede" (V.1207) right through and beyond the appointed time when Criseyde promised to return, and is finally giving in to despair and a desire to die. In great melancholy, he lies down to sleep and dreams he is walking through a forest. He sees a sleeping boar being kissed by Criseyde, who is lying in his folded arms (V.1240–41).

The next section of the poem presents the reader with a particularly copious multilingual experience. The Tuscan of Boccaccio's *Il filostrato* always at its back, Chaucer's English dips in and out of French (Troilus's long letter to Criseyde [V.1317–422]) and then, as Troilus goes back to

---

[63] Citations from *Troilus* are taken from Geoffrey Chaucer, *"Troilus and Criseyde": A New Edition of "The Book of Troilus,"* ed. B. A. Windeatt (London: Longman, 1984).

the dream to try to interpret it, turns fully to Latin, for all the manuscripts (except two) insert here a twelve-line summary of the *Thebaid*, mediated through the Trojan heroine of Greek tragedy, his sister Cassandra (V.1498).[64] From here, as we all know, the poem stutters and starts its way to the end, bemoaning the "diuversite" of English (1793–95); praying for comprehension way beyond English ("wher-so thow be or elles songe" [1797]); and finally rising, with Troilus, to a place just below the stars—so movingly discussed by Susan Crane two years ago in London—before finishing with the world's uncircumscribed creator.[65]

These details are very well known. But I want to suggest that there is more than a confluence of "sources" here; and more than a confluence of texts in different languages. Could it be that Chaucer's use of dream is setting up a very specific argument about language? *Troilus and Criseyde* is a love story. But could it also be a grammar story? And a multilingual story?

Criseyde's changeableness has made her many enemies by those who read the love tragedy in human terms (as we are invited to do many times in the poem). But what if we also understand her—like Beatrice, like Laura—as Polia, or the name and love of language? Like Polia she is both Latin and Greek; she is also Tuscan, French, and English. Always ambiguous, with more than one face,[66] she is perceived through a dream; she is killed (her heart is rent out of her body) and she survives. She is always "new," but, like Troilus, from the ancient past, and a

---

[64] The two manuscripts that do not have the Latin argument are British Library, MS Harley 2392 (H⁴) and Bodleian Library, MS Rawlinson Poet.163 (R).

[65] Susan Crane, " 'The lytel erthe that here is': Environmental Thought in Chaucer's *Parliament of Fowls*," *SAC* 39 (2017): 1–30.

[66] I refer here to Chaucer's cross-lingual punning rhyme on "ambages" (a word taken directly and seemingly for the first time into English from *Il filostrato*):

> And but if Calkas lede vs with ambages—
> That is to seyn with double wordes slye,
> Swich as men clepe a word with two visages
> (*TC*, V.897–99)

See Windeatt's note to the line; David Wallace, *Chaucer and the Early Writings of Boccaccio* (Cambridge: Boydell & Brewer, 1985), 122 and note; and, most recently, on Criseyde's face(s), Stephanie Trigg, "Chaucer's Silent Discourse," *SAC* 39 (2017): 31–56. Alastair Minnis revisits the term and points out its close relation (semantically and poetically) with "amphibologies" (*TC*, IV.1406), itself used in Vincent of Beauvais (and other commentators) to mean "duplicitous language" (Alastair Minnis, *The Cambridge Introduction to Chaucer* [Cambridge: Cambridge University Press, 2014], 41–42). There is not space to develop this further ethical direction here, but it is clearly an important undertow in the presentation of Criseyde.

permanent representation of the new and the liminal. She is a dead woman, but one who is constantly brought to life by the modern poet's love of her pagan, classical language. Troilus, the figure of constancy, dies; Criseyde, the figure of the endlessly mobile, survives. But both figures are dead *au temps de jadis*, and both are subject to the same mutual irony of death in life and life in death. Reading her, seeing her lying on the forest floor enfolded by the boar—Diomede—through a dream, we see a strange, hybrid dream-body. This is a figure of language, a visualization not of the multilingual per se, but of language's history as enfolded in a past present. If English is to speak a vernacular, it has to understand itself as expressing "a reciprocal and dreamy mirroring"[67] of itself in other languages; in dead languages but also living ones; in dead languages that survive through the transient, perishing vernaculars in which they are also being nourished and enfolded.[68]

But Criseyde is not only, or not yet, Polia. It's hard to place her chronology in any exact way on the inverted timeline I have traced because language histories do not lend themselves to such exactness, and because there are so many language histories resonating together, to use Wai Chee Dimock's thought-provoking term for semantic change.[69] Reading this sequence of texts back through two centuries and four languages has shown not only different snapshots of the relationship between vernacular and grammar, but also how those snapshots are themselves located within different chronologies in different histories, born of different negotiations with the past. I feel it is important to insist that this multiplicity of histories warns against any overriding teleology of linguistic change. What these texts share is that for vernacular to become Latin or for Latin to become vernacular is figured by love but also loss. Both Criseyde and Polia yield, but it is famously hard to pinpoint the moment when yielding occurs, or what exactly are the consequences. The subtlety of historic change between the two works (of which this lecture has barely scratched the surface) shapes the difference between these two narrative arcs. All we can properly identify is that love and loss are in intimate discord.

---

[67] Agamben, *The End of the Poem*, 49.

[68] I would argue this remains true of English in our own past present, a new Latin in its global reach and second-language dominance, that is constantly lost and renewed through change and exchange between pedagogies and rampant transient oral innovation.

[69] Wai Chee Dimock, "A Theory of Resonance," *PMLA*, 112, no. 5 (1997): 1060–71.

Returning to the present (although I would argue we have not actually left it in these readings), I would like to suggest that the medieval dream of language (as I have tried to transpose it back in time from the *Hypnerotomachia*) asks us to think of language as not easily or desirably reified into categories of naming and identifying. The current buzzword in modern bilingualism research is "translanguaging."[70] It responds to the contemporary realities of multilingualism in many parts of the world, including, but not of course exclusively, cities and much wider areas that were colonized by western cultures, such as Singapore, Hong Kong, Indonesia, India, South America. In such contexts language change is so rapid that our terms for what people speak are helplessly inadequate: to take just one example, Singapore Chinese English, or Chinglish, has now become New Chinglish. Linguistic identities are hard to pin down because people are so complexly multilingual, passing, as they speak, in and out of "identifiable" languages.

And this is not actually a modern phenomenon: my own maternal lingual context of "German"-speaking Switzerland throws up the interesting case of a region where even now the spoken language of Swiss German has no official written form, which can be shown by its multiple possible spellings, such as *Schwyzertüütsch*, *Schweizerdeutsch*, *Züritüütsch*, *Baslerdytsch*, and so on. Children are taught *Hochdeutsch*, or German, in school, but this is like learning a different language. Although unofficial written forms of the spoken languages exist now, a generation ago they were undreamed of. But the distance between official and unofficial is narrowing, and one might argue that this fluent mixture of linguistic identities for a modern Swiss maps onto the figure of language as it is given textual life through Criseyde: it produces a tension among several versatile vernaculars in a state of semi-orality, and their translation into a written but tensile form of linguistic authority.

Translanguaging identifies *itself* as a way of thinking about language that responds to the inadequacies of terms such as code-switching, heteroglossia, hybrid language practices, metrolingualism, and many others. I'm not sure whether our goal is to keep replacing labels with other labels, but the interest for me of this stimulating new work is that its premises have much in common, in fact, with linguistic cultures predating the late fifteenth century, where the lines between official and unofficial language use were much less clear than they became once

---

[70] Li Wei, "Translanguaging as a Practical Theory of Language," *Applied Linguistics* 39 (2018): 9–30.

vernaculars started to be more fully encoded in grammar books. As for Chaucer, whatever schooling he may have received, it has always seemed important to me that we think of him *out* of the schools. This makes him more like Villon's self-proclaimed image as rebel,[71] more like the mysterious Colonna—someone who had less of a pedagogic urge to promote his vernaculars than a literary and personal one. Pandarus, watching the emotionally destroyed Troilus, cites the same proverb as Villon: "ʒe, fare-wel al the snow of ferne ʒere" (*TC*, V.1176), which perhaps was in Rossetti's mind so many centuries later. Chaucer reminds us in this moment how the dream *of* language must always confront that desire *for* language to be univocal.[72] But as Ojibwe speakers know only too well, this can be a contorted and indeed agonizingly torturous experience. Language change is not always a process with which it is easy or desirable to identify. Looking back, I see in Villon, Dante, and Chaucer a sensitivity to the fine balancing act of understanding how history manifests itself in language change and yet how languages may suffer through historical change. Their poetic representations of language in the cause of love and longing keenly acknowledge the equivocations of change and its potential for profound pain.

---

[71] In fact, he got a bachelor's degree from the University of Paris in 1449 and a master's degree in 1452.

[72] Agamben notes the ambiguity of the genitival "of"; *The End of the Poem*, 60.

THE BIENNIAL CHAUCER LECTURE

The New Chaucer Society
Twenty-First International Congress
July 10–15, 2018
Victoria University, Toronto, Canada

The Biennial Chaucer Lecture

The Invention of Style

Maura Nolan
University of California, Berkeley

Abstract

Style is a rare word in Middle English. It has long been assumed that the concept of a writer's individual or personal style only developed during the early modern period. This paper traces the emergence of style in English writing from the fourteenth to the sixteenth century, performing textual analysis at both the macro and the micro level by using computer software (Voyant; Stylo for R; AntConc) in tandem with traditional close reading. Two major databases were deployed: first, a collection of 279 Middle English digital texts assembled by my research assistant, Imogen Forbes-Macphail, and second, the Middle English Glossarial Database created by Professor Larry Benson, which includes lemmatized texts of Chaucer and Gower's English corpora. The results show that the literary sense of "style" is introduced to the English literary tradition by Chaucer, by way of Petrarch, and then more fully explored by Lydgate, especially in his *Fall of Princes*. Using stylometry software (Stylo for R by M. Eder), the essay shows in a series of graphs how Chaucer and Gower's styles are distinct from one another, using principal components analysis, cluster analysis, a bootstrap consensus tree, and network analysis; these graphs also show a clear distinction between Chaucer's verse and his prose. I suggest that the difference between Chaucer and Gower is related to these writers' explicit gestures toward the "high style" (Chaucer) and the "plain style" (Gower). The final section of the paper returns to the larger question of *style* as the word

Many friends helped me during the course of my research on style and during the writing phase. My greatest debt is to Imogen Forbes-Macphail, my research assistant and collaborator; her brilliance and insight advanced my thinking and saved me from many errors. Amy Clark, Imogen, and I team-taught a graduate course in Medieval Studies and the Digital Humanities; Amy and Imogen taught me an enormous amount about this new field. Thanks are due to the students in that class for leaping into the unknown with me; their creativity and intelligence made the class and the research a constant source of pleasure. Ruth Evans, Ardis Butterfield, and Alex Gillespie kindly shepherded me before and after my talk at the New Chaucer Society in 2018. Micha Lazarus offered fitting advice about translating Aristotle. Dan Blanton, Andrew Cole, Steve Justice, Jill Mann, Jennifer Miller, and Paul Strohm generously read the paper in draft; all errors are, of course, my own.

Studies in the Age of Chaucer 41 (2019): 33–71, A1–A12
© 2019 The New Chaucer Society

appears in the Forbes-Macphail database, investigating more closely the large spike in usage that appears in the fifteenth century in Lydgate's poetry. By examining his use of personal pronouns and adjectives in conjunction with *style*, I show that Lydgate pioneered the notion of a writer's *personal* style, in contradistinction to the rhetorical levels of style (high and low) to which Chaucer and Gower refer.

Keywords

style; stylometry; digital humanities; Chaucer; Gower; Lydgate; fourteenth century; fifteenth century; classical rhetoric; *Canterbury Tales*; *The Clerk's Tale*; *The Squire's Tale*; *Fall of Princes*

We must pay attention to style, not as being right, but necessary.

Aristotle, *The Art of Rhetoric*, III.1.1404a[1]

[O]ne must examine what is fitting for an old man in the way that the scarlet cloak is appropriate for the young, for the same clothing is not suitable [for both].

Aristotle, *The Art of Rhetoric*, 3.1: 1405a[2]

THE ADVENT OF HUMAN MAKING surely marked the invention of style. Style is at root a series of repetitions that form a pattern. The human brain excels at noticing and classifying such patterns—the footprints of an animal species, or a rhizome characteristic of a plant genus, or the developmental stages of young children. As people began to make and decorate things (tools, clothes, paintings, carvings), they noticed habits and repetitions in each other's work, enabling them to identify

---

[1] This line is quoted from Eugene Garver's translation of the passage, in his "Aristotle's *Rhetoric* in Theory and Practice," in *The Oxford Handbook of Rhetorical Studies*, ed. Michael J. MacDonald (Oxford: Oxford University Press, 2017), 133–41 (138). Robert Bartlett's translation of the same passage reads "one should be concerned with [diction], not on the grounds that it is correct to do so, but on the grounds that it is necessary." See *Aristotle's Art of Rhetoric*, trans. Robert C. Bartlett (Chicago: University of Chicago Press, 2019), 158.

[2] *Aristotle's Art of Rhetoric*, trans. Bartlett, 162. Bartlett explains that the "scarlet cloak" refers to military garb worn by the Spartans and Persians, which would be appropriate for a young man but not an old man.

(for example) flint knappers' characteristic hammer impressions and thus their "styles." Noticing a pattern, however, is not the same as developing a theory. Not until classical Greece does a theory of style emerge in the West. That theory centers on the human arts of writing and speech. One of its central elements is Aristotle's notion of aptness (*to prepon*), captured in the simile of the scarlet cloak above, in which adornment is linked to age by being "fitting" or "appropriate."[3] This concept of aptness or *to prepon* highlights the connection between human expressivity—in writing, speech, clothing—and its sociality, the ways in which it conforms to or resists social norms. In part, it is the notion of *to prepon* that produces style's remarkable conceptual portability; style easily attaches to (is appropriate to, is fitting for) other ideas, such as "period," "nation," "genre," "gender," and the like. This conceptual promiscuity has made style both ubiquitous and elusive. To define style thus requires language sufficiently abstract to capture its vagaries. At minimum, style refers to a *mode or manner of human behavior or artifice*. It is a *way of acting or doing* that is *visible to an audience as a rule or pattern*.[4]

As a concept, style presents a conundrum something like the "wave-particle" structure of light: style refers both to a generalizing idea (like "Ricardian style" or "mathematical style") and to something particular (an individual's style, which is distinctive and unique to her or him or them). At times, it means both things at once. When we say about a person, "she is so stylish," we are referring both to a characteristic that distinguishes her from the ordinary and to the way in which this person identifies herself as part of a group (i.e., the stylish people, who wear

[3] A very helpful discussion of Book III of Aristotle's *Rhetoric* appears in Stephen Halliwell, "Style and Sense in Aristotle's *Rhetoric*, Bk. 3," *Revue internationale de philosophie* 47 (1993): 50–69. John Walt Burkett's dissertation, "Aristotle, *Rhetoric* 3: A Commentary" (Texas Christian University, 2011), contains a useful discussion of *to prepon* and its role in Aristotle's discussion of style; see 56–59, 64.

[4] A wide range of works on style in art history, critical theory, literary criticism, and even mathematics has influenced my formulation here; I cite only the most significant, including Charles Altieri, "Style," in *The Oxford Handbook of Philosophy and Literature*, ed. Richard Eldridge (Oxford: Oxford University Press, 2009), 420–41; Alfred Gell, *Art and Agency: An Anthropological Theory* (Oxford: Oxford University Press, 1998); Fredric Jameson, *Marxism and Form: Twentieth-Century Dialectical Theories of Literature* (Princeton: Princeton University Press, 1971); Leonard B. Meyer, "Toward a Theory of Style," in *The Concept of Style*, ed. Berel Lang (Ithaca: Cornell University Press, 1979), 21–71; D. A. Miller, *Jane Austen; or, The Secret of Style* (Princeton: Princeton University Press, 2003); Heinrich Wölfflin, *Principles of Art History*, trans. M. D. Hottinger (New York: Holt, 1932); Richard Wollheim, "Pictorial Style: Two Views," in Lang, *The Concept of Style*, 183–204.

the latest styles). Being stylish suggests both that she has a personal style and that she follows the dictates of fashion. Because style refers both to the general and the particular, it is an especially powerful concept with which to think about art. It allows us to make both historical and formal claims at the same time. To identify a period style or regional style or international style is to characterize art in historical terms. It is to suggest that art produced at a certain place or time is distinctive, with specific qualities that are linked to its context. At the same time, the history of style in a given period is a history of forms: the distinctive ways in which forms, patterns, and techniques are deployed over the course of time in a particular place. Thus we might say that the flying buttress is a feature of Gothic architectural style, along with pointed arches and rose windows. Similarly, the style of an individual artist consists of techniques and habits distinctive to her work. Those formal characteristics emerge from the elements of her particular history—the sum total of events, observations, ideas, and art to which she has been exposed—as they intersect with what might be called "big" history: those forms and contexts that define an epoch or a place.

The idea that there exists a style distinctive to particular writers, self-evident as it may seem, has not always obtained; as I will show, the notion of style was substantially in flux in the later Middle Ages, oscillating between a fixed and general understanding of style derived from classical rhetoric and a new model in which style was attached to particular writers. This latter model is commonly associated with popular narratives of western cultural history that identify the Renaissance as the moment at which modern individualism (in art, in philosophy, in politics, and more) came to the fore. Hence the renaming of the field "early modern," to reflect the unbroken history of the western subject after Shakespeare. There have been many corrections to and amendments of this narrative by medievalists, beginning with scholars such as Lee Patterson and David Aers.[5] At the same time, it is important not to become

---

[5] See Lee Patterson, *Chaucer and the Subject of History* (Madison: University of Wisconsin Press, 1992); David Aers, "A Whisper in the Ear of the Early Modernists; or, Reflections on Literary Critics Writing the History of the Subject," in *Culture and History, 1350–1600: Essays on English Communities, Identities, and Writings*, ed. Aers (New York: Harvester Wheatsheaf, 1992), 177–202. There have been so many of these corrections—ranging from whispers to shouts—that the field collectively wondered how a distinguished professor could rehearse that narrative as late as 2011. See Stephen Greenblatt, *The Swerve: How the World Became Modern* (New York: W. W. Norton, 2011).

so busy countering narratives of Renaissance exceptionalism that we forget what is distinctive about the medieval period. Examining the notion of style provides a vivid illustration of the unevenness of cultural change—the way in which modernity can flash up at one early moment and be gone for decades, or an early writer can, *sui generis*, produce a concept that later writers can hardly grasp. It is always tempting to challenge the narrative of Renaissance subjectivity by drawing a straight line from these early manifestations of change to later instances of their fulfillment. But doing so ignores the meandering nature of historical and cultural change—what might be called its "sinuosity," a term used in the study of rivers: the greater the sinuosity, the more the river meanders to get from the top to the bottom of the valley.[6] The general direction remains downward (or forward, in the case of history), but the flow at any given point on the river might seem to be traveling backward or sideways. Style is a case in point. Its conceptual development moves in a general direction, toward the notion of "personal style" or "a writer's unique style"—but not without various meanders that include a range of other definitions and uses.

The trajectory of this essay mirrors the sinuosity of style's development: it proceeds in a general way toward a specific goal, but with a number of digressions that map the unevenness of stylistic change. The larger picture that I paint here has been aided by various techniques of computer-based analysis, which I couple with more traditional close readings of English poets as they meander through the stylistic landscape of the later Middle Ages. Right from the start, I wish to thank my research assistant, Imogen Forbes-Macphail, a graduate student at Berkeley and occasional medievalist, who is currently working on a dissertation in the Victorian period. Imogen put together a database of 279 Middle English texts, forming a digital corpus that allowed us to ask a variety of questions about style and related concepts (for a complete list of the texts in the corpus, see Appendix I). I have also been working with Professor Larry Benson's Middle English Glossarial Database, which Professor Christopher Cannon kindly shared with me. That database includes the complete corpora of Chaucer and Gower, which have been tagged for parts of speech. This tagging enables a variety of

---

[6]See the definition of "sinuosity" as the "ratio of stream length to valley length" offered by the Environmental Protection Agency at their "Watershed Academy Web," under "Fundamentals of Rosgen Stream Classification System," https://cfpub.epa.gov /watertrain/moduleFrame.cfm?parent_object_id = 1265 (accessed April 2, 2019).

searches related to style. Professor Benson's database is one of the many valuable gifts he gave to Middle English scholars during his career; I hope that this essay repays him in some small way for his generosity to the field.

Developing a digital database of primary texts makes certain questions possible, most of which are based on the ordinary search function: text-analysis software is very good at advanced searches and at turning the results of such searches into visual form. As a result, I was able to map the use of the word *style* over the course of the four centuries included in our database (thirteenth–sixteenth), which produced the graph shown in Figure 1. As in all digital humanities scholarship, the real work lies in the preparation of the data; each text had to be accurately dated (as far as possible) so that the corpus could be subdivided into groups based on date. As a general principle, the date of composition for each text was preferred, though some exceptions were made when a manuscript date was the only temporal information available. The texts were grouped by quarter-centuries, so that 13a refers to any date between 1300 and 1324, 13b refers to 1325–49, and so on. Using a program available on the web called Voyant, I searched the corpus for the word *style* and its variants, using the spelling variations in both the *MED* and the *OED*.[7] In the resulting graph, the horizontal axis records

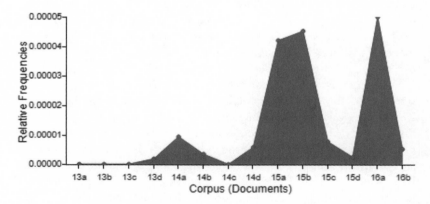

Fig. 1. The relative frequencies of "style" in the Forbes-Macphail Middle English Corpus, plotted over time, from 1300 to 1550, using the following list of variants: style|stile|styles|stiles|styele|styeles|styill|styills. The graph was created using Voyant Tools (https://voyant-tools.org/).

[7] Voyant is available here: http://docs.voyant-tools.org/ (accessed July 6, 2019). The site includes documentation and instructions for downloading and using the software.

the date of each group of texts chronologically, from 13a to 16b, while the vertical axis indicates the relative frequency at which *style* occurs in the corpus at a given point in time.[8] Voyant found 165 occurences of the term *style* in the database, as follows: 13d-1, 14a-4, 14b-3, 14c-0, 14d-10, 15a-48, 15b-63, 15c-13, 15d-2, 16a-19, 16b-2. As a point of comparison, I searched for the very similar word *manner* (using only the six most common variants: maner|maners|manere|maneres|manner|manners), which yielded 9,962 hits. "Style," therefore, represents only 1.63 percent of the total occurrences of *style* and *manner* together, making it a comparatively rare word in later Middle English.

This rarity must be kept in mind when the graphic result is analyzed, particularly because most of the occurences of *style* can be attributed to a tiny handful of writers. There are three peaks on the graph: the first, in the first quarter of the fourteenth century, represents 4 appearances of *style* in *Cursor mundi*. The second peak begins to rise at 14d and reaches its apex between 15a and 15b. This rise corresponds to the appearance of *style* in Chaucer's poetry and the subsequent efflorescence of *style* in Lydgate's oeuvre: 27/48 (56 percent) of the *style* occurrences in 15a can be found in Lydgate's poetry; even more dramatically, he is responsible for 49/59 (83 percent) of the *style* occurrences in 15b. The final peak, with 19 hits, includes 10 occurrences in Skelton's poetry, as well as occurrences in Barclay, Douglas, Dunbar, Wyatt, Rastell, and Watson.

The graph provides a portrait of a word as it emerges in language over several centuries; it is a top-down view that allows for some initial

---

For more information and analysis of Voyant, see Stéfan Sinclair and Geoffrey Rockwell, *Hermeneutica: Computer-Assisted Interpretation in the Humanities* (Boston, Mass.: MIT Press, 2016), as well as their website, http://hermeneuti.ca/ (accessed July 6, 2019). Some variants were eliminated after the initial search because the hits in our database for those variants were false positives (i.e., they meant something other than the literary "style"). In the following list, those variants that we eliminated are in bold; the remaining variants (style|stile|styles|stiles|styele|styeles|styill|styills) are in regular type. See *OED*, s.v. *style* (n. and v.): ME steyele, **styyl, stele, ME–15 still, ME stiel, styll**, ME–15 styill, **15 steill**, stylle, **15–16 steele**, ME–18 stile, ME– style; also 15–18 stile, 15 **Scottish styell**, 16 still(e, **Scottish stylle**, (17 **past participle stilen**). *MED*, s.v. *stile* (n.[2]): stīle . . . also **stīl, stille, stiel(e, stēl(e & (error) syill**.

[8] Note that the quarter-century spans represented by the points on the graph have variable numbers of texts in the database; some quarter-centuries have many more texts than others. Thus, Voyant calculates the *relative* frequency of occurrences of *style*, as shown by the vertical axis of the graph, on the left. It is worth noting that, even though we have compensated for the uneven distribution of data by using relative frequencies, the relative paucity of material in the earlier years does make the results for those years somewhat less reliable.

and very general conclusions about style that are based solely on frequency: how often and by whom the word is used. It also depends on the premise that the word *style* indexes an emergent concept: that when writers choose it, they are referring to a specific idea that is developing in Middle English, an idea that morphs and changes as the word is used and reused over time. Word-counting software can sketch the outlines of that idea, but in order to understand its development fully, we must descend from the bird's-eye vantage of the graph and look at individual uses, appropriations, and citations. The graph tells us that something is happening to the concept of style in the later Middle Ages; determining what that something might be requires something like a worm's-eye view: the view from inside and underneath the literary tradition.

To fully understand style from the bottom up, we must begin with traditional accounts of its meaning in Middle English. There is a long-standing assumption that the notion of style meaning "individual style" came into being in the sixteenth century as a result of the rediscovery of classical learning and the emergence of "self-fashioning" as a dominant concept.[9] Before that, style is presumed to refer to *stylus*, or pen (as in Trevisa's translation of Higden, "Seinte Barnabe his body was founde in a den . . . with þe gospel of Mathew þat he hadde i-write wiþ his owne stile"[10]); to the notion of style found in rhetorical handbooks (i.e., the levels of style from high to moderate to low), to which Chaucer refers in his mention of Petrarch in the *Clerk's Prologue*: "I seye that first with heigh stile he enditeth, / Er he the body of his tale writeth, / A prohemye";[11] and to "a step or set of steps for passing over a fence or wall,"

---

[9] A recent surge of interest in Renaissance eloquence and style has produced a number of revisionary studies; none, however, addresses the links between medieval style and early modern style. See Nancy Christiansen, *Figuring Style: The Legacy of Renaissance Rhetoric* (Columbia: University of South Carolina Press, 2013); Jeff Dolven, *Senses of Style: Poetry before Interpretation* (Chicago: University of Chicago Press, 2017); Sean Keilen, *Vulgar Eloquence* (New Haven: Yale University Press, 2006); Jenny Mann, *Outlaw Rhetoric: Figuring Vernacular Eloquence in Shakespeare's England* (Ithaca: Cornell University Press, 2012); Carla Mazzio, *The Inarticulate Renaissance: Language Trouble in an Age of Eloquence* (Philadelphia: University of Pennsylvania Press, 2009); Catherine Nicholson, *Uncommon Tongues: Eloquence and Eccentricity in the English Renaissance* (Philadelphia: University of Pennsylvania Press, 2014).

[10] *Polychronicon Ranulphi Higden monachi Cestrensis: Together with the English Translations of John of Trevisa and of an Unknown writer of the Fifteenth Century*, ed. Churchill Babington and Joseph R. Lumby, 9 vols, Vol. 5, Rolls Series 41 (London: Longman, 1865–66), 297.

[11] *CIT*, IV.41–43, in *The Riverside Chaucer*, gen. ed. Larry D. Benson, 3rd ed. (Boston, Mass.: Houghton Mifflin, 1987); further Chaucer citations are to this edition and are given in the text by fragment and line number or by title, book number, and line number.

which appears in the Squire's self-deprecating description of the marvelous knight who visits Cambuskyan's court: "Al be that I kan nat sowne his stile / Ne kan nat clymben over so heigh a style" (*SqT*, V.105–6).

The *MED* offers three further definitions of style: "a piece of written discourse . . . The subject matter of such a work, theme," as in *Cursor mundi*, "Now is good to go to oure style / Þat we haue left of a whyle / And turne to oure story aȝeyn;[12] "a way of life, manner, demeanor; also, behavior, conduct," as in Hoccleve's *Regiment of Princes*: "Allas, that kynges nobleye / Torne sholde into style of tirannye!" (4024);[13] and "a formal designation or title; also, the appellation defining a person's function or status," as in Fortescue's *Declaration*, "the said Kynge Charles shuld haue . . . the dignitie, stile, and name of Kinge of Fraunce."[14] These latter two definitions are suggestive because they discriminate between the behavior of an individual and an individual's official status or social function, both of which are grouped under the rubric "style."

The earliest uses of *style* reveal quite a lot about the way in which the term developed its English meaning. They demonstrate its origin in metonymy; since *style* comes from *stylus*, an instrument for writing, it is at root a literary term. Literary style predates the other kinds of style with which we are familiar—fashion, art, governance, and so on—and its early uses in English clarify precisely how this instrumental Latin term expanded over time to become a concept, with all of the flexibility of application that a concept implies.[15] I haven't forgotten the fact that *style* is a rhetorical term with a long history in Latin, but prior to the late fourteenth century, that rhetorical history is largely absent from

[12] *The Southern Version of Cursor mundi*, Vol. 1, ed. Sarah M. Horrall (Ottawa: University of Ottawa Press, 1978), p. 314, lines 8509–10.

[13] Thomas Hoccleve, *Hoccleve's "Regiment of Princes,"* ed. Charles Blyth (Kalamazoo: Medieval Institute Publications, 1999), lines 4024–25.

[14] Sir John Fortescue, *The Declaration Made by John Fortescu, Knyght, upon Certayn Wrytings Sent oute of Scotteland, ayenst the Kinges Title to the Roialme of Englond*, in *The Works of Sir John Fortescue, Knight, Chief Justice of England and Lord Chancellor to King Henry the Sixth*, ed. Thomas [Fortescue] Lord Clermont (London: Chiswick Press, 1869), 523–42 (529).

[15] For a comprehensive account of the process by which *stilus* was transformed into a prescriptive literary term—defining a specific mode of writing governed by rules—then expanded to a wide variety of human endeavors (art history in particular) in the eighteenth century, and subsequently (in the nineteenth century) into a term that defined a chronological phenomenon (a period style), and finally into a modern term meaning "originality; distinctiveness," see Willibald Sauerländer, "From Stilus to Style: Reflections on the Fate of a Notion," *Art History* 6, no. 3 (1983): 253–70.

English texts. Instead, we have a series of early appearances in *Cursor mundi*.[16]

> Grace haþ ȝyuen hir ȝiftis ȝore
> To vche dyuerse of þese bifore
> Matheu wroot al in ebru
> Þese oþere þre al in gru
> **Þe stile of Matheu watir was**
> And wyne þe lettre of lucas
> Marcus pagyn was like mylke
> And Iones hony swete as silke.[17]

In this passage, "stile" is being used as the tenor or ground of a metaphor: the writing of each of the four evangelists is compared with something to drink: Matthew's stylus to water; Luke's letter to wine; Mark's page to milk; and John's page to honey, "sweet as silk." This context makes it clear that "stile" refers to a writing instrument, which is parallel with letters and pages. In another passage, "style" metonymically refers to narrative:

> **Now is good to go to oure style**
> **Þat we haue left of a whyle**
> And turne to oure story aȝeyn
> To make hit hool & certeyn
> Dauid þat I red of here
> Was kyng & regned fourty ȝere.[18]

By extension, the stylus becomes the literary text; "going to our style" means returning to the main story from a digression. But even here,

---

[16] A quick note on the date of *Cursor mundi*: there are two manuscript traditions, one early and northern, the other later and southern. The *MED* cites the text by manuscript; in the EETS edition, four early manuscripts were printed in parallel. See *Cursor mundi (The Cursur of the World): A Northumbrian Poem of the XIVth Century in Four Versions*, ed. Max Kaluza, Heinrich Hupe, Hugo Carl Wilhelm Haenisch, and Richard Morris (London: K. Paul, Trench, Trübner, 1874–93). Our database includes the text of the Cotton Vespasian A.III manuscript, which I searched for appearances of *style* and its variant spellings. I also searched the five-volume Ottawa edition of the southern manuscripts for *style*, and turned up only one quotation that did not also appear in Cotton Vespasian A.III. For simplicity's sake, I have used quotations from the southern text. It should be remembered, however, that these quotations represent early fourteenth-century uses of the word.

[17] *The Southern Version of Cursor mundi*, Vol. 4, ed. Peter H. J. Mous (Ottawa: University of Ottawa Press, 1986), pp. 130–31, lines 21289–96.

[18] *The Southern Version of Cursor mundi*, Vol. 1, ed. Horrall, p. 314, lines 8509–14.

"style" specifically refers to *stylus*. The preceding passage describes how Solomon sits under David's tree, writing the sacred texts of Ecclesiastes, Proverbs, and Canticles, next to a marble stone inscribed with a writ that explains that the tree, which was the Tree of Life in Eden, will become Christ's cross. The *Cursor* poet describes the story of Adam and the tree-as-cross being "written in parchment," before saying "Now is good to go to *our* stylus"—as opposed to the pens of Solomon and the writer of the story of the tree.

The final example from *Cursor mundi* takes up the meaning defined by the *MED* as "formal designation or title":

> He is mon & makeþ him god
> to make men Ieue his wyle
> **He is no god nor goddis sone**
> **of him knowe we Þe stile.**[19]

In this scene two pardoners are indicting Jesus to Pilate, complaining that he has made himself a God to make men believe his tricks or deceptions. They say, "he is no God or God's son / of them we know the style"—i.e., we know the titles "God" and "God's son," and this man Jesus cannot claim them. "Stile" in this sense is a metonym for "stylus." It comes to have this meaning in official documents, when a king signs with a stylus and thereby "styles" himself with his title, king.

These three early uses of the term *style* illustrate the metonymic process by which the Latin word meaning "pen" expanded to include other meanings, such as "literary composition" and "formal title." Later in the fourteenth century, and especially in the fifteenth, that metonymic expansion continues. Chaucer uses the term *style* seven times in his oeuvre, all in the *Canterbury Tales*. Three of those uses refer to the kind of "stile" that is constructed over a fence, the first from *The Pardoner's Tale*:

> Whan they han goon nat fully half a mile,
> Right as they wolde han troden over a stile,
> An oold man and a povre with hem mette.
>
> (VI.711–13)

[19] *The Southern Version of Cursor mundi*, Vol. 3, ed. Henry J. Stauffenberg (Ottawa: University of Ottawa Press, 1985), p. 107, lines 16079–82.

And the second from the Thopas:

> Into his sadel he clamb anon,
> And priketh over stile and stoon
> An elf-queene for t'espye.
> (VII.797–99)

The third reference to a farmer's stile appears in *The Squire's Tale*, in tandem with a reference to rhetorical style. The other three uses of the word appear in *The Clerk's Tale*. These four uses of *style* in *The Squire's Tale* and *The Clerk's Tale* are all modified by the adjective *high*, as in "high style." The first of these uses appears early in *The Clerk's Prologue*, when the Host specifies the style in which the Clerk should tell his tale:

> Telle us som murie thyng of aventures.
> Your termes, youre colours, and your figures,
> Keepe hem in stoor til so be ye endite
> **Heigh style, as whan that men to kynges write.**
> Speketh so pleyn at this tyme, we yow preye,
> That we may understonde what ye seye.
> (IV.15–20)

The Host contrasts the high style with the plain style, describing the former as the style in which men write to kings and the latter as a style the pilgrims can understand. This use of the term "high style" marks a distinct shift from *Cursor mundi*'s uses of style. Chaucer clearly is familiar with the rhetorical tradition based on the works of Horace, Cicero, and Quintilian, which produced medieval poetic handbooks like Geoffrey of Vinsauf's *Poetria nova*. [20] He alludes to passages from Geoffrey twice, in Book I of *Troilus and Criseyde* (1065–71) and in *The Nun's Priest's Tale*. In this latter allusion, Chaucer parodies Geoffrey's lament for King Richard by writing a similarly histrionic lament for Chaunticleer in the

---

[20] Cicero, *Rhetorica ad Herennium*, trans. Harry Caplan (Cambridge, Mass.: Harvard University Press, 1954); Cicero, *Brutus: Orator*, ed. H. M. Hubbell, trans. G. L. Hendrickson (Cambridge, Mass.: Harvard University Press, 1939); Cicero, *On the Orator*, books I–II (Cambridge, Mass.: Harvard University Press, 1942); Horace, *Satires; Epistles; The Art of Poetry*, ed. and trans. H. Rushton Fairclough (Cambridge, Mass.: Harvard University Press, 1926); Quintilian, *Institutio oratoria*, trans. Harold Edgeworth Butler (Cambridge, Mass.: Harvard University Press, 1920–22). See also Geoffrey of Vinsauf, *Poetria nova*, trans. Margaret F. Nims (Toronto: Pontifical Institute of Mediaeval Studies, 2010).

high style (VII.3347–74). The high style to which the Host refers, with its colors, terms, and figures, is thus the Ciceronian grand style—precisely the style in which one writes to and about kings and rulers.

The Clerk responds to the Host's demand by saying, "I am under youre yerde" (IV.22), suggesting that he intends to write in the plain style. But right away he reveals that he will tell a tale he learned from a "worthy clerk" in Padua, "Fraunceys Petrak, the lauriat poete," whose "rethorike sweete / Enlumyned al Ytaille of poetrie" (IV.27–33). Petrarch, says the clerk, wrote the "prohemye" of his tale in the high style: "I seye that first with heigh stile he enditeth / Er he the body of his tale writeth / A prohemye" (IV.41–43).

This second reference to "style," as well as the introduction of Petrarch, marks a new development in the evolution of the concept in English. Petrarch writes extensively in his letters about style, including in the letter that contains the story of Griselda, in which he explains that his revision of Boccaccio's version of the story "retells it in another style":

Hanc historiam **stilo nunc alio** retexere visum fuit, non tam ideo, ut matronas nostri temporis ad imitandam huius uxoris pacienciam, que michi vix mutabilis videtur, quam ut legentes ad imitandam saltem femine constanciam excitarem, ut quod hec viro suo prestitit, hoc prestare deo nostro audeant.

[I decided to retell this story **in another** {style} not so much to encourage the married women of our day to imitate this wife's patience, which to me seems hardly imitable, as to encourage the readers to imitate at least this woman's constancy, so that what she maintained toward her husband they may maintain toward our God.][21]

Chaucer's adaptation of this passage, at the very end of *The Clerk's Tale*, pointedly includes its reference to style. The Clerk explains that

[21] Francis Petrarch, *Seniles*, XVII.3, printed in *Sources and Analogues of the "Canterbury Tales,"* Vol. 1, ed. Robert Correale and Mary Hamel (Cambridge: D. S. Brewer, 2002), 129. The translation is taken from Francis Petrarch, *Letters of Old Age*, Vol. 2, trans. Aldo S. Bernardo, Saul Leven, and Reta A. Bernardo (Baltimore: Johns Hopkins University Press, 1992), XVII.3. Bernardo et al. translate "stilo . . . alio" as "in another language," but though the translation is literally true (Petrarch translates Boccaccio's Italian into Latin), it does not give the true sense of "stilus"; see Charlton T. Lewis and Charles Short, *A Latin Dictionary: Founded on Andrew's Edition of Freund's Latin Dictionary* (1879; repr., Oxford: Clarendon Press, 1975), s.v. *stilus*, for the range of meanings for this word, including "pen" (II.A); "composing, composition . . . manner of writing, mode of composition" (II.B.1); "manner of speaking, mode of expression, style [in speaking]" (II.B.2). "Language" is not included.

Petrarch wrote the story not to suggest that women imitate Griselda, but to encourage all people to be "constant in adversitee" (IV.1146). He concludes with the third and final reference to "style" in the tale, which reiterates the point that Petrarch and style go together: "therfore Petrak writeth / This storie, which with heigh stile he enditeth" (IV.1147–48).

The Clerk's Tale is thus framed by two ideas: first that style refers to mode of writing, and second that there are multiple styles at work in the *Canterbury Tales*. By linking the notion of style to Petrarch, Chaucer both introduces the Ciceronian levels of style and begins to suggest that style has some relation to individual choice. As I will show in a moment, Petrarch comments in a crucial passage on the idea of individual style in relation to the imitation of past poets. That idea is lurking in Chaucer's final reference to style, which occurs when the Squire describes the speech of the knight who visits Cambuskyan's court:

> He with a manly voys seide his message,
> After the forme used in his langage,
> Withouten vice of silable or of lettre;
> And for his tale sholde seme the bettre,
> Accordant to his wordes was his cheere,
> As techeth art of speche hem that it leere.
> **Al be that I kan nat sowne his stile,**
> **Ne kan nat clymben over so heigh a style,**
> Yet seye I this, as to commune entente:
> Thus muche amounteth al that evere he mente,
> If it so be that I have it in mynde.
>
> (IV.99–109)

The Squire's pun on "style" is also a metaphor: we know the knight speaks in the high style because imitating it is compared to climbing over a high stile. The verticality inherent in the notion of stylistic levels from low to high is made real, expressed through the concrete image of climbing up steps and over a fence. The metaphor reminds us that a farmer's stile is also a border, a means of transgressing the boundary between one field and another. The Squire uses the phrase "climbing over" to describe the act of imitating the knight—going up and over the boundary between his speech and the knight's speech, which we recall is in a different language: the knight speaks "After the forme used in his langage." The style is both the border to be crossed and the means of crossing the border; if the speaker can climb high enough, he can move from one field to another, one language to another. The act of translation is also a stylistic act; not just the words, but their style, must cross over into the target language.

This claim might broadly be classed under the rubric of "decorum," the notion from classical rhetoric that the style of speech must be appropriate to the content, audience, and occasion.[22] The Squire has been reading rhetorical handbooks, like Geoffrey's *Poetria nova*, which gives instructions not only for rhetorical composition, but also for delivery—the "art of speche." Geoffrey explains: "In reciting aloud, let three tongues speak: let the first be that of the mouth, the second that of the speaker's countenance, and the third that of gesture. . . . The outward emotion corresponds with the inward; outer and inner man are affected alike."[23] This model of oratory, ultimately derived from Cicero and Quintilian, links the words of an oration to the demeanor of the speaker, arguing that they must be in accord in order for speech to be effective.[24] In Geoffrey's words, the "outward emotion corresponds with the inward," or in the Squire's, "Accordant to his wordes was his cheere." The connection made between a speaker's facial expression and his style of speaking is a key building block for the notion of an individual style, a style as unique to a writer as his face. This claim is not a teleological claim, with the idea of personal style as its end point; it is rather a claim about what can be thought and imagined at a given moment in time. When a writer like Chaucer uses the word *style* only four times, each time modified by the word *high*, it is clear that he means to highlight something specific—in this case, both the rhetorical tradition as the Clerk and Squire understand it and the humanist thought of Petrarch.

Petrarch offers a notion of individual style in a letter on literary invention written to Tommaso da Messina, which he begins by invoking Seneca's famous bee simile for literary invention and Macrobius's failure to

---

[22] Quintilian, *Institutio oratoria*, XI.1.57, p. 189.

[23] Geoffrey of Vinsauf, *Poetria nova*, 78–79.

[24] Quintilian, *Instituto oratoria*, XI.3, p. 281: "Nor is it wonderful that gesture which depends on various forms of movement should have such power, when pictures, which are silent and motionless, penetrate into our innermost feelings with such power that at times they seem more eloquent than language itself. On the other hand, if gesture and the expression of the face are out of harmony with the speech, if we look cheerful when our words are sad, or shake our heads when making a positive assertion, our words will not only lack weight, but will fail to carry conviction."

grasp its import.[25] Macrobius fails because he lacks an individual style: he does not transform Seneca's words (the flowers) into his own words (the wax and honey made by bees), but instead inserts Seneca's language unchanged into his text. Petrarch further argues:

This much however I affirm, that it is a sign of greater elegance and skill for us, in imitation of the bees, to produce in our own words thoughts borrowed from others. To repeat, let us write neither in the style of one or another writer but in a **style uniquely ours** although gathered from a variety of sources. That writer is happier who does not, like the bees, collect a number of scattered things, but instead, after the example of certain not much larger worms from whose body silk is produced, prefers to produce his own thoughts and speech— provided that the sense is serious and true and that his style is ornate.[26]

Whether or not Chaucer knew this particular letter, the image of bees gathering pollen and making wax and honey was familiar to English readers; Gower cites it as an image of writing in Book II of the *Vox*

---

[25] "Apes, ut aiunt, debemus imitari, quae vagantur et flores ad mel faciendum idoneos carpunt, deinde quicquid attulere, disponunt ac per favos digerunt et, ut Vergilius noster ait, liquentia mella / Stipant et dulci distendunt nectare cellas. . . . nos quoque has apes debemus imitari et quaecumque ex diversa lectione congessimus, separare, melius enim distincta servantur, deinde adhibita ingenii nostri cura et facultate in unum saporem varia illa libamenta confundere, ut etiam si apparuerit, unde sumptum sit, aliud tamen esse quam unde sumptum est, appareat" ("We should follow, men say, the example of the bees, who flit about and cull the flowers that are suitable for producing honey, and then arrange and assort in their cells all that they have brought in; these bees, as our Vergil says, 'pack close the flowing honey, / And swell their cells with nectar sweet' (*Aeneid*, i.432f.). . . . We also, I say, ought to copy these bees, and sift whatever we have gathered from a varied course of reading, for such things are better preserved if they are kept separate; then, by applying the supervising care with which our nature has endowed us,—in other words, our natural gifts,—we should so blend those several flavours into one delicious compound that, even though it betrays its origin, yet it nevertheless is clearly a different thing from that whence it came"). Seneca, *Moral Letters to Lucilius*, Vol. 2, trans. Richard Mott Gummere (Cambridge, Mass.: Harvard University Press, 1920), letter 84.

[26] Emphasis added. The Latin reads: "Sed illud affirmo, elegantioris esse solertiae ut, apium imitatores, nostris verbis, quamvis aliorum hominum, sententias proferamus. Rursus, nec huius stilum aut illius, sed unum nostrum conflatum ex pluribus habemus. Felicius quidem non apoum more passim sparsa colligere, sed quorumdam haud multo maiorum vermium exemplo, quorum ex visceribus sericum prodit, ex se ipso sapere potius et loqui, dummodo et sensus gavis ac verus, et sermo esset ornatus." See Francisci Petrarcae, *Epistolae de rebus familiaribus et variae*, ed. Iosephi Fracassetti (Florence: Felicis le Monnier, 1859), letter VII, pp. 58–59. For the English translation, see Francisco Petrarch, *Letters on Familiar Matters I–VIII*, trans. Aldo S. Bernardo (New York: Italica Press, 2014), Vol. 1, letter VIII.

clamantis.[27] Petrarch's insistence on the writer's "own thoughts and speech" as the measure of his poetry's quality—its elegance and skill—demonstrates that the notion of a unique style, particular to a given writer, was in the air as Chaucer wrote. He may not have used the word *style* in this way, but his references to Petrarch's writing about the concept show that it was available and thinkable for him.

Chaucer and Gower

It is a critical commonplace that Chaucer and Gower have markedly different styles of writing. Gower refers to *style* only once in the *Confessio Amantis* and his use of the term seems to harken back to *Cursor mundi*, rather than to embrace the Petrarchan model we saw in the *Canterbury Tales*. At the start of Book I, Gower comments on his enterprise in this way:

> I may noght strecche up to the hevene
> Min hand, ne setten al in evene
> This world, which evere is in balance:
> It stant noght in my sufficance
> So grete thinges to compasse,
> Bot I mot lete it overpasse
> And treten upon othre thinges.
> **Forthi the stile of my writinges**
> Fro this day forth I thenke change
> And speke of thing is noght so strange.[28]

Gower's reference to "stile" seems to fit nicely under the rubric offered by the *MED*, definition 1(b), "a piece of writing. . . . Or the subject matter of that writing, its theme." He plans to turn to "other things. . . . And speke of something that is not so strange." But what are these other things? What does Gower identify as "strange"—meaning "foreign; unfamiliar, unknown, remote"?[29] He begins with an image of

[27] "Lectus ut est variis florum de germine fauus . . . Doctorum veterum mea carmina fortificando / Pluribus exemplis scripta fuisse reor" (As the honey is gathered from the bud of various flowers . . . I think that my poems were written with the support of many examples from learned men of old). John Gower, *Vox clamantis*, II.Prol.78, in *The Complete Works of John Gower*, Vol. 4, *The Latin Works*, ed. G. C. Macaulay (Oxford: Clarendon Press, 1902).

[28] *John Gower: Confessio Amantis*, Vol. 1, ed. Russell Peck (Kalamazoo: Medieval Institute Publications, 2000), 1–10 (emphasis added).

[29] *MED*, s.v. *straunge*, def. 2(a).

height—"I may not stretch my hand up to the heavens"—which invokes a hierarchy of subjects, with "great things" up in the heavens, while "other things" are down below. "Great things" are "strange things"; turning away from "great things" is defined as "speaking of things not so strange"—in other words, "strange things" are things divine and far away, not of this earth.

Gower's use of "strange" to begin the *Confessio* recalls two passages in which Chaucer invokes the idea of "strangeness" as a way of introducing a poetic work. In Book II of *Troilus and Criseyde*, Chaucer's invocation links love, speech, and strangeness:

> Ye knowe ek that in forme of speche is chaunge
> Withinne a thousand yeer, and wordes tho
> That hadden pris, now wonder nyce and straunge
> Us thinketh hem, and yet thei spake hem so.
> And spedde as wel in love as men now do;
> Ek for to wynnen love in sondry ages,
> In sondry londes, sondry ben usages.
>
> (*TC*, II.22–28)

Like the *Confessio Amantis*, *Troilus and Criseyde* is about love. But love and speech in the former are familiar and universal, while in the latter they are historically contingent, changeable entities that become strange with the passing of time. Chaucer also invokes "strange things" at the start of the *Canterbury Tales*: "Than longeth folk to goon on pilgrimages / And palmeres for to seken straunge strondes" (I.12–13). The *Canterbury Tales* depict a pilgrimage; pilgrimages seek out the strange, much as the narrator in *Troilus and Criseyde* embraces the strangeness of the past. In contrast, Gower insists his work deals with the familiar, the day-to-day, the world that is close to home, not far away and "strange."

Chaucer links strangeness in love to strangeness in speech in *Troilus and Criseyde*. Gower similarly links the familiarity of love to a familiar and open kind of speech, which he identifies as "plein":

> I may you telle, if ye woll hiere,
> A wonder hap which me befell,
> That was to me bothe hard and fell,
> Touchende of love and his fortune,
> The which me liketh to comune

> **And pleinly for to telle it oute.**
> To hem that ben lovers aboute
> Fro point to point I wol declare
> And wryten of my woful care,
> Mi wofull day, my wofull chance,
> That men mowe take remembrance.
> (*Confessio Amantis*, I.66–76; emphasis added)

"Plein" is a word that appears many times in the *Confessio Amantis*; it is Gower's usual way of describing his mode of communication, or "telling it out." Coupled with his vertical image of the text descending from "strange" heavenly things to earthly "other things," Gower's reference to plainness clearly invokes the hierarchy of styles described by rhetoricians and evoked by Chaucer's references to Petrarch's high style. When Chaucer rewrites Petrarch he is clearly staking a claim for the vernacular as a medium for the high style; Petrarch revised Boccaccio's original from the vernacular into the Latin high style, thereby asserting the authority of Latin in the hierarchy of styles. When Chaucer revises Petrarch's revision, returning it to the vernacular, he translates its ornate, embellished quality into an equally ornate English style. But when Gower introduces his major English work by eschewing the "strange" and promising to speak "pleinly," his claim that he will "change the style of his writings" begins to look like an answer to this Petrarchan English mode—a rejection of the "straunge" that Chaucer embraces.

Computing Style

Up to this point, I have distinguished between Chaucer and Gower by examining their direct commentaries on style, which has suggested a familiar conclusion: Chaucer's style, at least at the moments in which he invokes the word *style*, is both courtly and Petrarchan—embellished, ornate, and high—while Gower's style is simple and plain. This observation is not new; it is to some extent a truism in Middle English literary criticism. In this section of the essay, I turn to an alternative means of assessing style: computer-based stylistics, also known as stylometry. Stylometry is the branch of the digital humanities that uses the power of the computer to study those features of literary style that are measurable: things like sentence length, vocabulary richness, and most frequent word usage. The last of these, most frequent word (MFW) usage, is typically used to determine author attributions, normally by comparing the works of multiple authors to the text whose authorship is in question. But you can also compare just two authors to see how distinct they are from each other, as I have done here for Chaucer and Gower (see Figure 2).

This graph was created using a program called Stylo for R, a stylometry program written for use with the R programming language, which

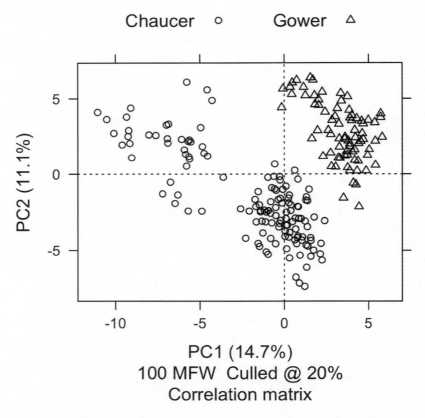

Fig. 2. The Middle English Glossarial Database was divided into 2,700-word chunks, which were labeled "Ch" or "Gow," based on the size of the smallest text (*Anelida and Arcite*). Chaucer's texts are represented by circles; Gower's texts are represented by triangles. Created using Stylo for R; an introduction to Stylo, with instructions for downloading the software package, can be found at https://sites.google.com/site/computationalstylistics/stylo.

performs unsupervised multivariate frequency analysis on a corpus or corpora of texts. In order to make the best possible comparisons, Chaucer and Gower's works were divided into chunks of 2,700 words, rather than relying on the variable sizes of different texts (*The Man of Law's Tale* versus *The Cook's Tale*, for example).[30] The 2,700-word chunks were labeled according to the following system. Gower's texts begin with "Gow," followed by the name of the individual poem and a number indicating which 2,700-word chunk is represented by the label; Chaucer's poetry begins with "Ch," followed by "P" for prose or "V" for verse, then the name of the individual text and a number (see Appendix II for a complete list of labels). We have chosen symbols for each poet: circles for Chaucer and triangles for Gower. Stylo uses the initial designation ("Gow" or "Ch") to assign the symbols to individual chunks, so it is easy to see which chunks cluster with which other chunks. For this search, we used the lemmas from the Middle English Glossarial Database, which eliminates the problem of variable spelling by substituting the dictionary headword for each occurrence of a given word.[31] As Figure 2 shows, Stylo has grouped Chaucer with Chaucer, and Gower with Gower. This grouping is not based on the program's recognition of different labels (i.e., Stylo does not automatically cluster "Gow" texts with other "Gow" texts and "Ch" texts with other "Ch" texts). Rather, Stylo first creates a list of MFWs; it then determines the frequencies of the MFWs in individual texts and normalizes them to create a final word list for analysis.[32] It then compares the results for individual texts and produces a graphic representation of the distances between texts, like the scatterplot in Figure 2.[33] That graph uses principal components analysis (PCA), which in the simplest terms allows a graph with many dimensions to be represented on two axes. The x and y axes do not refer to specific values; they

[30] The 2,700-word length was chosen based on the length of the shortest work under consideration, Chaucer's *Anelida and Arcite*, which allowed us to include the work as a separate text.

[31] The lemmatized corpora were used for all of the stylometry operations in this project involving MFW analyses; thus, any mention of MFWs in the Chaucer/Gower corpora in fact refers to "most frequent lemmas."

[32] What Stylo cannot account for is spelling variation or stylistic distinctions made on the basis of literary techniques. In the case of the Chaucer and Gower corpora, the problem of spelling variation has been solved for us by Larry Benson, who lemmatized the corpora, thereby producing standard spelling. Lemmatizing erases certain differences that are crucially important to medievalists, such as dialectal variation and syntactical choices; stylometric analysis cannot account for differences like these.

[33] Maciej Eder, Jan Rybicki, and Mike Kestemont, "Stylometry with R: A Package for Computational Text Analysis," *The R Journal* 8 (2016): 107–21.

are merely a way to visualize the distance between various texts. In other words, what matters in a graph like this are the relative distances between items, not their absolute positions on the graph.

This process adheres to one of the most basic principles of stylometry: the idea that authors distinguish themselves from other authors in their uses of small, non-load-bearing words, like "while" or "to" or "about." The "authorial signature" is thought to reside in these "function words" because they are less affected by the content of the work—its themes, perspectives, topics, and so on—than the words that represent the semantic heart of a text, largely nouns and verbs. As Hugh Craig and Arthur F. Kinney explain:

The heart of computational stylistics remains frequencies of common words. They are ubiquitous, abundant, and perform a wide range of syntactic functions. They can thus serve us as indicators of an unlimited range of stylistic effects, not as individual instances, but as a pattern or tendency, especially in combinations. . . . Common words account for most of the bulk of a text (typically, the fifty commonest words together represent three-quarters of all words used), but they are barely noticed by a reader, and might seem essentially only a framework for the rarer words, which are the ones we are conscious of. Most of the common words are function words, which have a grammatical job, and belong to closed classes that are only rarely added to. Lexical words by contrast have independent meaning and regularly go in and out of use.[34]

This notion of style is markedly different from the idea of style I examined in the previous section. I have already described the "wave-particle," individual versus general, problematic that characterizes the study of style. Stylometry raises a further definitional problem about style, in part because its primary use is for author attribution: distinguishing one author from another, resolving disputes about authorship, identifying the author of an unknown text, and the like. Stylometry's notion of an "authorial signature" that is revealed by function words conceals an important assumption about the relationship of writers to their style. That assumption might be summed up in a phrase attributed to the cubist painter George Braque, "One's style is one's inability to do

---

[34] Hugh Craig and Arthur F. Kinney, *Shakespeare, Computers, and the Mystery of Authorship* (Cambridge: Cambridge University Press, 2009), 12.

otherwise."[35] Or, in the words of Roland Barthes, "[S]tyle is always a secret . . . its secret is recollection locked within the body of the writer."[36] Both of these writers insist on the unintentional nature of style, the fact that it is unavailable to the writer herself. At the same time, it might fairly be objected that style, as literary criticism has traditionally understood it, depends entirely on intention: it is the very definition of a writer's self-conscious presentation as an artist. This meaning is encoded in the judgment that a work is "stylized" or "stylish," labels that point to a writer's self-aware performance of style.

Earlier in this essay, I suggested that style is a conundrum that sits on the axis between particular and general, between individual style and broader analytical notions of style. This distinction can now be made more precise by dividing each of these categories in two. The latter (broader notions of style) includes both *abstract style*—those considerations of style that are purely conceptual—and a series of more specific generalizations, as in a "period style," a "national style," a "gendered style," and so on. The former category, individual style, includes both *deep style* and *overt style*. *Deep style* is revealed by function words or other patterns, of which writers are not fully aware; it is the style on which author attributions in stylometry are based and the style theorized by writers like Barthes. *Overt style* denotes the self-conscious performance of style discernible in individual writers' works or oeuvres. Making these distinctions will enable the critical conversation about style to achieve a clarity that it has hitherto lacked; it will also enable interdisciplinary conversations among scholars working in fields whose presumptions about style differ (linguists, literary critics, art historians, architects, and so on), as well as conversations between practitioners, whose interest in overt style is particularly pointed, and those who analyze art, who often focus primarily on a general notion of style or on deep style.

Stylometry deals with deep style, because it relies on computing to see patterns that would be exceedingly difficult for individual persons to discern by reading texts. Another way to say this would be to say that human beings are distracted by content; computers are indifferent

---

[35] The source of this aphorism is somewhat mysterious; it was first quoted by the Australian writer Helen Garner, in her autobiographical "On Turning Fifty" (1992), in *True Stories: The Collected Short Non-Fiction* (Melbourne: Text Publishing, 2017), 157–60 (158). Craig and Kinney quote the phrase from Garner in their *Shakespeare, Computers, and the Mystery of Authorship*, 10.

[36] Roland Barthes, *Writing Degree Zero*, trans. Annette Lavers and Colin Smith (New York: Hill and Wang, 1967), 12.

to it. That indifference means that a software program does its work without preconceptions or nuance. Indeed, most of what stylometry does is simple counting: How often do certain words appear? What are the most frequent words in a corpus? How do those frequencies compare between corpora or texts? In the graph in Figure 2, Chaucer and Gower's texts have been plotted according to an MFW table. In the words of Stylo's creators, "The function code{stylo()} is meant to enable users to automatically load and process a corpus of electronic text files from a specified folder, and to perform a variety of stylometric analyses from multivariate statistics to assess and visualize stylistic similarities between input texts."[37] Stylo's analysis is "unsupervised," which does not mean that the user has no input into the process; users set various parameters, including (for example) the number of MFWs that will be analyzed, the nature of the n-grams (words or other groupings) to be identified, the kind of statistical process to be used, and more. The distinction between supervised and unsupervised machine learning is both central to the digital humanities and a source of controversy. Seth van Hooland and Mathias Coeckelbergs summarize this distinction as follows:

[O]ne of the main characteristics of unsupervised methods . . . [is] . . . their bottom-up generation of results, whereby it is not known a priori which form the results will take. By contrast, for supervised methods we have to first give correct examples as training input, thereby determining the structure of the output in the number of categories we assign the input data to. It is therefore [the case] that one of the most important tasks of supervised learning is classi-fication into a priori-designed categories, whereas that of unsupervised methods is clustering data together without knowing in advance what these clusters will represent. This makes unsupervised methods . . . suitable for dealing with large amounts of unknown data, to assist with tasks such as information retrieval or summarization.[38]

In our analysis of the Chaucer/Gower corpora, Stylo does not know that a particular chunk is associated with a given poet. Though the chunks are labeled, these data do not influence the unsupervised learning proc-ess; they merely tell Stylo to assign different colors to different labels

---

[37] Computational Stylistics Group, "stylo_howto," https://github.com/computation alstylistics/stylo_howto (accessed April 1, 2019).

[38] Seth van Hooland and Mathias Coeckelbergs, "Unsupervised Machine Learning for Archival Collections: Possibilities and Limits of Topic Modeling and Word Embedding," *Revista catalana d'arxivística* 41 (2018): 73–90 (78).

when graphing its results. As Van Hooland and Coeckelbergs describe, "[Stylo clusters] data together without knowing in advance what these clusters will represent." The results in Figure 2, showing Chaucer clustered with Chaucer, and Gower with Gower, therefore, confirm the validity of the MFW method for author attribution, at least in this case.

Principal components analysis produces graphs that are easy to visualize, but from which it is hard to extract details, because the actual links that produce the clustering of texts are hard to see. A simpler graph is produced by "cluster analysis," described by Maciej Eder as follows:

Hierarchical cluster analysis—as discussed in the present study—is a technique which tries to find the most similar samples (e.g. literary texts) and builds a hierarchy of clusters, using a "bottom-up" approach. What makes this method attractive is the very intuitive way of graphical representation of the obtained results: contrarily to the scatterplots as produced by multidimensional scaling or principal components analysis, where the goal is to interpret relative positions of several points settled on a rectangular plot, cluster analysis produces explicit links between neighboring items.[39]

Figure 3 shows a cluster analysis of the lemmatized Chaucer/Gower corpora, using the 100 most frequent words. From top to bottom, Chaucer's prose is in black; his poetry is in dark grey; and Gower's poetry is in light grey. It is immediately evident that Chaucer and Gower split apart very early on; the bracket on the far left (#1) represents the top level of the hierarchy of clusters. There is no confusion between the two: Chaucer clusters with Chaucer, and Gower with Gower. Moving down the hierarchy, the next major division separates Chaucer's prose from his poetry (bracket #2, second from the left: the series of texts rising up from the division with Gower). Bracket #3 next shows the division in Chaucer's poetry between the *Canterbury Tales* and *Troilus and Criseyde*, with the former on top and the latter underneath (though, as the larger, color-coded version of the graph shows [available online], two *Canterbury Tales* segments [CT_18 and CT_26] cluster with the *Troilus* segments). Other clusters and divisions emerge as the hierarchy of brackets descends; when the graph is viewed on a computer, it can be enlarged to make the connections between texts visible. For example, there is a

[39] Maciej Eder, "Visualization in Stylometry: Cluster Analysis Using Networks," *Digital Scholarship in the Humanities* 32 (2017), 50–64 (51).

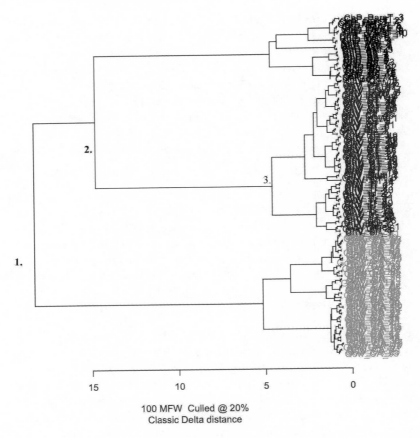

Fig. 3. Chaucer's prose is in black, his poetry is in dark grey, and Gower's poetry is in light grey. The first bracket on the left (#1) shows the distinction between Chaucer and Gower; moving to the right, the second bracket (#2) corresponds to the division of Chaucer's poetry from his prose. Bracket #3 marks the distinction between the *Canterbury Tales* and *Troilus and Criseyde*, though it is not absolute; two *Canterbury Tales* segments (CT_18 and CT_26) cluster with the *Troilus and Criseyde* grouping. Created using Stylo for R. For a scalable, color version, see http://newchaucersociety.org/pages/entry-sub/nolan-lecture.

clear cluster between *The Legend of Good Women* and the *Canterbury Tales* that appears when the reader zooms in on the labels. In cluster analysis, as opposed to PCA, the links between texts are easy to see and analyze; PCA provides a quick snapshot of the relations among texts, which can be useful for a "distant" portrait of the corpora of multiple writers.

One problem with cluster analysis is that different settings can produce radically different dendrograms. Eder describes how the fact that "a detailed inspection of multiple dendrograms generated for gradually increasing number of features (MFWs) shows that substantial rearrangements [of the dendrogram] might occur quite suddenly."[40] He cites the example of a cluster analysis of 66 English novels, in which a dendrogram based on 136 MFWs produces perfect author attribution, but at 137 MFWs the dendrogram is radically altered; Joseph Conrad's *Almayer's Folly* splits from the main Conrad cluster and joins a cluster with works of Rudyard Kipling. This formation is still in place at 969 MFWs, but at 970 MFWs *Almayer's Folly* rejoins the Conrad cluster.[41] This variability leads to the problem known as "cherry-picking," whereby scholars choose the dendrogram that best fits their thesis or overall analysis.[42] To avoid this problem, Eder suggests a technique known as a "consensus plot," which combines multiple dendrograms with different MFW limits:

This approach assumes that, in a large number of "snapshots" (e.g. for 100, 200, 300, 400, . . . , 1,000 MFWs), actual groupings tend to reappear, and apparent similarities are likely to remain accidental. The goal, then, is to capture the robust patterns across a set of generated snapshots. The procedure is aimed at producing a number of virtual dendrograms, and then at evaluating robustness of groupings across these dendrograms. If a given link—say, between Richardson's *Pamela* and Fielding's *Tom Jones*—turns out to appear frequently enough, it is reproduced on a consensus plot. In other words, several regular (yet virtual) dendrograms "vote" for the most robust links—the procedure summarizes the information on clustering from particular plots.[43]

A consensus plot limits the variation between dendrograms based on differing MFW lists by choosing only those links between texts that occur repeatedly, across a range of cluster analyses. We performed cluster analyses on the Chaucer/Gower corpora for 100, 200, 300, 400, and 500 MFWs, and then created a consensus tree for the results (Figure 4). The consensus tree confirms the results of the cluster analysis for 100

---

[40] Ibid., 54.
[41] Ibid., 54–55.
[42] See J. Rudman, "Cherry Picking in Nontraditional Authorship Attribution Studies," *Chance* 16 (2003): 26–32.
[43] Eder, "Visualization in Stylometry," 56.

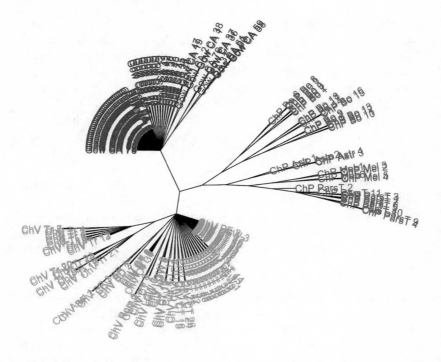

Fig. 4. A consensus tree in which Gower's works (top, in black), Chaucer's prose (right, in dark grey), and Chaucer's poetry (bottom, in light grey) cluster in three distinct groups. For a scalable, color version, see http://newchaucersociety.org/pages/entry-sub/nolan-lecture.

MFWs discussed above. The texts divide into three basic groups: the works of Gower (top center, in black), Chaucer's prose works (right, in dark grey), and Chaucer's poetry (bottom, in light grey) (see online for a color-coded, zoomable version of the graph).

Another solution to the problem of cherry-picking suggested by Eder is network analysis. This process uses the edge list generated by cluster analysis to create a visualization of the texts in the corpora in networked groups, as in Figure 5. In network analysis, an edge is the link between two nodes; a node, in the Chaucer/Gower example here, would be one of the 2,700-word segments of the corpora. An "edge table" is generated by Stylo during cluster analysis, produced by Eder's two-part algorithm, which is based on a series of comparisons between each node (or

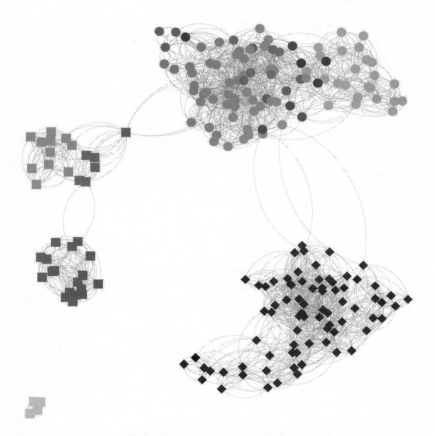

Fig. 5. A network analysis that clearly divides not only Gower's and Chaucer's works, but also distinguishes Chaucer's poetry from his prose (for a key to the color-coding, see Appendix III).

Gower—black diamonds, clustered together on the bottom right.

Chaucer's poetry—large cluster of greyscale circles on the top right.

Chaucer's prose—three clusters of greyscale squares in the middle and bottom left:

1. *The Parson's Tale* and *The Tale of Melibee*: light- and medium-grey squares, top left;
2. *Boece*: dark-grey squares, clustered at middle left;
3. *Treatise on the Astrolabe*: very light-grey squares, clustered at bottom left.

2,700-word segment) and all of the other nodes. This process of comparison produces a ranked list of connections for each segment, starting with the most similar other node (the "nearest neighbor") and proceeding through the list of nodes in descending order of similarity. The algorithm then establishes weighted connections between nodes (i.e., segments of texts) based on "a strong connection to its nearest neighbor (i.e., the most similar text), and two weaker connections to the 1st and the 2nd runner-up."[44] The second algorithm is based on the consensus tree technique described above; "[it] performs a large number of tests for similarity with different number of features to be analyzed (e.g. 100, 200, 300, . . . , 1,000 MFWs). Finally, all the connections produced in particular "snapshots" are added, resulting in a consensus network."[45] The end result is the edge table, which organizes the information produced by the two algorithms in a format that can be read by network analysis programs like Cytoscape.

The Cytoscape version of the graph shows much more clearly how the individual texts relate to one another. Gower's works are represented by black diamonds, tightly clustered together on the bottom right. Chaucer's texts cluster together in the same way they did in both the PCA graph in Figure 2 and the cluster analysis in Figure 3: prose (the three clusters of greyscale squares in the middle and bottom left) is distinguished from poetry (the large cluster of greyscale circles on the top right). The online version of this article presents a color-coded, zoomable version of this graph, in which much more detail can be seen; a key to the color-and-shape-coding can be found in Appendix III online. The color version shows Chaucer's poetry further divides into *Troilus and Criseyde* versus his other poems, primarily the *Canterbury Tales*, with other poetic works interspersed among the *Tales*. What can this graph tell us that the previous two (cluster analysis and PCA) could not? Through PCA we saw that Chaucer and Gower can be distinguished using stylometry. Cluster analysis specified the ways in which texts within the corpora were linked, creating a nested hierarchy of relationships that was easy to see. Network analysis shows vividly how certain texts are linked to others, and how others stand alone or in a small, isolated cluster. Thus Gower, in blue

---

[44] Ibid., 58.

[45] Ibid.; see also Maciej Eder, Jan Rybicki, and Mike Kestemont, " 'Stylo': A Package for Stylometric Analyses," pdf available at https://sites.google.com/site/computational-stylistics/stylo(stylo_howto.pdf), section 8.2., pp. 27–28.

diamonds, is connected to Chaucer by only a few links; his works are otherwise isolated. Chaucer's poetry is heavily interlinked, with multiple connections among the *Canterbury Tales*, *Troilus and Criseyde*, *The Legend of Good Women*, the dream visions, and the minor poems. However, his prose looks quite different. It appears as three comparatively isolated clusters: at top left (light grey and medium grey squares), *The Parson's Tale* and the *Melibee* cluster together; in the middle left (dark grey squares) appears *Boece*; and very isolated at the bottom left (very light grey squares) is the *Treatise on the Astrolabe*.

To return to the primary results shown by the graph, it is clear that Chaucer and Gower have distinctive styles based on MFWs; they are using sufficiently different lexicons to discriminate between them very reliably in a stylometric analysis. I would suggest that this difference reflects the distinction between Gower's plain style and Chaucer's more ornate style, features of their writing that both poets self-consciously highlight in their parallel story collections, the *Confessio Amantis* and the *Canterbury Tales*. Confirming this thesis would require more research and analysis; separating the two poets with MFW analysis tells us only that they are different, not precisely where those differences lie. Maciej Eder suggests that this limitation in authorship attribution via MFWs in fact points to the richness of the analytical material:

The difficulties with separating one specific signal suggest that a text (written or spoken) is a multilayer phenomenon, in which particular layers are correlated. These layers include authorship, chronology, personality, gender, topic, education, literary quality, translation (if applicable), intertextuality, literary tradition (e.g. sources of inspiration), and probably many more. Arguably, literary quality somehow depends on education, genre depends on topic, authorial voice is affected by chronology, gender affects personality, and so on. Some layers might be barely noticeable, and some others might become surprisingly strong. In authorship attribution, this complex system of uncontrollable layers is a problem of unwanted noise, and in literary-oriented computational stylistics, an opportunity to see more.[46]

There are two main lines of inquiry that the initial stylometric analyses of Chaucer and Gower suggest. The first is familiar to all medievalists: more close reading is needed to compare not only the two poets' direct comments on style, but also their modes of writing, particularly when

[46] Eder, "Visualization in Stylometry," 53.

narrating the same story. The second builds on the stylometric analyses we have already done to examine the MFW lists in relation to, for example, the parts of speech each poet uses most often or the etymologies of the words they choose (Germanic versus Romance). We have already begun to look at "bigrams" and "trigrams": these are groups of two or three words that regularly appear together, which might give us insight into Chaucer and Gower's stylistic choices. Many other possible avenues for analysis exist. For now, however, I will return to the initial graph I included, Figure 1, and the peak in uses of *style* that occurs in the work of Lydgate during the first half of the fifteenth century.

Fifteenth-Century Style

Neither Chaucer nor Gower used the word *style* with any frequency; among all of the other words in their corpora, *style* is a rare beast. I now turn to the second peak in the original graph I showed you—the extensive use of the word *style* by Lydgate and his imitators. Figure 6 shows what they look like in AntConc, a text analysis program, which is free to download on the web. There are 123 occurrences of the word *style* in the database from the fifteenth century. Of those, 29 refer to a farmer's stile; or to "steel," as in "hattes of stile" for helmets; or to the quality of being "still"; or to a rank or position, as in "the kynge his stile." Of the

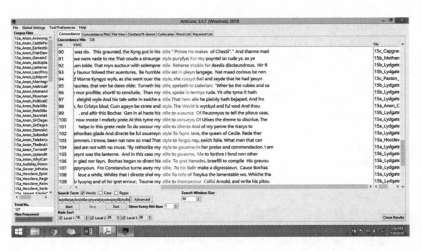

Fig. 6. The relative frequencies of "style" in the fifteenth century, as analyzed by AntConc. L. Anthony, AntConc (Version 3.5.8 [computer software]. Waseda University, Tokyo, 2019. Available at https://www.laurenceanthony.net/software.

remaining 94 uses of *style*, Lydgate accounts for 73 of them, or 78 percent. His closest competitor is Hoccleve, who uses the term 10 times, or 10 percent. The remaining uses come from figures such as Capgrave (3); Metham (3); Bokenham (1); Henryson (1); and texts such as the *Wars of Alexander* (1), the *Paston Letters* (1), and the corpus of political poems in Digby 102 and Douce 322 (1).

Of the 73 occurrences of *style* in Lydgate's fifteenth-century writing, 47 appear in the *Fall of Princes*; 19 appear in the *Troy Book*; and the remaining 7 appear in a range of texts, including the *Siege of Thebes*, *Temple of Glas*, *Complaint of a Lover's Life*, *Reason and Sensuality*, and *Pilgrimage of the Life of Man*. No doubt Lydgate uses the word many more times in his oeuvre, since our database does not include his *Lives of St. Alban and Amphibal*, the *Lives of St. Edmund and Fremund*, and the *Life of Our Lady*. These numbers illustrate how important the *Fall of Princes* is to understanding the development of the notion of literary style over the course of the fourteenth-through-sixteenth centuries, particularly since it was one of the most influential of his works during the early modern period. They also suggest that Lydgate understood the *Fall of Princes* to be doing a new kind of literary work, rooted in Chaucer, but reflecting his own synthesis of classical and continental sources.

I could begin this paper again at this moment, having cleared away the essential background to understanding Lydgate's use of *style*; it is a big topic, with many words to consider, just like everything Lydgate wrote. One way of getting at Lydgate's understanding of the word *style* is to examine the contexts in which he embeds it. Not surprisingly, those contexts—the words and phrases that surround *style*—repeat themselves over and over. Even less surprisingly, they repeatedly stage a dramatic scene that Lydgate found in his "master Chaucer's" poetry, in which the poet humbly defers to the past writer whose style he is imitating. Over half of Lydgate's references to style—50 out of 76, conservatively speaking—are also references to an author whose work he is translating: Boccaccio, primarily, since he provides the source for the *Fall of Princes*; but also Homer, Ovid, Dares Frygius, Jerome, Guido delle Colonne, and various "gramariens" and "rethoricyens." They typically take the following form:

> To whom I muste now my stile dresse,
> Folwen the tracis of Bochacius.
> (*Fall of Princes*, I.2409–10)[47]

---

[47] John Lydgate, *Fall of Princes*, 4 vols., ed. Henry Bergen, EETS e.s. 121, 122, 123, 124 (1924–27; repr., London: Oxford University Press, 1967); hereafter *FP*. Subsequent references will be in the text by title, book, and line number.

> Afftir thes forseid, rehersed in sentence,
> As Bochas procedeth in his stile.
>
> (*FP*, IX.1856–57)

In the first of these quotations, Lydgate is clearly referring to a stylus, "following the traces" of Boccaccio's pen. But in the second, "stile" appears in a prepositional phrase modifying the verb "procedeth." The import of both references is the same: Lydgate follows Boccaccio. But the stylus in quotation 2 has become abstract. To proceed *in* a style is to write in a certain manner. Style has become an entity with an inside and an outside, a mode that can be entered and exited. In other words, style has become a concept.

Throughout Lydgate's references to style, this split between style as an instrument—the stylus—and style as a concept persists. It is most evident in the relationship between the verbs and the adjectives that he associates with style. He uses strong, active verbs that assert his or his source's authorial agency and thus emphasize the instrumentality of their subject, style. Here is a sampling of the most frequently used verbs:

dressen ("to guide, steer, direct, control, govern"; 11 uses):[48] "Bochas in haste doth his stile dresse." (*FP*, VIII.1709)

directen (8 uses): "Bochas began to direct his stile." (*FP*, VII.74)

gien (2 uses): "Or who shall now my stile guy or lede?" (*A Complaynte of a Lovers Lyfe*, line 177)[49]

governen (2 uses): "And in this caas my stile to gouerne, / Me to forthre I fond non other muse / But, hard as ston, Pierides and Meduse." (*FP*, III.61–63)

More rarely, Lydgate uses verbs that suggest a more conceptual notion of style, as in:

avauncen (3 uses): "And Bochas heer doth his stile auaunce / Ful notabli with excellent langage." (*FP*, III.4649–50)

Avauncen means "to improve, further the development of, advance."[50] In this quotation, Lydgate modifies it with "Ful notabli" and tells us what

---

[48] *MED*, s.v. *dressen*, def. 8(a).

[49] *A Complaynte of a Lovers Lyfe*, in *Chaucerian Dream Visions and Complaints*, ed. Dana M. Symons (Kalamazoo: Medieval Institute Publications, 2004), 96.

[50] *MED*, s.v. *avauncen*, def. 2(b).

improved Bochas's style: "excellent langage." This quotation begins to suggest that style is more than a writing instrument or even the subject matter of the poem at hand; it proposes word choice as a component of style—much as stylometry looks for MFWs in making stylistic distinctions.

This expansion of the notion of style is accomplished in part by the addition of an adverb—a modifier that characterizes and qualifies the concept. Such modifiers work by applying qualities associated with other things or concepts to the object at hand, the stylus. Few modifiers actually apply to a pen *in propria persona*—perhaps "sharp," or "pointy," or "red," adjectives that describe the pen's material existence—and the addition of metaphor with modifiers like "Ful notabli" moves the concrete pen into the conceptual realm.

This point becomes even more evident when we look at Lydgate's uses of adjectives for style. They split into positive and negative groups: *humble* or *rude* versus *sovereign* or *golden*. All of the positive adjectives—*sovereign, solempne*, and *golden*—refer to the high style, and all refer to someone else's style—Ovid, Virgil, Dares, Guido delle Colonne, and especially Boccaccio. In these cases, the style being invoked is the high style as Chaucer introduced it in *The Clerk's Tale*—an impersonal mode that any poet can imitate. The negative adjectives function differently. With only a few exceptions—which in fact prove the rule, as I will show—all of these adjectives—*dull, rude, humble, bareyn, naked, bare, breef*, and *plein*—are preceded by the first-person possessive pronoun, *my*. All are self-referential, though it isn't always Lydgate who is speaking. All are expressions of inadequacy and ineptitude, almost always in relation to a figure of authority, classical or Italian. What does Lydgate mean when he describes his style in this way?

Lydgate's negative adjectives further subdivide into two groups. The first of these might be labeled "writerly inadequacy." It includes "dullness" (famously discussed by David Lawton in a groundbreaking essay) and "rudeness"; a "rude style" is thus one "lacking in intelligence, dull-witted" (*MED*, s.v. *rude*, defs. 2[a], 3[a, b]) or "uncouth, ill-bred," but also "unsophisticated, artless, simple." [51] The second group of negative adjectives—*humble, bareyn, naked, bare, breef*, and *plain*—is less pejorative and more descriptive. It looks very much like a set of words describing the plain style. *Bareyn, naked*, and *bare* all suggest an unembellished

[51] David Lawton, "Dullness and the Fifteenth Century," *ELH* 54 (1987): 761–99.

style, the opposite of Chaucer's style as Lydgate describes it in his prologue:

> My maistir Chaucer dede his besynesse,
> And in his daies hath so weel hym born,
> Out off our tunge tauoiden al reudnesse,
> And to refourme it with colours of suetnesse.
>
> (*FP*, I.275–78)

Lydgate contrasts this Chaucerian style with his intended style in the
Fall of Princes:

> Al this conceyuyd, I gan my stile dresse,
> Thouhte I wolde in my mater proceede;
> And for the mater abraid on heuynesse,
> Off fressh colours I took no maner heede,
> But my processe pleynli for to leede,
> As me sempte it was to me most meete
> To sette apart all rethoriques sueete.
>
> (*FP*, I.449–55)

Lydgate claims to be embracing the plain style, eschewing embellish-
ment and ornate language in favor of the "black and white" colors of
tragedy. But as every reader of the *Fall of Princes* is well aware, he does
no such thing. The text is full of amplification, Latinate diction, and
embellishments of all kinds. Why, then, does he make this claim?

The key to unlocking this mystery lies in the quotation above, beginning with "Al this conceyuyd, I gan my stile dresse." While making
this declaration, Lydgate uses a version of the first-person singular
pronoun—"I," "my," "me"—six times in seven lines. Recall, too, that
nearly all of the negative adjectives (from both groups) were modified
by "my"—"my rude style," "my plain style," "my dull style." All of
these references to himself—many more than in Chaucer, even factoring
in the differential of their productivity—suggest that Lydgate is seeking
a way to claim his own style. In Chaucer and Gower he found exemplars
of two vernacular styles, the high style and the plain style. The high
style is, as Chaucer tells us, for speaking to princes. The plain style is
the voice of Arion, the figure invoked by Gower at the end of his prologue to bring peace and heal division. In the *Fall of Princes*, this sense

of uncertainty is mediated by the relationship between Petrarch and Boccaccio, which Lydgate comments on extensively, particularly in the prologue to Book VIII. We have already seen in Chaucer's commentary in *The Clerk's Tale* that Petrarch and Boccaccio stand in for notions of style—Petrarch for Latin and the high style, Boccaccio for the low style and the vernacular. When Lydgate translates Boccaccio's Latin *De casibus virorum illustrium*, he is particularly compelled by its depictions of the writer's affect; Boccaccio represents himself as the humble follower of Petrarch, who reaches points of impasse and exhaustion and must be urged on by his mentor and friend, who appears wearing his laurel crown. Lydgate describes Boccaccio as he struggles to decide whether or not to continue with the eighth book of his text:

> Atwix[e] tweyne abidyng thus a while,
> What was to doone in doute he gan fleete,
> Halff withynne & half ouer the stile,
> Koude nat discerne to hym what was most meete,
> Til Fraunceis Petrak, the laureat poete,
> Crownid with laurer, grace was his gide,
> Cam and set hym doun bi his beddis side.
>
> (*FP*, VIII.57–63)

Boccaccio is "half within and half over the stile." On the one hand, "stile" here functions as a metaphor for indecision, for being caught between two courses of action—a metaphor we know as "sitting on the fence." On the other hand, Lydgate is clearly recalling the Squire's use of "stile" as a metaphor for literary imitation, when he claims he cannot "climb the high stile" of the mysterious knight visiting Cambuskyan's court. To Lydgate, Boccaccio is a figure for being caught between styles, between Petrarch's high Latin style and the low style of the vernacular he leaves behind to write *De casibus*.

Recalling for a moment the eloquence of the Squire's visiting knight, whose words were "Accordant to . . . his cheere," it becomes possible to see the link that Lydgate makes between style and affect. Throughout the *Fall*, he depicts his own emotional state in the same language and imagery he deploys for Boccaccio. For example, in the prologue to Book VI, Boccaccio is described in this way:

> Whil Bochas pensiff stood sool in his librarie
> With cheer oppressid, pale in his visage,
> Sumdeel abasshed, alone & solitarie.
>
> (*FP*, VI.15–17)

In the prologue to Book III, Lydgate gives us a portrait of himself:

> Thus be my-selff remembryng on this book,
> It to translate how I hadde vndirtake,
> Ful pale off cheer, astonyd in my look,
> Myn hand gan tremble; my penne I felte quake,
> That disespeired, I hadde almost forsake
> So gret a labour, dreedful & inportable,
> It to parfourme I fond my-silff so onable.
>
> (*FP*, III.43–49)

Over and over again, we hear about Lydgate's quaking pen and "pale . . . cheer" as he imagines the content of his tragedies expressed by his own body. Boccaccio's collapse in Book VIII is a similarly somatic and affective display of what it means to be "half within and half over the stile"—in other words, caught between the imperatives of contrasting styles. This image fires Lydgate's imagination because it so fully expresses his own sense of being half in and half out: being Chaucer's successor and imitator in creating an English high style, while simultaneously feeling the pull of the Gowerian plain style and the appeal of Latin learning. This tension between the high style and the plain style has a long future to come in English literature, starting with Wyatt and leading all the way up to the present, with detours in American literature and other literatures in English.

I said at the start of my talk that I would follow the history of style as a way of thinking about the concept of style. Tracing the articulation of the word *style* over 150 years is not the same as writing an account of medieval literary style. It is perfectly possible to write about Old English style or thirteenth-century style. The notion of style is not only contained in the word. But what following the word in English shows us is how a series of writers came to grips with an inherited idea, one transported from its classical origin to a new and very different environment. What Chaucer begins and Lydgate finishes is the cementing of a bond between the notion of style and the idea of the writer as a distinctive, bounded individual with an affective relationship to the text. Not a subject, I hasten to say, at least not in the new historical sense. The tension I identified at the start of the talk, between style as a general concept and as a particular and singular mode, is a tension newly apparent at the end of the Middle Ages. Lydgate's image of the writer with shaking hand and ghastly face vividly demonstrates the conceptual power of style even as it shows us a poet forging his own, particular style of expression. It shows us that the invention of personal style is not only a matter of writers having a style, but also of style having the writer.

Appendix I. List of Texts and Sources in the Forbes-Macphail Middle English Database

Sources

Each text is followed by a brief word or phrase in parentheses, which indicates the Internet source for the digital text we used in our database. The key to those designations is below, in alphabetical order. All web addresses were checked in May 2019 and were viable at that point.

1. (**Archive.org**): Internet Archive (https://archive.org/)
2. (**Bibliotheca Augustana**): Bibliotheca Augustana: *Litteraturae et artis collectio* (http://www.hs-augsburg.de/~harsch/augustana .html)
3. (**CMEPV**): Corpus of Middle English Prose and Verse, University of Michigan (https://quod.lib.umich.edu/c/cme/)
4. (**Doyle Macdonald**): Doyle Macdonald, "Viable Paradise: Fantasy and Science Fiction Writers' Workshop" (https://web .archive.org/web/20110607002812/http://www.sff.net/people /DoyleMacdonald/lit.htm)
5. (**EEBO**): Early English Books Online (https://eebo.chadwyck .com/home)
6. (**EEBO-TCP**): Early English Books Online Text Creation Partnership (https://www.textcreationpartnership.org/tcp-eebo/)
7. (**Gutenberg**): Project Gutenberg (https://www.gutenberg.org/)
8. (**Harvard**): Harvard's Geoffrey Chaucer Page (http://sites.fas .harvard.edu/~chaucer/special/lifemann/love/ep-cupid.html)
9. (**Luminarium**): Anniina Jokinen, Luminarium: Anthology of English Literature (http://www.luminarium.org/)
10. (**Otago**): Textbase of Early Tudor English, University of Otago, New Zealand (https://www.otago.ac.nz/english-linguistics /tudor/)
11. (**Poetry Nook**): Poetry Nook: Poetry for Every Occasion (https://www.poetrynook.com/poet/thomas-hoccleve)
12. (**Riverside**): WordHoard, Northwestern University (http://word hoard.northwestern.edu/userman/index.html)
13. (**TEAMS**): TEAMS Middle English Texts Series: A Robbins

Library Digital Project, University of Rochester (https://d.lib
.rochester.edu/teams)
14. **(Virginia)**: VIRGO on-line catalogue, University of Virginia
(https://search.lib.virginia.edu/catalog/uva-lib:463185)

List of Texts by Date

GENERAL PRINCIPLES FOR DATING

- Texts were dated within a quarter-century window, using the letters "a," "b," "c," and "d" to denote each 25-year bracket. Thus, a
  text in the first quarter of the fourteenth century would be labeled
  "14a"; a text in the last quarter of the twelfth century would be
  labeled "12d," etc.
- If the range of time during which a text could have been written
  was longer than 25 years, or crossed two 25-year brackets, we took
  the median date UNLESS there was good reason to believe that
  one quarter-century bracket was more likely than another. Thus,
  if a text was dated 1390–1414 and all dates within that range
  seemed equally plausible, we would average those dates to arrive
  at 1402; we would thereby arrive at a designation of "15a." However, if there was strong reason to believe that it was more likely
  that the text was written in the late fourteenth century (although
  it might still be possible that it was written in the early fifteenth),
  then we would label it "14d."
- If the date sat exactly on the boundary between two brackets (e.g.,
  1400), and there was no reason to assign it to an earlier or later
  bracket, we rounded up.

Thirteenth Century

13A: 1200–1225

The Katherine Group (TEAMS)
Layamon, *Brut* (CMEPV)
The Owl and the Nightingale (Bibliotheca Augustana)
Vices and Virtues (CMEPV)

13B: 1226–1250

Ancrene Wisse (TEAMS)
King Horn (TEAMS)
Liflade of St. Juliana (CMEPV)

13C: 1251–1275

Dame Sirith (TEAMS)
Early South English Legendary (CMEPV)
Floris and Blancheflour (TEAMS)
Iacob and Iosep (CMEPV)

13D: 1276–1300

Bevis of Hampton (TEAMS)
Havelok the Dane (TEAMS)
Lanfrank, *Science of Cirurgie* (CMEPV)
Robert of Gloucester, *Metrical Chronicle* (CMEPV)
Sir Tristrem (TEAMS)
South English Legendary: Life of St. Francis (TEAMS)
Stanzaic Life of Margaret of Antioch (TEAMS)

Fourteenth Century

14A: 1301–1325

Adam Davy's Five Dreams (CMEPV)
Cursor mundi (CMEPV) [Cotton Vesp. A.III]
Early South English Legendary: Life of Mary Magdalen (TEAMS)
King of Tars (TEAMS)
Robert Mannyng, *Handlyng Synne* (CMEPV)
Northern Homily Cycle (TEAMS)
Richard Coer de Lyon (TEAMS)
Stanzaic Guy of Warwick (TEAMS)

14B: 1326–1350

Amis and Amiloun (TEAMS)
Ayenbite of Inwit (CMEPV)

British Library, MS Harley 2253 (TEAMS) [created English-only version; excluded *King Horn*]
Earliest Complete English Prose Psalter (CMEPV)
The Gast of Gy (TEAMS)
Kildare Poems (CMEPV)
King Edward and the Shepherd (TEAMS)
Laurence Minot, *Poems* (TEAMS)
Lay Le Freine (TEAMS)
Long Charter of Christ (CMEPV)
Robert Mannyng, *Chronicle 1 and 2* (CMEPV)
Prick of Conscience (TEAMS)
Richard Rolle, *Prose Works* (CMEPV)
Richard Rolle, *Psalter* (CMEPV)
Sir Degaré (TEAMS)
Sir Orfeo (TEAMS)
Sir Owain (TEAMS)
Sir Perceval of Galles (TEAMS)
The Vision of Tundale (TEAMS)
William of Shoreham, *Poems* (CMEPV)
Ywain and Gawain (TEAMS)

14C: 1351–1375

John Arderne, *Treatises of Fistula in Ano* (CMEPV)
The Book of John Mandeville (TEAMS)
Geoffrey Chaucer, *Anelida and Arcite* (Riverside)
Geoffrey Chaucer, *The Book of the Duchess* (Riverside)
Geoffrey Chaucer, *The Parliament of Fowls* (Riverside)
Geoffrey Chaucer, *The Romaunt of the Rose* (Riverside)
Geoffrey de la Tour Landry, *Book of the Knight of La Tour-Landry* (CMEPV)
John of Hildesheim, *Three Kings of Cologne* (CMEPV)
Joseph of Arimathea (CMEPV)
Lybeaus Desconus (TEAMS)
Octavian (TEAMS)
Parlement of the Thre Ages (TEAMS)
Sir Eglamour of Artois (TEAMS)
Sir Isumbras (TEAMS)
Stanzaic Morte Arthur (TEAMS)

Wynnere and Wastoure (TEAMS)
The York Plays (CMEPV)

14D: 1376–1400

Alliterative Morte Arthur (TEAMS)
Jean d'Arras, *Melusine* (CMEPV)
Athelston (TEAMS)
The Awntyrs off Arthur (TEAMS)
The Bible: A Fourteenth-Century English Biblical Version (CMEPV)
Geoffrey Chaucer, *Boece* (CMEPV)
Geoffrey Chaucer, *Canterbury Tales* (Riverside)
Geoffrey Chaucer, *The House of Fame* (Riverside)
Geoffrey Chaucer, *The Legend of Good Women* (Riverside)
Geoffrey Chaucer, *Treatise on the Astrolabe* (CMEPV)
Geoffrey Chaucer, *Troilus and Criseyde* (Riverside)
John Clanvowe, *The Boke of Cupide* (TEAMS)
The Cloud of Unknowing (TEAMS)
Dispute between Mary and the Cross (TEAMS)
Emaré (TEAMS)
The Four Leaves of the Truelove (TEAMS)
Generydes (CMEPV)
Gest Hystoriale (CMEPV)
John Gower, *Confessio Amantis* (TEAMS)
Walter Hilton, *The Scale of Perfection* (TEAMS)
Julian of Norwich, *Shewings* (TEAMS)
Life of Soul (CMEPV)
John Lydgate, *Isopes Fabules* (TEAMS)
Minor Poems of the Vernon MS (CMEPV)
Pearl (TEAMS)
Piers Plowman, B-text (CMEPV)
Piers the Plowman's Crede (TEAMS)
The Pistel of Swete Susan (TEAMS)
The Pride of Life (TEAMS)
Purity (CMEPV)
Robert of Cisyle (TEAMS)
Short Charter of Christ (CMEPV)
The Siege of Jerusalem (TEAMS)
The Siege of Milan (TEAMS)

Sir Amadace (TEAMS)
Sir Gawain and the Green Knight (CMEPV)
Sir Launfal (TEAMS)
Sir Tryamour (TEAMS)
Thomas Usk, *Testament of Love* (TEAMS)
John Wyclif, *Apology for Lollard Doctrines* (CMEPV)
John Wyclif, *Select English Works* (CMEPV)

Fifteenth Century

15A: 1401–1425

John Audelay, *Poems and Carols* (TEAMS)
The Avowyng of Arthur (TEAMS)
The Brut (CMEPV)
The Castle of Perseverance (TEAMS)
Erle of Toulous (TEAMS)
Fifty Earliest English Wills (CMEPV)
Friar Daw's Reply (TEAMS)
John Gower, *In Praise of Peace* (TEAMS)
Thomas Hoccleve, *Epistle of Cupid* (Harvard)
Thomas Hoccleve, *Remonstrance against Oldcastle* (Poetry Nook)
Thomas Hoccleve, *Regiment of Princes* (TEAMS)
Thomas Hoccleve, *Series* (Poetry Nook)
Jack Upland (TEAMS)
James I of Scotland, *Kingis Quair* (TEAMS)
Lanterne of Light (CMEPV)
The Laud Troy Book (CMEPV)
Nicholas Love, *Mirrour of the Blessed Lyf of Jesu Christ* (CMEPV)
John Lydgate, *Beware* (TEAMS)
John Lydgate, *The Floure of Curtesye* (TEAMS)
John Lydgate, *Lyfe of Seynt Margaret* (TEAMS)
John Lydgate, *Reson and Sensuallyte* (CMEPV)
John Lydgate, *Siege of Thebes* (TEAMS)
John Lydgate, *Temple of Glas* (TEAMS)
John Lydgate, *Troy Book: Selections* (TEAMS)
Lyfe of Ipomydon (CMEPV)
The Marriage of Sir Gawain (TEAMS)
John Mirk, Selected Sermons (TEAMS)

Mum and the Sothsegger (TEAMS)

William Paris, *Life of St. Christina* (TEAMS)

The Plowman's Tale (TEAMS)

Rule of St. Benedict Northern Metrical (CMEPV)

Rule of St. Benedict Northern Prose (CMEPV)

Selections from the Middle English Metrical Paraphrase of the Old Testament (TEAMS)

Sir Cleges (TEAMS)

Sir Degrevant (TEAMS)

Sir Gawain and the Carle of Carlisle (TEAMS)

Sir Torrent of Portingale (TEAMS)

Stanzaic Life of Katherine of Alexandria (TEAMS)

The Sultan of Babylon (TEAMS)

The Tale of Beryn (TEAMS)

Twenty-Six Political and Other Poems from the Oxford MSS Digby 102 and Douce 322 (CMEPV)

Upland's Rejoinder (TEAMS)

Why I Can't Be a Nun (TEAMS)

15B: 1426–1450

The Alphabet of Tales (CMEPV)

Osbern Bokenham, *Life of St. Anne* (TEAMS)

The Book of Margery Kempe (TEAMS)

John Capgrave, *The Life of Saint Katherine* (TEAMS)

Complaint of a Prisoner against Fortune (TEAMS)

Dethe of James Kynge of Scotis (CMEPV)

Hymns to the Virgin and Christ (15b)

The King and the Hermit (TEAMS)

John Lydgate, *A Complaynte of a Lovers Lyfe* (TEAMS)

John Lydgate, *Fabula duorum mercatorum* (TEAMS)

John Lydgate, *Fall of Princes* (University of Virginia)

John Lydgate, *Guy of Warwyk* (TEAMS)

John Lydgate, *Mummings* (TEAMS)

John Lydgate, *Prohemy of a Mariage* (TEAMS)

John Lydgate, *The Pilgrimage of the Life of Man* (CMEPV)

John Lydgate, *St. Austin at Compton* (TEAMS)

John Metham, *Amoryus and Cleopes* (TEAMS)

Charles d'Orléans, *Fortunes Stabilnes* (TEAMS)

Reginald Pecock, *Repressor of Over Much Blaming of the Clergy* (CMEPV)
Prose Life of Alexander (CMEPV)
Richard the Redeless (TEAMS)
Richard Roos, *La belle dame sans merci* (TEAMS)
The Towneley Plays (CMEPV)
Two Fifteenth Century Cookery Books (CMEPV)
Simon Winter, *Life of St. Jerome* (TEAMS)

15C: 1451–1475

George Ashby, *Complaint of a Prisoner in the Fleet* (TEAMS)
The Assembly of Gods (TEAMS)
The Book of the Quinte Essence (CMEPV)
William Caxton, *The Game and Playe of the Chesse* (TEAMS)
The Chaucerian Apocrypha: A Selection (TEAMS)
   Included: "In February"; "O Merciful and O Mercyable"; "The Craft
   of Lovers"; "The Lover's Mass"; "I Have a Lady"; "O Mosy Quince";
   "Of Theyre Nature"; "Four Things that Make a Man a Fool"; "Eight
   Goodly Questions with Their Aunswers"; "Duodecim abusiones";
   "Prophecy"; Henry Scogan, "Moral Ballad"
   Not included: John Lydgate, *The Floure of Curtesye* and *Beware*; John
   Gower, *In Praise of Peace*
Craft of Deyng (CMEPV)
The Floure and the Leafe (TEAMS)
Sir John Fortescue, *The Governance of England* (CMEPV)
Thomas Malory, *Morte Darthur* (CMEPV)
Manking (TEAMS)
N-Town Plays (TEAMS)
Paston Family Letters (CMEPV)
Reginald Pecock, *Book of Faith* (CMEPV)
Pety Job (TEAMS)
Prose Merlin (TEAMS)
Register of Godstow Nunnery (CMEPV)
Register of Osney Abbey (CMEPV)
Saint Editha (CMEPV)
The Story of Asneth (TEAMS)
The Tournment of Tottenham (TEAMS)
Wars of Alexander (CMEPV)
The Wedding of Sir Gawain and Dame Ragnelle (TEAMS)

Wisdom (TEAMS)
Wisdom of Solomon (CMEPV)
York Corpus Christi Plays (TEAMS)

15D: 1476–1500

The Assemblie of Ladies (TEAMS)
The Babees Book (CMEPV)
Blanchardyn and Eglantine (CMEPV)
The Croxton Play of the Sacrament (TEAMS)
Dicts and Sayings of the Philosophers (TEAMS)
Everyman (TEAMS)
The Feast of Tottenham (TEAMS)
The Freiris of Berwick (TEAMS)
Robert Henryson, *Complete Works* (TEAMS)
The Isle of Ladies (TEAMS)
The Jeaste of Sir Gawain (TEAMS)
King Arthur and King Cornwall (TEAMS)
The Knightly Tale of Gologras and Gawain (TEAMS)
Lancelot of the Laik (TEAMS)
Lufaris Complaynt (TEAMS)
Lyf of the Noble and Cristen Prynce, Charles the Grete (CMEPV)
The Quare of Jelusy (TEAMS)
Right Plesaunt and Goodly Historie of the Foure Sonnes of Symon (CMEPV)
Rule of St. Benet Caxton Abstract (CMEPV)
Sir Gowther (TEAMS)
John Skelton, *Elegy on the Death of Henry Percy* (Luminarium)
The Squire of Low Degree (TEAMS)
The Tale of Ralph the Collier (TEAMS)
The Three Kings' Sons (CMEPV)
The Wallace (TEAMS)

Sixteenth Century

16A: 1501–1525

Alexander Barclay, *The Boke of Codrus and Mynalcas* (EEBO-TCP)
Gavin Douglas, *The Palis of Honoure* (TEAMS)
William Dunbar, *The Complete Works* (TEAMS)

A9

William Dunbar, *Tretis of the Twa Mariit Women and the Wedo* (TEAMS)
The Greene Knight (TEAMS)
Stephen Hawes, *The Conuercyon of Swerers* (Gutenberg)
Stephen Hawes, *Example Vertue* (EEBO-TCP)
Stephen Hawes, *Pastime of Pleasure* (Archive.org)
John the Reeve (TEAMS)
Thomas More, *Utopia* (Gutenberg)
John Rastell, *A New Commodye in English* (EEBO-TCP)
John Skelton, *The Bowge of Courte* (Luminarium)
John Skelton, *Chaplet of Laurel* (EEBO-TCP)
John Skelton, *Colin Cloute* (Luminarium)
John Skelton, *Phyllyp Sparowe* (EEBO-TCP)
John Skelton, *The Tunnyng of Elynour Rummyng* (Luminarium)
John Skelton, *Ware the Hauke* (EEBO)
The Turke and Sir Gawain (TEAMS)
William Walter, *Guistarde Sigismonde* (Otago)
Henry Watson, *King Ponthus* (EEBO)
Henry Watson, *Shyppe of Fooles* (EEBO)
Thomas Wyatt, *Poems* (Luminarium)

16B: 1526–1550

Anne Askew, *First Examination* (EEBO)
Anne Askew, *Later Examination* (EEBO)
John Bale, *Actes of Englysh Votaryes* (EEBO)
John Bale, *Examinacyon Death of Martyr John Oldecastell* (EEBO)
The Carle of Carlisle (TEAMS)
Robert Copland, *Seven Sorrows Women Have* (EEBO)
Leonard Cox, *Arte or Crafte of Rhetoryke* (EEBO)
Thomas Elyot, *Castel of Helth* (EEBO)
Thomas Elyot, *Pasquil the Playne* (EEBO)
John Heywood, *The Foure* (EEBO)
John Heywood, *Johan Johan* (Doyle Macdonald)
John Heywood, *A Mery Play betwene the Pardonere and the Frere . . .*
    (EEBO)
John Heywood, *Play of the Wether* (EEBO)
The History of Kyng Boccus (EEBO)
Hugh Latimer, *The Fyrste Sermon* (EEBO)
Thomas Lupset, *Dyenge Well* (EEBO)

Richard Morison, *A Remedy for Sedition* (EEBO)
Katherine Parr, *The Lamentacion of a Synner* (EEBO)
John Rastell, *The Pastyme of People* (EEBO)
Luke Shepherd, *Doctour Doubble Ale* (EEBO)
Luke Shepherd, *Upchering Messe* (EEBO)
Henry Howard, earl of Surrey, *Selections from Aeneid* (Luinarium)
Henry Howard, earl of Surrey, *Songs and Sonnets* (Luminarium)

Appendix II. List of Labels for Middle English Glossarial Database Segments Used in Cluster and Network Analyses

The database was divided into 2,700-word segments, based on the length of the shortest work (*Anelida and Arcite*). Each segment was labeled according to the following convention:

Author's name[+ optional verse/prose designation]_title of work_segment number

Chaucer

PROSE

ChP_Bo_1–18	*Boece*
ChP_Astr_1–4	*Treatise on the Astrolabe*
ChP_Mel_1–6	*The Tale of Melibee*
ChP_ParsT_1–11	*The Parson's Tale*

VERSE

ChV_Rom_1–3	*Romaunt of the Rose*
ChV_BD_1–3	*The Book of the Duchess*
ChV_HF_1–4	*The House of Fame*
ChV_Anel_1	*Anelida and Arcite*
ChV_PF_1–2	*The Parliament of Fowls*
ChV_TC_1–24	*Troilus and Criseyde*
ChV_SP_1–3	*Short Poems*
ChV_LGW_1–7	*The Legend of Good Women*
ChV_CT_1–49	*Canterbury Tales*

Gower

Gow_CA_1–76   *Confessio Amantis*
Gow_PP_1   *In Praise of Peace*

Chaucerian Humor

George Edmondson
Dartmouth College

Abstract

Taking as its starting-point the distinction Freud draws between outwardly directed comedy and inwardly directed humor, and as its Chaucerian proof-texts *The Prologue and Tale of Sir Thopas*, this essay reappraises Chaucerian humor as an all-encompassing mood, or *Stimmung*. Critical and un-affected, closer to melancholic reality-testing than to comedic boundary-creation, Chaucerian humor evacuates the authoritative position from which it originates—a position finally aligned, this essay argues, with that of the sovereign and the master. Where comedy works, in part, by reversing our expectations, Chaucerian humor works to reverse our expectation that we are doomed to suffer, whether at the hands of anarchic, tyrannical power; a cruelly demanding super-ego; or regimes of affective governance.

Keywords

Chaucer; humor; *The Tale of Sir Thopas*; Freud; psychoanalysis; *Stimmung*; biopolitics; sovereign; Harry Bailly; affect; mood; melancholia

THIS ESSAY TAKES UP THREE TERMS—health, humor, and paternalism—whose convergence in the figure of Chaucer remains comparatively under-theorized, despite the fact that each one has been studied, sometimes extensively, in isolation.[1] When and how that

I wish to thank the editors of *SAC*, both current and former, for their support and encouragement. I am grateful as well to the journal's two readers, whose criticisms and suggestions for revision improved every aspect of this essay. Special thanks are due to Peter Travis, who commented incisively on an earlier draft, and to Catherine Sanok, who brainstormed with me on a long train ride in the wrong direction.

[1] On the image of the healthy Chaucer, see Helen Phillips, "Chaucer and the Nineteenth-Century City," in *Chaucer and the City*, ed. Ardis Butterfield (Cambridge: D. S. Brewer, 2006), 193–210. On the subject of Chaucer's humor, see the essays collected in *Chaucer's Humor: Critical Essays*, ed. Jean E. Jost (New York: Garland, 1994); but see as well Morton W. Bloomfield, "Gloomy Chaucer," in *Veins of Humor*, ed. Harry

convergence began, whether in the years immediately following Chaucer's death or with the emergence of Chaucer studies as a distinct discipline, remains difficult to say. Arguably, one sees it taking shape already in Hoccleve's reverential depiction of Chaucer as his "maister": a figure whose rhetorical mastery is merely an extension of his overall self-mastery; a figure fundamentally sound, at peace with himself and with the world, secure enough in the "health of his spirit" that his default attitude could only be one of amused tolerance.[2] Indisputably, one begins to detect the convergence of health, humor, and (literary) paternalism, and its lasting effects upon our field, in the writings of such early professional Chaucerians as Caroline Spurgeon, Howard Patch, and George Saintsbury, all of whom link the question of Chaucer's mental and physical health to his "good-natured" humor, and his humor, in turn, to his exceptional status as the putative father of English poetry.[3] Even now, over a century later, the image of Chaucer bequeathed to us by those early critics—a Chaucer "whose distinguishing quality of mind

---

Levin (Cambridge, Mass.: Harvard University Press, 1972), 57–68. For the place of health and humor in popular constructions of "the most genial and humourful healthy-souled man that England has ever seen," see Steve Ellis (here quoting F. J. Furnivall), *Chaucer at Large: The Poet in the Modern Imagination* (Minneapolis: University of Minnesota Press, 2000), 17–31. The definitive statements on Chaucer's paternalism remain Lee Patterson, *Chaucer and the Subject of History* (Madison: University of Wisconsin Press, 1991), 13–22; A. C. Spearing, *Medieval to Renaissance in English Poetry* (Cambridge: Cambridge University Press, 1985), 88–110; and Seth Lerer, *Chaucer and His Readers: Imagining the Author in Late-Medieval England* (Princeton: Princeton University Press, 1993). Although Lerer's central argument in that work, that "Chaucer—as author, as 'laureate,' and as 'father' of English poetry—is a construction of his later fifteenth-century scribes, readers, and poetic imitators," undergirds my own, my aim here is not to revisit the question of Chaucer's paternalism as such but rather to disentangle the convergence of humor, health, and paternalism in the (retroactively constructed) figure of Chaucer (3). I would venture to say, moreover, that the construction of "father Chaucer" itself indicates that his inheritors understood the workings of Chaucerian humor all too well—or not at all.

[2] Thomas Hoccleve, *The Regiment of Princes*, ed. Charles R. Blyth (Kalamazoo, Mich.: Medieval Institute Publications, 1999), line 2077. Nicholas Perkins describes Hoccleve's representation of Chaucer as "a kind of gold standard in which Hoccleve can invest, [and that he] can bring to life in order to shore up his own poetic resources," and notes "the dual sense of rhetorical invention and generative value with which Hoccleve invests Chaucer, and which he by implication inhabits through Chaucer's textual/spectral presence." Nicholas Perkins, "Haunted Hoccleve? *The Regiment of Princes*, the Troilean Intertext, and Conversations with the Dead," *ChauR* 43, no. 2 (2008): 116–17.

I paraphrase Howard Patch, who writes of Chaucer that "the health of the poet's spirit is pervasive in all of his works, which exhibit nothing that from any point of view might be called morbid." Howard Rollin Patch, "The Idea of Humor," repr. in Jost, *Chaucer's Humor*, 23–38 (23).

[3] See, for example, Caroline Spurgeon, *Five-Hundred Years of Chaucer Criticism and Allusion, 1357–1900* (Cambridge: Cambridge University Press, 1925), cxxxv.

is a subtle, shifting, delicate and all-pervading humour"; a Chaucer whose humor makes up "the 'stuff and substance,' not merely of [his] intellect, but of his entire mental constitution"; a Chaucer whose humor, "the symptom of physical well-being," restrains him "from piercing into those depths of understanding where the tragic note must be heard and high seriousness is perpetually at home"—retains such a tenacious hold that the editors of a recent volume felt compelled to remind us that Chaucer, too, can be "dark."[4]

Given this state of affairs, one might reasonably assume that there have followed numerous studies devoted to Chaucer's humor, but that is not necessarily the case.[5] There exist innumerable articles, and several longer studies, devoted to Chaucerian comedy or to individual comedic works, and at least two books make a study of Chaucerian play; but we have tended to leave to one side the question of humor as something fundamental to Chaucer's makeup: a distinguishing quality of mind, an all-pervasive mood.[6] It is, however, along exactly such moody lines that this essay seeks to reevaluate Chaucerian humor. The primary aim of such humor, I mean to argue, is the one that Saintsbury touches upon when he describes a Chaucer "perpetually seeing the humorous side, not merely of his emotions but of his interests, his knowledge, his beliefs, his everything."[7] Expressing a mood that I will describe in these pages as critically melancholic, Chaucerian humor turns back upon its author in order to evacuate the very position of "father," which here will have to stand as a convenient proxy for Hoccleve's "maister" and, to borrow

---

[4] Ibid., cxxxviii; George Saintsbury, cited in Jost, *Chaucer's Humor*, 16; Howard Patch, cited in Jost, *Chaucer's Humor*, 24. Myra Seaman, Eileen Joy, Nicola Masciandaro, eds., *Dark Chaucer: An Assortment* (Brooklyn, N.Y.: punctum, 2012). I in no way dispute the assertion that Chaucer can be dark.

[5] "The bibliography on Chaucer's humor," notes Andrew Cole, "is not as extensive as one would expect." Andrew Cole, "Getting Chaucer's Jokes," in *Approaches to Teaching Chaucer's "Canterbury Tales,"* ed. Peter W. Travis and Frank Grady, 2nd ed. (New York: Modern Language Association of America, 2014), 62–66 (63).

[6] See, for example, Derek Pearsall, "The *Canterbury Tales* II: Comedy," in *The Cambridge Companion to Chaucer*, ed. Piero Boitani and Jill Mann, 2nd ed. (Cambridge: Cambridge University Press, 2003), 160–77; Peter W. Travis, *Disseminal Chaucer* (Notre Dame: University of Notre Dame Press, 2010); Cole, "Getting Chaucer's Jokes"; R. James Goldstein, "Chaucer, Freud, and the Political Economy of Wit: Tendentious Jokes in the *Nun's Priest's Tale*," in Jost, *Chaucer's Humor*, 145–62; Laura Kendrick, *Chaucerian Play: Comedy and Control in the "Canterbury Tales"* (Berkeley: University of California Press, 1988); Robert W. Hanning, *Serious Play: Desire and Authority in the Poetry of Ovid, Chaucer, and Ariosto* (New York: Columbia University Press, 2010); and the other essays found in Jost, *Chaucer's Humor*.

[7] Saintsbury, cited in Jost, *Chaucer's Humor*, 16.

from the language of contemporary political theory, sovereign.[8] Humor, or a humorous attitude, doesn't make Chaucer a father figure. On the contrary, one of this essay's implied arguments is that Chaucer's fifteenth-century inheritors invented a figure, "father Chaucer," that Chaucerian humor had already dissolved, not only as a figure, but as a structural position.[9] Rather, then, than treating Chaucerian humor as something to feel vaguely embarrassed about, and lest we misconstrue it at a time when "comedy has issues," we ought to understand it as the fundamental mood that helps make Chaucer a model, for anyone living under a regime of dispersed sovereign power, of health.[10]

[8] Structurally and functionally, linguistically and mythologically, legally and politically, the master, the father, and the sovereign all occupy the same exceptional position, as Kenneth Reinhard explains: "The signifier of the Father is 'sovereign' in its rule over the subject precisely insofar as it is the *exception* to the rules that govern the movements of signification"; or, "The primal father holds the place of the sovereign at the border of the law; both inside it, as its embodiment and the principle of its enforcement, and outside, the great exception, the one person who is not himself subject to prohibition, but freely enjoys"; or, "The sovereign is like the primal father in being stationed at the margins of the state he regulates; it is only insofar as there can be a radical exception to the law that the law can exist and be effective. The primal father and the sovereign occupy the position of extreme dictators whose word both violates the rule of the total state and promises its *totality*, closure, drawing a line between the inside and the outside." Kenneth Reinhard, "Towards a Political Theology of the Neighbor," in *The Neighbor: Three Inquiries in Political Theology* (Chicago: University of Chicago Press, 2005), 40, 42, 56. The matter is more than theoretical. In the *MED*, *fader*, def. 6; *maister*, def. 1; and *soverain*, defs. 1 and 2 shade into one another.

[9] My thinking here owes a profound debt to Spearing's argument in *Medieval to Renaissance in English Poetry*, which begins by noting that "Chaucer in his work nearly always presents the father unfavorably, either as absent or cruel" and that, furthermore, "he is unwilling to concede authority to his major poetic ancestors," and which culminates in the observation that Chaucer "is the first English poet to exist as an 'author,' the first to be known by name as the father of a body of work; and yet throughout his career he seems to be striving towards the culmination achieved in *The Canterbury Tales*, the relinquishment of his own fatherhood, the transformation of his work into a text [in the Barthesian sense of an 'anonymous, fatherless space']" (105–6). My only amendment to this interpretation is that even an absent, cruel father continues to occupy the position of sovereign exception, whereas the present essay aims to show how Chaucerian humor dissolves the position itself. Otherwise, I have not done much more than draw out the political implications of Spearing's reading by transposing it into a more contemporary theoretical key.

[10] See Lauren Berlant and Sianne Ngai, "Comedy Has Issues," *Critical Inquiry* 43 (Winter 2017): 233–49. In making reference to "a regime of dispersed sovereign power," I follow Giorgio Agamben's argument that "[T]he inclusion of bare life in the political realm constitutes the original—if concealed—nucleus of sovereign power. *It can even be said that the production of a biopolitical body is the original activity of sovereign power*. In this sense, biopolitics is at least as old as the sovereign exception." *Homo Sacer: Sovereign Power and Bare Life*, trans. Daniel Heller-Roazen (Stanford: Stanford University Press, 1998), 6 (emphasis in original). But see as well Eric Santner's description of our political situation as "a perpetual state of emergency/exception in which the boundaries

The Chaucerian text—scenario, really—that I will mostly focus on here, the prologue to *The Tale of Sir Thopas*, schematizes a particular configuration of power. In it, the "Chaucer" figure, diminutive and retiring, absorbed to the point of distraction, finds himself subjected to abuse by another figure at once vaguely tyrannical and vaguely ridiculous: the Host of the *Tales*, Harry Bailly.[11] As readers, we experience this scenario as amusing, and we understand that much of that amusement derives from the tension generated by the asymmetrical relation between the two figures involved.[12] But what is it that makes us register that tension as amusing in the first place? Why should a scenario built around tyranny and abuse be humorous at all?

To answer those questions, I turn to the crucial and, for our purposes, highly useful distinction Freud draws between jokes and the comic on one hand, and humor on the other.[13] I do so, in the first place, keenly aware that any turn to Freud risks putting off potential readers and yet buoyed by the conviction that the Freudian and Chaucerian texts overlap with and complicate one another, and particularly so on the matter

---

of the law have become undecidable" and the master's discourse "has been attenuated and dispersed across a field of relays and points of contact that no longer cohere, even in fantasy, as a consistent 'other' of possible address and redress." *On Creaturely Life: Rilke, Benjamin, Sebald* (Chicago: University of Chicago Press, 2006), 21–22.

[11] On the Host as tyrant, albeit one that gets reformed over the course of the *Tales*, see David R. Pichaske and Laura Sweetland, "Chaucer on the Medieval Monarchy: Harry Bailly in the *Canterbury Tales*," *ChauR* 11, no. 3 (Winter 1977): 184, 187. Judith Ferster also characterizes the Host as a kind of tyrant. See Judith Ferster, *Chaucer on Interpretation* (Cambridge: Cambridge University Press, 1985), 7, 144. On the Host as an object of ridicule and "figure of fun," see Barbara Page, "Concerning the Host," *ChauR* 4, no. 1 (Summer 1969): 3, 13. Ferster describes the Host as a dubious "ad hoc leader" who attempts to control a situation over which he has no authority and who in fact "has less than the control he claims" (7, 154). A more nuanced view of the Host as a mere governor (as opposed to a lord and governor) "seduced by his personal fantasy of the 'sovereign' or 'myghty man,'" and whose "tendency to confuse the visceral reactions of his own body with the interests of the corporate body he supposedly governs poses dangers for the *compagnye* throughout the Tales"—a figure against whom the pilgrim fellowship must remain on its guard—is found in David Wallace, *Chaucerian Polity: Absolutist Lineages and Associational Forms in England and Italy* (Stanford: Stanford University Press, 1997), 69, 70–71, 310.

[12] Bloomfield long ago observed that "the essence of Chaucer's humor comes out . . . in Chaucer's portrayal of himself," and particularly so in "the Chaucerian-persona strategy of answering a querulous objector." "Gloomy Chaucer," 61–62. Ordinarily, that "objector is assumed rather than portrayed" (62); but in the case of the Host, that objector is overbearingly present.

[13] Sigmund Freud, *Jokes and Their Relation to the Unconscious*, Vol. 8 of *The Standard Edition of the Complete Psychological Works of Sigmund Freud*, ed. and trans. James Strachey (London: Vintage Books, 2001), 236. Subsequent references to this edition will appear in the text.

of biopolitical subjectivity, to an extent that our field has been slow to recognize.[14] I turn to Freud, moreover, in respectful opposition to the approach, heavily indebted to the latest developments in cognitive studies, taken by Laura Kendrick in her own fascinating treatment of Chaucer's humor.[15] Freud was of course profoundly interested in cognition, or what he called "mental functioning." The difference is that contemporary cognitive studies, at least as Kendrick presents it, apparently proceeds from the assumption that mental functioning is directed only toward normative boundary creation and the securing of an integrated ego against external threats. Certainly there is some of that in Chaucer (and in Freud), but there is much less of it if we avoid making the fundamental error of confusing humor and the comic. Where Chaucer and Freud converge—and where the radical dimension of each comes through—is around the question of a split subject turned, not toward the outside world, but inward, against itself. Where Chaucer and Freud converge, in other words, is in their assumption of a split subject whose critical engagement with the world must first pass through a critical dismantling of itself. What makes Chaucerian humor humorous, and not just comic, is that it is directed against "Chaucer," which is to say, against one name for the ground of sovereign power.

Lastly, I turn to Freud in the hopes of clarifying the position, at once ambivalent, adjacent, and critical, of Chaucerian humor in relation to the field of affect.[16] Judged solely by the standards of medieval psychology (to say nothing of early Chaucer studies), Chaucer appears to have been a "well-disposed," if somewhat eccentric, subject, one whose "sensitive soul" was properly governed by his "intellectual soul."[17] Understood in those terms, humor becomes little more than an expression of Chaucer's capacity to impose reason upon feeling—to prevent his intellectual soul from being affected, too much, by the stirrings of his sensitive soul.

[14] With the notable exceptions of L. O. Aranye Fradenburg and Mark Miller.

[15] Laura Kendrick, "Humor in Perspective," in *Chaucer: Contemporary Approaches*, ed. Susanna Fein and David Raybin (University Park: Pennsylvania State University Press, 2010).

[16] For different, if equally illuminating, takes on the affective turn in premodern literary studies in particular, see Stephanie Trigg, "Introduction—Emotional Histories: Beyond the Personalization of the Past and the Abstraction of Affect Theory," *Exemplaria* 26, no. 1 (2014): 3–15; Holly Crocker, "Medieval Affects Now," *Exemplaria* 29, no. 1 (2017): 82–98; and Sarah McNamer, "Feelings," in *Oxford Twenty-First Century Approaches to Literature: Middle English*, ed. Paul Strohm (Oxford: Oxford University Press, 2007), 241–57.

[17] Crocker, "Medieval Affects Now," 84.

To rest there, however, is to risk reinforcing the very convergence of humor, health, and paternalism that the present essay hopes to recalibrate, and that the technique of Chaucerian humor itself works patiently to dismantle. True, when viewed from a certain perspective, humor begins to look suspiciously like a technique of affective governance: yet another tool available to those emotional regimes so central, as William Reddy has shown us, to the histories of human suffering.[18] We might, however, follow the lead of Spurgeon, Patch, and Saintsbury, and understand humor differently: as an all-encompassing mood, attunement, or disposition—in a word, as *Stimmung*.[19] Reducible to neither a feeling nor an emotion, humor is best understood as a form of critical attunement, a disposition in relation to regimes of emotional implantation, at least insofar as those regimes extend the combined reach of sovereign power and biopolitical governmentality. As Freud's work reminds us, moreover, humor as *Stimmung*—a disposition in relation to a world full of ugly feelings, a particular way of remaining attuned to suffering—holds a distinct advantage over such *Stimmungen* as boredom and anxiety. By differentiating humor from jokes and the comic, Freud could grasp its essential function as an un-affected attunement directed toward the neutralization of exactly those forces that thrive on the production and implantation of negative affect. If humor might really be understood as the expression of a well-disposed subject, a subject whose sensitive soul remains under the governance of their intellectual soul, it is only insofar as humor serves to counteract—to manage, as it were—the soul as Michel Foucault conceived of it: the soul as a technique of power, a disciplinary implantation, the prison of the biopoliticized body.[20] The

[18] "To a significant degree," Reddy explains in an interview with Jan Plamper, "suffering is organized and varies in surprising ways from one time and place to another. Normative 'emotives,' often prescribed, often repeated, can be used, up to a point, to change how we feel. Nonetheless there are (universal) limits to our plasticity in this regard, as well as a (universal) physiological substrate that is manipulated in such training. Learning the norms of a prevailing 'emotional regime' generally involves suffering under a certain discipline." See Jan Plamper, "The History of Emotions: An Interview with William Reddy, Barbara Rosenwein, and Peter Stearns," *History and Theory* 49, no. 2 (May 2010): 237–65 (241). It is my contention that Chaucerian humor disrupts the suffering engendered by that "certain discipline" required to enforce emotional regimes.

[19] For a concise overview of *Stimmung*, a word "virtually untranslatable" but conventionally rendered as "mood" or "attunement," and the central role it plays in the thought of both Heidegger and Walter Benjamin, see Ilit Ferber, "*Stimmung*: Heidegger and Benjamin," in *Sparks Will Fly: Benjamin and Heidegger*, ed. Andrew Benjamin and Dimitris Vardoulakis (Albany: SUNY Press, 2015), 67–93; but see in particular 74–77.

[20] Michel Foucault, *Discipline and Punish: The Birth of the Prison*, trans. Alan Sheridan (New York: Vintage, 1995), 29–30.

truly well-disposed subject, as psychoanalysis reminds us again and again, disorders itself so as to dissolve the paternal position. Where humor and health converge is around the preclusion of mastery.

The political implications of all this are best grasped by considering two different ways of accounting for the origin of affect. On the one hand, Brian Massumi argues that affects are, unlike emotions, prepersonal and (the inference follows) presubjective.[21] Eric Santner, meanwhile, describes most affect, and the negative affects (agitation, disorientation, boredom, cringingness) tied to what he calls "creaturely life," in particular, as stemming from an exposure to the sovereign ban and therefore as necessarily consequent to subjectification.[22] As such divergences suggest, the origin of affect remains a matter of theoretical dispute. Yet there is no dispute about the site of affect; both Massumi and Santner locate affect firmly in the unconscious.[23] Any intervention into our affective state must take place, then, in the unconscious or, to put the same thing differently, on the very ground of our split subjectivity. Charting a middle course across that murky terrain—a course halfway between Massumi and Santner, as it were—Chaucer shows us how to wrest affect away from the sovereign and lodge it in a time and place anterior to subjectification (and thus, as I will go on to explain, before the imposition of the reality principle and the ascendency of the superego). That, in and of itself, is a radical move, albeit one modestly pursued. Yet Chaucer's humorous masterstroke is to take this process one step further. For not only does his fictional relation, as pilgrim, to the Host of the *Tales* work to neutralize the latter's authority. Not only, then, does that relation extend the critique of tyranny and abusive

---

[21] Here I rely on E. Shouse, "Feeling, Emotion, Affect," *M/C Journal* 8, no. 6 (December 2005), http://journal.media-culture.org.au/0512/03-shouse.php (accessed June 4, 2019).

[22] Santner, *On Creaturely Life*, 12–15, 21–22. On the paradoxical logic of the sovereign ban as both banishment from, and abandonment to, the law, see Agamben, *Homo Sacer*, 28–29, 82–83, 104–11. But see as well Robert Mills's chapter on "Sovereignty," in *A Handbook of Middle English Studies*, ed. Marion Turner (Malden: Wiley-Blackwell, 2013), 269–83.

[23] Massumi: "Intensity is beside that loop, a nonconscious, never-to-conscious autonomic remainder. It is outside expectation and adaptation, as disconnected from meaningful sequencing, from narration, as it is from vital function. It is narratively delocalized, spreading over the generalized body surface, like a lateral backwash from the function-meaning interloops traveling the vertical path between head and heart." Brian Massumi, "The Autonomy of Affect," *Cultural Critique* 31 (Autumn 1995): 83–109 (85). Santner: "The so-called formations of the unconscious can be understood . . . as the specific modes of expressivity of creaturely life"; Santner, *On Creaturely Life*, 30.

authority carried out elsewhere in the *Tales*.[24] Chaucer's own self-positioning within the prologue to the *Thopas* teaches us how to arrest, through the power of absorption, the workings of the masterful position he himself occupies. What is more, he demonstrates how humor, understood neither as an affect nor as a disciplinary form of affective management but as an un-affected critical mood, provides us with one of the primary tactics for achieving that end. And in that he remains in sympathy with, even while staying several steps ahead of, Freud.

When Freud first takes up the subject of humor, in 1905's *Jokes and Their Relation to the Unconscious*, he does so under the auspices of an economic theory of psychical functioning predicated on an image of mental life governed by the dictates of the pleasure principle and striving to achieve equilibrium through the dynamic interplay of tension and discharge, repression and evasion. For the early Freud, the basic work of humor, work carried out by the humorist and imparted to the listener, reader, or spectator, consists of transforming unpleasurable emotions into an experience of pleasure, principally through the mechanism of humorous substitution. We err, Freud suggests, when we conflate humor with jokes and the comic; the one should really be understood as the inverse of the other two. Humor's "fending off of the possibility of suffering places it among the great series of methods which the human mind has constructed in order to evade the compulsion to suffer," writes Freud. He then continues: "Thanks to this connection, humour possesses a dignity which is wholly lacking, for instance, in jokes, for jokes either serve simply to obtain a yield of pleasure or place the yield of pleasure that has been obtained in the service of aggression."[25] We laugh at a joke or in the presence of the comic. But we look to the humorist for help in managing our own internal economy.

When Freud returns to the subject of humor in 1927, it is this question of humor's dignity and grandeur that mostly interests him. Now, though, he has at his disposal the so-called second topography of ego, id, and superego—that vaguely familial unit—and it quickly becomes evident that he means to enlist humor in his late-career project of shoring up the paternal superego. Humor can operate in one of two ways, according to Freud's (arguably reductive) estimation. More obviously, a

---

[24] See, for example, Wallace's chapters on the *Melibee*, *The Clerk's Tale*, and *The Manciple's Tale* in *Chaucerian Polity*, 212–98.

[25] Sigmund Freud, "Humour," in *Complete Psychological Works*, ed. and trans. Strachey, 21:159–66 (163). Subsequent references to this edition will appear in the text.

humorous attitude can be directed "towards other people" who are "made the object of humorous contemplation, as when a writer or narrator describes the behavior of real or imagined people" (21:161). In this attitude, suggests Freud, drawing an analogy that ought to make us immediately suspicious, the humorist stands in the same relation to his objects of contemplation as "an adult does toward a child when he recognizes and smiles at the trivialities of interests and sufferings that seem so great to it" (8:163). "Thus the humorist," concludes Freud, "would acquire his superiority by assuming the role of the grown-up and identifying himself to some extent with his father, and reducing the other people to being children" (21:163).

But what is it, Freud wonders, "that makes the humorist arrogate [the role of indulgent father] to himself" in the first place (21:163)? To answer this question, Freud asks the reader to recall "the other, probably more primary and important, situation of humour, in which a person adopts a humorous attitude towards himself in order to ward off possible suffering." If the humorist is to his subject as the indulgent father is to his child, then are we not justified in "saying that," in self-directed humor, "someone is treating himself like a child and is at the same time playing the part of a superior adult towards that child" (21:164)? The ego, Freud reminds us,

is not a simple entity. It harbours within it, as its nucleus, a special agency—the super-ego. Sometimes it is merged with the super-ego so that we cannot distinguish between them, whereas in other circumstances it is sharply differentiated from it. Genetically the super-ego is the heir to the paternal agency. It often keeps the ego in strict dependence and still really treats it as the parents, or the father, once treated the child, in its early years.

(21:164)

What we encounter in the "more primary and important" form of inwardly directed humor, Freud theorizes, is a complicated, quasi-familial dynamic whereby the paternalistic superego intervenes to keep the ego from being overwhelmed by affect, but only at the cost of the latter's deflation. "To the super-ego, thus inflated," avers Freud, "the ego can appear tiny and all its interests trivial; and, with this new distribution of energy, it may become an easy matter for the super-ego to suppress the ego's possibilities of reacting [to the provocations of reality]"

(8:164). What humor thus bestows on us is, among other things, an entirely different way of appraising the superego. "In other connections we knew the superego as a severe master," observes Freud. But now we have something else entirely. Now we have a superego willing to "condescend to enabling the ego to obtain a small yield of pleasure" (21:166). Now we have a superego that speaks "kindly words of comfort to the intimidated ego, a superego that, by means of humor, consoles the ego and protects it from suffering" (21:166). Now we have a super-ego that, like a wise and benevolent father (and Freud is quick to point out that a consoling superego "does not contradict its origin in the paternal agency"), says, whether directly to the humorist or, through the medium of the humorist, to others: "Look! here is the world, which seems so dangerous! It is nothing but a game for children—just worth making a jest about!" (21:166). Whereas a joke is "the contribution made to the comic by the unconscious," humor, Freud concludes, with that air of triumphalism known to exasperate even his most sympathetic readers, *would be the contribution made to the comic through the agency of the super-ego*" (21:165, italics in the original).

Two qualities make this inwardly directed form of humor quintessentially Chaucerian. One is that it bears a striking resemblance to medieval theories of an interiorized humoral economy—far more striking, one might argue, than does any outwardly directed comparison theory of comedy.[26] The other is that it goes hand in hand, as Simon Critchley points out, with melancholia. The "core insight" of Freud's humor paper, Critchley reminds us, "is that in humour I find myself ridiculous and I acknowledge this in laughter or simply in a smile."[27] Critchley then goes on: "Humour consists in laughing at oneself, in finding oneself ridiculous, and such humour is not depressing, but on the contrary gives us a sense of emancipation, consolation and childlike elevation."[28] Such elevation is not to be confused with inflatedness, however. On the contrary, "humour recalls us to the modesty and limitedness of the human condition, a limitedness that calls not for tragic-heroic affirmation but comic acknowledgement, not Promethean authenticity but a

[26] For an overview of those theories, which tend to locate the origin of laughter in one's sudden perception of superiority in comparison to another person, or of incongruity in another person's norm-violating behavior, see Kendrick, "Humor in Perspective," 139–42.

[27] Simon Critchley, *On Humour* (London: Routledge, 2002), 94.

[28] Ibid., 95.

laughable inauthenticity."[29] Its post-Romantic terminology notwith-standing, this is an account of humor entirely in keeping with a late medieval technique of humor—one developed in part, as Kendrick argues, by Chaucer and Deschamps—in which the "deregulation of humors" was "pretended and played deliberately for entertainment."[30] "Even though the humorist brought his humor to bear on others or the exterior world in order to amuse by highlighting their norm-violating contradictions," writes Kendrick,

the original sense of "humor" as something innate in the humorist lingered (and still does, although we no longer associate a sense of humor with imbal-anced humors). The humorist never forgets his "humorous" origins, that is, his own contradictory nature, and retains a capacity, even a tendency, deliberately to mock or provoke laughter at himself, as well as at others.[31]

Although we may wish to query whether the contradictory, deregula-tory nature of humor is pretended rather than revealed, the central point here remains an important one: for Chaucer and Deschamps no less than for Freud, humor is the outward expression of an internal economy gone awry.

That this has something to do with melancholia was intuited even by Deschamps, whose observation that "It's impossible to be very melancholy / when people laugh the ways they do these days" implies that humorous contemplation—of other people, in this case, although Deschamps was not above making himself the butt of the joke—offers the perfect way to drive off melancholy, as if the two dispositions were affected by the same stimuli or the one were the counterpart of the other.[32] And indeed this is exactly the point: The operations of humor can be described in terms of contradiction because they depend upon, and arise out of, the same split subjectivity, the same internal division between the ego and the superego, that gives rise, in Freud's model, to melancholia. For Freud, in fact, it is the enigmatic clinical phenomenon of melancholia that first affords us a clear view of "the constitution of the human ego,"[33] since it is in melancholia that we see how "one part

---

[29] Ibid., 102.
[30] Kendrick, "Humor in Perspective," 138.
[31] Ibid., 138.
[32] Ibid., 140.
[33] Sigmund Freud, "Mourning and Melancholia," in *Complete Psychological Works*, ed. and trans. Strachey, 14:237–58 (247). Subsequent references to this edition will appear in the text.

of the ego sets itself over against the other, judges it critically, and, as it were, takes it as its object" (14:247).

One can forgive Critchley for reading Freud's account of melancholia and concluding that, while "humour has the same formal structure as depression," "it is an antidepressant that works by the ego finding itself ridiculous" instead of despicable.[34] Humor is more, however, than just the inverse of melancholia: on one side, a kindly superego that helps the ego to see itself as an object of humorous contemplation; on the other, a cruel superego that punishes the ego as if it were an *abject object*.[35] Rather than two sides of the same coin, flipped by the same superego, wagered on by the same ego, humor and melancholia exist in a continuum on the order of a Möbius strip. Fundamentally, that continuum rests on what Freud calls reality-testing, and on the relationship between reality-testing and suffering. Like humor, which allows the ego to "refuse to be distressed by the provocations of reality, to let itself be compelled to suffer"—to insist, in fact, "that it cannot be affected by the traumas of the external world"—melancholia involves an extreme form of reality-testing: one that repudiates the reality of the so-called real world. Specifically, melancholia tests the reality that insists that the loved object is really, truly lost—the reality that mourning leads the healthy subject to accept, according to Freud—and rejects it in favor of preserving, not just the object as such, but the subject's love for the object and, more intriguing still, the conflict associated with one's ambivalence toward that object. Counterintuitive as it may sound, melancholia, like humor, allows us to test the reality that might say otherwise and declare, Look! the world is not such a bad place after all—because the loved object, far from being lost, persists as the encrypted, incorporated, utterly unconscious object of melancholia.

This brings us to an aspect of humor that neither Freud nor Critchley, in their strenuous efforts to identify a "mature," benevolently paternalistic superego, seems willing to confront. We, on the other hand, must confront it directly, as it forms the very core of what I am calling Chaucerian humor. Freud and Critchley both tend to assume that the suffering that melancholia and humor alike set out to manage comes from the outside. But that is only half right. For as Freud's own language suggests—in the joke-book, for example, when he describes the "defensive processes," of which humor is the highest, as performing "the task

[34] Critchley, *On Humour*, 101.
[35] Ibid., 97.

of preventing the generation of unpleasure from internal sources"
(8:233)—the principal reality that both humor and melancholia test
and reject is the reality of suffering assumed from the outside and yet
imposed from within: the suffering internalized, and then carefully
administered, by the "special agency" of the superego. Among the many
suggestive, seemingly incidental observations Freud makes in the 1917
essay "Mourning and Melancholia," two in particular stand out. One is
that the self-reproaches and complaints of melancholics "are really
'plaints' in the old sense of the word": "reproaches against a loved object
which have been shifted away from it on to the patient's own ego"
(14:248). The other is that the loss at the heart of melancholia is, unlike
the tangible loss of mourning, "a loss of a more ideal kind." Indeed,
writes Freud, the loss felt in melancholia is invariably affective and
intangible, extending "for the most part beyond the clear case of a loss
by death" and including "all those situations of being slighted, neglected
or disappointed" (14:251). But where Freud wants to attach those feelings to the object (which, having once been incorporated into the ego,
then becomes the target of the superego's wrath), it seems clear from
her plaints that the discontent of the melancholic is directed, not at the
lost object per se, but at the actions of the paternal agency—that is, the
superego—that led to the loss of the object in the first place. Whatever
quality one might have admired in a paternal agency that, to paraphrase
Freud, is genetically the progenitor of the superego, it vanishes once
that agency demands that the nascent subject give up the object—once,
that is, the ego is compelled to suffer. To put this another way: if what
the melancholic ego and the humorous ego both repudiate is the reality
imposed by the reality principle, then this can only mean that it is the
superego, as the force behind the reality principle, that so frustrates and
disappoints the melancholic ego, which has now had to give up two
ideals: the object and the trustworthy paternal agency.[36] And if it is also
the case, as Freud seems to suggest, that the ego and the superego are
but two parts of the self-same complex (the superego being the

---

[36] Freud's canonical definition of the reality principle can be found in "Formulations
on the Two Principles of Mental Functioning," in *Complete Psychological Works*, ed. and
trans. Strachey, 12:218–26. To wit: the developing mind having grasped that the "satisfaction by means of hallucination" allowed under the pleasure principle can never result
in the actual satisfaction of a need, "a new principle of mental functioning was thus
introduced; what was presented in the mind was no longer what was agreeable but
what was real, even if it happened to be disagreeable. This setting up of the *reality
principle* proved to be a momentous step" (12:219, italics in the original).

"nucleus" of, or a "precipitate" within, the ego), then this can only mean that the superego is made to stand in judgment of its own, anarchic actions. In a two-pronged gesture, melancholia first apprehends and archives the great wrong, the fundamental unpleasure, that humor then transforms into the pleasure of the jest. The ultimate incongruity that humor thus registers, reversing our expectation that we must accept suffering, is the gulf between justice and the reality imposed by the superegoic reality principle.

That is the gulf widened—like a smile or a fissure—by the inter-actions between the pilgrim Chaucer and the Host, Harry Bailly, found in the prologue to Chaucer's *Tale of Sir Thopas* and, to a lesser extent, in the link between that tale and the *Melibee*.[37] That the links interspersed among the *Canterbury Tales* enact some sort of "roadside drama" has long been recognized; but in this particular instance, it might be more accu-rate to say, at least at first, that the links in question stage the splitting of the subject essential to humor by placing Chaucer's pilgrim persona in the position of the infantilized ego, and the Host in the position of the cruel and demanding superego.[38] It may not seem that way initially. Having just resorted to japing in an effort to repudiate the reality (as it were) of the prevailing somber mood created by *The Prioress's Tale*, Harry appears to play the part of the benevolent, "fatherly" superego, the one that, "in humor, speaks such kindly words of comfort to the intimidated ego": "Look! here is the world, which seems so dangerous! It is nothing but a game for children—just worth making a jest about!" That may well be true of the world, of course. All the same, let us exercise some critical caution. One definition of *japen* is "to deceive," and in this case

[37] Kenneth Eckert argues persuasively that *The Tale of Sir Thopas* itself, and not merely its linking prologue, should be read as a parody directed at the Host. "Thopas' referentiality," he writes, "points not to an outside genre (romance) but intratextually toward Fragment VII/Group B² as an episodic move in the *Tales*. Just as the Miller–Reeve and Friar–Summoner rivalries help contextualize their respective tales as rejoin-ders, *Thopas* makes better sense as a requital to the Host." Kenneth Eckert, "Harry Bailly and Chaucer-Pilgrim's 'Quiting' in the *Tale of Sir Thopas*," *RES* 68, no. 285 (2016): 471–87 (472).

[38] Such splitting remains consistent with the peculiarly Chaucerian strategy of autho-rial self-fashioning described by Helen Cooper: "There is a famous cartoon of an animal head with two long appendages projecting from one side, which can be either the ears of a rabbit or the bill of a duck. It is easy to see it as either; but it is impossible to see it as both rabbit and duck at once. The picture confounds and combines those categories of 'both/and' as against 'either/or'; and Sir Thopas is Chaucer's duck-and-rabbit of a self-portrait." Helen Cooper, "Chaucer's Self-Fashioning," *Poetica* 55, no. 1 (2001): 55–74 (59).

the superegoic position, in the guise of the Host, effectively masks its aggression by making a jest.[39] True, that aggression will be revealed soon enough in the way that Harry's demanding, vaguely abusive treatment of the pilgrim Chaucer—"Approche neer, and looke up murily"—coerces good cheer (*CT*, VII.698).[40] But for the moment, the Host's humorous demeanor continues to obscure the way that he repeats, in a kind of infinite parodic regression, the first time he declared himself the sovereign exception.[41] Then he had made himself the sole judge of a tale-telling game of his own devising. Now he moves, once again in good Schmittian fashion, to supplant the miracle of the *Prioress' Tale* by declaring himself the japing, secular exception to the *Tale*'s lingering mood (*CT*, VII.691–93).[42] Truly, in this case, humor, to paraphrase Freud, serves an economic function, regulating the amount of energy—psychological, somatic, communal—to be expended upon a feeling that Harry, alone among the pilgrims, finds unpleasurable enough to want to manage it.

Taken altogether, then, the prologue to the *Thopas* presents us with a humorous staging of the very encounter whose lasting effects humor works to economize: the putative encounter between ego and superego, subject and sovereign, creature and creator. The suspension of the norm, coupled with the declaration of the state of exception; the creation of the subject through the ex-citing encounter with sovereign power; the substitution of the exception for the miracle: those essential elements of the sovereign ban are here firmly in place.[43] Yet it is exactly at this

---

[39] *MED* online edition, https://quod.lib.umich.edu/m/middle-english-dictionary/dictionary (accessed June 4, 2019).

[40] All references to Chaucer's work are to *The Riverside Chaucer*, gen. ed. Larry D. Benson, 3rd ed. (Boston, Mass.: Houghton Mifflin, 1987).

[41] Although she did not have the concept of the sovereign exception at her disposal, Barbara Page describes the Host in precisely those terms. She does so, moreover, by citing Ralph Baldwin's *Unity of the "Canterbury Tales,"* written in 1955. In that work, writes Page, "Baldwin has described in rather schematic terms how the Host is set off from the pilgrims who 'have been presented in the *clause*' ['and pilgrimes were they alle'] whereas 'the Host is presented and described outside the *clause*, in the Tabard. . . . The Host thereby is identified with the actual journey, but separated from the original pilgrims.'" Page, "Concerning the Host," 10–11.

[42] The reference is to Carl Schmitt, in *Political Theology*: "The exception in jurisprudence is analogous to the miracle in theology." *Political Theology: Four Chapters on the Concept of Sovereignty*, trans. George Schwab (Chicago: University of Chicago Press, 2005), 36.

[43] On the elements of the sovereign ban, see Santner, *On Creaturely Life*, 12–16, 24, 30–34.

point, the point at which the *Canterbury Tales* stages a roadside "dra-
medy" externalizing the generation of suffering from internal sources,
that the subtly revolutionary potential of humor asserts itself. "What
man artow?," Harry asks the pilgrim Chaucer, posing the central question of biopolitical production: *What form of life are you* (*CT*, VII.695)?
And in truth the pilgrim Chaucer is not much of a man, if by *man* we
mean a form of life sanctioned, and qualified, by the sovereign ban, a
life animated by the agitations and excitements tied to creatureliness, a
political life, a life of *bios*. Thus Harry's teasing, which, when stripped
to its barest elements, can best be described as a kind of profiling, continues, famously:

> "Thou lookest as thou woldest fynde an hare,
> For evere upon the ground I se thee stare.
> [. . .]
> This were a popet in an arm t'embrace
> For any woman, smal and fair of face.
> He semeth elvyssh by his countenaunce,
> For unto no wight dooth he daliaunce"
> (*CT*, VII.696–704).

It is all a game, of course, albeit a high-stakes one that determines,
according to how well one understands its rules and how deftly one
performs within it, a pilgrim's status as insider or outsider. And yet
the crucial point is that the pilgrim Chaucer remains unmoved, almost
oblivious; the provocations and petty abuses of the superegoic Host,
however facetious they may be, affect him not at all. "Hooste," he
replies, "ne be nat yvele apayd / For oother tale certes kan I noon, / But
of a rym I lerned longe agoon" (*CT*, VII.707–9). This is where the
humor of the scene resides: in the way that, to paraphrase Freud,
"[Chaucer] refuses to be distressed by the provocations of [fictitious]
reality, to let himself be compelled to suffer. He insists that he cannot
be affected by the traumas of the external world; he shows, in fact,
that such traumas are no more than occasions for him to gain pleasure"
(14:162). The Host, occupying the position of the sovereign superego,
demands affect. Pilgrim Chaucer, unlike the Pardoner, say, or the Miller
or the Monk, refuses to give him any.

In this way, Chaucer provides us with a welcome antidote to one of
the late-period Freud's more frustrating tendencies, which is his habit

of shoring up the superego by attributing to it more power, and more humanity, than it rightly deserves. Chaucer counteracts that sort of backsliding by splitting "himself," on the page, between a tiny, put-upon ego and a superegoic figure, the Host in this case, who is at best blustering and preposterous—"laughably inauthentic" in his attempts at executing authority—and at worst tyrannical and anarchic, imposing a rule that is unsolicited, inconsistent, and impossible to maintain.[44] Of this quintessentially Chaucerian tactic I will have more to say in a moment. At this point, however, the attentive reader is no doubt wondering whether the pilgrim Chaucer's apparent obliviousness in the face of unpleasant reality—the essence of humor, according to Freud—doesn't serve to prop up the superego, and to substantiate sovereign power more generally, in an especially subtle and insidious fashion. After all, if the pilgrim Chaucer, who is nothing more than one of the masks worn by the poet Chaucer (who may well be nothing more than one of the masks worn by the functionary Chaucer)—that is to say, both a stand-in for, and a creation of, the creator of the other Canterbury pilgrims and their tales—if the pilgrim Chaucer remains impervious to the needling of the poet Chaucer's creation, Harry Bailly, then doesn't that imply that the representatives of power remain immune to the criticism we might direct their way? Is Chaucer's humorous presentation of himself as tiny and unobtrusive merely another instance of japing, of deception: the last laugh of the "naïf Collector of Customs"?[45]

To such questions, Chaucer's performance provides a slyly subversive answer. Superficially, Chaucer appears to have it both ways. On the one hand, he gets to play, simultaneously, the role of "humorist"—the role of kindly and benevolent father to his creations, indulging in their eccentricities and peccadillos, even their outrages, without being affected by them—and the role of "satirist," representing reality in such a way as to sharpen the reader's critical judgment. In that, of course, Chaucer only serves to perpetuate a certain image of sovereign power, a certain style of mastery, by arrogating to himself the right to display forbearance, and to delegate judgment, as only power can. On the other

[44] Or, as Pichaske and Sweetland put it, "Harry Bailly is not the prototype of a good ruler. His government is tyrannical, uncharitable, willful, irresponsible, malicious, abusive, undignified, and most of all inept. . . . The Host-ruler's reactions are arbitrary, irrational, uncharitable, and unfair." "Chaucer on the Medieval Monarchy," 184–85.

[45] The observation that "a naïf Collector of Customs would be a paradoxical monster" is G. L. Kittredge's, cited by E. Talbot Donaldson, "Chaucer the Pilgrim," in *Speaking of Chaucer* (Durham, N.C.: Labyrinth Press, 1983), 2.

hand, by exposing his pilgrim persona to the petty cruelty of a super-egoic figure like the Host, Chaucer manages to land a double-blow, as it were, against the masterful position of the paternal superego by making the position as such, and all those who occupy it (including the Father of English Poetry), appear simultaneously petty and ludicrous (the Host) and tiny and harmless (Chaucer). This can only serve to drain the position itself of grandeur, transforming the "paternal agency" that Freud works so hard to aggrandize into an object, if not of pathos and derision, then at least of humorous contemplation.

Here again, though, we need to guard against deception. If Chaucer has managed, by re-splitting his already split subjectivity, to transform the superegoic position of Father into a protean paradox—a figure at once laughably tyrannical, pathetically tiny, and defiantly oblivious to the demands of the reality principle—then how are we ever to criticize the power personified, and administered, by the avatars of the paternal agency? Who would feel comfortable attacking a "popet"? Who would wish to brag about vanquishing Harry Bailly? Might it be, in fact, that Chaucerian humor works so well as to put its target out of reach? Perhaps. But I want to propose another way of reading the situation. I want to suggest that, embedded within the layers of Chaucerian humor, there can be found a simple, two-pronged strategy for counteracting power. First: it does no good to attack power directly, since it will always find a way to absorb defiance, if only by feeding off of the affect that spectacles of outrage inevitably provide but that humor, in its studied indifference, wisely withholds. Second: the best course of action is thus not to defy power or even to address it (through mockery, say) but to absorb its attentions so thoroughly as to arrest them. The best course of action, in other words, lies in remembering, as Chaucer manifestly does, an affinity we examined earlier and to which we must now return: the affinity between melancholia and humor.

The mourning process is not difficult to comprehend, according to Freud. Having first "shown that the loved object no longer exists," "reality-testing" then "proceeds to demand that all libido shall be withdrawn from its attachments to that object" (14:244). Understandably, this process, which gets "carried out bit by bit, at great expense of time and cathectic energy," can drag on, and it often arouses an opposition on the part of the ego "so intense that a turning away from reality takes place and a clinging to the object through the medium of a hallucinatory wishful psychosis" (14:244). In the end, though, concludes Freud, the fact remains "that when the work of mourning is completed the ego becomes free and uninhibited again," ready to transfer its libido to another object (14:245). In the meantime, the inhibitions and loss of interest in the outside world that mark the condition "are fully accounted for by the work of mourning in which the ego is absorbed" for the duration (14:245). No, there is no mystery to mourning. Melancholia, though, is different. In melancholia, the object-loss at the root of the affliction remains unconscious, and so, as Freud himself must admit, "the melancholic seems puzzling to us because we cannot see what it is that is absorbing him so completely" (14:246).

That puzzlement comes to mind as we make our way through the prologue to the *Thopas* and the "murrie wordes" that pass there between the pilgrim Chaucer and the Host. In a manner reminiscent of the intrigued (and somewhat bemused) Freud—the manner, that is, of the captivated would-be master—Harry cannot see what it is that is absorbing the distracted Chaucer so completely. All we know is that Chaucer's absorption manages to capture the attentions of the Host, who reacts, comically, by drawing a comparison: "He semeth elvyssh by his countenaunce / For unto no wight dooth he daliaunce." Setting aside how Chaucerian humor works here to perform a critique of the policing aspect of comic comparison, let us ask a more pressing question: What *does* absorb the pilgrim Chaucer, his eyes set intently on the ground like one who "woldest fynde an hare," so completely that Harry cannot make out what it is, either literally or figuratively? Consider the divergent associations of *hare* and *woldest*. The association of the hare with images of being hunted and hounded, of being prey to a more powerful predator—images, in short, of vulnerability and suffering—recall the suffering that both humor and melancholia refuse.[46] The association of

---

[46] "*Fynde an hare* is usually interpreted as a hunting figure," according to Beryl Rowland. More intriguingly, when the figure "is used as a technical term in the hunting treatises, the understanding is that dogs are employed in the hunt." Most intriguingly, "the idea that it was a bad omen to encounter a hare prevailed until the end of the nineteenth century" in England and elsewhere. "If the Host is thinking of the popular lore regarding the hare, he may imply that the expression on Chaucer's face is that of a man anticipating ill-luck." Or bringing it. Either way, the image of being absorbed in the earth and tied, vaguely, to bad omens and ill luck is a quintessentially melancholic one. Beryl Rowland, "Bihoold the murye wordes of the Hoost to Chaucer," *NM* 64, no. 1 (1963): 48–50. On the dog as an "emblem" of melancholia, see Walter Benjamin, *The Origin of German Tragic Drama*, trans. John Osborne (London: Verso, 1985), 152. I note as well that, according to the *MED*, the etymological root of "dogerel," as in the Host's complaint about the *Thopas* that "[t]his may wel be rym dogerel" (*CT*, VII.925), is *dogge*.

the hare with the "unruly" world of nature tempts us to accept, more-over, that suffering is just that: natural, inevitable, given. Then we recall that the hare is not in fact present, that it is "there" only as an effect of Harry's teasing language (and whatever forces they are that inform that language). The pilgrim Chaucer only looks as if he *woldest* find a hare; and it is that introduction of potentiality that makes all the difference, alerting us as it does to what might be called Chaucer's double uncon-sciousness. For as much as one of his eyes may be fixed on suffering, the other is fixed on a speculative, "as if" realm, an alternative to the reality of the reality principle that can only be accessed through the form of reality-testing, common to melancholia and humor, that repudiates the world as it is: unjust, diminished, missing the lost object. Pushed to the speculative outskirts of the *polis*, the melancholic humorist is left to pursue an "elvyssh" craft that, to a far greater extent than the other "elvysshe craft" practiced in the "suburbes," acts as the precondition for transformation.[47]

It is this quintessentially Chaucerian convergence of humor and mel-ancholia that Freud's and, following him, Critchley's emphasis on the benevolence of a "mature" superego tends to downplay; for such an emphasis misreads the dynamic between ego and superego under the melancholic workings of humor. Let us recall an image from before: that of humor and melancholia not as the inverse of one another but as a sort of Möbius strip—a continuous relationship staged, as I have been arguing, in the prologue to the *Thopas*. In "Humour" Freud notes, almost in passing, that "the grandeur" in humor (a grandeur, let us remind ourselves, lacking in jokes and the comic) "clearly lies in the triumph of narcissism, the victorious assertion of the ego's invulnerabil-ity" (21:162). Almost immediately, though, Freud turns around and betrays the ego by crediting its moment of triumph to the good graces of the superego (21:165). Yet if humor represents the triumph of the narcissistic ego, then it also represents the triumph of the melancholic ego. That, at least, seems to be the upshot of what Freud suggests toward the end of "Mourning and Melancholia," when he notes that melancholia is fundamentally narcissistic insofar as it involves a regres-sion of libido back into the ego in an effort to preserve love for the now incorporated object (14:257, 258). Recall, moreover, that what humor and melancholia both repudiate is not suffering in general but the suf-fering compelled by the superego's enforcement of the reality principle

[47] That would be alchemy, as the Canon's Yeoman reveals (*CT*, VIII.751, 657).

and its cruel abuse of the ego, specifically. To which we should add Freud's later observation (or is it a concession?), made in "The Ego and the Id," that the ego preserves, through incorporation and encryption, the object as a part of itself—that, indeed, the ego is a veritable archive of objects.[48] All of which prompts the question: Is the grandeur we detect in humor really due to the triumph of an ego consoled, in all its tininess, by an inflated superego?

The superego, as any reader of Lacan will be quick to tell you, gets off on the sufferings of the ego.[49] The superego needs the ego in the same way a sovereign needs cowering subjects. Like the sovereign, it thrives on the cultivation of particular affects, dread foremost among them. Yet Freud says something else about the melancholic ego: he says that "the complex of melancholia behaves like an open wound, drawing to itself cathectic energies . . . from all directions, and emptying the ego until it is totally impoverished" (14:253). If we understand humor and melancholia as working in tandem, then we can think of this as the opening gambit in their joint project: emptying the ego of all of the affect on which the superego might feed. The Freud of "Mourning and

---

[48] "We succeeded," writes Freud in "The Ego and the Id," "in explaining the painful disorder of melancholia by supposing that [in those suffering from it] an object which was lost has been set up again inside the ego—that is, that an object-cathexis has been replaced by an identification. At that time, however, we did not appreciate the full significance of this process and did not know how common and how typical it is. Since then we have come to understand that this kind of substitution has a great share in determining the form taken by the ego and that it makes an essential contribution to what is called its 'character.'. . .

"When it happens that a person has to give up a sexual object, there quite often ensues an alteration of his ego which can only be described as a setting up of the object inside the ego, as it occurs in melancholia; the exact nature of this substitution is as yet unknown to us. . . . At any rate the process, especially in the early phases of development, is a very frequent one, and it makes it possible to suppose that the character of the ego is a precipitate of abandoned object-cathexes and that it contains the history of those object-choices." Sigmund Freud, "The Ego and the Id," in *Complete Psychological Works*, ed. and trans. Strachey, 19:3–68 (28–29).

[49] As one of those readers explains: "For Lacan, the superego is located in the symbolic order and retains a close but paradoxical relationship to the law. As with the law, the prohibition operates only within the realm of culture and its purpose is always to exclude incest. . . . The law, in other words, is founded upon that which it seeks to exclude, or, to put it another way, the desire to break and transgress the law is the very precondition for the existence of the law itself. On the one hand, the superego is a symbolic structure that regulates the subject's desire, and, on the other, there is this senseless, blind imperativeness to it. . . . According to psychoanalysis, there is simply no way a subject can avoid the tension between the law and the desire to transgress it and this manifests itself as 'guilt.'" Sean Homer, *Jacques Lacan* (London: Routledge, 2005), 58–59.

Melancholia" sees this, the ego's utter abandonment to the object, as a grave problem. The Freud of "The Ego and the Id" would recognize that this is simply what the ego amounts to, an archive of identifications with incorporated objects. As such, the ego is left even more open to the ravages of the cruel and demanding superego. Just picture the struggle: the poor ego caught in the middle, absorbed by the object while trying to keep the superego off its metaphorical back. But as the fascination that Freud and Harry both have with the "ego"'s (i.e., the melancholic's and the pilgrim Chaucer's) absorption suggests, there can be another way of reading the situation. That would be the humorous reading, the one where the ego triumphs precisely *as* the archive of the object, where the ego and the object triumph together. They do so, however, not because the mature, benevolent, fatherly superego has decided to go easy on them. They do so because the superego, having been deprived of the affect to be drawn from a cowering, lacerated, endlessly suffering ego, is itself left emptied and enfeebled. The nobly indifferent ego of humor—humor, we now see, aided and abetted by melancholia—is simply so absorbed in, one might even say liberated by, the speculative realm of the object and the alternative to reality it preserves, that it leaves the superego nothing else to feed on, and nowhere else to direct its energies, other than the absorption of the ego. The ego in this way channels the attentions of the superego into the realm of the object and strands it there—there, where it is left too absorbed, too fascinated and preoccupied, to cause the ego any more suffering. Freud surveys the peculiar topography of humor and, being thoroughly absorbed himself, mistakes exhaustion for benevolence.

Chaucer's *Tale of Sir Thopas* could almost be read as a parable of this agonistic interplay between ego and superego—could, that is, if not for the fact that the whole thing also reads like a parody, even a burlesque, of the dynamic whereby suffering at the hands of the superego gets internalized. Granted, the elements that allow for a parabolic reading are there for the taking. To begin with, of course, there is the manner in which the tale traffics in the speculative and the fantastic, almost as if it were an exercise, in both form and content, in a reality-testing that repudiates suffering in favor of "serving an illusion," to paraphrase Freud (21:166). Sir Thopas retreats from the giant into the nursery-rhyme world of his castle; the pilgrim Chaucer retreats from the pushy Host into the fairy-tale world of romance; humor ensues. The tale rehearses, moreover, the basic structure of humor, with the childlike pilgrim Chaucer presenting himself as laughably inauthentic and tiny while at the same time presenting would-be superegoic figures such as the Host; the giant; or, for that matter, Chaucer himself as equally ludicrous. Give the tale a slight turn, however, and you quickly move beyond a parable, however humorous, of the agon between ego and superego to arrive at something far more radical: the Oedipal struggle itself rendered dainty and childlike—"cute," to borrow Wan-Chuan Kao's keyword for the tale—with Thopas "priking" out to confront the reality of castration, in the figure of the giant, only to decide *No thanks!* before scurrying back to the delicious comforts of home.[50] What is there left to say about such a confection that it hasn't already said about itself, all the while laughing up its sleeve?

In other words, the Chaucerian humor at work in the *Thopas* ends up dissipating even the operations that, according to Freud's model, make humor possible. At every turn, it seems, Chaucer undermines the traditional supports holding up his own position as future Father of English Poetry—every support for the mature superego that, as heir to the paternal agency, might condescend to console the tiny, frightened, childlike ego. Consider, for example, the matter of Sir Thopas's return home (*CT*, VII.838–56). When Freud describes humor as an economy in expenditure upon feeling—that is, as an internal mechanism for managing unpleasure—we should understand that to be a home economy: an *oikonomia* that, having emerged out of a paternal *oikos*, proves to be the *fons et origo* of suffering.[51] *The Tale of Sir Thopas*, true to itself, can

[50] Wan-Chuan Kao, "Cute Chaucer," *Exemplaria* 30, no. 2 (2018): 147–71. On the way in which *Sir Thopas* "burlesques all of the topoi of [the] primal scene of romance," further diminishing the "gigantomachia" that, in the conventional confrontation between hero and monster, already "maps the movement from gigantism of desire to libido in its socially sanctioned, Oedipalized, *miniaturized* circulation," see Jeffrey Jerome Cohen, *Of Giants: Sex, Monsters, and the Middle Ages* (Minneapolis: University of Minnesota Press, 1999), 100–112.

[51] The father of the family, as Marx, Freud, Lacan, and Foucault (for starters) well knew, stands at the gateway to modern economic and political thought. Foucault, for example, notes that the family, although sovereign in origin and grounded in the *patria potestas* of Roman law, constitutes the "cell" of the disciplinary archipelago. In the family structure, as Foucault reads it, the flat, isotopic politics of contiguity associated with discipline joins the hierarchical, asymmetrical politics of verticality associated with the sovereign. See Michel Foucault, *Psychiatric Power: Lectures at the Collège de France, 1973–1974*, ed. Jacques Legrange, trans. Graham Burchell (New York: Picador, 2006), esp. 82. See as well Panu Minkkinen, "Michel Foucault on Sovereignty and Law," in *Proceedings of the Eighth Annual Conference of the Association for the Study of Law, Culture and the Humanities* (2005): 1–19, esp. 9–10. For a fascinating treatment of the topic in relation to Chaucer's *Physician's Tale*, see Randy P. Schiff, "The Physician and the Forester: Vir-

only address this state of affairs in meandering, roundabout fashion. Thopas's retreat home does indeed appear to be what a particular critical tradition claims it to be: a retreat from painful reality, an escapist fantasy worthy of a child.[52] It is difficult, in fact, not to read the whole episode as a humorous indictment not only of the superegoic structure that makes humor possible but also of the beneficiaries and facilitators of that structure: the chivalric romances that imagine a retreat from the changing social and economic landscape of England, the aristocracy seeking ways "to transform itself from a loosely organized and permeable class into a hereditary caste defined by a distinctive lifestyle," the court poets who rehearse ideological fantasies for the benefit of their aristocratic audiences.[53] So, yes, the tale somehow manages to perform a humorous indictment of the very genre of which it itself, in its childish refusal to accept the harsh world as it is, provides the consummate example. Nevertheless, the implied childish question—the plaintive, petulant *But why?*—raised by the tale is not itself dissipated, even if the pretensions and presumptions of paternal power are. Why should we put up with suffering, especially when there is gingerbread waiting at home? Why should we accede to the demands of the superego, especially when one of its avatars goes by the name Sir Oliphaunt? Why should we accept our position as children in the middle, not simply of history, as Patterson would have it, but of the "guilt history" perpetuated by a superegoic reality principle?[54] The questions retain their exigency and dignity, even when asked in the voice of an errant child.

But of course Harry doesn't describe the pilgrim Chaucer only as

---

ginia, Venison, and the Biopolitics of Vital Property," in *The Politics of Ecology: Land, Life, and Law in Medieval Britain*, ed. Randy P. Schiff and Joseph Taylor (Columbus: Ohio State University Press, 2016), 82–103. On Chaucer's jokes as the currency of a specifically political economy, see Goldstein, "Chaucer, Freud, and the Political Economy of Wit."

[52] For a brief overview of that tradition, see Lee Patterson, "'What man artow?': Authorial Self-Definition in the *Tale of Sir Thopas* and the *Tale of Melibee*," in *Temporal Circumstances: Form and History in "The Canterbury Tales"* (New York: Palgrave, 2006), 97–128 (103–5).

[53] On these points, see ibid., 98.

[54] Ibid., 127–28. I take the understanding of all history as guilt history—a descent in which "whatever is prior has had something taken from it by what follows; or whatever is prior has withheld something from that which follows it"—from Walter Benjamin, as explicated by Werner Hamacher. See Werner Hamacher, "Guilt History: Benjamin's Sketch 'Capitalism as Religion,'" *diacritics* 32, nos. 3–4 (2002): 81–106 (82–83). It is my conviction that Chaucer, like every truly ethical writer, seeks to liberate both history and its subjects from guilt history.

small and childlike; he also describes him as "elvyssh." Here we should give credit where it is due and recognize that the pilgrims' Host detects something slightly dangerous and demonic about the "popet" not entirely in their midst, and with good reason: humor, with its capacity to change negative affect—and the negative affect generated by super-egoic suffering in particular—into a jest, is transformative in a distinctly "elvyssh" way.[55] This power of transformation is not simply a threat; it is a threat to the home economy in and upon which humor expends itself. Surely it is no coincidence that Chaucer directs the parody in the *Thopas* not only toward the cultural practices of a feudal aristocracy, as Patterson argues, but also toward the "homegrown" form of English tail-rhyme romance. The inwardly directed force of humor is here turned toward the home where Thopas retreats for comfort, the home associated not only with paternal power but with the language through which humor is able to express itself at all: humor turned against its own mechanisms, its own source, its own medium. And surely it is no coincidence that Chaucer directs his parody against the one thing that supposedly secures his place as the superegoic Father, at once determinative and inimitable, of English Poetry: his mastery of language. This is of course the big "joke" of the *Thopas*: Chaucer the maker recites some bad poetry, LOL.[56] Is such irony meant to assert Chaucer's mastery of English even further, assuming the cliché to be true that only a master-ful poet is capable of pulling off the trick of composing self-consciously bad verse? Or are we being invited to see how Chaucer deploys humor to make the very idea of a Father of English Poetry appear ludicrous, "laughably inauthentic," even before the fact: to deauthorize the idea of superegoic poetic authority at the very site of its origin—its *oikos*, if you will? No wonder Harry cuts the *Thopas*, which threatens to go on and on, short: Who knows where the *elvyssh* transformations of humor will stop (*CT*, VII.918)? Who knows what, if anything, will be left standing, once they have run their course? Not even *The Tale of Sir Thopas* itself, which at the formal level "seems to narrow away, section by section, towards nothingness," is immune to its own operations.[57]

---

[55] On the interconnections among transformation, alchemy, and "elvysshness," see Richard Firth Green, "Changing Chaucer," *SAC* 25 (2003): 27–52.

[56] On this point see Kao, "Cute Chaucer," 167.

[57] J. A. Burrow, " 'Sir Thopas': An Agony in Three Fits," *RES* 22 (1971): 54–58 (57). This is an observation elaborated upon by Katharine Jager, " 'Som deyntee thyng': Poetry and Possibility in Chaucer's *Tale of Sir Thopas*," *Medieval Perspectives* 24 (2009): 22–45 (38): "Organized into three fitts, of eighteen stanzas, nine stanzas, and four and a half stanzas, respectively, the poem progressively halves itself to the point of deletion.

That the *Thopas* could potentially go on indefinitely, the dissipating effects of its humor ending who knows where (the truncated tale's last line, "Til on a day—" [*CT*, VII.918], "gestures toward a future at which Thopas cannot possibly arrive," observes Jeffrey Jerome Cohen), seems entirely fitting for a tale prompted by Harry's reaction, pitched somewhere on the spectrum from annoyed to intrigued to fascinated, to a pilgrim who stares "for ever upon the ground."[58] Here we have, on the one hand, a stark depiction of the coercive techniques of power, with Harry stepping forward as the self-appointed enforcer of the reality of the reality principle. On the other hand, it is at the same site—the site where power makes its presence known—that humor tests the demands of that reality, rejects them, and thereby preserves the possibility of speculation, of a realm of the *woldest* wherein we might discover an alternative to the reality of suffering imposed by a superegoic guilt history. Herein lies the truly "elvyssh" dimension of this interlude, this injection of humor into what we might call, paraphrasing Freud, the *oikonomia* of pain: it puts us in contact with the transformative potentiality that shadows power, the uncanny Otherworld of natural historical turmoil made apprehensible to mortals through the convergence, like a portal opening up, of melancholia and humor.[59]

Once again it is Harry who calls this to our attention, when he complains that the pilgrim Chaucer's rhyming is "drasty" and "nat worth a toord" (*CT*, VII.923, 930). *Drasty* is typically glossed as meaning "crude" or "crappy," which captures its transpositional association with human waste. Yet the term can also refer, as Alan Gaylord points out,

---

This halving effect is accentuated in many of the manuscripts of the poem, which lay it out by separating the stanzas into consecutively smaller, bracketed sections, so that the tale looks as if it is dwindling away to nothing by the time it reaches the edge of the page."

[58] Cohen, *Of Giants*, 106.

[59] My use of the term *natural history* derives from Theodor Adorno's insight that the second nature created by "society's law of motion" results in "the negation of any nature that might be conceived as the first." Theodor W. Adorno, *Negative Dialectics*, trans. E. B. Ashton (New York: Continuum, 1973), 357. As Adorno, commenting on Walter Benjamin's own claims about the convergence of nature and history, observes, nature and history are present in each other: nature can only be "present as transience" in the history that has eradicated first nature (nature having no presence thereafter other than as a figure for transience), while history is present in nature "as something that has evolved and is transient" by virtue of having constantly to transform itself in response to the nature that it ceaselessly transforms. Theodor W. Adorno, *History and Freedom*, trans. Rodney Livingstone (Cambridge: Polity Press, 2006), 135. On the "economy of pain," see Freud, 'Mourning and Melancholia', 244.

to the dregs of wine.[60] Given that second association, it becomes all the more intriguing that Harry should use this particular word, *drasty*, to describe, not just the rhyming and the speech of a figure who will be accorded the mantle of Father of English Poetry based on his mastery of the language and the tongue, but the rhyming of a tale whose protagonist is given a glass of sweet wine after he runs back home in order better to prepare himself for combat, wine thereby being pressed into service as an image of home and comfort. Wine, dregs, waste, consumption, home: such associations cannot help calling to mind a vivid passage from Marx's *Capital*:

By the purchase of labor-power, the capitalist incorporates labor, as a living agent of fermentation, into the lifeless constituents of the product, which also belong to him. . . . The labor process is a process between things the capitalist has purchased, things which belong to him. Thus the product of this process belongs to him just as much as the wine which is the product of the process of fermentation going on in his cellar.[61]

The Tale of Sir Thopas, spiced through as it is with images of commerce and the consumption of luxury goods (including itself as a romance), presents us with a humorous take on the metabolic—the transformative, the fermentative—activities of the home economy that produced it, and that makes its humor possible.[62] It is best read, then, not as a deathly serious, but as a vitally humorous, commentary on the uncanny overlapping of the *elvyssh* and the economical, the natural historical and the *heimlich*. Simply put, humor's metabolic ability to transform affect into jest places in Chaucer's hands—in all our hands—the capacity to impoverish the paternal agency at the very source of its power, the home. "Listeth, lordes," "Yet listeth, lordes," "Now holde youre mouth, *par charitee*": so begin the tale's three fitts, as if Chaucer were calling upon an aristocratic audience, first to assume, then to seal up within themselves—in a word, to incorporate—an *unheimlich* poem that, at once wholly original and utterly derivative, equivalent to itself only

---

[60] Alan Gaylord, "Chaucer's Dainty 'Dogerel': The 'Elvyssh' Prosody of *Sir Thopas*," in Jost, *Chaucer's Humor*, 271–94 (273).

[61] Karl Marx, *Capital*, Vol. 1., trans. Ben Fowkes (New York: Penguin, 1990), 292.

[62] As both Kao and Jager point out, the poem is filled with what are essentially product placements. Kao, "Cute Chaucer," 163; Jager, "Som deyntee thyng," 39.

because it comprises materials other than its own, speaks the very language of self-estranging dissolution (*CT*, VII.712, 833, 891).[63] If humor is indeed an economy in expenditure upon feeling, then here we encounter, as Harry well perceives, the uneconomical waste product of that economy: a poem that retreats from history only then to fill the household with inoperative language.[64] And what is one supposed to do with this waste, these dregs, these *drasty* leavings? What is one supposed to do with this evidence of a natural historical process that continues to operate whether the owner of the wine cellar (is he an innkeeper, by any chance, or a courtier who received an annual "tonne" of wine in repayment for his services?) wants it to or not? "Why wiltow lette me / Moore of my tale than another man?," the pilgrim Chaucer asks Harry, and in the question one can detect an indictment, however indirect, of the arbitrariness of superegoic power (*CT*, VII.926–27). Why shouldn't the pilgrim Chaucer be allowed to tell the "beste rym" he knows (*CT*, VII.928)? Who is Harry to say otherwise? But of course Harry cannot allow it to continue, any more than fermentation can be allowed to continue unchecked: the metabolic properties of Chaucerian humor threaten to destroy the economy, the order, the history at whose head the paternal agency sits. They could, potentially, dissolve everything.

Would they even dissolve Chaucer? In his own reading of the tale, Jeffrey Cohen argues that "Sir Thopas and Chaucer in his own self-presentation embody diminishing masculinity in its attenuating extreme."[65] But Chaucerian humor does more than just diminish masculinity. Driving beyond the imaginary level of gender, Chaucerian humor instead dissolves the paternal position itself, and it does so by allowing

---

[63] Helen Cooper notes that the *Thopas* has "no single source or model," despite the fact that we can trace the lineage of every one of its clichés. What is more, her descriptions of the tale as profaned, anticlimactic, and drained ("The debasement starts at the level of vocabulary"; "It is insistently parochial, never seeking allusions beyond its own vernacular kind"; "It is a tale that makes its effect in part by the absence of all those other effects that ought to be there") make it sound like the consummate melancholic object, which it is. Helen Cooper, *The Canterbury Tales*, 2nd ed., Oxford Guides to Chaucer (Oxford: Oxford University Press, 1996), 301, 306–9.

[64] As John Finlayson puts it: "The parody [in the *Thopas*] is achieved, not by the simple mention of the stock elements . . . but by, first, their superfluity—in a short space Chaucer has crammed in almost more stock elements than are to be found in any but the worst Middle English romance—and, second, their lack of function. As in mock-heroic, it is the non-functional display of rituals which generates the parody in humor, not simply the rituals themselves." "Definitions of Middle English Romance," *ChauR* 15, no. 1 (Summer 1980): 44–62 (47).

[65] Cohen, *Of Giants*, 101.

that position to become utterly absorbed in—utterly engulfed by and abandoned to—the realm of the object.[66] Consider two images encountered in *The General Prologue* to the *Canterbury Tales*: those of the Miller's tufted nose and the Cook's ulcerous *mormal*. Both features could be read as instances where comic comparison—those hairs! that sore!—is used to put some distance between the human community and the humorous other; for both features metaphorically mark the characters who bear them as being a little more grotesque, a little closer to the natural world, a little less "human." We could, then, register the claim that the Miller and the Cook are being disparaged and leave it at that. Yet to do so would be to overlook how the two (quite prominent and memorable) features force us, at the very instance of making a comic comparison precipitated by an act of isolating judgment—an instance, in other words, when our attentions are fully absorbed by the humorous other—to acknowledge the intrusion, not merely into reality, but into the field of mental functioning by which we assess reality, of the real object.

It takes the insistence of two natural historical features, in other words, to clarify how humor, properly understood—and my argument here has been that humor is only properly understood as Chaucerian humor—provides us with a much-needed means of counteracting immunitarianism, as the term has been developed in the work of Roberto Esposito. The extent of Chaucer's immunitarianism—the question, that is, of just how much philosophical distance Chaucer took from the world and of what form(s) that distance assumed—is a question well worth pursuing for its own sake. But for the time being, I simply want to use that question as a way of emphasizing why it is so important to draw a distinction between the comedy in the *Canterbury Tales*, which often works through normative comparison, and the technique of Chaucerian humor, which, being self-directed, can seem like a rejection of the world and its problems when it is anything but that. Recall that humor arises out of our split subjectivity, our laughable inauthenticity. That split subjectivity, as Esposito has argued, is nothing less than the

---

[66] My thinking here is indebted to Lacan: "Unless we distinguish between the object *a* [the real object] and the i(*a*) [the ideal ego], we cannot form a conception of the radical difference that lies between melancholia and mourning. . . . Freud affirms—he's the one who says this—that, in melancholia, this process clearly doesn't come to a conclusion, because the object takes the helm. The object triumphs." Jacques Lacan, *Anxiety: The Seminar of Jacques Lacan*, Book X, ed. Jacques-Alain Miller, trans. A. R. Price (Cambridge, Mass.: Polity Press, 2014), 335.

manifestation, the proof as it were, of our having given the gift, the *munus*, of self-identity that makes us members of the community. Esposito's thesis, simply put, is that we lack the ability, as individuals, to constitute community with one another because, paradoxically, community has already constituted each of us from deep within. We have already given the gift, the *munus*, of self-identity that would allow us to constitute community as something properly our own, something belonging to us or something to which we belong. Community, argues Esposito, "determines us at a distance and in difference from our very selves, in the rupture of our subjectivity, in an infinite lack, in an unpayable debt, an irremediable fault."[67] Community expropriates us, makes us lack. Humor, then, is nothing less than an expression of one's belonging to the community, through the giving of the *munus* of authentic self-identity (this as opposed to jokes and the comic, which tend to work by demarcating the borders of community). What this also means, however, is that humor is emphatically not a species of immunitarianism, which, as Esposito argues, seeks to immunize or indemnify the individual against having to pay the *munus* that has already been paid: the *munus* of self-identity that opens one to community. Not only is humor predicated on the idea that one cannot, in fact, refuse to pay the debt to community of one's self-identity. Humor insists that we cannot, and perhaps should not, seek to immunize ourselves against *anything*— anything, that is, except the reality of suffering mandated by the superego. Our indebtedness, such as it is, lies elsewhere.

It is here, I think, that we can at last clearly delineate the thin line that separates humorous reality-testing from comic comparison. The latter, as Kendrick would argue, retains the paradoxical capacity to extend the reach of psychic tolerance by carefully demarcating the margins of community, alerting us to the intrusive, norm-violating presence of an *apolis* populated by the incongruous beasts and improbable gods of natural history.[68] Humorous reality-testing, I want to suggest, not

---

[67] Roberto Esposito, *Terms of the Political: Community, Immunity, Biopolitics*, trans. Rhiannon Noel Welch (New York: Fordham University Press, 2013), 15.

[68] "[M]edieval people were certainly aware of the humorous effect of incongruities created by selective exaggeration, visual as well as verbal," writes Kendrick. "We have many examples of this in the margins of Gothic psalters and books of hours, where the artist deliberately plays with magnification and disproportion. . . . [T]he marginal illuminator of a section of the Luttrell Psalter . . . produced humor from sudden perceptions of enormity, not by blowing up a true-to-life image . . . but by blowing up images of deliberately created incongruity, that is, fantastic babewyns combining parts of humans, beasts, insects, serpents, and plants. . . . Such babewyns are depicted dispropor-

only leads us, via a repudiation of objective loss that is at the same time an acknowledgment of subjective lack, to a preservation of the object; it goes one step further than the comic by expanding the reach of tolerance to include, not just the humorous other, designated as such through comic comparison, but the forces of potentiality and dissolution themselves. Like the comic, humor relies on judgment. Or, to be more specific, both modes enact *krísis*, understood in its ancient sense as a process of separation, selection, differentiation, and partitioning.[69] But where the comic judges in order to separate or demarcate, humor judges in order to test the reality it ultimately rejects. It is the difference, finally, between the Host, who is obsessed with classifications and with reckoning time, who never hesitates to judge but whose powers of judgment, most critics agree, are limited, and the pilgrim Chaucer, who does "noght elles but despendest tyme" and whose judgments on reality take the forms, first of a "disorderly, excessively wrought, and inconsistent" romance "every bit as lurching, indecisive, meandering, and irregular as its metrical form," then of a moral treatise designed to intervene in, partly by suspending through the accumulation of advice, the process of sovereign decision-making carried out in the *oikos* (*CT*, VII.931).[70]

---

tionately large as compared to other images on the page, as if they had been magnified or brought closer to show their disparate parts in greater detail, to evoke the sort of comic close-up that takes possession of and experiments with the substance and form of an object." Kendrick, "Humor in Perspective," 148–49.

[69] As Reinhardt Koselleck explains the origins of the term: "Κρίσις has its roots in the Greek verb χρίνω: to 'separate' (part, divorce), to 'choose,' to 'judge,' to 'decide'; as a means of 'measuring oneself,' to 'quarrel,' or to 'fight.' This created a relatively broad spectrum of meanings. In classical Greek, the term was central to politics. It not only meant 'divorce' or 'quarrel,' but also 'decision' in the sense of reaching a crucial point that would tip the scales. . . . But 'crisis' also meant 'decision' in the sense of reaching a verdict or judgment, what today is meant by criticism." Reinhardt Koselleck, "Crisis," trans. Michaela W. Richter, *Journal of the History of Ideas* 67, no. 2 (April 2006): 358–59.

[70] For discussions of the Host's obsession with reckoning time and also of his powers of judgment, see Page, "Concerning the Host"; Cynthia C. Richardson, "The Function of the Host in the *Canterbury Tales*," *TSLL* 12, no. 3 (Fall 1970): 325–44; and L. M. Leitch, "Sentence and Solaas: The Function of the Hosts in the 'Canterbury Tales,'" *ChauR* 17, no. 1 (Summer 1982): 5–20. The description of the *Thopas* comes from Eleanor Johnson, *Practicing Literary Theory in the Middle Ages: Ethics and the Mixed Form in Chaucer, Gower, Usk, and Hoccleve* (Chicago: University of Chicago Press, 2013), 128. On the *Melibee* as a tale "about advice" and about the paradoxical relation between advice and decision-making (Melibee "does not so much decide on mercy as decide to do whatever [Prudence] advises"), see Ferster, *Chaucer on Interpretation*, 19–21. Of the *Melibee*, Patterson writes that "throughout the Tale, Melibee is counseled to pause, to consider, to reflect, to examine his situation and himself. . . . Yet, as we have seen, as soon as Melibee is given an opportunity to make a decision on his own . . . he reveals the failure of this effort [on the part of Prudence to cultivate in him the habit of 'mature

Humor, we have seen, operates melancholically by redirecting attention into the realm of the object, a realm that I have described as natural historical. The *krísis* of humor—the *krísis* that repudiates the reality principle in favor of the potentiality of speculation—draws us into the realm of natural historical crisis: the realm of metabolism and fermentation, turmoil and endless dissolution.[71] More to the point, it draws the attentions of the superego into that same crisis and, in so doing, arrests the very agency charged with carrying out the decisionist *krísis* that grounds the reality of the reality principle. Subverting comic judgment no less than tragic suffering, humor leaves only itself.

---

self-reflection']." Patterson, "What man artow?," 118. But what Patterson regards as Prudence's failure, I regard as humor's success: the preclusion of sovereign decisiveness.

[71] Here I mean *crisis* in the more colloquial sense, derived from multiple sources (post-Enlightenment theories of history, eschatological expectation, economic instability, environmental catastrophe), as an unsettled time of continuous upheaval, permanent transition, revolutionary ferment, and structural realignment: nature permeated by history and history engulfed by natural forces. On the development of this meaning of *crisis* since the eighteenth century, see Koselleck, who warns: "'Crisis' is often used interchangeably with 'unrest,' 'conflict,' 'revolution,' and to describe vaguely disturbing moods or situations. Every one of such uses is ambivalent. . . . The concept of crisis, which once had the power to pose unavoidable, harsh and non-negotiable alternatives, has been transformed to fit the uncertainties of whatever might be favored at a given moment. Such a tendency towards imprecision and vagueness, however, may itself be viewed as the symptom of a historical crisis that cannot as yet be fully gauged." Koselleck, "Crisis," 398–99.

Dwelling with Humans and Nonhumans: Neighboring Ethics in *The Franklin's Tale*

Emily Houlik-Ritchey
Rice University

Abstract

In this article I propose a merger of neighbor theory with insights drawn from the clustered fields of ecocriticism, posthumanism, and new materialism to analyze Chaucer's representation of the ethical dilemmas appending the interrelation of humans and nonhumans. Theorists of the neighbor insist upon the productive potential of the ethical process to which the neighbor invites us: to acknowledge the transgressive alienation shared by self and neighbor, and then to love the neighbor by being willing to dwell in that uncomfortable space as we make ethical choices. Yet the basis for making ethical choices has become radically unstable in light of the ontological leveling that ecocriticism, posthumanism, and new materialism often insist upon, to say nothing of other constraints that limit human agency. Chaucer's *Franklin's Tale* elucidates the vexed nature of these dilemmas. I argue that Dorigen's troubled relationships with her husband, her would-be lover, and the sea-rocks together constitute an imbricated cluster of neighboring relationships in the tale. These neighbors confront Dorigen with a series of difficult and socially charged ethical demands to which she struggles to respond. Through Dorigen's intense affective expression, Chaucer interrogates the problems and potentialities of loving troublesome neighbors, whether those neighbors are human or nonhuman. Reading across these interrelations through the ethical framework of neighboring allows us to probe the possibilities and challenges for ethical human action in light of our new ontological frameworks.

Keywords

The Franklin's Tale; Geoffrey Chaucer; Dorigen; ethics; neighbor; human responsibility; nonhuman; ecocriticism

But whan she saugh the grisly rokkes blake,
For verray feere so wolde hir herte quake
That on hire feet she myghte hire noght sustene.
(Geoffrey Chaucer, *The Franklin's Tale*)[1]

---

[1] *FranT*, 859–61, in *The Riverside Chaucer*, gen. ed. Larry D. Benson, 3rd ed. (Boston, Mass.: Houghton Mifflin, 1987). All citations of Chaucer are from this edition.

Studies in the Age of Chaucer 41 (2019): 107–139
© 2019 The New Chaucer Society

I N HER PRESIDENTIAL ADDRESS to the New Chaucer Society (published in *Studies in the Age of Chaucer* in 2017), Susan Crane analyzes Chaucer's "preoccupation with how beings, including human beings, are interrelated on earth."[2] Such interrelations open, as Crane's analysis demonstrates, onto questions of ontology and ethics, as ontological theories of posthumanism and environmental thought seek new conceptions of being that "will better integrate human and nonhuman interests."[3] Such theorizing raises several challenging questions: first, how to assess nonhuman interests;[4] second, how to determine what human actions or inactions will "better integrate" those nonhuman interests with our own; and finally, how relationships among humans ethically impinge upon relationships between humans and nonhumans. If we approach these relationships from the vantage of neighborly ethics, we can pursue the last two questions even when we cannot definitively answer the first. In what follows, I will use *The Franklin's Tale* in concert with theories of neighboring to elucidate the dilemmas of interrelations among diverse beings.[5] Dorigen's vexed encounter with the "grisly rokkes blake" (*FranT*, 859) is one of Chaucer's most profound interrogations of human/nonhuman interrelation. It also functions as the hinge for her interrelations with two humans, impinging upon the ethical facets of her marriage with Arveragus and her potential romantic liaison with Aurelius. Her human relationships, in turn, affect her relationship with these rocks. Reading across these human and nonhuman interrelations through the ethical framework of neighboring, we can probe the

---

[2] Susan Crane, " 'The lytel erthe that here is': Environmental Thought in Chaucer's *Parliament of Fowls*," *SAC* 39 (2017): 3–29 (4).

[3] Ibid.

[4] Julian Yates's *Of Sheep, Oranges, and Yeast: A Multi-Species Impression* (Minneapolis: University of Minnesota Press, 2017) provides one of the most recent discussions of assessing nonhuman desires and interests. Work in this vein has frequently been speculative. See Bruce Holsinger's characterization of speculation as one of the "dominant modes" of object-oriented ontology: "Object-Oriented Mythography," *Minnesota Review* 80 (2013): 119–30 (120). Andrew Cole and Sandra Macpherson, working in different literary periods and intellectual traditions, have each offered critiques of work in this vein (Andrew Cole, "The Call of Things: A Critique of Object-Oriented Ontologies," *Minnesota Review* 80 [2013]: 106–18; Sandra Macpherson, "A Little Formalism," *ELH* 82, no. 2 [2015]: 385–405). For defenses of the approach, see Yates, *Of Sheep*; and Jeffrey Jerome Cohen, *Stone: An Ecology of the Inhuman* (Minneapolis: University of Minnesota Press, 2015).

[5] Crane, "The lytel erthe that here is," 28.

possibilities and challenges for ethical human action in light of our new ontological frameworks.

The last several years have seen a great deal of theoretical and analytical work by medievalists in the related realms of ecology and posthumanism.[6] Turning to early archives in order to elucidate the ways that, as Kellie Robertson has recently put it, "being is imagined as potentially circulating among categories rather than confined to a single step on the *scala naturae*," work in these fields continues to expose and redress the fiction of separation between humans and other living and nonliving entities, disrupting human-centric hierarchies and the (un)ethical systems based upon them.[7] Yet these theoretical moves have not fully resolved persistent ethical problems of human responsibility within these new ontological frameworks, nor attendant questions of desire, choice, and action. For even within lateral systems of relationality, choice is always present.

The Necessity of Choosing

In some ways, "bump[ing] the human from its sovereign ontological perch" has rendered ethical questions of desire and choice more complex and urgent.[8] Sharon O'Dair, for instance, has pointed out that ontological leveling is not inherently more ethical than a traditional humanistic framework, in that it provides a theoretical means of *abdicating* ethical assessment and action:

the fates of life sustaining, generative water and its creatures depend upon decisions humans make now. Neither Katrina nor Deepwater Horizon altered public policy about fossil fuel consumption. . . . Getting most people to care for the environment would constitute a significant advance. To suggest instead that they think of natural gas, tankers and shrimp as agents like them would prove disastrous.[9]

---

[6] See, for example, Cohen, *Stone*; Karl Steel, *How to Make a Human: Animals and Violence in the Middle Ages* (Columbus: Ohio State University Press, 2011); Randy P. Schiff and Joseph Taylor (eds.), *The Politics of Ecology: Land, Life, and Law in Medieval Britain* (Columbus: Ohio State University Press, 2015); Alfred K. Siewers, *Strange Beauty: Ecocritical Approaches to Early Medieval Landscape* (New York: Palgrave Macmillan, 2009); and, a bit earlier, Gillian Rudd, *Greenery: Ecocritical Readings of Late Medieval English Literature* (Manchester: Manchester University Press, 2007).

[7] Kellie Robertson, *Nature Speaks: Medieval Literature and Aristotelian Philosophy* (Philadelphia: University of Pennsylvania Press, 2017), 239.

[8] Crane, "The lytel erthe that here is," 27.

[9] Sharon O'Dair, "Water Love," *postmedieval* 4, no. 1 (2013): 55–67 (65–66).

O'Dair argues that the ethical urgency of climate change and species endangerment requires human judgments that run counter to the principles attending ontological leveling of matter, being, and scale. For O'Dair, selecting what to privilege is paramount, and the choices seem to her to be obvious: forms of life matter more than natural gas; clean water matters more than tankers; and faced with climate crisis, human agency ought not to be considered equivalent to that of shrimp. Ethics, in other words, may be in conflict with ontology here. If ethics is attendant upon forging "better" communities with other entities to integrate their interests with those of humans (neither inherently receiving priority), then achieving a more ethical relationality still requires human choice and action. While we might dispute the particular entities O'Dair selects for valuation here, from a theoretical stand-point we are nonetheless faced with the necessity of choice by some sort of rubric. Human choice, as well as being an inherently exclusionary move, is paradoxically also the "condition of possibility for any possible affirmation," as Cary Wolfe notes.[10] Julian Yates agrees: "To put things very directly, like it or not, 'we *must* choose, and by definition we *cannot* choose everyone and everything at once. But this is precisely what ensures that, *in the future, we will have been wrong*' and shall have to begin all over again."[11] Though some scholars have advocated for a "willing and ethical embracing of *all* beings, bodies, and relations,"[12] we cannot evade "the perverse necessity of choosing,"[13] even as we recognize that our decisions, caught in time and made in inadequate states of knowledge and agency, will be imperfect. Dorigen's experience over the course of *The Franklin's Tale* reveals precisely these insights. Choice thus remains both an imperative and a problem for Chaucerian, ecocritical, and posthuman ethics.

Human desires and fears influence our choices such that we tend to privilege, and act ethically by, those with whom we can identify (whether they are human or nonhuman). This is precisely why scholars decenter the human, and human frameworks, in new ontologies. Our capacity for identification is limited, and so a gap inheres in any ethical

---

[10] Cary Wolfe, *Before the Law: Humans and Other Animals in a Biopolitical Frame* (Chicago: University of Chicago Press, 2006), 103.

[11] Yates, *Of Sheep*, 23, quoting Wolfe (emphasis in original).

[12] Kathleen Coyne Kelly, "Lost Geographies, Remembrance, and *The Awntyrs off Arthure*," in Schiff and Taylor, *The Politics of Ecology*, 232–66 (236; emphasis in original).

[13] Timothy Morton, *Ecology without Nature: Rethinking Environmental Aesthetics* (Cambridge, Mass.: Harvard University Press, 2007), 193.

theory predicated on it.[14] Redressing this problem, Timothy Morton attempts to formulate an ethics in the face of non-identification through his conceptualization of "dark ecology" in *Ecology without Nature*. In the final section of that book, Morton demands an environmental politics that exhibits a radical love for things that we find "disgusting, inert, and meaningless"—in short, with precisely those nonhuman beings we don't (want to) identify with.[15] Consider my epigraph from *The Franklin's Tale*, where Dorigen looks down upon the "grisly rokkes blake" and her legs give out in fear. She does not love these rocks. She does not wish to act ethically by these rocks (she wishes, in contrast, that they would sink into hell). Morton insists that "the most ethical act is to love what is nonidentical with us."[16] Dorigen would seem, by this standard, to have an ethical duty toward those rocks despite her fear and her desire that they sink into hell. Chaucer gives extensive poetic attention to Dorigen's interrelation with the dangerous, persistent presence and then shocking absence of these grisly rocks, and in so doing this medieval poet interrogates precisely the ethical conundrum that preoccupies environmental and posthuman theorists. Through Dorigen, Chaucer makes legible the complexities and necessities of human choices within a mesh of relations humans cannot fully know or control, and in which human interests do not trump others. Dorigen's case exemplifies a further insight I wish to suggest: that we need to be able to think human relationality with the nonhuman in tandem with human relationality with other humans—to recognize that the interrelation of beings on earth happens in concert rather than isolation. As Dorigen's entangled relationships with her husband, the sea rocks, and Aurelius demonstrate, human–nonhuman relations in *The Franklin's Tale* are not discrete from human–human relations; rather, they impinge profoundly upon one another, necessitating an ethical framework that can negotiate the messy co-incidence and collision of human and nonhuman interests. Before turning to *The Franklin's Tale*, I will elaborate the theoretical conjunction I propose between an ecological love for the non-identical and ethical theories of love for the neighbor.

[14] For instance, Kelly proposes an ethics based upon mourning, arguing that grief grants subjectivity and agency to nonhuman others. She draws upon recent work by Judith Butler to this effect: Judith Butler, *Precarious Life: The Powers of Mourning and Violence* (New York: Verso, 2004). Yet this affective mode of ethics that Butler and Kelly propose necessarily omits anything and anyone we cannot identify as beloved and grieve-able. It therefore requires an ethical supplement.

[15] Timothy Morton, *Ecology without Nature*, 195.

[16] Ibid., 185.

Neighbor-Love and the Ethics of Non-Identity

For Morton, ethical responsibility is encapsulated in two related human actions: loving and "stick[ing] around."[17] In other words, Morton envisions an ethics whereby we do not limit our human responsibility, presence, and love to those entities with whom we are able to identify (seeing value in them only in human terms or seeing in them a ciphered view of our ideal, coherent selves). He suggests, rather, that we stick around with the discomfort arising when we cannot find common ground, loving the other in spite of our limited capacity for such identification. To take responsibility beyond the range of our identifications requires, as Morton has suggested, a radical vision of ethical love. It is terrifically difficult to do what Morton advocates; we need to formulate an ethics of loving the unlovable. The religio-ethical injunction to "love thy neighbor as thyself" poses, in Sigmund Freud's analysis, the same radical difficulties.[18] I therefore propose theories of the neighbor as an intervention into the problems of ethics that ecocriticism, posthumanism, and Chaucer have raised. Neighbor theory offers a mature discourse of ethics that has given us our thickest articulation of ethical relationality in the face of these dilemmas, having theorized precisely this juncture of non-identification, radical love, and ethical choice.

The fundamental premises of the neighbor in its psychoanalytic instantiation are that the self and the neighbor share an internal strangeness (or non-identification), and that the relation carries an ethical obligation of love. Kenneth Reinhard turns to the religio-ethical trajectory of the neighbor in Jewish scripture to explain its grounding of ethical love precisely in shared strangeness.[19] The ethics of neighboring appears

[17] Morton argues that we should "find ways to stick around with the sticky mess that we're in and that we are" (ibid., 188). This sticking around is ethical for Morton—a manifestation of love that "refuses to digest the object into an ideal form" (195). Ideal forms, in Morton's argument, reinstitute the very distance between human and nonhuman that ecocriticism seeks to eliminate.

[18] Sigmund Freud explores this difficulty in *Civilization and Its Discontents*, trans. James Strachey (New York: Norton, 1989), 56–59.

[19] The scriptural origin of the ethical injunction to love the neighbor may give some ecotheorists pause. This may seem, at first glance, like a return to an ethics of stewardship where humans occupy a privileged place of ethical responsibility toward the rest of the world. Rather than reinstating the human into an ontological hierarchy, I am interested in extending the range of human responsibility to include nonhumans as neighbors (a move in line with the semantic range of the Hebrew term for "neighbor" in the original Jewish scriptural injunction to love the neighbor, as I show below). The human remains my primary ethical actor throughout this study, precisely because we need to

as a religious commandment to "love thy neighbor as thyself," in Leviticus 19:18:[20] "Thou shalt not take vengeance, nor bear any grudge against the children of thy people but thou shalt love thy neighbor as thyself: I am the LORD."[21] Reinhard makes much of the reflexive logic of this commandment ("love thy neighbor *as thyself*"), which draws an affinity between self and neighbor via love—that is, the self's love for each that the commandment envisions. The obvious question that arises is, "But who is [our] neighbor?"[22] The perennial problem (as well as the potential) of neighbor ethics, this question has a grand tradition of interrogation within scriptural, theological, Talmudic, philosophical,

---

continue theorizing human ethical responsibility in a decentered context. My proposal to consider nonhumans as neighbors implies (partly on the basis of syntactic twists that Jesus introduces in the parable of the Good Samaritan [Lk 10:25–37]) that nonhumans, too, could be ethical actors. But for now, I leave the subject of nonhuman ethical responsibility for another day.

[20] This is the earliest appearance of that formulation in Jewish scripture. The ethics of the neighbor within scriptural contexts continues within Christianity and Islam. The Christian context, with its famous parable of the Good Samaritan, spurred a significant amount of exegesis and moral commentary among the early Church fathers that was influential into the Middle Ages. Augustine and Origen, among others, formulated allegories of salvation and moral exegesis based on this parable that became standard ways of interpreting it in the Christian Middle Ages (influencing English literary, scholastic, and liturgical writing). The Middle English *Mirror*, for instance, a lectionary and collection of associated prose sermons, draws upon such exegesis in its sermon for Luke 10:25–37. Aside from this focus on the parable of the Good Samaritan, other classical and medieval ethical discourses of the neighbor gained traction in the medieval period: especially the perspective that behaving ethically toward the neighbor constituted a remedy for envy (which can be found in the work of Aristotle and Thomas Aquinas, among others). This strain of thinking of the neighbor also influenced literary production in the late Middle Ages: texts that link envy and the neighbor include *The Man of Law's Tale* and *The Parson's Tale*, *The Book of Margery Kempe*, and William Langland's *The Vision of Piers Plowman*. These various classical, early Christian, and medieval discourses on the neighbor lie beyond the scope of my present argument insofar as my methodology is theoretical rather than historicist. For literary arguments that engage medieval ethics more broadly (i.e., beyond the neighbor), see Jessica Rosenfeld, *Ethics and Enjoyment in Late-Medieval Poetry* (Cambridge: Cambridge University Press, 2011); J. Allan Mitchell, *Ethics and Exemplary Narrative in Chaucer and Gower* (Rochester: D. S. Brewer, 2004); Eleanor Johnson, *Practicing Literary Theory in the Middle Ages: Ethics and the Mixed Form in Chaucer, Gower, Usk, and Hoccleve* (Chicago: University of Chicago Press, 2013); and Robertson, *Nature Speaks*.

[21] When citing Leviticus, I have used the same version of the Pentateuch that Reinhard does as he explicates the syntactic and ethical link among various scriptural injunctions: *The Soncino Chumash*, ed. A. Cohen (New York: Soncino Press, 1983). See Kenneth Reinhard, "The Ethics of the Neighbor: Universalism, Particularism, Exceptionalism," *Journal of the Society for Textual Reasoning* 4, no. 1 (2005), http://jtr.lib.virginia.edu/volume-4-number-1/the-ethics-of-the-neighbor-universalism-particularism-exceptionalism/ (accessed February 7, 2018).

[22] This is the question the lawyer puts to Jesus in Luke 10:29, in response to which Jesus tells the parable of the Good Samaritan.

and literary discourses.[23] The Hebrew word *re'a*, rendered "neighbor" in Leviticus 19:18, delivers ambiguity rather than clarity on the identity of this figure, as it is used scripturally in a wide variety of contexts for fellow human beings, as well as, I would note in particular, nonhuman animals.[24] That is, the original Hebrew injunction to love one's neighbor was not semantically restricted to a solely human context, though that is indeed how it has overwhelmingly been interpreted. Reinhard follows a line of Jewish commentators as far back as Nahmonides in the thirteenth century, who seek to clarify precisely this question of who the neighbor may be. Whether the neighbor was a fellow Jew or a stranger to the Jewish community has been one of the most urgent questions scriptural glosses have taken up. The very instability of interpretation in this regard becomes instrumental to neighbor theorists. Love of the neighbor (quoted above) is linked syntactically to another ethical injunction a handful of verses later: love of the stranger (Lv 19:33–34), which, among other similarities, includes and expands the same reflexive phrase, "as thyself": "33. And if a stranger sojourn with thee in your land, ye shall not do him wrong. 34. The stranger that sojourneth with you shall be unto you as the home-born among you, and thou shalt love him as thyself; for ye were strangers in the land of Egypt: I am the LORD your God." Reinhard elucidates the implications of the two ethical mandates in a passage that is worth quoting at length:

In the ethical space that opens in the nearness of Leviticus 19:18 to 19:34, the *ger* [stranger] dwelling among Jews is "like" the Jews only insofar as they were themselves *unlike* someone else, "strangers in the land of Egypt." The parallelism of the two commandments does not imply that the injunction to love the

---

[23] For an introduction to these scriptural, theological, and Talmudic discourses, see Reinhard, "The Ethics of the Neighbor"; Kenneth Reinhard, "Freud, My Neighbor," *American Imago* 54, no. 2 (1997): 165–95; Kenneth Reinhard, "Paul and the Political Theology of the Neighbor," in *Paul and the Philosophers*, ed. Ward Blanton and Heut de Vries (New York: Fordham University Press, 2013), 449–65. On the philosophical discourses of the neighbor, see Slavoj Žižek, Eric L. Santner, and Kenneth Reinhard, *The Neighbor: Three Inquiries in Political Theology* (Chicago: University of Chicago Press, 2005). The neighbor, in various guises, makes brief appearances in medieval literature, including *The Vision of Piers Plowman*, the *Canterbury Tales*, John Gower's *Confessio Amantis*, and *The Book of Margery Kempe*.

[24] *Re'a* signifies both Jews and Gentiles among the instances where it is used to refer to fellow humans. See Kenneth Reinhard, "Neighbor," in *Dictionary of Untranslatables*, ed. Barbara Cassin, translation ed. Emily Apter, Jacques Lezra, and Michael Wood (Princeton: Princeton University Press, 2014), 706–7.

neighbor is based on a common positive feature, practice, or ideal that all humanity shares, but rather that neighbor-love involves an element of essential *difference*, the fact that both the self and the neighbor are "strange," internally alienated from the larger group, whether that be Egypt or Israel, and that this structural parallel is the only absolute basis for their solidarity.[25]

The ethical solidarity forged by loving neighbors is not only a recognition of difference (a paradoxical affinity of disaffinity); rather, according to neighbor theory, the condition of difference itself is what makes solidarity and ethics possible by negating justifications based on shared positive features (e.g., identification). The structural repetition of the two Leviticus commandments "articulates a principle of neighbor-love based on structural *difference* . . . I am 'like' the neighbor only insofar as we each are *not-like* someone else, and the memory or fact of that alienation determines both myself and my neighbor as singular and self-different."[26] This is an ethical love based upon non-identification. The reader in Leviticus who is enjoined to love the neighbor or stranger thus bears all the hallmarks of strangeness carried by these figures.

To love such a figure as the self is to love (that is, to confront, choose, and dwell with) the very fact of strangeness, in the self as well as in the neighbor. The ethical subject cannot escape from their own sense of alienation from others. Concurrently, they cannot escape from their own sense of alienation from themselves. These are recognitions we often strive to avoid, for our own peace of mind. The ethical basis for love is precisely this recognition (however difficult) of shared self-alienation; the ethical course is to choose actions that serve such mutual strangeness rather than deny it. The linguistic links are also telling: Reinhard observes that the Arabic word for "neighbor" (*al-jar*) is related to Hebrew *gar* (to dwell) and to Hebrew *ger* (stranger).[27] The neighbor, in English, is "based on the prefix 'nigh-' (denoting proximity in time or space) and the suffix 'boor' (a dweller or place of dwelling, as in 'bower' or 'abode')."[28] The neighbor, then, is the proximate stranger with whom one must dwell. Neighborly relationships, in other words, rupture the coherence of the home and insular family: "the neighbor is not confined

---

[25] Reinhard, "The Ethics of the Neighbor" (emphasis in original).

[26] Reinhard, "Freud, My Neighbor," 172 (emphasis in original).

[27] Islam also refers to the neighbor as "a figure of special obligation and ambiguous determination" (Reinhard, "Neighbor," 706).

[28] Ibid.

to the exterior of the household; rather . . . the function of the neighbor is already located inside the house."[29] Reinhard continues, "like the English word 'boarder,' which derives both from the table on which we eat and the edge or margin that separates inside from outside," the neighbor is the internal stranger—the figure who "disturbs the home's tranquility and disrupts the very distinction between inside and outside on which the household is built."[30] This internal stranger manifests doubly within neighbor theory: within the neighbor (another creature who is both strange and proximate) *and* within the self (who is a stranger to oneself).[31] The shared strangeness of the self and the neighbor makes love of that figure so very difficult—as difficult as it is to love the most foreign aspects of ourselves. And we are charged to love this strange, unfathomable neighbor with no guarantees of reciprocity.

The nonreciprocal nature of neighbor-love occupies Freud in *Civilization and Its Discontents*. He exposes the incompatibility of ethics with reciprocity (an insight of neighbor theory that Jacques Lacan, Reinhard, and Slavoj Žižek articulate further).[32] The ethics of the neighbor are asynchronous and nonreciprocal. They have to be, Freud reasons, or we get caught up in the give-and-take of "well, I'll do this because I might get something from it" (e.g., a return, either of similar ethical behavior from the other, a sense of our own self-righteousness, a reward in heaven, or some other material/psychological good). Such, as Freud argues, is not ethics but the self-serving calculus of the pleasure principle. The other possibility is that we'll reason, "well, I'll do this for X because X is like me" (which centralizes and reinforces ourselves as being worthy of love). To avoid these ethical pitfalls, neighbor theorists reason,

[29] Kenneth Reinhard, "Toward a Political Theology of the Neighbor," in Slavoj Žižek, Eric L. Santner, and Reinhard, *The Neighbor: Three Inquiries in Political Theology* (Chicago: University of Chicago Press, 2005), 11–75 (36–37).

[30] Ibid., 37.

[31] I draw the phrase from the title of Julia Kristeva's *Strangers to Ourselves*, trans. Leon S. Roudiez (New York: Columbia University Press, 1991).

[32] Emmanuel Levinas also theorizes an asymmetrical ethics based upon the figure of the neighbor. The theorists upon whom I draw engage the work of Levinas, critiquing him on the point of particularity. Levinas famously locates the face of the other as an enabling site of ethical action/relations. Posthumanists have criticized and modified Levinas's insistence that this face be human (for instance, in Karalyn Kendall's "The Face of a Dog: Levinasian Ethics and Human/Dog Coevolution," in *Queering the Non/Human*, ed. Noreen Giffney and Myra J. Hird [Burlington: Ashgate, 2008], 185–204; and Steel's *How to Make a Human*]). Neighbor theorists have also objected to Levinas's emphasis on the face: Žižek, in particular, takes up this point: Slavoj Žižek, "Neighbors and Other Monsters: A Plea for Ethical Violence," in Žižek et al., *The Neighbor*, 134–90.

we must choose to love what we don't recognize and we must choose to do so without expecting any return. The neighbor, in fact, may *not* be bound by this duty, nor subject to this law. The neighbor, like the character of the Jew that John Gower imagines in "The Tale of the Jew and the Pagan,"[33] may in fact insist that he is bound by an entirely different ethical code.[34] Or the neighbor may recognize the same ethics but fail in their obligation nonetheless. Our responsibility, in either case, does not change. We remain persistently, unrelentingly responsible for "loving" our neighbors.

The relational complexities in these neighborly interactions are dense enough between humans, who share similarities as a species. When neighbor theory is applied to the nonhuman entities studied by ecocriticism and posthumanism, these fractures multiply, yet the same principles apply: the neighbor is opaque, different from us and yet proximate to us. We cannot know the desires of the (nonhuman) neighbor; we cannot assess with full clarity what lies in their interest. And the confrontation with them is likely to force us to confront anew our own self-alienation. Expanding the traditional conception of neighbors as fellow humans to include nonhuman neighbors permits us to articulate human responsibility amidst constraint, contingency, limited agency, and imperfect knowledge of the desires of the other, yet without insisting that humans are a privileged site of ethical responsibility or care. It therefore allows us more rigorously and productively to theorize the ethics attendant upon choice in a lateral system of entanglement and precarity. Precarity seems aptly to describe Dorigen's emotional state throughout much of *The Franklin's Tale*. I therefore turn now to Chaucer's work to analyze his literary take on the tangled ethical problems that arise in human–nonhuman relations, and the complex ways those relationships and interactions among humans impinge upon each other.

Dwelling with Chaucerian Neighbors

The sea rocks of *The Franklin's Tale* first come to our attention because Dorigen, our tale's heroine, does not like them: she famously laments

---

[33] "The Tale of the Jew and the Pagan" appears in Book VII of certain manuscripts of the *Confessio Amantis*. See Emily Houlik-Ritchey, "Fellows in the Wilderness: Neighborly Ethics in 'The Tale of the Jew and the Pagan,'" *South Atlantic Review* 79, nos. 3–4 (2014): 65–75.

[34] It always bears repeating that the fictional Jew of Gower's tale (who does not abide by neighbor ethics) is a literary construction that bears little resemblance to historical Jews and their ethics regarding the neighbor.

their very existence.[35] She connects the rocks' presence to her husband's absence; faced with both her distress about Arveragus and her fear of the rocks, she uses each to parse the other. She ultimately wishes for the rocks' absence (as Arveragus is absent, we might note); she then uses the rocks' continued existence as a means by which to block Aurelius's unwelcome proposition (which he likewise frames in terms of a tension between presence and absence). And the seeming absence of the rocks after the clerk has performed his "magyk natureel" (1125) renders Dorigen famously rock-like: she stands "astoned" (1339) in the face of Aurelius's victory crow. As this overview suggests, the relationship Chaucer imagines between Dorigen and the rocks impinges profoundly on her relationships with Arveragus and Aurelius, and, to borrow an insight from Robertson, "makes apparent the constitutive relations that exist even between rocks and humans."[36] The shifting presences and absences of these various neighbors in Dorigen's life drive the plot of the tale. Dorigen's relationship with the rocks, in other words, is the (not unproblematic) ethical hinge of her human relationships.

Chaucer sets up Dorigen and the rocks as neighbors in theoretically precise ways, the first aspect of which has to do with their proximity in the physical world. Dorigen lives right by the black rocks that affect her so dramatically: her "dwellyng," as Chaucer at one point describes it, "stood . . . faste by the see" (801, 847). The description of Dorigen's home is crucial, both in its physical location and in its lexicographical form. The substantive form "dwellying," operating grammatically as a noun, derives from a verbal action. Dorigen's place of residence is analogous to a state of being; this sense of activity is heightened also by the adverb "faste," which expresses the proximity of her home to the sea and its firm foundation. And like "dwellyng," the term "faste" paradoxically conjoins connotations of rapid movement with stasis. In the same sentence in which we learn that her castle stands on the brink of the ocean,

---

[35] Scholars have analyzed these rocks in a startling variety of ways; most such readings share an assumption that the rocks make legible Dorigen's human character. V. A. Kolve believes Dorigen overreacts, exaggerating the danger the rocks pose only to discover "how little wisdom and truth she derives from that image" (*Telling Images: Chaucer and the Imagery of Narrative II* [Stanford: Stanford University Press, 2009], 174). Gillian Rudd argues that Dorigen is an anthropocentric "landlubber" betraying "an assumption that nature is subservient to human whim" (*Greenery*, 142). Exceptions to this trend are the new materialist analyses of Robertson and Cohen: Kellie Robertson, "Exemplary Rocks," in *Animal, Vegetable, Mineral: Ethics and Objects*, ed. Jeffrey Jerome Cohen (Washington, D.C.: Oliphaunt, 2012), 91–121; and Cohen, *Stone*.

[36] Robertson, *Nature Speaks*, 239. On this subject see also Cohen, *Stone*.

we learn that Dorigen is physically active in this littoral geography: "And often with hire freendes walketh shee / Hire to disporte upon the bank an heigh" (848–49). Dorigen's "dwellyng" stands "faste" on that coast, yet in line with both words' semantic range, she herself is constantly moving in this tale, going to and from her home on the coast, the cliffs, the pleasure garden, and the street of the nearby town.[37] This is her neighborhood, and her movement in this social and physical space—the constant actions of *dwelling* here—are actions of neighboring, putting her into ethical relationships with the other beings of this community. Throughout the tale Dorigen demonstrates the ethical challenges of dwelling with difficult neighbors—those figures who confound the expectations she holds for them as well as her expectations for herself. Dwelling, in other words, is an ethical act of neighboring.

This is not the only Chaucerian context where dwelling takes on such a neighborly valence, as Aranye Fradenburg reveals in her analysis of the *Prologue* to *The Legend of Good Women*.[38] Human and nonhuman neighboring in *The Legend* provide a useful preliminary case of ethical dwelling (with a less grisly nonhuman neighbor, for one thing) that will help to elucidate the more complex case of Dorigen. In Fradenburg's analysis the sublime courtly lady Alceste emerges as neighbor to the restless narrator: "The beauty of the lady . . . and her arbitrary, capricious demands express the exactions of the ideal image, the impossibility of identifying with it fully"; that is, she marks the "intimacy of the 'I's' formation through the other, but also a limit, the "I"'s distance from itself, from the stranger within."[39] Such is the dynamic of neighboring, wherein the ambivalent relation of self (in this case lover/narrator) to other (in this case courtly lady/daisy) marks the internal strangeness of the self. What fascinates me most about this Chaucerian context, for

[37] While her movement and mobility are not those of Arveragus (who crosses the sea to other climes in pursuit of chivalric adventure), Dorigen is not, I argue, fixed in place in purely domestic spaces, as Andrea Rossi-Reder has suggested: "Male Movement and Female Fixity in the *Franklin's Tale* and *Il filocolo*," in *Masculinities in Chaucer: Approaches to Maleness in the "Canterbury Tales" and "Troilus and Criseyde,"* ed. Peter G. Beidler, Chaucer Studies 25 (Cambridge: D. S. Brewer, 1998), 105–16.

[38] L. O. Aranye Fradenburg, "Loving Thy Neighbor: *The Legend of Good Women*," in *Sacrifice Your Love: Psychoanalysis, Historicism, Chaucer* (Minneapolis: University of Minnesota Press, 2002), 176–98.

[39] Ibid., 186. Fradenburg argues that "The daisy in effect puts the narrator to sleep, in an alluring image of the repose man seeks in the objects of his desire; but this image points uncannily to the potential destructivity of desire with respect to the 'nothing I' of the subject, a destructivity from which the narrative then runs away" (191).

the present purposes, is the slippage between Alceste and the daisy, which inextricably imbricates neighborly relationality among humans (lover/courtly lady) with human/nonhuman relationality (narrator/daisy). Fradenburg herself does not address this human/nonhuman slippage in ecological terms, though she shows how neighborly the narrator's strange modes of dwelling turn out to be. The dreamer's ambivalence to the daisy that both does and does not become Alceste as the *Prologue* continues emerges through Chaucer's use of the Middle English word *dwellen*. Fradenburg's argument focuses on the narrator's restless movement; before Alceste appears, the narrator describes his obsessive resolution to keep looking at the daisy:

> . . . me thoghte I myghte, day by day,
> *Duellen* alwey, the joly month of May,
> Withouten slep, withouten mete or drynke.
> Adoun ful softely I gan to synke,
> And, lenynge on myn elbowe and my syde,
> The longe day I shoop me for t'abide
> For nothing elles, and I shal nat lye,
> But for to loke upon the dayesie.[40]

The narrator, though he seems to recline quite comfortably near the daisy, does *not* abide in the meadow the entire month of May without sleep, meat, or drink, but rather,

> For derknesse of the nyght, the which she [the daisy] dredde,
> Hom to myn hous ful swiftly I me spedde,
> To goon to reste, and erly for to ryse,
> To seen this flour to sprede, as I devyse.
> And in a litel herber that I have,
> That benched was on turves fressh ygrave,
> I bad men sholde me my couche make;
> For deyntee of the newe someres sake,
> I bad hem strawen floures on my bed.

> (199–207)

The narrator rushes home each night to recline on his flower-strewn turf "couche," creating a bed that mimics the daisy's meadow, in which he

---

[40] *LGW*, 175–82 (my emphasis). I quote from the F-text.

has been reclining all day. He then rushes back to look at the flower again the next day: "this flour that I so love and drede" (211). The narrator's ambivalence, legible not only in his movement (running toward, contemplating, running away from) but also in his affective relationship to the daisy (formed of love and dread), marks an imperfect corollary to the daisy's metaphorical love of the sun and dread of the night.[41] Through his own restless dwelling, in other words, he himself mimics the daisy's tracking of the sun, such that Peter Travis remarks, "the narrator almost turns into a daisy himself: his crepuscular stirrings at dawn and dusk, his subsolar motions to and from the daisy's bower, and the floral habitation of his own 'natural' bed translate him into a heliotrope, an andromorphic flower sensitive to the sun."[42] This is a narrator moved in extraordinary ways by the daisy and the sun, entangled in extraordinary ways with the daisy and the sun.

Furthermore, the narrator's re-creation of the meadow as his "couche" confounds the distinction between outdoor summer meadow and indoor human home that his daily commute at first implies. The "herber" where he sets up his turf bed is an orthographic form of two Middle English nouns, listed in the *Middle English Dictionary* as *hērbeȓ* (n.[1]), which signals a garden, a bower, an arbor, a grassy plot (or, figuratively, a garden of the heart, a garden of philosophy); and *herberwe* (n.), which signals a temporary or permanent dwelling place of various sorts: house, home, lodgings, inn, chamber, or campsite, as well as the hospitality associated with such temporary or permanent residency (it also figuratively signifies the dwelling of God in man). The narrator's re-creation of the flower-strewn meadow in his "litel herber" at his "hom," therefore tangles notions of human cultivation and wild growth, indoors and outdoors, permanence and transience, home and away, night and day.

Of this rich description, Fradenburg singles out the verb "Duellen" (*LGW*, 176) by which to parse the neighborly ambivalence of the dreamer's inconsistencies—inconsistencies that extend, as I have just shown, throughout the passage. As she points out, *dwellen* (v.) means to delay, to be tardy, as well as to take time, to linger. It means to restrain or pause, as well as to treat at length. It means to stay, to sojourn, to wait (with their implications of temporary stillness), as well as carrying the more permanent connotations of residing or inhabiting. It means to

---

[41] See Peter W. Travis, "Chaucer's Heliotropes and the Poetics of Metaphor," *Speculum* 72, no. 2 (1997): 399–427.

[42] Ibid., 411.

stand fast and endure, as well as to be contingent or to depend upon something. It means to survive and endure, or to be left as a remainder or residue. Fradenburg eloquently concludes: "When one dwells, one is either at home or away, or a bit of both: neighborly."[43] In the narrator's ambivalent love for the daisy, his restless dwelling instigates a series of entangled binaries that carry neighborly valences. This narrator's relationship with the daisy signifies the ambivalent perils and demands of neighboring in an ecological context where human and nonhuman interrelations exert pressure on each other.

The ecological implications arising from the affinity the narrator exhibits with the daisy whose sun-worshiping and turf-embedded behavior he so closely imitates are complex. On the one hand, the narrator's aesthetic contemplation and poetic invention hold the daisy continually at a distance (and here we might note that the daisy/marguerite was a traditional medieval figure of poetic invention itself—an aestheticization of a sort that Morton has critiqued as a distancing mechanism by which human poets and writers reify a separation between themselves and "Nature").[44] On the other hand, to the extent that the narrator spends as much time running *away* from the daisy as kneeling in rapt contemplation *before* it, and to the extent to which such activity "translate[s] him into a heliotrope," we might consider that Chaucer's suggestion of a strange affinity between the human and the floral forwards a neighborly relational ethics across the species boundary. Dwelling, in this literary passage, is a harbinger of such relational dynamics and their challenges in *The Franklin's Tale*.[45] Dorigen's relationships with her husband Arveragus, with the coastal rocks she lives near, and finally with her would-be suitor Aurelius also emerge through the neighborliness of dwelling, with its restless oscillations between presence and

---

[43] Fradenburg, *Sacrifice Your Love*, 191.

[44] This is one of the central arguments of Morton's *Ecology without Nature*.

[45] In *Ecology without Nature*, Morton critiques the concept of "dwelling" as bound up with the persistent suspension of "Nature" from the human, proposing his concept of *dark ecology* "against the affirmative talk of 'dwelling' and the false immediacy of ecomimesis" (ibid., 187). Morton shuns a concept of "dwelling" drawn largely from Martin Heidegger; in this line of thinking, "dwelling" signifies for Morton a positive, affirmative, static suspension of Nature. At the same time, Morton preserves a category of activity something like "dwelling": he advocates that we "stick around with the sticky mess that we're in and that we are" (188), seeking a way of "being with" the other that is critically engaged and active, that can capture the "perverse necessity of choosing" (193), and through which we can "love the other precisely in their artificiality" (195). I suggest, particularly for a medieval archive, the Middle English verb *dwellen* and its substantive form, *dwellyng*, do precisely this.

absence and its power to disrupt the binaries on which the characters organize their lives. Amidst such disruptions, the possibility of ethical action unfolds.

Married Neighbors

Dorigen's marriage constitutes the earliest neighborly relationship that the tale explores, and though this is a human relationship whose dynamics do not, initially, seem to invoke a wider ecological context, close attention to the neighborly dynamic here elucidates the later interrelations. Chaucer's depiction of Dorigen and Arveragus's marriage has proven to be one of the most provocative and befuddling aspects of this tale, if we are to judge from the range of critical opinions.[46] The linguistic and social tensions with which Chaucer describes their relationship, including literary and social conventions of love and marriage, result in a "complex and ambiguous marital relationship."[47] For instance, Jill Mann argues that "there are no fixed roles, no unalterable distribution of power [between Dorigen and Arveragus]; instead there is a ceaseless alternation of 'lordshipe' and 'servage.' "[48] Attending to the many repetitions of these two concepts, Mann concludes that Chaucer offers us "a doubling of roles: their constant alternation shows that each partner is *simultaneously* both dominant and subservient in the relationship."[49] In short, Mann interprets Dorigen and Arveragus's marriage as a flexible, accommodating ideal (though one that she acknowledges operates very differently and unequally in practice). Angela Jane Weisl registers the

[46] Margaret Hallissy and David Raybin, each commenting on Arveragus's surrender of "maistrie" in his marriage, come to opposite conclusions about the autonomy this provides Dorigen. Raybin takes seriously Arveragus's abdication of authority: "Arveragus proposes . . . that they share his sovereignty, insisting only that he retain the appearance of domination" (David Raybin, " 'Wommen, of kynde, desiren libertee': Rereading Dorigen, Rereading Marriage," *ChauR* 27, no. 1 [1992]: 65–86 [67]). Raybin's reading of the scene where Dorigen reveals her situation with Aurelius to Arveragus bears out his conviction, legible in what I've quoted here, of Arveragus's real commitment to Dorigen's autonomy (67–69). In contrast, Hallissy sees Arveragus's gestures of equality in marriage as empty: "Male dominance was a major assumption in medieval marriage . . . and Dorigen's language when she accepts Arveragus's promise shows that she knows this . . . he is still her hierarchical superior, and she is under his authority" (Margaret Hallissy, *Clean Maids, True Wives, Steadfast Widows: Chaucer's Women and Medieval Codes of Conduct* [Westport: Greenwood Press, 1993], 37).

[47] Hallissy, *Clean Maids*, 35.

[48] Jill Mann, *Feminizing Chaucer*, Chaucer Studies 30 (Cambridge: D. S. Brewer, 2002), 90.

[49] Ibid., emphasis in original.

same repetitions of service and lordship that Mann tracks but empha-sizes instead "how opposite the two terms are and how difficult to com-bine."[50] Chaucer's repetition of opposing terms registers, for Weisl, not flexibility, but impossibility: "The binary opposition created through this impossibility of articulation, the disjunction between courtly-love and marital power structures, between the public and the private, sets the conflict that underscores the rest of the tale."[51]

However diversely they interpret it, scholars have tended to agree on one aspect of the marriage: namely that the problem with the relation-ship Chaucer imagines for Dorigen and Arveragus at the opening of *The Franklin's Tale* hinges on the disconnect, if not flat-out contradiction, between courtly love and marriage conventions. Scholars frequently track the incompatibility of courtly love (with its privileging of male service in the private context of an intimate, often secret, relationship) and marriage (with its privileging of male authority within the public—religious, social, and legal—institution of marriage).[52] But framing it this way, as I think Chaucer's verse indeed encourages us to do, also deemphasizes the ways in which tensions about identity, power, and autonomy are rife *within* discourses of courtly love and medieval mar-riage themselves.[53] The tensions within each discourse are deep, rever-berating through the successive, competing, overlapping lenses by which Chaucer asks us to measure Dorigen and Arveragus's evolving relationship. Their marriage, in short, exhibits the indeterminacy theo-rists associate with neighborliness.

External/internal boundaries break down in Dorigen's and Arvera-gus's marriage—a breakdown reminiscent of Reinhard's point that the neighbor is already located inside the home: within a short span of lines, the suitor Arveragus becomes household intimate, who, strangely, can-not live for long with his wife "in quiete and in reste" (*FranT*, 760), but

---

[50] Angela Jane Weisl, *Conquering the Reign of Femeny: Gender and Genre in Chaucer's Romance* (Rochester: D. S. Brewer, 1995), 108.

[51] Ibid.

[52] A notable exception is Wan-Chuan Kao, who argues that rather than "a conflict between courtly love, in which women dominate, and secular marriage, in which men exert control," the tale insistently engages with shame via medieval conduct literature in ways that fundamentally disrupt firm divisions between public and private that courtly love and marriage seem initially to imply. "Conduct Shameful and Unshameful in *The Franklin's Tale*," *SAC* 34 (2012): 99–139 (137).

[53] See, for instance, Fradenburg's analyses of courtly ladies in *Sacrifice Your Love*; and Cathy Hume's argument about public and private aspects of medieval marriages in *Chaucer and the Cultures of Love and Marriage* (Rochester: D. S. Brewer, 2012).

feels compelled to leave her in order to "*dwelle* a yeer or tweyne / in Engelond" (809; my emphasis). He goes "To seke in armes worshipe and honour—/ For al his lust he sette in swich labour—/ And *dwelled* ther two yeer" (810–13; my emphasis). Arveragus's physical "dwelling" (801) may be the castle "nat fer fro Pedmark" (801) where he lives with Dorigen for a year "in blisse and in solas" (802), but his overriding desire is to dwell far from her, occupied not in married bliss, but rather in individual "labour" (812)—that is, the martial pursuit of his own honor.[54] Arveragus emerges here as a particularly neighborly kind of husband: more often away than he is home (a pattern that will continue throughout the tale), he dwells seldom in his dwelling. Arveragus's residence both at home and abroad disrupts not only the internal/external distinctions of the traditional home, but also the relational dynamics of Arveragus and Dorigen as a couple.

Within its first eighty lines, the tale dedicates significant energy to encouraging us to think of Arveragus and Dorigen in their relation to each other, foregrounding their ever fascinating, confusing courtship-turned-marriage accommodations. In the much-quoted passage on lordship and service, Chaucer asserts that "Thus hath she take hir servant and hir lord, / Servant in love, and lord in mariage. / Thanne was he bothe in lordshipe and servage" (792–94). Arveragus's relationship with Dorigen, in short, is one either of lordship or of service, or a bit of both: neighborly.[55] Read this way, their marriage foregrounds ethics: in this case the thorny ethics of loving each other on constantly shifting ground. The promises each has made to the other, as described by the Franklin, are incompatible, even before Arveragus chooses not to dwell with Dorigen all the time. The desire of the neighbor is indeterminate (for instance, a husband's promise to be both servant and lord obscures the state of his desire and how it may shift—as when he desires neither lordship nor service, but departure from home and wife). The ethics of the neighbor demands that one take responsibility for that indeterminate desire—to love and dwell with it without being able fully to assess or account for it. Arveragus's desire to leave catches Dorigen off-guard, at least if we judge by the extent of her grief, which is generally read

---

[54] In another instance of language doubling, Chaucer uses "labour" to describe Arveragus's love service to Dorigen at the opening of the tale (*FranT*, 732).

[55] Recall Fradenburg's analysis of the dreamer who rushes between the daisy and his home: "when one dwells, one is either at home or away, or a bit of both: neighborly" (*Sacrifice Your Love*, 191).

as excessive.[56] Arveragus's pursuit of chivalric honor is conventional to medieval romance, as is his departure from his wife to do so. Chaucer has here rendered the familiar strange by encouraging us to see it through Dorigen's intense affective response. Arveragus's desire to seek himself (his own honor/chivalric identity) rather than to live as part of a couple deeply informs Dorigen's relationships (equally indeterminate) with the rocks and then with Aurelius, the man Chaucer explicitly identifies as "hire neighebour" (961). Dorigen's desire through all of this remains equally difficult to pin down, as I will show.

Affinity with Rock

Dwelling as a mode of neighborly ethics becomes urgent in the tale precisely here, when Arveragus leaves and Dorigen's distress apparently defies all expectation. Her puzzled friends and she take to the cliffs "hire to disporte" (849). Instead of pleasure, this coastline provokes terror. Dorigen's speech, as several scholars have noted, exemplifies human anguish at the sight of something that makes no sense in human, philosophical, or divine terms.[57] The sight of the black rocks, stunning and yet impervious, and indeed dangerous to humans, overwhelms her:[58]

[56] Exemplifying such readings are Kolve, *Telling Images*; and Alcuin Blamires, *Chaucer, Ethics, and Gender* (Oxford: Oxford University Press, 2006).

[57] For readings of Dorigen's lament about the sea rocks that engage with scholastic conceptions of an ordered universe, see W. Bryant Bachman, "'To maken illusioun': The Philosophy of Magic and the Magic of Philosophy in the 'Franklin's Tale,'" *ChauR* 12, no. 1 (1977): 55–67; and Blamires, *Chaucer, Ethics, and Gender*, 161–62.

[58] It would be possible to read Dorigen's reaction here as an example of the premodern sublime. Edmund Burke (1729–97) describes the sublime as an affective response of "astonishment" (i.e., "that state of the soul, in which all its motions are suspended, with some degree of Horror") to the vast and overwhelming elements of nature, in *Philosophical Enquiry into the Origin of Our Ideas of the Sublime and the Beautiful* (Oxford: Oxford University Press, 1990), 53. Chasms and precipices are classic examples of places the sublime may be experienced, according to Simon Schama's studies of Burke's sublime, in *Landscape and Memory* (London: HarperCollins, 1995), 450. Analogous human reactions to nature have been noted in the medieval archive, though not always explicitly through the category of the "sublime." For instance, James Smith, though he is not speaking of *The Franklin's Tale*, points out that astonishment and horror in the face of a world that gives and takes human life with apparent indifference form a very common medieval attitude: "for medieval thinkers . . . the world shaped and thwarted the projected form of a human life . . . the response within the human heart? Anguish." James Smith, "Fluid," in *Inhuman Nature*, ed. Jeffrey Jerome Cohen (Washington, D.C.: Oliphaunt, 2014), 115–31, 199–20. Cohen might also easily have been talking about Chaucer's Dorigen and the sublime when he observes: "when the nature for which it offers an emblem marks utter difference from the human, stone arrives into thought limned by terror." "Introduction: Ecostitial," in Cohen, *Inhuman Nature*, i–x (iii).

> Another tyme ther wolde she sitte and thynke,
> And caste hir eyen dounward fro the brynke.
> But whan she saugh the grisly rokkes blake,
> For verray feere so wolde hir herte quake
> That on hire feet she myghte hire noght sustene.
>
> (*FranT*, 857–61)

Dorigen is frightened of this seascape and compelled by it into speech: she questions the rocks' very existence: "Why han ye wroght this werk unresonable?" (872), she cries out, explaining that she sees no value and much danger in them:

> For by this werk, south, north, ne west, ne eest,
> Ther nys yfostred man, ne bryd, ne beest:
> It dooth no good, to my wit, but anoyeth.
> Se ye nat, Lord, how mankynde it destroyeth?
> An hundred thousand bodyes of mankynde
> Han rokkes slayn, al be they nat in mynde.
>
> (873–78)

That she fears these proximate rocks, and sees no value in them for either human, bird, or beast, seems inescapably clear.[59] The culmination of her lament is to wish for the rocks' absence: "But wolde God that alle thise rokkes blake / Were sonken into helle for his [Arveragus's] sake! / Thise rokkes sleen myn herte for the feere" (891–93). On the one hand, we might read this moment as Joseph D. Parry has done, observing that "with Arveragus gone, the phenomenal world of the Franklin's romance fully unmasks itself as an inscrutable, dangerous, potentially disastrous environment to men and women."[60] To put this in Morton's terms, the black rocks form a dark ecology. Yet it is not exclusively a scene of horror and dislike. This moment registers, more complexly, as a neighborly context of affinity within disaffinity.

Dorigen's neighborly relationship with rock emerges in the dual

---

[59] Rudd argues that Dorigen exhibits "[a] view of the natural world [that] is not only anthropocentric but specifically androcentric, as she seeks to master and subdue the environment to what she perceives as the greater good" (*Greenery*, 143). I appreciate Rudd's analysis, though my own departs from it.

[60] Joseph D. Parry, "Dorigen, Narration, and Coming Home in the *Franklin's Tale*," *ChauR* 30, no. 3: 262–93 (265).

dynamic that she does not like them, and yet she is like them. Theoretically speaking, they are each non-identical with someone or something else: they are strange, resisting interpretation within common relational frameworks and thus disrupting the (social and ecological) contexts in which they are placed. Chaucer links Dorigen to rock through analogy: Dorigen is stone-like in the obduracy of her misery at Arveragus's departure:[61]

> Men may so longe graven in a stoon
> Til som figure therinne emprented be.
> So longe han they [her friends] conforted hire [Dorigen] til she
> Receyved hath, by hope and by resoun,
> The emprentyng of hire consolacioun.
>
> (830–34)

Chaucer, describing the continual efforts of her friends to comfort her, likens Dorigen to a stone engraved by her friends' consolation, until they carve her surface into the shape of their desire: a socially ingrained human desire that she be tranquil.[62] They do this because Dorigen's

---

[61] This extended link between Dorigen and stone is unique in Chaucer's oeuvre. For while on the one hand Chaucer quite likes the adjective "astoned" (which he uses in a wide range of texts, as a quick search through the quotation fields of the *MED* reveals), he does not usually go on to develop the implied metaphor behind the term in such detail as he does with Dorigen. For example, both Troilus and Pandarus are "astoned" at various points throughout *Troilus and Criseyde*, but these arresting descriptive references nonetheless remain discrete (see *TC*, I.274, II.427, III.1089, V.1729). Chaucer occasionally uses stones as a point of contrast from which to emphasize various aspects of humanity: so Harry Bailly rhetorically positions human storytelling in opposition to mute stone in *GP*, I.773–74. Cohen takes particular note of this moment, arguing that "stones are the taciturn, immobile, everyday objects against which the vivacious company defines itself" (Cohen, *Stone*, 48). And Troilus, in Book IV of *Troilus and Criseyde*, positions his affective capacity against what he sees as the emotionlessness of stone. Troilus declares that Pandarus "moost me first transmewen in a ston" before Criseyde's departure from Troy could cease to trouble him (*TC*, IV.467). If Harry Bailly conceives of stone as voiceless, Troilus conceives of stone as passionless. But Dorigen—so extensively likened to rock by Chaucer—is neither mute, nor passionless, nor still (at least not more than momentarily) in this tale. Her affinity with stone is quite complex.

[62] Chaucerians have long found the association between Dorigen and rock to be evocative, often citing the now infamous pun that Dorigen stands "astoned" in the wake of Aurelius's claim to have achieved a rock-free coastline (*FranT*, 1339). Taking the cue from Chaucer, Rossi-Reder claims that Dorigen's "rock-like fixity" symbolizes "her inflexible position as a medieval woman" ("Male Movement," 115). Specifying Dorigen's resistance to the consolation efforts of her friends, Mann remarks upon "the slow erosion of Dorigen's first intensities of suffering" (*Feminizing Chaucer*, 91). Dorigen's resistance to such change indicates, in the view of Francine McGregor, a durability in Dorigen, who in turn "makes the rocks the visible manifestation of her husband's absence," effectively "emprentyng" significance on "stoon"; Francine McGregor, "What of Dorigen?

misery has been excessive, transgressing social bounds. Chaucer describes her grief as a "derke fantasye" (844): "wepeth she and siketh, / As doon thise noble wyves whan hem liketh. / She moorneth, waketh, wayleth, fasteth, pleyneth" (817–19). Dorigen's friends "conforten hire in al that ever they may" (823), and they do seem to have some comforting influence upon her, although Chaucer renders this effect ambiguous through the tale's vacillations. For instance, is it her friends' comfort (that Chaucer imagines as engraving) that consoles her, or the letters we are told she receives from Arveragus (837–40)? Are we meant to understand the hope and reason by which she receives the "emprentyng" of consolation to be Dorigen's internal faculties, or the affective and rational desires of her friends? And how consoled is she? Chaucer gives us this analogy of consolation before Dorigen sinks in fear to the ground at the sight of the black rocks and the danger she feels they pose to Arveragus. The pleasure garden where her friends take her next is likewise ambiguous in its capacity to console Dorigen. On the one hand, it can soothe anyone "save Dorigen allone, / Which made alwey hir compleint and hir moone" (919–20); on the other hand, while she is there she appears to be able to "lete hir sorwe slyde" (924). Her grief comes and goes, sometimes disturbingly present and sometimes sliding away.

The image, then, of an engraved stone that Chaucer uses to render Dorigen's ambiguous affective state, is precisely aligned with the image of the rocky coast—a proximate place where her affective state impels her into a speech in which she cannot make sense of the rocks' presence. Both the rocks and Dorigen resist rational explanation in these moments: "reason" grinds away, working to imprint Dorigen-as-stone, while the rocks, despite the "argumentz" that "clerkes wol seyn," seem a "werk unresonable" (886, 885, 872). I argue, then, that Dorigen fears and loathes these rocks not because of their utter alterity, but because of their resonance with her own intense, indeterminate emotional state in the wake of Arveragus's departure. To the extent that she links the rocks (and her fear of them) to Arveragus's absence, we might wonder how much of this baffled rage and fear arises from the way Arveragus's desire to leave confounds her sense not only of him as husband, but of

---

Agency and Ambivalence in the 'Franklin's Tale,'" *ChauR* 31, no. 4 (1997): 365–78 (373). Most recently, taking a new materialist approach, Kellie Robertson and Jeffrey Jerome Cohen have each sought to understand the agency of the rocks themselves—specifically their capacity to "organize[] the human" (Robertson, "Exemplary Rocks," 108; Cohen, *Stone*, 49–53).

herself as wife—it is a situation where neither lordship nor service seems to apply. Arveragus's desire to leave tangles with the ships Dorigen watches "seillynge hir cours, where as hem *liste* go" (851; my emphasis). Ships go where they want, as does Arveragus. She has as little control over her husband's presences and absences as she later has over the rocks'.

Pleasurable Grief

Consider again Chaucer's construction of Dorigen's misery in her husband's absence: it is not only excessive but also transgressively pleasurable: she mourns "As doon thise noble wyves *whan hem liketh*" (818; my emphasis). Her intense grief is, on the one hand, rendered legible according to the generic conventions of intense love-longing (this is what noble wives do, we are told). On the other hand, this extraordinary claim arguably disrupts romance conventions as much as it invokes them. The grief of women of rank within romance plays certain structural roles, but though we often read women's grief as rhetorically and affectively savvy, this emotional distress is rarely, if ever, so explicitly positioned by poets as pleasurable to the women who grieve.[63] Dorigen, however, cries when she wishes to. The normalcy of Dorigen's grief, and her pleasure in indulging in this grief, are therefore at once asserted and interrogated. Her grief exceeds the explanations Chaucer has here given it, disrupting the expectations of her companions and the bounds of reason.[64] The proximate sea rocks track the ways Arveragus's absence disrupts Dorigen's already complicated female identity as, simultaneously, courtly lady (who receives service) and wife (who is obedient). As Wan-Chuan Kao has put it, "the rigidly demarcated identities of servant-lord and lady-wife are impossible to achieve."[65] We might say that Arveragus's absence has made him her neighbor twice over. Dorigen's obdurate, transgressive enjoyment of grief at once insists upon the importance and coherence of her marriage as well as symptomatizing

[63] Priscilla Martin briefly takes note of this valence of Dorigen's grief, conceding that the line "suggests indulgence as well as nobility of sentiment"; *Chaucer's Women: Nuns, Wives, and Amazons* (London: Macmillan, 1990), 127.

[64] Susan Crane notes that for medieval audiences, such an emotional response would have at once expressed Dorigen's femininity and subordinated it to rational masculinity; *Gender and Romance in Chaucer's "Canterbury Tales"* (Princeton: Princeton University Press, 1994), 247.

[65] Kao, "Conduct Shameful and Unshameful," 125.

its neighborly impossibility. Wishing the rocks away paradoxically both signals Dorigen's wish for Arveragus's safe return (which in her mind the absence of the rocks would seem to guarantee), and also rhetorically positions the rocks in an analogous position to Arveragus – that is, as absent. The desired absence of rock maintains Arveragus's literal absence at the forefront of her mind. Absence carries a complicated relationship to lack, a state on which desire depends. Though she prays, seemingly, for Arveragus's protection: "thilke God that made wynd to blowe / As kepe my lord!" (888–89), the Middle English verb *kēpen* (v.) can also mean to force to remain or stay, or to prevent from coming near. This could be read, in other words, as a transgressive desire that Arveragus stay away. The semantic ambiguity—the fact that "kepe" can be read various ways—reminds us that inasmuch as Dorigen's speech is a mode of grieving, it is contingent upon his absence. To the extent that the grief is pleasurable to her, then, she may transgressively be enjoying his absence.

Dorigen's grief and the "grisly rokkes blake" are excessive to the point of overdetermination. George Edmondson describes the neighbor's capacity to exceed signification as its "petrified unrest," a term I find particularly evocative in this instance.[66] Dorigen exemplifies petrified unrestfulness: paradoxically durable and yet subject to the inscriptions and interpretations of others, as well as to her own restless movement. The rocks, as Dorigen's neighbors, invoke her own transgressive desires. But they, as independent entities in their own right, are not reducible to that meaning. To be clear, Dorigen's encounter with rock does not, in my view, reveal what the rocks might be said to desire, or tell us anything much at all about the rocks on their own terms. Rather, the encounter brings them to both her and our attention as ethically relevant. What seems overridingly clear here is that Dorigen does not and cannot know these rocks fully (which, to give her some posthumanistic credit, she seems willing to admit, refusing to engage in human philosophical disputations on the subject). Just as Chaucer showcases that Dorigen does not know the rocks fully, he likewise showcases that she does not know herself or Arveragus fully either. *That* is the ethical insight neighboring elucidates. Dorigen will have to act toward her neighbors in the absence of such assuring knowledge. The

---

[66] George Edmondson, *The Neighboring Text: Chaucer, Boccaccio, Henryson* (Notre Dame: University of Notre Dame Press, 2011), 29.

narrative space that Chaucer gives to Dorigen's stone-like grief and to the fearful rocks in the first half of this tale is itself ethical in that it dwells in this uncomfortable and ambivalent space rather than rushing past it.[67]

Ethical Deliberation

To explore the ways dwelling can constitute the ethical action of neighbor-love, we must follow the tale's hinging movement to Aurelius. Though a majority of scholarship either argues or implies that Dorigen is not, by any sane measure, legitimately under obligation to Aurelius when he claims to have fulfilled her condition to remove the sea rocks,[68] many critics nevertheless consider that in making such a "rash" promise, Dorigen acted foolishly and unwisely.[69] I wish to propose another possibility: that making the removal of the rocks the "impossible" condition of her love is a deliberate ethical choice, one mindful of the neighborly dynamics at play. The choice is risky and, from the retrospective vantage of the tale's ultimate events, imperfect. But that is precisely the ethical dilemma—we are never able to make decisions from the vantage of their later outcomes, nor from a full assessment of the desires of all involved. From the perspective of neighbor theory, ethical love inherently incurs

[67] On the tale's compression and expansion of narrative time to focus upon Dorigen (an unconventional move for the genre), see Linda Charnes, " 'This werk unresonable': Narrative Frustration and Generic Redistribution in Chaucer's 'Franklin's Tale,' " *ChauR* 23, no. 4 (1989): 300–315.

[68] See Weisl, who argues that while Dorigen intends her impossible condition as a "no," the genre of romance and Dorigen's role as courtly lady make it impossible for her "no" to be heard and honored by either Aurelius or the tale; Weisl, *Conquering the Reign of Femeny*, 110–11. For an alternative reading, see Alison Ganze, " 'My trouthe for to holde: Allas, allas!': Dorigen and Honor in the 'Franklin's Tale,' " *ChauR* 42, no. 3 (2008): 312–29.

[69] The frequent scholarly characterization of Dorigen's promise as "rash" or "foolish" in otherwise diverse interpretations signals a loose consensus that in setting the condition "in pley" as she does, Dorigen is in some measure to blame for getting herself into the fix with Aurelius. Exemplifying such arguments are Kathryn Lynch, "East Meets West in Chaucer's Squire's and Franklin's Tales," *Speculum* 70, no. 3 (1995): 530–51; and Warren S. Smith, "Dorigen's Lament and the Resolution of the *Franklin's Tale*" *ChauR* 36, no. 4 (2002): 374–90. For readings that take seriously the possibility that Dorigen in some measure intends her impossible condition to be fulfilled, see John A. Pitcher, *Chaucer's Feminine Subjects: Figures of Desire in "The Canterbury Tales,"* New Middle Ages Series (New York: Palgrave Macmillan, 2012); and Elizabeth Robertson, "Marriage, Mutual Consent, and the Affirmation of the Female Subject in the Knight's Tale, the Wife of Bath's Tale, and the Franklin's Tale," in *Drama, Narrative and Poetry in the "Canterbury Tales"* (Toulouse: Presses universitaires du Mirail, 2003), 175–93.

risk (in part because it assumes that the interests of the neighbor and the interests of the self diverge in ways that cannot be foreseen); that risk does not eliminate responsibility. Dorigen makes a deliberate decision to continue dwelling with the rocks—a decision, in other words, to dwell in the uncomfortable state of self-realization that they incited. By banking on the rocks' presence, she recognizes that their ontological significance and their interests (whatever those may be) exist irrespective of her own desires. This choice is not reconciliation, but an ethical choice of cohabitation in a disturbing state of non-identification.

Dorigen's choice to offer a response founded on the grisly rocks' existence recognizes furthermore that Aurelius's desires are themselves neighborly. Dorigen is shocked when Aurelius finally confesses his love—"She gan to looke upon Aurelius" (979)—as though really seeing him for the first time: "'Is this youre wyl,' quod she, 'and sey ye thus?'" (980). Dorigen suddenly sees him differently—that is, as a man who carries this particular desire:

> So that I wiste it myghte youre herte glade,
> I wolde that day that youre Arveragus
> Wente over the see, that I, Aurelius,
> Hadde went ther nevere I sholde have come agayn.
>
> (968–71)

Both men who love Dorigen in this tale desire to leave her. Aurelius wants to join her husband in a permanent absence from Dorigen—his desire mimicking her husband's absenting actions. As Elizabeth Scala has argued, "From the very beginning (and recognized in this declaration itself) Aurelius has followed in the steps of Arveragus. Here he places himself hypothetically in Averagus's distanced position 'over the see.'"[70] Just as Dorigen has linked Arveragus's absence to the intrusive presence of those rocks, Aurelius's love-declaration of hypothetical absence links his desire for Dorigen to her much-bemoaned husband, and through him to the sea rocks that Dorigen wishes away "for his

---

[70] Elizabeth Scala, "'Ysworn . . . withoute gilt': Lais of Illusion-Making Language in the *Canterbury Tales*," special issue of *Etudes Epistémè* 25 (2014), http://revue.etudes -episteme.org (accessed July 15, 2019). Scala further argues that Arveragus "has been [Aurelius's] pursuit all along," noting that "the pains Aurelius suffers, his infamous 'penaunce', is [*sic*] exactly like the 'penaunce' suffered by Arveragus that moves Dorigen to pity and to marriage." In Scala's view, the episode thus "naturalizes Aurelius's claims on Dorigen's affections" and suggests a context for her dual answer.

[Arveragus's] sake" (892). Aurelius rhetorically participates in her grief, imagining himself, with Arveragus, as the absent and mourned beloved that will, paradoxically, make her "herte glade."[71] Aurelius has hit, uncannily (or so it may seem to Dorigen), upon the precise neighborly dynamic Chaucer sets up in the early part of the tale. Dorigen's impossible condition—the removal of the sea rocks that she declares would allow her to love Aurelius "best of any man" (997)—in effect meets this proposition on those neighborly terms. It works, of course, at many levels. She sets him an impossible task, the failure of which endorses his stated desire to be absent from her, and to the extent that his love-declaration is unwelcome to her, it might indeed make her "herte glade" if he were to go off and not return. Yet the transgressive enjoyment we have seen her take in mourning an absent beloved threatens to endorse Aurelius's desired affinity with Arveragus. To wish Aurelius away, as to wish the rocks away in the earlier passage, threatens to blur into a wish for him to be like Arveragus (and specifically, like Arveragus in the way that Arveragus most troubles Dorigen). To this extent, her condition recognizes and maintains (in an ethical, but also risky fashion) the socially transgressive aspect of Aurelius's declaration that seeks to flout the "trouthe" she has plighted Arveragus.[72] From another angle, her condition endorses Arveragus's desire to be absent, by staking her rebuff of an unwanted suitor upon the rocks that resonate her husband's desire to dwell elsewhere. Given that she effectively chooses the rocks over both men, perhaps Arveragus's continued absence is a price she is willing to pay to secure Aurelius's distance, suggesting that what she may most desire is for both men to stay away.

[71] The Tenth Commandment of the Jewish and Christian Decalogue enjoins men not to covet their neighbor's goods or wife. If Aurelius intends misdirection here, attempting to circumvent the fact that he is violating this social and religious prohibition, he initially fails, for Dorigen chides him explicitly for his temerity "to go love another mannes wyf" (*FranT*, 1004).

[72] This situation is yet more complicated because Aurelius's proposition, though flouting the social, legal, and religious institution of Dorigen and Arveragus's marriage vows, perfectly aligns with *fin'amors* expectations for an extramarital love plot. For instance, Felicity Riddy argues persuasively that the "vehicles of courtly utterance" conventionally allow Aurelius to demonstrate his "gentil" capacity to defer—perhaps perpetually—the consummation of his desire; for Aurelius to speak "feelingly of love . . . the woman must be unavailable." Felicity Riddy, "Engendering Pity in the *Franklin's Tale*," in *Feminist Readings in Middle English Literature: The Wife of Bath and All Her Sect*, ed. Ruth Evans and Leslie Johnson (London: Routledge, 1994), 54–71 (58–59). John A. Pitcher comes to similar insights about the role of desire's deferral in his monograph *Chaucer's Feminine Subjects*, as well as in his article " 'Word and werk' in Chaucer's *Franklin's Tale*," *Literature and Psychology* 49, nos. 1–2 (2003): 77–109. Elaine Tuttle Hansen

Chaucer has encouraged us to see an obdurate resistance to reason and persuasion in Dorigen herself and in her speech about those rocks. We can trace the unreasonableness (and, indeed, the transgressive enjoyment of being unreasonable) through Dorigen's use of the rocks to deflect Aurelius. She sets this condition, after all, "in pley" (988). Might she be signaling her enjoyment of being unpersuadable when she sets this condition?[73] The "playful" use of the rocks to augment a serious "no" signals the neighborly tensions that her marriage, her encounter with the rocks, and her conversation with Aurelius exude. But if so, then it comes wholesale—Dorigen cannot control which valences to bring along and which to exclude. These encounters are not tame, or safe. In reading Dorigen's choice to use those rocks to block Aurelius as an instrumental part of her ethical process, I do not mean to suggest that it was a "good" choice or the "right" choice. The ethics of the neighbor insists upon the imperative to take responsibility in a nonreciprocal situation amidst constrained knowledge: it does not offer an ethical playbook, nor does it promise that in loving the neighbor all will be well. Theorists of the neighbor insist upon the productive potential of the ethical process to which the neighbor invites us: to acknowledge the transgressive alienation shared by self and neighbor—and then to love the neighbor by being willing to dwell in that uncomfortable space and take responsibility for our choices.

"Astoned"

If Dorigen's actions regarding the black rocks are ethical in their acknowledgment of the neighborly strangeness amongst her human and nonhuman relationships, the clerk's actions toward the rocks are profoundly *un*ethical in their pragmatic, self-interested calculation. For the clerk only ever considers the rocks as a means to earn a thousand pounds that in turn become a means to demonstrate his noble generosity. His

---

likewise addresses the conventionality of Aurelius's love for Dorigen in *Chaucer and the Fictions of Gender* (Berkeley: University of California Press, 1992).

[73] This moment resonates with Boccaccio's *Il filocolo* (Chaucer's source for *The Franklin's Tale*), in which Boccaccio invokes Ovid's advice to lovers to persevere in wooing a woman because water eventually erodes rock. Chaucer's direct transformation of this image into a statement on the social pressure that can effect consolation, rather than on wooing a recalcitrant woman, can be seen, in my argument, to return obliquely to the analogy's original topic of love.

feat of "magyk natureel" that appears to remove the rocks may demonstrate his deep understanding of the astral influences upon beings and matter (in his ability not only to calculate or ascertain them but also to augment or manipulate those natural processes),[74] yet his motivation reveals his interest in the rocks to reside solely in their use-value to him.[75] Determined to maximize his profits, he sets a price equal to the sum total of Aurelius's wordly possessions and legacy;[76] by instigating this transaction the way they do, the two men reduce the tale's deliberate, complex ethical configurations to a calculating financial marketplace wherein Dorigen is no more than one more debtor.

When Aurelius confronts Dorigen with the completed task, ethics,

[74] The concept of "magyk natureel" in the late Middle Ages can encompass alchemy; astrology; illusion and spectacle; science and philosophy; and, in some of its grosser experiments, a Frankenstein-like reanimation of dead tissue, such as how to generate bees from the corpse of a calf, or vice versa (for a description of this experiment, see Maaike van der Lugt, "'Abominable Mixtures': The 'Liber vaccae' in the Medieval West, or the Dangers and Attractions of Natural Magic," *Traditio* 64 [2009]: 229–77 [236]). See also Nicolas Weill-Parot, "Astrology, Astral Influences, and Occult Properties in the Thirteenth and Fourteenth Centuries," *Traditio* 65 (2010): 201–30. The question of what is "natural" about "magyk natureel" is precisely the site of urgent debate about "the legitimacy and the limits of the manipulation of nature by artificial means" (Van der Lugt, "Abominable Mixtures," 232). It was a category of experiment and philosophy that threatened to confound the divides among understanding, manipulation, and transgression of natural processes. Dorigen describes Aurelius's success at removing the rocks as a "monstre" (*FranT*, 1344) that is "agayns the proces of nature" (1345). She expresses, in these comments, the paradox that is "magyk natureel," and why it was the source both of excitement and of anxiety among the learned in the Middle Ages. While never admitted as a university discipline, it remained the province of university-trained clerics, such as the clerk and his associates at Orléans in *The Franklin's Tale*. Chaucer nicely captures this ambiguity: Aurelius's brother recalls the student who "prively" leaves a book of "magyk natureel" upon his desk; this "felawe" is "a bacheler of lawe" studying "to lerne another craft" (1124–28).

[75] Working in concert with natural processes, the clerk effects, as Alexander N. Gabrovsky argues, a transmutation: he "fabricate[s] illusions and manipulate[s] the laws of natural science for gain"; *Chaucer the Alchemist: Physics, Mutability, and the Medieval Imagination* (New York: Palgrave Macmillan, 2015), 85. Reading the clerk from an ecocritical perspective that diverges from my own, Gillian Rudd argues that the clerk offers "a better role model" than Dorigen, for "apparent ability to control the natural world rests on his skilful use of predominant perceptions, without actually requiring him to alter the environment at all" (*Greenery*, 147). There is a general critical consensus that the clerk's actions rest upon scientific knowledge: Anthony E. Luengo, for instance, argues that all of the clerk's illusions are the result of stage magic, such that "what is done [to the rocks] is achieved by purely natural or scientific means"; "Magic and Illusion in 'The Franklin's Tale,'" *JEGP* 77, no. 1 (1978): 1–16 (12).

[76] It is clear from the way Chaucer describes the financial negotiations that the clerk is out, at least initially, for all the profit this little market will bear: "He made it straunge, and swoor, so God hym save, / Lasse than a thousand pound he wolde nat have, / Ne gladly for that somme he wolde nat goon" (*FranT*, 1223–25). Aurelius, initially cavalier about the price, faces shame and financial ruin when the time comes to

which became calculated financial transaction, becomes in turn a pledge of honor to which he insists that she is bound. In his anxiety that Dorigen might perhaps view this situation differently, he harps on her "trouthe" (1328), constantly backpedaling away from directing her course of action while simultaneously insisting that she lies under an obligation: "wel ye woot what ye han hight—/ Nat that I chalange any thyng of right / Of yow" (1323–25), and "Dooth as yow list, have youre biheste in mynde" (1335). His backhanded rhetoric, when he claims to "have do so as ye comanded me" (1333), effects this transformation and results in an entirely different mode of interaction from the earlier garden party where he approached her as a neighbor. His most fervent wish now is not to be, like Arveragus, far away from her, but that she recognize herself as indebted and keep her word.

Upon hearing Aurelius's parting shot, "But wel I woot the rokkes been aweye" (1338), Dorigen "astoned stood" (1339). She is stone-like once again, and again because of an intolerable absence. Both times, Chaucer's association of Dorigen with rock nestles against her intense emotive expression: "And hoom she goth a sorweful creature; / For verray feere unnethe may she go. / She wepeth, wailleth, al a day or two" (1346–48). Coincidence of language resonates across the two episodes where Chaucer likens Dorigen to rock. In both instances, her "verray feere" impedes the normal functioning of Dorigen's body, making it difficult to walk and to stand (1347, 860). Dorigen's grief at the disappearance of the rocks ("she wepeth, wailleth") reminds us of how she "wepeth" and "siketh" (817) at Arveragus's departure, invoking the miseries she earlier endured: "she moorneth, waketh, wayleth, fasteth, pleyneth" (819). Love-longing for the absent Arveragus transmutes in this later scene into something that sounds very like love-longing for the absent rocks, as she confronts the horror of losing Arveragus all over again another way. In other words, across the tale the rocks, whether present or absent, serve as the rhetorical site where Dorigen encounters neighborly strangeness. She returns home (to the site where the rocks *should* be) and grieves alone; in a Chaucerian move at once farcically redundant and grimly appropriate, Arveragus is again absent. We are back not quite where we started. The apparent removal of the rocks leaves Dorigen unmoored, without the ethical ballast she was relying

---

pay the debt in full: "Myn heritage moot I nedes selle, / And been a beggere; heere may I nat dwelle / And shamen al my kynrede in this place" (1563–65).

on when she answered Aurelius's neighborly love-declaration. Aurelius's desire, like Arveragus's before him, has proven to be unfathomable (as the neighbor's desire will always be), throwing her anew into a state of anguished, petrified unrest. Confronted with Aurelius's shifting desires, Dorigen can only envision a resolution encompassing "deeth or elles dishonour" (1358), which she proceeds to bewail at length. But while contemplating these options, what she actually does is dwell with this fraught neighborly situation. Dwelling in this affective mode, she in fact defers and resists responding to Aurelius on his newly contractual terms. Persistent and intense emotional expression does not solve her problems (neither here nor earlier in the tale), but it does serve as one of Dorigen's consistent means of dwelling with the uncomfortable ramifications of her neighbor relations—a form of action whose final (human) tragedy is that no one else is willing to dwell there with her.

In conclusion, Chaucer uses *The Franklin's Tale* to interrogate what it might mean to be called to ethical action toward one's human and non-human neighbors from a position of social constraint and self-alienation. In other words, there is a way in which the tale uses Dorigen to recognize that all creatures (even those with limited agency) are ethically responsible to their neighbors, and to query the unique ethical difficulties and opportunities that such constraint puts into motion. As O'Dair, Wolfe, and Yates have shown at the beginning of this article, choice is unavoidable for Dorigen. And though choice is necessary, all choices, inevitably made with limited knowledge, risk being wrong when viewed from a future stand-point. From this neighborly perspective, the Franklin's *demande* at the tale's end is quite ironic: "which was the mooste fre, as thynketh yow?" (1622).[77] "Fre" to whom?, we might well wonder, and, taking a cue from the term's other valences, "fre" from what? The necessity of choosing ethical action and the constraints of limited agency haunt the tale's final *demande* in their conspicuous absence.

An ethics of human/nonhuman relationality insists upon our ongoing obligation to our neighbors, even (and perhaps especially) when we dislike them; when we receive no benefit from them; when we cannot

---

[77] His question is a variation of the *demande d'amour* traditional in courtly contexts. Another, more typical example is the Knight's question at the end of the first part of *The Knight's Tale*, where he says, "Yow loveres axe I now this questioun: / Who hath the worse, Arcite or Palamoun? / That oon may seen his lady day by day, / But in prison he moot dwelle alway; / That oother wher hym list may ride or go, / But seen his lady shal he nevere mo" (*KnT*, 1347–52).

ascertain their interests clearly; when we operate amidst conditions of constraint; or when, confronted with them, our knees grow weak and our value systems simply fail. Resonant with O'Dair's fears about the ethical implications of ontological leveling, Sarah Stanbury has argued that Chaucer's poetic production provides humans a means of abdicating ethical obligations. She argues that Chaucer's representation of the nonhuman world, particularly in the figure of "Nature," imperils the notion, drawn from Jewish and Christian Scripture, of human stewardship over the created world. By "exonerating . . . human subjects from custodial responsibilities," Chaucer's literary representation "may have had dire historical consequences" for modern environmental exploitation.[78] Yet Dorigen is a site where Chaucer, in contrast, wrestles with human and nonhuman interaction as a persistent ethical problem, revealing that his literary meditations on the interrelations of diverse beings are not monolithic. For amidst difficult human interactions, Dorigen does not relinquish ethical responsibility to her nonhuman neighbors. Her ethical process of neighborly recognition, dwelling, and loving negotiates messily among human and nonhuman interests rather than instigating a hierarchy of ethical privilege that foregrounds humans. Reframing Dorigen as an ethical subject with neighbors both spousal and extramarital, both human and nonhuman, we can analyze and assess Chaucer's varied representations of the difficult relationships arising from these wide ecological neighborhoods. His work carries resonances for us in the twenty-first century: the difficulties and risks we run in choosing to love our neighbors, we learn from Dorigen, do not exonerate us from the urgent imperative and radical potential of doing so.

[78] Sarah Stanbury, "Ecochaucer: Green Ethics and Medieval Nature," *ChauR* 39, no. 1 (2004): 1–16 (13).

"The emprentyng of hire consolacioun": Engraving, Erosion, and Persistent Speech in *The Franklin's Tale*

Alastair Bennett
Royal Holloway, University of London

Abstract

When Dorigen's friends console her in *The Franklin's Tale*, the Franklin says that their words take effect in the same way that engraving makes an impression in a stone. This comparison recalls a similar analogy found in Boccaccio's *Il filocolo*, and cited there from Ovid's *Ars amatoria*, which holds that a lover's petitions will move his lady in time, just as dropping water hollows out hard rock. In the first part of this article, I trace the history of this analogy from the *Ovidius minor* to its appearances in the work of Chaucer's contemporaries. Ovid and his medieval inheritors recognized that the analogy could motivate many different kinds of persistent speech, from lovers' complaints to petitionary prayer, but they also sought to qualify its overstated claim that a speaker might reshape a listener's desires by sheer persistence, and to suggest instead that persistent speech might be a good in itself, an opportunity for creative expression and for the cultivation of virtue. In the second part, I argue that *The Franklin's Tale* continues to think in terms of this analogy as its characters test their own powers of persistent speech. Dorigen comes to reappraise it as she complains about the black rocks and discovers that stone can resist erosion and petition for a long time, but Aurelius goes to great lengths to avoid this kind of realization and to sustain the illusion the analogy encodes, that a persistent speaker can "emprent" his desires on other people.

Keywords

Chaucer; Ovid; Boccaccio; speech; complaint; preaching; prayer

WHEN DORIGEN MOURNS the absence of Arveragus early in *The Franklin's Tale*, her friends do "al hire bisynesse" to comfort her,

My thanks to Isabel Davis, Cath Nall, and the anonymous readers for *SAC* for their helpful comments on the earlier drafts of this article.

telling her "nyght and day, / That causelees she sleeth hirself" (*FranT*, V.827, 824–25).[1] The Franklin explains that, through these long endeavors, Dorigen's friends "emprent" their consolation on her, much as a craftsman might carve "som figure" in stone:

> By proces, as ye knowen everichoon,
> Men may so longe graven in a stoon
> Til som figure therinne emprented be.
> So longe han they conforted hire til she
> Recevyed hath, by hope and by resoun,
> The emprentyng of hire consolacioun.
>
> (V.829–36)

As he draws this analogy, the Franklin makes some confident claims about the power of persistent speech. Over time, he suggests, a speaker can "emprent" new attitudes and desires on even the most obdurate listener, like an artisan incising a resistant material. The "proces" of engraving supplies a figure for the kind of transformation that Dorigen's friends are trying to achieve—a clear, comprehensible metaphor for the way that consolation takes effect—and this figure, in turn, seems to hold out a promise to persistent speakers, reassuring them that, in the end, their words will make an impression.

With this image of "emprentyng," Chaucer reworks another widely disseminated figure for the power of persistent speech, where the speaker's words are compared to dropping water that hollows out a stone. This analogy features prominently in Menedon's story from Boccaccio's *Il filocolo*, Chaucer's most immediate source for *The Franklin's Tale*, and Boccaccio cites it from Book I of Ovid's *Ars amatoria*, another text that Chaucer knew well.[2] In both these contexts, the analogy refers to seduction rather than consolation. Ovid's *praeceptor amoris* offers reassurance to male lovers, promising them that women will respond to their petitions over time. Ovid deploys this analogy in a sophisticated and skeptical way: the *praeceptor* of the *Ars* acknowledges the power of this figure to motivate lovers, even in apparently hopeless circumstances, but he

---

[1] Chaucerian texts are cited from *The Riverside Chaucer*, gen ed. Larry D. Benson, 3rd ed. (Boston, Mass.: Houghton Mifflin, 1987).

[2] For a detailed bibliography on the sources of *The Franklin's Tale*, see Michael Calabrese, "Chaucer's Dorigen and Boccaccio's Female Voices," *SAC* 29 (2007): 259–92 (259 n. 1). See also, more recently, John Finlayson, "Invention and Disjunction: Chaucer's Rewriting of Boccaccio in the *Franklin's Tale*," *ES* 89 (2008): 385–402.

also draws attention to the qualifications it encodes, noting that the "proces" of erosion takes a long time. In his later poetry of exile, moreover, Ovid returned to this analogy, but with a very different understanding of what persistent speech could achieve. In the *Epistulae ex Ponto*, the persistent speaker continues his complaint even after the stone is worn away, discovering his own capacity for endurance even as he comes to realize that his words may never take effect. Ovid's medieval readers, who were trained to read his works in a complex, mutually qualifying relationship to one another, might find a nuanced account of persistent speech, the desires that animate it, and the effects it achieves, in his evolving treatment of this analogy.

The image of water dropping on stone recurs with its own insistent force in medieval texts of many different kinds.[3] If Chaucer was responding to Boccaccio's citation of Ovid in the first instance, he would also have been conscious of the wide dissemination of this figure in a range of discourses, from love poetry to sermons. This analogy retains a strong association with courtship and seduction, offering hope to rejected lovers, but it also works to encourage other kinds of persistent speech, including preaching, instruction, and prayer. Texts in these different traditions often sought to theorize or to dramatize the realizations that emerged in Ovid's repeated engagements with this figure; lovers and preachers alike found ways to harness the persuasive power of the analogy, while also qualifying its claims about persistent speech and its effects. Medieval *praeceptores* used the figure to encourage long loveservice and persistent prayer, but they also invited their students to recognize that these activities brought their own rewards, enabling the cultivation of "noblesse" and *longanimitas*, which might ultimately displace the rewards the analogy seems to promise.

---

[3] For partial lists of this figure in medieval and early modern English sources, see Walter W. Skeat, *Early English Proverbs: Chiefly of the Thirteenth and Fourteenth Centuries, with Illustrative Quotations* (Oxford: Clarendon Press, 1910), 10 (no. 24); Bartlett Jere Whiting and Helen Wescott Whiting, *Proverbs, Sentences, and Proverbial Phrases from English Writings Mainly before 1500* (Cambridge, Mass.: Harvard University Press, 1968), 145 ("D412, Little drops thirl (*pierce*) the flint on which they often fall"); and Morris Palmer Tilley, *A Dictionary of the Proverbs in England in the Sixteenth and Seventeenth Centuries* (Ann Arbor: University of Michigan Press, 1950), 174 ("D618, Constant dropping will wear the stone"). Hans Walther, *Proverbia sententiaeque latinitatis medii aevi*, 5 vols. (Göttingen: Vandenhoeck and Ruprecht, 1963–67), 2.1:686 lists a Latin proverbial form: "5599a: Dicit Aristoteles: lapidem cavat ultima gutta." While Skeat traces the figure to the *Epistulae ex Ponto*, both the Whitings and Tilley argue that it derives from Job 14:19, where the effects of water on stone figure the experience of tribulation; none of these lists mentions the *Ars amatoria*.

The analogy between speaking and engraving, rehearsed in the voice of the narrator and applied to the endeavors of Dorigen's friends, has a broader significance for *The Franklin's Tale* as a whole. This tale is populated with persistent speakers: over the course of the narrative, both Dorigen and her unwanted suitor Aurelius will speak long passages of petition and complaint, addressing audiences who are hostile, inscrutable, or simply absent. Some of their speeches are briefly described, but others constitute long, lyrical interludes in the dramatic action. The analogy with "emprentyng" stone expresses the hopes and assumptions that sustain the speakers of this tale in "al hire bisynesse." This "figure" appears in a dense cluster of sententious, proverbial expressions at the start of the narrative, concerned with mastery in marriage and with the need for patience, and, like them, it voices claims that will come under scrutiny as the story unfolds. Some of the tale's most memorable episodes take up and reconfigure the image of "emprentyng" stone, as Dorigen directs her complaint against the black rocks around the coast and when she challenges Aurelius to remove them, "stoon by stoon." Over the course of the Franklin's story, I argue, Dorigen will come to understand how this "figure" works, negotiating its deceptive claims about the "proces" of erosion and the power of persistent speech, but Aurelius will continue to demand the rewards it seems to promise, the power to "emprent" his desires on other people.

"Gutta cauat lapidem"

In the first book of the *Ars amatoria*, the *praeceptor amoris* tells the young men of Rome that they should carry on writing to their ladies even if the ladies return their letters without reading them. He argues that women will succumb to persistent suitors, just as rings and plowshares are worn down by constant use, and stones are hollowed out by dropping water:

> ferreus assiduo consumitur anulus usu,
> > interit assidua uomer aduncus humo.
> quid magis est saxo durum, quid mollius unda?
> > dura tamen molli saxa cauantur aqua.
> Penelopen ipsam, persta modo, tempore uinces.
> > (Ovid, *Ars amatoria*, I.473–77)

144

[An iron ring is worn by constant use, a curved share wastes by constant ploughing of the ground. What is harder than rock, what softer than water? yet soft water hollows out hard rock. Only persevere; in time, you will overcome Penelope herself.][4]

In Menedon's story from the *Filocolo*, Tarolfo attempts to court a married *donna* who repeatedly rejects his advances. When she ignores his messages, he takes encouragement from the *praeceptor*'s words: "Ma già per tutto questo Tarolfo di ciò non si rimanea, seguendo d'Ovidio gli amaestramenti, il quale dice l'uomo non lasciare per durezza della donna di non perseverare, però che per continuanza la molle acqua fora la dura pietra" (19–22) ("But through all this Tarolfo still did not stop, following the teachings of Ovid who said that a man should not stop persevering because of a lady's hardness, since by persistence soft water works its way through hard rock").[5] The *praeceptor*'s injunction to persevere, "persta modo," becomes an axiom for Tarolfo in this story: it sustains him not only in these early efforts at seduction but also in his later trials, when he takes up the impossible task his lady sets for him, to plant a garden for her that blooms in January as though it were May.[6] In *The Franklin's Tale*, where Chaucer reimagines Menedon's story as a Breton *lai*, he also recasts this figure for persistent speech, replacing Ovid's image of erosion with an image of engraving and applying it to the consoling speech of Dorigen's friends. The tale suggests that the analogy might also apply to Dorigen's persistent speech, as she echoes her friends' entreaties with her own, ongoing complaint, and the history of

[4] Text from Ovid, *Amores; Medicamina faciei femineae; Ars amatoria; Remedia amoris*, ed. E. J. Kenney (Oxford: Clarendon Press, 1961); translation adapted from Ovid, *"The Art of Love" and Other Poems*, trans. J. H. Mozley, rev. G. P. Goold, Loeb Classical Library 232 (Cambridge, Mass.: Harvard University Press, 1929).

[5] Text and translation from Robert R. Edwards, "The Franklin's Tale," in *Sources and Analogues of the "Canterbury Tales,"* ed. Robert M. Correale and Mary Hamel, 2 vols. (Woodbridge: Brewer, 2002–5), 1.211–65 (220, 221).

[6] Modern editions of Chaucer, following Skeat, claim that Tarolfo cites the later instance of this image of water dropping on stone from Ovid's *Epistulae ex Ponto*, and that this, in turn, is the ultimate source of the Franklin's image of carving and "emprentyng." See, for example, *The Complete Works of Geoffrey Chaucer*, ed. Walter W. Skeat, 2nd ed., 7 vols. (Oxford: Clarendon Press, 1899–1900), 5.389; *The Riverside Chaucer*, 897; Geoffrey Chaucer, *The Canterbury Tales*, ed. Jill Mann (London: Penguin, 2005), 952. As editors of Boccaccio have long been aware, however, Tarolfo is citing the *Ars*, where this figure applies directly to the experience of lovers: see Giovanni Boccaccio, *Opere minori in volgare*, Vol. 1, *Filocolo*, ed. Mario Marti (Milan: Rizzoli, 1969), 475 n. 4. See also the discussion in Richard L. Hoffman, *Ovid and the "Canterbury Tales"* (Philadelphia: University of Pennsylvania Press, 1966), 169.

this figure, extending back to Boccaccio and Ovid, affirms its relevance to the lovesick petitions of Aurelius, too.

This chain of citations links *The Franklin's Tale* to Ovid's *Ars* and positions its account of persistent speech in part as a response to Ovid's figure of water drops eroding stone. Yet, the significance of this figure was complicated, in turn, by its treatment elsewhere in the *Ovidius minor*, and in other medieval writing that appropriated and redeployed it. As he makes this local allusion to his immediate sources, Chaucer also enters a much larger discourse about persistent speech, the desires that motivate it, and the effects it can achieve.

The passage from Book I of the *Ars* reveals the important role of repeated practice, or *usus*, in Ovid's text, as Colin Fewer has argued.[7] In the first two books, the *praeceptor* encourages his male readers to cultivate and inhabit a lover's persona, rehearsing the artificial techniques of seduction until they come to seem like "second nature."[8] The same techniques can be applied to seduction itself: through the persistent application of artistry, the *praeceptor* argues, men can subject women to their own desires. "What the *magister* audaciously promises in *Ars amatoria*," Fewer writes, "is that the desire of others is capable of being produced and domesticated through practice, by repetition and habituation."[9] The imagery of water dropping on stone figures the gradual effects of *usus* in both these contexts, Fewer contends, showing how long, reiterative practice can transform the will. This is the promise that consoles Tarolfo in *Il filocolo* and that encourages Dorigen's friends early in *The Franklin's Tale*. Indeed, Fewer, who discusses the Franklin's version of this analogy alongside other, similar metaphors in *Troilus and Criseyde*, notes that the language of "proces" that appears here is often found in Chaucer in contexts "that recall the Ovidian imagery of shaping the will through practice."[10]

Even as he advances his audacious claims about *usus*, however, Ovid's *praeceptor* introduces some ironic qualifications. In a hyperbolic flourish, he evokes Penelope, who resisted many suitors during the long decade

---

[7] Colin Fewer, "The Second Nature: *Habitus* as Ideology in the *Ars amatoria* and *Troilus and Criseyde*," *Exemplaria* 20 (2008): 314–39 (322–23).

[8] On the cultivated identity of the lover in the *Ars*, see Robert R. Edwards, *The Flight from Desire: Augustine and Ovid to Chaucer* (New York: Palgrave Macmillan, 2006), 40–42.

[9] Fewer, "Second Nature," 323.

[10] Ibid., 327–28.

when her husband Ulysses was absent: "Penelopen ipsam . . . tempore uinces" ("in time, you will overcome Penelope herself"). Penelope's long endurance suggests what the analogy with erosion already implies: that cultivating another person's desires through repeated practice will be a long and drawn-out process.[11] Her story hints at the scale of the lover's task, the length of time he may have to persist. Similar forms of qualification and ambiguity surround the use of this analogy in Boccaccio and Chaucer. In the *Filocolo*, Tarolfo proves himself to be a committed student of Ovid's *praeceptor* and a firm believer in his claims about the power of habituation and persistent speech; his elaborate efforts serve not only to win his lady, but also to prove the arguments about persistent speech that underpin the analogy from the *Ars*. Yet, his turn to magic to achieve his impossible task might itself seem to call these arguments into question; ultimately, in Menedon's story, repetition and habituation are insufficient to provoke and direct the *donna*'s desires. The narrative of *The Franklin's Tale* casts doubt on the analogy between speaking and "emprentyng" almost as soon as the narrator evokes it. After he affirms the power of persistent speech to "emprent" consolation on its listeners, the Franklin suggests that Dorigen's sorrow "gan aswage" because she had temporarily exhausted herself ("She may nat alwey duren in swich rage"), calling the agency of her friends into question (V.836). In the following lines, moreover, Dorigen resumes her complaint and her friends resume their efforts to console her, the promised reward for their efforts deferred into the future.

In their original context, the *praeceptor*'s claims about *usus* were bound up with the larger ironic project of the *Ars amatoria*. Treating the subject matter of love elegy in the form of a didactic poem, Ovid satirized both traditions, offering an urbane comment on Roman morality through the juxtaposition of Augustan poetic genres. The *Ars* suggests that a lover might learn to master the experience of love through the cynical application of craft, and, at the same time, that the forms of self-discipline

---

[11] Addressing female readers in Book III, the *praeceptor* invokes Penelope as a paradigm of chastity: "est pia Penelope lustris errante duobus / et totidem lustris bella gerente uiro" (III.15–16) ("yet Penelope is chaste, though for ten years her lord was wandering and fighting for as many years"). On these lines, and their relation to the passage in Book I, see *Ovid: Ars amatoria, Book 3*, ed. and trans. Roy Gibson, Cambridge Classical Texts and Commentaries 40 (Cambridge: Cambridge University Press, 2003), 93.

that were prized in didactic poetry might be exploited for sexual gratification.[12] The analogy with water dropping on stone provides a pre-
existing intertextual link between these traditions: Tibullus used it to
encourage rejected lovers in his elegies, much as Ovid's *praeceptor* does,
while Lucretius, in his *De rerum natura*, groups the hollow stone with a
worn-down ring and plowshare, to show the effects of erosion.[13] These
are texts that Ovid knew and that he cites repeatedly in the *Ars*.[14] As
Alison Sharrock has noted, moreover, this figure not only links the
didactic and amatory traditions, but also suggests that instruction and
seduction might work in similar ways.[15] The lover persists with his lady
much as the *praeceptor* persists with his student, and his own experience
of instruction supplies a source of encouragement as he takes up the role
of seducer. When Tarolfo remembers the words of Ovid in the *Filocolo*,
he takes encouragement not only from the analogy itself, but also from
the way his own desires were formed through subjection to Ovid's
praeceptor.

[12] For introductions to the *Ars* that consider its complex and subversive relationship
to love elegy and didactic poetry, see Patricia Wilson, "*Praecepta amoris*: Ovid's Didactic
Elegy," in *Brill's Companion to Ovid*, ed. Barbara Weiden Boyd (Leiden: Brill, 2002),
141–65; and Roy Gibson, "The *Ars amatoria*," in *A Companion to Ovid*, ed. Peter E.
Knox (Oxford: Wiley-Blackwell, 2009), 90–103.

[13] In the elegies of Tibullus, the speaker says: "sed ne te capiant, primo si forte
negabit, / taedia . . . longa dies molli saxa peredit aqua" (I.iv.15–18) ("He will refuse at
first, but don't become worn down! . . . Long days let gentle water eat through rock");
Tibullus, *Elegies*, ed. Robert Maltby, trans. A. M. Juster (Oxford: Oxford University
Press, 2012), 20, 21. Lucretius describes the ring, the plowshare, and the stone in Book
I at lines 312–14: "anulus in digito subter tenuatur habendo, / stilicidi casus lapidem
cavat, uncus aratri / ferreus occulto decrescit vomer in arvis" ("a ring on the finger is
thinned underneath by wear, the fall of drippings hollows a stone, the curved plough-
share of iron imperceptibly dwindles away in the fields"); Lucretius, *De rerum natura*,
trans. W. H. D. Rouse, rev. Martin Ferguson Smith, 2nd rev. ed., Loeb Classical Library
181 (1982; repr., Cambridge, Mass.: Harvard University Press, 1992), 26, 27. The
analogy itself predates both Tibullus and Lucretius; the earliest written record of it
survives in a fragment of epic poetry attributed to Choerilus of Samos, who wrote at
the end of the fifth century BCE. See *Choerili Samii reliquiae*, ed. P. Radici Colace (Rome:
Bretschneider, 1979), 79–82.

[14] For Ovid's debts to Tibullus, see Robert Maltby, "Tibullus and Ovid," in Knox, *A
Companion to Ovid*, 279–93. Ovid's intertextual engagement with Lucretius was complex
and extensive. For a comprehensive list of his allusions and quotations, see Anton Zing-
erle, *Ovidius und sein Verhältniss zu den Vorgängern und gleichzeitigen römischen Dichtern*
(Innsbruck: Wagner, 1869–71), 2.12–47 (the passage on water and stone is identified
on page 14); for a discussion of references in the *Ars amatoria* specifically, see Marion
Steudel, *Die Literaturparodie in Ovids "Ars amatoria"* (Hildesheim: Olms-Weidmann,
1992), 40–76, who addresses this passage at 63–64.

[15] Alison Sharrock, *Seduction and Repetition in Ovid's "Ars Amatoria" 2* (Oxford: Clarendon Press, 1994), 21–23; and see also Edwards, *Flight from Desire*, 40–41.

Amatory didacticism was not necessarily incongruous in medieval culture, and the extent to which medieval readers recognized the original ironies of the *Ars* remains a matter for debate. Marilynn Desmond has argued that, while the juxtaposition of elegiac and didactic modes had a subversive edge for the first readers of the *Ars*, the use of this text to teach Latin composition in the medieval schoolroom served to naturalize the idea that a "pedagogical imperative" attached to the experience of love, that "the onset of *amor* must be attended by instruction."[16] The *Ars amatoria*, which circulated in Latin and in several vernacular translations, was often evoked as a kind of authority in medieval love literature where, as Suzanne Conklin Akbari writes, "[t]he Ovidian art of love" served as "the foundation of a court centred on service to the 'dieu d' amors.'"[17] It also provided inspiration for erotodidactic works such as Andreas Capellanus's *De arte honesti amandi* and the *Roman de la Rose*, both of which borrow from it directly. Desmond argues that medieval writers took Ovid's didacticism seriously in texts like these, imagining him as a cleric of love ("Venus clerk," as Chaucer calls him in *The House of Fame*, line 1487).[18] The familiarity of Ovid's *Ars*, and of the genre of erotodidactic writing, did not preclude skeptical responses to this text, however. Vincent Gillespie contends that at least some of the medieval *praeceptores* who engaged with the *Ars* were as "subtle and self-aware" in their handling of it as Ovid was in writing it.[19] Sharrock argues that medieval readers "understood the irony of the

---

[16] Marilynn Desmond, "Venus's Clerk: Ovid's Amatory Poetry in the Middle Ages," in *A Handbook to the Reception of Ovid*, ed. John F. Miller and Carole E. Newlands (Oxford: Wiley-Blackwell, 2014), 161–73 (164). On the study of Ovid in medieval grammar schools and universities, see also Ralph J. Hexter, *Ovid and Medieval Schooling: Studies in Medieval School Commentaries on Ovid's "Ars amatoria," "Epistulae ex Ponto," and "Epistulae Herodium"* (Munich: Bei der Arbeo-Gesellschaft, 1986); and Vincent Gillespie, "From the Twelfth Century to c. 1450," in *The Cambridge History of Literary Criticism*, Vol. 2, *The Middle Ages*, ed. Alastair Minnis and Ian Johnson (Cambridge: Cambridge University Press, 2005), 145–235 (186–206).

[17] Suzanne Conklin Akbari, "Ovid and Ovidianism," in *The Oxford History of Classical Reception*, Vol. 1, *800–1558*, ed. Rita Copeland (Oxford: Oxford University Press, 2016), 187–204 (198).

[18] Desmond has argued consistently that students and teachers alike "accepted [the] didactic rhetoric [of the *Ars*] without attending to its irony" in the medieval schoolroom; "Venus's Clerk," 162. See also Marilynn Desmond, *Ovid's Art and the Wife of Bath: The Ethics of Erotic Violence* (Ithaca: Cornell University Press, 2006), 36–37; and Marilynn Desmond, "Gender and Desire in Medieval French Translations of Ovid's Amatory Works," in *Ovid in the Middle Ages*, ed. James G. Clark, Frank T. Coulson, and Kathryn L. McKinley (Cambridge: Cambridge University Press, 2011), 108–22 (109–10).

[19] Gillespie, "From the Twelfth Century to c. 1450," 187.

poem perfectly well, even if the manner in which such irony played out for their culture was different from that of the Augustan age."[20] The treatment of the *praeceptor*'s analogy between persistent speech and water dropping on stone, first in the *Filocolo* and then in *The Franklin's Tale*, but also more broadly in the medieval works of amatory and moral instruction, itself reveals a questioning attitude to his didactic methods. If medieval readers no longer recognized the inherent ironies of erotodidaxis, they nevertheless perceived the mercurial qualities of this particular teaching voice.

The lessons of the *Ars amatoria* were further complicated for medieval readers by the poem's relationship to Ovid's biography and to his later writing. Medieval *accessūs* to Ovid explained that the *Ars* created a scandal in Rome that led to the poet's exile, and that his later works were part of a long and unsuccessful attempt to restore his reputation.[21] The *Remedia amoris*, in particular, was intended to counteract the *Ars*, explaining how to guard against the "illicitum amorem" it had encouraged; in this text, as Fewer observes, repeated *usus* allows the lover to "unlearn" the *praeceptor*'s lessons.[22] For medieval readers, Ovid's teachings about love emerged from the contradictory *duplex sententia* of these texts and not from either in isolation. This situation accounts for what Alastair Minnis has called the characteristic "elasticity" and "pliancy" of the *Ovidius minor* in the hands of medieval interpreters.[23] Ovid's exile poetry was implicated in the same biographical narrative, which was also rehearsed in *accessūs* to the *Fasti*, the *Amores*, the *Tristia*, and the *Epistulae ex Ponto*.[24] Readers who were trained to interpret the *Ars* and

[20] Alison Sharrock, " 'Naso magister erat—sed cui bono?' On Not Taking the Poet's Teaching Seriously," in *Knowledge, Text and Practice in Ancient Technical Writing*, ed. Marco Formisano and Philip van der Eijk (Cambridge: Cambridge University Press, 2017), 112–37 (132).

[21] For examples of this narrative, see the twelfth-century *accessūs* edited as *Accessus ad auctores, etc.*, by R. B. C. Huygens (Leiden: Brill, 1970), 19–54, and translated in *Medieval Literary Theory and Criticism c. 1100–c. 1375*, ed. Alastair Minnis and A. B. Scott with David Wallace (Oxford: Clarendon Press, 1988), 15–36. See also Fausto Ghisalberti, "Mediaeval Biographies of Ovid," *Journal of the Warburg and Courtauld Institutes* 9 (1946): 10–59 (12); Alastair Minnis, *Magister amoris: The "Roman de la Rose" and Vernacular Hermeneutics* (Oxford: Oxford University Press, 2001), 11, 37; and Gillespie, "From the Twelfth Century to c. 1450," 186–87.

[22] Quotation from *Accessus ad auctores*, 34, line 11; see Fewer, "Second Nature," 323.

[23] Minnis, *Magister amoris*, 39, 102.

[24] The *accessus* to *Ex Ponto* says "Dicitur et hunc librum in Ponto insula Scithiae composuisse, quo missus erat in exilium ab Octaviano Cesare propter librum quem scripserat de amore, per quem corruptae fuerant romanae matrone" ("This book is said to have been composed in Pontus, an island in Scythia, where Ovid had been exiled by Octavian Caesar because of the book he had written about love, which had been the means of

the *Remedia* as part of a mutually qualifying dialogue were also encouraged to notice moments in these later poems when Ovid returned to images from the *Ars* and used them to lament his altered circumstances.[25]

Ovid revisited the image of water dropping on stone for precisely this purpose on at least two occasions in his letters *ex Ponto*. In his letter to Atticus from the second book, he employs this figure to describe the effect of his ongoing misfortunes: "utque caducis / percussu crebro saxa cavantur aquis, / sic ego continuo Fortunae vulneror ictu" ("as the falling drops by their constant force hollow the rock, so I am wounded by the steady blows of fate") (II.vii.39–41).[26] In the next lines, he likens his heart to a plowshare, ground down by repeated *usus*, in a sustained engagement with the language of the *Ars*. The poet himself is subject to the effects of erosion here, as his capacity for hope is worn away by his relentless experience of suffering. In a letter to Albinovanus from the fourth book, however, Ovid distinguishes his own situation from that of the stone, the ring, and the plowshare. While other materials wear away, the poet himself endures:

> gutta cavat lapidem, consumitur anulus usu,
>   atteritur pressa vomer aduncus humo.
> tempus edax igitur praeter nos omnia perdet.
>
> (IV.x.5–7)

[Drops of water hollow out a stone, a ring is worn thin by use, the hooked plough is rubbed away by the soil's pressure. So devouring time destroys all things but me.]

As he revisits this figure from the *Ars amatoria*, Ovid tacitly acknowledges the resemblance between his own campaign of letter writing and

---

corrupting Roman matrons"). "Accessus Ovidii de Ponto," in *Accessus ad auctores*, ed. Huygens, 34–35, lines 10–13, translated as "Introduction to Ovid, *From Pontus*," in Minnis, Scott, and Wallace, *Medieval Literary Theory*, 25–26 (26).

[25] See K. Sara Myers, "Ovid's Self-Reception in His Exile Poetry," in Miller and Newlands, *Handbook to the Reception of Ovid*, 8–21. Michael Calabrese describes how, in the *Tristia*, Ovid "summons images and scenes from his earlier love poems and 'metamorphizes' them into dark, sorrowful conceits that reflect his downfall and woe"; Michael Calabrese, *Chaucer's Ovidian Arts of Love* (Gainesville: University Press of Florida, 1994), 13.

[26] Text and translation from Ovid, *Tristia; Ex Ponto*, trans. Arthur Leslie Wheeler, rev. G. P. Goold, 2nd ed., Loeb Classical Library 151 (Cambridge, Mass.: Harvard University Press, 1988).

the strategies of seduction he had recommended to lovers in his guise as
the *praeceptor amoris*. In both cases, a persistent speaker appeals for pity
and continues sending messages when they have no discernible effect.
Writing from exile, however, the poet has come to a new understanding
of his earlier analogy with water dropping on stone: he has discovered
that people can withstand persistent speech for longer than a stone
withstands water. At the same time, his long endeavors have also
revealed his own capacity to endure, to carry on speaking and writing
in hopeless circumstances. In this sense, lived experience and self-
observation have affirmed what the *praeceptor*'s allusion to Penelope had
seemed to imply. The speaker's resilience comes into view, even as his
earlier claims about persistent speech, figured through the analogy with
dropping water, begin to break down.

From its first appearance in the *Ars*, moreover, the analogy contains
an invitation to observe the real effects of water dropping on stone and
to consider what they might reveal about the power of persistent speech.
When the *praeceptor* echoes Lucretius, he allows that his claims about
the natural world might be tested against scientific observation, and
that such observation might complicate his arguments from analogy.
While the *praeceptor* evokes the hollow stone and the worn-down ring
and plowshare as unambiguous phenomena that provide tangible support for his arguments, Lucretius describes them as the visible signs of
invisible processes, noting that erosion itself is impossible to see: "haec
igitur minui, cum sint detrita, videmus; / sed quae corpora decedant in
tempore quoque, / invida praeclusit specimen natura videndi" ("These
we observe to be growing less because they are rubbed away; but what
particles are separated on each occasion, our niggardly faculty of sight
has debarred us from proving") (I.319–21). For Lucretius, the effect of
dropping water on stone remained elusive, constantly evading direct
observation. Although Lucretius's poem was largely unknown to medieval readers, the observation about dropping water and its effect on stone
could be found in scientific writing throughout the Middle Ages.[27] Seneca quoted both *De rerum natura* and the *Ars amatoria* as related authorities on the way water-drops hollow out stone in his *Naturales quaestiones*

---

[27] On the survival of *De rerum natura* in the Middle Ages, see Michael Reeve, "Lucre-
tius in the Middle Ages and Early Renaissance: Transmission and Scholarship," in *The
Cambridge Companion to Lucretius*, ed. Stuart Gillespie and Philip Hardie (Cambridge:
Cambridge University Press, 2010), 205–13. Large claims have been made for the sig-
nificance of its rediscovery by the Italian humanist Poggio Bracciolini; see Stephen
Greenblatt, *The Swerve: How the Renaissance Began* (London: Vintage, 2012).

(4b, 3–5), a text that influenced many medieval authors, including Robert Grosseteste and Roger Bacon in England.[28] The image of water dropping on stone was also presented as a scientific observation in Bartholomeus Anglicus's *De proprietatibus rerum*; John Trevisa, in his Middle English translation, preserves a version of the line from the letter to Albinovanus in Latin: "And þogh a drope be moste nesshe, ȝit by ofte fallynge he persiþ and þrilleþ þinge þat is wel harde, as þis verse seiþ: *Gutta cavat lapidem non vi set sepe cadendo*; þat is to menynge 'a drope þrilleth þe stone nouȝt by strength but by often fallynge.' "[29] The particular ambiguities that emerge from Ovid's allusion to Lucretius were lost to the Middle Ages, but the sense that the analogy might be tested, reinforced, or supplemented by reference to the natural world, as represented in this tradition of scientific writing, was not.

When Chaucer's late medieval contemporaries took up this figure of water dropping on stone, they exploited its power to encourage long endeavors, forms of *usus* that might cultivate a noble identity, or foster spiritual virtues. As they did so, however, they sought to preserve the qualifications that emerge from Ovid's use of the figure, retracing the realizations that unfold across the *Ovidius minor*. Thomas Usk's *Testament of Love*, a work that combines amatory instruction with Boethian dialogue, illustrates the careful deployment of this figure in an erotodidactic context. In the third book, Love invites Usk to imagine his devotion to Margery as a tree, which takes root in his heart with the assent of his free will. "[G]ood servyce" forms the trunk, which grows "by longe processe of tyme" (III.vi.698–99); the branches are the words of his petitions, spoken "in voice of prayer in complaynyng-wise used" (III.vii.811–12); and Margery's "grace" is the fruit that grows on them.[30] Yet, when Usk imagines this "grace" as "rewarde for my longe travayle," Love insists that he cannot change Margery's disposition by

---

[28] Seneca, *Natural Questions*, trans. Thomas H. Corcoran, 2 vols., Loeb Classical Library 450, 457 (Cambridge, Mass.: Harvard University Press, 1971–72), 2.46–49. On the medieval reception of this text, see H. M. Hine, "The Younger Seneca: *Natural Questions*," in *Texts and Transmission: A Survey of the Latin Classics*, ed. L. D. Reynolds (Oxford: Clarendon Press, 1983), 376–78; and Winston Black, "The Quadrivium and Natural Science," in Copeland, *Classical Reception*, 77–94 (84–85).

[29] *On the Properties of Things: John Trevisa's Translation of Bartholomaeus Anglicus' "De proprietatibus rerum,"* ed. M. C. Seymour et al., 3 vols. (Oxford: Clarendon Press, 1975–88), 1:675. In *Bartholomaeus Anglicus and His Encyclopedia* (Aldershot: Ashgate Variorum, 1992), 151, the editors point to Job 14:19 as the source of this quotation.

[30] Thomas Usk, *The Testament of Love*, ed. R. Allen Shoaf (Kalamazoo: Medieval Institute Publications, 1998). Love elaborates the metaphor of the tree in III.v–vii.

his own efforts, since any "grace" he receives "cometh not of thy deserte, but of thy Margarytes goodnesse and virtue alone" (III.vii.876–80). Even as she commends love-service as an opportunity to cultivate noble virtues, then, Love withholds the promise that Ovid's *praeceptor* makes to his students, denying Usk the power to "emprent" his desires on Margery through his own persistent efforts. As this part of the dialogue draws to a close, she offers him two examples to encourage him in his ongoing service: the axe that slowly fells a tree, and dropping water that hollows out a stone; "So ofte must men on the oke smyte tyl the happy dent have entred, whiche with the okes owne swaye maketh it to come al at ones. So ofte falleth the lethy water on the harde rocke tyl it have thorowe persed it" (III.vii.870–72). The images of carving and erosion run counter to the metaphor of arboreal growth that structures this dialogue (will the tree flourish or be cut down?); in combination, they serve to promote the "longe processe" of love-service itself, while creating ambiguity about its final outcome. Indeed, as he reflects on his own experience, Usk identifies complaint itself as a source of satisfaction and enjoyment, saying that the lover who "dare complayne" with "hope of . . . grace to be avaunced" is "joyed" and "greatly eased" (III.vii.816–19); the experience of habituation offers its own rewards.

In lyric poetry of the kind Aurelius composes for Dorigen, speakers rediscover the lessons of the letter to Albinovanus as they follow the advice of the *Ars amatoria*. In Petrarch's *rime* "Aspro core et selvaggio," for example, the lover despairs of moving his lady, but recalls that drops of water can gradually work through stone—"che poco humor già per continua prova / consumar vidi marmi et pietre salde" ("I've seen a little liquid's constant trial wear solid stone and marble quite away")—and concludes that his own tears and prayers might soften her heart in a similar way (lines 10–13).[31] The image of dropping water occurs to him as he watches his own tears, which are themselves an expression of his love-service, a continuation of his verbal complaint. Self-observation provokes a memory of the *Ars amatoria*, which encourages the speaker to persist, but it also offers the insights of the letters *ex Ponto*, as the speaker affirms his own capacity to endure. A similar act of self-observation plays out in Gower's Balade XVIII. At the start of this poem, the lover challenges the *praeceptor*'s analogy, observing

---

[31] *Petrarch's Songbook: Rerum vulgarium fragmenta*, ed. Gianfranco Contini, trans. James Wyatt Cook (Binghamton: Medieval and Renaissance Texts and Studies, 1995), 308–10 (original text), 309–11 (facing translation).

that, while "Les goutes d'eaue qu cheont menu / L'en voit sovent percer la dure piere" ("Little drops of water that fall often are able to pierce the hard stone") (lines 1–2), his own petitions leave his lady unmoved: "Com plus la prie, et meinz m'ad entendu" ("The more I pray, the less I am heeded") (line 7).[32] Yet this complaint, addressed as much to the *praeceptor amoris* as to his lady, itself forms the basis of the poem that follows, and recurs as the refrain at the end of each stanza. In the final quatrain, the speaker considers the poem he has written, the material evidence of his own persistence, and resolves to send it to his lady as a "lettre," as though following the *praeceptor*'s advice in the *Ars* (lines 21–25). This poem dramatizes the moment when a speaker discovers the purpose of Ovid's analogy, displaying his cultivation as a lover and asserting his own powers of persistence, even as he abandons the fantasy of transforming his lady through his long efforts.

Similar negotiations can be found in the literature of religious instruction. Here, writers deployed the analogy with dropping water to encourage persistent devotion, only to reveal that persistence was a good in itself. In a sermon for Holy Week, for example, Peter Comestor combines a quotation from the letters *ex Ponto* with a maxim adapted from St. Augustine and a verse from the Psalms as he encourages his listeners to persevere in love: "Habe charitatem, et fac quidquid vis: omnia difficilia facilia sunt amanti. Gutta cavat lapidem. Exspecta Dominum, viriliter age, et confortabitur cor tuum" (Have charity and do whatever you want: all difficult things become easy through love. Drops of water hollow out a stone. Expect the Lord, act manfully, and let your heart take courage).[33] In his commentary on Luke 18:1–8, meanwhile, Bonaventure compares the efficacy of persistent prayer ("efficaciae orationis instantia") to the power of dropping water that hollows out a stone: "Gutta cavat lapidem, non vi, sed saepe candendo" ("A drop of water hollows out a stone, not by force but by steady dripping"); prayer will

---

[32] John Gower, *The French Balades*, ed. and trans. R. F. Yeager (Kalamazoo: Medieval Institute Publications, 2011), 84–87.

[33] Peter Comestor, "Sermo XVI in Hebdomada poenosa," in *Patrologia latina*, ed. J.-P. Migne, 221 vols. (Paris: Migne, 1844–64) (hereafter *PL*), 198, col. 1767. Peter quotes Ovid's *Ex Ponto* alongside Psalm 26:14, and a maxim derived from Augustine's sermon on 1 John 4:4–12. The phrase "Dilige, et quod vis fac" from Augustine's sermon was recast as "Habe caritatem, et fac quidquid vis", perhaps by Ivo of Chartres, and was often quoted in this form in the twelfth century. See John F. Benson, "Consciousness of Self and Perceptions of Individuality," in *Renaissance and Renewal in the Twelfth Century*, ed. John F. Benson and Giles Constable with Carol D. Lanham (1982; repr., Toronto: University of Toronto Press, 1991), 293 n. 93.

incline God to mercy, just as the widow's entreaties move the hard-hearted judge in Luke's parable.[34] For Comestor and for Bonaventure, the analogy between persistent speech and dropping water promises rewards that might really come to pass, in the form of divine assistance and salvation. However, it also serves to encourage forms of effort that are virtuous in themselves and that transform the condition of the soul. Comestor, in particular, echoes the literature of amatory instruction, extolling the transformative power of love, which enables the Christian to perform impossible tasks. A sermon from the English Wycliffite cycle names the virtue that this kind of *usus* produces, using Ovid's analogy to promote *longanimitas*, one of Paul's twelve fruits of the Holy Spirit (Gal 5:22–3): "Þe seuenþe fruyȝt of þis spiriȝt is *longlastynge* in uertues, for þe drope persiþ þe stoon not bi ones but bi longlastyng."[35]

Henry Suso's mystical dialogue *Horologium sapientiae* explicitly appropriates Ovidian amatory instruction and repurposes it as a guide to ascetic devotional practice. Wisdom explains that religious contemplatives should emulate the "lovers of þis worlde," who remain "bisye and abydynge" in their love-service, even as they endure the "turnynge abowte of þe whele of love." The contemplative, too, should be a "feruent lover," who persists in his devotion despite the "comynge and goynge" of mystical experience.[36] Wisdom quotes repeatedly from the *Ars amatoria*, recasting the *praeceptor*'s advice to lovers for his own disciple. He tells him that "Love is a maner of knihthode" ("militiae species amor est" [*Ars*, II.233]), which requires courage and commitment, and

---

[34] Bonaventure, "Commentarius in evangelium S. Lucae," XVIII.ix, in *Doctoris Seraphici S. Bonaventurae opera omnia*, 10 vols. (Quaracchi: College of St. Bonaventure, 1882–1902), Vol. 7 (1895), 451. Translation from *The Works of St. Bonaventure*, Vol. 8, *Commentary on the Gospel of Luke*, trans. Robert J. Karris, 3 vols. (St. Bonaventure, NY: Franciscan Institute Publications, 2001–2004), 3.1713.

[35] "Dominica xiiii post Trinitatem, Epistola: Sermo 44," in *English Wycliffite Sermons*, ed. Anne Hudson and Pamela Gradon, 5 vols. (Oxford: Clarendon Press, 1983–96), 1.663 (emphasis in original).

[36] Karl Horstmann, "Orologium sapientiae; or, *The Seven Poyntes of Trewe Wisdom*, aus MS Douce 114", *Anglia* 10 (1888): 323–89 (335). I have silently expanded the contractions and modernized the punctuation. For the Latin text, see *Heinrich Seuses "Horologium sapientiae,"* ed. Pius Künzle (Freiburg: Universitätsverlag, 1977); and for a modern English translation from the Latin see Henry Suso, *Wisdom's Watch upon the Hours*, trans. Edmund Colledge (Washington, DC: Catholic University of America Press, 1994). In this part of the *Horologium*, Suso explains the comings and goings of mystical experience as part of the *ludus amoris*, the "game" or "play" of love, which heightens a lover's desire and allows him to prove his resolve, drawing from Hugh of Saint Victor's *Soliloquium de arrha animae*.

he reassures him that "continuele trauayle ouercomeþ alle þinges," citing the effect of water-drops falling on stone: "For what is softere þanne
water, or harder þanne stone? And ȝit by ofte fallynge and smytynge of
water þe stone is persede."[37] The travails of the spiritual lover should
include insistent prayers, analogous to the lover's complaint: Wisdom
tells the disciple to "preye and aske ofte-siþes, and leue not."[38] Suso
draws attention to the moment when the comparison breaks down:
unlike the stern and savage ladies who confront courtly lovers, he
observes, God takes delight in the speaker's petitions and will be quick
to answer them.[39] At the same time, however, he affirms that, for lovers
and contemplatives alike, the long effort of love-service brings its own
rewards.

Other religious texts, however, cite the analogy from a different
source, attributing it to the desert fathers. The image of water dropping
on stone appears as a figure for persistent speech on two occasions in
the *Verba seniorum*, a collection of anecdotes and exchanges that records
the wisdom of the fathers and that often circulated in the Middle Ages
with the *Vitas patrum*, an anthology of their lives.[40] In Book V, the abbot
Poemen tells the abbot John that frequent exposure to the word of God
will stir the fear of God in a hard heart, just as dropping water works
its way through stone; Pimenion uses the analogy to make the same
point to an unnamed questioner in Book VII (V.xviii.16, VII.xxix.1).[41]
The exchange between Poemen and John was anthologized in medieval
resources for preachers: the late thirteenth-century *Liber de similitudini-
bus et exemplis*, for example, contains an exemplum "De abbate Johanne

---

[37] Suso, *Orologium sapientiae*, ed. Horstmann, 335–36.

[38] Ibid., 336.

[39] Suso writes that "in alle þis worlde is none fowndene þat is so liht to be askede of
and preyede, so redye to hir and so godelye to answere, as is sche þis þin most goddelye
spowse"; ibid.

[40] The Latin *Verba seniorum* was translated from the systematic version of the Greek
Apophthegmata patrum, which derives in turn from a Coptic oral tradition; the earliest
texts were produced in late fifth-century Palestine, and the monks whose wisdom they
record were active in Lower Egypt from the 330s to the 460s. See William Harmless,
S.J., *Desert Christians: An Introduction to the Literature of Early Monasticism* (Oxford: Oxford
University Press, 2004), 169–71. For general introductions to the *Apophthegmata patrum*
see Harmless, *Desert Christians*, 167–273; and Douglas Burton-Christie, *The Word in the
Desert: Scripture and the Quest for Holiness in Early Christian Monasticism* (Oxford: Oxford
University Press, 1993), 76–103. On the medieval transmission of the *Verba seniorum*,
see Columba M. Batlle, *Die "Adhortationes sanctorum patrum" ("Verba seniorum") im la-
teinischen Mittelalter* (Münster: Aschendorff, 1972).

[41] *De vitis patrum libri quinque, sex, septem, sive Verba seniorum*, PL 73. For the exchange
between Poemen and John, see col. 983; for the words of Pimenion, see col. 1050.

et lapide et aqua et duricia cordis."[42] It also appears in surviving sermons: in a Middle English sermon from Bodleian Library, MS Laud Misc. 706, the preacher rehearses it to console those members of his audience who might struggle to follow his argument and so conclude that listening to preaching is "a spending and wastyng of tyme."[43] In this version, an "hold fadyr" promises a "ʒong man" that "the ardnes and the dolnes" of his wit will be "parchit" by "ofte heryng of the word of God," just as "a harde stone whas parchyd whyt softe watur be ofte dropyng of reyne."[44]

These borrowings from the *Verba seniorum* reveal the application of this figure to persistent teaching and instruction, a connotation that was always present in Ovid's *Ars*. The desert fathers also echoed Ovid's invitation to test the claims that underpin the analogy through direct observation of the natural world. Abbot Poemen even suggests that John might stage an experiment in order to see the process of erosion for himself:

Natura aquae mollis est, lapidis autem dura est; et si vas aquae plenum pendeat supra lapidem, ex quo assidue stillans gutta cadat in lapidem, perforat eum; ita et sermo divinus lenis est, cor autem nostrum durum; audiens ergo homo frequenter divinum sermonem, aperitur cor ejus ad timendum Deum.

(V.xviii.16)

[The nature of water is soft, the nature of stone is hard; but if a bottle is hung above a stone letting water drip down, it wears away the stone. It is like that

---

[42] See J.-Th. Welter, *L'exemplum dans la littérature religieuse et didactique du Moyen Age: La Tabula exemplorum secundum ordinem alphabeti; Recueil d'exempla compilé en France à la fin du XIIIe siècle* (Geneva: Slatkine Reprints, 2012), 80, no. 298; and Frederic C. Tubach, *Index exemplorum: A Handbook of Medieval Religious Tales*, FF Communications 204 (Helsinki: Suomalainene Tiedeakatemia, 1969), no. 4636. Karris, *Commentary on the Gospel of Luke*, 1713 n. 43, suggests that Bonaventure may have found the analogy in the *Verba seniorum*, rather than in Ovid.

[43] Oxford, Bodleian Library, MS Laud Misc. 706, fol. 149v. I cite the text of this sermon from Patrick Horner, "An Edition of Five Medieval Sermons from MS Laud Misc. 706," Ph.D. diss. (State University of New York, Albany, 1975), 111–46 (119). On the sermons in this manuscript, see also Veronica O'Mara and Suzanne Paul, *A Repertorium of Middle English Prose Sermons*, 4 vols. (Turnhout: Brepols, 2007), 3.2183–194 (this sermon is summarized as Bodl/Laud 706/002); Patrick Horner, "Benedictines and Preaching in Fifteenth-Century England: The Evidence of Two Bodleian Library Manuscripts", *Revue bénédictine* 99 (1989): 313–32; and Siegfried Wenzel, *Macaronic Sermons: Bilingualism and Preaching in Late-Medieval England* (Ann Arbor: University of Michigan Press, 1994), 173–77.

[44] Horner, "Five Medieval Sermons," 119–20.

with the word of God; it is soft and our heart is hard, but if a man hears the word of God often, it will break open his heart to the fear of God.][45]

Isolated in the desert, Poemen and Pimenion were uniquely placed to observe such natural processes as they unfolded over time. This kind of knowledge was directly related to their ascetic practice. This was the wisdom the recluse could offer the preacher, recasting the analogy with water dropping on stone as a comment on the slow, incremental process of instruction, rather than a promise of immediate transformation.

The analogy between persistent speech and water dropping on stone, which in turn informs the image of engraving and "emprentyng" in *The Franklin's Tale*, emerged from the *Ovidius minor* as an elusive, ambivalent kind of wisdom, qualified by the complex ironies of the *Ars amatoria*; by the invitation to observe the process of erosion in nature; and by the evidence of lived experience, prefigured in the allusion to Penelope and affirmed by the poet in his later exile poetry. The medieval writers who appropriated this analogy either discerned these complexities in Ovid or rediscovered them for themselves, balancing the questionable promise that a speaker might reshape his listener's desires through his own efforts against the evident power of this figure to sustain worthwhile endeavors and to enable the cultivation of virtue. Preachers and poets alike promote the analogy as wisdom to use but not necessarily to believe, a figure that encouraged worthwhile endeavors by promising deferred, intangible, or illusory rewards.

The Franklin's Tale, "stoon by stoon"

The analogy with "emprentyng" stone that appears near the start of *The Franklin's Tale* signals Chaucer's engagement with a long tradition of writing about persistent speech and its consequences. Taking up Boccaccio's reference to Ovid in his immediate source, Chaucer offers an expansive reply, which responds to the evolving significance of this analogy in the *Ovidius minor* and to its treatment in the work of his own contemporaries. *The Franklin's Tale* presents persistent speech of many kinds— clerical consolation, preacherly instruction, lovers' complaints, and petitionary prayer—linking together the discursive contexts where Ovid's analogy was cited and theorized. It describes the "proces" by

---

[45] *Verba seniorum*, PL 73, col. 983. Translation from *The Desert Fathers: Sayings of the Early Christian Monks*, trans. Benedicta Ward (London: Penguin, 2003), 191.

which speakers might come to understand how this analogy works, testing its claims about speech and stone against their own experience, but it also asks what happens when a persistent speaker resists this kind of realization and demands instead the rewards that the analogy seems to promise, the power to reshape another person's desires through long, reiterative effort.

The analogy with engraving forms part of a cluster of proverbs and sentences that appear early on in *The Franklin's Tale* and that inform the subsequent development of its narrative. They include another Ovidian aphorism, "Love wol nat been constreyned by maistrye" (*FranT*, V.764), a version of *Metamorphoses*, II.846–47, "non bene conveniunt nec in una sede morantur / maiestas et amor," as well as Boethian sentences on the instinctive desire for freedom and an injunction to lovers to "Lerneth to suffre" (*FranT*, V.777).[46] This cluster of *sententiae* is organized around a central, proverbial claim about the power of patience, which the Franklin attributes to "clerkes," and which is glossed in one manuscript with its Latin form, "pacientes vincunt": "Pacience is an heigh vertu, certeyn, / For it venquysseth, as thise clerkes seyn, / Thynges that rigour sholde nevere atteyne" (V.773–75).[47] The Franklin's analogy with engraving, which appears shortly after this sententious passage in the tale, echoes the proverb "pacientes vincunt" in its claim that persistent speech will "conquer" resistant listeners, transforming their desires through habituation and repeated *usus*, but the forms of speech it seems to encourage might as easily take the form of "rigor"—with its connotations of obduracy, fixity, and violence—as of patience, with its links to sufferance and forbearance.[48] Understanding this analogy will itself require patience, a willingness to test its claims against lived experience,

---

[46] Ovid, *Metamorphoses*, trans. Frank Justus Miller, rev. G. P. Goold, 3rd ed., 2 vols., Loeb Classical Library 42–43 (1977; repr., Cambridge, Mass.: Harvard University Press, 1994). Chaucer would also have encountered this aphorism in the *Roman de la Rose*, where it forms part of the advice of Friend to the lover; see Guillaume de Lorris and Jean de Meun, *Le Roman de la Rose*, ed. Félix Lecoy, 3 vols. (Paris: Librairie Honoré Champion, 1965–70), lines 9409–12. For a reading of *The Franklin's Tale* as a meditation on these lines from Ovid, see Gregory Heyworth, *Desiring Bodies: Ovidian Romance and the Cult of Form* (Notre Dame: University of Notre Dame Press, 2009), 121–40.

[47] London, British Library, MS Egerton 2864 (En³). For a transcription of the text, see Stephen Bradford Partridge, "Glosses in the Manuscripts of Chaucer's *Canterbury Tales*: An Edition and Commentary," Ph.D. diss. (Harvard University, 1991), V-5.

[48] Compare *MED*, s.v. *pacience*, defs. 1 and 2; and *MED*, s.v. *rigour*, esp. def. 2. On the distinction between these terms, see Jill Mann, *Feminizing Chaucer*, new ed. (Cambridge: Brewer, 2001), 89–90.

to revisit them over time. Learning to suffer in *The Franklin's Tale* involves making the proper use of proverbial wisdom like this.

The figure of "emprentyng" stone appears in a scene where amatory complaint and clerical instruction are in open competition. While Dorigen laments the absence of Arveragus, her friends attempt to console her, countering her complaints with appeals and petitions of their own. Dorigen articulates her suffering in a wide range of expressive modes, from wordless weeping to elaborate speech, and the tale describes them with an asyendetic list of terms, which suggests their insistent, repetitive quality: "She moorneth, waketh, wayleth, fasteth, pleyneth" (V.819). Her friends display similar forms of tenacity and resourcefulness in their replies: they appeal to her reason, telling her "nyght and day / That causelees she sleeth hirself" (V.824–25); they plead with her, "on knees, for Goddes sake," to abandon her "derke fantasye" (V.844); and they "prechen hire" (V.824), offering instruction and illustrative examples. The tale hints at the preacherly content of these exhortations when Dorigen relents for a moment, as though accepting her friends' argument that all "was for the beste" (V.846), a proverbial recasting of Romans 8:28, "omnia cooperantur in bonum" ("all things work together unto good"). When the Franklin refers to the long "proces" of their speech, moreover, he uses a term that describes the *processus* or development of a scholastic sermon.[49] In doing so, he maps the procedures of habituation onto the recursive, exegetical forms of this discourse, which returns to and elaborates on the same *thema*, much as a lover derives new complaints from the same subject matter. As it opposes complaint and consolation, the tale affirms the close resemblance between these two forms of persistent speech. Each provides opportunities for the cultivation of virtue and an occasion for the masochistic enjoyments of self-denial: through her long commitment to complaint, Dorigen confirms her place among "thise noble wyves" (V.817), while her friends display their own form of preacherly "noblesse" as they work to console her.[50]

[49] For the specialized sense of this term in preaching, see H. Leith Spencer, *English Preaching in the Late Middle Ages* (Oxford: Clarendon Press, 1993), 111 and n. 130. Spencer, *English Preaching*, 110–11, shows that preachers would describe the structure of their sermons using this kind of technical terminology, importing Latin terms into Middle English, and that attentive listeners absorbed these terms into their own vocabulary.

[50] Tison Pugh has argued that Arveragus assumes the role of the Lacanian courtly lady in this part of the poem, inflicting arbitrary cruelty on Dorigen through his motiveless absence and occasioning her long complaint: *Chaucer's (Anti-)Eroticisms and the Queer Middle Ages* (Columbus: Ohio State University Press, 2014), 30–64; I would add that

The Franklin describes "The emprentyng of [Dorigen's] consolacioun" at the point when she seems to succumb to her friends' entreaties, before taking up her complaint again in the subsequent lines (V.834); voicing the analogy in this moment, where complaint and consolation provoke and sustain one another, he reveals its applicability to both forms of persistent speech.

As Dorigen continues her complaint, however, she comes to a new understanding of the analogy between persistent speech and "emprentyng" stone. Walking by the sea, she considers the "grisly rokkes blake" around the coast (V.859) and, imagining that they might shipwreck Arveragus on his return, she prays to God to drag them down into hell. These related acts of observation and expression place different kinds of pressure on Ovid's *praeceptor*'s arguments about the powers of speech and the properties of stone. Dorigen sees the rocks surrounded by water, but sees no evidence of the water wearing them away. Instead, she reflects on their capacity for endurance, tracing their effects on human beings through a long, destructive history that extends beyond her own memory into the distant past: "An hundred thousand bodyes of mankynde / Han rokkes slayn, al be they nat in mynde" (V.877–78). The rocks inhabit a slow, geological time—what Jeffrey Jerome Cohen has called "lithic time"—that exceeds the limits of a human life and so also the human capacity for observation.[51] Erosion, too, takes place on this timescale, lasting longer than the history Dorigen can recall. In her prayer to God, Dorigen tries to remove the rocks through an act of persistent speech, as though the corresponding terms in Ovid's analogy were interchangeable. The rocks, however, remain unmoved: they resist the force of her petitions just as they resist the force of the waves.

This encounter reframes the implications of Ovid's analogy and of the Franklin's, placing the promised rewards for persistent speech out of reach of any individual speaker. Even as she comes to this realization,

---

Dorigen performs a similar role for her friends, prolonging their suffering by resisting their petitions.

[51] Jeffrey Jerome Cohen, *Stone: An Ecology of the Inhuman* (Minneapolis: University of Minnesota Press, 2015), 198–99. Both Cohen and W. A. Davenport have linked these rocks to the standing stones of ancient British history, drawing attention to their ancient condition. See W. A. Davenport, *Chaucer, Complaint and Narrative* (Woodbridge: Brewer, 1988), 180–81; and Cohen, *Stone*, 198–200. John B. Friedman, "Dorigen's 'grisly rokkes blake' Again," *ChauR* 31, no. 2 (1996): 133–44, argues that the rocks in the tale refer to the prehistoric menhirs that stand on the coast of Brittany as a reminder of the ancient past.

however, Dorigen also displays and affirms her own capacity for endurance. Her ongoing prayer, marked out in one manuscript as "the complaynte of dame Dorigen," forms the first of the tale's lyric interludes, where the claims of first-person expression outweigh the claims of narrative.[52] Her tenacity in the face of the implacable rocks creates opportunities for creative expression: she echoes the Franklin's first description of the "grisly rokkes blake" in her own voice, transforming it into a refrain, which appears in amplified and abbreviated forms ("thise grisly feendly rokkes blake," "thise rokkes blake") and she extrapolates an elaborate challenge to God's providential design from her observations about the dangers they pose, in a remarkable act of rhetorical invention (V.859, 868, 891). In this pivotal scene, Dorigen takes up the invitation that was always present in this analogy, in Ovid and in the wisdom of the desert fathers, testing and qualifying its confident claims by considering the real effect of water on stone. At the same time, like Ovid in exile, she discovers her own capacity for perseverance, finding new opportunities for creative expression as she addresses the impervious rocks.

Dorigen's persistence in this scene is closely linked to her intransigence, her resistance to the entreaties of her friends. As she observes the rocks, she restates her indifference to their preacherly petitions. Imagining that "clerkes" might try to account for the rocks as part of God's creation, she rejects their arguments, which contain an echo of her friends' insistent claim that Arveragus's absence was "for the beste" (V.846):

> I woot wel clerkes wol seyn as hem leste,
> By argumentz, that al is for the beste,
> Though I ne kan the causes nat yknowe.
> But thilke God that made wynd to blowe
> As kepe my lord! This my conclusion.
> To clerkes lete I al disputison.
>
> (V.885–90)

This outspoken rejection of "argumentz" and "disputison" itself forms part of Dorigen's complex response to Ovid's analogy. The claim about persuasive speech that informs this analogy is shown to be insufficient, even misleading, when qualified by the evidence of Dorigen's direct

---

[52] This gloss appears in Bodleian Library, MS Arc. Selden B. 14 (Se). See Partridge, "Glosses in the Manuscripts," V-5.

experience, and Dorigen, at this point of realization, alleges the evidence of her own situation against the promises the analogy seems to make. Perhaps Ovid's *praeceptor*, "Venus clerk," is himself among the "clerkes" to whom she offers her reply. These lines also anticipate the difficulties that Dorigen will face when she tries to communicate what she has learned, however. These are lessons that emerge over time, in dialogue with lived experience, and that cannot be simply expressed as clerical "argumentz."

With the introduction of Aurelius, *The Franklin's Tale* turns its attention to the kind of speaker whom Ovid addresses in books I and II of the *Ars amatoria*. A "lusty squier" and "servant to Venus," Aurelius loves Dorigen "best of any creature" (V.937–39). His long and fruitless love-service is modeled on Tarolfo's attempts to seduce the married *donna* in Menedon's story from *Il filocolo*, a task inspired and sustained by the *praeceptor*'s advice. Courting Dorigen in her husband's absence, however, he also resembles the suitors of Penelope, whose trials seem to undercut, or at least to qualify, the *praeceptor*'s assertions about the power of persistent speech. When he first appears in the tale, Aurelius expresses his "wo" in lyric poetry, performing "layes, / Songes, compleintes, roundels, virelayes" for Dorigen (V.945, 947–48); here, Chaucer introduces another mode of first-person speech that was associated with the figure of water dropping on stone, like a lover's lament, petitionary prayer, and preacherly consolation. This asyndetic list of poetic forms recalls the list of terms that described Dorigen's sorrowful expression earlier in the tale and hints again at the persistent way Aurelius returns to the same "matere," prolonging his sufferings as he articulates them (V.947).[53] It also suggests that Aurelius has made his suffering the occasion for

---

[53] This inventory of poetic forms has a literary tradition of its own. In Gower's *Confessio Amantis*, for example, Amans confesses that "I have ofte assaied / Rondeal, balade and virelai / For hire on whom myn herte lai / To make" (I.2726–29), listing some of the forms Aurelius employs, while, in *The Legend of Good Women*, Alceste remembers the "balades, roundels, virelayes" that Chaucer has composed in praise of love (F 423, G 412). The constitution of *La cour amoureuse* adds *compleinte* to this list, condemning lovers who compose "dittierz, complaintes, rondeaux, virelays, balades, [ou] lays" that disparage women, and so does Lydgate when, in the *Fall of Princes*, he praises Chaucer for his "Compleyntis, baladis, roundelis, virelais / Ful delectable" (I.353–54). See John Gower, *Confessio Amantis*, ed. Russell A. Peck, 3 vols. (Kalamazoo: Medieval Institute Publications, 2001–4), I.174; and *La cour amoureuse dite de Charles VI*, Vol. 1, *Etude et édition critique des sources manuscrites*, ed. Carla Bozzolo and Hélène Loyau (Paris: Léopard d'Or, 1982). These lines from *La cour amoureuse* are cited, translated, and discussed in Carolyn P. Collette, *Rethinking Chaucer's "Legend of Good Women"* (Woodbridge: York Medieval Press, 2014), 57–58.

sophisticated, creative expression: "compleinte" appears here alongside demanding forms such as the rondel and the *virelai*, where, as James Wimsatt has observed, the principles of "repetition and accumulation" produce ornate and elaborate patterns.[54] As Jenni Nuttall has recently noted, however, these forms are often identified with juvenilia in Chaucer's poetry and with the self-regarding naïveté of inexperienced lovers.[55] For Aurelius, perhaps, the process of habituation has only just begun.

Certainly, Aurelius has still to recognize this process of habituation as a source of satisfaction in its own right. As he composes his poems, he continues to complain that his words have no effect on Dorigen. Turning from the *Ars* to the *Metamorphoses*, he likens himself to Echo, who "dorste nat telle hir wo" to Narcissus, a persistent speaker who never obtained her desires and who, with a prayer to Venus, finally wore herself away (V.951–52).[56] At a crucial turning-point in the tale, Aurelius abandons his "general compleynyng" and openly declares his "entente," petitioning Dorigen, "reweth upon my peynes smerte" (V.945, 959, 974). Rather than persisting with his own lyrical expression, to the point where he might discover the real significance of Ovid's analogy, he demands the power to "emprent" his desires on others that the *praeceptor* had promised, the ability to reconfigure Dorigen's will through his own persistent speech.

In her reply, Dorigen searches for a way to share her own understanding of Ovid's analogy with Aurelius. First, she flatly refuses him, resisting his efforts at subjection and declaring her loyalty to Arveragus: "Ne shal I nevere been untrewe wyf / In word ne werk, as fer as I have wit; / [. . .] / Taak this for fynal answere as of me" (V.984–87). Then she presents him with an impossible task, like the task the *donna* demands from Tarolfo, challenging him to remove the rocks from around the coast:

> "Aurelie," quod she, "by heighe God above,
> Yet wolde I graunte yow to been youre love,

---

[54] James I. Wimsatt, *Chaucer and His French Contemporaries: Natural Music in the Fourteenth Century* (Toronto: University of Toronto Press, 1991), 110.

[55] Jenni Nuttall, " 'Many a lay and many a thing': Chaucer's Technical Terms," in *Chaucer and the Subversion of Form*, ed. Thomas A. Prendergast and Jessica Rosenfeld (Cambridge: Cambridge University Press, 2018), 21–37 (31–32).

[56] Elizabeth A. Dobbs, "Re-Sounding Echo," *ChauR* 40, no. 3 (2006): 289–310 (291), links this reference to Echo to the earlier analogy with "emprentyng" stone, as related Ovidian allusions concerned with speaking and interpreting.

> Syn I yow se so pitously complayne.
> Looke what day that endelong Britayne
> Ye remoeve alle the rokkes, stoon by stoon,
> That they ne lette ship ne boot to goon—
> I seye, whan ye han maad the coost so clene
> Of rokkes that ther nys no stoon ysene,
> Thanne wol I love yow best of any man;
> Have heer my trouthe, in al that evere I kan."
>
> (V.989–98)

Aurelius accuses Dorigen of capricious, motiveless cruelty, demanding "Is ther noon oother grace in yow?" and declaring his task "an inpossible!" (V.999, 1009). Yet, Dorigen's challenge is no senseless ordeal. Rather, it seeks to recreate for Aurelius the circumstances in which she had come to reevaluate the claims of the analogy herself. Dorigen invites Aurelius to confront the material realities of the black rocks and consider the time it would take to wear them away, "emprentyng" or eroding them, "stoon by stoon." She also presents an opportunity for him to continue his complaint and so to arrive at a mature understanding of persistent effort, the virtues it cultivates, and the satisfactions it entails. Recognizing the onset of *amor* in her young suitor, Dorigen also perceives his need for instruction and assumes the role of *praeceptor* herself. Rather than instructing him directly, however, she works to prolong his endeavors, so that the full significance of Ovid's analogy might emerge in his own experience over time.

There are early signs that Dorigen's strategy has been successful, as Aurelius resumes his complaint, moving from lyric poetry to petitionary prayer and calling on Apollo and Lucina to cover the rocks with a high tide. Like Dorigen's lines on the black rocks, Aurelius's prayer forms a long, lyrical interlude in the narrative, marked out in the Ellesmere manuscript (El), and in British Library, Additional MS 35286 (Ad[3]), as "The compleint of Aurelius to the goddes and to the sonne," and it expresses a similar desire, to remove the rocks from around the coast.[57] There are signs, too, that Aurelius is discovering the pleasures of deferred gratification, as he asks the gods to create a flood that will "endure yeres twaine" before he finally declares to Dorigen that "the rokkes been aweye" (V.1062–64).

---

[57] See Partridge, "Glosses in the Manuscripts," V-5.

Through the intervention of his brother, however, Aurelius finds a way to prolong the fantasy that he might still habituate Dorigen to his own desires, avoiding the direct encounter with stone that Dorigen had sought to engineer for him. Remembering his school days in Orléans, where "yonge clerkes . . . been lykerous / To reden artes that been curious," Aurelius's brother takes him to meet another clerk, still resident in the city, who can create the illusion that the rocks have disappeared (V.1119–20). The clerk displays his skills to Aurelius, conjuring scenes of hunting and hawking; jousting and dancing; and, finally, an image of Aurelius and Dorigen dancing together, as though promising the ultimate fulfillment of his desires. The cathedral school at Orléans was renowned as a center for the study of classical authors, and the Orléanais masters Arnulf, William, and Fulco produced some of the most influential medieval commentaries on Ovid's work.[58] The curious "artes" the clerk has read include books of "magyk natureel" (V.1125) but also, surely, the *Ars amatoria*; indeed, his skillful manipulation of Aurelius's fantasies might seem to figure his mastery of that text. When Dorigen set Aurelius his impossible task, she proposed a course of study that would allow him to move beyond the deceptive promises of the *Ars* and discover what Ovid had learned in his letters *ex Ponto*. Aurelius's brother, however, invites him to return to Orléans, where "yonge clerkes" have learned to prolong the fantasies of the *Ars* itself. Like Tarolfo in Menedon's story, Aurelius resorts to magic and illusion in an effort to validate the *praeceptor*'s claims, seeking to avoid the encounter with nature that would qualify them: rather than confront the material reality of stone, he remains in the clerk's study, "ther as his bookes be" (V.1207 and cf. 1214), and indulges ephemeral illusions, which are quickly "voyded," disappearing when he "clapte his handes two" (V.1195, 1203).

Criticism on *The Franklin's Tale* has often returned to the "rash promise" that forms part of Dorigen's challenge to Aurelius, her pledge to love him if he can "remoeve alle the rokkes" from around the coast (V.993).[59] Bonnie Wheeler argues that Dorigen is "constrained . . . [by

---

[58] On the school of Orléans and the Orléanais commentators, see Frank T. Coulson, "Metamorphoses in the School Tradition of France," in Clark et al., *Ovid in the Middle Ages*, 48–82 (50–59); and Wilken Engelbrecht, "Fulco, Arnulf, and William: Twelfth-Century Views on Ovid in Orléans," *Journal of Medieval Latin* 18 (2008): 52–73. Fulco wrote commentaries on the *Ars amatoria* and the *Remedia amoris*, while Arnulf wrote commentaries on the *Ars*, the *Remedia*, and *Ex Ponto*.

[59] On the literary and legal contexts for the "rash promise," see Alan T. Gaylord, "The Promises in *The Franklin's Tale*," *ELH* 31, no. 4 (1964): 331–65; and Richard

the] rhetorical codes" of courtly love, which provide no way to refuse Aurelius: "[a] woman who is chosen as a beloved is allowed myriad delaying techniques, but postponement is as close as she can come to a final *no*," she writes.[60] Susan Crane, too, contends that the discourse of *fin' amors* restricts what Dorigen can say, so that she "finds herself ventriloquizing encouragement" even as "she attempts refusal."[61] For Michael Calabrese, by contrast, this moment reveals the reckless excesses of Dorigen's language, which play out in her characteristic tendency to "endless amplification"; Calabrese argues that Dorigen lacks the "self-mastery and rhetorical cultivation" prized in the ladies of the *Filocolo* and other Italian *novelle*, who often bring lovesick men sharply to their senses with their incisive wit.[62] I suggest, however, that Dorigen's difficulties arise from the elusive qualities of Ovid's analogy, whose lessons resist direct communication and whose promises encourage dangerous illusions about the power of persistent effort. Dorigen's "rash promise" to Aurelius is, after all, the same promise that Ovid's *praeceptor* makes to his students, refashioned as a lover's ordeal. She places herself at risk, promising her own subjection as an incentive for his continued efforts, in the hope that these efforts will teach their own lessons in time. When Dorigen steps into the role of *praeceptor amoris*, offering Aurelius this lesson in love, she stakes her own honor on the efficacy of this pedagogical strategy, a level of personal investment that was never required from the *praeceptor* of Ovid's *Ars*.

Dorigen's difficulties are compounded in this moment by the very habits of persistent speech that the analogy serves to encourage. Her reply to Aurelius is insistent and reiterative; she refuses him, then restates her refusal in another form, then elaborates on the terms of this new refusal. As she reiterates her challenge, Dorigen creates ambiguity around its conditions: in line 993 Aurelius must physically remove the rocks, but lines 995–96 allow that he might find a way to conceal them instead. Dorigen knows that the lessons of this analogy are only available from long experience and cannot be communicated as clerical

---

Firth Green, *A Crisis of Truth: Literature and Law in Ricardian England* (Philadelphia: University of Pennsylvania Press, 1999), 293–335.

[60] Bonnie Wheeler, "Trouthe without Consequences: Rhetoric and Gender in Chaucer's *Franklin's Tale*," in *Feminea medievalia I: Representations of the Feminine in the Middle Ages*, ed. Bonnie Wheeler (Cambridge: Academia Press, 1993), 91–116 (106).

[61] Susan Crane, *Gender and Romance in Chaucer's "Canterbury Tales"* (Princeton: Princeton University Press, 1994), 65.

[62] Calabrese, "Chaucer's Dorigen and Boccaccio's Female Voices," 266, 272. Calabrese here responds directly to Wheeler and Crane.

"argumentz": to learn them, Aurelius must observe the effects of his own complaint and consider the realities of stone. Even so, her language begins to resemble clerical consolation, echoing the preaching of her friends, as she urges Aurelius to "Lat swiche folies out of youre herte slyde" (V.1002). Aurelius seems to recognize a clerical aspect to the impossible task she sets for him when he calls it "an impossible," a form of ingenious argumentation, a realization that in some ways foreshadows his later journey to Orléans.[63] The generosity of Dorigen's response is confounded by the duplicity and ambivalence of the *praeceptor*'s analogy, the deceptive way it teaches, and the dangerous desires it provokes. Her own capacity for persistent speech serves to exacerbate these problems, as she communicates her lesson in a mode that Aurelius is bound to resist.

When the clerk of Orléans performs his trick and Aurelius announces that the rocks are "aweye," Dorigen declares it a "monstre," a "merveille," and "agayns the proces of nature" (V.1344–45). This clerical illusion challenges the lessons she has learned from her encounter with the rocks and makes it difficult for her to reaffirm them. In his effort to obtain the rewards that the *praeceptor* seems to promise, Aurelius has removed the natural evidence that qualifies his claims: the "proces" of erosion, with its comment on the "proces" of habituation, is no longer available for observation. As Dorigen understands her situation, she must now either keep the promise the *praeceptor* had made to male lovers, subjecting herself to Aurelius's desires, or end her own life: "oonly deeth or elles dishonour; / Oon of thise two bihoveth me to chese" (V.1358–59).

Dorigen responds with the longest passage of first-person speech in the tale, glossed in El and Ad[3] as "The compleynt of Dorigene ayeyns Fortune."[64] Petitionary prayer evolves into preacherly consolation as, "wrapped" in the "cheyne" of Fortune (V.1356), Dorigen draws out a

---

[63] Kyle Mahowald argues that Aurelius recasts the nature of the challenge when he identifies Dorigen's task as "an impossible." Dorigen intends the task as a form of *adynaton*, insisting by hyperbole that she will never grant Aurelius's request, yet Aurelius will come to treat it as a scholastic *impossible*: a proposition that runs counter to common-sense assumptions about the world, but that may yet be proved true by ingenious argument. Kyle Mahowald, " 'It may nat be': Chaucer, Derrida, and the Impossibility of the Gift," *SAC* 32 (2010): 129–50. Mahowald draws definitions of the scholastic *impossible* from Roy J. Pearcy, "Chaucer's 'An Impossible' ('Summoner's Tale' III, 2231)," *N&Q* 14 (1967): 322–23.

[64] Partridge, "Glosses in the Manuscripts," V-7.

long *catena* of interrelated stories that bear on her own situation, listing virtuous women who chose death over dishonor.[65] Kara Gaston reads Dorigen's complaint as an attempt to "buy time," postponing the choice between "deeth" or "dishonour" that Aurelius presses on her.[66] Although she gestures ahead to the conclusion she will reach ("I wol conclude that it is bet for me / To sleen myself than been defouled thus" [V.1422–23]), she also defers the moment of her death through the accumulation of examples. I would add that Dorigen's complaint is also an attempt to reaffirm her hard-won understanding of Ovid's analogy between dropping water and persistent speech, recovering the lessons that Ovid learned in his letters *ex Ponto*. Although she can no longer see the rocks, or observe the "proces" of erosion, she can observe her own resilience and her capacity for creative invention as she carves out this time for herself. The stories of these other women extend into something like "lithic time." Like the history of the rocks themselves, they exceed what Dorigen herself can imagine or remember: "Mo than a thousand stories, as I gesse, / Koude I now telle as touchynge this mateere" (V.1412–13). Linking her story to theirs, Dorigen amplifies her own claim to stony endurance. At the same time, she demonstrates her resilience by resisting the conclusions of these narratives; although she addresses these stories "to herself" (V.1352), Dorigen never moves herself to action. The tale avoids staging a single moment of realization, turning away from Dorigen as her speech continues: "Thus pleyned Dorigen a day or tweye, / Purposynge evere that she wolde deye"

[65] Mary Carruthers, *The Book of Memory: A Study of Memory in Medieval Culture* (Cambridge: Cambridge University Press, 2008), 259, explains the *catena* as a metaphor for a particular technique of memorial composition, where each remembered text "pulls other texts and sayings with it" as the speaker brings it to mind. On the *catena* as an image for associative groupings in the memory, see also Carruthers, *Book of Memory*, 78 and 143, and for a related manuscript border illustration see 322.

[66] Kara Gaston, "The Poetics of Time Management from the *Metamorphoses* to *Il filocolo* and *The Franklin's Tale*," *SAC* 37 (2015): 227–56 (227). Gaston stresses the creativity involved in this endeavor, linking Dorigen's *compleinte* to the magician's spell in the *Filocolo*, and to Medea's spell in Ovid's *Metamorphoses*, both of which might seem to reorganize time by analogy with poetic craft. Kathryn L. Lynch, "East Meets West in Chaucer's Squire's and Franklin's Tales," *Speculum* 70, no. 3 (1995): 530–51, has also argued that Dorigen buys time with her complaint. Lynch, who reads *The Franklin's Tale* in part as a response to the exotic orientalism of *The Squire's Tale*, proposes that Dorigen's examples serve a similar purpose to Shahrazad's stories in the *Thousand and One Nights*, providing a way "to avoid death by passing the time." Yet, for Lynch, the "awkwardly recursive" quality of Dorigen's complaint limits its creative potential. She writes: "the exempla are sterile, mechanical, nothing more than the expanded version of 'She moorneth, waketh, wayleth, fasteth, pleyneth'" (548).

(V.1457–58); holding the *praeceptor*'s promises in tension with the lessons of the letters *ex Ponto*, she continues to cultivate and perform her "noblesse." It seems significant, however, that, late in her speech, she evokes the example of Penelope, whose introduction in the *Ars amatoria* first seemed to complicate the *praeceptor*'s claims about the power of habituation: "What seith Omer of goode Penalopee?," she asks; "Al Grece knoweth of hire chastitee" (V.1443–44).

The turn to illusion has very different consequences for Aurelius. When he first encounters Dorigen on his return from Orléans, Aurelius resumes his complaint, lamenting his "peyne" and appealing for "routhe" (V.1318–19). His intention, however, is to claim the rewards the *praeceptor* had promised and that Dorigen had reformulated in her challenge to him. But when Dorigen and Aurelius meet in the garden, Aurelius is moved to "routhe" by Dorigen's sorrowful condition and releases her from her promise "in fewe wordes," recognizing his request as a kind of "cherlyssh wrecchednesse" (V.1520, 1525, 1523). Dorigen's distress reveals the shortcomings of Aurelius's strategy: rather than engage in a long, persistent effort to alter Dorigen's desires, he has forced her to submit to him against her will. Although the narrator himself declares this a "gentil dede," it soon becomes clear that the satisfactions of habituation are now denied to Aurelius; this affirmation of "gentilesse" seems as richly ironic as anything in Ovid's *Ars* (V.1543). Avoiding the encounter with stone that Dorigen sought to engineer for him, he has missed his opportunity to cultivate a lover's "noblesse," and his chance to understand the implications of Ovid's promise as they might unfold in his own experience. While Dorigen returns to resume her role as a noble wife, Aurelius is left to worry about money, debating how he can afford to pay the clerk of Orléans.

The image of water dropping on stone, as a figure for the power of persistent speech, formed a small but complex part of Ovid's legacy to the Middle Ages. Ovid's medieval readers saw the great utility of this analogy, its power to encourage and sustain persistent effort and enable the cultivation of virtue, but they also recognized the potential for risk in its overstated promises about habituation, its implicit claim that, through persistence, a speaker might "emprent" their desires on a resistant listener. Ovid himself had surrounded this figure with qualifying ironies when he presented it to lovers in the *Ars amatoria*, and medieval *praeceptores*, too, encouraged careful responses to this analogy, urging their readers to appreciate the virtues that developed through long persistence, *longanimitas*, and "noblesse," and to see these as goods in themselves. *The Franklin's Tale* affirms that Ovid's analogy can motivate many kinds of persistent speech, from lovers' complaints to friendly consolation and petitionary prayer, and it demonstrates the kinds of creative expression that are possible in these interrelated modes. Yet, the tale also offers warnings about the destructive desires this analogy encourages and about its peculiar capacity to elude the *praeceptores* who use it, escaping the strategies of qualification and containment that Ovid and his medieval inheritors deployed. While Dorigen comes to a mature understanding of this figure, discovering the rewards and satisfactions of complaint even as she recognizes the difficulty of "emprentyng" stone, Aurelius is never able to abandon the fantasy of "emprentyng" his desires on Dorigen, and goes to elaborate lengths to sustain it, against the evidence of his own experience. The tale invites its readers to consider what happens when a lover demands the rewards that Ovid's *praeceptor amoris* tries to defer, and it never loses sight of the implications these promises have for the lady the lover desires. While Ovid's *praeceptor* makes casual promises about the subjection of women in order to motivate the habituation of men, Dorigen reveals what is at risk in these promises when she makes them about herself.

The sustained engagement with the image of "emprentyng" stone that plays out in the narrative of *The Franklin's Tale* is, in part, an exploration of the desires that motivate persistent speakers, and the benefits that accrue from persistent speech. Yet, it also constitutes an investigation into how people live with and learn from familiar wisdom, whose meanings emerge in dialogue with lived experience. As it thinks about this ancient, Ovidian figure, so often rehearsed and adapted in other medieval texts, *The Franklin's Tale* shows how maxims and aphorisms might take on new significance or impart new knowledge in new experiential contexts. As its claims about habituation lose their initial force, and the value of persistence emerges as a good in itself, this analogy offers a particularly dramatic demonstration of the way that familiar wisdom might unfold new meanings in time.

In Agincourt's Shadow: Hoccleve's "Au treshonorable conpaignie du Iarter" and the Domestication of Henry V

Carl Grey Martin
Norwich University

Abstract

Thomas Hoccleve's commitments to the Lancastrians did not allay his reservations about the pretensions of chivalry: title, *prouesse*, conquest. Only months after the English victory at Agincourt in October 1415, and amidst planning for Henry V's expansion of the campaign for French territory, Hoccleve publicly articulated his concerns in a two-part poem addressed "au tres noble Roy H. le quint . . . & au tres honorable conpaignie du Iarter." Invoking Constantine and Justinian, the work is a plea to the premier knights of the realm to focus their energies on suppressing English heresy—and thus to redefine English aristocratic identity as a means for orthodoxy and security *within* the insular realm. In this paper I decisively date Hoccleve's little-known Garter poem to spring 1416; perform a close reading of its "domesticating" anti-Lollard emphasis; and explore the implications of the poem's originating circumstances and its major themes for anti-imperialist attitudes under the rule of the iconic warrior-king.

Keywords

Thomas Hoccleve; Henry V of England; Agincourt; Oldcastle; Lollards; imperialism; chivalry; ideology; Hundred Years War; Lancastrians; Order of the Garter

And so nowe men suppose that the Kyng wil fro henys forthe make were yn France; for Normandie is alle hys. . . . More write y not at thys tyme; bote y

This project received essential support from the Norwich University Offices of Academic Research and Faculty Development, whose granting of an independent study leave allowed me to enjoy a 2016 Mayers Fellowship at the Huntington Library, San Marino, California. Thanks to Sean Field, Charles-Louis Morand-Métivie, and Andrea Tarnowski for inviting me to share two early versions of the paper in 2015; to Charlie Briggs, Ian Cornelius, John Fyler, Maureen Jurkowski, Alex Mueller, Jennifer Sisk, Paul Strohm, Craig Taylor, and Peter Travis for their advocacy and/or reading of multiple drafts; and to the *SAC* readers and editors for their guidance.

prey yow ye prey for us that we may come sone, oute of thys unlusty sound-yours [soldiers'] lyf, yn to the lyf of Englond.[1]

The literary work gives the measure of a difference, reveals a determinate absence, resorts to an eloquent silence.[2]

A S ANNE CURRY REMINDS US, "It is easy to get carried away by Agincourt."[3] And yet Thomas Hoccleve, privy clerk and noted enthusiast of the king whose fame is so closely tied to this battle, and to whom Hoccleve dedicated his *Regiment of Princes*, seems not to have been. To support that counterintuitive assertion, I assign a post-Agincourt date for the short, two-part occasional poem described by Hoccleve himself as "balades . . . fais au tres noble Roy H. le quint . . . & au tres honorable conpaignie du Iarter."[4] A bold plea to the English nobility to protect the realm from religious heterodoxy, the "balades" infuse religious encouragement with trenchant criticism of knightly mores. By localizing this work's antiheretical affect and vocabulary, with its pronounced echoes of the contemporaneous 1415 poem-homily known as "To Oldcastle" (a direct address to the jail-breaking Lollard Sir John Oldcastle, Baron Cobham), the essay then explores the political implications of that dating. These support the ongoing "reappraisal" of Hoccleve's intellectual independence and non-Chaucerian literary dimensions.[5]

---

[1] "T. F. to his Fellows and Friends in England, from Evreux, A.D. 1420," *Original letters, Illustrative of English History; Including Numerous Royal Letters: From Autographs in the British Museum, and One or Two Other Collections; with Notes and Illustrations*, second series, Vol. 1, ed. Henry Ellis (London, 1827), 77–78. Christopher Allmand, *Henry V* (Berkeley: University of California Press, 1992), 130, reassigns this letter to John Feelde, March 1419.

[2] Pierre Macherey, *A Theory of Literary Production*, trans. Geoffrey Wall (London: Routledge & Kegan Paul, 1978), 79.

[3] Anne Curry, "After Agincourt, What Next? Henry V and the Campaign of 1416," in *Conflicts, Consequences and the Crown in the Late Middle Ages*, ed. Linda Clark (Woodbridge: Boydell, 2007), 23–52 (23).

[4] San Marino, Huntington Library, MS HM 111.

[5] Albrecht Classen, "Hoccleve's Independence from Chaucer: A Study of Poetic Emancipation," *FCS* 16 (1990): 59–81 (59). Important contributors to this revaluation include J. A. Burrow, "Hoccleve and Chaucer," in *Chaucer Traditions: Studies in Honour of Derek Brewer*, ed. Ruth Morse and Barry Windeatt (Cambridge: Cambridge University Press, 1990), 54–61; Nicholas Watson, "Censorship and Cultural Change in Late-Medieval England: Vernacular Theology, the Oxford Translation Debate, and Arundel's Constitution of 1409," *Speculum* 70 (1995): 822–64 (848–49); Ethan Knapp, *Bureau-*

Hoccleve's persona has been thoroughly conflated with deference to Henry V's interests. His work clearly assisted the Lancastrians' much-sought "objectivization of opposition in a sufficiently vivid form to permit a reciprocal stabilization" of their shaky rule.[6] Nonetheless, his sour address to the fellowship erodes the common characterization of Hoccleve as "congenial to the claims and prerogatives of Lancastrian kingship"—even at its most charismatic.[7] To be specific, unlike "To Oldcastle" this poem both rejects secularizing tendencies within English chivalry and is conspicuously silent on the subject of France precisely at a moment—early 1416—when advocacy for more war could not have been more conducive to King Henry's highest military and ideological designs.

Caution and disillusion about war were, after all, active and fully compatible with Hoccleve's pessimistic worldview—as well as artistically alluring.[8] England had suffered decades of costly foreign war, and even the military successes of Edward III won short-lived political gains and imposed a much-resented tax burden.[9] In both cases French conquest threatened to appear as a squandering of domestic wealth as well as an abrogation of domestic duty. Poets, including those working within the Troy- and Arthur-haunted alliterative tradition, therefore produced evocative works deeply worried by imperialism and energized by the conviction that much political crisis derives from "the volition of aristocrats" pushed akilter by "the contingent and entropic force of events."[10]

---

cratic Muse: Thomas Hoccleve and the Literature of Late Medieval England (University Park: Pennsylania State University Press, 2001); Andrew Cole, Literature and Heresy in the Age of Chaucer (Cambridge: Cambridge University Press, 2008), 103–14; and Jenni Nuttall, "Thomas Hoccleve's Poems for Henry V: Anti-Occasional Verse and Ecclesiastical Reform," Oxford Handbooks Online (Oxford University Press, 2015), https://www.oxfordhandbooks.com/view/10.1093/oxfordhb/9780199935338.001.0001/oxfordhb-9780199935338-e-61 (accessed January 18, 2016).

[6] Paul Strohm, England's Empty Throne: Usurpation and the Language of Legitimation, 1399–1422 (New Haven: Yale University Press, 1998), 2, 81–82.

[7] Paul Strohm, "Hoccleve, Lydgate and the Lancastrian Court," in The Cambridge History of Medieval English Literature, ed. David Wallace (Cambridge: Cambridge University Press, 1999), 640–61 (657).

[8] Larry Scanlon, "Nothing but Change and Variance: The Problem of Hoccleve's Politics," ChauR 48, no. 4 (2014): 504–23 (508).

[9] R. H. Britnell, The Commercialisation of English Society, 1000–1500 (Cambridge: Cambridge University Press, 1993), 185. See also Michel Mollat, The Poor in the Middle Ages: An Essay in Social History, trans. Arthur Goldhammer (New Haven: Yale University Press, 1986), 214.

[10] James Simpson, Reform and Cultural Revolution: 1350–1547, The Oxford English Literary History 2 (Oxford: Oxford University Press, 2002), 86. Important scholarship

Hoccleve duly adopted, therefore, what James Simpson describes as "the prudential voice" to produce a modest yet resonant accompaniment to those big, bitter narratives from the north.[11] Within that moralistic generic framework, "To Henry V and the Company of the Garter" confronts the English nobility with its capacity for a pious—even officious—exertion of prowess on their traditional domains at a time of turbulence.[12] This would mean hunting down homegrown heretics who were, moreover, redefining an "Englische nacioun" for themselves.[13] The enemy was a reformist movement inspired by the wide-ranging scholarship of John Wyclif that in one instance during Henry V's early tenure, January 1414, assumed a loosely militarized aspect under the putative direction of Oldcastle, who was made to embody the imminent threat of which the much-absent Henry V would become the embodied destroyer.[14] It was, for Hoccleve, a time when the chivalric elite needed to be brought home.

Circumstances and Date of Composition

It can be admitted that, as an eight-stanza, sixty-four-line brace of poems, Hoccleve's "balades au tresnnoble Roy H. le quint . . . et au treshonorable conpaignie du Iarter" seem a modest work. The "balades" actually comprise a single text, which for the sake of brevity will be referred to hereafter as "To the Garter Knights." The poet chose for this (as for other ballads of similar theme and audience) the eight-line

---

on turn-of-the-century English pacifism and anti-imperialism includes R. F. Yeager, "Pax poetica: On the Pacifism of Chaucer and Gower," *SAC* 9 (1987): 97–121; Ben Lowe, *Imagining Peace: A History of Early English Pacifist Ideas* (University Park: Pennsylvania State University Press, 1997); Andrew Lynch, " 'Manly cowardyse': Thomas Hoccleve's Peace Strategy," *MÆ* 73 (2004): 306–23; Rory Cox, *Wyclif on War and Peace* (Woodbridge: Boydell, 2014); and Sebastian Sobecki, " 'Ecce patet tensus': The Trentham Manuscript, *In Praise of Peace*, and John Gower's Autograph Hand," *Speculum* 90 (2015): 925–59.

[11] Simpson, *Reform*, 263.

[12] For social unrest under the Lancastrians, see Allmand, *Henry V*, Chap. 14; and Edward Powell, *Kingship, Law, and Society: Criminal Justice in the Reign of Henry V* (Oxford: Clarendon Press, 1989), Part 3.

[13] Jill C. Havens, " 'As Englishe is comoun langage to oure puple': The Lollards and the Imagined English Community," in *Imagining a Medieval English Nation*, ed. Kathy Lavezzo (Minneapolis: University of Minnesota Press, 2004), 98. For an overview of the related topics of the "national mythologies extant in medieval English culture itself" and the many "rhetorics of Englishness" (xiii), see Kathy Lavezzo's Introduction to this volume, vii–xxxiv.

[14] Knapp, *Bureaucratic Muse*, 138.

"monk" stanza, "known as the double croisée in French" but otherwise not "conform[ing] to the French type."[15] These appear uniquely as the fifth item in San Marino, Huntington Library, MS HM 111, a holograph collection datable to 1422–26 of mostly short poems, many of them addressed to specific high-ranking persons.[16]

The work can be summarized as a compact call to arms to the Garter that designates its head, King Henry, as the inheritor of the burden of imperial Roman antiheresy—subject matter explored the year before in the more diffuse "To Oldcastle." The circumstances of the composition of the "balades" are little known, but an accurate dating of the text must account for its response to three externalities, examined in order of their textual prominence: (1) Garter ceremonies; (2) heresy/Lollardy; and (3) Sigismund and the Council of Constance. As I seek to show, no *single* one of these can determine a date. To begin with the holograph itself, we may note that the sequence of HM 111's poems, according to John M. Bowers, is unrelated to "chronology of composition."[17] With little help from Hoccleve himself, scholars have offered only modest clarification within the last century. No explanatory attention was paid to these "balades" in F. J. Furnivall and Israel Gollancz's edition.[18] With some care J. H. Wylie assigned this "stirring call" to 1414, and Richard Firth Green likewise suggests a date "not long after" Henry's accession.[19] According to J. A. Burrow the text "was no doubt occasioned by a gathering of the Order of the Garter, either that on 23 April 1414 or the particularly grand assembly on 24 May 1416," while Paul Strohm

---

[15] John Burrow, "Hoccleve and the Middle French Poets," in *The Long Fifteenth Century: Essays for Douglas Gray*, ed. Helen Cooper and Sally Mapstone (Oxford: Clarendon Press, 1997), 35–49 (38).

[16] For more on HM 111's design and audience, see John M. Bowers, "Hoccleve's Huntington Holographs: The First 'Collected Poems' in English," *FCS* 15 (1989), 27–51; John J. Thompson, "Thomas Hoccleve and Manuscript Culture," in *Nation, Court, and Culture: New Essays on Fifteenth-Century English Poetry*, ed. Helen Cooney (Dublin: Four Courts Press, 2001), 81–94; and David Watt, *The Making of Thomas Hoccleve's "Series"* (Liverpool: Liverpool University Press, 2013), Chap. 1.

[17] Bowers, "Hoccleve's Huntington Holographs," 36.

[18] *Hoccleve's Works: The Minor Poems in the Huntington Library MS. HM 111 (Formerly Phillipps MS. 8151), the Durham Univ. MS. Cosin V. III. 9, and Huntington Library MS. HM 744 (Formerly Ash-Burnham MS. Additional 133)*, ed. Frederick James Furnivall and Israel Gollancz (London: Oxford University Press, 1970).

[19] James Hamilton Wylie, *The Reign of Henry the Fifth*, 3 vols. (Cambridge: Cambridge University Press, 1914–29), 1:318–19; Richard Firth Green, *Poets and Princepleasers: Literature and the English Court in the Late Middle Ages* (Toronto: University of Toronto Press, 1980), 184.

has proposed "1414–16."[20] Contrarily, Linne R. Mooney, in an exhaustive analysis of pertinent Hoccleve-related documents, poetic and official, proposes *no* textual activity by Hoccleve from September 1415 to December 1416, a span that, for her, could "mark the period of Hoccleve's illness."[21] Ethan Knapp without explanation dates the poem to 1416, but Vincent Gillespie supports this year on grounds to be considered here.[22] Finally and most recently, Jenni Nuttall links it to "one of the annual Garter assemblies at Windsor, most likely in 1414," as does Chris Given-Wilson.[23] Curiously, however, most of the dates proposed bookend the events surrounding the symbolically immense Agincourt campaign, of which Hoccleve's poem—composed within a field of ideological and social coercions—makes no explicit mention. As Bowers does with the *Canterbury Tales*, I entrust "the unsaid and the barely said" in Hoccleve's poem with forensic importance.[24]

"Yow, Lordes of the Garter": Meetings of the Order, 1414–16

Accurately dating the text will require, first, some alignment of its composition with an annual meeting of the Order. This fellowship received special attention from Henry V (himself elected in 1399), likely from the start of his reign. According to Elias Ashmole (1617–92), "How this Noble *Order* flourished from its Foundation to the time of *Henry* V. no Account can be given, since the Annals thereof are wanting to his Reign; but then it appears to have been in considerable Splendor."[25] Indeed, in

---

[20] John A. Burrow, *Thomas Hoccleve* (Aldershot: Variorum, 1994), 21; Strohm, *England's Empty Throne*, 184.

[21] Linne R. Mooney, "Some New Light on Thomas Hoccleve," *SAC* 29 (2007): 293–340 (307).

[22] Ethan Knapp, "Thomas Hoccleve," in *The Cambridge Companion to Medieval English Literature 1100–1500*, ed. Larry Scanlon (Cambridge: Cambridge University Press, 2009), 191–203 (199); Vincent Gillespie, "Chichele's Church: Vernacular Theology in England after Thomas Arundel," in *After Arundel: Religious Writing in Fifteenth-Century England*, ed. Vincent Gillespie and Kantik Ghosh (Turnhout: Brepols, 2011), 3–42 (39).

[23] Nuttall, "Anti-Occasional Verse," 2; Chris Given-Wilson, *Henry IV* (New Haven: Yale University Press, 2016), 397.

[24] John M. Bowers, *Chaucer and Langland: The Antagonistic Tradition* (Notre Dame: University of Notre Dame Press, 2007), 160–61. On the impact of Agincourt, see Strohm, "Hoccleve, Lydgate and the Lancastrian Court," 642; Anne Curry, *Agincourt: A New History* (Stroud: Alan Sutton, 2006), 32; Allmand, *Henry V*, 18; Robert J. Meyer-Lee, *Poets and Power from Chaucer to Wyatt* (Cambridge: Cambridge University Press, 2007), 64; Derek Pearsall, "Hoccleve's *Regement of Princes*: The Poetics of Royal Self-Representation," *Speculum* 69 (1994): 386–410 (400).

[25] Elias Ashmole, *The History of the Most Noble Order of the Garter* (London, 1715), 411.

Henry's hands the Order would be molded from a mere "source of honorific patronage" into an instrument for the personal consolidation and militarization of his best knights.[26]

D'A. J. D. Boulton explains that "meetings of the Order were held at the prescribed time and place in most of the years between 1349 and 1520" notwithstanding "lacunae in the accounts," and he refers to "four feasts in the reign of Henry V for which records survive."[27] No document exists confirming a 1414 meeting of the Garter. On the other hand, while 1415 seems to be the least popular year assigned by scholars (only Strohm allows for it), a well-planned meeting of the Garter is surely to have taken place that year if, as Lisa Jefferson argues, "the earliest extant statutes of the Order must . . . be dated to 22 April 1415, and not to the reign of Edward III" as previously assumed. The tenth of these statutes ordained that "chacun an, la vigile Sainte George, soit faicte une assemblé de tous les compaignons de Saint George seurnommez au dit Chastel de Wyndesore qui sont dedens la terre ou dehors qui venir y pourront."[28]

Since April 23—St. George's Day—was the prescribed occasion for the ceremony, it is notable that Henry that very month summoned his lords to announce an end to negotiations with France, with the result that "indentures for the army were drawn up and sealed on 29 April."[29] Knowing Henry's mind for organization, we must conclude that a failure to coordinate the feast—the first obligated by the Order's own statutes—that month would be improbable. Indeed, Burrow's unexplained omission of 1415 could derive not from any assumed hiatus of the Order but rather from the perceived discrepancy between Henry's observable preparation for war that spring and the poem's outright neglect of the matter. That is, if "To the Garter Knights" had been

[26] Hugh E. L. Collins, *The Order of the Garter, 1348–1461: Chivalry and Politics in Late Medieval England* (Oxford: Clarendon Press, 2000), 119.

[27] D'A. J. D. Boulton, *The Knights of the Crown: The Monarchical Orders of Knighthood in Later Medieval Europe, 1325–1520* (New York: St. Martin's Press, 1987), 151. On the ritual importance of the meetings and of members' attendance, see T. Tolga Gumus, "A Tale of Two Codices: The Medieval Registers of the Order of the Garter," *Comitatus* 37 (2006): 86–110 (93–95).

[28] Lisa Jefferson, "MS Arundel 48 and the Earliest Statutes of the Order of the Garter," *EHR* 109 (1994): 356–85 (356–57, 377–78). Jefferson will subsequently conclude, adducing other circumstances, that "a feast of the Order was held in 1415, as we know from the Wardrobe Accounts" (373).

[29] Curry, *Agincourt*, 49. See also Jefferson, "MS Arundel 48," 373; and Allmand, *Henry V*, 72, 78.

written in early 1415, it (unlike the war-conscious "To Oldcastle") entirely resisted the excitement around the invasion of France for which Parliament had agreed a subsidy the previous November.[30]

No compelling circumstances for the composition of such a grave address to the Order obtained in 1415 after April, which brings us to the following spring, when there would be *plenty* to celebrate and commemorate. In the aftermath of Agincourt, Sigismund, king of Germany and Hungary (to whom I shall return), later to succeed as Holy Roman Emperor, would be inducted to the Garter fellowship on a postponed date in May 1416. As an anonymous *Brut* chronicler records:

This same yeer cam Sigismund, þe emperour of Almayn, into Englond forto speke with King Harri, to trete of certayn thyngiz touching þe pees of Englond and of Fraunce, and also for the welfare and vnite of alle holi chirche. And þe king and his lordis mette with him at Saint Thomas Wateryng, withoute Suthwerk, and him receyued with greet reuerence and worship, and brouȝte him into London, and fro thennez to Westmynstre, and þere he was loggid in þe paleis atte kyngis coste. And þat same tyme, þe king yaf him þe liverey of þe garter.[31]

Thomas of Elmham's *Liber metricus de Henrico Quinto* notes the ceremony's collective chivalric significance: "De Festo Sancti Georgii in quo Imperator eligitur in militiae fraternitatem, et cum debitis insigniis installatur."[32]

In embracing Sigismund (hosted, at much expense, from May to August), Henry was looking forward, but he was also gazing back, for Sigismund's election to the Order coincided with four nominations related to the campaign that culminated in the heroics of Agincourt. According to the *Gesta Henrici Quinti*,

during these solemn ceremonies the same supreme prince the emperor was first elected and then admitted into the fraternity of the knights [in fraternitatem militum], four other nobles [alii nobiles quatuor], too, being received into the same by virtue of their diligence in arms, in place of those others who . . . had

---

[30] Curry, "After Agincourt," 27, 42–43.

[31] *An English Chronicle 1377–1461: A New Edition Edited from Aberystwyth, National Library of Wales, MS 21068 and Oxford, Bodleian Library, MS Lyell 34*, ed. C. William Marx (Rochester, N.Y.: Boydell, 2003), 45.

[32] *Elmhami liber metricus de Henrico Quinto*, in *Rerum Britannicarum medii ævi scriptores*, ed. C. A. Cole (London: Longman, 1858), 77–166 (88).

died during that year on behalf of the commonalty; and they received the insignia of installation, our king, as sovereign of that college of knights, presiding.[33]

These "alii nobiles quatuor," elected between August and October 1415, were Sir William Harrington (d. 1440), a banner-bearer at Agincourt;[34] William de le Zouche, fourth Lord Zouche of Haryngworth, who died November 1415 after serving in Calais and as judge of the Southampton plotters (thereby providing a vacancy for Sigismund);[35] Sir John Holland, earl of Huntingdon, who also sat on the plotters' tribunal and fought at Harfleur and Agincourt;[36] and Richard de Vere, eleventh earl of Oxford (d. 1417), who served in France with the king as well.[37]

By all accounts the battle of October 25, 1415, was impressive not merely for the unlikely odds of English victory but for the intense association of that victory with the physical presence of the king—"[God's] own soldier," according to the *Gesta* (89)—who led an English expeditionary force—"that little band [paucitate illa]"—into enemy territory to defeat a much larger French host comprising "the very pick and most sturdy of warriors [tot electissimos et robustissimos milites]" (91). In the song known as the "Agincourt Carol," which, argues Helen Deeming, may be confidently connected to the London pageantry of November 1415, we hear of Henry's intrepid frontline action:

> Than went hym forth owr kyng comely
> In achyncourt feld he fauth manly
> Thorw grace of god most mervelowsly
> He had both feld and victory[38]

---

[33] *Gesta Henrici Quinti: The Deeds of Henry the Fifth*, ed. and trans. Frank Taylor and John S. Roskell (Oxford: Clarendon Press, 1975), 133; hereafter cited parenthetically by page number.

[34] Rosemary Horrox, "Harrington, William, Fifth Baron Harrington (c. 1392–1458)," in *Oxford Dictionary of National Biography* (Oxford: Oxford University Press, 2004) (hereafter *ODNB*). The *ODNB* indicates 1417 for his election to the Garter, but both Ashmole, *History* (508), and Collins, *Order* (293), place Harrington before Sigismund in their election lists. Ashmole declares, just before the elector list for Henry V's reign, "These that follow are Marshalled in an exact Series of their Elections" (508).

[35] Eric Acheson, "Zouche [de la Zouche] Family (per. c. 1254–1415), Magnates," in *ODNB*.

[36] R. A. Griffiths, "Holland [Holand], John, First Duke of Exeter (1395–1447)," in ibid.

[37] Helen Castor, "Vere, John de, Twelfth Earl of Oxford (1408–1462), magnate," in ibid.; Wylie, *Henry the Fifth*, 2:89; Collins, *Order*, 126.

[38] Helen Deeming, "The Sources and Origin of the 'Agincourt Carol,'" *Early Music* 35 (2007): 23–36 (24); hereafter cited parenthetically by line number.

Likewise the *Gesta*: "Nor do our older men remember any prince ever having commanded his people on the march with more effort, bravery, or consideration, or having, with his own hand, performed greater feats of strength in the field [seu qui manu propria se virilius gerebat in campo]" (100–101).

That Feast of St. George would have been an excellent opportunity not only to reaffirm how, in Richard W. Kaeuper's words, "a good king was a good knight and could cleave helmets and thrust lances with the best" but also to publicize Henry's holy and self-mortifying characterization of the battle.[39] The piety associated with Agincourt might have enticed even Hoccleve. On that rainy October morning Henry was said to have ordered each man to "put a litill porcion of erthe in his mouth" and then announced "with an high vois, 'In þe name of Almyȝti God and of Saint George, auaunt banner! And Saint George this day thyn help!' "[40] And to cap it all, the *Gesta* recounts, after a punishing campaign punctuated by formal expressions of devotion, in November 1415 Henry would enter London under the stern but approving visage of "a most beautiful statue of St. George, in armour save for his head," and fully accoutered: "And to its right hung his triumphal helm, and to its left a shield of his arms of matching size. With his right hand he held the hilt of the sword with which he was girded, and with his left a scroll which extended over the ramparts, containing these words: *Soli deo honor et gloria*" (105). Armed but bareheaded, the soldier-saint of England perfectly symbolized Henry's projected image, mitigating fears that military achievement might come at the cost of weakened devotion.

Notwithstanding their many noteworthy circumstances, there is no official account of the 1416 proceedings, but Henry surely made the most of an occasion when supporters and comrades were fêted. He even insisted that his military retinue be present, summoning all nobles in the realm "to reside in the city during the Emperor's stay" (while taking the precaution to ban knights' and esquires' carrying of weapons in the city), as well as "forbidding any lord, knight, or esquire to cease his attendance upon the King before the close of the solemn Feast of St. George or afterwards without special permission."[41] Spring 1416 would

---

[39] Richard W. Kaeuper, *Chivalry and Violence in Medieval Europe* (Oxford: Clarendon Press, 1999), 103.

[40] *English Chronicle 1377–1461*, 44.

[41] *Calendar of Letter-Books Preserved among the Archives of the Corporation of the City of London at the Guildhall*, Vol. I, ed. Reginald R. Sharpe (London: n.p., 1909), 160, 161.

therefore also be the prime moment for Hoccleve, verbally or via manuscript, to address the prestigious, morally freighted gathering.

"The heresies bittir galle": Lollard Threats, 1414–16

Despite the happy occasion, however, the mood of "To the Garter Knights" is imperative, the diction antagonistic, the meter jumpy. It redepicts a realm whose religious troubles had been scrutinized in the 512-line poem "fee au temps q*ue* le R*oi* H*enri* le V*t* . . . feust a hampton sur son primer passage vers harflete [Harfleur]"—our "To Oldcastle."[42] This work will function as our *terminus post quem* not only for its title (placing us squarely in the summer of 1415) but also for specific textual references to the upcoming campaign. Just as pertinent, Hoccleve's encouragement in "To Oldcastle" that Sir John renounce the Lollards on whom his error is blamed would presuppose the possibility of his actually escaping conviction for heresy. On that point we know that a general pardon, to include "all rebels, felons, &c., who severally sue for charters of pardon before Michaelmas Day next," was issued to the sheriffs on December 9, 1414.[43] Since this pardon followed two—issued March 28 and May 20, 1414—that had *excluded* Oldcastle, we can be confident that "To Oldcastle" was indeed composed in the summer of 1415, when a deadline for clemency was likely approaching.[44]

Because Oldcastle was most notorious for the so-called Lollard uprising of January 1414 at St. Giles, it could be inferred that "To the Garter Knights" was composed for the annual assembly that would coincide

---

[42] Huntington Library, MS HM 111.

[43] Ibid., 1:132. This writ can be traced to a royal act dated November 6, 1414, as recorded in the *Fœdera, conventiones, literæ, et cujuscunque generis acta publica, inter reges Angli;ae, et alios quosvis imperatores, reges . . . ab anno 1101, ad nostra usque tempora, habita aut tractata . . . In lucem missa de mandato nuperæ Reginæ*, Vol. 9, ed. Thomas Rymer, 2nd ed. (London, 1729), 170–71.

[44] *Calendar of Letter-Books*, I:xxi (based on Rymer's *Fœdera*). Powell, *Kingship*, 163, claims that the December 1414 pardon was revoked in March 1415, but Hoccleve perhaps anticipated a renewal of terms, as Henry V generally preferred pardons to prosecutions in order to raise revenue through fines and to direct noble offenders' "aggressive energies into his foreign wars" (229). Apropos of his strategy, according to John A. F. Thomson, "Oldcastle, John, Baron Cobham (d. 1417), soldier, heretic, and rebel," in *ODNB*, and Strohm, *England's Empty Throne* (86), a personal pardon was also issued to Oldcastle in December 1415—although such a pardon does not appear in the second edition of the *Fœdera*. The *Calendar of Letter-Books*, however, contains a writ dated November 24, 1416, that renews the terms of the pardon granted during the king's "second year" (169). On the sequence of pardons and their sources, see Cole, *Literature and Heresy*, 106–8.

with new anti-Lollard legislation inspired by those very "grandes rumours, congregacions et insurreccions cy en Engleterre, par diverses lieges le roi," namely those "del secte de heresie appellee Lollardrie."[45] Indeed, "To the Garter Knights" contains an exhortation to Henry to ensure that no subject be allowed "Of the feith to despute more or lesse / Openly among peple," instructing him, "Makith swich lawe/ & for aght may befalle / Obserue it wel."[46] Nonetheless, these April statutes are largely concerned with the laicization of investigation and arrest, as well as with their after-the-fact mechanics—forfeiture, jail delivery, empanelment, clerical jurisdiction. Powerless to *block* subversive speech, publication, or assembly per se, the statutes allow the targeting of those people assistant to the promotion and dissemination of Lollardism.[47]

Hoccleve's reference to "swich lawe" testifies instead to the elusive, frustrated aim of more than a decade's legal efforts, most recently the 1409 Constitutions' attempts to prevent all unlicensed preaching and unauthorized publishing of Wyclif or scriptural translations.[48] This stanza merely urges the king to broadcast and execute more forcefully extant duties and powers in a general antiheresy spirit. For as "To Oldcastle" itself concedes, such control over religious "despute" would still not be realized more than a year *after* the St. Giles rising. Heresy, Ian Forrest explains, "often happened in secret and its psychological roots were buried in the depths of the mind," so it can be no surprise that, since the rise of Wycliffism in the 1380s, the effort at extirpation was a long, alternating series of failures and recommitments.[49]

[45] *The Parliament Rolls of Medieval England, 1275–1504*, ed. Chris Given-Wilson (Leicester: Scholarly Digital Editions, 2005), Henry V, 1414 April, iv.24.

[46] Huntington Library, MS HM 111, lines 27–28, 30–31; hereafter cited parenthetically by line number. Unless there is a significant divergence from the holograph, my transcriptions of this poem and "To Oldcastle" rely on *Hoccleve's Works*, ed. Furnivall and Gollancz, alongside *Thomas Hoccleve: A Facsimile of the Autograph Verse Manuscripts: Henry E. Huntington Library, San Marino (California), MSS HM III & HM 744; University Library, Durham (England), MS Cosin V.III.9*, ed. J. A. Burrow and A. I. Doyle, EETS s.s. 19 (Oxford: Oxford University Press, 2002). Punctuation changes are indicated by brackets.

[47] Secular officers shall have "plein poair d'enquerer de toutz yceux qe teignent ascuns errours ou heresies come Lollards, et queux sont lour maintenours, recettours, fautours, susteignours, communes escrivers de lieux sibien de lour sermons comes de lour escoles, conventicles, congregaciouns et confederacies" (*Parliament Rolls*, Henry V, 1414 April, iv.24).

[48] For details on the Constitutions, see Watson, "Censorship and Cultural Change in Late-Medieval England."

[49] Ian Forrest, *The Detection of Heresy in Late Medieval England* (Oxford: Clarendon Press, 2005), 1. Forrest refers to the 1414 legislative effort as "essentially a restatement of the lapsed provisions of 1406," which targeted those who preached, published, and

Internal evidence matters here too. If, as Forrest suggests, "Henry's anti-heresy activity petered out fairly quickly," with a steady issuance of pardons beginning in early 1414, it is hard to account for what I shall show to be the poem's palpable annoyance with the "flour / Of Chivalrie" (5–6), for at *that* moment the Garter would have had its renewed authorization and mission, as yet unembarrassed by their ineffectiveness. More compelling yet, although the Lollard-minded Parliament of spring 1414 would have coincided with that year's Garter meeting, there seems little rationale for Hoccleve's having appealed so summarily, as well as so *obliquely*, to the Garter without even mentioning the reputed knight-ringleader who had, according to Walsingham, "summoned and hired them [the rebels] at his own expense."[50] Comparatively sedate, the poem fails to resonate with the tension that produced a February 10 imposition of a London-wide curfew "under penalty of forfeiture of life and property" and, on May 15, a reaffirmation of the Statute of Northampton "forbidding riots and conventicles and the carrying of arms" in the presence of the king's ministers.[51]

"Our worthy kyng and cristen Emperour": Sigismund and the Council of Constance, 1414–16

Emperor-elect Sigismund would prove an irresistible model and Christian brother-in-arms for Henry. In assisting the English king's self-fashioning as geopolitical peacemaker and strict justiciar in regard to France, while confirming a pan-European united front against heresy, he would also make a unique Garter knight. Under Sigismund's direction, the Council of Constance had gathered on November 1, 1414, with the threefold task of "seeking unity under one pope; . . . extirpating heresy; and . . . promulgating reform."[52] The heresy problem was of immediate concern to Sigismund, as the most prominent foe of the day was the barbative Bohemian excommunicant Jan Hus (c. 1371–1415).

---

held views contrary to the "foye Catholike," or promoted the Church's temporal disendowment (45). See *Parliament Rolls*, Henry IV, 1406 March, iii.584. Moreover, Archbishop Henry Chichele would try to overhaul Arundel's "ground-breaking 1414 statute" with his own promulgation of preemptive investigative machinery in July 1416 (Forrest, *Detection*, 46).

[50] The *"Chronica maiora" of Thomas Walsingham, 1376–1422*, trans. David Preest, ed. James G. Clark (Woodbridge: Boydell, 2005), 394.

[51] *Calendar of Letter-Books*, I:122, 125.

[52] Allmand, *Henry V*, 238. See also Wylie, *Henry the Fifth*, 2:239.

His preaching sustained Wyclif's arguments against priestly mediation of sacraments and churchly temporalities, with no less than "an extensive re-structuring of christian society" at its center.[53]

Condemned at the Council's fifteenth session, Hus burned while Henry's galleys, destined for Normandy, were loaded up at Southampton.[54] Indeed, that execution could be the referent of Hoccleve's jibe in "To Oldcastle" that "Some of thy fetheres weren plukkid late, / and mo shuln be" (257–58).[55] The loss would have been painful for Sir John, who had personally written in 1410 to a Hussite noble, Wok of Waldstein, and in 1411 to King Wenzel of Bohemia, both regarded by the Englishman "as comrades in the battle to free the Church from the clutches of the priests of Antichrist and to return it to its pristine state of apostolic poverty."[56] Alternatively, Hoccleve invokes here Wyclif himself: ahead of Hus's fatal conviction, his books were ordered to be burned, his corpse despoiled.[57]

The matching of names, terms, and phrasing across "To Oldcastle" and "To the Garter Knights" suggests that events in Constance that summer dominated Hoccleve's thought for many months to follow— just as the king envisioned military success in France. Attesting to that influence, "To the Garter Knights" contains not only multiple references to the Roman imperial dynasty but also a pun on the location of the in-session Council.[58] In the international context of the Council's ongoing work, and in the immediate manuscript context of HM 111 (prepared for "devout readers preoccupied with . . . orthodox reform"[59]), both texts express a hoped-for renewal of Roman *auctoritas*, a "Church Militant" buttressed by "a sense of historical antiquity and doctrinal stability."[60] Our poet is careful in his choice of imperial exemplars. All have strong credentials as battlers of heresy on behalf of a strong state imbued with

[53] Michael Wilks, "*Reformatio regni*: Wyclif and Hus as Leaders of Religious Protest Movements," *Studies in Church History* 9 (1972): 109–30 (116).

[54] Allmand, *Henry V*, 242.

[55] Nuttall, "Anti-Occasional Verse" (4), hints at this possibility without providing the instance, while Cole, *Literature and Heresy* (235 n. 21), posits a reference here to Oldcastle's 1413 arrest.

[56] Powell, *Kingship*, 146.

[57] Allmand, *Henry V*, 241–42.

[58] Gillespie, "Chichele's Church," 39.

[59] Watt, *Hoccleve's "Series,"* 45.

[60] Gillespie, "Chichele's Church," 25, 26.

that "theocratic grandeur" so attractive to the Lancastrians.[61] The emperors are "model instances of the relationship between ecclesiastical and imperial power and between spiritual and temporal jurisdictions"; furthermore, their expansionism goes unremarked, supporting Nuttall's observation that the poet's selection attempts "both to encourage royal action and yet to determine the limits of such intervention."[62]

Hoccleve's desire for military constraint is implied by verse that conflates Hoccleve's own king with Sigismund—presumably sitting amongst his new Garter brethren—as in the apostrophe to "Our worthy kyng and cristen Emperour" (26), which, Gillespie posits, was "framed to embrace Henry and Sigismund in a single address and as co-workers in a common cause."[63] David Watt concurs, insisting, "Hoccleve is not, as has been thought, addressing Henry V with two titles."[64] Yet the moniker "cristen Emperour" can encompass *both* Sigismund and Henry. Furthermore, Hoccleve's semantic slippage was central to his poem's purpose, as he sought to promote their identification. Nonetheless, and setting aside Hoccleve's own double-address "title" to the poem (omitting Sigismund), we find that the opening salutation

> To yow welle of honur and worthynesse
> Our right cristen kyng/ heir & successour
> Un to Iustinians deuout tendrenesse
> In the feith of Ihesu, our Redemptour
>
> (1–4)

offers an appositive series in which "Our right cristen kyng" is the third item (after "yow" and "welle"), followed immediately by a lineal link with Justinian, and then by "yow lordes of the garter" (5), which completes the echo of the dual-addressee title. If "Our right cristen kyng"—a clear reference to Henry, reiterated at line 44—can claim an emperor's mantle as "heir," the roles can be conflated—as they are in line 26 with that epithet "Our worthy kyng and cristen Emperour."

---

[61] Lee Patterson, "Making Identities in Fifteenth-Century England: Henry V and John Lydgate," in *Acts of Recognition: Essays on Medieval Culture* (Notre Dame: Notre Dame University Press, 2010), 120–54 (139).

[62] Nuttall, "Anti-Occasional Verse," 6, 7.

[63] Gillespie, "Chichele's Church," 39.

[64] Watt, Hoccleve's "Series," 45.

It is conceivable that, by that fourth stanza, Hoccleve's vision broadens, and he generously acknowledges both monarchs (as grammar and context certainly allow) and their efforts. Ultimately, however, neither sovereignty eclipses the other. Writing during an epoch that J. H. Burns associates with monarchical crisis, Hoccleve would be unlikely to suggest any subordination of Henry's power to Sigismund's—nor would it make much sense to invite Sigismund to exercise his powers in England. While the affirmation of "your Constance" may indeed speak to both rulers, Hoccleve advocates English "*imperium* as embodying a fullness or plenitude of royal power . . . which belongs at any one time uniquely to one ruler" (in the sense of "rex in regno suo imperator est"), a distinction reaffirmed by the singular apostrophe "Lige lord" at the start of the second stanza.[65] The Lollards were an English affair, and Hoccleve would be unlikely to affirm *romanitas* to England's detriment.

Some generations earlier, Charles V of France's self-identification as "most Christian king" went largely unchallenged by "foreign powers, whether adversaries of the Valois or not." These included Emperor Charles IV himself, who ahead of his January 1378 visit to Paris was expressly forbidden by his hosts to wear the imperial insignia within the borders of the French kingdom.[66] Henry V would have acted no differently before his guest. Few monarchs conceded their powers, "territorial in their basis," to others, whether popes or kings.[67] Hoccleve sought to enhance the Henry–Sigismund affinity, pushing the former away from territorial contests without impinging upon Henry's "imperial" self-image. To this latter end, Henry at the very same Garter ceremony presented Sigismund with the Lancastrian signature "SS collar," which (like the Garter itself) symbolically made Sigismund a retainer within the Lancastrian affinity.[68] Fully aware that the momentum for war was growing, Hoccleve sought to redirect, not block, Henry's militancy,

---

[65] J. H. Burns, *Lordship, Kingship, and Empire: The Idea of Monarchy, 1400–1525* (Oxford: Clarendon Press, 1992), 5, 13.

[66] Jacques Krynen, " 'Rex christianissimus': A Medieval Theme at the Roots of French Absolutism," *History and Anthropology* 4 (1989): 79–96 (81); František Šmahel, *The Parisian Summit, 1377–78: Emperor Charles IV and King Charles V of France*, trans. Sean Mark Miller and Kateřina Millerová (Prague: Karolinum Press, 2014), 182–83.

[67] Forrest, *Detection*, 111. On the limits of papal authority in England, see Allmand, *Henry V*, 257–59; as well as Gillespie, "Chichele's Church," 10.

[68] Allmand, *Henry V*, 105–6. In return, Henry received from Sigismund an object "purported to be the heart of St. George, no ordinary present" (106). See also Given-Wilson, *Henry IV*, 393–96.

linking it horizontally to a nobleman of comparable rank (more *primus inter pares* than overlord) facing similar heretical threats to sovereignty.

Whereas Henry sought in Sigismund "an important ally on France's eastern flank," an Anglo-French *settlement* was central to the grand vision of Sigismund, who in 1412 had warned the English "not to become embroiled in France."[69] It was precisely in April 1416, as ships were being readied for Sigismund's journey to England, that the worsening situation at Harfleur was debated in Parliament. Under French blockade, the isolated port had for months lacked sufficient food and supplies.[70] But if Henry intended anything more than the maintenance of the garrison at Harfleur, the presence of the reconciliatory Sigismund would be an impediment. "If there was a chance at peace, or at least a temporary cessation of hostilities, then the Commons could not be asked, nor would they grant, any further subsidies," Curry explains.[71]

In the uncertain political context of early 1416, therefore, Hoccleve's sangfroid would support Curry's insistence that victory at Agincourt did not guarantee broad English support for, or even expectation of, the reinvasion of France. As Curry reminds us, many of the contemporary accounts of Henry's broader French aims on which we rely *postdate* his entrenchment in Normandy and the Treaty of Troyes, making them vulnerable to a "deterministic stance" that might retrospectively underplay the fears, risks, and contingencies surrounding the early phase of Henry's wars.[72] A less provocative path guided by Sigismund and based on the 1360 Brétigny–Calais treaty was still possible, enabling the consolidation of a wider front on behalf of orthodoxy. The 1416 Garter assembly, like Hoccleve's poem for that occasion, testifies to an opportunity for English royal self-assertion that would mirror Sigismund's own.

A New "aart of chiualrie"

"To the Garter Knights" not only neglects to reflect upon what was widely seen as an astounding military success, one credited to God,

---

[69] Allmand, *Henry V*, 240; Given-Wilson, *Henry IV*, 497.

[70] Curry, "After Agincourt," 32–33; Allmand, *Henry V*, 104, 107. For details of the preparations, see *Calendar of Letter-Books*, I:161–64.

[71] Curry, "After Agincourt," 34.

[72] Ibid., 23. For estimations of the risks posed by Henry's expeditions, see Allmand, *Henry V*, 167; Curry, *Agincourt*, 15, 52, 56, 60, 114; Knapp, *Bureaucratic Muse*, 138; Powell, *Kingship*, 163, 253.

embellished with Georgian trappings, and conferring special honor on—and promising further power to—Henry. Following new financial commitments by the Commons in November 1415 in support of his "ius corone Anglie ad regnum Francie" (*Gesta*, 122–23), the work also fails to build support for the *next* phase of the campaign, which Henry would finalize only at the end of 1416.[73] Whereas Henry desired an aggrandizement of recent English achievement in France, Hoccleve's "To the Garter Knights" omits any promotion or even memorialization of the Norman invasion, especially as a portal to further action there.

Nevertheless, both "To the Garter Knights" and its close predecessor "To Oldcastle" are exhortations, admonishing and encouraging English knightly audiences. Another homology is the double address itself, with a single auditor (Oldcastle/Henry V) followed by his respective affinity (Lollards/Garter knights), although in both texts the two halves reference *both* parties. The relative synchronicity of texts implied by these likenesses also highlights an important difference of outlook and, thus, a definite *sequence*: "To the Garter Knights," more confident in its address and with a greater concentration of theme, is effectively a précis, as well as a post-Agincourt revision, of its tract-like predecessor. Most important here, the earlier text replicates chivalric conventions; the latter revises them.

"To Oldcastle" condemns the eponymous outlaw for his heresy, becoming an opportunity to refute Lollard tenets and to urge Lord Cobham to return to his proper chivalric identity: "O Oldcastel/ how hath the feend thee blent / Where is thy knyghtly herte/ art thow his thral?," Hoccleve asks (98–99). "Now syn the feend hath youen thee a fal / Qwyte him, let see, ryse up & slynge him doun" (102–3), he adds; and again, "Ryse vp a manly knyght, out of the slow / Of heresie" (105–6), as if the two states are inherently incompatible. A true knight should seek the *vita activa*, but if he insists on reading, Hoccleve recommends texts befitting a nobleman bound for Normandy:

> Clymbe no more/ in holy writ so hie!
> Rede the storie of Lancelot de lake
> Or Vegece of the aart of Chiualrie,
> The seege of Troye/ or Thebes/ thee applie
> To thing þat may to thordre of knyght longe!
> (194–98)

[73] Curry, "After Agincourt," 27.

If, Hoccleve adds, it would please Oldcastle to "rede of auctoritee" (201), he suggests what Ruth Nissé describes as the "historical-romance canon of the Old Testament"—that is, the bloodletting in "Iudicum," "Regum," "Iosue," "Iudith," "Paralipomenon [Books of Chronicles]," and "Machabe" (203–5).[74] The common denominator among these diverse works is, rather, that none is "more pertinent to Chiualrie" (208).

Hoccleve saw the upcoming French campaign as preferable to heresy and rebellion by its keeping knights away from theology. Consequently, "To Oldcastle," though composed on the point of Henry's disembarking, appears indifferent to the *purpose* of the French expedition, insisting on muscular feudal service as its own end:

> Looke how our cristen Prince, our lige lord,
> With many a lord & knyght beyond the See
> Laboure in armes,/ & thou hydest thee
> And darst nat come/ & shewe thy visage!
> O fy for shame/ how can a knyght be
> Out of thonur of this rial viage?
>
> (499–504)

Since "the lak of feith/ hath qwenchid his manhode" (287), the only thing needed is for Oldcastle to join the campaign "in armes" and all will be well with him again. But Hoccleve strains here between an autotelic chivalry shorn of all "higher" meaning, and the impossibility of any true knightly practice operating outside a specific ethos. Indeed, Hoccleve elsewhere in the same poem cites Augustine's warning,

> Thogh þat an heretik for Crystes name
> Shede his blood/ & his lyf for Cryst forgo,
> [It] Shal nat him save.
>
> (42–44)

For Hoccleve, even Christ-like self-sacrifice requires proper religious disposition, which cannot, he insists, be substituted with voluntary self-negation conferred in combat *ipso facto*.[75]

---

[74] Ruth Nissé, " 'Oure fadres olde and modres': Gender, Heresy, and Hoccleve's Literary Politics," *SAC* 21 (1999): 275–99 (295).

[75] Yeager, "Pax poetica," 105.

Hoccleve will not reproduce this vagary in his subsequent text. Old-castle's syllabus, meant to encourage a "radically literal, anti-interpretive model of reading," shows up Hoccleve's striking contrast of approach to the threat of Lollardy before and after the Agincourt campaign.[76] "To the Garter Knights" will suggest that the spiritual stakes are much higher than those that in 1415 faced Oldcastle. Garter militarism, hardly analogous to Arthurian or pagan models, must be more rarified. This expectation applies to the king himself. Whereas the "Carol" exults at how under Henry's command at Agincourt "dukys and erlys lorde and barone / Were take and slayne and þat wel sone" (21–22), Hoccleve begins with nebulous praise of the king. Rather than depicting the preeminent knight as the destroyer of obstinate French *chevaliers*, he situates the Lancastrian within a specific tradition of centralized Roman Christianity, calling him

> heir & successour
> Un to Iustinians deuout tendrenesse
> In the feith of Ihesu
>
> (2–4)

before extending and enhancing the patrimony by likening Henry to

> Constantyn, thensaumple and the mirour
> To princes alle, in loue & buxumnesse
> To holy chirche.
>
> (10–12)

Hoccleve's references to the Roman past suggest knowledge of the fourteenth-century *Chronicles of Rome*, a translation of "the principal handbook of imperial and papal history for theologians and canon lawyers," the *Chronicon pontificium et imperatorum*: therein Constantine I is not only said to have obstructed "þe erresy of þe Aryanes" with "þe

---

[76] Nissé, "Oure fadres olde and modres," 297–98. Watt, *Hoccleve's "Series,"* argues, contrarily, that the full list would enable Oldcastle to "read ethically" about imperfect knights "in order to amend accordingly" (128)—but that would not fully justify inclusion of "Vegece," the *Epitoma rei militaris*, a well-known work of organization, tactics, and morale. On the *Re militari* as an ethical work to the extent that it reinforced a knight's "obedience to his lord and willingness to serve the public good," see C. T. Allmand, *The "De re militari" of Vegetius: The Reception, Transmission and Legacy of a Roman Text in the Middle Ages* (Cambridge: Cambridge University Press, 2011), 269. Cole, *Literature and Heresy*, explores Hoccleve's charitable investment in Oldcastle's chivalric "accordance with the secular virtue of mercy" (105) and opportunity for redemption.

conselle of Nycene" but is noted for "þe gret reuerence þat he dude to þe clergie."[77] Although both Constantine and Justinian, the great codifier for whom "deviants must be corrected or eliminated," had their own military credentials, these emperors were, in the milieu of the *Chronicles*, chiefly associated with statist ideological consolidation, benevolent or coercive as it might be.[78]

"To Oldcastle" also refers to both Constantine, a "christen Emperour/ whos worthynesse / Desdeyned nat to holy chirche obeye" (218–19), and to Justinian, who exercised "swich cheertee / To holy chirche" (433–34) by protecting its property ("goodes" [435])—just as the 1406 statutes advocated.[79] Furthermore, "To Oldcastle" invokes Justinian on a theological point central to "To the Garter Knights"—to see "þat no wight haue hardynesse . . . / Of the feith to despute more or lesse / Openly among peple" (25–28) through strong "lawe" (30). In Hoccleve's accounting, the Thracian

> Made a lawe deffending euery man,
> Of what condicion or what degree
> Þat he were of nat sholde hardy be
> For to despute of the feith openly.
>
> (187–90)[80]

With its law-and-order preoccupations, "To the Garter Knights" mitigates the kinetic language of chivalric glory with benevolent, stately epithets for Henry (notwithstanding some contrary effects):

---

[77] *The Chronicles of Rome: An Edition of the Middle English Chronicles of Popes and Emperors and The Lollard Chronicle*, ed. Dan Embree (Rochester, N.Y.: Boydell, 1999), 1–2, 53–54.

[78] "Justinian I," in *The Oxford Dictionary of the Classical World* (Oxford: Oxford University Press, 2007) (hereafter *ODCW*).

[79] "To Oldcastle" also includes Theodosius (I), who "as a lamb, to holy chirche obeide" (54). The *Chronicles* are content to record that Theodosius, "for his gret vertues, was wel iloved of þe heþen, & many, þoruʒ his styrryng, lefte her mawmetes [idols] & turned hem to Crist," the emperor being so "mylde & mercifulle" (59). While Theodosius's overall military success is debatable, "his religious policies mark a significant step in the developing alliance between Church and State, and were greeted with delight by Augustine" ("Theodosius I," in *ODCW*). As already noted, Hoccleve cites "Seint Austyn" in "To Oldcastle" on the dangers of "heresie or scisme" (34).

[80] As Hoccleve puts it earlier, "Lete holy chirche medle of the doctrine / Of Crystes laws, & of his byleeue, / And let alle othir folke there-to enclyne / And of our feith noon argumentes meeue" (137–40).

> o verray sustenour
> And piler of our feith, and werreyour
> Ageyn the heresies bittir galle,
> Do foorth, do foorth, continue your socour
> Holde vp Crystes Baner , lat it nat falle!
>
> (12–16)

Hoccleve's ideal is protective ("socour") as well as aggressive ("werre-your"), with clear Crusader associations ("Do foorth", "Crystes Baner"). But there will be no journey *outremer*. Hoccleve's poem concerns *England*, to which Henry had safely sailed with his tried, tired men that November, to be "receyued with moche ioie and worship."[81] His imperial discourse is unexpectedly constrained, almost parochialized. Horizons retract markedly in the face of imminent, devilish menace:

> And yit, this day the feendes fikilnesse
> Weeneth fully to cacche a tyme & hour
> To haue on vs, your liges, a sharp shour
> And to his seruiture/ vs knytte and thralle.
> But ay we truste in yow our protectour;
> On your constance we awayten alle.
>
> (19–24)

Through such ominous diction "heresy is set on its feet and sent walking in the land."[82] Meanwhile the dynamic warrior king is reimagined, his prowess tempered with loving attention to his endangered but "trusting" childlike "liges." Against the devil's "fikilnesse" Hoccleve poses Henry's homely, prophylactic "constance." The king's centrifugal aggression, Hoccleve implies, must be replaced with centripetal wariness.[83]

To make manifest his inner steadfastness ("*your* constance") while advancing the transnational league (with Sigismund) against heterodoxy

---

[81] *English Chronicle 1377–1461*, 45.

[82] Strohm, *England's Empty Throne*, 184.

[83] If "sharp shour" echoes a phrase from the *Regiment*—"What sorwe lamentable / Is causid of your werres sharpe shoures[?]" (5329–30)—appearing in a far-sighted lament on the Anglo-French conflict, then Hoccleve redeploys a phrase that captures the incalculable costs of inter-Christian discord more broadly. For the text, see Thomas Hoccleve, *The Regiment of Princes*, ed. Charles R. Blyth, TEAMS (Kalamazoo: Medieval Institute Publications, 1999), available at http://d.lib.rochester.edu/teams/text/blyth-hoccleve-regiment-of-princes (accessed July 27, 2019).

("your [C]onstance"), the future colonizer of continental territory is urged to become the destroyer of lawlessness and aberrance within. According to Nuttall, Hoccleve "positions the king not as a military or chivalric figure . . . but as an imperial defender of faith, characterized by obedience and subordination to ecclesiastical authority."[84] All the same, a uniquely localized, even vulnerable, kingly identity is projected as he is urged,

> Makith swich lawe/ & for aght may befalle,
> Obserue it wel/ ther to been yee dettour.
> Dooth so/ and god/ in glorie shal yow stalle.
>
> (30–32)

Perhaps with an allusion to his former flirtations with the Lollard scene, the king is reminded that he remains "dettour" to a higher *iudicium*. The first half of the poem thus ends by affirming Henry's own subjection, as he is made the direct object ("yow") in the final conditional clause: "god in glorie shal yow [in]stalle" only *if* his juridical duty is met.[85] But whereas in "To Oldcastle" Hoccleve had reminisced of knights "in tymes þat be past / When they had tendrenesse of hir office," "stidefast" yet docile to the priest who "hem goostly fedde, & yaf hem the notice / Of Chrystes lore" (209–14), "To the Garter Knights" omits all mention of prelates. And while the former poem affirmed that "moche is a popes auctoritee / Aboue a kynges might" (313–16), the latter attempts a *synthesis* of royalty and spirituality, whose transcendent point of reference is God alone.

Advising a realignment of chivalric militarism with local need, Hoccleve at this point shifts to the "treshonorable conpaignie du Iarter" itself as the auxiliary to the "tresnoble" monarch. This juxtaposition—anticipated in the plural "balades" of the manuscript rubric—should remind us of the formal splittings in Hoccleve's other major poems, including the *Regiment of Princes*, "To Oldcastle," and the *Series*. Lee Patterson notes, for example, that the holograph of "To Oldcastle" is also

---

[84] Nuttall, "Anti-Occasional Verse," 5, 7.

[85] *OED*, s.v. *stall* (v.[1]). The earliest recorded usage listed is none other than this very poem of Hoccleve's, here dated 1415. Nuttall, "Anti-Occasional Verse," reads here a reference to Henry's "physical installation in his individual stall as sovereign of the Garter" (4–5), but the term would have been used at any annual meeting. Its function in "To the Garter Knights" is metaphorical: becoming a Garter knight will not in itself defeat heresy.

organized into two roughly equal sections, the first addressing Oldcastle directly and the second "the heretics who have led him astray," with "a large initial at line 273, encouraging the reader to notice a redirection in the theme of the poem at that point."[86] Likewise, both equal parts of "To the Garter Knights" begin with illuminated capitals, the first only slighter darker and more elaborate than the second.

Since the text's purpose is to unite king and coterie for disciplined religious struggle, the break between the "balades"—marked with the large capital in "Yee"—attests to a fissure in the aristocratic sociopolitical fabric that the poem seeks to suture (hence, the opening and closing stanzas addressing the Order *as one*). Furthermore, Hoccleve's addressing the knights in the first stanza as "lordes of the garter, flour / Of Ch*ival*rie, as men yow clepe & calle" (5–6), implies another division, that between the Garter knights' essence and their clichéd ascriptions, hinting at a gap between reality and appearance.[87] The following plea, "The lord of vertu, and of grace Auctour, / Grante/ the fruyt of your loos nat appall*e*!" (7–8), verges upon insult, implying that the renown earned from secular achievements could redound upon them.

This second half of the poem is similarly hesitant about the "proper" application of chivalric attributes. The insistence on duty conveys the idea of a delinquent noble corpus:

> Yee lordes eek shynynge in noble fame
> To whiche approp[r]ed is the maintenance
> Of Crystes cause[:} In honour of his name
> Shoue on/ & putte his foos to the outraunce!
> God wolde so, so wolde eek yo[u]r ligeance:
> To tho two prikkith yow your duetee:
> Who so nat keepith this double obseruance
> Of meryt & hono*ur*/ nakid is he.
>
> (33–40)

The verse is trochaic, the images dynamic, but the action is not entirely the knights': "ligeance" is personified as having volition, while the knights, steed-like, are spurred by "duetee." Whether any of them will fulfill this role is in question. Doubt is reinforced by Hoccleve's single

---

[86] Lee Patterson, " 'What is me?': Hoccleve and the Trials of the Urban Self," in *Acts of Recognition*, 84–109 (101).

[87] Yeager, "Pax poetica," 115–16, considers such knightly pretension.

marginal note for the poem (in the same brown ink, the letters roughly half the size of the verses), which begins just to the right of the word "ligeance": "*Quorum* Rex illa*m*/ iustissi*m*am p*a*rtem/ tenet" (of which the king holds that most rightful part). The annotation suggests, just at the moment of a fuller address to the Garter, the company as an incomplete accessory to Henry's primacy.

As elsewhere in his work, Hoccleve espouses fears of "a deviation from the selfhood prescribed by society," in this case among the most potent secular power.[88] To inspire their rectification, Hoccleve offers the warning that those who cannot sustain the "double obseruance / Of meryt & hono*ur*/ nakid is he," purposively alluding in the next stanza to the Garter's motto *Honi soit qui mal y pense*:

> Your style seith/ þ*a*t yee been foos to shame.
> Now kythe [make known] of your feith, the p*er*seu*er*ance
> In which an heep of vs arn halt & lame.

> (41–43)

Here "style," meaning at once "appellation," "manner," and "behavior," connotes empty honorifics, or perhaps the effeminate courtly clothes and mannerisms that Hoccleve derided in the *Regiment*.[89] For emphasis, Hoccleve produces the repetition of "foos" in the preceding stanza (36) where it obviously designates the heretics, while reminding us, through eye rhyme, of the knights' doubtful "loos" (8). Against such decadence, the Garter knights must enact their "feith" and not just their manpower. As Andrew Lynch shows, Hoccleve's critique of aristocratic masculinity combined scorn for "prowess in fighting, love *par amour*, conspicuous consumption, and concern for public status."[90] His worry would have been even stronger if he had inherited any sense of "the overweening territorial, sexual, and temporal, in a word terrestrial, dispensation of the monarchy and aristocracy" that, according to Francis Ingledew, adumbrated the Garter's founding.[91] "The Order's rich mantles and collars," Nuttall paraphrases, "are insignificant and as if nonexistent if the Garter Knights do not overcome Christ's heretical foes."[92]

---

[88] Patterson, "What is me?," 102.
[89] *OED*, s.v. *style* (n.); Nissé, "Oure fadres olde and modres," 282.
[90] Lynch, "Manly cowardyse," 308.
[91] Francis Ingledew, *"Sir Gawain and the Green Knight" and the Order of the Garter* (Notre Dame: Notre Dame University Press, 2006), 157.
[92] Nuttall, "Anti-Occasional Verse," 4.

Hoccleve brings to his depiction of the Garter knights as supercilious, modish, and unready an unflattering comparison: with the "heep" of commoners—Hoccleve presumably included—who, albeit "halt & lame," make up a part of the social whole. This adjectival phrase is the poem's only hint of the authorial impotence—physical, psychic, social— that pervades an oeuvre full of "aggressive self-denigration."[93] Otherwise, the poet commands, no less than he entreats, his noble auditors. Indeed, defeating this subtle antagonist will require enlisting the whole people of the realm, with their monarch at the apex:

> Our Cristen kyng of Engeland & France,
> And yee, my lordes, with your alliance,
> And othir feithful peple þat ther be,
> Truste I to god, shul qwenche al this nusance,
> And this land sette in hy prosperitee.
>
> (44–48)

More vigilance than valor is required, it seems, to defeat *mescreance*.

It's a bold reconceptualization of Henry's Garter, at once "a perpetual chivalric memorial to Edward III's continental ambitions" and a tool "to cultivate a body of tried and trusted soldiers who were to be the mainstay" of his French campaigns—as mentioned in "To Oldcastle."[94] Less sympathetic to these goals in 1416, Hoccleve stresses close cooperation ("your alliance") between king and knights without excluding "othir feithful peple þat ther be," all while avoiding references to action abroad. All that we hear of the Continent—*France*—is contained in a formulaic holdover deriving from Henry IV that might just as well assure us that it need *not* be fought for.[95] Whatever the Garter knights have recently achieved—and the still glossy "fruyt of your loos" suggests the feats of honorees such as Sir William Harrington and Sir John Holland at Agincourt itself—is behind them.

---

[93] Knapp, "Thomas Hoccleve," 193.

[94] David Green, *The Hundred Years War: A People's History* (New Haven: Yale University Press, 2014), 36; Hugh Collins, "The Order of the Garter, 1348–1461: Chivalry and Politics in Later Medieval England," in *Courts, Counties and the Capital in the Later Middle Ages*, ed. Diana E. S. Dunn (New York: St. Martin's Press, 1996), 155–80 (170).

[95] Given-Wilson, *Henry IV*, 332. As the nouns in the phrase were reversed to produce a new "national" center of gravity, the epithet does not, for Given-Wilson, necessarily possess the colonial valence associated with the transnational aggregation and administration of disparate territories (as inherited by Henry IV and actively sought by Henry V); on this difference, and England's "disintegrating empire," see Chap. 15.

An "yle" of "hethenesse"

As Kathy Lavezzo suggests, "images of a cohesive nation" tend to arise from situations experienced as large-scale threats to community.[96] Attending to the home front, Hoccleve's third stanza begins, "This yle, or [ere] this, had been but hethenesse, / Nad been of your feith the force and vigour" (17–18). His topographic phrasing not only supports Jill Havens's claim, in a related context, "that the *peoples* occupying the island of England were ready to think of themselves as separate, linguistically and spiritually, from the Continent"; it also demonstrates that Hoccleve's depiction of a crisis-ridden realm employed the same discourse as that of his enemies, the Lollards, who linked "personal salvation . . . to the greater interests of the English nation and its continuity and stability."[97] With a pun on *hethen* (OE *hæþ*), suggesting a land wasted by heterodoxy, Hoccleve marks traditional geographical boundaries—and the people defined thereby—at a time when Henry's political aspirations in France blurred them.[98] Consequently, his repurposed Company of the Garter will muster not on distant *campagnes* but in the English countryside, towns, and parishes to weed out dissenters and plotters.

A linkage of spiritual evil with *lèse majesté* provided the perfect target, or pretext, for Hoccleve's rededicated Garter knights.[99] It is precisely because, as the *Gesta* presents it, Oldcastle sought "to overthrow both the spiritual and the temporal estate [in subversionem status utriusque mucronis]" (2–4) that Lollardy could be depicted as an attempt against "the very source of established order."[100] As the English Chronicler captures the events of early 1414:

And þis same yere were take L[oll]ardez and heretikes þat hadded purposed throgh her false treson to have slayn þe kynge and *the lordes spirituell and temporell* and destroye[d] all the clergie off þe reame. But the kynge, as Godde wolde, wasse warned of þer false purpose and ordenaunce, and wente into Fikettis

---

[96] Kathy Lavezzo, *Angels on the Edge of the World: Geography, Literature, and English Community, 1000–1534* (Ithaca: Cornell University Press, 2006), 33.

[97] Havens, "As Englishe is comoun langage," 100, 107.

[98] Patterson, "Making Identities," 143–44; Derek Pearsall, "The Idea of Englishness in the Fifteenth Century," in Cooney, *Nation, Court, and Culture*, 15–27 (21).

[99] See Margaret Aston, "Lollardy and Sedition 1381–1431," *Past & Present* 17 (1960): 1–44.

[100] Allmand, *Henry V*, 280.

Felde *beside London*, and Maister Thomas Arundell, Archbisshope of Caunturbury, *toke with hym a notable peple and lete kepe the weyes aboute London.*[101]

The true extent of the crisis that elicited the king's "bold, expeditious ride with few troops from Westminster to Clerkenwell" remains questionable, the uprising itself, according to Pearsall, "greatly exaggerated and certainly stage-managed."[102] Nonetheless, such an event (whether, in Richard Rex's revealing formulation, "coup or demonstration"[103]) multiplied opportunities for any sign of heterodoxy to trigger stern reaction by lay and ecclesiastical powers because the danger was seen not only as an abstract, scholarly one.

In this panicky spirit did the 1414 Lollard statutes drafted a few months later represent Lollardy as a threat not merely to orthodoxy but to "all manner of governance, and ultimately the laws of the land" (item XII). Their terms included a directive enabling all offices of government, from chancellor to justice to municipal bailiff, "de mettre leur entire peyn et diligence d'oustier, et faire oustier, cesser, et destruier, toutz maners heresies et errours appellez vulgairement Lollardries."[104] This codifying of secular bodies as the arm of a churchly "thought police" is subsequently enhanced by item XIII, a statute that facilitates the arrest, restraint, and interrogation of "trespassours ou maffesours [malefactors]," and then, more broadly and redundantly, by item XIV, emphasizing "diverses murdres, homicides, robberies, batteries, assemblees de gentz en graunde nombre par manere d'insurrection, et de diverses autres rebellions et riotes"; this establishes the right for the king or his chancellor to issue orders of arrest for fugitives in "diverses bois et lieux covertez et disconuz, et aillours."[105]

Thus the 1414 statutes seize every opportunity to raise and conflate dangers, running swiftly from the arcane "heresies et errours" perpetrated by Wycliffites to the palpable but no less mysterious "lieux covertez et disconuz" held by ne'er-do-wells. Such a comprehensive evil

---

[101] *English Chronicle 1377–1461*, 42 (emphasis added).

[102] Maureen Jurkowski, "Henry V's Suppression of the Oldcastle Revolt," in *Henry V: New Interpretations*, ed. Gwilym Dodd (Woodbridge: Boydell, 2013), 103–29 (126); Derek Pearsall, "Crowned King: War and Peace in 1415," in *The Lancastrian Court: Proceedings of the 2001 Harlaxton Symposium*, ed. Jenny Stratford (Donington: Shaun Tyas, 2003), 163–72 (164). See also Jeremy Catto, "Religious Change under Henry V," in *Henry V: The Practice of Kingship*, ed. G. L. Harriss (Stroud: Alan Sutton, 1993), 114–15.

[103] Richard Rex, *The Lollards* (Houndmills: Macmillan, 2002), 85.

[104] *Parliament Rolls*, Henry V, 1414 April, iv.24.

[105] Ibid., Henry V, 1414 April, iv.25, 26.

demands a community-wide synthesis of effort, with lay and priestly figures "working hand-in-hand," along with the involvement of everyday people acting as informers and witnesses.[106] In "To the Garter Knights," likewise, Hoccleve redefines elite militarism so that it need not be associated primarily with mass mobilization, armed encampment, siege, and *chevauchée*. The concerted "programme of law enforcement" urged by Henry and articulated in Parliament's actions, with the fusion of treason and heresy at their core, implied that any secular juridical response to social disorder was also effectively hallowed, bonded to "Crystes cause" (56).[107]

Hoccleve's strategy involved sustaining the atmospherics for that new militarism, which would require as much watchfulness as aggression. Central to this project was, unsurprisingly, the figure of Oldcastle, who becomes a blend of the bandit and the sophistical demon. According to the *Gesta*, he not only commanded "those turbulent people who throughout divers parts of England had been grievously afflicted by such a malignant disease [turbine populi, quem per diversas partes Anglie pestis huiusmodi inviscarat]" (2–4) but also, "devot[ing] himself to Satan, from that time on lurked in holes and corners [in antris et latibulis latitavit] out of the sight of men, and indeed still does, like another Cain, a vagabond and a fugitive upon the face of the earth [vagus et profugus super terram]" (8–9).[108]

But how does an English nobleman sporting the Garter insignia fight a sprite like this? Such a figure, to be bested by faith and contrition, as in a psychomachia, could risk obviating the nobility's military purpose entirely. Wary of that possibility, Hoccleve's "To the Garter Knights" could be said to reimplement the infernal dramatics of January 1414 with his own dense network of deixes and metaphors. In the *Gesta*'s account of the 1414 uprising, for example, we hear how "on the next day after the king had moved to his palace of Westminster [January 9],

---

[106] Patterson, "What is me?," 97. See also Forrest, *Detection*, 237–39.

[107] Powell, *Kingship*, 141. As a result of this thickened veneer of religiosity, the less spectacular, indeed quotidian, violence inherent in feudal society is advanced. Even more so since this lay–religious arrangement also confers quasi-military associations on the clergy, as when the *Gesta* refers to Archbishop Arundel, "than whom from olden times no man has been found braver in fighting Christ's battles [strenuior in preliis Christi] and opposing seditious men" (*Gesta*, 4–5).

[108] "To Oldcastle" imagines something similar, with persistent references to "dirknesse" (lines 15, 24, 384, 478) and devils, and a touch of the same physical immediacy, as when Hoccleve implores Oldcastle, "Do by my reed / it shal be for thy prow: / fflee fro the ffeend" (239–40).

this same *raven of treachery* ["idem corvus perfidie": Oldcastle]—with those *his crows* who, as arranged, were to flock to him from almost every part of England—*there in the neighborhood of the city*, next to St. Giles Hospital (which is *within a mile of the palace*), resolved to take the field by night" (7–9, emphasis added). We find a similarly menacing being in the second half of "To Oldcastle," where the knight's doomed conspirators, who eventually will be "enhabited with Sathanas" (280), assail the narrow path of virtue before retreating

> to halkes [and] to hernes
> As yee [Oldcastle] doon/ þat holden the feendes syde,
> Whiche arn of dirknesse the lanternes.
> (282–84)[109]

There too, since the Lollard threat is both spiritual and physical, it is scarcely visible yet tangible, like a "disease" or "pestilence" (5 and 9), and yet creaturely, with Oldcastle "the raven of treachery" leading his locust-like "crows" as well as, fox- or snake-like, "lurk[ing] in holes and corners" (9).

Furthermore, the *Gesta* observes that Oldcastle, "this enemy and subverter of the Church," "swollen with the list to dominate," and hence "easily deformed into a beast," would be divinely "root[ed] out like barren trees [arbores steriles]" (11). Likewise, in the penultimate, seventh, stanza Hoccleve provides metaphorical references to *wood* (a pun) and *root* (sustaining the earlier pun on *heth*), a burst of georgics suggesting that Henry's knights should locate and eradicate the human equivalents of invasive weeds ready to spoil the crop:

> Conqueste of hy prowesse is for to tame
> The wylde woodnesse of this mescreance
> Right to the roote/ rype yee þat same!
> (49–51)

His agricultural diction, blazoned by consonance, evokes (to a horrid end) the resurgent vegetal imagery of Chaucer's *General Prologue*. We

---

[109] *OED*, s.v. ° *halke* (n.). Both *halke* and *hern* can mean "corner," "nook," "recess," "hiding-place." *Halke* appears again near the end when Hoccleve warns, "yee feendes, yee / In the dirke halke of Helle shul descende" (477–78), the images recalling the "diverses bois et lieux covertez et disconuz" in the 1414 statute. Hoccleve's formulation "lanterne of dirknesse" also cancels the presumption of the Lollard tract *Lanterne of Liȝt*.

have already seen this construction, when the king was directed to "where errour / Spryngith alday,/ & engendrith rumour" (28–29). Redeploying the vision of England as "hæþ," Hoccleve suggests that a land of plenty and nourishment (cf. "the fruyt of your loos" [8]) will be overrun and desolated. Counteracting it demands a bloody husbandry. So in urging the Garter fellowship to "rype" out the "roote" Hoccleve uses a verb that in the fifteenth century could mean not only to "rifle" and "rummage" but also to "search out" and "plough/dig up."[110]

In short, in accordance with the new antiheresy legislation, the Garter will use its powers and its weapons to search and seize—but within the symbolic framework of cleansing the land. "Analogies of contagion, infection, botanical invasion, and poison," Forrest writes, "were pervasive in anti-heretical texts in all periods and places."[111] It is apropos in this respect that the "multifaceted patronage" and martyrology of the Garter's figurehead, St. George, encompass activities that contrast significantly with his militarism: according to Jonathan Good's cultural history, Ælfric, the eleventh-century archbishop of York, wrote an Anglo-Saxon Passion of St. George in which, uniquely, the captive before death prays for rain-showers to replenish a scorched earth—one of a number of agricultural associations perhaps tied to his name, "from geos and ergon, mean[ing] 'earth-worker,' or farmer."[112]

In Hoccleve's hands such natural associations complement the chivalric. In a culture that celebrated the reenactment of Christ's agonies, an elite, ascetic militarism like that of St. George, famed for his "heroic resistance to torture for the sake of Christ," will not only enhance collaboration between lay and Church law but will also counteract the sinful tendencies of temporal existence, so that healing occurs both inwardly and socially.[113] After all, Lollard disturbances were, it was thought, exacerbated by age-old honor-based violence among the nobles, especially in northern shires, where under Henry V's tenure we find "a political and social vacuum at local level waiting to be filled."[114] To that end Hoccleve's concluding emphasis falls not on the Garter knights' capacity for violence per se but on their self-awareness and discipline:

[110] OED, s.v. ripe (v.[2]).
[111] Forrest, Detection, 155.
[112] Jonathan Good, The Cult of Saint George in Medieval England (Woodbridge: Boydell Press, 2009), 4, 31–32.
[113] Ibid., 32.
[114] Allmand, Henry V, 315.

> Sleepe nat this/ but for goddes plesance
> And his modres/ & in signifiance
> Þat yee been of seint Georges liueree,
> Dooth him seruice and knyghtly obeissance!
> ffor Crystes cause is his, wel knowen yee.
>
> (52–56)

Partnership and solidarity, vertical and horizontal, are the lesson. Hoccleve presents the fusion of St. George and Christ in a way that "bond[s] meritorious suffering to all licit, loyal service to kin and lord" while mitigating prowess with forbearance:[115]

> Stif stande in þat/ & yee shuln greeue & grame
> The fo to pees/ & norice of distaunce;
> That now is ernest/ torne it in to game.
>
> (57–59)

The implication is that inner strength (e.g., Henry as "pillar") can mean the defeat of the foe who (in another pun) is not only smashed to *pieces* but also brought to *peace*, his "distaunce" (discord) made "game."[116] All that remains is a reinstatement of the fundamental principles that will seal this collaboration:

> Dampnable fro feith were variance!
> Lord lige/ & lordes, haue in remembraunce,
> Lord of al is the blissid Trinitee,
> Of whos vertu/ the mighty habundaunce
> Yow herte & strengthe in feithful vnitee! Amen!
>
> (60–64)

The Order of the Garter is loaded with spiritual vigor, ready for action but momentarily restrained.

Thomas as Tragedian

Rosemary Horrox writes of a king's need to "impose dispute resolution on the great men of the realm" just as the king required the noblemen

---

[115] Richard W. Kaeuper, *Holy Warriors: The Religious Ideology of Chivalry* (Philadelphia: University of Pennsylvania Press, 2009), 113.
[116] *OED*, s.v. *piece* (n.).

to act as "his chief advisors, his military commanders, his most powerful agents in the localities."[117] Hoccleve's twin appeal to king and Garter knights attempts a similar mediation. In the joined "balades" the aristocratic monopoly of violence is "organically" diffused throughout the peerage even as the competitive, secular tendencies of the fellowship are checked. In this double movement Henry's popularized piety is extended to enhance his affinity, while the decentralized, conservative influence of the landed aristocracy mitigates the solipsistic, risk-taking compulsion behind aggressive kingship.[118] Even so, while the preponderance of Hoccleve's doubt in the poem concerns the king's subordinates, Henry's own persona is dulled within the context of aristocratic egotism marking the Garter brotherhood.

"By long tradition one of the positive characteristics expected of a king was that he should be a soldier," Allmand writes.[119] Henry V would successfully embody the ruler as the physical guarantor and model of duty, order, and justice, in a way that, for different reasons, neither his father (thwarted crusader) nor Richard II (dishonorable pursuer of peace with France) had managed. Nonetheless, waging war must align with that "bone et jouste Governance" marking so much official Lancastrian discourse. "Englishmen wanted their kings to return victorious from battle," Kaeuper cautions, "yet they no less expected them to settle their disputes with neighbours, and to hear their plaints against royal officers, to provide a central administration and in the process to insure a tolerable level of public order."[120] Dedicated to the soldier's life, however, Henry V "spent less than half his reign in England, and much of that in active preparation for war."[121] After Agincourt he mobilized

---

[117] Rosemary Horrox, "England: Kingship and Political Community, 1377–c. 1500," in *A Companion to Britain in the Later Middle Ages*, ed. S. H. Rigby (Oxford: Blackwell, 2003), 224–41 (233).

[118] Such an organic vision falls within what Simpson calls "the Aristotelian vernacular tradition" (*Reform*, 224), wherein the human body is a powerful analogue for society, and where political life is founded upon obligatory and complementary material practice. See also Stephen H. Rigby, "Aristotle for Aristocrats and Poets: Giles of Rome's *De regimine principum* as Theodicy of Privilege," *ChauR* 46, no. 3 (2012): 259–313.

[119] C. T. Allmand, "Henry V the Soldier, and the War in France," in Harriss, *Henry V*, 118–35 (118).

[120] Richard W. Kaeuper, *War, Justice, and Public Order: England and France in the Later Middle Ages* (Oxford: Clarendon Press, 1988), 129.

[121] Edward Powell, "The Restoration of Law and Order," in Harriss, *Henry V*, 53–74 (53). Like G. L. Harriss, "The Management of Parliament," in Harriss, *Henry V*, 137–58 (146), Allmand, *Henry V* (376), notes Henry's absenteeism, making inexplicable his epilogue's melancholic musing that Henry's administrative and juristic achievements "at home" went largely unrecorded in the chronicles (442).

his countrymen's moral and material support for two more campaigns, in 1417 and 1421, and repeatedly took center stage—until a relentless cycle of grueling and increasingly static sieges brought exhaustion and fatal illness, leaving his realm with an infant heir.

In 1416 Hoccleve could not predict the worst outcomes of Henry's obsessive relocation to Normandy. Taxation, debt, property seizures, conscription, and the years-long relocation of the king and his warrior nobles abroad would threaten public order, trade, fiscal resources, international relations, and even Englishness.[122] Hoccleve could, however, certainly anticipate the widening scope of Henry's desire. Venting his frustration with chivalric vainglory, in "To the Garter Knights" he urges knightly ferocity—but as a redirection of post-Agincourt incitements toward action abroad. With an irony that would perhaps have shocked the author, this poem testifies to an "existential shift" traceable to figures such as Wyclif himself, during whose career "war began to be understood as a violation of the state of peace rather than as constituting a natural state of being in itself."[123] In January 1395 a Lollard bill condemning war was posted at both Westminster Hall and St Paul's Cathedral, while John Clanvowe observed bitterly in *The Two Ways* that "þe world holt hem worshipful þat been greet werryours and fiȝteres and þat distroyen and wynnen manye londis."[124] Gower's *In Praise of Peace* urged the just-crowned Henry IV to reestablish Richard's truce with France rather than aggravate the turmoil at hand.[125] Even the alliterative epic *Morte Arthure* serves up competing tyrannies, waves of knightly gore, and cumulative civilian desolation.[126]

[122] Recognition of the human toll and vanishing revenues that were required of voluntary, large-scale violence eventually came—"even at the moment of most prepossessing success in France" (Strohm, *England's Empty Throne*, 85). On the tapering-off of funds consistent with the Commons' restrictions on direct taxation for defensive purposes only, see Harriss, "Management of Parliament," 144–51. See also Craig Taylor, "Henry V, Flower of Chivalry," in Dodd, *Henry V*, 217–48 (232); and Pearsall, "Crowned King," 167.

[123] Cox, *Wyclif*, 96.

[124] Allmand, *Henry V*, 284; V. J. Scattergood, "*The Two Ways*: An Unpublished Religious Treatise by Sir John Clanvowe," *English Philological Studies* 10 (1967): 33–56 (47). Notably, Rex, *Lollards*, ignores Lollards' attitudes to war.

[125] Sobecki, "Ecce patet tensus," 935.

[126] Michael Prestwich, *The Three Edwards: War and State in England, 1272–1377* (New York: St. Martin's Press, 1980), 211; Lowe, *Imagining Peace*, 125–26; Geraldine Heng, *Empire of Magic: Medieval Romance and the Politics of Cultural Fantasy* (New York: Columbia University Press, 2003), Chap. 3. Symbolically, the epic nears its close with an image of the southwestern coastline of England, having been abandoned by Arthur, resisting his low-tide landing.

Of course, scholars have long situated Hoccleve within a metropolitan, Chaucerian milieu, far from the "markedly clerical" and provincial alliterative tradition whose poets "attended to the treachery, destruction, and sacrifice of the innocent that served as the origin for English claims to empire."[127] On the other hand, as Ralph Hanna and Bowers remind us, prominent alliterative works, as well as their authors, circulated among the courts and offices of Chaucer's London.[128] More to the point, "To the Garter Knights" itself is a modestly alliterative little poem—a surprising designation only if our concept of the tradition means "prioritizing unrhymed long-lines" above that wider thematic investment among vernacular clerks in "*gesta*" and "governance."[129]

Although, as Judith Jefferson argues, Hoccleve was a careful adherent to rhymed iambic pentameter, we can note this poem's energetic clusters of consonantal stress (as well as some "half-line" caesuras).[130] Carefully placed, they recall the recherché alliteration that Chaucer employed for the tumultuous tourney scene in *The Knight's Tale*. Hoccleve's imitative gesture in such a verse, a bastardized alliteration, not only conveys the resonance of knightly aggression, however; it also sustains, stylistically, Nuttall's argument that his aspirations and affiliations were primarily ecclesiastical and only secondarily Lancastrian: "Hoccleve was not an official poet or proto-laureate, but rather, at least in some parts of his diverse literary career, a clerical commentator, occupying in verse a position analogous to that of a preacher, prayer-giver, adviser, or educator. This is a less familiar Hoccleve to us at present, but one who is ripe for future research."[131] That said, Nuttall's assumption that Hoccleve's moralizing verse should be appraised independently of its utility for the Lancastrians omits to consider the *dialectic* of kingly and churchly apparatuses as co-dependent instruments of hegemony. Hence Hoccleve's insistence on the figure of the emperor, a hybrid but in the last resort a temporal power.

---

[127] Alex Mueller, *Translating Troy: Provincial Politics in Alliterative Romance* (Columbus: Ohio University Press, 2013), 222, 228.

[128] Ralph Hanna, "Alliterative Poetry," in Wallace, *The Cambridge History of Medieval English Literature*, 488–512 (509–11); Bowers, *Chaucer and Langland*, 15.

[129] Hanna, "Alliterative Poetry," 504.

[130] Judith A. Jefferson, "The Hoccleve Holographs and Hoccleve's Metrical Practice: More than Counting Syllables?," *Parergon* 18 (2000): 203–26. Accentual consonance is decisive at lines 1–3, 6, 9, 18, 19, 21, 26, 32, 35, 41, 43, 50–51, 56–57, 61.

[131] Nuttall, "Anti-Occasional Verse," 9. See also Classen, "Hoccleve's Independence," 70; and Burrow, "Hoccleve and Chaucer," 56.

Hoccleve asks the king and Garter not to lay down arms but to wield them suitably against heathenish dangers to the realm, naturalizing a warrior elite that shall "greeue & grame / The fo to pees." Indeed, Hoccleve's religiosity had not prevented him from preparing in 1415 eighteen documents relating to indentures and advances in order to secure the commitment of Henry's commanders, or from urging participation in that same campaign in "To Oldcastle."[132] As Lynch summarizes, Hoccleve at once "counsels against war, yet praises chivalry in war. Because right sometimes has to be maintained by force, courage in battle is a necessity, for the good of the king's people and the Church."[133] He does, however, significantly depart from other poets, including the author of the contemporaneous *The Crowned King*, whose critique of the costs of war nonetheless hesitates to imagine the renunciation of adventurism:

> Cherissh thy champyons and chief men of armes;
> And such as presoners mowe pike [despoil] with poyntes of werre,
> Let hem [welde] that they wynne and worthyly hem thonke;
> And such as castels mowe cache, or eny clos tounes,
> Geve hem as gladly—than shalt thou gete hertes.[134]

For this alliterative poet, a monarch must manage the distribution of booty with largesse, not avarice, while the conventional practices—siege, slaughter, seizure, ransom—are accepted.

More astutely, Henry carefully sought to rationalize and sanctify most aspects of the war on the Valois, but such justification could not be easily squared with a legalistic conflict waged on the other side of the Channel, and therefore doubly reminiscent of Edward III (whose disappointing 1359–60 Normandy campaign prompted the "insular" literary reorientation in which Langland thrived).[135] Hoccleve would argue that the nobility could do better, for itself and the realm, by facing off with devilish plots in the courts and counties. Only months before, the Southampton plotters, intentionally or not, turned attention from French guile with a dramatic reminder that the dynastic question remained unsettled, reawakening "fears that the Welsh might rise in

---

[132] Mooney, "Some New Light on Thomas Hoccleve," 310.

[133] Lynch, "Manly Cowardyse," 310.

[134] *The "Piers Plowman" Tradition: A Critical Edition of "Pierce the Plowman's Crede," "Richard the Redeless," "Mum and the Sothsegger," and "The Crowned King,"* ed. Helen Barr (London: J. M. Dent, 1993), 203–10, lines 94–98.

[135] Bowers, *Chaucer and Langland*, Chap. 2.

alliance with the Scots and the fugitive Sir John Oldcastle."[136] "To the Garter Knights" aggravates the nightmare of Henry's ship of state foundering in the gale of chivalric ambition with dread that the absence of the warrior nobility would bring more social and spiritual delinquency.

True to his image, Hoccleve "serves the ends of monarchical survival"—but indirectly.[137] "The Prince, like his father, viewed the Lollards as an opportunity rather than a threat," Strohm explains, "and Hoccleve was fully complicit in the interested invocation of anti-Lollard sentiment at crucial junctures in both reigns."[138] But a crucial difference between the kings' and the poet's *bête noire* would emerge over the course of the younger Henry's early reign. Both kings had attempted to make Lollardy a pretext for their rule following Richard's overthrow. Yet after 1414 Henry V could not put the genie back in the bottle. Contrary to his intentions, this double threat to Crown and Church continued to menace the land, especially in the guise of Oldcastle, *just* as Henry planned to leave England again. Contrary to his reputation as "a tame political counsellor," Hoccleve was not doing his master's bidding in 1416 by reminding all of the lurking danger that they had vivified.[139] Indeed, his material situation at that time reflected a changed reception. Whatever post-*Regiment* recognition came to Hoccleve, "all this was over, for whatever reason, soon after 1415, and by 1419 Hoccleve was looking for a new patron."[140] Indeed, if "the *Regiment* could have been seen as a dissenting document" on the subject of foreign war, perhaps Hoccleve's intervention in "To the Garter Knights" was nothing less than a reminder to the king of an earlier affront.[141]

---

[136] Powell, *Kingship*, 200.
[137] Simpson, *Reform*, 263.
[138] Strohm, *England's Empty Throne*, 182–83.
[139] Lynch, "Manly cowardyse," 306.
[140] Pearsall, "Hoccleve's *Regement of Princes*," 410.
[141] Lynch, "Manly cowardyce," 316.

Listening for Lyric Voice in Sermon Verses and *The Book of Margery Kempe*

Ann Killian
Ohio Dominican University

Abstract

Preachers valued poetry, not only for its affective power, but also for its capacity to signal changes in voice. Verses embedded in sermons audibly mark passages wherein the preacher ventriloquizes the voice of Christ or scripts a prayer for congregants to use. This essay analyzes the verses in a macaronic sermon for Good Friday on the theme *Amore langueo* to show that preachers deployed vernacular poetry as a stylistic marker of "familiar conversation," or intimate speech. It demonstrates the success of this preacherly strategy by identifying traces of sermon verses in *The Book of Margery Kempe*. Kempe attended sermons often enough to have acquired an intuitive understanding of their formal composition and rhetorical techniques. Kempe's *Book* participates in sermon culture by incorporating themes and forms related to the genre. Stitched into *The Book*'s prose is a web of poetic verses, which have generally passed unnoticed in Kempe scholarship. Kempe composed these embedded verses in imitation of preacherly discourse. The lyrics represent her prayer dialogues with Christ as a kind of intimate speech, befitting her relationship with him as beloved daughter and bride.

Keywords

sermon verses; macaronic sermons; Good Friday; *Amore langueo*; Margery Kempe; intimate speech; dalliance; familiar conversation

Poetic verses in sermons serve a rhetorical as much as a mnemonic function. This point has been made by Siegfried Wenzel and Alan

This essay has benefited from the attention of many generous readers. In particular, I would like to thank Ardis Butterfield, Alastair Minnis, Jessica Brantley, and members of the Yale Medieval Colloquium. I appreciated the opportunity to present this material at the 2018 Annual Meeting of the Medieval Academy of America. I am grateful to the journal's two anonymous readers, who offered detailed and helpful comments, and to the current and former editors of *SAC* for their support. Any remaining errors are my own.

Fletcher, both of whom cite the example of Christ's appeal from the cross.[1] In Latin and macaronic sermons from late medieval England, preachers embedded lyrics that give voice to Christ as part of a rhetorical strategy to move audiences toward conversion of heart. How effective was this strategy, and what evidence do we have, apart from the sermon texts themselves, that might help us assess how audiences responded? In this essay I argue that we can see traces of sermon verses in *The Book of Margery Kempe*, a text produced collaboratively by a laywoman and her clerical amanuensis. My aim is twofold: to show, first, that preachers valued vernacular poetry as a stylistic marker of "familiar conversation," or intimate speech; second, that *The Book of Margery Kempe* participates in sermon culture by incorporating themes and forms related to the genre. Traces of sermon performances in Kempe's text invite us to rethink how we talk about the literary sources of a work composed by a laywoman who, though "not lettryd" (4290), rehearses Scripture with an ease that astonished medieval clerics and incited charges of heresy.[2]

Medieval preachers deployed a gamut of rhetorical tropes in their efforts to capture audiences' goodwill. Preaching manuals recommend the use of exempla, insisting that their concrete narrative content proves especially persuasive to lay audiences.[3] Lyrics similarly arrest listeners' attention by evoking particular human experiences. Although the manuals lack an explicit theory of poetics, Rita Copeland has offered this assessment: "Preaching sought to capture the emotional capacity of poetry by turning to its concrete, affective language."[4] Vernacular

---

[1] Siegfried Wenzel's extensive scholarship changed the field's understanding of sermon verses. Whereas scholars had assumed their function to be primarily mnemonic, Wenzel made a case for their structural and rhetorical importance to sermon composition; see Siegfried Wenzel, *Preachers, Poets, and the Early English Lyric* (Princeton: Princeton University Press, 1986), 13–15. On popular sermons "both as a host for, and also a generator of, vernacular lyric poetry," see Alan J. Fletcher, *Late Medieval Popular Preaching in Britain and Ireland: Texts, Studies, and Interpretations* (Turnhout: Brepols, 2009), 273–305 (292).

[2] Citations by line number from *The Book of Margery Kempe*, ed. Barry Windeatt (Woodbridge: D. S. Brewer, 2004).

[3] On preachers' use of vernacular styles and speech genres to make clerical learning accessible to lay audiences, see Claire M. Waters, *Angels and Earthly Creatures: Preaching, Performance, and Gender in the Later Middle Ages* (Philadelphia: University of Pennsylvania Press, 2004), 57–72.

[4] Rita Copeland, "Pathos and Pastoralism: Aristotle's Rhetoric in Medieval England," *Speculum* 89, no. 1 (2014): 96–127 (127). Nicolette Zeeman notes the lack of an explicit poetic theory from medieval England and discusses the implications for scholarship on Middle English lyrics in "The Theory of Passionate Song," in *Medieval Latin and Middle English Literature: Essays in Honour of Jill Mann*, ed. Christopher Cannon and Maura Nolan (Cambridge: D. S. Brewer, 2011), 231–51.

poetry earned its place in sermon culture by moving the audience to feel. Preachers relied on poetry to express affect through direct address, such as Christ's requests for loving compassion.[5]

To assess the reception of sermon verses among lay audiences, I turn to *The Book of Margery Kempe*. Completed in 1436, *The Book* relates the conversion and spiritual experiences of an illiterate laywoman from Norwich who, though a burgess's wife and mother, devotes herself to pilgrimage and prayer. A large part of the text records memorial accounts of Kempe's mental dialogues with Christ.[6] Kempe describes Christ's manner of speaking to her by thought as a kind of "dalyawns," or intimate conversation.[7] In David Lavinsky's view, the term "dalyawns" expresses her "fervent, even childlike celebration of a loving and compassionate Jesus" and her "state of figurative betrothal to the incarnate Jesus."[8]

Kempe seems to have assimilated this intimate conversational style through hearing the language of others. Mikhail Bakhtin's theory of speech genres proves helpful in thinking through the process by which an individual comes to adopt a generic style.[9] To construct an individual

[5] Siegfried Wenzel has posited that "the tendency to establish an intimate emotional relationship between two characters finds its fullest realization in several dialogue lyrics" between Christ and his mother at the Crucifixion, and even that "utilization of the dialogue form was the work of preachers" (*Preachers*, 48, 50).

[6] On Kempe's spiritual colloquies with God, see Barbara Zimbalist, "Christ, Creature, and Reader: Verbal Devotion in *The Book of Margery Kempe*," *Journal of Medieval Religious Cultures* 41 (2014): 1–23.

[7] *MED*, s.v. *daliaunce* (n.). When Christ first "ravishes" her spirit, he demands that Kempe leave the "byddyng of many bedys," or recitation of formulaic prayers, in favor of speaking to him by thought just as he speaks to her (523–24).

[8] David Lavinsky, " 'Speke to me be thowt': Affectivity, *Incendium amoris*, and the *Book of Margery Kempe*," *JEGP* 112 (2013): 340–64 (357). Noting that colloquies with God are "rarely found in the hagiographic and didactic literature upon which the *Book* draws," Lavinsky looks instead to the influence of Walter Hilton's model of contemplative *daliaunce*, which he contrasts with Richard Rolle's physical and material signs of union with God (341).

[9] Mikhail M. Bakhtin, "The Problem of Speech Genres," in *Speech Genres and Other Late Essays* (Austin: University of Texas Press, 1987), 60–102 (78). (This essay provides an overview for a book project he never completed.) Applying Bakhtin's insights to medieval literature, Nancy Mason Bradbury has argued that proverbs embedded in larger works mark a crucial change in voice, one set off as if by virtual quotation marks; see "The Proverb as Embedded Microgenre in Chaucer and *The Dialogue of Solomon and Marcolf*," *Exemplaria* 27 (2015): 55–72 (56). Ardis Butterfield has drawn on Bakhtin's theory of dialogic discourse to frame her analysis of "inset songs" and refrains in thirteenth-century French poetry; see *Poetry and Music in Medieval France: From Jean Renart to Guillaume de Machaut* (Cambridge: Cambridge University Press, 2002), 130–31. On "embedded songs" in Chaucer's *Troilus and Criseyde*, see Ardis Butterfield, " 'Mise-en-page' in the 'Troilus' Manuscripts: Chaucer and French Manuscript Culture," *HLQ* 58 no.1 (1995): 49–80.

utterance, a speaker necessarily absorbs the words of others, with the result that even the most intimate speech is an act of creative quotation.[10] The tension between typicality and individuality becomes evident in Bakhtin's implication that intimate utterances involve self-revelation:

> Intimate genres and styles are based on a maximum internal proximity of the speaker and addressee (in extreme instances, as if they had merged). Intimate speech is imbued with a deep confidence in the addressee, in his sympathy, in the sensitivity and goodwill of his responsive understanding. In this atmosphere of profound trust, the speaker reveals his internal depths.[11]

Intimate speech, expressive of a deep rapport between speaker and addressee, describes well the tone of Kempe's dialogues with Christ in prayer. Pervasive marital imagery conveys the intensity of their communion.[12] More even than husband and wife, Christ and Kempe cannot be parted asunder because they address one another by thought.

Sermon performances, however, are likely the context in which Kempe first heard the voice of Christ addressing her in English. Sermons also would have provided her with verse prayers to use in responding to Christ's address. Kempe attended sermons often enough to have acquired an intuitive understanding of their formal composition and rhetorical techniques. Stitched into *The Book*'s prose is a web of poetic verses. This poetic language has generally passed unnoticed in Kempe scholarship, though Rebecca Krug has recently argued that *The Book* "uses verbal phrases drawn from other books," including proverbs, lyrics, and "scriptural tags," as sources of affirmation.[13] I contend that

---

[10] Bakhtin defines speech genres as "typical forms of construction" with conventions that govern the utterances of individual speakers; see "The Problem of Speech Genres," 87–89.

[11] Ibid., 97.

[12] For example, Christ likens himself to a husband who, having wed his wife, "thynkyth that he is sekyr anow of hir and that no man schal partyn hem asundyr, for than, dowtyr, may thei gon to bedde togedyr wythowtyn any schame er dred of the pepil and slepyn in rest and pees" (7188–91). So it stands between them. Christ then thanks Kempe "for alle the tymys that thu hast herberwyd me and my blissyd modyr in thi bed" (7207–8). Kempe's meditative practice domesticates the metaphorical relationship of bridegroom to bride, as she welcomes Christ into the most private space in her home.

[13] Rebecca Krug, *Margery Kempe and the Lonely Reader* (London: Cornell University Press, 2017), 110–28 (110). Krug cites devotional lyrics among the texts familiar to Kempe, though she does not elaborate on the form or circumstances in which Kempe would have encountered them (124–25). The occurrence of rhyming couplets was first noted in Robert Karl Stone, *Middle English Prose Style: Margery Kempe and Julian of Norwich* (The Hague: Mouton, 1970), 84–88.

Kempe composed the embedded verses in imitation of preacherly discourse. These lyrics represent her prayer dialogues with Christ as a kind of intimate speech, befitting her relationship with him as beloved daughter and bride.[14]

Poetic Voice in the *Amore langueo* Sermon

Late medieval sermons offer more than scriptural exposition and moral dogma. They comprise a repository of guidance in the art of prayer. Not only would preachers begin and end sermons by leading the congregation in reciting the Pater and Ave; sermon texts also insert versified prayers at structural divisions to mark points of transition. These prayers provide "scripts" for individuals to adopt when speaking to God.[15] Although embedded in a larger discursive genre, they are formally constructed for easy excerption, so that members of the congregation might remember and reiterate the words after the sermon performance.

Appreciating the pragmatic function and rhetorical power of embedded verse prayers requires an understanding of scholastic-sermon form.[16] H. L. Spencer and Siegfried Wenzel provide comprehensive overviews of the subject in their studies of the massive corpus of sermon literature produced in medieval England.[17] While homiletic sermons comment on the liturgical readings designated for Sundays and feast days, a scholastic sermon takes a single scriptural verse as its theme (*thema*). Because the theme can be lifted from anywhere in the Bible, it is necessary to explain why the theme is appropriate to the occasion of its delivery. The

---

[14] My account builds on Zimbalist's study of *The Book*'s "participatory" devotional speech. Zimbalist considers the textual representation of speech to be an innovative literary strategy that presents Kempe as an exemplary figure. Kempe's imitation of Christ's speech becomes, in turn, worthy of imitation by the reader; see Zimbalist, "Christ, Creature," 3–4. I would maintain, however, that this rhetorical construction of Kempe's exemplarity was modeled by and implicitly theorized in sermon writing.

[15] Jessica Brantley, *Reading in the Wilderness: Private Devotion and Public Performance in Late Medieval England* (Chicago: University of Chicago Press, 2007), discusses lyric poems as prayer "scripts" for devotional performance. Sarah McNamer, *Affective Meditation and the Invention of Medieval Compassion* (Philadelphia: University of Pennsylvania Press, 2010), reads devotional literature as "scripts" for generating the historically constructed emotion of compassion.

[16] Also known as modern, thematic, or university sermons, though the assumption that they were only delivered before academic audiences is mistaken; see Wenzel, *Preachers*, 61–62.

[17] H. Leith Spencer, *English Preaching in the Late Middle Ages* (Oxford: Clarendon Press, 1993); Siegfried Wenzel, *Latin Sermon Collections from Later Medieval England: Orthodox Preaching in the Age of Wyclif* (Cambridge: Cambridge University Press, 2005).

sermon writer then uses each word of the theme to generate the division (*divisio thematis*) that will divide the sermon into parts. These parts may be further subdivided by distinctions, each supported by its own scriptural quotation. Citation of patristic authorities or illustration by *exempla* can further embellish this framework. Writers would often highlight these structural elements—theme, division, subdivision, distinction, translated or quoted authority—by rendering them in verse, either Latin or vernacular.

Countering the assumption that sermon verses functioned solely as mnemonic devices, Wenzel has argued that "a good number were used not to help remember certain matters but to summarize, to furnish structure, or to create rhetorical emphasis."[18] He identifies four principal rhetorical aims: structural control, verbal concordance, variation, and decoration. To punctuate and ornament the sermon, the writer could use maxims, proverbs, proof texts, "message verses," and verse prayers.[19] I am particularly fascinated by the instances Wenzel classifies as message verses:

These items do not so much prove a point by authority as address an imaginary or real audience whom they warn or frighten or console. They have, in other words, a strong emotional appeal. . . . [In addition to] exclamations or appeals in *exempla*, message verses include inscriptions reportedly found on such objects as rings, boxes, paintings, and statues. I would also place in this group appeals spoken by Christ on the cross or by the preacher calling attention to him, which address the audience with *behold*, *see*, *think*, or a similar command.[20]

Message verses seek to express emotion and move the audience toward an affective response—the experience of either fear or comfort.

Missing from Wenzel's account, however, is the centrality of voice to the examples listed. When the preacher exhorts the audience in the imperative, the speech act of direct address calls the audience into relationship with Christ.[21] In the other three cases, the message verses signal

---

[18] Siegfried Wenzel, *Verses in Sermons: "Fasciculus morum" and Its Middle English Poems*, Mediaeval Academy of America Publication 87 (Cambridge, Mass.: Mediaeval Academy of America, 1978), 125.

[19] Wenzel, *Preachers*, 80–81. Rita Copeland flags "the use of maxims or proverbs to punctuate and divide sermons [as] a basic technique of both Latin and vernacular preaching," in "Pathos and Pastoralism," 108.

[20] Wenzel, *Preachers*, 81.

[21] On addressivity as a key feature of the lyric genre, see Jonathan D. Culler, *Theory of the Lyric* (Cambridge, Mass.: Harvard University Press, 2015), which proposes a trans-

a change in voice, as the preacher ventriloquizes another speaker—whether exemplary character, Christ, or written inscription (i.e., entextualized speech). The literary invention of another's speech was known in medieval rhetoric as *ethopoeia*, the "imitation of the character of a proposed speaker."[22] In scholastic sermons, that inventive work is often marked by poetic language—meter, rhyme, and parallel syntax. The formal shift from prose to verse—which an audience would hear during the sermon's delivery—places ventriloquized speech in audible quotation marks.[23] The poetic form of message verses achieves the effect that "air quotes" do in oral presentations today.

The context of oral performance raises the question of language. How did preachers deliver sermons that were written down in Latin or in a mix of Latin and English? Wenzel maintains that late medieval sermons should be treated "as literary texts written out to serve preachers for study or as guidelines which could be adapted in actual delivery to whatever audience a preacher had before him."[24] The same sermon might be delivered either in Latin or in the vernacular, depending on whether the preacher were addressing a clerical, lay, or mixed audience.[25] Alternatively, a sermon might be delivered twice, first in Latin,

---

historical theory of lyric based on common aspects of the genre: addressivity, present temporality, hyperbole, and ritualistic elements such as rhythm and repetition. Culler emphasizes the performative character of lyric as a kind of speech act or ritualistic event (34–38).

[22] Ingrid Nelson, *Lyric Tactics: Poetry, Genre, and Practice in Later Medieval England* (Philadelphia: University of Pennsylvania Press, 2017), 39. Nelson contends that the concept of voice theorized by medieval rhetoricians, by distinguishing between literary voice and speaking subject, allows the lyric "I" to encompass multitudes. "Lyric readers, performers, and audiences" who find themselves in similar circumstances or affective states can perform the utterance as their own (32).

[23] Bradbury, "The Proverb as Embedded Microgenre," draws on Bakhtin to show that, in medieval literature, smaller genres embedded in longer works have "sharply defined boundaries" that "serve as generic frames, identifying the incorporated form and linking it to the performative tradition from which it arose. As virtual quotation marks, they draw attention to crucial changes in voice" (56). Bradbury focuses on the proverb: "In Middle English works, textual markers such as 'Men seyn' or 'I have herd say' identify proverbs, distinguish them from the surrounding context, and affirm their wide circulation among speakers and writers" (58–59). We see these features in sermon texts as well, but message verses are further distinguished from the surrounding context by their poetic form (though proverbs too were often rendered as verse). The performative context of public preaching makes this formal distinction more important.

[24] Wenzel, *Preachers*, 19.

[25] Siegfried Wenzel, *Macaronic Sermons: Bilingualism and Preaching in Late-Medieval England* (Ann Arbor: University of Michigan Press, 1994), 119–23.

then in the vernacular. Macaronic sermons may even have been preached in bilingual form. Wenzel concludes, "That English verses found their way into the literary texts shows us again how important a place poems held in late medieval preaching."[26]

A Good Friday sermon on the theme *Amore langueo* demonstrates beautifully how medieval preachers deployed poetry to represent diverse voices.[27] This macaronic sermon text, extant in four manuscript witnesses, exemplifies the use of English verse to fulfill various structural and aesthetic purposes.[28] The sermon writer takes his theme from the Song of Songs, that great biblical repository of intimate speech: "Amore langueo," in English, "Y morne fore loue" (64). These words, he explains, indicate the intense, languishing love Christ shows for humanity on Good Friday, the liturgical memorial of his Crucifixion.[29] To characterize Christ as a languishing and tormented lover, the writer ventriloquizes his complaint. The words he attributes to Christ come,

---

[26] Wenzel, *Preachers*, 19.

[27] Wenzel has published the text and a translation from Oxford, Balliol College, MS 149 (fourteenth century), with variants from Oxford, Magdalen College, MS 93 (late fifteenth century); Dublin, Trinity College, MS 277 (fifteenth century); and Cambridge University Library, MS Kk.IV.24 (first half of the fifteenth century). See Wenzel, *Macaronic Sermons*, Appendix B, 212–67. Middle English verse items are listed in Julia Boffey and A. S. G. Edwards, *A New Index of Middle English Verse* (London: British Library, 2005), nos. 541.8, 830, 834, 847, 1140, 1271, 1332, 1551, 1975, 2256, 3433 (hereafter *NIMEV*). They count as prose a final item listed in Carleton Fairchild Brown and Rossell Hope Robbins, *The Index of Middle English Verse* (New York: printed for the Index Society by Columbia University Press, 1943), no. 1269.8 (hereafter *IMEV*).

[28] Wenzel, *Macaronic Sermons*, notes that variant readings among the four witnesses affect the English material. One manuscript "frequently renders words and phrases that are part of the divisions in Latin, though here and there this rendition is in turn supplemented with an interlinear gloss in English" (212–13). Literary analysis must take into account such variation among multiple copies of what we might consider the same text or work. The situation becomes more complicated when one tries to draw wider inferences about the composition of macaronic sermons as a genre. Although Wenzel found substantive variety in the amount of English used across the forty-three macaronic sermons he studied, use of the vernacular "for glosses, translated or quoted authorities, and parts of the division, subdivision, or distinctions" is common, and writers frequently rendered the *divisio thematis* in verse. The observations I offer here about the use of verse to mark changes in voice must therefore be taken as tentative in relation to the corpus of macaronic sermons, and the larger genre of sermons with verses.

[29] Wenzel, *Preachers*, cites the *Amore langueo* sermon as a model of "how to recount the whole Passion narrative within the structure of a scholastic sermon," in contrast to a linear-chronological account (147–48). Holly Johnson has discussed this sermon in *The Grammar of Good Friday: Macaronic Sermons of Late Medieval England* (Turnhout: Brepols, 2012), 61–66, 73, 78–80, 126–27. Johnson argues that these macaronic Good Friday sermons from late medieval England complement the liturgical ritual by both "educating audiences in the meaning of Good Friday" and "seeking to draw audiences into the immediate moment in which the Passion is re-presented" (11).

not from the Gospel, but from Psalms. While undergoing the Passion, "potest Christus querelare et dicere cum Psalmista, 'Miser factus et curuatus sum', etc. **Y am disseset and al for-schende, / Sori and sykande and alle to-rent**" (333–37; "Christ may well complain and say with the Psalmist, 'I have become wretched and a cripple', etc.").[30] The sermon writer represents Christ in torment, quoting Psalm 37:7, which is then translated as an English couplet. By reiterating the psalmist's cry, Christ fills the subject position of the lyric "I." In response, the audience is enjoined to recite a four-line English verse prayer: "Lorde þat suffrydist harde turment / And on \the/ rode were alle to-rent, / Let me suffri wo and pyne, / Þat Y may be on \of/ þine" (361–64). The verses, while not isosyllabic, generally have four beats. Rhyme and parallelism are regular features. By rendering Christ's speech and the audience's response using first-person pronouns, the sermon writer gives voice to multiple speakers. These verses express the speakers' respective emotions on the particular occasion of Good Friday: first Christ, forlorn and sorry, and then each member of the Christian community, asking to suffer likewise in compassion with him. In both instances, the sermon writer exploits the affective resources of poetry.

Whereas Wenzel distinguishes between verses that serve a structural function, those that translate authoritative quotations, and message verses, these diverse uses of poetry are actually linked by their role in signaling changes in voice. Even verses that render proof texts or mark the end of a section serve simultaneously to imagine the speech of different persons—Christ, preacher, individual believer—under specific conditions. We see this dual functionality displayed in the sermon protheme, which begins by declaring Good Friday both "a blisful day" and "a carful day" (45).[31] It is a sorrowful day, the writer explains, because Christ the innocent was killed, "et {ita impletur} illud quod ipse dicit per prophetam in Psalmo: 'Deficit in dolore vita mea', etc." (56–57; "And thus is fulfilled what he himself said through the prophet in a psalm: 'My life has ended in pain', etc."). The quoted verse, Psalm 30:11, is then translated: "My lyue y hynde in sorwe and wo / Man to hyme from ys fo" (58–59). The psalm quotation lends scriptural authority to the claim that Good Friday is "a carful day." Yet the rhetorical

---

[30] I follow Wenzel's convention of typing in bold the English phrases within the macaronic sermon text and include Wenzel's modern English translation of the Latin.

[31] For analysis of language switching in this sermon, see Ardis Butterfield, "Fuzziness and Perceptions of Language in the Middle Ages. Part 3, Translating Fuzziness: Countertexts," *Common Knowledge* 19, no. 3 (2013): 446–73 (455–62).

aim of the Middle English couplet has more to do with voice than the fact that it translates a proof text. In these verses, Christ speaks familiarly as the lyric "I."

The sermon writer's shift to verse implies that poetry was considered a discourse especially well suited to conveying voice and affectivity. I want to distinguish between the exegetical sense in which Christ can be said to have spoken the psalm verse ("quod ipse dicit per prophetam in Psalmo"), and the literary sense in which Christ speaks in the form of a lyric. Whereas the former consists in quoting an extant text, the latter involves generating something new. Medieval exegetes understood the Bible in its totality to constitute the Word of God, so Christ can be said to have inspired the psalmist to write every word of Psalms; that is, he spoke through the prophet by means of divine inspiration. Additionally, the psalmist can be interpreted as a type of Christ in the allegorical sense of scriptural exegesis. Thus the figural meaning of the psalm is fulfilled by Christ's suffering and death. By citing the psalm verse, the sermon writer makes a theological point: that the Bible can signify in both the literal sense, as the words of the psalmist, and in the allegorical sense, as the words of Christ. But the translation of the psalm verse into vernacular poetry is a rhetorical exercise that exceeds the demands of the sermon's exegetical discourse. It represents what Christ might hypothetically have said to express the depth of his sorrow while dying—quite a challenge for the lyric "I" to convey.

The layering of voices produced through figural exegesis is displayed to stunning effect in the introduction to the sermon *materia* (or the antetheme), where the theme is thrice identified as the speech of Christ:

[D]icit nobis hodie Christus: *Amore langueo* (17; "Christ says to us today, '*I languish with love*'").

Vnde in persona Christi sic languentis dicit sponsus, Canticorum 2: "Adiuro vos, filie Ierusalem, vt <cum> inueneritis dilectum meum nuncietis michi, quia *amore langueo*" (23–25; "Hence, in speaking like Christ, who thus languishes, the lover of Canticles 2 says, 'I charge you, daughters of Jerusalem, to tell me when you find my beloved, for *I languish with love*'").

Christus potest hodierna die dicere veraciter, *Amore langueo* (41; "Christ can truly say today, '*I languish with love*'").

The second formulation is particularly interesting for the way it presents the relationship between the two biblical speakers—literally, the lover, and allegorically, Christ. Yet Christ is said to have spoken the words first: "Hence, in speaking like Christ, who thus languishes, the lover of Canticles 2 says. . . ." The sermon writer insists that, even though Canticles is historically the older text, it is the lover who speaks like Christ, not Jesus who quotes Canticles. The temporal emphasis on all three occasions is striking. These words not only belonged to Christ before they were voiced by the lover of Canticles, but they were also implied when Jesus said on the cross, "I thirst."[32] Moreover, the sermon writer insists, Christ speaks these words today, on Good Friday, the liturgical ritual that re-presents the historical event of Christ's Passion, making it real again in the present tense.

But when the theme is rendered in English for the first time (in the protheme, after the couplet translating Psalm 30:11), the speaking voice changes dramatically:

Si ergo nos sicut homines grati cogitauerimus ex vna parte quantum gaudium per Christum lucrati sumus, tenemu[r] eum intente diligere; et si cogitauerimus ex alia parte materiam doloris, tenemur languere. Et ista sunt illa duo verba que dixi vobis in principio, et sunt scripta in libro amoris: *Amore langueo*. Anglice: **Y morne fore loue.**

(60–64)

[If we therefore, like grateful people, think on the one hand how much joy we have gained through Christ, we must love him intently; and if, on the other hand, we think about his pain, we must languish. And these are the two words I told you in the beginning, and they are written in the Book of Love: *amore langueo*. In English: "**I mourn for love.**"]

Having first heard Christ speak through the lyric "I," the audience is now prompted to respond by thinking about the pain he expressed and by feeling a reciprocal, languishing love. The theme, rendered in a simple English line, is identified as a quotation from Song of Songs, but here the words express what "we" the audience should feel. The sermon writer clarifies, "Et possunt ista verba esse verba Christi hodierna die ad genus humanum, et e conuerso generis humani ad Christum" (65–66; "These words can be [considered as] Christ's words spoken today to

---

[32] "Et pro certo langu[et] amore . . . Igitur clamat Christus 'scicio', et si non verbo amore langueo" (18–19; "And certainly he languishes with love . . . hence Christ exclaims, 'I thirst', even if he does not literally say, 'I languish with love' ").

mankind, and conversely they can be [considered as] mankind's words to Christ"). While Christ and the lover of Canticles can be said to speak the same words for typological reasons, Christ and the audience can be made to speak the same words through verbal artistry.

The writer accomplishes this rhetorical distinction between Christ's speech and the individual Christian's response by rendering the theme as two separate couplets. First, "Nam Christus poterit hodie veraciter dicere generi humano '*Amore langueo*', quasi diceret: **Y morne for loue Þou may se, / Þat makide me deye for Þe**" (66–69; "For Christ could truly say to mankind today 'I languish for love', as if he were saying . . .). This couplet does more than provide a vernacular paraphrase or gloss; the poet has imagined what words would befit Christ to speak at the moment of death in a direct appeal to humankind. The phrase "quasi diceret," which equates the theme with this vernacular couplet, marks the latter as a rhetorical invention—specifically, a poetic invention. The sermon writer proceeds with the rhetorical exercise, next adapting the theme to the character of humankind, Christ's spouse. Each individual member of the audience is invited to identify with this character, "quia quilibet nostrum tenetur hodie dicere Christo '*Amore langueo*'" (71; "for each one of us must say to Christ today, 'I languish with love'"). While the theme remains constant, humankind's speech is represented by a new couplet: "For loue of Iesu, my swete herte, / Y morne and seke wyþ teres smert" (73–74). Again, Latin theme and English verses are linked by the phrase "quasi diceret," indicating that the sermon writer has imagined how a person might answer Jesus' appeal from the cross. The two English couplets, derived from the same Latin verse, become two halves of a dialogue, as Jesus calls and the individual speakers respond together as one congregation.

The subjunctive mood of "quasi diceret" marks each couplet as rhetorical ornament and poetic invention. It signals both a change of voice and a shift into vernacular idiom. To render the universal Latin theme diversely as the utterances of multiple speakers, the sermon writer turns to poetry, the discourse of emotional appeal. The Middle English verses represent the speech of Jesus as familiar, even lovingly intimate, and script a response appropriate to anyone in the audience. The paired couplets launch a dialogue that runs throughout the sermon, alternating between the two speakers. These lyric poems express in familiar terms what spiritual love for and compassion with Jesus feel like: desire for an absent sweetheart or grief for a lover in pain. They model how love of Christ can be conceived through words.

Scholars have inferred that preachers embedded rhyming couplets and rhythmical quatrains into sermons, not only to ease recall during delivery, but also to ensure the audience could remember them.[33] Their formal containment as units marked by end rhyme seems designed to facilitate excerption and reiteration in other performative contexts. But manuscript copies of sermon texts cannot tell us whether embedded verses successfully took root in the hearts of lay congregants. We must look elsewhere for evidence of such reception and recirculation among the laity.

Preacherly Discourse in *The Book of Margery Kempe*

The Book portrays Margery Kempe as an ardent sermon enthusiast. Her emotional response to public preaching sparks dramatic conflict on several occasions. No matter how many sermons Kempe attends, her appetite for God's word only intensifies. Impelled by an insatiable hunger, she prays:

Alas, Lord, as many clerkys as thu hast in this world, that thu ne woldyst sendyn me on of hem that myth fulfillyn my sowle wyth thi word and wyth redyng of Holy Scriptur, for alle the clerkys that prechyn may not fulfillyn, for me thynkyth that my sowle is evyr alych hungry. Yyf I had gold inow, I wolde gevyn every day a nobyl for to have every day a sermown, for thi word is mor worthy to me than alle the good in this werld.

(4778–84)

Kempe's conversation with people she meets while traveling demonstrates how thoroughly she digested readings from Scripture, whenever she had the opportunity to hear them. More than one cleric is dismayed by the fluency with which "sche spekyth of the Gospel" (4209). But Kempe consumes the biblical Word as preachers served it up, baked into a discourse with particular rhetorical ingredients.

Kempe learned the tricks of the preacher's trade well enough to produce sermonic speech of her own. She demonstrates masterful use of an exemplum by skillfully relating a tale about a priest, a pear tree, and a bear when she appears before the archbishop of York at Cawood (4215–

---

[33] Fletcher, *Late Medieval Popular Preaching*, 277.

56). Accused of illicit preaching, Kempe famously defends herself: "I preche not, ser; I come in no pulpytt. I use but comownycacyon and good wordys, and that wil I do whil I leve" (4213–14). As Alastair Minnis has explained, Kempe is citing the canonical distinction between public and private speech.[34] While women were not permitted to address the church publicly from the pulpit, it was considered appropriate for them to teach others privately in familiar conversation (*familiariter colloquendo*). The thirteenth-century preaching manual by John of Wales, O.F.M., insists that such private speech often proves more persuasive than public preaching. He therefore urges pastors to engage parishioners in "mutually edifying conversation" in addition to delivering sermons.[35] By calling her speech merely "comowynycacyon and good wordys," Kempe emphasizes its private nature, thereby protecting herself from ecclesiastical censure. But what she retells in private, she might have first heard on an occasion of public preaching. The exemplum she passes on, which conveys pointed moral critique through a humorous metaphor, would fittingly amplify a sermon. The tale's popular register marks it as a kind of common literary inheritance, proper to familiar conversation, but that could be used strategically in public preaching.

Alternatively, Kempe might be reiterating a tale she first heard in conversation with one of her many confessors. Either way, it exemplifies a particular, "preacherly voice" that Kempe imitates throughout *The Book*. Here I seek to build on the argument in Felicity Riddy's provocative essay "Text and Self in *The Book of Margery Kempe*."[36] Riddy draws

---

[34] Alastair Minnis, "Religious Roles: Public and Private," in *Medieval Holy Women in the Christian Tradition, c. 1100–c. 1500*, ed. Minnis and Rosalynn Voaden (Turnhout: Brepols, 2010), 47–81.

[35] On John of Wales's *Communiloquium*, see Waters, *Angels and Earthly Creatures*, 70.

[36] Felicity Riddy, "Text and Self in *The Book of Margery Kempe*," in *Voices in Dialogue: Reading Women in the Middle Ages*, ed. Linda Olson and Kathryn Kerby-Fulton (Notre Dame: University of Notre Dame Press, 2005), 435–53 (436). Riddy first critiques Lynn Staley's distinction between the author "Kempe" and the character "Margery," because it divorces the literary work from any connection to a particular woman's life experiences. See Staley, *Margery Kempe's Dissenting Fictions* (University Park: Pennsylvania Press, 1994). Riddy then critiques Nicholas Watson's attempt to distinguish between autobiographical passages written by Margery Kempe and later additions by *The Book*'s second scribe, her confessor, in "The Making of *The Book of Margery Kempe*," in Olson and Kerby-Fulton, *Voices in Dialogue*, 395–434. Krug, *Margery Kempe*, adopts Riddy's model of collaborative writing (15–16), as does Rory G. Critten, *Author, Scribe, and Book in Late Medieval English Literature* (Woodbridge: D. S. Brewer, 2018), who analyzes *The Book*'s "fractured presentation" of Kempe as simultaneously an example for emulation and a unique individual (76–110).

attention to the polyvocality implicit in *The Book*'s genesis. According to the Prologue, Kempe first consulted with her adult son both to compose and to write down her life story while caring for her infirm husband.[37] Later, Kempe reviewed the text with her confessor, who read it back to her, rewrote it, and continued the story up to the present day. Riddy describes this process of remembering, relating, writing, and rewriting as "relational." *The Book* "arose out of and was embedded in social interaction: people meeting and talking at a particular time in a particular place."[38] Rather than ascribe *The Book*'s multiple languages to different authors (such as the second amanuensis, probably Kempe's confessor Robert Spryngolde), Riddy explores the effects of its various discourses, including the "preacherly voice" reproduced in the text.[39]

As an example of this "preacherly discourse," Riddy cites "the defense of Margery's roaring" at the end of Chapter 28.[40] Following a description in the past tense of Kempe's violent bodily reaction to meditating upon the Passion, the narrative voice shifts into exhortative mode: "It is nowt to be merveyled yyf this creatur cryed and made wondirful cher and cuntenawns, whan we may se eche day at eye bothe men and women" weeping over the loss of worldly goods or the parting of friends (2281–83). "How meche mor myth thei wepyn" if their friends had been taken with violence, as Jesus was (2292). It is an offense to God that we unworthy wretches will neither have in mind our Savior's death, nor support the Lord's own secretaries (2302–6).[41] Use of the first-person plural in this passage situates the speaker in community with the audience of readers, yet the hyperbolic contrast between how people do behave (badly) and how devout Christians ought to behave presumes the speaker's authority to issue correction. By taking up a stance at once within and above the community, this voice occupies the role of teacher and preacher. Provocatively, Kempe inhabits this speaking position by issuing correction to her contemporaries and, later, by authoring her *Book*.

---

[37] Sebastian Sobecki identified the first amanuensis as Kempe's son in " 'The writyng of this tretys': Margery Kempe's Son and the Authorship of Her Book," *SAC* 37 (2015): 257–83 (257).

[38] Riddy, "Text and Self," 435.

[39] Ibid., 437.

[40] Ibid.

[41] On the Latinate vocabulary of this passage, see Watson, "The Making of *The Book of Margery Kempe*," 403. On the prophetic connotation of the word "secretaries," see Diane Watt, *Secretaries of God: Women Prophets in Late Medieval and Early Modern England* (Woodbridge: D. S. Brewer, 1997), 1–2.

I find this concept of "preacherly discourse" compelling and will argue that we see it elsewhere in *The Book*'s imitation of rhetorical practices drawn from sermon composition and delivery: selecting a theme, drawing distinctions, deploying proverbs and aphorisms, and signaling changes in voice through poetic form. Margery Kempe's familiarity with these techniques should hardly surprise. She certainly heard enough sermons to have picked up a preacherly accent. *The Book* recounts her attendance at one delivered on a Palm Sunday:

And it was custom in the place ther sche was dwellyng to have a sermown on that day, and than, as a worschepful doctowr of divinité was in the pulpit and seyd the sermown, he rehersyd oftyntyme thes wordys, "Owr Lord Jhesu langurith for lofe." Tho wordys wrowt so in hir mende whan sche herd spekyn of the parfyte lof that owr Lord Jhesu Crist had to mankynde and how der he bowt us wyth hys bittyr Passyon, schedyng hys hert blood for owr redempcyon, and suffyrd so schamful a deth for owr salvacyon, than sche myth no lengar kepyn the fir of lofe clos wythinne hir brest. . . . And so sche cryed ful lowde and wept and sobbyd ful sor as thow sche schulde a brostyn for pite and compassyon that sche had of owr Lordys Passyon.

(6203–16)

The meaning of Jesus' death for Christian eschatology is a fitting topic for a sermon on Palm Sunday, when the Passion narrative from one of the synoptic Gospels is read during the liturgy. Rather than give a homily on the Gospel text—translating and explicating the whole pericope—this doctor of divinity seems to have given a scholastic sermon on the theme "Owr Lord Jhesu langurith for lofe." These words likely render the scriptural verse "Amore langueo," the very theme of the Good Friday sermon discussed above. While we cannot know whether Kempe witnessed a delivery of this particular sermon, she must have heard sermons similarly ornamented with vernacular poetry.[42]

The English rendition of the sermon theme stuck in Kempe's memory thanks to its linguistic form. In translating "Amore langueo" as

[42] Extant collections of macaronic sermons were produced by Franciscans in Norfolk, the county in which Kempe lived. (She mentions attending sermons by itinerant friars.) Ralph Hanna has localized one such fifteenth-century collection to "a West Norfolk Franciscan ambit," arguing that the verses contained therein circulated among Franciscan centers throughout Norfolk, Lincolnshire, and Yorkshire. See Ralph Hanna, "Verses in Sermons Again: The Case of Cambridge, Jesus College, MS Q.A.13," *Studies in Bibliography* 57, no. 1 (2005): 63–83 (68).

"Owr Lord Jhesu langurith for lofe," the preacher shifts into the third person and introduces ornamental alliteration. Having heard the alliterating pair *langur**/*lofe* uttered in this context (and perhaps elsewhere), Kempe assimilated it into her own language. Earlier in the text, in the description of her first imaginative meditation on the life of the Virgin, *The Book* recounts how Kempe imagines herself traveling with Mary and providing for her needs, all the while praying about different topics. Weeping with desire for heaven, she yearns to be delivered out of this wretched world; then, "Ower Lord Jhesu Crist seyd to hir mende sche schuld abyden **and languren in lofe**" (609–10). The text switches from a narrative description of the content of Kempe's prayer to a memorial record of the dialogic communication she experienced with Christ. The sentence of indirect discourse telling us that Christ spoke to her mind introduces the following direct address: "For I have ordeyned the to knele befor the Trynyte for to prey for al the world" (611–12). Christ speaks the words "languren in lofe," but they describe the affective state of love-longing that Kempe will experience.

In Barry Windeatt's edition of *The Book of Margery Kempe*, the gloss on "languren in lofe" refers to mystical interpretations of Canticles 2:5 and cites Richard Rolle's *Incendium amoris*, Walter Hilton's *Scale of Perfection*, *The Cloud of Unknowing*, and Julian of Norwich.[43] The first two are named in *The Book* itself as texts Kempe had read to her (4818–21), and she recalls speaking in person with Julian (1336).[44] She may well have picked up the phrase from works such as these. But her own text provides evidence that she also encountered the alliterating word-pair in a sermon and adopted it into her intimate style of speaking with Christ in prayer.

We need not ascribe the phrase "languren in lofe" to any one source. The point is that Kempe's *Book* speaks in the language of both advanced spiritual treatises and popular preaching. Highlighting only one of these discourses, as Windeatt's footnote does, obscures this richly resonant discursive play. A more expansive reading would recognize that both genres—contemplative treatises and sermons—are drawing upon a

[43] Rolle glosses the quotation "Amore langueo" in two of his English treatises, *Ego dormio* and *The Form of Living*. *The Book* does not mention Kempe's reading of Rolle's English writings.

[44] In Chapter 58, Kempe befriends a young priest who "red to hir many a good boke of hy contemplacyon and other bokys, as the Bybyl wyth doctowrys therupon, Seynt Brydys boke, Hyltons boke, Boneventur, *Stimulus Amoris*, *Incendium Amoris*, and swech other" (4818–21).

common poetic language. Although modern scholars strongly associate the affect of love-longing with the hermit of Hampole, Rolle developed this imagery from a tradition of Latin and vernacular lyrics about longing for Christ as an absent lover.[45] Rolle's own writing makes use of homiletic and lyric discourses, especially in his vernacular treatises intended for female and lay readers, which feature embedded poems.

Alongside the writings of Rolle and the lives of continental holy women, editors have cited the pseudo-Bonaventuran *Stimulus amoris* and *Meditationes vitae Christi*—both works in the meditative tradition of imagining oneself as a participant in the lives of Christ and the Virgin—as important influences on *The Book of Margery Kempe*.[46] Neither *Meditationes vitae Christi* nor an English translation is explicitly named, however, and traditional methods of source criticism have only taken us so far. In the introduction to his edition, Windeatt explains:

No very exact verbal or substantial resemblances link the *Book* with the Latin *Meditationes* or the influential early fifteenth-century English translation by Nicholas Love, the *Mirror of the Blessed Life of Jesus Christ*, although—as annotations to this edition show—Kempe's approach in contemplating Christ's life recurrently converges with that in the *Meditationes* or Love's *Mirror*; it would be remarkable if it did not.

(12)

Windeatt's claim is persuasive, but he fails to consider the equally plausible explanation that Kempe was introduced to the practice of imaginative meditation—and the language used to describe this activity—through preaching. Passion meditation features prominently in macaronic sermons from late medieval England, as Wenzel's analysis has shown.[47] Most commonly composed for the Sundays of Lent, Good Friday, and Easter, macaronic sermons tend to emphasize repentance

---

[45] See Rosemary Woolf, *The English Religious Lyric in the Middle Ages* (Oxford: Clarendon Press, 1968), 159. Rolle's *Incendium* earns an explicit citation in *The Book* as part of its strategy to associate Kempe with the textual authority of a well-known spiritual author. Following *The Book*'s directive, scholars have looked for textual echoes of Rolle's writings and idiosyncratic spiritual experience in Kempe's language (Lavinsky, "Speke to me be thowt," 342–48). Albeit that Rollean influence is certainly discernible, critical focus on it has forestalled consideration of other, more popular discourses familiar to Kempe, such as the homiletic and lyric.

[46] For a succinct overview of Kempe's knowledge of the *vitae* of continental holy women, see Windeatt's introduction to *The Book of Margery Kempe*, 9–18.

[47] Wenzel, *Macaronic Sermons*, 66.

and Passion meditation to a greater extent than other Latin sermons. Holly Johnson has shown that Good Friday sermons make Passion meditation into a "public and communal" activity by "creat[ing] and sustain[ing] meditative moments that draw their audiences into an imaginative realm in which Christ is presently suffering."[48]

Margery Kempe fully entered into such moments of public meditation. Moreover, her *Book* rewrites these meditations and expertly interprets them in a preacherly voice. Consider the description of a procession on Ascension Thursday:

On the Holy Thursday, as the sayd creatur went processyon wyth other pepil, sche saw in hir sowle owr Lady, Seynt Mary Mawdelyn, and the xii apostelys. And than sche beheld wyth hir gostly eye how owr Lady toke hir leve of hir blysful Sone, Crist Jhesu, how he kyssed hir and alle hys apostelys and also hys trewe lover, Mary Mawdelyn. **Than hir thowt it was a swemful partyng and also a joyful partyng**.

(5851–57)

The final sentence engages in exegetical activity, commenting on the imagined scene as a preacher would interpret the Gospel passage. *The Book* mimics a preacherly voice, drawing a distinction to generate material while ornamenting the language with parallelism. It bears a striking resemblance to the protheme of the *Amore langueo* sermon, which describes Good Friday as both a "blisful" and a "carful" day (45).

Like a sermon writer ventriloquizing Christ on the cross, Kempe deploys poetic verse to signal acts of quotation, differentiate among multiple speakers, and distinguish spoken utterances from narrative prose. Her preacherly use of poetic language can be seen most clearly in the case of an embedded utterance that appears twice, though with slight variations.[49] Near the end of Book I, Christ quotes words that Kempe has previously addressed to him in supplication: "Lord, for thi wowndys smerte, drawe alle my lofe into thyn hert" (7307–8). These two lines form a couplet linked by end rhyme ("smerte"/"hert"), with

[48] Johnson, *The Grammar of Good Friday*, 49, 29.
[49] Krug, *Margery Kempe*, discusses instances of the rhyming pair *smert/hert*, which occurs in several poetic works, including "Jesus lord that madest me," the Holy Name prayer attributed to Richard Caister, one of Kempe's confessors (120–24). In Kempe's *Book*, Krug argues, it reappears at moments when Kempe is struggling to relinquish love toward people other than Christ.

regular meter. Earlier in *The Book*, the same two lines appear in expanded form: "Lord, for alle thi wowndys smert, drawe al the lofe of myn hert into thyn hert" (5412–13). Although the utterance no longer divides into two metrically equal halves, the form of the couplet is still audible thanks to internal rhyme.[50]

What is fascinating about these two textual fragments is the complexity with which they are embedded in Kempe's mental dialogue with Christ. Let's look at the earlier instance in context:

Dowtyr, I have drawe the lofe of thin hert fro alle mennys hertys into myn hert. Sumtyme, dowtyr, thu thowtyst it had ben in a maner unpossybyl for to ben so, and that tyme suffyrdyst thu ful gret peyne in thin hert wyth fleschly affeccyons. And than cowdyst thu wel cryen to me, seying, "Lord, for alle thi wowndys smert, drawe al the lofe of myn hert into thyn hert."

(5408–13)

Christ speaks the couplet, but the verb "seying" marks it as a quotation of what Kempe could, in the past, have said to him. Christ assures Kempe that, at this stage of her spiritual journey, she has given him all her love. In the past, he recalls, she had doubted it were possible not to feel any affection toward other persons. At that time, she could have cried out in prayer, adopting the lyric voice. The hypothetical mood of "cowdyst" suggests that Christ is engaged in a rhetorical exercise, composing verses to characterize the speech of a person enduring fleshly temptation, in this case, Kempe.

The couplet reappears when Christ recalls how Kempe once complained to him about the harshness of her confessor: "And than thu crydist to me wyth al thin hert, 'Lord, for thi wowndys smerte, drawe alle my lofe into thyn hert.' And, dowtyr, so have I do" (7306–8). The past tense of "crydist" implies that Kempe really did speak this verse prayer, but under different circumstances of duress. That the same

---

[50] This example raises the thorny question of what counts as verse, much less poetry. Differing approaches to identifying Middle English verse have resulted in two separate reference tools: *NIMEV*, and the open-access *Digital Index of Middle English Verse*, ed. Linne R. Mooney et al., www.dimev.net (accessed July 20, 2019). The latter includes a number of items that were either deemed prose or not included in *NIMEV*; many of these are short texts embedded in sermons. For a critique of the bibliographical methodology established by Carleton Brown and R. H. Robbins, editors of the original *IMEV*, see Ralph Hanna, "The Verses of Bodleian Library, Ms Laud Misc. 77," *N&Q* 63, no. 3 (September 2016): 361–70 (363).

poetic utterance can be vocalized appropriately on various occasions reflects the flexibility of lyric voice.

In these two instances, is Kempe reiterating a couplet she actually heard delivered by a preacher? If so, we might explain the textual variation between the two as the result of faulty memory, in which the remembered speech has become distorted in the act of quotation. Or Kempe may be adapting the verse prayer, picked up from a sermon, to her own prose text. While these explanations seem plausible, I want to suggest instead that Kempe might have invented this verse prayer by practicing a preacherly mode of composition. That is, Kempe not only heard sermon verses and remembered them; she also learned to compose rhyming couplets to mark a change of voice. We need not account for these preacherly poetic compositions by attributing them to Spryngolde, Kempe's confessor and amanuensis, whom she undoubtedly heard preach. Rather, we might see Kempe and Spryngolde as participating in a shared sermon culture, equally familiar with the homiletic appropriation of vernacular lyric discourse.

All of *The Book*'s embedded verses formally highlight acts of quotation or direct address. Where rhyming couplets appear in the prayer dialogues, they do so as reiterations of Kempe's words, reported back to her by Christ. *The Book* mimics the preacherly use of poetry to script prayers for the audience. Like the phrase "quasi diceret" in the *Amore langueo* sermon, Christ's hypothetical phrase—"And than cowdyst thu wel cryen to me, seying . . ."—presents the following couplet as a poetic invention that might be recited by other persons desiring to feel greater love for Christ in his suffering. *The Book* offers the verse prayer to readers who can inhabit the lyric "I" themselves. Kempe's voice in prayer thus becomes exemplary, modeling how to address Christ in an intimate style.[51]

These poetic quotations emphasize Christ's indwelling presence within Kempe. Riddy has explained the dialogic interplay between Christ's voice and Kempe's as a figure for Kempe's "internally fragmented" selfhood: "Jesus's voice is part of an internal dialogue that runs through the *Book*; his utterances and the discussions the 'creatur' has

---

[51] On the exemplarity of Kempe's voice, see Zimbalist, "Christ, Creature," 17. On the "intimate" voice of Jesus in fifteenth-century dialogues, including *The Book of Margery Kempe*, see Rebecca Krug, "Jesus' Voice: Dialogue and Late Medieval Readers," in *Form and Reform: Reading across the Fifteenth Century*, ed. Shannon Gayk and Kathleen Tonry (Columbus: Ohio State University Press, 2011), 110–29.

with him are a means whereby the protagonist speaks to, for, and about herself" (446).[52] In the modern psychoanalytic framework invoked by Riddy, Christ's speech gives expression to Kempe's experience of the divine within herself. We can also understand Kempe's practice of representing Christ's voice in terms of Latin rhetorical theory. In an analysis of classical treatments of character (*ethos*), C. Jan Swearingham has emphasized "the Latin rhetorics' model of conversation with and emulation of imaginary persons, and the promotion of character that is imagined and fabulated in a literary and aesthetic sense."[53] Their procedures for inventing rhetorical voice encouraged orators to imagine conversing with and imitating the speech of persons worth emulating, with the goal of growing more like them. "The Roman concept of edifying imitation, the imitation of sublime exemplars superior to oneself, is rich in conceptions of virtue."[54] Authors such as Cicero and Quintilian considered the invention of literary voice to be an exercise in cultivating a virtuous character.

Kempe would have gained indirect exposure to this rhetorical tradition of "edifying imitation" through her encounters with literate culture. Whereas Riddy sees Christ's voice working to represent Kempe's self, Latin rhetoricians would contend that, by imaginatively speaking in Christ's voice, Kempe actively becomes more like him. I do not think these two perspectives necessarily conflict. Kempe seeks to identify herself with Christ; her writing practice furthers this end as much as the devotional practices of bodily abjection described in *The Book*. This identification of Kempe with Christ achieves its fullest expression in his quotation of her verse prayers. When Christ reiterates Kempe's words, their voices merge in an apotheosis of intimate dalliance.

Contributing to the intricacy of this internal dialogue, in a few instances Christ uses poetic language to express Kempe's thoughts or emotions in the second person, while addressing her directly. Rather than using the past tense to quote words that Kempe (could have) said, these phrases appear in the present or future tense to announce Kempe's

[52] In a footnote, Riddy cites Sarah Beckwith, "Problems of Authority in Late Medieval English Mysticism: Language, Agency, and Authority in the Book of Margery Kempe," *Exemplaria* 4 (1992): 171–99 (180), on the subject of Kempe's book as "both God and herself."

[53] C. Jan Swearingen, "Ethos: Imitation, Impersonation, and Voice," in *Ethos: New Essays in Rhetorical and Critical Theory*, ed. James S. Baumlin and Tita French Baumlin, 1st ed. (Dallas: Southern Methodist University Press, 1994), 115–48 (124–25).

[54] Ibid., 125.

affective state at that moment or in time to come. At one point Christ reassures her, "Thu schalt be fulfyllyd of al maner lofe that thu coveytyst. Than schalt thu blysse the tyme that thu wer wrowte and the body that the hath bowte. He [the Father] schal joyen in the and thu in hym wythowtyn ende" (1663–66). The phrase, "blysse the tyme that thu wer wrowte / and the body that the hath bowte," yields a metrical couplet when excerpted from the surrounding prose. In a more ambiguous case, in Chapter 32, Christ promises Kempe a future blessing: "And so schalt thu don, dowtyr, and al thi wepyng and thi sorwe schal turnyn into joy and blysse, the whech thu schalt nevyr mysse" (2672–74).[55] The shape of an embedded couplet can be discerned if one squints a bit: "schal turnyn into joy and blysse, / the whech thu schalt nevyr mysse." The rhythm is awkward but the rhyming words link the two phrases together. Do these textual fragments qualify as verse? I would suggest they at least point to Kempe's familiarity with the homiletic use of poetry to emphasize acts of direct "I–thou" address.

Traces of verse marking changes in voice also appear within Kempe's imaginative meditations. On Easter Day, she sees Christ appear to his mother after the Resurrection and say, "Der Modyr, my peyne is al agoo, and now schal I levyn for evyr mo" (6621–22).[56] In this metrical, end-rhymed couplet, Christ occupies the subject position of the lyric "I" to address his mother directly. An actual dialogue takes place as Kempe meditatively accompanies the Virgin through her son's Passion:

And hir thowt sche herd owr Lady cryin anon wyth a lament-
   abyl voys and seyd:
"John, wher is my sone Jhesu Crist?"
And Seynt John answeryd agen and seyd:
"Der Lady, ye wetyn wel that he is ded."
"A, John," sche seyd, "that is to me a careful reed."

                            (6571–76)

The phrases, " 'ye wetyn wel that he is ded' . . . 'that is to me a careful reed,' " make up a metrical, end-rhymed couplet when excerpted from

---

[55] Citing the *blysse/mysse* rhyme pair, Krug, *Margery Kempe*, suggests that Kempe was familiar with the MS Harley 2253 lyric, "Swete Ihesu, now wil I synge" (124–25).

[56] Kempe echoes this phrase in an imaginative meditation on Ascension Thursday, when she sees Christ rise up into heaven, leaving her behind: "Hir thowt that al hir joy was ago" (5865).

the vocatives and narrative marker "sche seyd." These poetic effects highlight the shifts among the multiple voices in play.

The Book not only juxtaposes individual voices in dialogue; Kempe also deploys the powerfully communal voice of the proverbial utterance.[57] One embedded proverb appears in the speech of Christ, who, like a preacher, quotes the saying as a pithy summation of folk wisdom. In Chapter 32, Christ signals explicitly that he is citing a common proverb: "Tyme schal come whan thu [Kempe] schalt holdyn the ryth wel plesyd, for it schal be verifyed in the, the comown proverbe that men seyn, 'He is wel blyssed that may sytten on hys wel-stool and tellyn of hys wo-stool'" (2669–72).[58] Verbal parallelism and rhyme underscore the proverb's presumed authority as common-sense knowledge. The proverb fits Kempe's experience of social rejection into a paradigmatic understanding of how the world works: woe will turn to well.[59] Another proverbial saying is invoked to pronounce on the controversy between the Parish Church of St. Margaret, Lynn and its Chapel of St. Nicholas: "The paryschenys whech pursuyd weryn rygth strong and haddyn gret help of lordshyp, and also, the most of alle, thei wer ryche men, worshepful marchawntys, and haddyn gold anow, whech may spede in every nede, and that is rewth that mede schuld spede er than trewth" (1899–1903). The final clause, "whech may spede . . ." forms a five-line metrical unit linked by two rhyme endings: "spede"/"nede"/"mede" and "rewth"/"trewth." The proverbial utterance lends gravity to the moral judgment delivered upon the sale of church prerogatives. Concluding with an aphorism has the effect of imparting collective wisdom shared by the community.[60]

[57] As "items of common-sense knowledge," proverbs bring the weight of communally shared wisdom to bear on questions of right conduct. For a sociolinguistic analysis of proverbial form and usage, see Steven Shapin, "Proverbial Economies: How an Understanding of Some Linguistic and Social Features of Common Sense Can Throw Light on More Prestigious Bodies of Knowledge, Science for Example," *Social Studies of Science*, 31, no. 5 (2001): 731–69 (743). On proverbs in thirteenth-century Parisian sermons, see Franco Morenzoni, "Les proverbes dans la prédication du XIIIe siècle," in *Tradition des proverbes et des exempla dans l'Occident médiéval/Die Tradition der Sprichwörter und Exempla im Mittelalter: Colloque fribourgeois 2007/Freiburger Colloquium 2007*, ed. Hugo O. Bizzarri and Martin Rohde (Berlin: De Gruyter, 2009), 131–49.

[58] Windeatt notes, "No other Middle English instance is recorded (Whiting 1968: W194)" (*The Book of Margery Kempe*, ed. Windeatt, 184).

[59] Shapin, "Proverbial Economies," asserts: "[P]roverbs are resources for *creating* scenes of observation and action, for making situations recognizable as situations of a certain kind" (739). Which proverb one chooses to name the type of situation determines how one acts; thus, "proverbs help to constitute their referential realities" (740).

[60] On proverbs and citation, see Butterfield, *Poetry and Music*, 243–45. She likens refrain-citations to proverbs, in that both are "a form of common language," or "everybody's way of speaking" (243).

The rhyming phrases embedded in Kempe's prose imitate the use of poetic verses and proverbs in preaching. Evidence that she heard lyrics read in other contexts comes from *The Book*'s quotation of a single phrase that also appears in two important lyrics of the late fourteenth century. After a vision in which Kempe sees Christ's feet above her and finds, upon reaching for his toe, that it feels like flesh and bone, her response is described: "And than sche thankyd God of al, for thorw thes gostly sytys hir affeccyon was al drawyn into the manhod of Crist and into the mynde of hys Passyon" (7022–24). The phrase "thankyd God of al" resembles the varying refrain of a Vernon lyric, "Ever thank God of all."[61] Chaucer's *balade Truth* contains the same words: "Forth, pilgrim, forth! Forth, beste, out of thy stal! / Know thy contree, look up, thank God of al" (18–19).[62] As a refrain, this phrase encapsulates the moralistic tone that pervades the Vernon lyrics and unites them as a series.[63] In Chaucer's hands, the exhortation ripples with jocularity, as his suggestion that his reader is a beast puns on the name of the *balade*'s addressee, Philip de la Vache ("cow").[64] In Kempe's *Book*, the exclamation rings with heartfelt thanksgiving. These tonal shifts reflect the flexibility of lyric voice, which encourages the practice of creative quotation. The phrase "thank God of al" is a sign of verbal artistry precisely because it sounds popular and colloquial. The Vernon lyricist, Chaucer, and Kempe all appropriate it in strategic deployments of vernacular sincerity.

The traces of poetry in *The Book of Margery Kempe* invite us to listen more attentively to the variety of speech genres woven into Kempe's prose. *The Book* demonstrates a fluency in preacherly discourse and a familiarity with its use of verse, yet neither sermons nor lyrics have been acknowledged as important literary influences on Kempe's style. Scholars have paid more attention to the discourse of spiritual discernment, with its technical vocabulary and elitist register, than to the popular discourse of preaching, which has led to a narrowed perception of *The*

[61] Carleton Brown, *Religious Lyrics of the XIVth Century* (Oxford: Clarendon Press, 1924), 157–60, no. 105.

[62] *The Riverside Chaucer*, gen. ed. Larry D. Benson, 3rd ed. (Boston, Mass: Houghton Mifflin, 1987), 653.

[63] On the Vernon lyric series, see John Burrow, "The Shape of the Vernon Refrain Lyrics," in *Studies in the Vernon Manuscript*, ed. Derek Albert Pearsall (Cambridge: D. S. Brewer, 1990), 187–99; and John J. Thompson, "The Textual Background and Reputation of the Vernon Lyrics," in Pearsall, *Studies in the Vernon Manuscript*, 201–24.

[64] On the pun, see David Lawton, *Voice in Later Medieval English Literature: Public Interiorities* (Oxford: Oxford University Press, 2017), 34.

Book's masterful polyvocality.[65] One reason for this critical omission is *The Book*'s own silence concerning vernacular sources. It lists several Latin theological treatises as the reading matter that at once informs and authorizes Kempe's religious experience, but the only vernacular text explicitly acknowledged is "Hyltons boke," presumably the *Scale of Perfection*.[66] Nevertheless, her frequent and enthusiastic attendance at sermons suggests that preaching likewise shaped Kempe's development of an intimate style for prayer. Failure to appreciate Kempe's assimilation of preacherly discourse led critics throughout the mid-twentieth century to acknowledge *The Book*'s invocation of Rolle and other Latin writings, yet to deny Kempe a place alongside the canonical medieval English mystics out of discomfort with *The Book*'s code-switching. In a manner distinct from Rolle, Hilton, Julian, and the *Cloud*-author, Kempe shifts fluently between the technical language of a spiritual writer and the popular idiom of a preacher. Yet her most distinctive voice remains that of daughter and bride, dallying in intimate conversation with Christ.

This voice becomes available for adoption by readers through Christ's preacherly use of direct address in the prayer dialogues. *The Book* strives to represent Kempe's mental speech as exemplary, an aim we see clearly when Christ quotes one of her prayers in the form of an embedded verse couplet. This lyric mode invites readers to vocalize the prayer as their own utterance, in the same way that preachers offered versified prayer scripts to their audiences. I have argued that sermons provided the likeliest literary model for Kempe's entextualization of her mental dialogues with Christ. Her use of the term dalliance reflects, I think, how she perceived the homiletic ventriloquizing of Christ's speech. In the kind of scholastic sermons Kempe would have heard, preachers audibly distinguished Christ's voice from their own by shifting into poetic verse form. Exploiting the multimodality of lyric voice, they deployed message verses that function both typologically and rhetorico-poetically to

---

[65] Carol M. Meale has made a similar argument about the limited range of source materials acknowledged by editors of *The Book of Margery Kempe*. She finds textual evidence pointing to the influence of dramatic performances, especially the York Corpus Christi plays, on Kempe's visualizations of Christ's life; see " 'This is a deed bok, the tother a quick': Theatre and the Drama of Salvation in the *Book* of Margery Kempe," in *Medieval Women: Texts and Contexts in Late Medieval Britain. Essays for Felicity Riddy*, ed. Jocelyn Wogan-Browne et al. (Turnhout: Brepols, 2000), 49–67.

[66] See n. 44 above. The only work of Rolle's cited by Kempe is the Latin *Incendium amoris*.

move audiences to feel. These embedded lyrics render Christ's voice in an intimate register. This conclusion stems, not from modern assumptions about the vernacular as an intrinsically colloquial register, but rather from listening for echoes of preacherly discourse in *The Book of Margery Kempe*.

"It is a brotherhood": Obscene Storytelling and Fraternal Community in Fifteenth-Century Britain and Today

Carissa M. Harris
Temple University

Abstract

This article traces the early history of the explicit sexual verbs *swyve* and *fuck* in fifteenth-century England and Wales and provides a thorough overview of their origins and contexts, including *swyve*'s censorship in early manuscripts of the *Canterbury Tales*. It argues that obscene sexual storytelling is central to performances of masculine identity in same-sex textual communities, including letters among the younger Paston brothers; British Library, MS Harley 3362, a school notebook circulated among Cambridge students; and National Library of Wales, MS Peniarth 356B, a shared schoolbook from a Welsh Cistercian grammar school. This article explores the role of *fuck* and *swyve* in fostering fraternal bonds in homosocial discursive communities—particularly among men who are subordinate in some way, such as students and young, unmarried men subject to maternal authority—and shows how these terms can function to affirm male supremacy, authorize violence against women as well as other men, and encourage misogyny. It investigates these obscenities' pedagogical implications for teaching about sex, gender, consent, and power, drawing connections to the sharing of obscene narratives and images in all-male virtual spaces in the twenty-first century.

Keywords

masculinity; Chaucer; Paston letters; manuscripts; misogyny; obscenity; censorship; consent; pedagogy

ACCORDING TO A WARRANT issued by the State College Police Department in March 2015, a private Facebook group restricted to members of the fraternity Kappa Delta Rho at Pennsylvania State University circulated unauthorized sexual images of female students over

Studies in the Age of Chaucer 41 (2019): 239–266
© 2019 The New Chaucer Society

the course of several months. The virtual group's 144 members shared photographs "of nude females that appeared to be passed out and nude or in other sexual or embarrassing positions," and "it appears from the photos provided that the individuals in the photos are not aware that the photos had been taken."[1] Other photos depicted "strippers hired by the fraternity for a party."[2] Fraternity members added obscene narratives to the images: one wrote, "For all freshmen who don't know the background story I used to mercilessly fuck this chick when I was a freshman."[3] By "know[ing] the background story," the fraternity's younger members gain greater belonging in the group, and they learn the sexual scripts that their older peers expect them to perform. Another member boasted next to a photo of a woman, "I banged her lol [laughing out loud]."[4]

In an interview shortly after the group's existence was revealed, one anonymous Kappa Delta Rho member cast his brothers' actions as lighthearted fun and downplayed their violence by calling them "the humorous, albeit possibly misguided, antics of a bunch of college kids."[5] He said, "Everybody fools around, everybody makes jokes." Underscoring the homosocial nature of the group's actions, he declared, "It's an interfraternity thing and that's that," adding, "It is a brotherhood." His choice of the terms "inter-fraternity" and "brotherhood" illustrates the context as well as the purpose of the group's obscenity-sharing: by transgressing together within an all-male group, fraternity members set the terms for their shared vision of masculine identity and strengthened their bonds with one another. By invoking the ideal of a closed homosocial space, he claimed that the group's actions were harmless: "How

---

[1] The full warrant and affidavit of probable cause from the State College Police Department is available via Holly Otterbein, "Police: PSU Frat Posted Photos of Nude Unconscious Women on Facebook," *Philadelphia Magazine*, March 17, 2015, http://www.phillymag.com/news/2015/03/17/police-psu-frat-posted-photos-of-nude-unconscious-women-on-facebook/ (accessed July 13, 2019); this quotation occurs on page 2 of the affidavit.

[2] Affidavit of probable cause, page 1.

[3] Erin McCarthy and Anna Higgins, "'What I Hear Is that You Aren't Listening': Fraternities, Alcohol and Sexual Assault on College Campuses," *The Daily Collegian* and *The Cavalier Daily*, April 3, 2015, http://www.collegian.psu.edu/news/campus/article_42737bd2-d9be-11e4-a717-4ff4eba61251.html (accessed July 23, 2019). A cursory Google search of the phrase "mercilessly fuck" attests to its status as pornographic convention.

[4] Ibid.

[5] Holly Otterbein, "Member of Penn State's Kappa Delta Rho Defends Fraternity," *Philadelphia Magazine*, March 18, 2015, http://www.phillymag.com/news/2015/03/18/member-of-penn-states-kappa-delta-rho-defends-fraternity/ (accessed July 13, 2019).

240

would it [hurt anyone] when it's kept within . . . an entirely private group of 144 people?," he asked. As Mairead Eastin Moloney and Tony P. Love note, "the creation of a 'boys only' space is just as much about keeping women (down and) *out* as it is keeping men *in* (and in line)."[6] Here, this fantasy of "keeping men in" "an entirely private group" enabled the fraternity members to argue that their actions hurt no one as long as the group's gendered exclusivity remained intact.

Behaviors such as those by the Penn State students can be viewed as the result of new technologies that enable the swift, widespread dissemination of words and images.[7] However, these practices of teaching masculinity and building fraternal community through obscene storytelling stretch back to the Middle Ages, where they took place in letters and schoolbooks circulated among men. Whereas digital technology allows obscene narratives and images to metastasize rapidly across space, medieval manuscripts allowed these obscenities, and other men's responses to them, to accrue over time to much the same effect, as both technologies enable the creation of homosocial bonds. By tracing usages of the word *swyve*—the most explicit sexual verb in Middle English—and exploring its relationship to *fuck*, I argue that both verbs facilitated same-sex bonding and instruction in fifteenth-century England and Wales through their transgression and attention-grabbing shock value. In each of the examples that I discuss here, obscenities occur within close-knit, all-male textual communities of men who are subordinate in some way: correspondence among the unmarried Paston brothers, who express bitter resentment at being subject to their mother's authority; a schoolbook copied by a "puer" (boy) at a Welsh Cistercian grammar school; and a notebook circulated among Cambridge students in the fifteenth-through-seventeenth centuries. The obscenities function as a way for men in precarious positions—due to youth, unmarried status, or subjection to maternal or pedagogical authority—to bolster their own power, to build bonds with their peers, and to establish dominance over women as well as other men who are not members of their group. The terms operate as tools to teach a version of manhood that affirms male supremacy; encourages misogyny; prizes strong ties among those

---

[6] Mairead Eastin Moloney and Tony P. Love, "#TheFappening: Virtual Manhood Acts in (Homo)Social Media," *Men and Masculinities* 21, no. 5 (2018), 603–23 (610; emphasis in original).

[7] Nicola Henry and Anastasia Powell, *Sexual Violence in a Digital Age* (New York: Palgrave Macmillan, 2017).

who perform masculinity according to group norms; and condones violence against other men as well as women, often under the guise of lighthearted humor. These medieval examples shed light on the role of sexual storytelling in fostering synchronic fraternal bonds and teaching lessons about power and consent, they show how men used obscene language to alleviate anxieties regarding their place in the patriarchal order, and they carry important implications for understanding how obscenities shared among men can function in our own time.[8]

Swyve and *Fuck* in Context

This essay traces two intertwined histories: of the obscene verbs *swyve* and *fuck*, and of their centrality to modes of gendered textual community-building under pressure that persist to this day.[9] I categorize both terms as obscene, which I define as words referring to genitalia or sexual acts that are subject to cultural regulation.[10] The sense of taboo attached to these terms is demonstrated by the fact that they were sometimes written in code, scraped from the vellum page with knives, or replaced with more decorous terms by fifteenth-century scribes and readers.

The Middle English *swiven* (to fuck) survived nearly unaltered from the Old English verb *swifan*, which meant "to sweep, glide, revolve, move back and forth, move in a course."[11] Its early multivalence is illustrated by its usage in the Exeter Book riddles, where it characterizes a

---

[8] I am grateful to Sarah Salih for helping me to develop and clarify my argument here.

[9] I use Carolyn Dinshaw's definition of "community" as "some sort of social grouping that is not a conventional kinship group" but that nonetheless is frequently named using the language of brotherhood; *Getting Medieval: Sexualities and Communities, Pre- and Postmodern* (Durham, N.C.: Duke University Press, 1999), 22. On the inherently homosocial nature of medieval English masculine identity, see Derek G. Neal, *The Masculine Self in Late Medieval England* (Chicago: University of Chicago Press, 2008), 7.

[10] For an overview of obscenity in late medieval England, see Nicole Nolan Sidhu, *Indecent Exposure: Gender, Politics, and Obscene Comedy in Middle English Literature* (Philadelphia: University of Pennsylvania Press, 2016), 1–32. I focus on sexual obscenity rather than scatological or religious obscenity, although the latter, which typically entailed swearing by God's body parts, was connected with youthful masculinity in late medieval English culture. For more on this, see Miriam Gill, "From Urban Myth to Didactic Image: The Warning to Swearers," in *The Hands of the Tongue: Essays on Deviant Speech*, ed. Edwin D. Craun (Kalamazoo: Medieval Institute Publications, 2007), 137–60.

[11] *MED*, s.v. *swiven* (v.).

young bondswoman's movements of preparing ox-leather and pleasuring herself with a leather dildo.[12] Here the dildo is the speaking object operated by the woman's "hygegalan hond" (wanton hand), declaring, "swifeð me geond sweartne" (she turns me in the dark) (12a, 13a).[13] In another riddle from the same collection, *swifan* names the gliding motion of a ship at sea (*searoceap swifan* [to move skillfully crafted merchandise]).[14] By the later Middle Ages, *swiven* had become solely sexual, save for one example in which the phrase "swyve / A bareyn tree to childe" names the action of making a tree fruitful in the fifteenth-century Middle English translation of Palladius's *De re rustica* (c. 1440).[15] The non-corporeal valences of *swyve* either vanished entirely or were displaced onto *swivel*, *swifan*'s newly coined non-obscene descendant, which meant "a fastening or coupling device for a cart."[16]

Swiven's sexually explicit status is attested by its frequent censorship and alteration in fifteenth-century manuscripts of Geoffrey Chaucer's *Canterbury Tales*. In London, British Library, MS Harley 7333 (c. 1425–75), copied by a group of Augustinian canons at St. Mary de Pratis Abbey in Leicester, one scribe replaces four "swyve"s from Fragment I's bawdy fabliaux with the more decorous terms "served," "dyght," "pleyed with," and "edyght."[17] The canons omit *The Wife of Bath's Prologue and Tale* and *The Shipman's Tale* altogether, and someone later cut

[12] For more on this riddle's sexual implications, see Glenn Davis, "The Exeter Book Riddles and the Place of Sexual Idiom in Old English Literature," in *Medieval Obscenities*, ed. Nicola McDonald (York: York Medieval Press, 2006), 39–54; Sarah L. Higley, "The Wanton Hand: Reading and Reaching into Grammars and Bodies in Old English Riddle 12," in *Naked before God: Uncovering the Body in Anglo-Saxon England*, ed. Benjamin C. Withers and Jonathan Wilcox (Morganton: West Virginia University Press, 2003), 29–59; and Nina Rulon-Miller, "Sexual Humor and Fettered Desire in Exeter Book Riddle 12," in *Humour in Anglo-Saxon England*, ed. Jonathan Wilcox (Cambridge: D. S. Brewer, 2000), 99–126.

[13] *Old English Riddles of the "Exeter Book*," ed. Craig Williamson (Chapel Hill: University of North Carolina Press, 1979), no. 10.

[14] Ibid., no. 30.7a.

[15] In this instance, translated from the Latin *uberantur*, the Victorian editor has written "thryve" and then in a footnote added "swyve *auctor dicit*," indicating his sense of taboo regarding the word even when it is not used to name human sexual activity. *The Middle-English Translation of Palladius "De re rustica*," ed. Mark Liddell (Berlin: E. Ebering, 1896), XI.89.

[16] "*MED*, s.v. *swivel* (n.); *Dictionary of Medieval Latin from British Sources* (hereafter *DMLBS*), s.v. *swivelum* (n.). This term first appears in accounting records from Canterbury in 1294.

[17] Barbara Kline provides a thorough study of the manuscript in "Scribal Agendas and the Text of Chaucer's Tales in British Library MS Harley 7333," in *Rewriting Chaucer: Culture, Authority, and the Idea of the Authentic Text, 1400–1602*, ed. Thomas A. Prendergast and Barbara Kline (Columbus: Ohio State University Press, 1999), 116–

out the folios containing the bawdy pear-tree scene at the end of *The Merchant's Tale*.[18] The copyist of *The Reeve's Tale* expended inordinate effort upon censoring the "swyve" that Aleyn utters when voicing his plan to rape Malyne by substituting a more decorous synonym *and* changing the couplet's rhyme scheme, rewriting the offending line as well as the one preceding it. Whereas the standard text of the tale reads, "'For, John,' seyde he, 'als evere moot I thryve, / If that I may, yon wenche wil I swyve'" (I.4177–8), this copyist has written, "For Johan saide, 'Thanne als have I reste to nyght, / Yf that I may, the wenche here wolle I dyght.'"[19] His strenuous efforts to avoid writing "swyve" illuminate the verb's illicit status, and the altered couplet entails a brief, perplexing switch in speaker from Aleyn to John. The term occurs during a moment of boasting and sexual one-upmanship between the two young men, linking it to the fifteenth-century examples that I discuss later.[20]

Fuck, the closest synonym for *swyve*, originates from a cluster of Germanic words meaning "to strike, to beat, to breed cattle" and "to copulate."[21] Its earliest English appearance is in the form of a man's name,

---

44, esp. 126–27; also Timothy A. Shonk, "BL MS Harley 7333: The 'Publication' of Chaucer in the Rural Areas," *Essays in Medieval Studies* 15 (1999): 81–91. For these substitutions, see MS Harley 7333, fols. 56r, 59r, 59v. Kline notes that all four substitutions are copied by the same hand, which she christens Hand #3, suggesting that this copyist had a particular aversion to *swyve*. This scribe also copied *The Cook's Tale*, where "swyved" is written in a different fifteenth-century anglicana hand in slightly darker ink *over* an erasure, suggesting that the obscenity-averse scribe had originally copied a more decorous substitution (fol. 60r). The "swive" in *The Manciple's Tale*, copied in a hand that Kline christens Hand #4, remains unchanged (fol. 115r); Kline, "Scribal Agendas," 123.

[18] The page stubs from the censored folios of *The Merchant's Tale* are clearly visible between fols. 72 and 73.

[19] BL, MS Harley 7333, fols. 58v–59r; *The Riverside Chaucer*, gen. ed. Larry D. Benson, 3rd ed. (Boston, Mass.: Houghton Mifflin, 1987).

[20] For more on how *swyve* functions to foster competitive masculine communities in the *Canterbury Tales* as well as in the comic impotence poem *Lyarde* (c. 1430–50), both of which feature it seven times, see Carissa M. Harris, *Obscene Pedagogies: Transgressive Talk and Sexual Education in Late Medieval Britain* (Ithaca: Cornell University Press, 2018), Chap. 1 and conclusion.

[21] *OED*, s.v. *fuck* (v.); Roger Lass, "Four Letters in Search of an Etymology," *Diachronica* 12 (1995): 99–111; Anatoly Liberman, *Analytic Dictionary of English Etymology* (Minneapolis: University of Minnesota Press, 2007), 78–87; Jesse Sheidlower, *The F-Word*, 3rd ed. (Oxford: Oxford University Press, 2009), ix–xi, 83. *Fuck* does not appear as a sexual verb in the *MED*, and its first *OED* quotation is dated ante 1500, with the next dated ?ante 1513. However, the examples I cite below suggest that it was indeed used in a sexual sense during the later medieval period, and its scarcity in the dictionary record can be attributed to more recent editorial reactions to its obscenity.

"Roger Fuckebythenavele," in a 1310 Chester court roll.[22] This colorful surname, a compound of a verb, preposition, definite article, and noun, appears seven times in the roll during 1310 and 1311, as Roger evaded arrest for a serious unnamed offense and was subsequently outlawed. Paul Booth suggests that it translates to "fuck through the navel" or "fuck next to the navel."[23] Richard Coates argues that a 1373 Bristol charter referring to "Fockynggroue" constitutes another sexual usage of the term, suggesting that the location was known as a site for copulation.[24] The use of obscenities in surnames and place names shows that these terms were perhaps viewed as taboo chiefly in their literary context, as those are the only examples that show signs of censorship.[25] The earliest literary uses of *fuck* occur in two fifteenth-century schoolbooks circulated among groups of men, and one of these instances is written in code.[26] Even though we are still in the process of understanding precisely how prevalent *fuck* was in Middle English, these examples attest to its existence and accompanying discursive power. Through their illicit status—evidenced by the fact that they were frequently censored or altered—*fuck* and *swyve* functioned as tools for community-building particularly in pedagogical contexts, as they were used to share bawdy narratives and to teach lessons about gender, sex, consent, and power.

The examples that I discuss here illustrate how obscene storytelling functions as a "manhood act" that some men—including provincial gentry, university students, fraternity brothers, and Cistercian schoolboys—perform under pressure to signify a masculine self and to build gendered discursive communities.[27] This is especially important for men who are

[22] Paul Booth, "An Early Fourteenth-Century Use of the F-Word in Cheshire, 1310–11," *Transactions of the Historic Society of Lancashire and Cheshire* 164 (2015): 99–102.

[23] Ibid., 100.

[24] Richard Coates, "*Fockynggroue* in Bristol," *N&Q* 54, no. 4 (2007): 373–76. In 1528, the phrase "O d[amned] fuckin abbot" was written in the margins of Oxford, Brasenose College, MS VII next to a criticism of the "false" abbot of Osney on fol. 62v. Edward Wilson, "A 'Damned F. . .in Abbot' in 1528: The Earliest English Example of a Four-Letter Word," *N&Q* 40, no. 1 (1993): 29–34.

[25] Malcolm Jones discusses obscene surnames in "Sex, Popular Beliefs, and Culture," in *A Cultural History of Sexuality in the Middle Ages*, ed. Ruth Evans (New York: Berg, 2011), 139–64.

[26] See my discussion of MSS Harley 3362 and Peniarth 356B below. For the relationship between *fuck* and masculine community in Middle Scots flytings produced at the sixteenth-century Stewart court, see Harris, *Obscene Pedagogies*, Chap. 2.

[27] For more on how "manhood acts" function socially to signify a masculine self, see Michael Schwalbe, *Manhood Acts: Gender and the Practices of Domination* (Boulder, Colo.: Paradigm, 2014).

disempowered in some way—as students in the process of proving masculinity or as unmarried sons subject to their widowed mother's authority—because their verbal aggression illuminates the uncertainty of their position in relation to other men with whom they are vying for dominance. This tale-telling serves as a form of pedagogy, teaching the men who witness it about group norms and shared behavioral codes, and it enables these not-quite-men to claim a place in the hierarchy by asserting dominance over women.

In their analysis of manhood acts on Twitter in response to the massive nonconsensual leak of female celebrities' intimate photos in August 2014, Moloney and Love identify "creation of homosocial, heterosexist space," "sexualization of women," and "humor as a tool of oppression" as "manhood acts commonly employed to signify elevated membership in the heterosexist hierarchy."[28] Nicola Henry and Anastasia Powell likewise argue that technology enables groups of men to "facilitate the construction of particular masculine identities based on collective participation in the objectification of women, sexism, misogyny, and permissive attitudes toward non-consensual sex."[29] While these scholars focus on virtual spaces in the twenty-first century, many of their insights regarding gender, power, and shared discourse can also be applied to premodern textual communities created by letters exchanged and notebooks shared within networks of men. The members of these groups cloak their lessons in laughter, using humor as a tool to downplay the violence in the stories that they share with one another, as when the anonymous Kappa Delta Rho member claimed that his peers' online actions were "funny to some extent," "just satire," and "just . . . fooling around."[30]

"As kompany requereyd": Obscene Storytelling among the Paston Brothers

The brothers John II, John III, and Edmond II Paston exchanged dozens of letters between Norfolk, London, and Calais during the mid-to-late

[28] Moloney and Love, "#TheFappening," 606.

[29] Nicola Henry and Anastasia Powell, "Embodied Harms: Gender, Shame, and Technology-Facilitated Sexual Violence," *Violence against Women* 21 (2015): 758–79 (770).

[30] Otterbein, "Member of Penn State's Kappa Delta Rho Defends Fraternity." For more on sexual humor as a tool of power and oppression, see Moloney and Love, "#TheFappening," 616–17; Mary Jane Kehily and Anoop Nayak, "'Lads and Laugh-

fifteenth century, and their correspondence demonstrates obscenity's role in teaching the "requere[ments]" of masculine "kompany." Although the brothers focus primarily upon business affairs, family matters, and local news in their letters, they also exchange bawdy tales and jests: they marvel at a man whose "pyntell [penis] is asse longe as hys legge"; they rib one another about two women whom they call "the hoorys [whores]," with John II mockingly telling John III, "I remember not ther names; ye knowe them better than I"; and they share lurid tales that illuminate obscenity's role in shaping gendered communities.[31]

In a 1472 letter sent from the family estate at Mautby in Norfolk to his elder brother John III in London, Edmond Paston II laments that their mother Margaret fired his beloved servant Gregory. He expresses heartfelt affection for Gregory, declaring, "I am he that is as sory to departe from hym as any man on lyve [alive] from hys servant . . . [for] he is as true as any on lyve."[32] He explains why Margaret fired Gregory, claiming he was punished unfairly for a night of harmless fun:

Yt happyd hym to have a knavys loste, in pleyn termes to swhyve a quene; and so dyd in the konynere-closse [rabbit warren yard]. Yt foretunyd hym to be a-spyed be ij plowemen of my modyrs, whyche werene as fayne as he of that matere, and deseyred hym to have parte; and as kompany requereyd, seyd not nay, jn so myche that the plowemen had here alle a nythe in there stabylle and Gregory was clene delyverd [completely rid] of here and, as he swhereys, had not a do wyth here wyth-in my modyres place. Not wyth-standdyng my modyre thynkkys that he was grownd of that matere.[33]

Edmond performs several feats of linguistic manipulation to remove agency from Gregory's actions while at the same time granting him control over the woman's body. He portrays his servant's choices in passive terms: "yt happyd hym to have a knavys loste," he relates, using an

ter': Humour and the Production of Heterosexual Hierarchies," *Gender and Education* 9 (1997): 69–87; Sara Ahmed, *Living a Feminist Life* (Durham, N.C.: Duke University Press, 2017), 261–62.

[31] *The Paston Letters and Papers of the Fifteenth Century*, ed. Norman Davis, 3 vols. (Oxford: Oxford University Press, 2004), 1:415, 443–44. Neal analyzes the "pyntell" passage in *The Masculine Self*, 132–35, and Colin Richmond discusses the brothers' penchant for "men's locker-room talk" in *The Paston Family in the Fifteenth Century: Endings* (Manchester: Manchester University Press, 2000), 33–34.

[32] Davis, *Paston Letters and Papers*, 1:636.

[33] Ibid., 1:635. See also Neal, *The Masculine Self*, 160–62. Richmond briefly discusses both Paston examples that I analyze here in *The Paston Family*, 34 n. 55.

impersonal construction invoking chance and luck, and casting Gregory as a victim of uncontrollable desire linked to transgressive lower-class masculinity.[34] Edmond names Gregory's sexual partner as "a quene," a derogatory term meaning "a lowborn woman" or "a harlot" that frequently functioned as "a term of abuse."[35] By naming her in this way, Edmond categorizes her as a "common woman" whose status confers universal consent and removes the possibility of rape, a rhetorical move whose chilling implications soon become clear.[36]

When Gregory and the woman are spotted by two of his fellow employees, the incident takes a disturbing turn. The plowmen witness their peer having sex and ask him if they may "have parte" in the encounter, construing intercourse as something that men do together as a communal enterprise, as "parte[s]" of a group, and invoking a collective sexual subjectivity in which men share in each other's bodily pleasures.[37] The men's mutual enjoyment is reinforced by Edmond's use of the phrase "as fayne [desirous of, delighted] as he" to describe the plowmen's reaction to the sight, equating Gregory's corporeal pleasure with his peers' joy in witnessing it.[38] By representing intercourse as homosocial identification and perpetuating this vicarious thrill by relating the tale to his brother, Edmond demonstrates how one man's sexual actions provide gratification for his peers that can be savored through repeated retelling.

The woman is depicted as having no agency at all in Edmond's narrative, illustrated by the plowmen's choice to seek consent from Gregory rather than from her. Gregory grants consent on her behalf "as kompany requereyd," casting Gregory's choices as compelled by the rules of gendered community and implying that shared access to the woman's body cements the three men's bond with one another. This phrase draws on "kompany'"s valences of "intimate association with others," "companionship," and "fellowship" to suggest that their shared homosocial code "requere[s]" (demands, requires, commands) Gregory to privilege

---

[34] *MED*, s.vv. *happen* (v.[1]), defs. 1 and 2; *knave* (n.[1]), defs. 1, 2, 3.

[35] *MED*, s.v. *quene* (n.[1]), def. 1(b).

[36] Ruth Mazo Karras cites one case from Ipswich in which "Hugh Moon was accused of raping Alice Hill, and in the same court session Alice Hill was accused of being a common whore with Hugh Moon and others. Several other cases also follow this pattern." *Common Women: Prostitution and Sexuality in Medieval England* (Oxford: Oxford University Press, 1996), 101.

[37] *MED*, s.v. *part* (n.), def. 2(b[a]).

[38] *MED*, s.v. *fain* (adj.), defs. 1(a), 3.

his peers' desires over all else.[39] Edmond's use of "requereyd," and his claim that Gregory "seyd not nay" to his peers' demand, illuminate the implicit violence underlying this type of "kompany" and illustrate how it subordinates its participants.

By designating the woman as a "quene," Edmond leaves open the possibility that the men are simply haggling over the price of a sex worker for the night, but the term's semantic elasticity sheds light on how this version of masculinity imagines women's consent: as a "quene," her consent is assumed not to matter, showing how her bodily agency can be denied by affixing the name of "quene" to her. She cannot say no, for her status as "quene" at once renders her *yes* eternal and removes the need for it altogether. In telling the tale to his brother 135 miles away, Edmond both "has parte" in his servants' sordid night and invites his brother to join the "kompany," as the men are united by powerful bonds—between Gregory and the plowmen, between Gregory and Edmond, between Edmond and John III—that cross class lines.

Edmond, who is unmarried and living at home at the time, insists that his widowed mother is responsible for rupturing his bond with Gregory. He complains bitterly that "my modyre hathe causyd me to putte Gregory owte of my servyse," his use of "causyd" portraying Margaret as exercising power over him, and uniting himself with Gregory and the plowmen as equally subordinate to her overbearing matriarchal authority.[40] He places her in sharp opposition to the homosocial fellowship marked by sexual exploits and shared stories, and he portrays himself and Gregory as victims of her domestic tyranny, their obscene storytelling pointing to their precarious masculinity and serving as a tool for challenging that precarity. This sentiment is common in the brothers' letters, as when John III writes a long letter of complaint from the family home to John II in the same year: "Many qwarellys ar pyekyd to get my brodyr E[dmond] and me ought of hyr howse. We go not to bed unchedyn lyghtly [unrebuked]," he laments, invoking the misogynist stereotype of the chiding shrew and depicting himself as united with "my brodyr E" against their mother's sharp-tongued domination in "hyr howse."[41] The obscene story's circulation, from Gregory to Edmond to John, binds the men to one another and functions as a rebellion against Margaret's killjoy matriarchal authority: through telling the

[39] *MED*, s.vv. *compaignie* (n.), def. 3(a); *requeren* (v.), def. 1(c, e).
[40] *MED*, s.v. *causen* (v.), def. 2(a).
[41] Davis, *Paston Letters and Papers*, 1:576.

tale of the incident that offended his mother so grievously, Edmond defies her and seeks to preserve his bond with Gregory by begging his brother to hire him.

The Paston brothers use *swyve* once elsewhere in their letters, illustrating its capacity to unite some men and to assert power over others. In August 1478, John II writes to his younger brother John III from London with a graphic rape narrative:

Yonge William Brandon is in warde [custody] and arestyd fore thatt he . . . by force ravysshyd and swyvyd an olde jentylwoman, and yitt was nott therwyth easyd but swyvyd hyr oldest dowtre and than wolde have swyvyd the othere sustre bothe, wher-fore men sey fowle off hym, that he wolde ete the henne and alle her chekynnys; and som sey that the Kynge entendyth to sitte [pass judgment] uppon hym, and men seye he is lyke to be hangyd.[42]

Unlike the woman in the previous letter, whose potential rape is elided by Edmond's choice to name her as a "quene," here the victims' social status as a "jentylwoman" and her daughters, along with the modifiers "by force" and "ravysshyd," render their assaults nameable as such and generate shared outrage among "men." John uses "swyvyd" three times, one for each of Brandon's acts of violence. Here the obscenity serves to unite a group of men—John II, "the Kynge," and the "men" who disparage Brandon and express their belief that he will be hanged—against another man, and it also asserts their gendered power in comparison to the victimized women. John applies a metaphor of ravenous consumption to the attack, casting Brandon as the predator who "wolde ete the henne and alle her chekynnys," who steals and devours another man's feminized property. The tale of the three women's trauma is shared freely among men, emphasized by John II's twofold use of the phrase "men seye" to characterize its circulation. The Paston brothers' personal rivalry with the Brandon brothers, also from a Norfolk gentry family, colors John II's narrative—just one month previously, John III referred

---

[42] Ibid., 1:512. I have not been able to find mention of this case in legal records, but on March 28, 1484, a "General Pardon" was issued "to William Brandon the younger, 'gentilman,' alias esquire, son of William Brandon of the county of Norfolk, knight, of all offenses committed by him before 27 March." In *Calendar of the Patent Rolls Preserved in the Public Record Office: Edward IV–Richard III, AD 1476–1485* (London: Mackie, 1901), 423. Brandon was eventually killed by Richard III's forces in the Battle of Bosworth Field; Davis, *Paston Letters and Papers*, 2:594. For more on Brandon see Colin Richmond, *The Paston Family in the Fifteenth Century: Fastolf's Will* (Cambridge: Cambridge University Press, 1996), 124 n. 65.

to William Brandon (1456–85) and his brother as "my gretest enmy-eys" and reported having "gret wordys" with them—and his threefold use of "swyvyd" serves as a verbal weapon against his younger peer.[43]

The Paston brothers use *swyve* to foster fraternal community in spite of the geographical spaces that separate them, and to cement alliances with other men, just as the men in the examples I discuss below use it to create same-sex communities across time. Edmond uses obscene storytelling to ally himself with John II, Gregory, and the two plowmen against the matriarchal authority of Margaret Paston, whereas his brother John II uses it to unite with the king and the men of London against his hometown rival. In the former case, men in subordinate posi-tions affiliate themselves with other disempowered men, whereas in the latter case, obscene storytelling enables John II to join with other, more powerful men against his "gretest [enmye]." Acknowledging the explicit nature of "swhyve" by characterizing it as "pleyn termes," the Paston brothers deploy it to convey lessons about power, consent, social status, and culpability: they teach that women categorized as "quenes" do not possess the power to say no to sex, whereas gentlewomen who are assaulted deserve men's collective empathy and outrage.

"Wode" Women and "Wys" Men in MS Peniarth 356B

My next two examples are more explicitly pedagogical, showing how obscenities copied in fifteenth-century schoolbooks played an integral role in the intertwined processes of acquiring proficiency in Latin gram-mar and learning codes of masculine behavior. Christopher Cannon dis-cusses how schoolbooks in later medieval Britain drew from a common body of popular pedagogical texts but were largely "improvisatory," as schoolboys copied short Latin texts or proverbs into their notebooks before translating them into the vernacular, blurring the lines between schoolroom translation and literary creation.[44] These schoolbooks typi-cally contained a mixture of grammatical treatises and translation exer-cises, as pupils wrote down the rules of grammar and tested their knowledge of those rules through pedagogical exercises, just as they copied the tenets of misogynist masculinity and wrote down obscene

---

[43] Davis, *Paston Letters and Papers*, 1:568.

[44] For an overview of late medieval English schoolbooks like the two manuscripts I discuss here, see Christopher Cannon, *From Literacy to Literature: England, 1300–1400* (Oxford: Oxford University Press, 2016), 41–83.

verses.[45] Marjorie Curry Woods observes that "sexual imagery is omnipresent in the texts used to teach Latin to medieval boys, and rape is a common narrative vehicle in these texts."[46] She argues that the rape narratives popular in the classroom curriculum required young boys to identify with the perspective of both perpetrator and victim as they underwent the twin processes of learning Latin and masculinity.[47] Both Woods and Cannon note that Claudian's *Rape of Proserpina* was central to the grammar school curriculum, surviving in numerous thirteenth- and fourteenth-century English schoolbooks similar to the ones I discuss below.[48] We can see a comparable phenomenon in the case of Penn State's Kappa Delta Rho: the "freshmen" in the virtual group, depicted as the audience of at least one obscene narrative, are taught by their older peers' stories that it is laudable "to mercilessly fuck . . . chick[s]" at the same time that they are subjected to violence from those peers in the form of hazing. Housed within academic institutions, fraternities such as Kappa Delta Rho portray themselves as "communities . . . committed to . . . academic achievement" and "brotherhood" at the same time that they share obscene material, just as medieval men shared obscene verses while attending all-male schools and learning Latin together.[49] In both cases, these communities are marginalized within the larger patriarchal order on account of their status as not-quite-men, and their misogynist obscenities can be read as a defensive reaction against actual or perceived disempowerment: the grammar school students were subject to corporeal violence by their masters, while the Penn State students are part of an academic institution whose ratio of male to female students has fallen from 5:2 to 6:5 since the 1950s, enabling

[45] Cannon lists thirty-one medieval schoolbooks in ibid., 61–62.

[46] Marjorie Curry Woods, "Rape and the Pedagogical Rhetoric of Sexual Violence," in *Criticism and Dissent in the Middle Ages*, ed. Rita Copeland (Cambridge: Cambridge University Press, 1996), 56–86 (58); also Marjorie Curry Woods, *Classroom Commentaries: Teaching the "Poetria nova" across Medieval and Renaissance Europe* (Columbus: Ohio State University Press, 2010), 60–65.

[47] Woods, "Rape and the Pedagogical Rhetoric of Sexual Violence," 61–62. For more on the role of racy or sexually violent material in the grammar school curriculum, see Neal, *The Masculine Self*, 158–59; Ruth Mazo Karras, *From Boys to Men: Formations of Masculinity in Late Medieval Europe* (Philadelphia: University of Pennsylvania Press, 2003), 77–78.

[48] Cannon, *From Literacy to Literature*, 65, 163.

[49] "Office of Fraternity and Sorority Life," http://studentaffairs.psu.edu/hub/greeks/ (accessed July 23, 2019).

their actions to be construed as a backlash against gender-integrated education and a violent reinforcement of all-male spaces.[50]

Obscenity's capacity to teach masculine conduct is central to Aberystwyth, National Library of Wales, MS Peniarth 356B (1460s–1480s), a monastic schoolbook. The manuscript's compiler and main scribe was Thomas Pennant, who served as abbot of Basingwerk Abbey, a Cistercian foundation in north Wales, from 1481 to 1522.[51] Pennant fathered three illegitimate sons, including one named Thomas who became vicar of Holywell, and another, Nicholas (b. 1495), who succeeded him as abbot. He oversaw a revival of the abbey's fortunes, as he was renowned for his patronage of Welsh bards, architectural improvements, and lavish hospitality to guests. Although Pennant copied the bulk of the manuscript's contents, it contains eight hands in total, including six from the mid-to-late fifteenth century and two from the first half of the sixteenth century, as it continued to circulate among the abbey's monks in the decades before its dissolution in 1537.[52] It consists of 192 paper and parchment leaves, and contains Middle English and Latin grammatical texts; proverbs; English glosses on Latin words; prayers; and English, Latin, Welsh, and macaronic verses.[53] The manuscript evidence

[50] For more on schoolboys and physical violence see Ben Parsons, "Beaten for a Book: Domestic and Pedagogic Violence in *The Wife of Bath's Prologue*," *SAC* 27 (2015): 163–94. On Penn State's gender ratios in the 1950s and 2017–18, see Michael Bezilla, *Penn State: An Illustrated History* (University Park: Pennsylvania State University Press, 1985); https://libraries.psu.edu/about/collections/penn-state-university-park-campus-history -collection/penn-state-illustrated-3 (accessed July 13, 2019); and "Admission and University Statistics," https://admissions.psu.edu/apply/statistics/ (accessed May 26, 2018). I am grateful to Sarah Salih for pointing me in this direction.

[51] For a description of the manuscript and its contents, see David Thomson, "Aberystwyth, National Library of Wales, MS Peniarth 356B," in *A Descriptive Catalogue of Middle English Grammatical Texts* (New York: Garland, 1979), 114–31. For more on Pennant and his book, see Janet Burton and Karen Stöber, *Abbeys and Priories in Medieval Wales* (Cardiff: University of Wales Press, 2015), 46–50; Arthur Jones, "Basingwerk Abbey," in *Historical Essays in Honour of James Tait*, ed. J. G. Edwards, V. H. Galbraith, and E. F. Jacob (Manchester: Manchester University Press, 1933), 169–78 (175–76); Ceridwen Lloyd-Morgan, "Manuscripts and the Monasteries," in *Monastic Wales: New Approaches*, ed. Janet Burton and Karen Stöber (Cardiff: University of Wales, 2013), 209–27 (215); William Marx, "Peniarth 356 (*olim* Hengwrt 209)," in *The Handbook of Middle English Prose, Handlist XIV: Manuscripts in the National Library of Wales (Llyfrgell Genedlaethol Cymru), Aberystwyth* (Woodbridge: D. S. Brewer, 1999), 40–42.

[52] For a list of the hands and their respective dates, see Thomson, "MS Peniarth 356B," 115; for its later circulation history, see 131.

[53] The schoolbook's grammatical texts include John of Garland's *Distigius* and *Synonyma et equivoca*; Oxford grammar master John Leyland's *Comparacio*, *Informacio*, and *Accedence*; Cato's *Distichs*; Donatus's *Ars minor*; and multiple anonymous treatises on

suggests that Pennant began compiling the schoolbook as a boy learning Latin in the 1460s, probably at a grammar school attached to Basingwerk Abbey.[54] Pennant writes the colophon "Thomas Pennant bonus puer [good boy]" on fols. 45r and 135r, and David Thomson argues that a list of students' names, weekly attendance tallies, and school fees on fol. 95r–v indicates that he may have served as schoolmaster before he became a monk.[55] Pennant continued to copy didactic texts as he transitioned from student to teacher, rendering the codex an extraordinary pedagogical document of both learning and instruction spanning several decades.[56]

At the top of fol. 149v in the midst of a collection of Latin proverbs alongside their renderings in English, Pennant copied a short, obscene poem as a translation exercise:

> Women were wode and sweryn by the rote [error for "rode"]
> That thay swylde fuc ne men.
> Men were wys and turnyd her gerys
> And sowyvud ham.
> Femine de mentes fuerunt & per cruculas iuraverunt
> Quod omnes homines stupaverint mares erant sapientes
> & gesturas cambientes illas deflorarent.

[Women were out of their minds and swore by the cross
That they would block all men (from having sex with them). Men were wise
And, changing their conduct, deflowered/raped them].[57]

These verses, which have gone virtually unnoticed by scholars until now, are significant for understanding the history of obscenity in English.[58]

---

orthography. For editions of the Leylond treatises, see *An Edition of the Middle English Grammatical Texts*, ed. David Thomson (New York: Garland, 1984).

[54] Thomson, "MS Peniarth 356B," 130–31; David Thomson, "Cistercians and Schools in Later Medieval Wales," *Cambridge Medieval Celtic Studies* 3 (1982): 76–80.

[55] Thomson, "Cistercians and Schools," 79–80.

[56] Thomson, "MS Peniarth 356B," 130.

[57] Thomson christens this portion of the manuscript "Section O," comprising "a collection of proverbs in English, Latin, and Welsh" on fols. 148–51. These folios are in Pennant's hand (ibid., 129).

[58] The Middle English quatrain does not appear in the *Digital Index of Middle English Verse* (hereafter *DIMEV*), and is printed elsewhere only in a brief, erroneous footnote in *William Dunbar: The Complete Works*, ed. John Conlee (Kalamazoo: Medieval Institute Publications, 2004), 367 n. 13. The Latin has never been printed until now. Thomson includes only the first English line in his description of the manuscript ("MS Peniarth 356B," 129).

As one of the rare early literary examples of *fuck* they provide valuable insight into its usage and show that it was used interchangeably with *swyve*. The quatrain contrasts the "wode" women who refuse intercourse with the "wys" men, who ignore their nonconsent and penetrate them anyway, and uses alliteration to underscore the gendered contrast between "wode" and "wys." "Wode" contains valences of recklessness, anger, foolishness, and insanity, whereas "wys" denotes prudence, discretion, and cleverness in addition to more negative connotations of deviousness and cunning.[59] The verses represent women's choice to "fuc ne men" as a rash decision resulting from an unsound mind, implying that feminine sexual willingness is the reasonable norm, and they depict ignoring women's refusals as a clever choice. Pennant translates "sowyvud" from *deflorare*, a verb meaning "to deflower (sexually), to ravish" whose valences range from loss of virginity to rape.[60] By using the obscenity to translate a term with strong connotations of violation, Pennant implies that sexual force is permissible when women withhold their consent. He translates "fuc ne" from *stupare*, meaning "to block or stop (a gap, breach, passage)" and "to obstruct, impede, hinder," exchanging the women's non-obscene declaration of nonconsent for a sexually explicit one and trading a verb denoting women's preventing men's sexual incursion for one signifying women's deliberate choice not to copulate with men.[61] By translating *stupare* and *deflorare* as "fuc ne" and "sowyvud," Pennant both emphasizes women's sexual agency and elides the original verses' sexual violence.

Pennant's obscene pedagogical exercise highlights women's sexual agency in order to teach readers its foolishness and futility, using humor to produce the quatrain's punchline: "wode" women make sworn declarations regarding their bodies, only to be put in their place by "wys" men. In an unusual moment of gendered sexual-grammatical agency, Pennant depicts women as agents of the verb "fuc," which does not happen elsewhere until the seventeenth century.[62] As Ruth Mazo Karras notes, sexual activity was understood in the Middle Ages as something

---

[59] *MED*, s.vv. *wod* (adj.), defs. 1(a), 3(b, d); *wis* (adj.), def. 2(a, c).

[60] *DMLBS*, s.v. *deflorare* (v.), def. 1(b).

[61] *DMLBS*, s.v. *stuppare* (v.), def. 2.

[62] The next recorded use of *fuck* with a feminine agent occurs in *As I Went to Westminster Abbey* (c. 1610): "She's a damn'd lascivious Bitch / And fucks for half-a-crown." In *Bawdy Verse*, ed. E. J. Burford (New York: Penguin, 1982), 63. *The Dictionary of the Older Scots Tongue*, which goes to 1700, does not cite any examples of *fuk* with a feminine agent.

that one person—typically a man—did to another person even when it was initiated by a female partner, rendering this example extremely unusual.[63] Pennant's brief attribution of agency to women is immediately reversed in the next couplet: women become the butt of the joke and the object of the verb, as men successfully "sowyv[e]" them in the end. Pennant's use of "sowyvud" in the final line returns agency to the wily men, as he deftly restores their dominance by rendering "sowyvud" with men as the agents and women as the objects. Overcoming women's sworn "no" and their assertion of bodily sovereignty is the quatrain's punchline.

Pennant copies the verses alongside proverbs such as "Better ys late then never," "Loke or thu speke and thynke or thu speke," and "The wod hath erys the fylde syght."[64] This lends them didactic authority, as does his inclusion of them in a codex whose primary purpose was the teaching and learning of Latin. On the same folio as his bawdy verses, Pennant copies proverbial instructions addressed to a "ffelow" (companion), translated from the Latin vocative noun *socie* (companion, comrade), imagining a pedagogical community in which men teach and learn from one another.[65] The manuscript bears signs of heavy use and circulation among the monks at Basingwerk Abbey—scribbles, decorative flourishes, linear glosses, marginal notes, and drawings in different inks and hands—that bolster the abbey's status as a textual community where "manhood acts" are performed for the "ffelow[s]." The codex shows how monastic schoolboys—disempowered by youth and subject to corporal punishment from other men—could use obscenity to assert power by emphasizing men's sexual domination of women.

Restricted Access: Pedagogical Community in BL, MS Harley 3362

Swyve and *fuck* are also copied together in BL, MS Harley 3362 (c. 1475), a university student's school notebook annotated by successive

---

[63] Ruth Mazo Karras, *Sexuality in Medieval Europe: Doing unto Others*, 3rd ed. (New York: Routledge, 2017), 4–6.

[64] The first two proverbs (Bartlett Jere Whiting and Helen Wescott Whiting, *Proverbs, Sentences, and Proverbial Phrases: From English Writings Mainly before 1500* [Cambridge, Mass.: Belknap Press, 1968], L98; and *DIMEV*, 3173) are copied along with others on MS Peniarth 356B, fol. 148v. The third (*DIMEV*, 5532), copied on fol. 149v, also appears in MS Harley 3362, fol. 5r.

[65] MS Peniarth 356B, fol. 149v: "ffelow yff thu haste the kybe / Tell hyt not to wyde" (Companion, if you have chilblains, do not broadcast it too widely).

generations of scholars throughout the sixteenth and seventeenth centuries.[66] The early modern readers augmented the miscellany's contents, added additional glosses and references, and underlined or drew manicules next to words they viewed as noteworthy, showing how the notebook's textual and pedagogical community developed over time. Martha Rust notes that "a systematic study of Harley 3362 has yet to appear in print, but through the piecemeal efforts of a number of scholars, its intriguing contents and literary ramifications have come to light."[67] My discussion of the manuscript's obscenity and gender politics shows how it portrays misogyny as a rite of passage, and obscenity as a strategy for gaining a foothold in the patriarchal system by exerting power over the bodies of women as well as rival men.

The original scribe seems to have begun compiling and copying the ninety-one-leaf paper codex as he gained greater proficiency in Latin grammar and vocabulary, and his English translations become markedly more accurate as the notebook progresses. The manuscript, which Julia Boffey characterizes as "a scrappy student notebook" and "a pedagogical anthology," sheds light on the process of learning both Latin and a specific brand of misogynist masculinity.[68] It is heavily corrected, particularly at the beginning, with numerous strikethroughs, additions, expunction, and words written in superscript by later readers. It is nonetheless extremely orderly, as the original scholar's hand is neat and regular, his "i"s are carefully dotted, and his pages are ruled, while later readers have added cross-references to link different texts in the manuscript. This orderliness contributes to the notebook's sense of textual community, enabling its knowledge to be marked, cross-referenced, shared, and understood by others long after it has left the hands of its original scribe.

---

[66] For more on Harley 3362, see Julia Boffey, "The Manuscripts of English Courtly Love Lyrics in the Fifteenth Century," in *Manuscripts and Readers in Fifteenth-Century England: The Literary Implications of Manuscript Study*, ed. Derek Pearsall (Cambridge: D. S. Brewer, 1983), 3–14 (13–14), and Julia Boffey, *Manuscripts of English Courtly Love Lyrics in the Later Middle Ages* (Cambridge: D. S. Brewer, 1985), 25, 89, 192; Martha Rust, "An Exposition of Women's Names in British Library Harley MS 3362," *JEBS* 9 (2006): 141–48; *A Catalogue of the Harleian Manuscripts in the British Museum*, 4 vols. (London: British Museum, 1808–12), 3:20; Ad Putter, "The French of English Letters: Two Trilingual Verse Epistles in Context," in *Language and Culture in Medieval Britain: The French of England c. 1100–c. 1500*, ed. Jocelyn Wogan-Browne with Carolyn Collette, Maryanne Kowaleski, Linne Mooney, Ad Putter, and David Trotter (York: York Medieval Press, 2009), 397–408 (397, 401).

[67] Rust, "An Exposition of Women's Names," 141.

[68] Boffey, *Manuscripts of English Courtly Love Lyrics*, 89.

Harley 3362's chief contents are Latin grammatical exercises—proverbs, riddles, and epigrams drawn from the popular corpus of scholastic *sententiae*—with occasional Middle English glosses and translations, underscoring its primary function as a pedagogical document, an aid for gathering and retaining knowledge. It contains popular educational texts such as Robert Grosseteste's *Stans puer et mensam* and *Ut te geras ad mensam*, two didactic treatises on table manners and appropriate conduct addressed specifically to young men; verses on the evils of drunkenness and the virtues of good wine; John of Garland's *Synonyma et equivoca*, a thirteenth-century treatise on synonyms; riddles; misogynist verses; and a trilingual pair of courtly love lyrics.[69] The manuscript features at least five scribal hands: the original fifteenth-century student hand, a second fifteenth-century hand, a sixteenth-century secretary scrawl, a spiderlike seventeenth-century hand responsible for several page headings and a corrective gloss of *stuprum* (licentious behavior) on fol. 65v, and another seventeenth-century hand that used a crude brown crayon-like implement to underline derogatory material about women and to write "John Garland" throughout the manuscript.[70] The longevity of this scribal conversation is remarkable, demonstrating obscene misogyny's capacity to foster bonds among men across time. In addition to their shared focus on correcting one another's Latin and disparaging women, the notebook's many hands betray a mutual interest in sexed bodies. The original student-scribe wrote "Genitalia non habet ille" (That man does not have genitals) as the first line on fol. 37v, while a different fifteenth-century hand wrote the same statement in the upper-right margin of the page. A third, later hand directs the reader to fol. 14r, where they have underlined another "genitalia non habet ille," written by the first scribe, and added a marginal cross-reference pointing the reader back to fol. 37v. With its multiplicity of hands reinforcing the notebook's pedagogical misogyny and emphasis on corporeality, Harley 3362 sheds light on how men learned from one another in a textual community spanning three centuries.

A two-line Latin couplet on the notebook's original parchment cover

[69] For *Stans puer ad mensam*, see Servus Gieben, "Robert Grosseteste and Medieval Courtesy-Books," *Vivarium* 5 (1967): 47–74; for the riddles, see Andrew Galloway, "The Rhetoric of Riddling in Late-Medieval England: The 'Oxford' Riddles, the *Secretum philosophorum*, and the Riddles in *Piers Plowman*," *Speculum* 70, no. 1 (1995): 68–105 (98–101); and the pair of love epistles is discussed in Putter, "The French of English Letters."

[70] See fols. 6r, 23v, 79v.

(fol. 1v) announces the compilation's inordinate interest in women. It concludes with the proverbial phrase "et femina mutat" (and woman changes), illustrating the popular stereotype of women's inherent instability prominent in proverbs such as "the nature and wyll of women is varyable and lightely chaunged."[71] "Mulier," a synonym for *femina*, is written just above it. This act of double glossing signals the codex's focus on women's mutability and sexual duplicity and showcases the scribe's proficiency in learning Latin terms for women that he can wield in a disparaging fashion. Since Harley 3362 is a pedagogical document, a product of the all-male university context where boys learned how to be men, its pervasive misogyny is unsurprising.[72] However, it occurs in Harley 3362 with particular virulence, in both proverbs and poetry. The original student-scribe copied multiple versions of a popular Latin poem called "Versus de femina," whose misogyny Carolyn Dinshaw labels "obsessive," and the notebook's later readers cross-reference these poems with one another so that they can be located and read together more easily.[73] These poems' respective thirteen and thirty lines open with the word "Femina" followed by a different disparagement: women fabricate lies, women feign tears, women are incurably jealous, women are the font of all evils, women are brimming with poison, women conquered the mighty David and the wise Solomon with their wiles. These didactic poems about feminine wickedness are addressed to a masculine "te" (you), performing a model of same-sex pedagogy in which men educate their peers about women. The codex's cross-temporal misogyny, expressed by students who were subject to male authority in the classroom as well as in the dormitory hall, is a tool for men in subordinate positions to bond with their peers and to assert their masculine identities by claiming dominance over women.

[71] This and other proverbs on women's changeability are listed under Whiting and Whiting, *Proverbs*, W526.

[72] Karras, *From Boys to Men*, 79.

[73] Dinshaw designates the longer poem, which exists in numerous versions, as "the paradigmatic poem of the medieval antifeminist tradition" and discusses it in *Chaucer's Sexual Poetics* (Madison: University of Wisconsin Press, 1989), 6, 190–191 n. 8. One of the pieces in Harley 3362 begins, "Femina fallit adam ; victus sunt in arbore quedam" (fol. 35v), and is cross-referenced by later readers with the poems beginning "Arbore sub quadam dictavit clericus adam" (fol. 32v) and "Femina vicit Adam ; victus fuit arbore quadam" (fol. 35r). For the Latin original, see S. G. Owen, "A Medieval Latin Poem," *EHR* 2, no. 7 (1887): 525–26; also R. E. Kaske, " 'Clericus Adam' and Chaucer's 'Adam Scriveyn,' " in *Chaucerian Problems and Perspectives: Essays Presented to Paul E. Beichner, C.S.C.*, ed. E. Vasta and Z. P. Thundy (Notre Dame: University of Notre Dame Press, 1979), 114–18.

This antipathy toward women is prevalent in the proverbs that the student copies, such as "Ille lavat lateres ; qui custodit mulieres" (He washes bricks [i.e., labors in vain], who guards women) and "Est impossibile ; quo femina sit sine bile" (It is impossible for a woman to be without poison/hostility).[74] He writes "Femina fax Sathane" (Woman, torch of Satan) a total of three times.[75] On fol. 7v he copies a popular Latin proverbial distich interlined with its English translation as a pedagogical exercise:

> Quo graciliores . pise es plures ponuntur ad ollam .
> The smellere pesyn the mo to the pot .
> Quo mulier est pulcrior es magis viciosa .
> The fayrere womman the more gygelot . or strumpet .[76]

To flex his vocabulary muscles and make his point just as he did on the book's cover with his derogatory double-glossing of "femina" and "mulier," the student adds "or strumpet" next to "gygelot." "Gygelot" and "strumpet" are synonymous—both derogatory terms meaning a sexually transgressive woman or harlot—and thus their double usage is unnecessary, serving only for the student to show off how many terms for sex workers he knows.[77] By copying multiple sexually disparaging words for women, the student reinforces the codex's prevailing stereotype of women's incontinence, and he demonstrates his knowledge of the lexicon of misogyny to his schoolmates who inherit the manuscript. Elsewhere he copies multiple proverbs about *meretrices* (whores), writing that it is as impossible to whiten a crow with water as it is to make a sex worker "munda" (morally pure).[78]

On fol. 24r, the student copies a set of anticlerical macaronic satirical

---

[74] BL, MS Harley 3362, fol. 18v.

[75] BL, MS Harley 3362, fols. 7r, 35v, 36v.

[76] *DIMEV*, 5467; Whiting and Whiting, *Proverbs*, P102. The Middle English version of this proverb survives in at least four manuscripts, including BL, MS Sloane 1210, a fifteenth-century pedagogical miscellany of proverbs, vocabulary lists, and grammatical texts that shares numerous affinities with Harley 3362 and Peniarth 356B.

[77] *MED*, s.vv. *gigelot* (n.), def. 1(a); *strumpet* (n.), def. 1(a).

[78] MS Harley 3362, fol. 14v: "Balnea cornici ; quid prosunt vel meretrici. / Nec meretrix munda; nec cornix alba fit unda" (What good are baths to a crow or a whore? / Neither a whore nor a crow is made white with water); fol. 32v: "presbiter qui gaudes meretrices qualiter audes" (You, priest, who take pleasure in whores, how do you dare?). The latter is a variation on the more popular "Tangere qui gaudes meretricem qualiter audes" from BL, MS Lansdowne 762, fol. 99r, and Bodleian Library, MS Laud Misc. 23 (SC 655), fol. 112v.

verses attacking the local Carmelite friars.[79] The verses, delineated from one another with brackets in the right margin and marginal notations on the left, disparage local friars and contain multiple references to Ely, a cathedral city seventeen miles northeast of Cambridge. The first consists of six macaronic lines comparing friars to plant and insect pests and closing with the declaration, "For non that her ys . lovit flen flyyes ne freris"; the second is a macaronic quatrain critiquing the Carmelites' sexual predation; and the third is a Latin couplet about Ely. The most intriguing thing about the second is that the scribe has rendered its obscenities in code. He writes,

Fratres Carmeli navigant in a both apud Eli.
Non sunt in celi quia gxddbov xxkxzt pg ifmk.
Omnes drencherunt quia sterisman non habuerunt,
Fratres cum knyvys goth about and txxkxzv nfookt xxzxkt.

[Carmelite brothers sail in a boat near Ely.
They are not in heaven, because fuccant {they fuck} wivys of Heli.
All of them drowned, because they did not have a steersman.
Brothers with knives go about and swivyt mennis wyvis.]

The student encodes "swivyt" and "fuccant" using a popular scholarly system of alphabetic encryption that was commonly used in medieval universities to hide solutions to riddles.[80] The obscenity in each of these half-lines prompts his shift into cipher, illustrating precisely where he crosses the threshold between permissible and transgressive speech. These two half-lines are the only place in the manuscript where the student uses this code. Even though it is rudimentary at best, the code nonetheless renders the obscenities most legible to other university-educated men, restricting it to an elite textual community of male readers from similar educational backgrounds while also playfully drawing

[79] *Flen flyys and freris* (*DIMEV*, 1324). The first four lines only are copied onto a damaged folio in Bodleian Library, MS Digby 196, fol. 196v. The verses are printed, with some errors in transcription, in *Reliquiae antiquae*, ed. Thomas Wright and James Orchard Halliwell, 2 vols. (London: William Pickering, 1841–43), 1:91–92. This passage is discussed briefly by Coates, "*Fockynggroue* in Bristol," 374; Melissa Mohr, *Holy Shit: A Brief History of Swearing* (Oxford: Oxford University Press, 2013), 151–53; and Sheidlower, *The F-Word*, 83, although none has analyzed its sexual politics.

[80] Dieter Bitterli, *Say What I Am Called: The Old English Riddles of the Exeter Book and the Anglo-Latin Riddle Tradition* (Toronto: University of Toronto Press, 2009), 72–74.

attention to both obscenities. This illustrates how *fuck* was used synony-mously with *swyve* and demonstrates that the two terms were under-stood as equally illicit. The cipher also functions as a technology of nonconsensual reading, as it compels readers to dwell on the obscenities and participate actively in making them intelligible before they fully understand the nature of what they are reproducing. The scribe's usage carries an implicit lesson about women's agency: they are the objects of the verbs, not the agents. Their agency is further diminished by the poet's choice to name them as "mennis wyvis" and "wivys of Heli," which enables the obscenities to stage sexual competition between friars and local "men."

The plural noun "Fratres" (brothers, friars), which could denote a blood relationship, membership to a religious order or an urban guild, or a relationship between equals, is copied at the beginning of two of the four lines, its repetition and placement on the manuscript page underscoring the close-knit fraternal bonds at work in the poem.[81] The Carmelite "fratres" "fuc[k]" and "swiv[e]" women together, with the Latin plural ending of "fuccant" and the alliterating "f"s emphasizing this sense of collectivity. Bawdy humor is a means of articulating compe-tition, as the men of the university mock their Carmelite classmates for drowning and landing in hell—punning on "Heli," as Coates notes—because of their copulation with "mennis wyvis."[82] With the lascivious friars' damnation as the verses' punchline, the "wyvis" become collateral, their bodies serving as conduits for men's rivalries—between friars and laymen in Ely, between Cambridge students and Carmelites—with one another. The poem is not about the women at all, but rather about conflicts among men, with obscenities serving to structure those con-flicts. The references to Carmelites suggest an additional rivalry poten-tially at play here: there was no Carmelite foundation at Ely, but one was established at Cambridge in 1251, where Carmelites attended the university before receiving licenses to preach and hear confessions throughout the diocese of Ely, which included Cambridge.[83] This raises the possibility that the student who compiled the manuscript viewed

---

[81] *DMLBS*, s.v. *frater* (n.).

[82] Coates, "*Fockynggroue* in Bristol," 374.

[83] Bruce P. Flood, Jr., "The Carmelite Friars in Medieval English Universities and Society 1299–1430," *Recherches de théologie ancienne et médiévale* 55 (1988): 151–87; also "Friaries: Carmelites, Cambridge," in *A History of the County of Cambridge and the Isle of Ely*, Vol. 2, ed. L. F. Salzman (London: Victoria County History, 1948), 282–86, which contains a reference to seven Carmelites being licensed in Ely in 1375.

the local "fratres Carmeli" as rivals and deployed the obscene verses as a means of asserting power over them, as the poem accuses them of preying upon married women and imagines their mass-drowning in the streams and fens surrounding "Heli."

The manuscript's sixteenth- and seventeenth-century readers interpreted these verses as comic, illustrating how bawdy humor can be used to legitimize women's exploitation and to authorize violence against other men, as we see in the case of the drowned friars. One of the codex's later readers wrote "Carmina Iocosa" (Jocular Songs) in large letters in the upper margin of the page, interpreting the verses' salacious content and their macaronic, encoded form as humorous and enjoyable. This marginal note expresses one reader's response to them and directs others to interpret them similarly, drawing upon "Iocosa'"'s valences of "playful," "sportive," "jocose," and "delightful" to minimize the violence and objectification at work in the poem.[84] This rendering of these verses as a sportive jest reflects the early modern readers' larger responses to the notebook's contents, as they both notice and reinforce its pervasive misogyny. Folio 35v, one of the most woman-hating pages in the manuscript, contains a total of four men's hands. The original student-scribe copies two Latin poems about the evils of women, a thirteen-line version of the popular *Versus de femina* and an eighteen-line poem titled *Exposicio nominum mulierum*; the second hand writes in the upper margin, "De feminis vide plura folio proximo" (Concerning women see many things on the next folio); a third underlines "De feminis" for emphasis, further highlighting the codex's focus, and adds, "vidz. folium proximum .b. & 64" (namely, the verso of the next folio and 64); and a fourth uses red ink to underline the title *Exposicio nominum mulierum* and the name "Mergereta."[85] One reader adds a manicule next to the beginning of the *Exposicio*, a catalogue of eighteen women's names with corresponding derogatory glosses.[86] This later addition and underlining of "De feminis," coupled with the cross-references to other misogynous material, shows that the codex's early modern readers echoed its fifteenth-century compiler in viewing "feminis" as an important category in the notebook. H. J. Jackson notes that "marginalia can be used to construct and to

[84] *DMLBS*, s.v. *jocosus* (adj.).

[85] These references direct readers to the longer version of *Versus de femina* on fol. 36v and *Arbore sub adam* on fol. 32v.

[86] Rust examines this poem's complexities in "An Exposition of Women's Names in British Library Harley MS 3362," and provides a transcription and translation on 142.

monitor identity," and here the schoolbook's readers are actively constructing gendered textual identities in response to its pedagogical material.[87] This single page contains input from four men regarding women's evils, each confirming and perpetuating the misogyny in the original pieces, forming a transhistorical gendered community. By cross-referencing the poems with one another and providing an easy guide for others to locate them, the early modern readers enable their shared antifeminism to be accessed and learned more easily, as one also writes "De feminis" in the upper margin of fol. 36v. They underline *mulier* (woman), *femina* (woman), and *uxor* (wife) when those terms are used disparagingly, as well as longer lines such as, "Si capis uxorem diceris habere dolorem" (If you take a wife, you will say that you have sorrow).[88] In response to the popular Pauline instruction "bonum est hominem mulierem non tangere" (it is good for a man not to touch a woman), one reader underlines "non tangere" for emphasis.[89] Readers draw manicules next to misogynist content, such as the proverbs "Femina fax Sathane," "Uxorem duxi . sed semper postea luxi" (I married a wife, but I mourned forever after), and "Omnino amans cecus" (Every [male] lover is blind).[90] The textual evidence shows male readers responding to the manuscript's misogyny just as its pedagogical material teaches them to do: they enthusiastically express their disapproval of women and marriage, using bold underlining and accusatory pointing fingers to show that they have learned their lessons well. This textual community's members connect with one another across generations, laugh at shared jests, and affirm antifeminist teachings together.

"We can still come together as brothers": Present-Day Implications

These examples from the fifteenth century shed light on obscenity's role in teaching lessons about masculinity and asserting power by men in positions of patriarchal precarity, as all three show men who are disempowered in some way—as unmarried sons subject to maternal rule, as schoolboys, as students—using *swyve* and *fuck* to share sexual narratives

[87] H. J. Jackson, *Marginalia: Readers Writing in Books 1700–2000* (New Haven: Yale University Press, 2001), 91.
[88] MS Harley 3362, fol. 37r.
[89] MS Harley 3362, fol. 16v. See 1 Corinthians 7:1.
[90] MS Harley 3362, fols. 7r, 3v, 10v.

within all-male groups. These texts are important for understanding how obscenities function today in same-sex pedagogical communities to teach their members shared codes of behavior and to make a bid for social power.

Like the three medieval examples of men who use obscene storytelling as a means of ameliorating the insecurities of masculinity under pressure, the Penn State brothers are not quite men. Instead, they are students subordinate to institutional authority and to senior members of the fraternity, and many are financially dependent on their parents. In the investigation that Penn State conducted after Kappa Delta Rho's private Facebook group was revealed, the university found that, in addition to the photos and tales shared online, "pledges . . . were made to create stories containing pornographic images and a 'sex position of the day.' "[91] Those who wished to join the fraternity were required to demonstrate their ability to share obscene stories with the group, illustrating how sexual storytelling played an integral role in sustaining bonds of brotherhood among its members. In addition to this compulsory storytelling, the university found that "members . . . used demeaning language to describe females"; "cultivated a persistent climate of humiliation for several females"; and violently hazed pledges, including forcing them to "participate in boxing matches" with one another.[92] The fraternity members taught new initiates how to perpetuate their group's brand of masculinity through creating obscene narratives, engaging in compulsory misogyny, and inflicting violence upon one another, just as Harley 3362's contents taught generations of university students about misogynist masculinity and rivalry with other men. The pledges' mandatory creation of daily pornographic stories for their brothers' enjoyment illustrates how sexual storytelling functioned as a manhood act necessary for inclusion in the brotherhood, while their imperative to engage in physical conflict with each other illustrates the violence suffered by all who belong to those types of communities.

Penn State's Kappa Delta Rho, which is only one example of all-male online groups caught sharing nonconsensual images of nude women in recent years, sheds light on the ongoing usage of obscenity in homosocial groups to perpetuate misogyny, to teach models of aggressive

---

[91] "University Officials Withdraw KDR Fraternity Recognition for Three Years," May 26, 2015, http://news.psu.edu/story/358692/2015/05/26/university-officials -withdraw-kdr-fraternity-recognition-three-years (accessed July 13, 2019).
[92] Ibid.

masculinity, to use humor to trivialize women's degradation, and to commodify narratives of sexual coercion in service of fostering bonds of brotherhood.[93] It illustrates the necessity of understanding how obscenity can assert gendered selfhood, betray masculine anxieties, and reaffirm domination over women in all-male spaces, as all these examples feature narratives where women's consent is compromised, ignored, overridden, or violated outright. By examining the dynamics of twenty-first-century virtual groups alongside the Paston brothers' letters, the Welsh monks' schoolbook, and the Cambridge students' notebook, we can see how these practices of obscene storytelling as strategies for forcibly securing precarious masculine identities stretch back across many centuries, strengthening fraternal bonds and teaching their participants codes of sexual conduct that favor coercion and compromised consent.

[93] In March 2017, news broke that an all-male closed Facebook group of 30,000 current and former US Marine Corps members had shared thousands of nude photos of their female peers without the women's consent or knowledge. The group's members referred to the photos as "wins," invoking a model of competition with other men grounded in women's violation. This can be interpreted as part of a larger backlash against the inclusion of women in the armed forces, as some male service members sought to assert their power in response to the perceived threat embodied by sharing ranks with women. Dave Philipps, "Inquiry Opens into How a Network of Marines Shared Illicit Images of Female Peers," *New York Times*, March 6, 2017, https://www .nytimes.com/2017/03/06/us/inquiry-opens-into-how-30000-marines-shared-illicit-im ages-of-female-peers.html (accessed July 13, 2019). In July 2017, another closed Facebook group containing over 18,000 male marines and featuring new photos was exposed. The group's description stated, "we can still come together as brothers on a page that is just for us and share the camaraderie that makes us Marines." Kyle Jones, "Marines Revenge-Porn Page Resurfaces with New Explicit Images of Female Servicemembers," *New York Times*, July 12, 2017, http://nytlive.nytimes.com/womeninthe world/2017/07/12/marines-revenge-porn-page-resurfaces-with-new-explicit-images-of -female-servicemembers/ (accessed July 13, 2019).

Defending Images in Pecock's *Repressor*: *Caritas*, the Absent Friend and the Sense of Touch

Katie L. Walter
University of Sussex

Abstract

Reginald Pecock's defense of orthodox practices in the *Repressor of Over Much Blaming of the Clergy* is grounded in the biblical commandment to love God, which, following Thomas Aquinas's thoroughly Aristotelianized theology, is understood as "a friendship of man and God." Images are key tools—proxies for forms of presence—in the dual processes of learning and recollection that are needed to mediate friendship with God. In this context, the efficacy of physical images derives from the structures of human memory and imagination, which are reliant on sensory perception: physical sight thus aids the imaginative work of making present something that is absent. The paradigm of *caritas* as friendship surfaces powerfully in the *Repressor*'s defense of images: Christ is the absent friend, an image of whom offers a form of presence essential to imagining, and so to loving, him. Aristotelian friendship's emphasis on presence and proximity, however, underpins Pecock's advocacy of the value of the physical image not just in terms of its appeal to the sense of sight, but also to the sense of touch: love for a friend, ordinarily fostered by presence and completed in touch, is mediated between God and man not only by seeing but also through touching an image. That Pecock's arguments about the lawfulness of image-use culminate in a powerful defense of those who caress and kiss images registers not only the strength of Lollard objection to touching images in fifteenth-century controversy, but also the under-recognized importance of touch to medieval understandings of memory, cognition, and love.

Keywords

Reginald Pecock; *Repressor of Over Much Blaming of the Clergy*; images; *caritas*; friendship; touch; sight; Aristotle; Thomas Aquinas; Lollardy

My thanks to the anonymous readers for *SAC*, and to Sebastian Sobecki and Sarah Salih for their careful readings of this essay; to Eva von Contzen for guidance on translations from Latin; and to audiences at Cornell, Oxford, and Cambridge, whose comments have been valuable in shaping my argument.

Thow shalt loue the Lord thi God of al thin herte, and of al thi soule, and of alle thi strengthis.

Deuteronomy 6:5[1]

IN PART 1 OF THE *Repressor of Over Much Blaming of the Clergy* (c. 1449), Reginald Pecock outlines in detail the foundations on which his defense of orthodox practices against Lollard attack will be built. The last of these foundations, which he terms "general profis," comprises three rules from which he draws four conclusions.[2] The first is grounded in the biblical commandment of *caritas*, first articulated in the Pentateuch but established as the Great Commandment in the New Testament, that a man should (in Pecock's modified rendering) "loue God and drede God with al his herte, soul, and strengthe."[3] The second conclusion is that a man must "bithinke and remembre" seven matters: who God is, the "benefetis" he gives to man, the punishments he dispenses, the articles of his law and service, how man should serve God in these points, man's natural frailty and disposition to sin, the sins and their remedies. The third conclusion is that active knowledge of these seven matters is a prerequisite for the first: "the remembraunce and mynde taking upon these vij. maters is so necessarie a meene into the loue and drede of God, that withoute meditacioun and mynde vpon hem or upon summe of hem no man schal loue God and drede God in eny while with al his herte, soule, and strengthe."[4] A man cannot love God "with al his herte, soule, and strengthe," so the syllogism demonstrates, without having in mind some part of the knowledge of him encompassed in those "vij. maters." This command to love God thus requires a knowledge of him that is hard work to obtain, not least because God is materially absent. In the *Repressor*, Pecock argues that the particular difficulty of knowing God in order to love him can be

---

[1] *The Holy Bible, Containing the Old and New Testaments, with the Apocryphal Books*, ed. Josiah Forshall and Frederic Madden (Oxford: Oxford University Press, 1850).

[2] Reginald Pecock, *The Repressor of Over Much Blaming of the Clergy*, ed. Churchill Babington, Rerum britannicarum medii aevi scriptores 19 (1860; repr., Wiesbaden: Kraus, 1966), 110.

[3] Ibid., 113–14. Pecock offers a subtle rewriting of scriptural authority here by combining the injunction to "drede God" with the command to love him.

[4] Ibid., 114.

overcome through the dual labors of learning and recollection. But such is man's natural frailty that he cannot recall and keep in mind these matters without the help of the following "weies or meenes": reading or hearing Scripture and other writings; hearing sermons; "biholding upon picturis or purtraturis or graued werk or coruun [carven] werk"; and visiting places where holy men did or do dwell, or where their relics and "relifis [remains]" are housed.[5] The fourth conclusion is thus that the problems of God's absence and man's forgetfulness are partly counter-acted not only through teaching and the written word, but also through physical actions and material objects that mediate, or become proxies for, forms of presence. The efficacy of these means is predicated on an understanding of the reliance of human cognition on sensory perception. Pilgrimages, sacred relics, and images (paintings, portraits, engravings, sculptures)—though highly suspect to Lollards—are all, Pecock posits, tools key to the work of learning and remembrance that generates the knowledge of God necessary to obey the greatest biblical command-ment.[6] As such, they operate not only through an appeal to sight, but also, as this essay explores, to the sense of touch.

The algorithm of knowledge, remembrance, and love, upon which the *Repressor*'s arguments against Lollardy rest, is also the explicit foun-dation of a number of Pecock's surviving works that have the broader aim of offering orthodox instruction in the vernacular for laity and clergy alike (*The Donet*, 1443–49; *The Reule of Crysten Religioun*, 1443; and *The Folewer to the Donet*, 1453–54).[7] Since, as the *Reule* makes clear, "love may not be had anentis [toward] eny persoone wiþoute knowing had afore vpoun þe same persoone," Pecock's works systematically tabu-late and categorize the knowledge necessary to know God in order to love him.[8] In these works (though not explicitly in the *Repressor*), the

---

[5] Ibid.

[6] This claim is repeated elsewhere in Pecock's works. See, for example, Reginald Pecock, *The Reule of Crysten Religioun*, ed. William Cabell Greet, EETS o.s. 171 (1927; repr., Millwood, N.Y.: Kraus, 1987), 244.

[7] Two other works survive, *Poore Mennis Myrror* (c. 1443–49) and *The Book of Faith* (c. 1456). On Pecock's target audience in his works, see further Mishtooni Bose, "Reli-gious Authority and Dissent," in *A Companion to Medieval English Literature and Culture*, ed. Peter Brown (Oxford: Blackwell, 2007), 40–55.

[8] Pecock, *Reule*, 2. *The Donet*, for example, organizes the knowledge necessary for Christian life into four tables, explicitly related to the strands of the commandment to love God, neighbor, and self. See further Kirsty Campbell, *The Call to Read: Reginald Pecock's Books and Textual Communities* (Notre Dame: University of Notre Dame Press, 2010), e.g., 22, for outlines of the various modes of categorization employed across Pecock's works.

Christian imperative to love God, but also, per the second part of the commandment of *caritas*, to love one's neighbor as oneself, is expressed as friendship and the kind of love required as "freendful" or "freendly."[9] Charity itself is defined as "not ellis þanne an habit or a dede of freendly louyng to god, or a wel willing to god aboue alle þingis, and to alle oþire resonable and sauable creaturis in god and for god."[10] Pecock's thinking thus follows Thomas Aquinas, who influentially expounds charity in the *Summa theologiae*, in a thoroughly Aristotelianized understanding, as "a friendship of man and God."[11]

The requirements of *caritas* thus to some extent underpin Pecock's entire literary project, and its expression as friendship is central to works such as the *Donet*, the *Folewer*, and the *Reule*.[12] While the paradigm of friendship for *caritas* is left largely implicit in the *Repressor*, it surfaces

[9] The instances are numerous. See Reginald Pecock, *The Donet*, ed. Elsie Vaughan Hitchcock, EETS o.s. 156 (1921; repr., New York: Kraus, 1971), e.g., 28, 36, 37, 42, and passim. For the *Reule*, see for example, 239, 241, 242, 496, and passim.

[10] Pecock, *Donet*, 109.

[11] Thomas Aquinas, *Summa theologiae*, gen. ed. Thomas Gilby, 60 vols. (London: Blackfriars, 1975), 2a2ae q. 23, art. 1 (34:6–7). Aquinas deals with the theological virtue of charity as friendship extensively in 2a2ae, qq. 23–46, where, as the translator notes, he understands charity as "whole-hearted love of God" that includes love of self and neighbor as set out in the biblical commandments (34:xviii). Nathan Lefler gives a thoroughgoing account of Aquinas's theology of friendship and its debt to Aristotle in *Theologizing Friendship: How "Amicitia" in the Thought of Aelred and Aquinas Inscribes the Scholastic Turn* (Cambridge: James Clarke, 2014). On the influence of Aquinas on Pecock, see further Campbell, *The Call to Read*, e.g. 12–13, Chap. 5. See also Mishtooni Bose, "Two Phases of Scholastic Self-Consciousness: Reflections on Method in Aquinas and Pecock," in *Aquinas as Authority*, ed. J. J. van Geest (Leuven: Peeters, 2002), 87–107.

[12] As Pecock explains in the *Donet*, Christ's "two tables" are threefold, defining an ethics of love toward God, self, and neighbor. Fulfillment of the command in these three areas means that the "remenaunt" of God's law will also be fulfilled (Pecock, *Donet*, 17; see also Pecock, *Reule*, e.g., 240). It is this threefold application of Christ's commandments that governs Pecock's categorization of the whole of God's law into three tables understood to encapsulate all "eendal" moral virtues. A fourth table (placed first) contains the "meenal" virtues. These "meenal" virtues accord with the seven matters that the *Repressor* and the *Reule* set out as the means to fulfilling the commandment to love wholeheartedly; these seven matters, in turn, can be reduced to Christ's two tables and are comprehended fully in Pecock's four tables. The four tables are intended to encapsulate and ultimately replace the existing multiple tabulations relating to God's law, such as the Decalogue, the cardinal virtues, the Seven Deadly Sins, and so on. The *Donet* lays out the four tables; the *Folewer*, intended as an extension of the *Donet*, gives an extended justification of the four tables in Part 2. Both the seven matters and the four tables will teach that God is worthy to be loved with the love of friendship above all others, and instruct how to love God, self, and neighbor with the pure love of friendship. See, for examples, Pecock, *Reule*, 239; Reginald Pecock, *The Folewer to the Donet*, ed. Elsie Vaughan Hitchcock, EETS o.s. 164 (1924; repr., Millwood, N.Y: Kraus, 1981), 194, and passim.

compellingly in his defense of images. Pecock's long discussion of images in the *Repressor* culminates in the idea of Christ as an absent friend, an image of whom offers the Christian a form of presence essential to meeting the difficult demands of charity.[13] Pecock sets out the argument thus:

Ech man hath nede forto haue gode affecciouns anentis [toward] Crist, as upon his best freend; and this freend ȝeueth [gives] not to us his presence visibili; wherfore it is profitable to ech man for to ymagine this freend be present to us bodili and in a maner visibili. And sithen herto serueth ful weel and ful myche the ymage of Crist crucified.[14]

The need for love ("gode affecciouns") for Christ the friend is potentially compromised by the absence of presence—that is, by the absence of sensibles: "this freend ȝeueth not to us his presence visibili." An imagined image, supported by a physical "ymage of Crist crucified," however, can serve to mediate friendship with Christ. The underlying logic here follows that of the "general profis" of Part 1, which establishes images as one of the "meenes" or instruments through which a man is able to recollect the knowledge required to obey the commandment to "loue the Lord thi God of al thin herte." As I suggest in this essay, Pecock's use of the figure of Christ as friend in his defense of images is the logical extension of an Aristotelianized understanding, worked out across his corpus, of the command to love God. But so too is it rooted in an Aristotelianized theory of the operation of the imagination and of sensory perception, and of their key roles in mitigating absence and mediating presence. Together, Aristotelian theories of friendship and of sensory perception provide Pecock with his most affectively charged arguments as to why Christians need images.

Pecock's broader defense of images is thus framed with a particular set of concerns: the human desire for presence and the problem of absence; the role played by imagination and memory in making that which is absent present; and, finally, imagination's and memory's a-priori reliance on sensory perception. Orthodox defenders of images justify the use of physical images in part on the grounds that they act as a stabilizer for

---

[13] The analysis of this episode in this essay builds on my earlier discussion made in "Reading without Books," in *Spaces for Reading in Later Medieval England*, ed. Mary C. Flannery and Carrie Griffin (New York: Palgrave, 2016), 115–31.

[14] Pecock, *Repressor*, 269.

the sense of sight, and so also for the imaginative and memory practices at the heart of late medieval piety.[15] As Shannon Gayk has described, Pecock similarly advocates images as props for vision and visual images drawn in the imagination.[16] Pecock's engagement with Aristotelian friendship, however, with its emphasis on presence and proximity, also facilitates his advocacy of the value of the physical image's appeal to the sense of touch. If a reader accepts his reasoning as to why an image enables a man to love Christ in his absence, Pecock says in concluding his defense of image use, then he or she also has "sufficient ground forto excuse fro blame" those who "touche with her hondis the feet and othere parties and the clothis of ymagis, and wolen thanne aftir sette to her visage and to her iʒen and to her mouthis her tho hondis."[17] The utility of the image—and specifically the three-dimensional image, with "parties" and "clothis"—is not therefore just in the visual image it affords to the sense of sight, but also in the tangible experience it mediates to the sense of touch: the same logic that allows a Christian to use an image as a proxy to see Christ in his absence, allows that he or she use it likewise to touch him. Pecock's intervention in the controversy over images thus moves beyond the traditional terms of the written word versus the visual image, or of images as *libri laicorum*, to the relationship of material images to mental ones, and thereby out to a broader consideration of the structures of human cognition and sensation.[18] By thinking about the problem of images through the figure of the friend, Pecock makes a powerful claim: in substituting for that which is absent, the image mimetically offers presence in ways that structure an ethics central to *caritas*, not just of vision, but also of touch.

Pecock's *Repressor*

The *Repressor* targets a group of the laity that have fallen into error; more specifically, "tho erring persoones of the lay peple whiche ben clepid

[15] See Kathleen Kamerick, *Popular Piety and Art in the Late Middle Ages: Image Worship and Idolatry in England 1350–1500* (New York: Palgrave, 2002), e.g., 158.

[16] Shannon Gayk, *Image, Text, and Religious Reform in Fifteenth-Century England* (Cambridge: Cambridge University Press, 2010), 167. Cf. the discussion of Thomas Hoccleve, Chap. 2.

[17] Pecock, *Repressor*, 270.

[18] See Chapter 5 in Gayk, *Image, Text, and Religious Reform*, e.g., 156, on Pecock's contribution to the debate on the relationship of the visual image to the written word, and on images as books for the illiterate.

Lollardis."[19] Following the general proofs of Part 1, Parts 2–5 of the *Repressor* offer the "special maner" of proofs with which Pecock defends the eleven "gouernauncis of the clergie" attacked by Lollards.[20] The first of these governances, "hauyng and vsing of ymagis," pertains to a more general use of images in Christian practice; the second, concerning pilgrimages "to dyuerse bodies and bonys of Seintis" and "to ymagis of Crist crucified and of Marie and of othere Seintis," attends to pilgrimage and the more specific role of images and relics as the object of pilgrimage.[21] For Lollards, Christians who venerate "dead" images run the risk of falling into idolatry, as well as of erring in belief. While some Lollards allow the use of a "pore crucifix" (as did John Wyclif) on the grounds that Christ took bodily form, images of the Trinity are instead held to lead to misunderstandings of the nature of God.[22] Another source of anxiety was the imputation of miraculous powers to images themselves. From a Lollard perspective, the proclivity displayed by some for touching images is evidence both of belief in their inherent power (which might be conveyed through touch) and of idolatry. One early fifteenth-century Lollard text thus registers unease at the spectacle of Christians clinging to images, caressing and kissing them, as if they were really those they represent: some "lewid folc . . . cleuen sadly strokande and kyssand þese olde stones and stokkis, layyng doun hore grete offryngis . . . as ȝif þei weren Crist and oure Lauedy and Ion Baptist and Thomas of Caunterbery and siche oþer."[23] Such tactile habits not only misdirect

---

[19] Pecock, *Repressor*, 127–28. On the *Repressor's* imagined audience, see further Campbell, *The Call to Read*, 28; and Bose, "Religious Dissent," 41. "Lollardy," of course, represents a more diverse (and sometimes conflicting) set of beliefs and practices than suggested by the use of a single term for heterodoxy in the late fourteenth and early fifteenth centuries.

[20] Pecock, *Repressor*, 4. The eleven are: image use, pilgrimages, Church ownership of property, the hierarchy of priests, the authority of the pope, "dyuersite and nouelte" in strictness and forms of religious rule, prayer to saints, the cost of furnishing church interiors, practices concerning signs and sacraments, oath-swearing, and the use of the death sentence. On Lollard and orthodox beliefs see further Margaret Aston, *England's Iconoclasts*, Vol. 1, *Laws against Images* (Oxford: Clarendon Press, 1988); and for Lollardy in Pecock's works in particular see Kantik Ghosh, "Bishop Reginald Pecock and the Idea of 'Lollardy,'" in *Text and Controversy from Wyclif to Bale: Essays in Honour of Anne Hudson*, ed. Helen Barr (Turnhout: Brepols, 2005), 251–65.

[21] Pecock, *Repressor*, 136, 175.

[22] Margaret Aston, *Lollards and Reformers: Images and Literacy in Late Medieval Religion* (London: Hambledon Press, 1984), 136–41 (for Wyclif's views see, e.g., 138).

[23] London, British Library, Additional MS 24202, fols. 26–28v, edited in *Selections from English Wycliffite Writings*, ed. Anne Hudson (Toronto: University of Toronto Press, 1997), 87.

affection, but also time, money, and materials—away from God and from charitable giving to the poor, who are living images of Christ, to the clergy and the Church.[24] In broad terms, the defense Pecock makes in the *Repressor* against these and other Lollard conclusions about images is a conventional one: Scripture, reason, and moral law (the threefold authority Pecock tests each governance against) do not forbid, but rather approve, that images be used—not, as Lollards fear, as objects of worship, but as "rememoratijf or mynding signes."[25] Having established the lawfulness of image use for the purpose of recollection and remembrance, Pecock then proceeds to detail fifteen Lollard objections to these two governances, before refuting each objection in turn. That his arguments about the lawfulness of image use culminate in a powerful defense of those who caress and kiss images registers not only the strength of Lollard objection to touching images, but also the under-recognized importance of touch to medieval understandings of memory, cognition, and love.

Three particular Lollard objections (13–15) form a unit that Pecock notes need special attention in refuting: by praying to, bowing to, or kissing a cross, a person takes the cross to be a god.[26] While these actions may be performed by a Christian in private devotion, they are all variously mandated in liturgy: one prays to the cross, for example, when the hymn *Vexilla regis prodeunt* (*The Banners of the King Advance*) is sung in the Passion week; one bows to a cross in the Palm Sunday procession; and one kisses a cross (as the culmination of creeping to it) on Good Friday. Pecock is thus concerned to "assoile" (resolve or refute) these objections because some "wijters" (blamers or critics, i.e., Lollards) are "out of eese [disturbed]" when they must participate in these communal performances.[27] To explain the way in which prayer to a cross does not automatically make a god of it, Pecock makes recourse to "colouris of rethorik": Scripture uses (as everyday speech does) figurative language, such as the synecdoche and the metonym, which shows how we can address the cross but in fact be directing our petition or worship to Christ.[28] To answer "the xiiij^e. and xv^e. argumentis to gidere vndir

---

[24] See further Gayk, *Image, Text, and Religious Reform*, Chap. 1, for a nuanced discussion of the spectrum of Lollard beliefs about images. See also *Selections from English Wycliffite Writings*, ed. Hudson, e.g., 27.

[25] See, e.g., Pecock, *Repressor*, 136–37.

[26] Ibid., 207. Objection 13 is detailed at 199–202; 14 at 202–7; and 15 at 207–8.

[27] Ibid., 207.

[28] Ibid., 255–67. On Pecock's detailed arguments on rhetoric see further Gayk, *Image, Text, and Religious Reform*, e.g., 175–80.

oon"—that is, the charges that bowing to and kissing an image makes a god of it—Pecock first sets out three rules. It is here, perhaps unexpectedly, though entirely in line with the logic of the requirements of *caritas*, that the paradigm of friendship surfaces.

The first of these rules is that:

a man schal haue more feruentli hise affecciouns and loues anentis his loued freend, whanne and whilis thilk freend is at sumwhile present personali with him and bisidis him, than he schal haue, if the freend be absent alwey and not personali present with him.[29]

The axiom on which Pecock's argument rests predicates the affection necessary for friendship on presence: a man loves his beloved friend more "feruentli" when the friend is "present personali [i.e., bodily]," "bisidis him," than he does if the friend is "absent alwey." The second supposition is that if a man's friend is absent then in order to "encrese his gode affecciouns" toward the friend, the next best thing to bodily presence is imagining him to be present: "so it is, that thilk present beyng of the freend, grettist aftir his bodili visible presence, is his presence in ymaginacioun."[30] The third supposition is that "It is esier forto ymagyne a thing absent to be present in an other thing lijk therto, than withoute eny other thing lijk therto. Forwhi euery thing lijk to an othir thing bringith into ymaginacioun and into mynde better and liȝtir and esier the thing to him lijk, than the thing to him lasse lijk or vnlijk."[31] A physical image aids the difficult process of making present something that is absent in the imagination; the more like this image is to the thing it signifies, the easier and more precise is this imaginative work. The first and second of these rules thus posit the paradigm of friendship as central to Pecock's defense of performative, liturgical practices involving images; the second and third of these rules situate that defense further in imaginative and sensory theory. Yet these rules, at first, might

[29] Pecock, *Repressor*, 267. A number of scholars have discussed this passage. Aston, *Lollards and Reformers*, 185–86, offers a summary of Pecock's claims, helpfully noting that here Pecock expounds "the devotional values of imagining, inner visualising . . . which lay behind the theory and practice of medieval religious art" (n. 175). W. R. Jones, "Lollards and Images: The Defense of Religious Art in Later Medieval England," *Journal of the History of Ideas* 34, no. 1 (1973): 27–50, notes Pecock's use of the trope of the absent friend, but does not elaborate upon it (41 n. 73). See also Alastair Minnis, "Affection and Imagination in 'The Cloud of Unknowing' and Hilton's 'Scale of Perfection,' " *Traditio* 39 (1983): 323–66 (362).

[30] Pecock, *Repressor*, 268.

[31] Ibid.

seem a misdirection: they do not directly address the Lollard objections (to bowing to or kissing an image) that they are employed to answer. What the paradigm of friendship crucially provides, however, is the evidence, first, that bodily presence, perceptible to the senses, is the condition for generating love (as the second supposition clarifies: "If the freend were bodili visibili present, thilk presence were best forto gendre the seid affeccioun");[32] further, that the imagination serves as a virtual space for approximating presence, which, in turn, arouses love; and, finally, that imaginative practices, supported by sense perception of an image, generate love not for the image but for the person of whom the image is a likeness. This paradigm thus further puts center-stage in the discussion of image use what is also at the heart of the commandment of *caritas*—love—but it does so in a way that makes it inextricable from the logic implicit in the notion of presence.

Pecock's thinking here is thoroughly Thomist. In the *Summa*, Aquinas writes that love "derives its species from its object, but its intensity from the lover . . . when the question is one of intensity, we must look to the man who loves. By this test a man loves those closest to him."[33] Species (from the Greek denoting "what a thing looks like") are, as Robert Pasnau explains, "likenesses of the things they represent." There are three kinds of species: in the air (species *in medio*); in the sense organs (sensible species); and in the intellect (intelligible species).[34] Species are thus generated by the object but received in the perceiver in the act of perception. Just as a person is able to see a stone because of the presence of "the species of the stone in his eye," so a person is able to love another through perceiving and cognizing their species.[35] It is this, as Thomas goes on to explain, that effects a kind of mutual indwelling or union of the lover and the beloved ("Cognitively, the person loved, Y, is said to dwell in the lover, X, in the sense that he is constantly present in X's thoughts").[36] Love, then, cannot arise without presence and perception, but its intensity derives instead from the person who loves (just as clear

---

[32] Ibid.

[33] Aquinas, *Summa theologiae*, 2a2ae q. 26, art. 7 (ed. Gilby, 34:138–39).

[34] Robert Pasnau, *Theories of Cognition in the Later Middle Ages* (Cambridge: Cambridge University Press, 1997), 16. Pages 11–18 provide an excellent introduction to cognition and the role of species in Thomist thought.

[35] The useful comparison with Aquinas's explanation of how species operate in sight (Aquinas, *Summa theologiae*, 1a q. 89, art. 6) is noted by the translator (ed. Gilby, 34:138 n. c).

[36] Aquinas, *Summa theologiae*, 1a2ae q. 28, art. 2 (ed. Gilby, 19:92–93).

vision of a stone depends, not on the stone's species, but on "the eye's visual power"). This, then, accounts for the importance of proximity in determining the strength of love felt for another. In the *Repressor*, Pecock takes this Thomist logic further: the nearer one is to the friend the more love is aroused; the closest one can be to another is to be touching.

Engaged as the *Repressor* is with the precise terms of Lollard arguments, the kinds of images Pecock requires his reader to view through the lens of friendship are, of course, predominantly (though not exclusively) three-dimensional ones. As Margaret Aston notes, "The imagery seen as proscribed by the law was primarily three dimensional: the works of carvers in wood and stone . . . Lollards were certainly critical of the work of contemporary painters, but in directing the main burden of their criticism at image-*worship* they had in mind sculpture—'the craft of graving'—more than painting."[37] While this concern partly stems from Old Testament prohibitions concerning graven images, it also lies in the three-dimensional image's different claim to realness in comparison with a flat, two-dimensional one.[38] If for Lollards this sculptural quality, in approximating greater lifelikeness, might lead the viewer down the dangerous path of crediting the image with liveliness, for Pecock (though he acknowledges that images may indeed at times miraculously seem alive) an image's lifelikeness works less to animate the image than the imagination, by providing tools for sensory perception.[39] Such sculptural images, niched in the fabric of churches and used in liturgical performances, offer visible presence to the sense of sight, but they also can be reached out to and touched. The paradigm established by these three rules thus has staggering implications for Pecock's

[37] Aston, *Lollards and Reformers*, 146.

[38] The prohibition against graven images is given, for example, in the second commandment of the Decalogue recorded in Exodus 20 and Deuteronomy 5. On Lollard objections to images, see further Richard Marks, *Image and Devotion in Late Medieval England* (Stroud: Sutton, 2004), 2. On the medieval association of three-dimensional images with "reality," see Michael Camille, *The Gothic Idol: Ideology and Image-Making in Medieval Art* (Cambridge: Cambridge University Press, 1989), 41.

[39] The miraculous animation and agency of some images are touched on by Pecock; see *Repressor*, 153–54, 157. For thinking around vivacity or aliveness and images, see further Sarah Stanbury, *The Visual Object of Desire in Late Medieval England* (Philadelphia: University of Pennsylvania Press, 2008), e.g., 26–27; and Sarah Stanbury, "The Vivacity of Images: St. Katherine, Knighton's Lollards, and the Breaking of Idols," in *Images, Idolatry, and Iconoclasm in Late Medieval England: Textuality and the Visual Image*, ed. Jeremy Dimmick, James Simpson, and Nicolette Zeeman (Oxford: Oxford University Press, 2002), 131–50. On the links between sculpture and imagination, see further Camille, *Gothic Idol*, 45, where he recounts Hugh of St. Victor's discussion of sculpture compared with painting in the *Didascalion*.

theory of images: not merely "rememoratijf or mynding signes," images are mediators of the perception of presence at the heart of friendship; and just as the desire to be in the presence of a friend is completed in an embrace or a kiss, so too is the imaginative work of making an absent friend present completed in touching an image. In revising the function of images thus, Pecock simultaneously exposes the problem of absence, which images are used to counteract, to be all about *caritas*.

Aristotle's *Nicomachean Ethics*

The Middle Ages inherit several classical theories of friendship—principally via Cicero's *De amicitia* and Aristotle's *Ethica Nicomachea*—and develop, in part under the influence of Augustine, Christian ideas of spiritual friendship (as in the writings of Aelred of Rievaulx and Bernard of Clairvaux) as well as of friendship with God (as in the work of Robert Grosseteste and Thomas Aquinas).[40] It seems, however, that it is Aristotle's theory of friendship, with its emphasis on presence and proximity, that motivates Pecock's recourse to the figure of the absent friend in his defense of image use in the *Repressor*.[41] The *Nicomachean Ethics*, translated into Latin by Robert Grosseteste around 1240, details Aristotle's philosophy of friendship in Books VIII and IX.[42] While Pecock does not explicitly cite Aristotle in his discussion of the figure of the absent friend, his familiarity with the *Ethics* is evidenced by his citation of both Grosseteste's translation of the *Ethics* and Thomas Aquinas's commentary on it elsewhere in the *Repressor*.[43] And, as already noted,

[40] James McEvoy, "Ultimate Goods: Happiness, Friendship, and Bliss," in *The Cambridge Companion to Medieval Philosophy*, ed. A. S. McGrade (Cambridge: Cambridge University Press, 2003), 254–75, outlines friendship in Augustine. For Aelred of Rievaulx, see Lefler, *Theologizing Friendship*; and for Bernard of Clairvaux, see Shawn Madison Krahmer, "The Friend as 'Second Self' and the Theme of Substitution in the Letters of Bernard of Clairvaux," *Cistercian Studies Quarterly* 31, no. 1 (1996): 21–33. On the influence of Aristotelian friendship on Grosseteste's theology of salvation, see James McEvoy, "Robert Grosseteste on the Cross and Redemptive Love," *Recherches de théologie et philosophie médiévales* 66, no. 2 (1999): 289–315 (e.g., 297–98).

[41] Cicero's model of friendship does not, as Aristotle's does, require personal acquaintance. See Julian Haseldine, "Understanding the Language of *Amicitia*: The Friendship Circle of Peter of Celle (c. 1115–1183)," *Journal of Medieval History* 20 (1994): 237–60 (240).

[42] Grosseteste also writes a commentary on the *Ethics*. See James McEvoy, "Grosseteste's Reflections on Aristotelian Friendship: A 'New' Commentary on *Nicomachean Ethics* VIII.8–14," in *Robert Grosseteste: New Perspectives on His Thought and Scholarship*, ed. McEvoy (Brepols: Turnhout, 1994), 149–68.

[43] On the influence of Aristotle on Pecock's works, see further V. H. H. Green, *Bishop Reginald Pecock: A Study in Ecclesiastical History and Thought* (Cambridge: Cambridge University Press, 1945), 84–87. Hitchcock notes some "points of likeness" between Pecock and Aristotle in her commentary on *Folewer*, and gives Jessie Flemming's assess-

Aristotelian friendship finds profound expression in the thinking of Aquinas, who is an important authority for Pecock.[44] While the *Ethics* has little to say on the subject of images, it provides particularly powerful avenues for thinking about the binaries of presence and absence in terms of the interplay of sensory perception and affection.

Aristotle establishes that friendship is not only "necessary" ("without friends no one would choose to live") but also "noble."[45] While the paradigm of friendship structures relationships from the domestic (parent–child, man–wife) to the political (ruler–subject, nation–nation), perfect friendship is that between equals. Aristotle defines perfect friendship as "the friendship of men who are good, and alike in virtue; for these wish well alike to each other *qua* good, and they are good in themselves."[46] The conditions for perfect friendship are therefore grounded in virtue, equality, and likeness—the friend is "another self"—as well as in reciprocity of feeling and mutual well-wishing, to the extent that one friend is prepared to sacrifice himself for the other ("the good man . . . does many acts for the sake of his friends and his country, and if necessary dies for them").[47] For such a friendship between equals to arise, however, both time and familiarity are required: "one must . . . acquire some experience of the other person and become familiar with him, and that is very hard."[48] Thus perfect friends, in Aristotle's estimation, live together; such proximity is what makes love for the friend possible. We might thus summarize the central tenets of Aristotelian friendship, as the late fifteenth-century *Catholicon anglicum* does Middle English "Frende," in four Latin glosses: "amicus [loved one], necessarius, proximus [nearest, next], alter ego."[49] Most significant for Pecock's thinking about images is that the "amicus" must be "proximus."

As Aristotle makes clear, proximity and presence themselves, of course, are all to do with sensory perception. Embedded in the *Ethics'* discussion of friendship is, accordingly, another of perception, where Aristotle is at pains to posit not just perception but the *recognition* of

---

ment of the closer relationship of Pecock to Thomas Aquinas than to Aristotle (Pecock, *Folewer*, ed. Hitchcock, 230).

[44] See n. 11 above.

[45] Aristotle, *Ethica Nicomachea (Nicomachean Ethics)*, 1155a.1, trans. W. D. Ross, in *The Basic Works of Aristotle*, ed. Richard McKeon (New York: Random House, 1941), 935–1126 (1058–59).

[46] Aristotle, *Ethica Nicomachea*, 1156b.3 (trans. Ross, 1061).

[47] Aristotle, *Ethica Nicomachea*, 11169a.8 (trans. Ross, 1087).

[48] Aristotle, *Ethica Nicomachea*, 1158a.6 (trans. Ross, 1064).

[49] *Catholicon anglicum: An English–Latin Wordbook*, ed. S. J. H. Herrtage and H. B. Wheatley, EETS o.s. 75 (1881; repr. Millwood, N.Y.: Kraus, 1987), 142.

perception ("he who sees perceives that he sees, and he who hears, that he hears," etc.) as lying at the core of self-consciousness and ultimately of happiness: a man "needs, therefore, to be conscious of the existence of his friend . . . and this will be realized in their living together."[50] The perception of the presence of the friend is thus necessary, not only in order for friendly feelings to arise but also for those feelings to be sustained:

Those who live together delight in each other and confer benefits on each other, but those who are asleep or locally separated are not performing, but are disposed to perform, the activities of friendship; distance does not break off the friendship absolutely, but only the activity of it. But if the absence is lasting, it seems actually to make men forget their friendship; hence the saying "out of sight, out of mind."[51]

Somewhat problematically for the medieval reception of the *Ethics*, however, the human possibility that friendship might survive (temporary) absence or distance is not one Aristotle affords to God, nor does he allow perfect friendship to exist between God and man on the grounds of inequality: "Much can be taken away and friendship remain, but when one party is removed to a great distance, as God is, the possibility of friendship ceases."[52] As Jacques Derrida observes on this passage in *The Politics of Friendship*:

Presence or proximity [proximité] are the condition of friendship, whose energy [énergie] is lost in absence or in remoteness. Men are called "good" or "virtuous" from the vantage point of aptitude, possibility, *habitus* (*kath'éxin*), or in act (*kat'enérgeian*). It is the same for friendship: friends who sleep or live in separate places are not friends in act (*ouk energousi*). *The energy of friendship draws its force from presence* or from *proximity*. If absence and remoteness do not destroy friendship, they attenuate or exhaust it, they enervate it.[53]

Derrida's reading of the *Ethics* usefully articulates the condition of presence for the "energy"—activity, but also force or potency—constitutive

---

[50] Aristotle, *Nicomachean Ethics*, 1170a.9 (trans. Ross, 1090). On medieval reception of Aristotle's ideas about happiness and their dependency on sensory perception, see Jessica Rosenfeld, *Ethics and Enjoyment in Late Medieval Poetry: Love after Aristotle* (Cambridge: Cambridge University Press, 2013), 135–49.

[51] *Nicomachean Ethics*, 1157b.5 (trans. Ross, 1063).

[52] *Nicomachean Ethics*, 1159a.7 (trans. Ross, 1066).

[53] Jacques Derrida, *The Politics of Friendship*, trans. George Collins (London: Verso, 1997), 222 (emphasis in original).

of Aristotelian friendship. If friendship is generated and nurtured through living together and through sensory perception, how can man (in the here and now) be friends with God? While medieval thinking asserts instead that friendship with God is necessary and possible, Aristotelian friendship, in making proximity or presence the condition of friendship, poses the question of how love for God is to be maintained and acted out at a distance and in his absence.[54] Christ's Incarnation is key to medieval answers to this problem, but so too, as the *Repressor* demonstrates, are images.

Images and Absence

While Aristotelian qualities of perfect friendship—the friend is "another self," prepared to sacrifice his life for his friends—might be particularly suggestive for analogy with Christ, as they are elsewhere in scholastic and vernacular theology, Thomas Aquinas's theology of friendship, as Nathan Lefler summarizes, is "transcendent": that is, it is more interested in friendship with God "in his essence" than with the person of Christ.[55] It is Aristotle's condition of equality for friendship in the *Ethics*, however, that motivates, in Lefler's words, Aquinas's "brief, lapidary formulation of the theology of friendship in brazenly christological terms."[56] In Book IV, Chapter 54 of the *Summa contra gentiles*, Thomas posits that friendship between man and God in his essence is made possible through Christ's Incarnation:

since friendship consists in a certain equality, things greatly unequal seem unable to be coupled in friendship. Therefore, to get greater familiarity in friendship between man and God it was helpful for man that God become man, since even by nature man is man's friend; and so in this way, "while

---

[54] See further Caroline White, "Friendship in Absence: Some Patristic Views," in *Friendship in Medieval Europe*, ed. Julian Haseldine (Stroud: Sutton, 1999), 68–88, for Patristic engagement with the idea of absence.

[55] Lefler, *Theologizing Friendship*, 117–20. For example, Robert Grosseteste takes up the notion of the friend as the "alter ipse" (the other self) in developing his theology of salvation. John Lydgate's poem "A Freond at Neode" shows that Christ's death for mankind provides the superlative example of friendship; and the fifteenth-century *Mirour of Mans Saluacioun* describes Christ's loss of blood in the Crucifixion itself as a "friendly" act.

[56] Lefler, *Theologizing Friendship*, 119.

we know God visibly, we may [through Him] be borne to love of things invisible."[57]

Incarnation, then, effects a kind of equality, a "familiarity," between God and man necessary in Aristotelian terms for perfect friendship. Inextricably in Aquinas's thinking here, however, the equality effected by the Incarnation also entails presence—not only bringing God down to earth, but making him perceptible to human, bodily senses: knowledge of God in his visible, human form leads us to love of God in his essence. While Aquinas is thinking about the Incarnation and not about images at this point in the *Summa contra gentiles*, it is precisely this catenation that grounds the orthodox claim, commonly made in the medieval period, that making images of God is lawful: the same move in which Incarnation makes friendship between God and man possible also makes God visible and representable.[58]

According to orthodox defenses of images, then, Christ's Incarnation authorizes bodily representations of the divine. But if the Incarnation is fundamentally about making God present and perceptible to man, because of Christ's Resurrection and Ascension the fullness of this presence is deferred until a future moment: Christ is, for the time being, bodily absent.[59] Thus one function of images, as Roger Dymmok suggests in his Latin, anti-Lollard treatise *Liber contra errores et hereses lollardorum* (c. 1396), is to offer a material remnant of, or a substitute for, bodily presence:

when a man has loved something fervently, he desires its presence; and therefore, since we rightly owe the saints of God to be worshipped and venerated

[57] Thomas Aquinas, *Summa contra gentiles*, gen. ed. Jospeh Kenny, O.P. (New York: Hanover House, 1955–57), Book IV, *Salvation*, trans. Charles O'Neil, Chapter 54, §6. See Marko Fuchs, "*Philia* and *Caritas*: Some Aspects of Aquinas's Reception of Aristotle's Theory of Friendship," in *Aquinas and the "Nicomachean Ethics,"* ed. Tobias Hoffmann, Jörn Müller, and Matthias Perkams (Cambridge: Cambridge University Press, 2013), 203–19.

[58] Influentially elaborating a connection made by earlier writers, John of Damascus cites the Incarnation as authorizing the making and use of images in his eighth-century defense of icons, *On the Divine Images: Three Apologies against Those who Attack the Divine Images*, trans. David Anderson (Crestwood, N.Y.: St. Vladimir's Seminary, 1980), e.g., 23–26. Fourteenth- and fifteenth-century discussions of images commonly continue to cite this argument; on its longer history, see further Alain Besançon, *The Forbidden Image: An Intellectual History of Iconoclasm* (Chicago: University of Chicago Press, 2000), 115–23; and Stanbury, *The Visual Object*, e.g., 21, specifically for English examples in the fourteenth and fifteenth centuries.

[59] On Christ's "imminent disappearance," see Amy Knight Powell, *Depositions: Scenes from the Late Medieval Church and the Modern Museum* (New York: Zone, 2012).

by means of the honours that are due to them, because we cannot have the persons themselves present, we are advised at least to come near to their relics and images in order to worship them.[60]

Images and relics, in the form of body parts or objects that have been touched by or worn on the body, offer material points of connection with an absent God and absent saints, love for whom manifests itself as a desire for presence, for nearness to them. At heart, then, image-making addresses the human need for something of the divine to be made available to the senses. As David Freedberg remarks, the aim of "[medieval meditative] forms that depend on real images for the production of mental ones" is precisely "to grasp that which is absent."[61] What Dymmok imagines as presence, however—being near to a material relic or image—though not without active potential (as a locus for worship, but also for healing, for spiritual transformation, etc.), is a far cry from that defined by Aristotle and implied by Pecock, as the energy of living together. As the *Repressor* demonstrates, it is the mnemonic function of images that becomes key for enabling a different kind of presence—one that is an active, lived-out performance.

Since, as Aristotle suggests, long absence might not only enervate love but lead to forgetting, images are also justified to remind Christians of those they ought to love and serve—in other words, as goads to the activity of remembrance. In his fifth principal conclusion on image use in Part 2 of the *Repressor*, Pecock thus points out that, in ordaining the Sacrament of the Altar in which bread and wine are made flesh and blood, Christ himself instituted Christian use of signs and symbols for precisely the purpose of remembrance: "Crist ordeyned in the newe lawe visible sacramentis to be take and vsid as seable rememoratijf signes of Crist, and of his passioun and deeth, and of his holi lijf."[62] Since Christ ordained the use of "seable" signs in the form of bread and wine, Pecock

---

[60] *Rogeri Dymmok, Liber contra XII errores et hereses Lollardorum*, ed. H. S. Cronin (London: published for the Wyclif Society by Kegan Paul, Trench, Trübner, 1922), 193: "cum homo aliquid feruenter amauerit, eius presenciam desiderat; et ideo, cum sanctis Dei merito affici debeamus et eos debitis honoribus uenerari, quia personas ipsas in presenti habere non possumus, saltem ad eorum reliquias uel ymagines adorandus accedere monemur" (the English translation is my own).

[61] David Freedberg, *The Power of Images: Studies in the History and Theory of Response* (Chicago: University of Chicago Press, 1989), 161.

[62] Pecock, *Repressor*, 163.

concludes, then images that are likenesses of him must also be permissible. The grounds for this claim lie in medieval sign theory.[63] If it is lawful and expedient to use a sign that is not like the thing it signifies, it must also be to use one that is like, or more like, that which it signifies:

Forwhi the likenes of a signe to his significat, (that is to seie, to the thing signified bi him,) wole helpe the signe forto signifie and forto make remembraunce the bettir upon the thing signified; but so it is, that ymagis graued, coruun, or ʒut ben more lijk to Crist and to his passioun, than ben the sacramentis whiche Crist ordeyned.[64]

Images of Christ that are graven, carved, or cast ("ymagis graued, coruun, or ʒut"), Pecock somewhat audaciously claims, are therefore more efficacious signs of him than the sacraments, their particular present-making power notwithstanding. Here, Pecock seeds the principle of likeness that he returns to in his claim that an "ymage of Crist crucified" can best mediate friendship with an absent Christ: likeness helps the sign signify and better enables remembrance. This principle is so crucial because of how human memory operates.

Medieval memory work, as Mary Carruthers demonstrates, is not a neutral, merely intellective process of recollection, but a fully embodied, affective one that is all about "making present."[65] Staged in the imagination and reliant on prior sensory perception, it is this imaginative making present that enables the virtual performance of friendship with God

---

[63] St. Augustine influentially lays out the thinking that forms the foundation of medieval sign theory, for example, in *De doctrina Christiana*. For the development of sign theory in the high medieval period, and especially its implication for questions of absence and presence, see Brigitte Miriam Bedos-Rezak, "Medieval Identity: A Sign and a Concept," *American Historical Review* 105, no. 5 (2000): 1489–1533; for the later medieval period, see further Arthur Ross, *Medieval Sign Theory and "Sir Gawain and the Green Knight"* (Toronto: University of Toronto Press, 1987).

[64] Pecock, *Repressor*, 163. Cf. Augustine of Hippo, *On Christian Doctrine*, trans. D. W. Robertson, Jr. (New York: Liberal Arts Press, 1958), 61: "It is true that everyone seeks a certain verisimilitude in making signs so that these signs, in so far as is possible, may resemble the things that they signify. . . . Where pictures or statues are concerned, or other similar imitative works . . . no one errs when he sees the likeness, so that he recognizes what things are represented." On the role of likeness, see further Heather Madar, "Iconography of Sign: A Semiotic Reading of the *Arma Christi*," in *ReVisioning: Critical Methods of Seeing Christianity in the History of Art*, ed. James Romaine and Linda Stratford (Cambridge: Lutterworth Press, 2014), 115–31 (e.g., 124–25).

[65] Mary Carruthers, *The Book of Memory: A Study of Memory in Medieval Culture* (Cambridge: Cambridge University Press, 1990), e.g., 275. Carruthers notes the derivation of the Latin verb *representare* from *praesens*, meaning "presence in time."

that must, in Pecock's thinking, accord with a Christian's external actions. Pecock's broadly Aristotelian understanding of the nexus of sense perception, imagination, and memory is central to his image theory and, in fact, is foundational to his whole literary project. The *Donet*, the *Folewer*, and the *Reule*, for example, each predicate vernacular instruction in theology on a prior knowledge of what man is and on an understanding of the interrelation of body and soul. Pecock thus sets out at the start of each of these works the operation of the five outer wits (sight, hearing, smell, taste, and touch) and their cerebral processing by the five inner wits (common wit, imagination, fantasy, estimation, and memory).[66] The *Donet* explains that the office of the senses is "forto knowe bodili þingis in her presence, and whilis þei ben in kynde"; the inward wits, instead, work to know such things when they are absent.[67] As Pecock's multiple accounts all reiterate, the imagination plays a key role in the cognitive capacity to make something that is absent to the senses present in the mind, and further, in Pecock's account, in storing (along with memory) "alle þe same now seid knowingis wiþ her fundamentis [foundations, bases], whiche ben called 'similitudis,' 'liknessis,' or 'ymagis' of þingis, *þat þei falle not soon aweie*."[68]

Precisely what these "similitudis," "liknessis," or "ymagis" are is made clearer in the *Folewer*, which builds on the foundation of sensory knowledge given in the *Donet* by detailing more fully the optical theory of intromission.[69] This theory is an extension of medieval thinking around the notion of species, at the heart (as we have seen) of Thomist understandings of cognition. The "likeness" (also referred to in optical theory as "species") of an object is impressed into the eyeball, whence the "spiritis"—a bodily spirit that performs the offices of the soul—carries it into the sinews (or nerves): the eye thus "seeþ and knowiþ þe þing whos liknesse is so receyuyd into þe iȝe."[70] That likeness is then conveyed

---

[66] See, for example, Pecock, *Donet*, 8–11; Pecock, *Folewer*, 20–30; and Pecock, *Reule*, 37, and passim.

[67] Pecock, *Donet*, 9.

[68] Ibid., 10 (my emphasis).

[69] See Mishtooni Bose, "Vernacular Philosophy and the Making of Orthodoxy in the Fifteenth Century," *NML* 7 (2005): 73–99; for Pecock's knowledge of optical theory, see 88–93. David C. Lindberg, *Theories of Vision from Al-Kindi to Kepler* (Chicago: University of Chicago Press, 1976), offers a detailed history of medieval optical theory, and the theory of intromission in particular. Chapter 7 details its place, not only in science and philosophy, but also in theology.

[70] Pecock, *Folewer*, 39. See Michael Camille, "Before the Gaze: The Internal Senses and Late Medieval Practices of Seeing," in *Visuality before and beyond the Renaissance: Seeing as Others Saw*, ed. Robert Nelson (Cambridge: Cambridge University Press, 2000),

further "bi office of spiritis" into the forehead, where it is impressed first lightly in the common wit and then more deeply in the imagination, by which likeness the inner wits "knowe þe same þing" as the eye perceived. The way in which a likeness of an object sensed is brought into the body by means of *spiritis* and impressed in the imagination supports the logic of Pecock's claim that the more like an image is to the thing it signifies the easier it is to do cognitive work with it; it also discloses a material aspect to imaginative "making present." Likenesses—whether first brought into the mind through the eye or through any other organ of sense—are called up from the store in memory to stock the images required in the process of imagining.[71] Doing this without the aid of any physical image is hard work, as Pecock points out in the *Repressor*. If a man seeks to recall what he has heard preached or read in church previously, for example,

it schal be to him miche gretter labour for to laboure so in his brayn bi taking mynde and for to withinneforth calle into mynde without siȝt of the iȝe withouteforth vpon ymagis what he bifore knewe and thouȝte vpon, than it schulde be to him if he biholde bi iȝe siȝt upon ymagis or other peinting according to his labour. And aȝenward, bi biholding upon ymagis or upon such peinting his witt schal be dressid and lad forthe euener and more stabili and with myche lasse peyne and labour, than forto wrastle withinneforth in his owne ymaginaciouns withoute leding withouteforth had bi biholding upon ymagis.[72]

The cerebral struggle involved in calling into mind "withinneforth," without an external image "withouteforth" looked upon by the eye, is amply reflected in Pecock's convoluted syntax. But the essential point is a simple one: images, especially those that are like that which they signify, make the devotional work of memory easier and less painful, but also less error-prone—a man's wit shall be "dressid [guided, directed] and lad forthe euener and more stabili"—by making present to the sense of sight an image upon which inner sight can found its images in the imagination.

197–223, on the intromission model of vision, the importance of the principle of likeness, and the role of the "species" in bridging "the physical gap between the object and the sense organ" (208).

[71] Cf. Pecock, *Folewer*, 39–40, on the operation of the other senses in comparison with sight.

[72] Pecock, *Repressor*, 214.

What motivates Pecock's thinking here, and throughout his discussion of the senses, imagination, and memory, is a recognition of man's natural frailty. It is because "mankinde in this lijf is so freel" that "seable" signs are needed in addition to "heereable" ones: man's ability to recall and remember rightly is affected by labor, study, old age, and sickness (when "his heed is feeble for labour or studie bifore had or for sikenes or for age"), and humans are prone to forgetfulness.[73] The sixth opening conclusion on pilgrimages offered by Pecock in Part 2 of the *Repressor* makes clear just what is at stake in man's tendency to forget: if Christ's life and Passion are not remembered, "thei schulen not be reckid [regarded]," and "sithen al thing which is not had in mynde of a man is, as toward eny thing which he schulde do ther with or ther bi, deed or lost or not being."[74] Not remembering Christ might mean it is as if he were dead, lost, or even as not having existed at all.

The parallel sixth conclusion on images identifies this problem of forgetfulness more specifically as the central issue for *caritas*. Here Pecock reminds the reader of what he has set out in the *Repressor*'s opening: that each man (and woman) is commanded to "loue God and drede God, that he mai therbi be hertid and strengthid in wil forto serue God"; he therefore must "ofte thinke vpon tho thingis and meenis, whiche schulden stire him forto loue God and drede God." And yet: "forto so ofte remembre we ben ful freel and forȝeteful."[75] The memory work central to obeying the biblical commandment to love God, neighbor, and self is potentially compromised by man's natural frailty. As Aquinas acknowledges in his discussion of charity in the *Summa*, although God is of himself "supremely knowable . . . on account of the feebleness of our knowledge, which has to depend on things of sense, we do not find him so."[76] For Pecock, as we have seen, images are part of the solution to man's dependency on sense perception.

Significantly, then, it is in the context of this reminder of the command to "loue God and drede God" that Pecock first invokes the figure of the absent friend (though he does not use the term "friend," the analogy is implicitly one of friendship). Referring to the authority of reason ("doom of resoun allowith"), Pecock argues it is permissible

---

[73] Ibid., 209; 213; e.g., 165.
[74] Ibid., 182.
[75] Ibid., 165.
[76] Aquinas, *Summa theologiae*, 2a2ae q. 24, art. 2 (ed. Gilby, 34:38–39).

forto make and haue for us silf and for othere men ymagis of men and wom-men, that tho men and wommen be therbi the oftir thouȝt upon, and therfore be therbi the more loued and the better serued, and that the more be doon and suffrid of us and of othere biholders, for as miche as we bithenken tho persoones or the ensaumpling of the persoones so representid bi the ymagis, and that the more be doon and suffrid for her sake of us silf and of othere men seing the same ymagis with vs.[77]

Just as an image of an absent friend enables another to think about (or imagine) them often, and thus better love and serve them, so too, Pecock claims, does an image of God or a saint. The Latin treatise (writ-ten between 1385 and 1395) known variously as *De tolerandis imaginibus* or *De adoracione ymaginum*, attributed to Walter Hilton, similarly argues that images are permissible "because sometimes a friend, who absences himself from his friend, is in the habit of giving him an image as a memento, so that he can remember the absent friend by looking at the image."[78] Pecock's accumulative thinking around friendship and images in the *Repressor*, however, goes much further than does Hilton's brief recourse to it in *De tolerandis imaginibus*.[79] In Pecock's second, extended use of the figure of friendship fifteen chapters later, Christ becomes the absent friend we are recalling, friendship with whom is the central requirement of the greatest biblical commandment. And just as an image as a memento facilitates the imaginative making present of an absent friend necessary to perform and sustain the activity of friendship (love, service, and even sacrifice), so too does an image of Christ enable the memory work central to meeting the demands of *caritas*.

Christ the Absent Friend

Like Thomas Aquinas's, Pecock's theology of friendship is concerned principally with friendship with God in his essence. The turn to Christ

---

[77] Pecock, *Repressor*, 164–65.

[78] *Walter Hilton's Latin Writings*, ed. John H. Clark and Cheryl Taylor, 2 vols., Ana-lecta Cartusiana 124 (Salzburg: Institut für Anglistik und Amerikanistik, 1987), 199: "Quia interdum amicus se absentans ab amico, aliquod signum recordatiuum ad ami-cum suum transmitter solet, ut per intuitum signi recordetur asbentis amici." The English translation is my own. For a detailed summary of this treatise, see J. H. Clark, "Walter Hilton in Defence of the Religious Life and of the Veneration of Images," *Downside Review* 103 (1985): 1–25. See further Minnis, "Affection and Imagination," 361.

[79] See further Marks, *Image and Devotion*, e.g. 18, for ways Pecock goes beyond other defenses of the image.

as friend in the *Repressor* is (like Aquinas's in the *Summa contra gentiles*) exceptional and all the more compelling as a result. Pecock arrives at the idea of Christ the friend, as I have sought to explicate in this essay, as the culmination of his thinking around *caritas* as friendship predicated on presence, and around the role of the imagination, memory, and the senses in making present something that is absent. From this perspective, Pecock's thinking about images in terms of the presence necessary for friendship in the *Repressor* is entirely consonant with a broadly Aristotelian understanding of the role of the senses and imagination in making present what is absent. Having set out the paradigm for friendship in the form of three rules at the opening of Chapter 20 of Part 2 of the *Repressor* Pecock proceeds thus (as already outlined above):

Ech man hath nede forto haue gode affecciouns anentis Crist, as upon his best freend; and this freend ȝeueth not to us his presence visibili; wherfore it is profitable to ech man for to ymagine this freend be present to us bodili and in a maner visibili. And sithen herto serueth ful weel and ful myche the ymage of Crist crucified, whilis and if the biholder ymagineth Crist to be streiȝt abrode bodili thoruȝ the bodi of the same ymage, heed to heed, hond to hond, breste to breste, foot to foot.[80]

In our second look at this passage, we should first note the invocation of the commandment of *caritas* ("Ech man hath nede forto haue gode affecciouns anentis Crist"), its expression as friendship ("as upon his best freend"), and the way it steers Pecock's argument: images are imbricated profoundly in fulfilling the fundamental requirements of Christian living. Christ the friend is not visibly present, and yet as the first rule has established and as Aristotle emphasizes, presence is the condition for the arousal of love and its increase. This, as Aquinas emphasizes in his account of charity in the *Summa*, is rooted in "dwelling together," which concept (as the translator notes) "is given its full and active force . . . . *Convivere, conversatio, communicatio, participatio* are key-words for the association which is the basis of friendship."[81] The condition of cohabitation for friendship is likewise drawn out by Pecock in the proofs he gives of the first rule:

This reule is openli trewe bi experience. Forwhi, (not withstonding a man talke and speke of his freend at the mete table or in sum other place, and haue as

[80] Pecock, *Repressor*, 269.
[81] Note to Aquinas, *Summa theologiae*, 2a2ae q. 23, art. 1, ed. Gilby (34:5 n. b).

good affeccioun as he can haue upon the same freend in such absence,) ȝit if in the meene while the freend come into him personali and sitte doun with him, he schal haue miche gretter affeccioun vpon the seid freend than he hadde in the freendis absence.[82]

The "mete [dinner] table" becomes a kind of paradigmatic space for practicing friendship: for sitting and talking together in person, or, in the friend's absence, for sitting and talking *about* the friend. The problem thus implicitly raised is: How is Christ to be loved above all others, if those others are present and he is absent?[83] Imagining Christ to be "present to us bodili" goes some way to countering this problem, not least since, as the second rule has established, the presence of something in the imagination, though inferior to bodily presence, is nonetheless a real form of presence with a materially felt aspect that enables love. This imaginative memory work is aided best by using an image of Christ crucified, because, as established by the third rule, it bears a direct likeness to that which it represents.

It is this insistence on the importance of the sign's likeness to what it signifies that leads Pecock to reject, earlier in the *Repressor*, the Lollard argument "that ech Cristen man is a perfiter and a fuller and a spedier [that is, "efficacious," but also "exact"] ymage of Crist than is eny stok [piece of wood] or stoon graued."[84] In so doing, Pecock closes down the possibility (at the heart of Lollard arguments against images) that the energy required for friendship with Christ might derive from proximity to one's neighbor. Listing three conditions required in order to be a perfect, full, and efficacious image of Christ, Pecock reiterates firstly that the greater degree of likeness there is, the greater is the claim of one thing to be the perfect image of another.[85] The second condition is that the image must be ordained to signify something in particular. The third is that the image must signify singly (using a sign that signifies multiply will mean its likeness to Christ will suffer interference from its likeness to something else). Pecock therefore concludes:

---

[82] Pecock, *Repressor*, 267.

[83] Aquinas, in the *Summa theologiae*, asserts that since charity is caused by God it cannot, in this sense, cease or be diminished (2a2ae q. 24, art. 10), but he acknowledges that man's reliance on sense perception to know God creates a problem (2a2ae q. 27, art. 4), ed. Gilby (34:62–69, 171–73).

[84] Pecock, *Repressor*, 219. On man as a true image of God, see further Aston, *Lollards and Reformers*, e.g., 155–59.

[85] Pecock, *Repressor*, 219–20.

no Cristen man now lyuyng hath these iij. condicions anentis the persoon of Crist in his manhode, as hath a stok or a stoon graued into the likenes of Crist hanging on a cros nakid and wounded . . . except whanne a quyk man is sett in a pley to be hangid nakid on a cros and to be in semyng woundid and scourgid. And this bifallith ful seelde and in fewe placis and cuntrees.[86]

Notably, then, a living man acting out the part of Christ in the Crucifixion, as might be seen in a mystery play, trumps images. But since this, at least according to Pecock, happens seldom and in only a few places, three-dimensional images that *represent* Christ crucified are the next best thing.[87]

The utility of an image's likeness is further extended in Pecock's detailing of the precise way in which a Christian should use the image in the imagination in relation to the physical image: an image is particularly efficacious in making present an absent Christ, "whilis and if the biholder ymagineth Crist to be streiȝt abrode bodili thoruȝ the bodi of the same ymage, heed to heed, hond to hond, breste to breste, foot to foot." What, though, does Pecock mean by this? "[S]treiȝt abrode" suggests both the idea of extension (*MED*, s.v. *strecchen* [v.{1}] gives "stretched out" as one possibility for "streiȝt abrode (forth)"), as well as of straightness or directness. One way of understanding the imaginative process Pecock describes, then, is as follows: in looking at the image that gives physical sight, the Christian needs also to see the real Christ stretched through or over this image in the imagination. That the past participle of the verb *strecchen* (as the *MED* attests) might be rendered "streiȝt" implies precisely this kind of stretching (so "streiȝt abrode," in this reading, would mean "stretched across"). In this sense, there is some overlap with the common use of Middle English *strecchen* to refer to Christ's body on the cross, of which examples in medieval literature are plentiful, or with Christ's own act of stretching down from the cross to

---

[86] Ibid., 221.

[87] The question of whether London had comparable biblical play cycles to, for example, York or Coventry remains under discussion. There are records of a biblical drama performed at Clerkenwell (just outside London) between 1384 and 1409. Anne Lancashire, *London Civic Theatre: City Drama and Pageantry from Roman Times to 1558* (Cambridge: Cambridge University Press, 2002), suggests this was a continuous, regular tradition of playing the biblical cycle. Lawrence M. Clopper, "London and the Problem of the Clerkenwell Plays," *Comparative Drama* 34, no. 3 (2000): 291–303, believes instead that these were one-off performances. But in either case, the evidence disappears after 1409, so whether such plays were regularly being performed in London at the time Pecock was writing remains uncertain.

embrace the penitent sinner as his friend, as recounted in an exemplum drawn upon in Good Friday sermons.[88]

Another complementary way of understanding what Pecock is describing, however, is according to the more specific terms of the operation of sensory perception. As an adjective (derived from the same verb *strecchen*), "streiȝt" also means "straight" or "direct," and so recalls the vernacular vocabulary for describing the optical lines (conveying species) understood to stretch from an object to the eye in the theory of intromission (so, in this second reading, "streiȝt abrode" would mean something like "straight through"). Underpinning the cognitive process that maps an image of Christ in the imagination to a physical image is thus a sensory one predicated (quite literally) on straight lines. The encyclopedia *On the Properties of Things*, translated into Middle English by John Trevisa around 1398, thus records, following the authority of Aristotle, that sight is made "by straite lynes vpon þe whiche þe liknes of þe þing þat is iseyne comeþ to þe siȝt."[89] When a viewer sees an image of the crucified Christ, the lines conveying the image's likeness to sight connect Christ in the imagination with the physical image: head to head, hand to hand, breast to breast, foot to foot.

By describing, and so teaching, a form of imagining predicated on the operation of sight, in which a virtual image of Christ is "streiȝt abrode bodili thoruȝ the bodi" of a physical image, Pecock is at pains to show the material connection between interior and exterior that orients how liturgical performances should be understood: external actions (such as processing with, praying and bowing to, or kissing images) should be contiguous with an imaginative process that aims to make Christ in some sense really present. Attentiveness to this contiguity between interior presence and external acts, achieved through this imaginative practice, is what staves off idolatry by properly directing worship and love to God. Such contiguity, not only of the external with the

---

[88] On this motif, see Margaret Aston, "Lollards and the Cross," in *Lollards and Their Influence in Late Medieval England*, ed. Fiona Somerset, Jill C. Havens, and Derrick G. Pitard (Woodbridge: Boydell, 2003), 99–113; and Sara Lipton, " 'The sweet lean of his head': Writing about Looking at the Crucifix in the High Middle Ages," *Speculum* 80 (2005): 1172–1208. See Lipton's discussion of Rupert Deutz (1179). Exempla collections tell of how, on Good Friday, Christ leaned down from the cross to embrace a penitent sinner; see Gwenfair Walters Adams, *Visions in Late Medieval England: Lay Spirituality and Sacred Glimpses of the Hidden Worlds of Faith* (Leiden: Brill, 2007), 149 for examples.

[89] *On the Properties of Things: John Trevisa's Translation of Bartholomaeus Anglicus' "De proprietatibus rerum,"* ed. M. C. Seymour et al., 3 vols. (Oxford: Clarendon Press, 1975–88), 1:109. Lines are understood also to be bent or refracted.

interior image, but also of external action with imagined action, in facilitating a kind of virtual living together, is thus key to performing the activity of friendship necessary to *caritas*. Indeed, as Pecock observes, such was the "oolde practik of deuoute Cristen men." Thus, in Palm Sunday processions when the cross was bowed to, devout Christians "helden hem silf forto meete bodili and presentli with Crist" in the imagination. Likewise, in creeping to the cross on Good Friday, "aftir her ymaginacioun" they "crepiden to the persoon of Crist, which bi her ymaginacioun was bodili streiȝt forth with the bodi of the ymage." And in kissing the feet of the image on the cross, they did so, "not as that the feet of the ymage weren al that thei there kissiden, but that ther with thei kessiden the feet of Crist whom thei ymagineden to be there in bodili maner present."[90] In these further iterations of, or steps in, imagining Christ to be "bodili streiȝt forth with the bodi of the ymage," the lines established between the imagined image and the physical one through vision are first paralleled by the physical extension of the viewer's body toward the image in the act of bowing and then, finally, replaced with the body itself in the act of touching.

We might think that vision is unique in its reception of species cast out from an object, but, as Pecock notes, all the senses are understood to bring likenesses into the body in essentially similar ways. *On the Properties of Things* further suggests that all the inner senses, located in the brain, are connected to each of the sense organs, and so in some way to all objects of sense through lines: "hit is comyn and general to all þe vttir wittis þat fram þe innere wit, þat hatte *sensus comunis* 'þe comyn witte,' comeþ as it were lynes out of þe middle þerof to eueruche singular vttir wit and makeþ it parfite."[91] Thus, in the act of kissing the feet of an image of Christ while imagining kissing the feet of Christ, it is touch itself that establishes the material connection (the lines conveying species) between image and imagination, making them contiguous. The imagined and the actual are thus traversed through touch, creating presence and arousing love.

Touching Images

Pecock asserts that the same imaginative and sensory processes at work in the "practik" of Christians in the past should likewise underpin current devotional and liturgical uses of images.[92] In the closing stages of

[90] Pecock, *Repressor*, 269–70.
[91] Trevisa, *On the Properties of Things*, 1:119.
[92] On liturgical use of images, see further Marks, *Image and Devotion*, e.g., 160–61.

Part 2 of the *Repressor*, Pecock thus returns the reader to contemporary liturgical performances involving images and touch (those which cause Lollards to feel "out of eese") with a reformed understanding of their value: the process of making Christ present in the imagination in order to love him wholeheartedly must be matched in external action and is completed in touch.

Liturgical performances such as the Palm Sunday procession and Good Friday creeping to the cross are, of course, collective instances of remembrance that aim at a kind of making present even while they might embody (and even, as Amy Knight Powell suggests, prefigure) absence.[93] In the Palm Sunday procession, re-presenting Christ's entry into Jerusalem, the sacrament—the real presence of Christ in the form of bread and wine—is processed outside and then brought into the church. As Eamon Duffy describes:

> The clergy and people entered the church, passing under the shrine with the Sacrament, and then the whole procession moved to its culminating point before the Rood-screen. All through Lent a great painted veil had been suspended in front of the Crucifix on the Rood-screen. This veil was now drawn up on pulleys, the whole parish knelt, and the anthem "Ave Rex Noster" was sung, while the clergy venerated the cross by kissing the ground.[94]

On Good Friday, commemorating Christ's Passion, a crucifix is unveiled (this time, in three stages), culminating in the custom of creeping to it: as Duffy describes, "Clergy and people then crept barefoot and on their knees to kiss the foot of the cross." Afterwards, the consecrated Host is symbolically "buried" in the Easter sepulchre.[95] Deposition rites associated with Holy Week, as Powell describes, sometimes also used an articulated Christ with moving body parts to reenact his burial.[96] Scholars

---

[93] On the role of the liturgy in collective remembrance and making present, see further Carruthers, *The Book of Memory*; and Mary Carruthers, *The Craft of Thought: Meditation, Rhetoric, and the Making of Images, 400–1200* (Cambridge: Cambridge University Press, 1998). On the idea of absence in medieval Deposition images and their prefiguration of Reformation iconoclasm, see Powell, *Depositions*. On paraliturgical performances, such as plays, and presence, see further Sarah Beckwith, "Absent Presences: The Theatre of Resurrection in York," in *Medieval Literature and Historical Inquiry: Essays in Honor of Derek Pearsall*, ed. David Aers (Cambridge: Brewer, 2000), 185–205 (e.g., 185).

[94] Eamon Duffy, *The Stripping of the Altars: Traditional Religion in England, 1400–1580* (New Haven: Yale University Press, 1992), 25.

[95] Ibid., 29.

[96] On such moving Christs, see Powell, *Depositions*; Laura Varnam, "The Crucifix, the Pietà, and the Female Mystic: Devotional Objects and Performative Identity in *The Book of Margery Kempe*," *Journal of Medieval Religious Cultures* 41 no. 2 (2015): 208–37.

have thoroughly documented the ways in which three-dimensional images are thus used, along with the material space and fabric of a church, to emphasize visual spectacle in liturgical performance in the medieval period.[97] More recent scholarship has begun to recognize the ways in which even objects seen in this context also operate in conjunction with haptic experience. Jacqueline E. Jung and Joanne E. Ziegler, for example, find (respectively) that devotional engagements with rood screens and *pietà* sculptures should be understood in a tactile frame.[98] But material objects situated in churches, more than just appealing to a sense of touch, also invite literal acts of touching. As Caroline Walker Bynum highlights, devotional objects were often constructed precisely to "call attention to their materiality by means both obvious and subtle": some were thus designed in such a way as to impel "viewers to experience greater tactility as they penetrated to deeper soteriological significance"; others, however, explicitly "enjoined the worshipper to kiss them."[99]

The explicit invitation made in the context of the liturgy to touch images is in part so objectionable to Lollards, as Pecock summarizes, because in so doing people "beren hem silf and gourene hem silf as thei wolden bere hem and gouerne hem, if thilk thing were God hem silf"; indeed, if God were himself visibly present, they could not make "meker or louʒer [lower, humbler] or deuouter submission."[100] For Pecock, however, this is precisely the point. Since contiguity between imagination's images and physical ones results in an approximation of Christ's presence—he is, in some way, really present—then the desire to touch mouth, eye, and hand to that of the physical image logically

[97] On traditional emphasis on the visual in scholarship, see Gayk, *Image, Text, and Religious Reform*, 167; Suzannah Biernoff, "Carnal Relations: Embodied Sight in Merleau-Ponty, Roger Bacon and St Francis," *Journal of Visual Culture* 4, no. 1 (2005): 39–52 (e.g., 40). Liz James, " 'Seeing is believing, but feeling's the truth': Touch and the Meaning of Byzantine Art" (9) notes: "Scholars tend to treat religious services as essentially visual elements in which the congregation functions as spectators. . . . Worship, however, is a participatory act and so touch plays as great a role as vision."

[98] Jacqueline E. Jung, "The Tactile and the Visionary: Notes on the Place of Sculpture in the Medieval Religious Imagination," in *Looking Beyond: Visions, Dreams, and Insights in Medieval Art and History*, ed. Colum Hourihane (Princeton: Index of Christian Art, 2010), 203–40; Joanna E. Ziegler, *Sculpture of Compassion: The Pietà and the Beguines in the Southern Low Countries c. 1300–c. 1600* (Brussels: Brepols, 1992), e.g., 64. See also the essays collected in *Sculpture and Touch*, ed. Peter Dent (Farnham: Ashgate, 2014) for the long tradition associating sculpture with touch.

[99] Caroline Walker Bynum, *Christian Materiality: An Essay on Religion in Late Medieval Europe* (New York: Zone, 2015), 24.

[100] Pecock, *Repressor*, 202.

follows. If a reader thus finds friendship a persuasive paradigm for legitimizing looking at images of Christ, so too, Pecock argues, will it justify touching images of him.

Imagine, Pecock urges his reader, Christ were walking on earth in a great crowd of people,

and thou myȝtist come so nyȝ that thou schuldist touche with thin hond hise feet or his hond his breste or his cheke or hise clothis, and woldist therbi gendre to thee bi so myche the more affeccioun anentis him than if thou myȝtist not so touche him or his clothing, (euen riȝt as we han experience that oon persoon gendrith more loue to an other, if he biclippe him in armys, than he schulde, if he not come so nyȝ to him and not biclippid him,)—it muste nedis folewe, if thou ymagine Crist or an other Seint for to be bodili streiȝt thoruȝout the bodi of the ymage, that thou schalt gendre, gete, and haue bi so miche the more good affeccioun to God or to the Seint, that thou dost to him touching him in the ymage as bi ymaginacioun.[101]

Aquinas emphasizes in the *Summa*: "charity grows, not by one charity being added to another, but by being intensified in its subject."[102] Here, Pecock reminds us yet again that such intensification of charity is most profoundly achieved in touch: a person engenders more love for another if he "biclippe [embrace] him in armys" than if he merely sees him. In emphasizing the connection of touch and love (and so, by extension, of touch and *caritas*), Pecock suppresses other reasons to touch images, such as healing or to obtain holy properties or virtues.[103] More particularly, Pecock's "imagine this" instance recalls the Gospel account of the woman suffering a "flux of blood," who, standing in a crowd, dares to reach out and touch the hem of Christ's clothing in the hope that she might be healed.[104] The healing potential of touching Christ's clothes (via an image of Christ) is here side-stepped. Instead, Pecock stresses again the proximity necessary to the energy of friendship. Acknowledging that Christ's presence *would* generate a desire to touch him leads us to accept that the perception of presence (achieved through the process of mapping an interior image onto an exterior one) would likewise make

---

[101] Ibid., 271.

[102] See Aquinas, *Summa theologiae*, 2a2ae q. 24, art. 5 (ed. Gilby, 34:48–49).

[103] See further on touch's transformative potential, for example, C. M. Woolgar, *The Senses in Late Medieval England* (New Haven: Yale University Press, 2006), 29.

[104] The account is given in Matthew 9, Mark 5, and Luke 8.

us want to reach out and touch the physical representation. So important and so natural is this point for Pecock that he makes recourse not to one but to three further illustrations from the paradigm of friendship, each of which is compelling in its affective charge.

First comes Pecock's boldest analogy: with the desire of those who love each other to be joined as one. Pecock invokes this analogy following on from the example of friendship being maintained at a distance and in absence through intermediaries: "thou woldist be weel plesid, if thi freend, whom thou louest and which loueth thee, wolde sende to the a cosse [kiss] or an handling or a biclipping or eny other bodili touching bi a meene persoon receyuyng thilk cosse, handling, biclipping, or othere touching of him immediatli, and delyueryng to thee as fro him mediatli." Just as a man derives pleasure from receiving a kiss, an embrace, or another bodily touch "bi a meene persoon," who first receives it and then delivers it "mediatli," so too is it "coueitable," Pecock argues, for a man to obtain through an image a touch (with his face, eyes, or mouth) of the feet, mouth, hand, or breast of Christ. The use of the material image as a proxy for physical presence is thus explained as natural:

namelich sithen the nature of loue bitwixe persones [is] forto be a moving in to oonyng and ioynyng tho persoones to gidere, in so miche that if tho persoones miȝten make euereither of hem forto entre into the ful hool persoon of the other of hem and forto be streiȝt thoruȝ out the bodi or persoon of the other of hem, than were had a greet entent and purpos into which her loue enclyneth.[105]

By this point in the imaginative process that makes the external image contiguous with the imagined Christ we have moved far from mapping or stretching and far from optical lines, into a physical overlaying and "entering into" of bodies: love for another inclines one to desire to touch and to match—more than this, collapse—every part of one's own body into the other's.[106]

---

[105] Pecock, *Repressor*, 271–72. On the role in Aquinas's account of the apprehension of species in effecting a union between those who love each other, see *Summa theologiae*, 1a2ae q. 28.

[106] Here Pecock seems to be drawing on the notion of the friend as another self, developed in monastic traditions of spiritual friendship, rather than sexual union, though this too is a possible interpretation. On the friend as another self in monastic traditions, see Krahmer, "The Friend as a 'Second Self.'"

With this powerful example, a reader might ask why Pecock thought two more were necessary. He next sketches a profoundly beautiful instance from the friendship paradigm of parent and child: "if a man loue a child," he notes, "he wole sette his cheke to the cheke of the child, his iȝe to the childis iȝe, his forhede to the childis forhede, his nose to the childis nose, and therbi the more loue is gendrid anentis the child."[107] Through this analogy, I suggest, Pecock seeks both to assert the naturalness of the desire to touch and to cut off the potentially dangerous suggestion of the erotic in his assertion that the love between friends, as modeled in medieval accounts of spiritual friendship, inclines them to union. Such distancing is underscored in Pecock's final example, which comes from the paradigm of the lord and servant: is it not also the case, he asks, that a man who is loved particularly by a lord "mai be admyttid for to come so nyȝ that he lie with the lord in oon bed? And if he mai not be admyttid into so greet nyȝnes, ȝit if he mai be admittid for to ligge in the same chambir with the lord, certis therbi schal good loue and affeccioun be gendrid."[108] With this last excessive example, Pecock thus seems to hope (though we might judge that he fails) to rein in the excess of affect that his insistence on the validity of touching an image of Christ has provoked. If the desire for presence experienced through touch is universal to love in all its forms, as is implied by Pecock's examples taken from the friendship of lord and servant, of father and child, and between equals, then meeting the difficult demands of *caritas* might also legitimately require it.

Pecock's sustained engagement with the figure of the absent friend in his defense of the use of images in the *Repressor* thus very clearly shows that what is at stake (for him) is the problem Christ's absence causes for sensory perception and for imagination. In pursuing the logic of friendship with Christ, Pecock shows the debate about images to be not only about vision, or about ways of seeing, but also about touch, and about the imaginative practices that should engage these sensory processes. In his insistent return to the imaginative process in which Christ is "streiȝt thoruȝout the bodi of the ymage," Pecock establishes not only a sense of touch but an actual experience of touch as the grounds for approximating presence. Since Christ is absent, imagining touching him is the next best thing to his real presence, but

[107] Pecock, *Repressor*, 272.
[108] Ibid.

imagination (under the feeble conditions of the human mind) needs physical images. If, when viewing and simultaneously touching an image, a man maps the imagined image onto the physical one, the sense of touch gives real solidity to imagining—making vividly present Christ the friend.

"Far semed her hart from obeysaunce": Strategies of Resistance in *The Isle of Ladies*

Boyda Johnstone
Borough of Manhattan Community College, CUNY

Abstract

The fifteenth-century poem *The Isle of Ladies* has received little critical attention up to this point. At once dream vision and romance, it tells the tale of a narrator whose trancelike dream carries him into an island populated by women that is gradually and violently conquered by a marauding regiment of knights. Scholars have generally viewed the poem, as per its conclusion, as a masculinist victory that celebrates feminine oppression. Reading more sensitively between the lines of the action unearths a narrative of covert feminist resistance, horizontal alliances, and strategies for surviving a patriarchal regime. The opening frame of the poem, which delineates the power of half-sleep rather than full immersion into dream, trains readers in reading doubly for both the men's victory and the women's dissent.

Keywords

resistance; women; *The Isle of Ladies*; Christine de Pizan; dreaming; romance; sleep; reader response; same-sex desire; female friendship; utopias; book history; modern reception

AMALE POET FALLS into a stupor and dreams of an island inhabited by women, guarded by walls of glass. He is enchanted by this new land and its lovely ladies, yet frightened; the women behave courteously toward him, but expressly request his departure, conspiring to imprison him until they are suddenly interrupted by the arrival of

Many thanks to Jocelyn Wogan-Browne and Sarah Salih for their consistent feedback and assistance through the various stages of this process, and to the anonymous readers of *SAC* for their clarifying comments on this article.

the queen with a knight who has mistreated her. The women refocus their energies on the offending knight before the island is suddenly invaded by thousands of the knight's compatriots who systematically override the ladies' rules and customs, establishing an alternative patriarchal history and imprinting their ordinances into a new rule of law. The women, armed only with decorous language and courteous custom, cannot defend themselves against the men's physical violence and military clout, though in private they find solace in reading and composing romances and lays, a practice the dreamer himself engages in as he straddles the gendered lines of battle. A failure by the men to fulfill their promise to return for the royal wedding in time leads the women to fear they have been too "lyghtly conquest" (1662) upon which they starve themselves and die out of grief and remorse, later to be revived by a magical herb.[1] All, including the dreamer and his lady, are intermarried by the end before the dreamer awakens and is anguished to discover his lady is gone.

Plot summaries are not neutral. The way a story gets told can have a significant impact on its reception, and brief synopses of long, complex poems such as this anonymous 2,200-line late fifteenth-century romance *The Isle of Ladies* have the inevitable consequence of obscuring nuance and poetic texture, the layers of emotion that are so complexly intermingled in the provisional and disorienting logic of dreams. The modern edition most often consulted for this poem, Derek Pearsall's 1990 TEAMS edition, tells a different version of the story than I do here. Pearsall does not comment upon the emotional bonds among the women or their attempts to resist the cruelties of the men through reading and circulating literary production. He has elsewhere called the poem a "flimsy airy fantasy" so perhaps we should not be surprised that he views *The Isle* as "vague, obscure, and confused," with thin stylistic texture.[2] Relying on Pearsall's summary as a framing motif might pit

---

[1] *The Isle of Ladies*, 1662, in *"The Floure and the Leafe," "The Assembly of Ladies," and "The Isle of Ladies,"* ed. Derek Pearsall (Kalamazoo: Medieval Institute, 1990). Despite its flaws, I cite line numbers from Pearsall's edition in this article. Other editions of *The Isle of Ladies* include *A Critical Edition of "The Isle of Ladies,"* ed. Vincent Daly, The Renaissance Imagination 29 (New York: Garland, 1987); and *The Isle of Ladies; or, The Ile of Pleasaunce*, ed. Anthony Jenkins (New York: Garland, 1980). *The Isle of Ladies* appears only in two sixteenth-century manuscripts: Longleat House, MS 256 and British Library, Additional MS 10303.

[2] Derek Pearsall, introduction to *The Isle of Ladies*, 63–67 (63). The phrase "flimsy airy fantasy" comes from Derek Pearsall, "The English Chaucerians," in *Chaucer and Chaucerians: Critical Studies in Middle English Literature*, ed. D. S. Brewer (Alabama: University of Alabama Press, 1966).

readers against the female side of the gender dynamic in the poem. Regarding the author, he asserts that:

Nothing indeed needs to be known, since the poem is perfectly transparent as an allegory of sexual repression and fulfilment. It is a dream of male desire, in which the skill of women in deflecting men's sexual drive with "fayre wordes" (741), enigmatic smiles (883–92), and vague non-committal promises (642–78), their skill in managing the world of mannered politeness, in which reputation or *name* is everything (see 529, 557, 1666), is overcome by the power of the God of Love, who operates here, as in the *Roman de la Rose*, exclusively to the furtherance of male sexual desire.[3]

It is impossible to ignore the ultimate victory of the men in the poem, but I hope in this article to contribute to an ongoing critical effort to position women's voices and concerns at the center rather than the periphery of medieval literary culture.[4] I aim to show that "perfect transparency" is a highly reductive, if not downright dangerous, attitude to take toward a tale that remains the victim of scholarly neglect. Underneath the dominant contours of its overarching narrative lies a narrative of female resistance, solidarity, mutual care, and even potentially same-sex desire and sexual bonds. In what follows, I will show that the framing of the poem as a half-dream is crucial in learning to approach the narrative through a divided, ambivalent lens (as does the dreamer), and I will demonstrate, by comparing this dream to another female-dominant vision by Christine de Pizan, that *The Isle* could be considered a "negative utopia" in its emergent possibilities. I argue that rather than necessarily reifying male domination, the poem may also showcase the women as the ideological heroines of the queendom turned kingdom, pitting horizontal structures of female networks against the vertical forces of patrilineal conquest. In other words, while there is a dominant narrative of male victory, there is also a subtext of female victimhood, and it is the underacknowledged latter to which this article will give voice.

---

[3] Pearsall, 'Introduction,' 65.

[4] On this topic see Liz Herbert McAvoy and Diane Watt, eds., *Women's Literary Culture and Late Medieval English Writing, ChauR*, special issue, 51, no. 1 (2016); on the invisible efforts of medieval women to support and circulate literature and documentary records, see Jocelyn Wogan-Browne, " 'Invisible Archives?': Later Medieval French in England," *Speculum* 90, no. 3 (2015): 653–73.

The Poem as Half-Dream

The Isle of Ladies is not a poem often mentioned in critical conversations on late medieval dream literature, even though it has much to say about the afterlife of Geoffrey Chaucer's poetry and the form and import of dreaming.[5] Until the nineteenth century *The Isle* was thought to be the work of Chaucer, known in the seventeenth century as *Chaucers Dreame* and appearing in Longleat House, MS 256 under the title "The temple of glasse / Compiled by geoffray / Chaucer."[6] Nineteenth-century philologists then dismissed *The Isle*'s rhyme scheme as un-Chaucerian, and it was more or less banished from critical consideration for centuries, viewed as derivative vis-à-vis the robust Chaucerian canon. Few scholars beyond Pearsall have commented upon the question of antifeminism within the poem, acknowledging instead the "sense of uneasiness about interpreting the text and a tendency to admit that one is essentially baffled by it."[7] Manfred Markus remarks that the "style is unsophisticated, 'unbookish in the extreme,' and in many ways popular to rural," and he attributes this stylistic inadequacy to the poem's status as a satirization of courtly love, using the frame of the ironic dreamer.[8] Part of his evidence is based on his sense that the plot has no purpose and that "the plot of our romance clearly reveals that 'isles of ladies' do not function": two claims that seem to be in conflict.[9] While satire may be at play, I aim here to question Markus's latter claim concerning purpose, and complicate our pat approach to the poem as silencing female voices at the end.

On the surface, the poem follows some of the conventions of Breton *lais* and love visions in its reliance on magic for plot devices and its recounting of a single episodic adventure,[10] but the linear romance tale

---

[5] Other critical undertakings of this poem include Annika Farber, "Usurping 'Chaucers Dreame': *Book of the Duchess* and the Apocryphal *Isle of Ladies*," *SP* 105, no. 2 (2008): 207–25, which explicates the textual history of the poem as well as its contested modern reception; Kathleen Forni, "'Chaucer's Dreame': A Bibliographer's Nightmare," *HLQ* 64, nos. 1–2 (2001): 139–50, which unpacks the early print affiliations of *The Isle* with *The Book of the Duchess* and John Lydgate's *Temple of Glass*; and Manfred Markus, "'The Isle of Ladies' (1475) as Satire," *SP* 95, no. 3 (1998): 221–36.

[6] Farber, "Usurping 'Chaucers Dreame,'" 207, 210. The Longleat title amalgamates the work of Chaucer with the later dream vision of John Lydgate, the *Temple of Glass*.

[7] Farber, "Usurping 'Chaucers Dreame,'" 215.

[8] Markus, "'The Isle of Ladies' (1475)," 229, 234.

[9] Ibid., 236.

[10] Daly, introduction to *A Critical Edition of "The Isle of Ladies,"* 44. For other medieval women-centric communities, see Lisa M. Bitel, *Land of Women: Tales of Sex and Gender from Early Ireland* (Ithaca: Cornell University Press, 1996), 161.

form is sutured with the individuated mode of the dream vision. In dream visions our focus as readers is filtered through the dreamer's movements and responses, registered by frequent perception cues such as "I thought" or "I saw." The poem's framing turns out to be deeply significant here as the narrator goes to great pains to observe that the dream is not even fully experienced:

> And in my thowghtes, as I laye
> In a lodge out of the waye,
> Beside a well in a foreste,
> Wher after huntinge I toke reste,
> Nature and kynd so in me wrought
> That halfe on slepe thay me browght,
> And gan to dreme, to my thinkinge,
> With minde of knowledge leke wakinge.
> For what I dreamed, as me thought,
> I sawe it, and I slepte nought.
>
> (17–26)

The dream is positioned at the beginning of the poem as only half-dream, one that the dreamer can see and understand as though he is awake rather than lying in the inertia of repose. Dreaming "[w]ith minde of knowledge leke wakinge" opens up an epistemological register that combines the best parts of sleeping and waking respectively: the receptivity of sleep and the processing capabilities of wakefulness, recalling Aristotle's appraisal in "On Dreams" that often a dreamer will mistake the dreamed objects for the things themselves.[11] The collocation of "[n]ature and kynd" helps him achieve a perfect convergence of self and surroundings and indeed activate his lucid cognitive state. Sometimes understood as synonymous, nature and kynd are technical terms that draw from contemporary physiological theories of dreaming. John Trevisa's fourteenth-century translation of Bartholomaeus's *De proprietatibus rerum*, for example, describes how sleep gathers "kinde" heat inward, and ejects that which is "vnpure and rawe, and quietiþ and comfortiþ the vertues of felinge and of mevinge."[12] He claims that if digestion fails

[11] Aristotle, "On Dreams," trans. J. I. Beare, in *The Complete Works of Aristotle*, Vol. 1, ed. Jonathan Barnes (Princeton: Princeton University Press, 2014), 729–35.

[12] *On the Properties of Things: John Trevisa's Translation of Bartholomaeus Angelicus De Proprietatibus Rerum. A Critical Text*, ed. M. C. Seymour et al. (Oxford: Clarendon Press, 1975), 1:333.

and the body is made moist and cold, then there is less "kinde" heat, and if the body fattens and the heart is comforted, the humors become temperate and heat is produced again. The *MED* defines *natur(e* (n.) as referring specifically to the physical properties of created beings, while *kinde* (n.) is a more expansive term, pointing to "[t]he aggregate of inherent qualities or properties of persons, animals, plants, elements, medicines, etc; essential character." In her recent study of *kynde* in *Piers Plowman*, Rebecca Davis asserts that the term "encompasses nature in the broadest sense, indicating the cosmos as a whole as well as the inherent qualities of its individual components, persons, animals, plants, and inanimate things."[13] Others have argued that the pseudo-Aristotelian understanding of " 'kynde' knowing" accrued ethical dimensions in the twelfth and thirteenth centuries, when the sensate body was thought to harbor innate structures of knowledge in contrast with learned or acquired knowledge.[14] I propose that "nature" in *The Isle of Ladies* refers to the dreamer's physical body as well as his contiguous waking environment, while "kind" refers to intangible characteristics that inhere within his mind and his soul that merge with his environment during sleep, including his alert perceptions. The combination of both marks the merging of internal seeing and physical environs that activates his state of half-sleeping ("thay me browght").[15] As the dreamer seems to meld with his environment, physical, spiritual, and immaterial realities interpenetrate to produce the ideal circumstances for his liminal experience of swooning. Further, "kind" may reach beyond the textual confines of the scenario to include readers within these complex layers of porous liminality; "kynde," after all, comes from the Old English *cynd*, a cognate of *cyn*, meaning "kin" or "people," and so invokes notions of kinship and its obligations.

The prologue expounds on the broader significance of the dreamer's cognitive state:

[13] Rebecca Davis, *"Piers Plowman" and the Books of Nature* (Oxford: Oxford University Press, 2016).

[14] James Wade, "Romance, Affect, and Ethical Thinking in a Fifteenth-Century Household Book: Chetham's Library, MS 8009," *NML* 15 (2013): 255–83 (259).

[15] Ad Putter observes that the forthcoming dream is "ambiguously poised between the disturbed sleep of the lover and the spiritual vision," because spirits were believed to live in wells; "Fifteenth-Century Chaucerian Visions," in *A Companion to Fifteenth-Century English Poetry*, ed. Julia Boffey and A. S. G. Edwards (Woodbridge: D. S. Brewer, 2013), 143–55 (151). Putter aims to show that fifteenth-century dream visions have merit on their own terms, not just as extensions of or tributes to their Chaucerian heritage.

who that dremes and wenes he see,
Much the better yet may hee
Wit what, and of home, and where,
And eke the lesse it wol him deare
To think I se thus with myne eyne!

(43–47)

That is to say, those who process their dreams while lying alert and awake—those who dream lucidly—will absorb more active knowledge from the dream than if they were fully unconscious, while also achieving a higher degree of detachment, remaining unperturbed that such fantastic events are occurring. The dreamer in fact inhabits the same subject position as readers themselves: he can see his dream with as much presence of mind as though he were awake, though he is caught within a sequence of events over which he has little control. Dreaming and reading are hermeneutically similar practices, as Peter Schwenger has explored; both involve the partial suspension of active faculties of thinking and feeling.[16] What the dreamer experiences, then, this paradoxical hermeneutic positioning of receptivity (dreaming) and agency (waking) at the same time, is akin to what readers are meant to experience as they approach the following vision. This is significant because it is not so "perfectly transparent" how the poem is meant to be read, and whose side we are meant to be on.

My approach here, then, echoes Helen Barr's notion of "interpretive polarity" in the *The Prioress's Tale*; she argues that readers, depending on their values, tendencies, and philosophies, may make contradictory inferences from the poem and leave with oppositional—or uneasily reconciled—responses.[17] Medieval readers were perhaps more attuned to polarizing readings of a text than we assume, accustomed to multifarious meanings and numerous layers of possibility. *The Isle*'s dreamer himself illustrates this by wavering between gendered camps and becoming caught in various degrees of indecision throughout the poem. Through the device of half-sleeping, the prologue of *The Isle* encourages readers to develop ambivalent patterns of thought as they encounter a poem where their allegiances too might be profoundly divided. Readers,

---

[16] See Peter Schwenger, *At the Borders of Sleep: On Liminal Literature* (Minneapolis: University of Minnesota Press, 2012).

[17] Helen Barr, "Religious Practice in Chaucer's *Prioress's Tale*: Rabbit and/or Duck?," *SAC* 32 (2010), 39–65.

rather than searching for a single overarching message, must learn to think and see doubly, weighing the relative ease and strength of the ladies' patterns of governance and communication against the authoritarian regime the men establish upon arrival.

There is one final point to be made about the dream-vision prologue, which is that it implies there are political advantages to couching such controversial material in the realm of a dream, even just a half-dream. A conventional humility topos gestures toward the diplomatic nature of the distancing effect of dream narratives, as the narrator proclaims he will tell the tale:

> As holly as I cane devise
> In playne Englishe, evell writton;
> For slepe wrightter, well ye weten,
> Excused is, thowghe he do mise [amiss],
> More then on that wakinge is.
>
> (58–62)

A straightforward interpretation of this passage takes it as a disclaimer on the author's talent for a poem written "In playne Englishe," rather than in the more elevated French or Latin, by a writer who is only half-awake.[18] But it also implies that "writers of sleep" achieve greater cover for their ideas than those who present real historical events and transparent philosophical arguments, and should not be held responsible for the contents of the dream with which they were visited.[19] "Slepe wrightter" has a potentially double meaning: it can be translated as "sleepy writer" or as a "writer of sleep," either a groggy author who has only recently awakened from his extraordinary dream or, tantalizingly, a member of a broader category of authors who specialize in sleep narratives. In the former case, it is significant that the narrator of the poem is not only half-awake while he is dreaming—reading the vision presented to him—but also half-asleep while he is writing, again emphasizing the themes of liminality and uncertainty. The aside "well ye weten" suggests that what he is saying is broadly understood, a slight nudge to the

[18] This very phrase becomes somewhat of a refrain throughout the poem, such as when the dreamer's lady gives her consent "in playne englyshe" (1242) or the knight explains his marital plans "in playne englyshe" (1452) to the people in his land.

[19] See Kathryn Kerby-Fulton, *Books under Suspicion: Censorship and Tolerance of Revelatory Writing in Late Medieval England* (Notre Dame: University of Notre Dame Press, 2006), 21.

reader that establishes a known subtext. Stylistic inadequacies should be forgiven, and the author should not be held responsible for any potentially objectionable material—a subtle acknowledgment that there may exist some objectionable material to ignore.

A "prisoner adventurus" in *The Isle of Ladies*

The double-seeing of the prologue is a key feature of the poem itself, in which the half-dreamer and others are frequently caught between two variant and sometimes contradictory versions of the story—a dream that causes the dreamer both "paine and . . . pleasaunce . . . axes and heale [fever and health]" (34–35). The queen of the island is extolled as one who "nothinge used [practiced] but faythe and trothe" (115), and before the knights arrive, the women of the island live in happy harmony, with "Richesse, hele, beauwty, and ease" (133), able to conjure anything they desire into existence: "with everye thinge that hem might please, / Thynke, and have, hit cost no more" (134–35). As with other late medieval dream-vision poems, such as *The Floure and the Leafe*, the setting of the island of ladies intertwines art and nature: golden weathervanes "ay turninge / Entuned [in tune with one another]" (77–78), artificial birds signing in tandem (78), towers carved "of a suite [in the same fashion] like flowers" (81), and playing and dancing ladies "of one age 7 / They semed all" (95–96). Industry and toil are left at bay within the Ovidian women's world whose pristine nature portends future complications. Subtle details unsettle the idyllic climate: the towers are "[o]f uncothe [foreign, unknown] colours," and the walls of glass that surround the island are "[u]ncothe and straunge to beholde" (75), recalling both the temple of glass and the mountain of ice in *The House of Fame*. These details could be read as underscoring the unnaturalness of the ladies' land, or simply its curious and awe-inspiring qualities. The twinning of artifice and nature, auspicious and inauspicious imagery, accords with the paradoxes of an overall dream invested in the productive collocation of opposites and double seeing.

More paradoxical dualities appear as the dreamer experiences "joyous doubte" and "dowble paine" (779) when named the servant of the lady, "[t]hat what to do, ne what to sayne / Wist I not ne what was the best" (880–81), uncertain whether he should trust the new authorities:

> Suer an unsurest of that rowte [crowd].
> Right as myn hart thowght it were,

> So more or lesse woxe my fere,
> That yf one thowght made it well,
> Annother shente yt everye deale[.]
> (894–98)

Here the dreamer experiences not a seamlessly liminal state of medial consciousness, but profound, unstable ambivalence regarding whether he should be grateful to be paired with such a virtuous lady or rue the superseding of the rules of the island by the newly landed men. He wavers between fear and solace, both sure and unsure; while his gender would mark him as a member of the dominant class, he also knows he doesn't belong there, minutes before being asked by the ladies to leave. The paralysis caused by the onset of major decisions or a shift in the plot echoes the suspension between activity and inactivity marked by the half-waking state at the beginning, and the dreamer's divided response asks readers at least initially to harbor two equally true but conflicting accounts of the tale within our own apprehension of the poem. The poem thus activates what Barbara Newman calls a hermeneutics of *both/and* that prevails throughout medieval culture.[20] Pain and pleasure, fever and health collide for the dreamer rather than meld together, producing a poetics of uncertainty that demands we embrace the paradox inherent in a poem framed by waking sleep.

For readers, this ambivalence becomes an interpretive framework through which to approach the complicated narrative of male domination that follows. While some readers may applaud the knights' ascendancy, others may pick up on details that cast the women as pitiable victims whose weapons of defense are feeble and ineffectual; as the queen proclaims, "woman is a feble wyght / To rere a ware agayne a knyght" (469–70). Although the ladies prove themselves capable administrators of their own land, they can scarcely defend themselves against the men who arrive kitted out in the full accoutrements of the militia—and their attempts to do so become almost comical. At a loss upon glimpsing the ten thousand advancing ships of men and realizing they will be destroyed, for example, the women endeavor to defend themselves from the men's invasion of the island using one of their only tools of power, language: "best was shette ther yattes [gates] faste, /

---

[20] Barbara Newman, *Medieval Crossover: Reading the Secular against the Sacred* (Notre Dame: University of Notre Dame Press, 2013), 7.

And arme them all in good langauge, / As they had done of old usage, / And of fayre wordes make ther shoot" (738–41). Here the female discourse of courtesy is tested and found inefficacious, highlighting the structural limitations of the ladies' means of defense. Courtesy is meant to elevate and refine, an effect we see in such romances as *Sir Gawain and the Green Knight*, but here it is figured as mere words, impotent in its confrontation with men and their weaponry. Perhaps this is a satirical moment, as Markus would suggest. But regardless, the ladies' unsuccessful attempt to propel decorous words over walls of glass at a large fleet of ships populated by thousands of angry knights—a detail that some may be tempted to pass over as obscure or confusing—arguably stands as one of the most literalized dramatizations of male versus female power in late medieval literature.

Amidst the upheaval of the knights' arrival, the women are internally loyal, struggling desperately to maintain the ties that the alien men are in the process of unraveling. Readers are given persistent access into the women's own subjectivity and affective responses to the invasion. For example, the queen relays a story of being abducted by a knight who claims her as his: "[a]nd [he] sayd, thowgh he me never had sene, / Yet had I longe his lady bene" (385–86). She faints and can "feld neyther live, ne brethe" because of the "sodeyne paine" of being forcibly stolen (394, 396); in the knight's own words, "in myn armes I had her faste" (631), gesturing toward a possible undercurrent of rape.[21] The knight then swoons and begs mercy, causing the queen to apologize for upsetting him, yet in a single arresting line we are informed that she expresses secret resistance to his rule inside her heart: "Far semed her hart from obeysaunce" (678). At the same time, she maintains her plan to expel the knight from the island and worship him from afar. Giving us insight into the women's defiant interior state in contradistinction to their external acquiescence could have the effect of swaying readers to the ladies' side while witnessing ever-expanding waves of heartless colonization.

Once the rest of the men arrive, the God of Love disregards the lofty

---

[21] There has been much recent and ongoing critical interest in misogyny and rape within medieval literature. See for example Suzanne M. Edwards, *The Afterlives of Rape in Medieval English Literature* (Basingstoke: Palgrave Macmillan, 2016); Carissa M. Harris, "Rape Narratives, Courtly Critique, and the Pedagogy of Sexual Negotiation in the Middle English Pastourelle," *JMEMSt* 46, no. 2 (2016): 263–87; and Caroline Dunn, "The Language of Ravishment in Medieval England," *Speculum* 86, no. 1 (2011): 79–116.

status of the queen and resorts to physical violence in order to render her his servant: "He thawght the quene sonne [soon] shuld obye / And in his hannd he shoke his bowe / And sayd right sone he wolde be know" (780–82). While being shot by Cupid's bow is a well-known metaphorical image, in this context it foregrounds the uneasy boundaries between love and sexual violence that undergird courtly conquests in many medieval romances, as well as popular iconographic imagery such as the assault on the Castle of Love.[22] Cupid's arrow causes a wound that will last many years, an act that leads the queen to kneel before him and offer a formal bill of apology for allegedly mistreating the knight who had abducted her, evidence of her systematic psychological manipulation. This moment marks the God of Love's stated intention to "withein that Ile / Be lord and syr, bothe est and west," deeming it his "new conquest" (933–34). With unflinching swagger, the God turns to the crowd of women and declares himself lord, eliciting no whisper of protest from the stunned crowd: "Was ther non 'ney,' ne wordes none, / But very obeysaunt semed eche one" (968). As with the queen's heart above, the *seeming* obeisance of the women raises the possibility that their external compliance does not match with private submissiveness, and even as the knights inaugurate a new regime, the women continue to find ways to resist privately.

One of the first actions by the newly landed knights is to rewrite the "old custome . . . Wiche hathe continewed many yere" (238–39) of the island's feminine history, replacing it with an alternative origin story. An attendant to the God of Love stands in front of an assembly of knights and ladies and, after underscoring the authoritative mandate that "no debate / Ofte ne goodlye might be used" in order to maintain peace and "one accorde" (1004–5, 1009), recounts a new history of the "lustye Ile" (1023):

> All the astate in little while
> Reherse, and hollye every thinge
> [. . .]

---

[22] A fourteenth-century roundel decorated with scenes of the attack on the Castle of Love, for example, is held in the Cloisters Collection in New York (accession no. 2003.131.1). The image of the God of Love, or Cupid, as more tyrannical than benevolent as a master has precedent in classical and medieval literature, for example in Ovid's *Loves* (*Amores*) and John Clanvowe's *The Boke of Cupide, God of Love*, or the Prologue to *The Legend of Good Women*, in which the God of Love has been seen as a stand-in for Richard II. See Theresa Tinkle's *Medieval Venuses and Cupids: Sexuality, Hermeneutics, and*

And everye wele [benefit], and every wo,
And for what cause eche thinge was so,
Well shewed he there, in easye speche;
And how the syke had nede of leche
And who that whole was and in grace,
He told playnelye how eche thinge was.
(1024–25, 1027–32)

Love's attendant not only tells the story of the island in "playne" terms, as though its customs and heritage are easily reducible to a single speech, but also diagnoses its ailments and requirements, positioning the knights as the emancipators of the "syke [in] nede of leche" and discrediting the women's own account of their origins. The women's own language and testimonies are rendered illegitimate—just as the queen's account of her abduction is summarily discarded—while their land is being systematically taken away from underneath them. This is not simply a geographic conquest, in other words, but also a psychological and an ideological one. The dreamer marvels at the rhetorical effect of the God of Love's words, imbued with the power of an official seal ("For every thinge he sayd there / Semed as it insealed were" [1015–16]), and breaching the dreamer's consciousness to the extent that he experiences flashbacks of the speech whenever he's alone, as though suffering from residual trauma: "where I be, me thinke I here / Him yet alwaye, when I my one [on my own] / In any place may be allone" (1020–22). The psychological imprint of the God of Love's words on the dreamer recalls the prologue's claims that half-sleeping allows for enhanced perception because those who dream and think they see will better digest the contents of the dream. The dreamer's half-consciousness suggests the God of Love's words have attained the efficacious force of the God's own arrows as they plant themselves deeply within the dreamer's memory—but as we will see, this mental domination does not mean he too has been won over.

An Unraveling City of Women

The Isle of Ladies, with the men not only colonizing the present state of the city but also radically altering its past, is an inverted version of the

---

English Poetry (Stanford: Stanford University Press, 1996) for more on the widely unstable and varied depictions and significations of Cupid and other amatory gods.

most famous medieval account of a city inhabited by women: Christine de Pizan's early fifteenth-century French text *Le livre de la Cité des Dames* (*The Book of the City of Ladies*). Christine, whose works were well known in England, built much of her career around intervening in the masculinist history of letters and exposing its omissions, errors, moral injustices, and gender-based violence.[23] Her most direct intervention comes in the form of what is now known as the *querelle de la Rose*, a precursor to the *querelle des femmes* which would extend into the Renaissance. In a series of letters to and responses from the Parisian intellectual establishment that she later released in the form of dossiers, Christine positions herself as a distinguished disputant in a public debate with major contemporary male voices, with the support of Jean Gerson, chancellor of the University of Paris. Her *Epistres sur le débat du "Roman de la Rose"* roundly condemns the misogyny she perceives in Jean de Meun's extension of the *Rose*, a French dream vision of vast popularity of which there are hundreds of extant manuscripts. Other poems, such as her *Epistre au Dieu d'Amours* (1399) and *Dit de la Rose* (1402), similarly engage in reshaping and rewriting the *Roman de la Rose* from the perspective of women. Centering women's experiences and oppression were Christine de Pizan's chief concerns throughout her extensive literary output.[24] Other texts,

---

[23] Christine's works were popular in England and she had strong ties and crosscurrents there. *La Cité des Dames* is included in BL, MS Harley 4431, which was brought to England and presented to Jacquetta of Luxembourg by John, duke of Bedford, and there exists a printed 1521 translation of the *Boke of the Cyte of Ladyes*, suggesting it is possible that the author of *The Isle of Ladies* was familiar with this text in either its French or its English form (see the recent edition by Hope Johnston, *Boke of the Cyte of Ladyes*, trans. Brian Anslay [Tempe: ACMRS, 2014]). Henry VIII of England owned a woven panel containing the "City of Ladies," though these lost tapestries were produced in the sixteenth century and thus unfortunately too late for this study; see Susan Groag Bell, *The Lost Tapestries of the City of Ladies: Christine de Pizan's Renaissance Legacy* (Berkeley: University of California Press, 2004). For more on Christine's circulation in England see Stephanie Downes, "A 'Frenche Booke Called the Pistill of Othea': Christine de Pizan's French in England," in *Language and Culture in Medieval Britain: The French of England, c. 1100–c. 1500*, ed. Jocelyn Wogan-Browne et al. (Woodbridge: York Medieval Press, 2009), 457–68; James C. Laidlaw, "Christine de Pizan, the Earl of Salisbury and Henry IV," *French Studies* 36 (1982): 129–43; and Jennifer Summit, *Lost Property: The Woman Writer and English Literary History, 1380–1589* (Chicago: University of Chicago Press, 2000), Chap. 2.

[24] Kevin Brownlee, "Discourses of the Self: Christine de Pizan and the *Romance of the Rose*, in *Rethinking the "Romance of the Rose,"* ed. Kevin Brownlee and Sylvia Huot (Philadelphia: University of Pennsylvania Press, 2016), 234–61. See also Rosalind Brown-Grant, *Christine de Pizan and the Moral Defense of Women: Reading beyond Gender* (Cambridge: Cambridge University Press, 2004), esp. Chap. 1 on the *querelle de la Rose*; and Renate Blumenfeld-Kosinski, "Christine de Pizan and the Misogynistic Tradition," *Romanic Review* 81, no. 3 (1990): 279–92.

such as *Le livre du chemin de long estude* (*The Book of the Path of Long Study*), have Christine following a Cumaean Sibyl throughout the world and its celestial spheres, using Dante's *Divine Comedy* as a model.

But the most explicit text by Christine de Pizan that the author of *The Isle of Ladies* may have drawn upon in his construction of an initially women-governed city is *Cité*, which concludes the way *The Isle* begins. It is thus useful at this point to take a detour through this poem in order to attain a better sense of the landscape of feminine allegorical thought operative at the time. Christine, wishing to counter her frustration and internalized contempt upon encountering the misogynist, male-authored narratives of the past, sets out to build an allegorical city founded on and populated by "all ladies of fame and women worthy of praise."[25] We are told that after confronting Matheolus she falls into a "stupor [etargie]" (I.1.1), a word that evokes Aquinas's distinction between *admiratio* and *stupor*.[26] True to Aquinas's assessment, her stupor causes her to become fearful and overcome, proving a hindrance to further inquiry into the reasons behind the conspicuous omission of women from the master narrative of history and literature. Her stupor morphs quickly into self-hatred, the inverse of the productive energy generated by *admiratio*: "And I finally decided that God formed a vile creature when He made woman, and I wondered how such a worthy artisan could have deigned to make such an abominable work which, from what they say, is the vessel as well as the refuge and abode of every evil and vice" (I.1.1). Christine's head bows and rests on the arm of the chair where she sits as she, like the *Isle*-dreamer, *almost* drifts off into sleep's oblivion. The scene abruptly shifts when a ray of light falls into her lap and three regal ladies present themselves to her, announcing that they know her to possess a "great love of investigating the truth through long and continual study" (I.3.1) and have arrived to bring Christine "out of the ignorance which so blinds [her] own intellect" (I.2.2). After

[25] Christine de Pizan, *The Book of the City of Ladies*, rev. ed., trans. Earl Jeffrey Richards (New York: Persea, 1998), I.3.3.

[26] According to Aquinas, "He who is amazed shrinks at present from forming a judgment of that which amazes him, fearing to fall short of the truth, but inquires afterwards: whereas he who is overcome by stupor fears both to judge at present, and to inquire afterwards. Wherefore amazement [*admiratio*] is a beginning of philosophical research: whereas stupor is a hindrance thereto" (*Summa theologiae*, 1a2ae q. 41 art. 4 ad. 5). See also Karma Lochrie's discussion of this passage, in "Sheer Wonder: Dreaming Utopia in the Middle Ages," *JMEMSt* 36, no. 3 (2006): 493–516 (497); and see Patricia Clare Ingham's investigation of *curiositas* in *The Medieval New: Ambivalence in an Age of Innovation*, Middle Ages Series (Philadelphia: University of Pennsylvania Press, 2015).

experiencing another wave of fear, Christine is able to assume a position of *admiratio* that penetrates through the mental fog: "Having stood up out of respect, I looked at them without saying a word, like someone too overwhelmed to utter a syllable . . . but continued to keep my gaze fixed on them, half-afraid and half-reassured by the words which I had heard, which had me reject my first impression" (I.3.1).

Like the dreamer in *The Isle of Ladies*, Christine does not fall entirely asleep. Like the dreamer, her response is split, "half-afraid and half-reassured." Her erect posture illustrates the respectful commitment to openness and truth integral to *admiratio*, as does her silence, marking her awareness that this expectant moment must involve listening, not speaking. If she were entirely reassured at this stage, there would be no need for the subsequent methodical exegesis of the literary past that unfolds across 3 lengthy parts and 136 chapters. She here models a stance of vulnerability, humility, and openness that allows for the unfolding of productive inquiry. Readers are meant to trace her mental path through this construction; as Betsy McCormick has argued, "Christine creates a textual city to serve as an artificial memory system that will train the ethical memory of her female reader."[27] Christine's book links together the allegorical community of the goddesses; the new fellowship of noble ladies she reanimates from the dust of the past; and the present and future women readers who participate in their own imaginative construction of the distinguished city, offering shelter to fellow "ladies who have been abandoned for so long, exposed like a field without a surrounding hedge, without finding a champion to afford them an adequate defense" (I.3.3). By the end of the book, when the "New Kingdom of Femininity" has been established, Christine gives instruction to readers in managing the real world, which remains controlled by men.

If the author of *The Isle* were familiar with *Cité*, perhaps they took Christine's ending-point as a starting-point.[28] Both the ladies of Christine's New Kingdom and the ladies initially inhabiting *The Isle* are nonviolent versions of the ancient Amazonian women whom Reason extols

[27] Betsy McCormick, "Building the Ideal City: Female Memorial Praxis in Christine de Pizan's *Cité des Dames*," *Studies in the Literary Imagination* 36, no. 1 (2003): 149–66 (153).

[28] My argument here directly counters that of Markus, who asserts that the *Isle* author "seems to ridicule the feminist viewpoint most prominently topicalized in Chaucer's *Wife of Bath's Tale* and also in Christine de Pizan's *Cité des Dames*" ("'The Isle of Ladies' (1475) as Satire," 236).

near the beginning of her genealogy. Like the fabled women warriors, who as Christine recounts position themselves in hidden ambushes in order to trick and capture male invaders, the women of *The Isle* devise crafty (albeit unsuccessful) tactics to keep their island free from male contamination.[29] Christine's New Kingdom, populated by women of the past within the architectural space of the reader's memory, is self-sufficient, unbeholden to the seed of men, like the paradisiacal kingdom of ladies operative at the beginning of *The Isle*.

But Christine's early fifteenth-century New Kingdom of Femininity is entirely dismantled in our late fifteenth-century English poem, and what is important to take away from this discussion is the negative possibilities this undoing opens up. Rather than providing shelter, the boundaries of the city are breached. *The Isle of Ladies* and Christine's *Cité* both contain half-sleeping narrators exemplifying the powers of *amplificatio* as they witness a vision that is drawn out of the realm of spiritual visitation into a secular courtly dream context, but the later English text substitutes construction with destruction, complicating the moral injunctions of Christine's text and leaving the ending susceptible to readers' own personal weighing of alliances. Rather than incorporating other women into the imagined city through the procedural mnemonics of mental construction, *The Isle* asks readers, with their 'interpretive polarity' as per Barr, to form their own ethical determinations about what kind of city they themselves want to construct in their minds, and perhaps in a future, more-just world: one dominated by military force, alternative histories, and the muffling of dissenting views, or one ruled with care, solidarity, and compassion. I propose that the open-ended nature of *The Isle* instantiates what Karma Lochrie calls "negative utopia," in which rather than pointing directly to the present and building a vision of the way the world should be—as in Christine—the ideological grounding of the poem uses the tool of double-seeing to unlock a new "vision of social justice," perhaps one organized more around the textual philosophy of the women.[30] The heightened awareness enabled by the

---

[29] Tales of the Amazons are recounted in *Le livre de la Cité des Dames*, I.16–I.19.

[30] Lochrie, "Sheer Wonder," 509. Lochrie builds off Ernst Bloch's term "utopian function," which "designate[s] that surplus of ideology that becomes known and conscious through an application of hope" (495). Her work addresses the problems around discussing medieval utopia when the term was not in existence before Thomas More's 1516 titular text. See also Russell Jacoby's distinction between blueprint and iconoclast utopianist traditions in *Picture Imperfect: Utopian Thought for an Anti-Utopian Age* (New York: Columbia University Press, 2005).

dreamer's paradoxically half-sleeping condition at the beginning becomes a key conduit for the negative utopian function: the dreamer does not inhabit his dream with full abandon, but remains open to processing and reevaluating what is seen and felt around him. In *The Isle of Ladies* we have a dystopian universe from which, as enacted by the dreamer-narrator who is also a reader of the dream, negative-utopian thinking can emerge.

Horizontal Female Networks

So far I have argued that *The Isle of Ladies'* half-sleeping frame activates a hermeneutic ambivalence that is enacted by a dreamer who wavers between siding with the conquerors or siding with the conquered, with the possible intertext of *Le livre de la Cité des Dames* encouraging a similar mode of feminist reenvisioning. Worth underscoring further are the networks and desires sustained by the women even after the men have succeeded in silencing them. The internal interactions among the women are characterized by affection, attachment, and physical and intellectual pleasure—perhaps even of a sexual nature. Their relationships exhibit what Judith M. Bennett might call "lesbian-like" behavior, a term encompassing female affiliations that work against heteronormative standards: "women whose lives might have particularly offered opportunities for same-sex love; women who resisted norms of feminine behavior based on heterosexual marriage; women who lived in circumstances that allowed them to nurture and support other women."[31] By this definition, the women inhabiting the island can be seen as lesbian-like: they nurture and support each other; they initially resist the normative requirements of heterosexual marriage; and they present models

---

[31] Judith M. Bennett, " 'Lesbian-Like' and the Social History of Lesbianisms," *Journal of the History of Sexuality* 9, nos. 1–2 (2000): 1–24 (9–10). While sodomy applied to both male and female same-sex relations, men were more frequently charged for it than women, and in the absence of language to describe lesbian bonds and desire it is safe to assume that female homosexual behavior was frequently practiced but rarely documented. For the relatively small body of scholarship on medieval female lesbianism (relative to that of male homosexuals) see Helmut Puff, "Same-Sex Possibilities," in *The Oxford Handbook of Women and Gender in Medieval Europe*, ed. Judith M. Bennett and Ruth Mazo Karras (New York: Oxford University Press, 2013), 379–95; Karma Lochrie, "Between Women," in *The Cambridge Companion to Medieval Women's Writing*, ed. Carolyn Dinshaw and David Wallace (Cambridge: Cambridge University Press, 2003), 70–90; and Francesca Canadé Sautman and Pamela Sheingorn, eds., *Same Sex Love and Desire among Women in the Middle Ages*, New Middle Ages (New York: Palgrave Macmillan, 2001).

of same-sex care, love, and potentially queer desire. The queen's unnamed lady-friend, who doubles as the dreamer's lady, serves as her physician, savior, and perhaps even lover, reviving her with a magic apple and entreating the knight to return the ladies to their homeland, thus serving as mediatrix between the queen and the knight.[32] The queen describes the lady as "leche of all my smart [hurt]," who "from great paine succourte myn harte" (507, 508). Pearsall notes that the term "leche," or "physician," is "usually thought appropriate to the relationship of a lady to her lover," such as when Troilus describes Criseyde as "[h]is hertes lif his lust / his sorwes leche" (*TC*, II.1066–67), or when the God of Love later in *The Isle* commands the queen "to be his leche" (778). The lady physically restores the queen's affliction of her heart, suggesting an intimately loving bond between them. A later moment in the tale, when a dead bird is revived by a magic herb delivered by a fellow bird, echoes this feminine resuscitation scene, and supplies more evidence for a queer reading of the poem: this vignette recalls the twelfth-century "Eliduc" by Marie de France, which has been discussed by scholars as a medieval lesbian narrative.[33] In this lay, a dead female weasel is revived by a flower delivered by her mate, who is probably also female, echoing the main romance storyline in which Eliduc's wife, Guildeluec, revives the dead maiden Guilliadun by placing a flower in her mouth, much like the lady resuscitating the unconscious queen in *The Isle*. Guildeluec seems to fall in love with Guilliadun at first sight, and the two women end up living out their days together in a nunnery.

The intimacy between queen and lady seems to transcend the platonic and enter the physical—an interpretation that to disavow, I contend, reflects modern heteronormative paradigms while foreclosing what appears quite simply within the poem. When they are reunited after the lady's journeys, we are told that:

> the quene so hartelye glad
> Was, that in sothe shuche joyes she hadd

[32] At the risk of vagueness, I refer to the dreamer's love interest as simply 'lady' in order to resist the impulse to identify the unnamed women in the poem as possessions of men.

[33] See "Eliduc," in *The Lais of Marie de France*, trans. Glyn S. Burgess and Keith Busby (New York: Penguin, 2003), 128 n. 1. On the same-sex relations in "Eliduc" see also Lochrie, "Between Women," 83. The women are the unassuming center of a lay that should properly be called "Guildeluc and Guilliadun," despite the continued practices of modern editions, for we are informed at the beginning that the lay "was first called *Eliduc*, but now the name has been changed, because the adventure upon which the lay is based concerns the ladies" (111).

> When the shipe approched lannde,
> That she my ladye on the sannde
> Met, and in armes so constrayne,
> That wonder was beholde them twayne
> Whiche, to my dome, duringe twelve oures,
> Nether for heat ne watery showers
> Departed not; ne companye,
> Savinge themselfe, bode none them bye,
> But gave them leaysure, at their ease,
> To reherse joye and diseace,
> After the pleasure and corrages
> Of ther younge and tender ages.
>
> (2019–32)

The two women clasp each other's bodies, though readers are not told for exactly how long this physical contact continues; we do know they remain together outside on the beach for twelve hours, to the exclusion of all others. Pearsall glosses the noun "corrages" as "stirrings of the spirit," but "cor-" comes from the Latin for "heart" and thus transcends the spiritual; the *MED* indicates that other possible definitions include sexual desire and lust (*corage* [n.]). "Heart-stirrings" would be a more suitable gloss on "corrages," with possible sexual undertones, given the physical nature of their dalliance. If Lochrie and others have bemoaned the relative lack of overt references to female homosexual behavior in medieval literature and records, here we seem to have an unequivocal picture of same-sex love and intimacy. While some might see this moment as serving a larger picture of eventual male domination, at the very least it splits the focus between male and female heroes, offering suggestive if not explicit possibilities for alternative relationship models based on feminine bonds. The joys and sorrows the friends recount to one another carve out an underlying emotional narrative of loss and sustenance that the dominant narrative of the knights' conquest attempts (and fails) to suppress, and readers are keyed into a receptive mentality by the dreamer's "wonder" to "beholde them twayne." In a way this moment serves as the emotional climax of the entire poem, powered by an almost frenzied awareness that the women are about to be separated and consigned to heterosexual couplings.

The pair's fierce loyalty and self-sacrificial nature contrasts with the men's constant need for geographic and interpersonal advancement within a vertical system of power, silencing, and submission. When the lady decides to leave the island, frustrated with the new regime, the queen is so distraught that she offers up her crown (she "offered ther to resyne [resign] / To my ladye, eight tymes or nyne" [1117–18]), valuing her friendship with the lady more than her own regal status—but the lady insists that the queen's chief allegiance should be to the land. Alexandra Verini has proposed that according to classical paradigms, friendships between men are characterized by sameness and uniformity; by contrast, as she explores in Christine de Pizan and Margery Kempe, relationships between women tend to be more fluid and generative, involving horizontal networks of reciprocity among groups of unrelated friends and neighbors rather than depending on immediate, equitable returns.[34] In *The Isle*, these horizontal relations between women, even across uneven and divergent social boundaries, can offer relief from the violent vertical models of male–female bonds, and masculine discourse and repression. That the dreamer himself weeps often when he remembers the love between queen and lady suggests that we, too, are meant to be moved by the bonds between women in this poem.

Literary Practice and the Role of the Dreamer

There is one final piece of the puzzle here. The dreamer—who, as we recall, is both waking and sleeping at the same time, lying in a swoon for much of the dream, initially encountering the dream with "joyous doubte," and thus manifesting the oppositional forces of polarization—serves as a mediator of both male and female practices within the island, thus enhancing further his liminal status. His experience of *admiratio* renders him susceptible to new modes of being, becoming, and feeling, rather than the regressive blockage formed by *stupor*. Though we see the dreamer experiencing divided alliances and responses, avoiding imprisonment via his gendered affiliation with the knights and bowing to the God of Love's injunction to marry a lady who does not seem to love him, more and more he falls into step with the behavior of the women in the dream. The clearest way his increasing affiliation with the women becomes visible is through the dynamics of literary practice: away from the domineering regime of men and the legalistic discourse they stamp

[34] Alexandra Verini, "Medieval Models of Female Friendship in Christine de Pizan's *The Book of the City of Ladies* and Margery Kempe's *The Book of Margery Kempe*," *Feminist Studies* 42, no. 2 (2016): 365–91.

into the land, the ladies escape to their rooms, where "to reade old romansys / Hem occupied for ther pleasaunces, / Some to make virleyes and leyes / And some to other diverse pleyes" (973–76; MED, s.v. *virelai* [n.]). As is well known, medieval women were strong patrons and enthusiasts of romance literature.[35] While the men establish an autocratic regime ruled by a single rewritten historical narrative, the women embrace the diversionary and escapist powers of creativity, finding solace within spaces unmonitored by men by entering other imaginative worlds. They are not only readers but also composers of romance tales, producing lays that are often circulated orally, and thus contrasting the rigid forms of the men's discourse with the freer and unconstrained version of female oral circulation. The dreamer proves himself to be a man of poetry and romances alongside the women's covert literary practices, following suit after they disperse to compose their own lays, and himself "to . . . a romaunse toke," becoming lost in the narrative until the sun rises (977). His siding with female practices here holds even higher significance when we recall that he is the reader, the narrator, and the 'slepe wrightter' of the romance we are currently reading, which is also a dream cultivated for the consumption of dreamer and reader alike. The very nature of this dream-tale, pitched to readers as a partial dream and existing in the world of fantasy and romance, is antithetical to the authoritarian discourse of the men who have landed on the island.

The lady actually elects the dreamer as a preserver and conduit of the women's story, fast being overwritten and erased by the alternative narrative of the knights:

> And of the quene, and of the Ile,
> She taled with me longe while,
> And of all that she there had sene,
> And of th'astate, and of the quene,
> And of the ladyes, name by name,
> Two owres or mo, this was her game.
>
> (1273–78)

Sharing the history of the island with the dreamer, including naming each of the ladies and detailing her affairs with the queen, serves as a means of preserving a lost queendom, imprinting the dreamer's

---

[35] See Corinne Saunders, "Affective Reading: Chaucer, Women, and Romance," *ChauR* 51, no. 1 (2016): 11–30.

receptive, half-waking mind with specifics that are in the process of being erased. The dreamer agrees to enter into a pact of secrecy and proves his ultimate allegiance by withholding the details of her message even from readers, "for eak the othe, that I have swore, / To breke me were bet unbore" (1253–54). By blocking us from accessing the full forgotten realm of the women, the dreamer underscores its essential unknowability in contrast to the "playne" discourse of the knights, who render the land legible yet shallow, lacking in the captivating mysteries of dream. Yet he translates some of the women's origin story for us now in the form of this narrative, allowing space for an alternative reading of the tale that upholds the women as the romance's true heroes, valiant and crafty and systematically silenced, even as he shifts their dependency on oral forms of textual transmission into the permanence of written form.

Never to be firmly aligned with one camp or the other, an anguished dreamer at the end of the poem reverts back to enacting some of the qualities of the knights. He prays, upon waking, that "of [his] dreame the substaunce / Might turne once to cognisaunce [knowledge, awareness], / And cognisaunce to very preve" (2193–95). The terms "cognisaunce" and "preve" both stem from legal discourse: the former, according to the *MED*, was used to identify the "hearing and trying of a case at law," and the latter means, among other things, "[o]bserved or recorded evidence supporting a statement, an assertion, accusation, or a claim," as well as a test of the quality of the evidence and an examination generally.[36] The dreamer thus desires to transpose the "substance" of his dream into something akin to the factual and incontrovertible nature of legal proceedings, the definitive discourse enforced by the dreamed island's men. He wants this airy fiction to become reality, the partial continuity with the real world to become whole. But by the final Envoy, the dreamer seems to have resigned himself to the insubstantial nature of his future encounters with his dreamed lady, instructing his heart as follows: "When you shall slepe, have ay in remembraunce / The image of her whiche may withe lookes softe / Give the blysse that thou desyers ofte" (2226–28). The poem ends as the dream began: the dreamer achieving only partial access to an immaterial world, simultaneously lying in bed and blissfully present with his lady, who only exists in the buried recesses of his mind.

[36] *MED*, s.vv. *conissaunce* (n.), *preve* (n.).

Additionally, at the end of the vision, all that remains of the dream is "one [on] the walles old portrature" of hunting scenes (2172), a two-dimensional representation that can scarcely live up to the ostensibly real experience he has enjoyed. It is significant that the description of the walls appears only here, at the end of the poem, after the dreamer awakens; in the dream visions that surely constitute some of the *Isle*-author's sources, such as the *Roman de la Rose* and Chaucer's *The House of Fame* and *The Book of the Duchess*, the content of the walls and/or stained glass serves to inspire the material of the dream—the "curiouse portreytures" of *The House of Fame* denote the cryptic wall decorations that signal to Geffrey he has landed somewhere exceptional. Here, the trace-remains of the dream imprinted in the walls are upheld as substandard imitation, an insubstantial copy, of what was a vividly felt event—even as the image of "hurte deare full of woundes" (2174) evokes the dreamer's own love-pain. The end of the poem conjures in readers a desire to reenter the isle of women, to reexperience the perilous adventures of the dreamer, in the same way that one often pines to return into a pleasurable dream after it has ended. Dreaming and reading, after all, are two versions of the same experience: the suspension of waking, rational thought to become caught up in a narrative brought from elsewhere, an escapist jaunt to which the ideal response should be receptivity and a willingness to allow oneself to be transformed, as the *Isle*-dreamer is.

While the men transform *The Isle of Ladies* into an island of men, underneath the surface lies a feminist tale of refuge, sisterhood, and creative play. Using the guiding device of half-sleep at the beginning, the poem opens negative utopian space for critical assessment of structural inequalities between the sexes, highlighting the women's internal loyalties, horizontal networks of care, and creative literary outlets. While it is possible to read it as a narrative of male conquest and thus satisfying Pearsall's sense of it as a "dream of male desire," I hope to have shown that the poem has much more nuance than he gives it credit for. Readers who yearned for the same misogynist triumph as that presented in the *Roman de la Rose* would not likely pick up on the feminist subtext, reading for mere confirmation of their own viewpoints and treating the poem as dismissively as many scholars have today. And if challenged on any topically objectionable material within the fanciful romance they have produced, the unnamed "slepe wrightter" could always rest easy upon the old adage that it was all just a dream.

324

REVIEWS

Elizabeth Archibald, Megan G. Leitch, and Corinne Saunders, eds. *Romance Rewritten: The Evolution of Middle English Romance; A Tribute to Helen Cooper*. Cambridge: D. S. Brewer, 2018. Pp. xii, 295. $99.00.

That *Romance Rewritten* is the second tribute to Helen Cooper in less than three years testifies both to the importance of Cooper's work and to her generous collegiality. The earlier book, *Medieval into Renaissance* (2015), celebrated her often pioneering work on bridging the supposed gap between two periods now seen as continuous; this one turns to the study of romance, another field on which Cooper has left her mark. Frequent references to her *English Romance in Time* show that the new volume's focus on the transformations of romance conventions and motifs is inspired by and indebted to the innovative recasting of romance motifs as memes in her influential study. There is some thematic overlap between the two collections, though only Megan Leitch appears in both, here as one of the editors and author of the lucid and informative introduction, informed throughout by Cooper's idea that romance memes are central to understanding a genre that is intertextual by default.

Neil Cartlidge's characteristically witty opening chapter on romance "mischief" begins by reexamining long-established critical commonplaces about romances as "ideologically conservative, morally normative" providers of "wish-fulfillment fantasy" (27). While such views, most influentially formulated by Eric Auerbach and Northrop Frye, have long been silently ignored by romance specialists, they still color attitudes to the genre by scholars less familiar with it. More damagingly, they produce readings that disregard what texts say in order to make them fit preconceptions about what they should be saying. To such readings Cartlidge opposes his spirited analysis of "tonal dissonance, contrived incongruity or calculated provocation" (30) in romances, with special emphasis on the often deprecated *Sir Tristrem*.

Marcel Elias looks to specific historical contexts to account for how central motifs (hostile challenger, noble Saracen, ambivalent hero) are reconfigured in fourteenth-century English Charlemagne romances, compared to their French antecedents. Reacting against some excessively one-sided accounts of romance Saracens in recent criticism, he draws attention to pervasive "gestures towards parallelism" (53) in texts in which the virtuous Saracen, to take just one example, is often a foil for Christian shortcomings, a vehicle for self-criticism that at times questions the core elements of knightly morality.

The first section, "Romance Disruptions," concludes with Christopher Cannon's incisive argument for the centrality of comedy to Malory's *Morte Darthur*. Cannon turns on its head a long tradition of reading humor in the *Morte* as intrusive, arguing instead that Malory's "dark" comedy is a shadow of his "most pessimistic understanding of chivalry" (70). Bringing in Buster Keaton's style of slapstick as a surprisingly apt parallel, he shows Malory's comedy to be a matter of perspective: what makes a situation humorous is the "clarity with which it glimpses the terrible outcome that has been narrowly avoided" (69). In this light, the inveterate joking of a Dinadan is more clearly seen as "a form of ethical judgment," even "a kind of goodness" (78).

A point implicit in Cannon's analysis takes center stage in Jill Mann's illuminating rereading of Chaucer's *Knight's Tale*: narrative meaning greatly depends on how the action is cut up, when it ends, but also when and how it begins. Scholars have studied beginnings less often than endings, yet, as Mann notes, beginnings "implicitly suggest causes of which the stories are effects" (89), thereby directing how we read them. Like Cannon, Mann is interested in the way comedy and tragedy are determined by what follows an event but also by the perspective from which the event is described. Mann is excellent on the deliberate haphazardness of narrative links between events in Chaucer's tale, and the tale's general narrative "open-endedness" (89). She analyzes Arcite's death and its aftermath as a bravura display of shifts in style and tone, each carrying its own meaning while contributing to a sustained exploration of the co-existence of intractably clashing elements in human experience.

While these first four essays are broader in their implications, the two more narrowly focused chapters that follow, by R. F. Yeager and Elizabeth Archibald, will be read with pleasure and profit by students of Gower (Yeager) and Malory (Archibald). Trying to account for Gower's decision to conclude *Confessio Amantis* with the story of Apollonius of Tyre, Yeager speculates persuasively that the choice may reflect Gower's wish to influence the young Richard II by offering him a model of how a clueless young man becomes a responsible, even admirable, monarch. Revisiting the complex question of Malory's sources, Elizabeth Archibald aligns herself with James Wimsatt in arguing that Malory read the Post-Vulgate cycle much more carefully than other critics have been willing to concede. Familiarity with it can explain several of his more puzzling narrative choices, whether he is simply imitating elements of the French cycle or reacting against its moralizing bent.

Rounding off the section on "Romance and Narrative Strategies," Barry Windeatt offers a very helpful "gestural lexicon" (133) of Middle English romance. Remarking on how easily modern readers can "misread" references to gestures as expressions of emotion and endue them with psychological implications they may not have, he explains that, for medieval authors and writers, characters' body language acted as a "token of the type of . . . situation" (134) being narrated. It is not realistic—think of "simultaneous group swoonings" (147)—nor does it require description or elaboration, because "simply to record that familiar body language was enacted had its own sufficient emphasis and completeness of meaning" (149). In a chapter romance scholars will likely bookmark and revisit, Windeatt catalogues facial expressions, gazes and looks, posture, hand gestures, embraces, kisses, weeping, sighing, swooning, and laughing in twenty romances representing a cross-section of the genre.

"Romance and Spiritual Priorities," the next part, opens with an elegant essay by Marco Nievergelt, out to correct excessively black-and-white readings of "spendthrift knight" romances such as *Sir Cleges*, his main focus. Rather than reducing ideals to wealth, as has been argued, these romances articulate a complex and sophisticated dynamic between economics and salvation. Nievergelt builds on Ad Putter's work on the "metaphysics of *largesse*" in *Sir Amadace* to present a series of exemplary close readings in support of his interpretation of *Sir Cleges* as a carefully orchestrated "theological romance" (156), its formal features and Christmastide setting perfectly suited to its subtle expression of "the paradox and mystery" of incarnational theology. In this poem, which Nievergelt, echoing Helen Cooper, aptly describes as "conventional" in a nonpejorative sense, the Nativity functions as the "paradigm of all further human acts of charity, humility, courtesy, and *largesse*" (157).

Miriam Edlich-Muth studies the transformations of the swan-children story from the twelfth-century Latin prose *Dolopathos* to the fourteenth-century Middle English verse romance *Chevalere Assigne*. While illustrating "the persistence of romance 'memes'" (173), the process also shows how recontextualized memes can be at odds with the frameworks they operate in. Edlich-Muth's chief example is the clash between *Chevalere Assigne*'s simplified moral universe, where Christian didacticism has replaced magical logic, and motifs retained from the story's earlier, less moralizing incarnations.

Wrapping up this section is Corinne Saunders's convincing argument that Malory was more engaged with inner experience than he is usually given credit for. That the *Morte* asks troubling questions about agency, providence, and destiny has often been commented on; less frequent are readings that, like Saunders's, highlight Malory's kinship with "some of the greatest devotional writing of his age" (192). Saunders is particularly concerned with visionary experience, and excellent at unpacking, in a series of illuminating close readings, Malory's exploration of "the nature and limits of *avision*" (200) and his engagement "with the possibility of celestial vision in an uncertain world" (206).

The book's last part, on late romance, takes us to the sixteenth and nineteenth centuries. Ad Putter successfully rescues *The Court of Love* from a critical attitude tending half toward oblivion, half disparagement. While for C. S. Lewis late examples of a genre are stereotyped and boring, Putter points out that lateness "also makes things possible" by giving writers access to "the resources of a rich poetic legacy." If *The Court of Love* is an "exuberantly witty poem and a genuine *tour de force* of allegorical writing" (209), this is partly because its author can draw on Lydgate, Chaucer, Charles d'Orléans, and *The Romaunt of the Rose*, among others.

Julia Boffey and A. S. G. Edwards shed light on the evolving market for printed romance in the sixteenth century by looking at *The Squire of Low Degree*, first printed by Wynkyn de Worde in 1520. Unusually concerned, for a romance, with "material aspects of social and economic mobility" (232), this generically unstable text and its "capacity to encompass other modes" (240) may have suggested to de Worde that "the commercial appeal of [romance] might be extended in different directions" (229) even as other printers seemed to be losing interest in the genre. Andrew Lynch, whose essay closes the collection, examines attitudes to medieval chivalry in popular novels by Walter Scott and

Charlotte M. Yonge, whom he shows hesitating to endorse it whole-heartedly. Approaching them through their treatment of "youth at war," Lynch notes, for example, that both keep their young heroes out of scenes of warfare. Similarly, both find medieval Catholicism a danger-ous temptation. But although Yonge's attachment to the surface glamour of medieval chivalry is "shallow" (250) and she, like Scott, acknowledges and tries to counter its "hyperbole and extravagances" (Scott's words), both authors still manage "to indulge them in a different guise" (256).

There is not a single weak link in this excellent collection. All contri-butions share an interest in romance, generic transformation, and rewriting more broadly, while displaying a rich diversity of approaches and preoccupations. *Romance Rewritten* is easy to recommend not only to scholars of romance, but to students of Chaucer, Gower, Malory, sixteenth-century printing, or nineteenth-century medievalism as well. It is a handsome, excellently edited book, a fact worth mentioning in a world of plummeting production standards, where proliferating typos, solecisms, and inaccuracies so often get in the way of reading pleasure. (I counted fewer than a dozen minor slips in nearly 300 pages.)

With two tributes already out, covering two important areas of Coop-er's scholarship, can we hope for a third one, entirely devoted to Chaucer studies, another field on which Cooper's influence has been significant?

IVANA DJORDJEVIĆ
Concordia University, Montreal

CANDACE BARRINGTON, BRANTLEY L. BRYANT, RICHARD H. GOD-DEN, DANIEL T. KLINE, AND MYRA SEAMAN, eds. *The Open Access Companion to the "Canterbury Tales," 2017.* https://opencanterbury tales.dsl.lsu.edu/.

Chaucer companions appear in cycles, a slew of them cropping up every decade or so. As the last round of companions came out in the mid-2000s, the time is ripe for a fresh spate. What counts as "new" for a companion varies widely, running the gamut from minor revisions of a previous edition to entirely original content. Less frequently addressed is the question of genre: companions typically consist of chapters governed by particular theoretical approaches (feminist Chaucer, postcolonial Chaucer, etc.), genres (Chaucer's dream visions, Chaucer and romance), or related topics (Chaucer and the Italian tradition, love and marriage in Chaucer). The persistence of this format attests to its value: rarely does one read a companion from start to finish, and a clear organizational apparatus allows readers quickly to identify chapters of interest. Every once in a while, though, a companion offers a surprisingly fresh format, as is the case with *The Open Access Companion to the "Canterbury Tales"* (*OACCT*). This is a companion that makes good on its tagline—"A new way to learn about old books"—in smart and groundbreaking ways.

Perhaps its most impressive innovation is in the publication format. As its title suggests, the *OACCT* is a completely online, noncommercial resource, freely available to all. Remarkably, no presses were involved in this companion's making; at a time when academic publishing has entered troubled waters, this project demonstrates how scholars can work outside traditional publication venues and practices. Moreover, print companions necessarily offer readers a snapshot of a particular moment in Chaucer scholarship. This online companion, by contrast, is intended to be ever evolving; at the time that I am writing this review, the editors have plans to add additional material, including pedagogical resources and "reader contributions."

The *OACCT* specifically addresses itself to university-level, first-time readers of Chaucer. As of this writing, it consists of a user's guide; twenty-nine essay chapters, each devoted to a particular Canterbury tale, plus one on the Host and frame; and six reference chapters, providing cultural, linguistic, and biographical background. With the stated goal of "combin[ing] the dynamism of recent scholarship with pedagogical flexibility," the editors solicited essays that are "question-oriented," are of "cross-historical interest," and engage with "current critical approaches." This is a tall order, but one that the companion achieves. Its essays are by and large excellent, offering the reader—and reviewer—an embarrassment of riches. I therefore single out a few essays as representative of the quality of the whole.

Reference chapters are organized by standard topics—"English Society 1340–1400: Reform and Resistance," for example—with one exception: "What Does It Mean to Read a Medieval Text?," a collection of twelve short essays curated by Moira Fitzgibbons and addressing readers' emotional, intellectual, and imaginative responses to Chaucer. "Readers" here include professors, novelists, video-game designers, a high-school student, and a rapper, among others. The reference chapters are lively and accessible. Simon Horobin, for example, in "Chaucer's Middle English," provides an admirably clear, undergraduate-friendly introduction to Chaucer's English. Kathleen E. Kennedy's "Everyday Life in Late Medieval England" runs through the typical day of fourteenth-century Englanders and provides an array of memorable details: for example, that medieval people wore fur on the inside, rather than the outside, of garments, to maximize warmth.

For me, the knockout reference chapter is Alexandra Gillespie and Julianna Chianelli's "Manuscripts of the *Canterbury Tales*." Tackling their topic with verve, the authors counter popular misconceptions about the Middle Ages (nobody could read, there were no books, etc.), guide readers through the "bookishness" of the *Canterbury Tales*, and explain why that bookishness matters. Particularly fascinating is their section on associations among books, the human, and the divine: "manuscripts," the authors observe, "are at once vehicles for God's truths *and* signs of original sin, and they are intimately connected by that first sin to medieval thinking about sexuality and gender" (paragraph 18). An additional credit to Gillespie and Chianelli is that they present their complex, wide-ranging ideas in a student-friendly format, using transitions such as "But what does this have to do with writing and books?" (paragraph 17) to anticipate readers' questions and guide them toward main points.

Essay chapters follow the tried-and-true tale-plus-topic format but eschew its usual predictability. As noted in their user guide, the editors devised a list of topics but invited individual contributors to choose the topic for their assigned tale. The results are often eclectic: "The *Monk's Tale:* Disability/Ability," by Jonathan Hsy, for example, or "The *Friar's Tale*: Animals and the Question of Human Agency," by Karl Steel. Each essay-chapter consists of three sections: "Tools," providing whatever background (historical, theoretical, etc.) the author deems necessary; "Text," the analysis of the tale in light of its topic; and "Transformation," which invites further thinking about the tale through questions, connections to present-day phenomena, and suggested further reading. Transhistorical connections are not confined to the "Transformation" section; authors propose such connections throughout their essays, and this is one of the companion's real strengths. Special recognition here goes to Carissa M. Harris, Kim Zarins, and Emily Steiner, all of whom address Chaucer's more controversial and challenging material—rape and justice in *The Wife of Bath's Tale*; nonbinary bodies in *The Pardoner's Tale*; Jews and anti-Semitism in *The Prioress's Tale*. While the authors could use historical distance to side-step controversy, they instead invite transhistorical comparison openly to confront it.

To give a sense of what the essay-chapters have to offer, I wish to delve into a few in more detail, beginning with Emily Houlik-Ritchey's "Emotion, Feeling, Intensity, Pleasure, and the *Franklin's Tale*." Houlik-Ritchey frames her essay with an intriguing comparison between Marianne Dashwood of Jane Austen's *Sense and Sensibility* and Dorigen of *The Franklin's Tale*; "both of these literary characters," Houlik-Ritchey notes, "don't just feel sorrow in the absence of their beloveds, but *encourage* or stimulate that emotion" (original emphasis, paragraph 1). To explore the aesthetic, social, and gendered implications of this cultivated sorrow, Houlik-Ritchey provides a remarkably cogent introduction to the field of emotion studies, deftly presenting emotions as cognitive, affective, and somatic processes that traverse the personal and public divide. Equipped with these concepts, Houlik-Ritchey returns us to her primary texts, where her keen eye for detail transforms seemingly stock portrayals of female sorrow into moments of surprising significance. This essay is a beautiful demonstration of thinking in action; one question leads to another and another, and although Houlik-Ritchey points us in the direction of answers, she doesn't provide them, thus achieving the open-ended analysis that the companion promises. Despite its erudition, this essay is accessibly eloquent; one gets a strong sense of Houlik-Ritchey as a reader, which, for this companion's aims and audience, works well; her enthusiasm models what we hope to inspire in students.

In "Subsistence (Land and Food) in the *Squire's Tale*," Alexis Kellner Becker eschews the usual points of entry for the tale (exoticism, talking birds) and even the tale itself to begin with the Franklin's interruption of the Squire and offer of land to the value of £20 for a son more like him. While this interruption is often noted, its specific terms are not, leading Becker to pose some intriguing questions: "[W]hat does this tale have to do with land and its value? Why, in response to this tale in particular, is the Franklin thinking about these things?" (paragraph 1). These questions launch Becker's assessment of status-based perspectives on land and food, within and beyond *The Squire's Tale*, and allow her to revisit standard points of interest in unexpected ways. For example, she extends discussion of the tale's birds from the lovelorn falcon to the swans and herons consumed at Cambyuskan's feast. In Tartarye, Becker argues, people don't just talk to birds, they eat them, and the fact that the Squire is so utterly oblivious to this point says something about his privileged removal from food production. In this light, the Franklin's interruption can be interpreted as a figurative appropriation of squandered resources. In the closing questions of her "Transformation" section, Becker invites readers to seek out other instances in the *Canterbury Tales* that connect class, subsistence, and narrative, asking, in another example of her incisive attention to the seemingly mundane, why the two pilgrims of *The General Prologue* most involved in food production, the Cook and the Ploughman, receive no tale.

As outstanding as the *OACCT* is, I wish to make one comment that is less a criticism than an observation to bear in mind as this companion and other student-centered resources continue to develop. As noted above, the companion aims to be question-oriented and open-ended; in their original guidelines for contributors, the editors cheekily note that "any student trying to plagiarize from these chapters should still need to do a lot of thinking and writing to have a coherent paper or argument." Many of the essay chapters do, however, present coherent arguments, presumably because providing a strong model of analysis without argumentative direction is hard. I do not think this is a problem; these chapters beautifully illustrate close reading and literary scholarship for student readers. In fact, in a few cases, open-ended chapters struck me as less compelling than their more argument-driven counterparts, perhaps because, in conformance with the editors' directive, contributors were holding themselves back. Taken as a whole, however, the *OACCT* is a tremendous achievement, one for which anyone interested in reading, teaching, or researching Chaucer should be eminently grateful.

LYNN SHUTTERS
Colorado State University

HEATHER BLATT. *Participatory Reading in Late-Medieval England.* Manchester: Manchester University Press, 2018. Pp. 272. $120.00.

In the Invocation to Chaucer's *House of Fame*, the narrator articulates a program of reading, and not a very subtle one. There, he blesses those who "take hit wel and skorne hyt noght" (I.91) and curses any who, "thorgh malicious entencion," "presumpcion," "hate, or skorn," "or vilanye" (among other unsavory attributes), "mysdeme hyt" (I.93–97). The passage is one of my favorites in all of Chaucer: it is funny, and it makes explicit the relationship between author and reader, and the interpretative space between them. This passage also illustrates the importance of Heather Blatt's primary argument in *Participatory Reading in Late-Medieval England*: that works of the late fourteenth, and especially fifteenth, centuries foreground the importance of the reader in shaping them. They do so, according to Blatt, in four main ways: through "emendation invitations" (Chapter 1); "nonlinear reading" (Chapter 2); "materiality" (chapters 3 and 4); and, finally, "temporal reading" (Chapter 5). Blatt's argument essentially suggests that we think about moments such as the one in *The House of Fame* a bit more seriously than I have done, in any case—as moments that identify readers as wielding the kind of authoritative power we typically ascribe to writers alone. In reading this book, I often thought of Chaucer and this passage, and the extent to which its humor (and maybe even anxiety) bespeaks a cultural awareness in the period of how much various readers could influence meaning. Blatt's ideas, in other words, are very interesting and fruitful to think with.

Blatt splits *Participatory Reading* into two parts: the first, "Participatory Discourse," outlines ways in which writers themselves invited or anticipated readerly participation in the texts they constructed. Chapter 1, "Corrective Reading," focuses on what Blatt calls the "emendation invitation," a moment in the text in which, by asking the reader either to correct mistakes or, alternatively, to refrain entirely from doing so, a writer acknowledges the reader as a creative, corrective, or unwelcome collaborator. Blatt turns to several lines in *Troilus and Criseyde*, *Troy Book*, and Thomas Norton's *Ordinal of Alchemy* to show the differences between Chaucer's restricted invitation, Lydgate's open invitation to correction, and Norton's closed approach: a "highly restrictive model that also allows Chaucer's version to be identified as a hybrid example of the emendation invitation, partly open" (35). Blatt asks us to understand these instances as more than topoi (30), and rather as moments in which we can see (not assume) the author to be considering readerly collaboration and textual creation. Why these representative examples and not others serve to structure the chapter remains somewhat uncertain, however, and a rationale for the appendices (which include other examples of emendation invitations and of nonlinear texts) would have been very helpful in this respect, too.

Chapter 2, "Nonlinear Reading," similarly focuses on the rhetorical structure of several texts, suggesting that the authors of the *Orcherd of Syon*, *Titus and Vespasian*, and the *Siege of Thebes* invite their audiences to engage in nonlinear reading, thereby shaping and constructing the text's meaning, which is not limited to some kind of overarching authorial plan. This is a fascinating and important point; certainly, when I engage with texts such as the *Orcherd of Syon*, I do not necessarily consider the ways it might, in inviting readers to dip into the text where and as often as it suits them, elicit nonlinearity (the first kind of nonlinear reading Blatt identifies). Blatt goes on to suggest two other kinds of nonlinear reading: performed nonlinearity (*Titus and Vespasian*) and hybrid linearity, combining "elicited and performed modes of nonlinearity" (Lydgate's *Siege of Thebes*) (71). This chapter is most convincing in its engagement with the *Orcherd*, though here and throughout the book one wants more direct engagement with the primary texts themselves. This matters particularly because Blatt's claim that nonlinear reading—and indeed, every kind of participatory reading she identifies in this book—explores the "tension between freedom and control" inherent in late medieval literary culture (74) is an important and timely one. At the same time, in this chapter, it is sometimes not entirely clear what nonlinearity entails: is *Titus and Vespasian* nonlinear because it is episodic? Because it is linked thematically rather than temporally, juxtaposing Jerusalem's destruction with Pilate's suicide (77–78)? So, too, *Titus and Vespasian*, the *Siege of Thebes*, and the *Orcherd* are seldom quoted from; for the reader unfamiliar with these works, this may be a difficult argument to follow.

Part 2, "Evoking Participation," moves from the rhetorical world of the text itself to the spatial and architectural world surrounding it, considering how this three-dimensional world inevitably affects readerly engagement. Chapter 3, "Reading Materially," focuses on Lydgate's "Soteltes for the Coronation Banquet of Henry VI"; the argument is an interesting one, calling our attention as it does to the architectural surroundings of what Blatt helpfully calls an "extracodexical" text: "a written work that circulates outside the boundaries of the familiar codex" (106). This term surely deserves adoption and is a hugely useful one for thinking about even, say, moments *within* written works that feature extracodexical texts (I'm thinking here of Chaucer's dream visions, for instance). The "Soteltes" chapter calls our attention to the surroundings of Henry VI's coronation feast, where the soteltes—objects at feasts, often consisting of food, that themselves served narrative and rhetorical purposes, including in this case actual verse—would have been introduced. Blatt argues that this environment—the Great Hall at Westminster—would have inflected the way those in attendance would have interpreted and interacted with the soteltes, which is an intriguing idea, if necessarily speculative.

Chapter 4, "Reading Architecturally," continues with this focus on the material world, and here Blatt turns her attention explicitly to texts that were written on walls—the focus of chapters 3 and 4 is, in many ways, architectural, and they work well together as a reminder of the spatial contexts in which we all encounter literary works. But, as with Chapter 3, this chapter forgoes examining the texts at hand in favor of imaginatively reconstructing what we can about the spaces these texts—the Percy wall texts and Lydgate's *Daunce macabre*—once occupied. The issue here is that both structures (the medieval St. Paul's Cathedral and the Percy estates) are now gone; we can imagine what it may have been like to encounter poetry and didactic verses in these environments, but we cannot know. As in Chapter 3, this speculative reasoning is often inspiring and fruitful, particularly insofar as we can imagine Lydgate's text interacting with and deriving meaning from the Pardon Churchyard and the ornate tombs that were probably located there (144–45). At the same time, even this reasoning is limited by what we do not know; and it is also limited by what Blatt herself points out: that the Pardon Churchyard was not accessible to the "general public" (145); it is not therefore clear what "readers" she is imagining in the space (which, in the context of this argument, matters quite a lot). In both Chapters 3 and 4, that is, a key question is left unanswered: what do we do with extracodexical works that literally no longer exist? How do we imagine these works and what their effects on their audiences may have been? These questions are crucial as we think about medieval reading practices—that Blatt's chapter demands we ask them is one of the central contributions of this book. Engaging more fully with the poetry itself would have undoubtedly helped to think through issues like these.

The last chapter, "Reading Temporally," dovetails with Chapter 2, "Nonlinear Reading," in that both chapters take up the "effects of time on human lives" (167). Chapter 5 calls our attention to "multiplicities of temporality": sacred and secular, linear and circular, among others (168), and to how these temporalities inform reading practices. Blatt yokes together temporal reading and attentiveness in a lovely meditation on how the length of a text (in abridgments, 174) or even the amount of time we spend with it helps to shape meaning. It is not always clear what the terms here and elsewhere mean, though—Blatt introduces "participatory temporality" (175), which seems to mean readerly interaction with a text on their own time (a crucially important idea). So, too, this chapter postpones engagement with primary texts until about halfway through: *Thomas of Erceldoune's Prophecy*, Eleanor Hull's *Commentary on the Penitential Psalms*, and Thomas Norton's *Ordinal of Alchemy*. How texts invoking prophecy differ in their temporal usages from texts that invoke temporal participation through, say, the framework of salvation history (such as Hull's text) could have been more fully explored.

Blatt does not engage with reader response theory explicitly, but this critical mode encapsulates a central challenge of her book: that there is no easy way to gather evidence about readerly performance from the texts themselves. Unless we have records of reading, we can glean the readerly models that the texts seem to suggest, but not how they were actually read. Interestingly, the book invites the kind of "participatory reading" from the modern scholar in some of the same ways the texts considered invite completion, correction, and projection from their original audiences. A real boon of this work, in other words, is the extent to which it highlights the ways in which all creative output (scholarly or not) is, to some extent, collaborative. *Participatory Reading* offers innovative contexts in which to understand late medieval writing; these are questions we absolutely should be thinking about, and Blatt's intervention is an important one. I have glossed over Blatt's reliance on theories of digital media throughout this book because she is at her best when she is engaging in her own innovative readings of late medieval culture—"extracodexical" is one such instance—rather than when she summarizes digital media theory and superimposes it on the texts she discusses. This is not to say medieval manuscript culture does not benefit from this kind of engagement, but rather that Blatt's own voice is sometimes overshadowed, which is really unfortunate. That said, the ideas here will no doubt influence how we continue to think and write about late medieval literary culture, and I very much look forward to seeing how this book shapes the ensuing conversation.

ROBYN MALO
Purdue University

KENNETH BLEETH, ed. *Chaucer's "Squire's Tale," "Franklin's Tale," and "Physician's Tale": An Annotated Bibliography 1900–2005.* Chaucer Bibliographies 9. Toronto: University of Toronto Press, 2017. Pp. xxvi, 570. $133.00.

Reviewers of Variorum Chaucer fascicles have observed that readers know what to expect in each of those volumes. The same is true for the Chaucer Bibliographies series, the ninth volume of which has now appeared. Having reviewed Monica McAlpine's bibliography of *The Knight's Tale* (*SAC* 15 [1993]: 229–32), I certainly had a fair idea of what I would find upon opening Kenneth Bleeth's excellent addition to the Toronto series. Indeed, most Chaucer scholars have the same anticipations, but since they also have expectations of book reviews, let me begin by providing the requisite thumbnail sketch of the contents of Professor Bleeth's volume.

Because the book treats more than one tale, and because two of the tales, those of the Squire and the Franklin, constitute a single "fragment" or "group," Bleeth deploys the following system of organization in the first fifth of his book. He puts the introductions to *The Squire's Tale* and *The Franklin's Tale* in sequence (3–19 and 20–33, respectively). Each of these is divided into topics. For *The Squire's Tale*, he includes the categories of "Source Study," "Genre," "Teller and Tale," "Orientalism and the Exotic," "Magic, Science, and Technology," and "*The Squire's Tale*, Part 2." Last in this sequence is "The Tale as Fragment," itself subdivided into two sets of bullet points. The first set surveys opinions on the story's incompleteness as expressed before 1990. The second set summarizes responses to these earlier assessments, positive and negative. Following this section is the introduction to *The Franklin's Tale*, which identifies the following topics: "Sources and Analogues," "*The Franklin's*

Tale and the Marriage Debate," "The Teller and the Tale," "Characterization," "Astrology and Magic," "Setting," and "Six Passages" (each
passage a focus of commentary). In all of these sections, Bleeth paints
with a broad brush and supplies cross-references (bold-face entry numbers) where summaries of the individual treatments are to be found.
Then follows a joint section on "Editions and Modernizations" (34–59),
which treats the two tales as a unit. Thereafter, Bleeth lists and summarizes publications focused on "Sources, Analogues, and the Posterity of
The Squire's Tale" (60–82). Next appears "*The Franklin's Tale*: Sources,
Analogues, and Later Influence" (83–111). In each of these last three
sections, as in the general surveys of criticism that follow, items are
arranged chronologically; items published in the same year are presented in alphabetical sequence.

Given the careful subdivisions of most of the sections mentioned
above, it is surprising that the section on "Editions and Modernizations"
has no subdivisions at all; mere chronology and alphabetization are its
principles of arrangement. The editor has, I think, missed an opportunity. It would be easy to introduce categories. One could simplify the
model employed in Eleanor Hammond's *Chaucer: A Bibliographical Manual* (1908). By separating the thirty-six comprehensive editions (including editions both of the complete works and of the *Canterbury Tales*
alone) and the eighteen more-or-less complete translations (of the works
or of *CT*), one could more readily see the relative prominence of *The
Squire's Tale* and *The Franklin's Tale* over the last hundred or so years.
There are twenty-six editions of selected works; *SqT* and *FranT* appear
in six of them, *SqT* without *FranT* in seven, and *FranT* without *SqT* in
thirteen. Sifting further, one finds seven editions dedicated to *SqT* alone
and eight to *FranT* alone. Among translations of selected works, there
are four that have both *SqT* and *FranT*, seven with *SqT* but not *FranT*,
and eighteen with *FranT* but not *SqT*. Furthermore, there are three free-
standing translations of *FranT* (items 76, 94, and 119), and one (item
44, omit the erroneous "the" from the title as printed) that includes *The
Clerk's Tale* but otherwise only non-Chaucerian material. In counterbal-
ance, one notes the exclusive pairing of *SqT* and *The Tale of Sir Thopas*,
in an edition (item 69) and in a translation (item 66). This reorganization also reveals that in the late nineteenth and early twentieth centuries, *SqT* enjoyed more attention than did *FranT*. Thus, the era of
admiration for *SqT* can be extended a bit further than was indicated by

Don Baker at the start of his Variorum edition of *SqT*. Incidentally, my proposed reorganization reveals one outlier: item 114, Stephen Partridge's dissertation, which was an edition of manuscript glosses. Probably the index should include an entry for "Glosses," with a cross-reference to Partridge.

Bleeth's general survey of criticism of *SqT* occupies pages 112–207. The first section covers items published between 1889 and 1949 (items 373–448); each of the next five sections covers a decade of scholarship (items 449–74, 475–503, 504–63, 564–643, 644–706). Items 707–46 appeared between 2000 and 2005. Bleeth then adds a sort of appendix containing fourteen items published between 2006 and 2013, all focused on the field of animal studies as it bears upon the Canacee–falcon episode. This arrangement allows one to see both the expansion of scholarship in general and the concomitant growth of interest in *SqT* during the twentieth and twenty-first centuries. A separate section (208–17, items 758–94) focuses on the *Squire–Franklin Link* (V.673–708). The survey of general criticism of *FranT* (218–413) has a similar structure to that used for *SqT*, but without an appendix. Its much greater length testifies to the modern eclipse of *SqT*, despite the increased commentary devoted to it.

The Physician's Tale of course suffered no such eclipse because its star was never bright enough to gain much attention. Not surprisingly, in Bleeth's bibliography it occupies much less space than either *SqT* or *FranT*. Bleeth's introduction to the tale occupies pages 414–19; the sections on "Editions and Modernizations" (420–30) and "Sources, Analogues, and Later Influence" (421–40) follow. The general survey of criticism (441–516) has the same structure as that of *FranT*. While examining entries for *PhyT*, I was mindful of two things. One is a letter that Professor Bleeth sent to Paul Ruggiers in 1992; it provided eight pages of corrections to the Variorum edition of *PhyT*, mostly corrections of typographical errors but also of several more substantive matters. Paul and I were impressed by Professor Bleeth's attention to detail, and his document was a sobering reminder that even good scholars can be overwhelmed by the demands of large, detailed projects, and that editorial supervision must be stringent. The second matter that occurs to me is a point that I made in 1993 (see above): I concluded that the Toronto Bibliographies and the Variorum Chaucer are not so much rival projects as complementary ones. And it is in that spirit that I make my final remarks.

What strikes me about the Toronto Bibliography series is its prefer-
ence for general characterization of each recorded item of scholarship
and criticism. There is little effort to show specific comments on the
particulars of a given text. Also, the introductions present the historical
relation of readings of a text in a somewhat abstract fashion, with lists
of item numbers that readers must consult to arrive at a more nuanced
construction of scholarly debate. This arrangement requires a fair
amount of flipping around—rather like reading Chaucer before glosses
and notes came to be printed on the text page. Such presentation, I
think, is more useful for teachers than for scholars. Also, as I stated in
1993, the "real" organization of a Toronto Bibliography is in its very
elaborate index. But this vantage-point simply reverses the polarity of
difficulty, as one must flip from the back of the book to the individual
entries. Setting such demerits aside, I find that Bleeth's tome does fill
some gaps in the Variorum volumes on *SqT* and *PhyT*, just as those
volumes fill gaps in his work. Scholars would do well to consult all of
these resources.

DANIEL J. RANSOM
University of Oklahoma

VENETIA BRIDGES. *Medieval Narratives of Alexander the Great: Transnational Texts in England and France.* Studies in Medieval Romance.
Cambridge: D. S. Brewer, 2018. Pp. 319. $99.00 cloth; $24.99
e-book.

To frame her book's subject—texts about Alexander the Great composed between the mid-twelfth and mid-fourteenth centuries in northern France and the British Isles—Venetia Bridges turns in her
introduction and conclusion to Chaucer's *Monk's Tale*. There, while cata-
loguing those poor souls on the bottom of Fortune's wheel, the Monk
not only characterizes Alexander's nature ("gentil," "worthy"), but the
nature of Alexander's "storie": "so commune . . . That every wight that
hath discrecioun / Hath herd somwhat or al of his fortune" (*MkT*,
VII.2658, 2631–33). Bridges reads these lines straight in her introduction, as evidence that Alexander's story, "so commune," was both widely
known and ordinary—the latter condition being largely a function of

the former. In her book's conclusion, she posits an alternative and can-
nier reading of these lines, for her work in the intervening pages makes
clear that while Alexander may have been a ubiquitous figure in northern France and Britain, no single, "commune" story about him circulated in the medieval period: a fact Chaucer must have known, even if
his Monk did not. Occupying a space between epic and memory, the
medieval renderings of Alexander, Bridges asserts, interacted with or
interrupted various presents: geographical, political, linguistic, material.
"What is the range of meanings," she queries in her introduction, "in
which Alexander participates in literary contexts during the twelfth and
thirteenth centuries? How do these meanings relate to cultural identities
as they form and re-form in this period of swift change and innovation?" (2). Her book's five chapters attend to these questions by contextualizing and interrogating Latin, French, Anglo-Norman, and
Middle English narratives of Alexander within their various milieux and
through a series of very fine readings.

But the Monk's language quietly raises another issue Bridges concerns herself with throughout this book, namely the handling of Alexander narratives not only in the medieval period, but in modern
scholarship. Bridges calls into question a series of binaries that, she
argues, have so incrementally come to structure the study of romances
generally, and romances about Alexander specifically, that they often go
unquestioned and untested: history and fiction; Latin and the vernacular; local and global; "us" and the "other." She pushes back against the
scholarly reading of vernacular romances as expressions of identity and
proto-nationalism. We are in thrall to this mode of analysis, she suggests, at least partly because of how easily it maps onto disciplinary
boundaries.

Bridges advocates for a "transnational" lens because, she writes, of
the scope it offers. Boundaries are visible, but so too is the terrain on
either side of them, the "local" and its opposite. One gets the strong
sense that Bridges's keenest interest lies not in the book's textual field
of Alexander, but in the theoretical possibilities of a transnational
approach to that field and the possibilities it offers for the productive
(dis)organization of scholarship more broadly. The repeated suggestion
of those possibilities proves to be the book's most promising and most
challenging aspect. On the one hand, Bridges urges us to imagine a
new textual approach that prioritizes texts' movements across a range
of boundaries and among multilingual networks. Her book is rich with

important analysis: new readings of both key and previously overlooked passages demonstrate the ways in which authors grappled with their historical inheritance, or lack thereof, and Bridges's acute contextualizing of that inheritance evinces the recognition that medieval authors' predilection for crossing boundaries—whether linguistic, political, temporal, or generic—is often at odds with how we circumscribe their texts in our own work. Yet, on the other hand, the book itself stops short of proposing in detail or fully embodying a "transnational" mode of scholarship. Each chapter takes up the findings of the previous chapter(s) for the sake of comparative analysis, but in its overall structure—chapters divided in terms of geographical provenance, language, or contemporaneously produced texts—it obeys the distinctions it seeks to undermine. Bridges thus addresses a transnational approach often only implicitly, through intricate readings, or on the periphery, by drawing the reader's attention back to the idea of a transnational praxis at the conclusion of each chapter.

All chapters are divided into sections and subsections, so the following summaries aim to give an overview of the book's arc, rather than a comprehensive account of each chapter. Throughout, Bridges tracks what she calls the "debate" over *translatio studii* and the "poetics of *translatio*" that each text develops. The medieval concept of *translatio studii*—used to explain and sanction the inheritance of historical, non-Christian narratives—has been adopted in modern scholarship to describe transmission, and it provides the main framework within each chapter for discussion of narrative inheritance and its ethical stakes. The concept of *translatio* also gets at the crossing of various boundaries necessary for a transnational scholarship, though it has rarely been extended to include modern reception on a continuum, a move Bridges does not explicitly make, but that would follow naturally from her book's arguments.

With Chapter 1, Bridges looks at the prehistory of the medieval romance tradition, mining Alexander the Great's "antique" tradition for the raw material that constituted the medieval inheritance of Alexander. Any ancient "knowledge," she clarifies, cannot be divided neatly according to a binary of "history" and "fiction," for there was never one single "historical" account of Alexander, but rather a proliferation of texts and identities. The chapter surveys the fragmentary (often, Bridges notes, an overly generous description) remains of the Alexander corpus produced between the fourth century BCE and the fifth century CE. The balance of the book's chapters grapple with the presences, absences, and historicity of that corpus.

Chapter 2 moves forward in time to twelfth-century northern French poems about Alexander, the Latin *Alexandreis* and the French *Ylias*. (The reader should be aware that Appendix 2 consists of summaries for each medieval text discussed.) In this and the following chapter, Bridges situates the poems in their milieux; investigates their part in the construction of a multilingual, complexly political and religious identity in northern France; and demonstrates each text's "poetics of *translatio*." Chapter 3 focuses on the twelfth-century French *Roman d'Alexandre* and the *Roman de Troie*, as well as Chrétien de Troyes's *Cligès*. Here, Bridges introduces the concept of "anxious romance" as a means of understanding how and what choices of *translatio* were made and unmade in each text.

Chapters 4 and 5 turn to Britain and its vernaculars. It is here that Bridges's model of a transnational scholarship is most successful. Chapter 4 challenges the idea of a strictly Anglo-Norman, "insular Alexander" by looking closely at two late twelfth-century texts—Thomas Kent's *Roman de toute chevalrie* and, surprisingly, the *Roman de Horn*—and by looking back to Chapter 2's continental texts for relationships among the insular and continental. The multidimensional analysis of the *Roman de toute chevalrie*, a text Bridges calls "intellectual romance," is perhaps her finest work in the book and, if expanded at key points, could have constituted an entire chapter on its own. For instance, a brief discussion of the text's Anglo-Norman Text Society edition, which separates the Anglo-Norman *ur*-text from later additions of continental material, could have been extrapolated to consider the processes of medieval and modern inheritance. The situation Bridges describes surely exemplifies medieval readers' disregard for the boundaries we ascribe in our textual criticism, and in doing so addresses the problems and stakes of a transnational approach for medieval writers and readers and our inheritance of their books. Chapter 5 remains in Britain to query the axiomatic belief that Middle English romances are primarily sites of multifaceted, local identity-formation. In her analysis of the fourteenth-century *Kyng Alisaunder*, *Of Arthur and of Merlin*, and the *Seege or Batayle of Troye*, Bridges largely eschews the scholarly triumvirate for Middle English romance—language, literature, nation—to show, for example, *Kyng Alisaunder*'s disinterest in those themes and affinities with continental materials.

In addition to fresh readings of Alexander narratives, Bridges's most important contributions are the new terms ("anxious romance," "intellectual romance") by which she organizes—or, better, disorganizes—notions of the genre, and her repeated calls to question settled scholarly practice. It is left to the reader to imagine what a fully rendered transnational scholarship might look like. Nevertheless, with this book Bridges clears a path for new approaches to medieval literary study and maps ways of getting there. Put otherwise, the questions Bridges poses in her introduction about how medieval writers handled the ethical challenges of historical inheritance can be read as likewise directed at us as we strive to define the global Middle Ages in theory and praxis.

MARISA LIBBON
Bard College

JOHN BUGBEE. *God's Patients: Chaucer, Agency, and the Nature of Laws.* Notre Dame: University of Notre Dame Press, 2019, Pp. xvii, 477. $55.00.

God's Patients: Chaucer, Agency, and the Nature of Laws brings two of the greatest writers of the Middle Ages—Bernard of Clairvaux and Geoffrey Chaucer—into meaningful dialogue for the first time. While John Bugbee stops short of claiming Bernard's direct influence on Chaucer (despite the fact that the twelfth-century mystic is referenced by Chaucer ten times), he makes a powerful argument for the poet's far-reaching, nuanced adoption of a spiritual model that Bernard had helped to embed in medieval culture—a model of what Bugbee calls "conjoint" or "cooperative" agency. The human will moved by this ideal finds that patient and watchful submission to God's will mysteriously leads it to conform freely to God's providential plan; for such a will, passivity, or more accurately "receptivity," mysteriously becomes an opportunity for collaborative action with God.

Bugbee develops this idea via a structure of argument that itself mirrors the dialogue he is tracing in Chaucer's poetry between the human and the divine, moving smoothly back and forth between theory and doctrine (both medieval and modern), between concepts of will and of

345

law, and interleaving new readings of Chaucer that grow in persuasiveness as the reader's appreciation of the ideal of shared agency deepens. Bugbee's writing is beautifully crafted on the sentence level as well as in its overall structure of argumentation. The book begins in Chapter 1 on the ground in the poetry, with a comparison of Griselda and Custance—two Chaucerian women who are often read as alike in their submissiveness—revealing Griselda's will to be forced, even mechanical, as she "continually promises for the future what she continually fails to achieve in the present" (67). Custance, in contrast, refrains from oaths in the style of Griselda, demonstrating what Bugbee calls "drift as mastery" (79). Drawing on Chaucer's small changes in his sources, Bugbee demonstrates that one character serves as a negative example of purposeless abjection while the other inspires human imitation by making herself a willing channel for the divine, establishing patience as strength.

In Chapter 2, we learn that "conjoint agency" informs a mode of reading appropriate to medieval texts as well as a style of spiritual patience. Following Hans-Georg Gadamer's typology of reading stances, which arrays Enlightenment, Romantic, and historicist methodologies against an ideal of "dialogic" reading, Bugbee suggests that a mere suspension of disbelief is insufficient for full apprehension of a work of art with spiritual aspirations. The reader must engage in a "dialogue of presuppositions" (103) within which she risks genuine persuasion and change. This might be understood as reading like Custance rather than like another unsuccessful Chaucerian interpreter discussed here: Theseus in *The Knight's Tale*. Constrained within a limited, pagan world, Theseus admirably opens himself to experience, but when life delivers repeated disappointment and frustration he remains unable to internalize its lesson—that, absent a Christian God, he lacks the unilateral power to halt the interruptions of chance. The reader is now in a position to see the importance of Bernard's understanding of agency, which stipulates that the human will is both active and passive in its receptiveness to the divine. Bugbee elaborates on this mystical "theory of action" (127) in Chapter 3, citing extensively from Bernard's doctrinal treatises.

In the typology that emerges, Theseus, Griselda, and Custance differ according to how perfectly they subordinate their wills to God. Partly because the first two have bound themselves to earthly masters, Custance alone engages in spiritually "conjoint agency." But what of other Chaucerian characters who clearly seek to perform God's will? What of the "holy anomaly" St. Cecilia, in *The Second Nun's Tale*, with her "fiercely independent agency" (157)? In Chapter 4, Bugbee acknowledges that there is nothing "cooperative" or "conjoint" about Chaucer's Cecilia. Indeed, Chaucer has manipulated both the hagiographic genre and Cecilia's individual story to emphasize her independent agency or "active sanctity" (151). Unlike other saints of the time, she does not regularly refer her power back to its heavenly source. Additionally, Chaucer splices together his own two sources in a fashion that minimizes Cecilia's debt to the divine. The story as told in the *Legenda aurea*, which Chaucer adheres to through line 348, weakens Valerian and Tiburce, while pressing Cecilia "toward pure and self-grounded agency" (164–65). The poet then turns abruptly to a "Franciscan abridgement" of the tale (163), whose elisions enable him to maintain his steady focus on Cecilia rather than on the brothers or on a model of Christian sacrifice that is shared among all believers. Other details and small changes also bear out the argument that Chaucer deliberately underscores Cecilia's ferocious self-confidence, and thus undermines her value as a model for the Christian who strives to serve as a cooperative conduit for God's will.

Bugbee's discussion of *The Second Nun's Tale*, while persuasive in the main, ultimately succumbs to a certain "bottom-up" (311) rigorist mode of analysis foreign to the rest of this superb book. This mode is most troublesome in his discussion of the *Prologue*. It is unclear why Bugbee puts much weight on the *Prologue*, as earlier he had announced that he would be bracketing the role of narrators (22–27), a decision that excused him from reconciling framing material with their tales. One might question this strategy—can one fully understand the Man of Law's or Clerk's tales without addressing the introductions or interruptions from their narrators?—but this arrangement has had the advantage of freeing Bugbee to make inferences based "on indicators internal to the tales themselves" (27). With *The Second Nun's Prologue*, though, the reference to Bernard (*SNT*, 30) sweeps away caution and draws Bugbee into an unusually tendentious inspection of the invocation to Mary (*SNT*, 29–84); that invocation pairs poorly with the Cecilia of the *Tale*, "who does not match Mary in a single category" (195). With this "glaring mismatch" between the *Prologue* and the *Tale* now clearly in view, Bugbee is tempted to a highly speculative and admittedly unprovable biographical solution that situates the invocation early in Chaucer's career, "a decade or more" before the tale (201). Bugbee himself seems to acknowledge that the evidence here is somewhat forced ("the hypothesis makes for an excellent story," he confesses [202]); his candor on this point is refreshing and consistent with the study's trustworthy voice.

Chapter 5 ("Law Gone Wrong: The Franklin's and Physician's Tales") introduces Part 2 of *God's Patients* ("Will and Law"). If "Will" is the forward-facing concept of this book—inviting a gracious cooperative relationship between human and divine—that relationship is framed by its mirroring, rear-facing image, "Law"—those duties to which the obedient soul is strictly subject. The Franklin's and Physician's tales, adjacent to one another in the Ellesmere order, dramatize the suffering that flows from an oath or law with a patently unjust consequence. Courtly in tone, *The Franklin's Tale* ultimately celebrates forgiveness, while *The Physician's Tale* culminates in a father's merciless beheading of his innocent daughter. But both present a quandary to critics, since the "central problem" in each is a "faulty law," which readers are "coached" to question even as the characters within the tales go along as if the underlying justness of a demand were irrelevant to their dilemmas (234).

Again, Bernard supplies a solution. In Chapter 6, Bugbee returns to the twelfth-century mystic, now in his writing on the Rule of St. Benedict. While not an antinomian, Bernard clearly disfavors the "mindless following of orders" (260), allowing rather for context, intention, and a hierarchy of laws. What Thomas Merton might call "openness to the hidden will of God" (255) Bernard accommodates in a paradox of obedience that, in the saint's words, frees the "bountiful will . . . toward everything that is enjoined . . . into infinite freedom" (169). Here emerges the great reward of "conjoint agency": not subservience but joyful participation in a structure of laws that places love, or *caritas*, at its center (272). We are now, in Bugbee's Conclusion, well positioned to appreciate his universalist claim: that "conjoint agency" is more than a theme within Chaucer's poetry but, because it informs the ethics and epistemology of the work at such a deep level, a mode of reading and thinking that we must sincerely entertain in order to experience that poetry as it was intended.

Bugbee flirts with but ultimately skirts whether such a commitment to "reading Chaucer religiously" (306) implies "that the cooperative ideal has some claim to being true" (314). His invitation of modern mystics such as Thomas Merton and Simone Weil into the discussion inclines him in this direction. But he strongly suggests that we all read as something—whether as atheists (95–100), as Protestants (or

Protestant-inspired rationalists) (308–13), or as non-rigorist "contemplatives." Only the last leaves room for the "relaxed tension" (315) that E. Talbot Donaldson identifies as required for genuine dialogue with a text from the past. For the humanities, and especially those fields that take the past as their subject, there is no issue that matters more right now. Nothing poses a deadlier challenge to the relevance of medieval or Chaucer studies than our modern tendency to appropriate early periods as reflections of momentary concerns or to read back into them misleading progressive or reactionary narratives. Bugbee's compelling interpretations remind us that the Middle Ages was a subtle, generous, and philosophically sophisticated time, worthy of deference and genuine respect for its own first principles.

KATHRYN L. LYNCH
Wellesley College

DAVID K. COLEY. *Death and the "Pearl" Maiden: Plague, Poetry, England.* Columbus: Ohio State University Press, 2019. Pp. xi, 220. $99.95 cloth; $19.95 e-book.

"In vain does one look for a parallel from an English quill to the long and moving descriptions of the Black Death given by Boccaccio and by Machaut." Siegfried Wenzel's statement in "Pestilence and Middle English Literature" (1982) becomes for David Coley a challenge to locate in the four poems of the Cotton Nero A.x manuscript (but not *Saint Erkenwald*) literary traces of the bubonic plague, even if nothing like the graphic representations in the *Decameron* and *Judgment of the King of Navarre*. It is indeed deeply mysterious why the outpouring of vernacular poetry in the second half of the fourteenth century should have remained persistently silent about the devastating trauma of the Black Death, which killed upwards of 62 percent of England's population during its first outbreak during 1348–50 and returned periodically, with similar mortality rates, in 1361 and thereafter.

Coley has produced a book of such originality, so much rooted in gripping historical and smart theoretical texts, and so much written against the grain of traditional interpretation, that it is a real page-turner. This is true despite the fact—or because of the fact—that the

Pearl-poet is such an unlikely writer to investigate. Nowhere does he provide even glimpses comparable to Langland's "pokkes and pestilences" in *Piers Plowman* (B XX.97–107) or Chaucer's Death who "hath a thousand slayn this pestilence" in *The Pardoner's Tale* (*PardT*, VI.675–82). Vance Smith and Aranye Fradenburg assist with insights into the ways in which trauma leads to historical as well as personal amnesia, forcing responses that negotiate between acknowledgment and suppression, between the need to speak and the denial of events too painful to speak about. What emerged instead was "a literary witness defined less by verisimilitude and directness than by oblique referentiality, linguistic play, and allusive embodiment" (6). Literary responses to trauma, when not marked by silence and inarticulacy, were expressed "in ways that are deferred, submerged, deflected, or unrecognized—in ways that are resistant to transparent narrative representation" (15).

Most persuasive is the opening chapter on *Cleanness* where a string of biblical holocausts are deployed, starting with Noah's Flood and proceeding to the destruction of Sodom and Gomorrah, then Jerusalem, and finally Babylon. These repetitions are themselves symptomatic of trauma. "The poem's three Old Testament exempla produce a pattern of violence, survival, silence, witness, and memory that reiterates, in its compulsive repetition, a key pattern that trauma theorists recognize in survivors, as well as in modern and postmodern literature written out of trauma" (47). Lot's wife, frozen and deprived of emotion and voice, becomes both witness and victim of the catastrophic event, repeating in miniature the Sodomites' sin of disobeying God. Greatly exceeding his scriptural sources, the poet lavished shocking visual details on the carnage of Jerusalem's women and children and the butchery of Babylon's sleeping citizens, all of these passages legible as displaced memories of the physical ravages visited upon English plague victims whom he must have seen dead and dying.

What *Cleanness* left implicit, London, British Library, MS Sloane 965's Latin treatise made explicit by comparing the devastation of the plague to God's punishment for sinfulness in exactly the same biblical instances: Noah's Flood, Sodom and Gomorrah, and Lot's wife (47–48). These Old Testament precedents had become such commonplaces in chronicles and sermons such as those of Thomas Brinton that *Cleanness* may be considered a "plague poem" in which these unspeakable events, never indeed spoken outright, stood powerfully before readers.

The next chapter on *Pearl* proceeds on the dubious assumption that the Pearl-Maiden died of the plague. Whatever her identity or true cause of death, she nonetheless represented singly what England had suffered collectively in the 1361 visitation known as "the mortality of children." Coley demonstrates how a "pestilential lexicon" of *spot*, *clot*, *moul*, *bolnen*, and *bele* infiltrated the dream vision's language to create subliminal unease throughout. The challenging compound *slepyng-slaȝte*—literally "sleeping-slaughter"—becomes a haunting expression for a plague death. Coley makes a telling point that the medicinal flowers and herbs at the poem's beginning, especially ginger, were routinely prescribed for plague victims, and the unexpected August setting, instead of the customary springtime opening, was meaningful because August was the month when outbreaks of the Black Death would usually peak. The dream censors the actual cause of death while softening the intensity of trauma, personal as well as communal, with its visions of a paradisal landscape and its spotless, gorgeously attired dream-figures. Even the 144,000 brides of Christ in the New Jerusalem had an indirect impact: "Such a multitude of heavenly souls, I would suggest, could not help but bring to mind the scores of thousands killed by a disease so virulent the living were not able to bury the dead" (87).

The chapter "Flight and Enclosure in *Patience*" poses the question why Jonah, not Job, was chosen as an example of the Christian virtue, and it answers the question by showing how his reactions to the prospect of the divine extermination of Nineveh paralleled men's typical responses to the arrival of the plague. Flight was one instinctive response, as enacted by the *Decameron*'s young people who flee plague-ravaged Florence for the healthier environs of the countryside. Another reaction was enclosure as a form of self-quarantine from contagion. Jonah begins with a panicky flight overseas toward Tarshish, and then he finds himself in a series of enclosures, first below deck on the ship, then for three days inside the whale, and finally in his woodbine-covered hut. By disobeying a direct command from God to go on a mission, Jonah reenacts the negligence of fourteenth-century priests who would not do their duties of ministering to the plague's sick and dying for fear of catching the disease themselves. Even the random-seeming detail of the hut's window "on þe norþ syde" (line 451) picked up a detail from medical treatises recommending north-facing windows for fresh air to avert infection. These same medical treatises recommended sweet-smelling flowers such as the woodbine also to keep away the plague.

Jonah tries to avoid his own martyrdom in a story that gestures to a contingent universe where extermination is always on the horizon, never present. It is a narrative of anxiety over a proximate future with grisly suffering always on its cusp. If God is angry, his anger can be assuaged by "prophylactic prayer." The destruction of Nineveh is indeed averted when the entire population enacts extreme penance, even the king exchanging his royal robes for a hair-shirt and ashes, paralleling the extreme practices of the Flagellants who appeared in England during the 1349–50 outbreak of plague. The poet again found in the Ninevites a ready-made biblical example invoked by preachers such as Archbishop Sudbury for a sinful population freed by prayer from divine retribution like the pestilence.

Coley works hard at identifying the impact of plague in *Sir Gawain and the Green Knight* and succeeds best when discussing Morgan le Fay as an example of a dowered "plague widow" who had inherited wealth, status, and power in the aftermath of male deaths. Lady Bertilak's campaign of seduction also fits: "female licentiousness was posited as both cause *and* effect of the Black Death" (136). Just as the pestilence would run its course with each cycle finally returning to normalcy, Gawain's visit to Hautdesert, where gendered hierarchies are reversed, comes full circle with his wholesome return to Arthur's male-ruled Camelot. The chapter's argument falters, however, when Gawain's nick in the neck is compared to the emblematic neck pustules on victims of the Black Death, and even the fatal arrow through the neck of St. Sebastian, the patron saint of plague sufferers (151–56).

The concluding chapter searches for other literary cases as well as explanations as to why there were not others as explicit as Lydgate's fifteenth-century "Doctrine for Pestilence." Discussion of *The Book of the Duchess* loses persuasion because based on two assumptions open to challenge—first that Blanche of Lancaster died of the plague (we don't know) and second that John of Gaunt actually commissioned the elegy (it seems unlikely) so that Chaucer needed to proceed with gentle tact by not specifying the gruesome symptoms that killed her.

Unlike Latin and the continental vernaculars, English was a language inadequate for describing the enormity of human losses and their emotional aftermath for survivors. Was the absence "a kind of fourteenth-century English stiff upper lip" (168)? Was it simultaneously the case that writers felt it inappropriate, even vulgar, to describe the plague in Middle English *and* that they were always producing pestilential discourses whether or not they wanted to? If Theodor Adorno was right

that "to write poetry after Auschwitz is barbaric," perhaps for Englishmen who had survived the defining trauma of the fourteenth century,
writing poetry about the Black Death was unbearable.

JOHN M. BOWERS
University of Nevada Las Vegas

SONJA DRIMMER. *The Art of Allusion: Illuminators and the Making of
English Literature, 1403–1476.* Philadelphia: University of Pennsylvania Press, 2018. Pp. 352. 27 color plates, 97 black-and-white
illus. $59.95.

Written with verve and energy, Sonja Drimmer's new book is an excellent contribution to a vital, discipline-wide conversation about the
importance of visual images in late medieval manuscripts. But, as Drimmer argues, very little attention has been paid to the visual apparatus
of manuscripts that transmit late medieval secular English literature.
Art historians have ignored this material for aesthetic reasons, while
literary historians have neglected its distinct contribution to the way
ideas of literature were produced in late medieval England. In filling
this lacuna, Drimmer's study aims to do for the agency of medieval
illuminators what reception studies has done for the agency of the scribe
and the reader, by placing them at the center of a discussion, rather than
its periphery. Drimmer's cleverly constructed chronological boundaries
(1403–76) highlight her distinctive emphasis on the blend of material,
ideological, and literary histories. These seventy-three years—defined
by the founding of the Stationers' Company and the first text printed
by Caxton—bracket the major waves of manuscript production that
"made" Middle English literature in the literal sense, as workshops created the physical objects that would define the incipient tradition.

The book begins with a close reading of an image in a manuscript of
Lydgate's *Fall of Princes* from which Drimmer derives the idea that late
English literary manuscripts construct authorship as part of an "occupa-
tional continuum" (9) that includes commentator, compiler, translator,
and scribe. Illuminators are part of the same "culture of adoption and
adaptation as their scribal and authorial counterparts" (10). Drimmer
offers an abbreviated but effective account of why we need to take what

she calls an "offramp" from the word-and-image approach that has prevailed in medieval studies of visual material. Her chosen term of art, "allusion," has the benefit of immediate recognition, but it also has a long legacy that was superseded by notions of "intertextuality" in literary studies. Literary scholars will have to "un-think" some of this history in order to approach her study on its own terms, defined by her critique of related concepts in art history. In her account, "intervisuality" is too focused on reception and "visual translation" too wed to the notion that the visual image "translates" the word-text. While "allusion" will not likely regain currency in her sense, her introduction defines a balanced approach to the role that illuminators play in responding to higher-order concepts drawn from vernacular literary culture, rather than merely illustrating a text.

Chapter 1, "The Illuminators of London," anchors the study in the material world of fifteenth-century London workshops. Pushing away from the "master craftsman" model of conventional art history, Drimmer's astute reading of the archival records privileges anonymity, collaboration, shared expertise, and improvisation over divisions of labor among bookbinders, illuminators, and scribes. This chapter passes through vexing questions of aesthetics (critiquing scholarly identification of illuminators) and paleography (treating Scribe D, newly controversial in Middle English studies). But it also provides an invaluable synthesis for literary scholars to think about the bustling world of London bookshops, where decentralized and hybrid practices produce a radically contingent manuscript object, rather than a reified aesthetic object.

The contingencies of reproduction, adaptation, and reuse are then applied in the rest of the book to notions of authorship (Part 2) and history (Part 3). In the three chapters on images of Chaucer, Gower, and Lydgate, which will generate the greatest interest among readers of this journal, Drimmer argues that illuminators struggle to invent visual forms to represent the complexity of authorial self-representation in English vernacular writing. Her arguments focus on the diversity of models upon which illuminators drew, but also highlight the material evidence of changes, hesitations, and reworking of images in the physical objects. In her analysis of an image of a seated Chaucer with his hand on his head, for example, she focuses on the scraping, overlaid paint, and a shift in brushwork that reflect indecisions in his understanding of authorship (66–68). This approach shifts the focus from the "meaning" of author-portraits to the "making" of the author by a limner befuddled with his task.

In Chapter 2, "Chaucer's Manicule," Drimmer argues that the paucity of images depicting English authors writing—only one in the entire tradition—"discloses unease with the protean category of the vernacular author" (58), and draws our attention to his "contingent authority" (61). Amid the variety, however, Drimmer identifies the common iconographic thread of Chaucer's manicule, which links images of Chaucer in manuscripts of the *Canterbury Tales* with the famous portrait tradition that derives from Hoccleve's *Regiment of Princes*. This deictic gesture— pointing at text—constructs Chaucer as a reader as much as an author, and sets up her astute reading of Speed's frontispiece to the 1598 edition, in which the hand points back to the authorial self. Drimmer's excursus on Hoccleve's Chaucer portrait as a "surrogate for a chantry tomb" (74) will be of great interest, especially to those who have read Bridget Whearty's recent article on the "construction of community" in and through images of commemoration in fifteenth-century literature (*SAC* 40 [2018]: 331–73).

Chapter 3, "Gower *in Humilitatio*," similarly focuses on the difficulty of visually representing Gower as an author of a multilingual, hybrid text. Noting the range of representations of the author-figure as a youth (aligned with Amans) and an old man (aligned with the biographical Gower), Drimmer argues that the problems illuminators faced derive from an understanding of Gower's authorship as a "negotiable presence" based on "the author's renunciation of his agency" (87). In many of these images, however, she identifies one visual solution: arms crossed over the chest, a simple gesture of humility that alludes to Marian iconography of the Virgin as a model of self-sacrifice. These images cast Amans (and, indirectly, Gower) as a willing confessional subordinate submitting to a higher power.

Chapter 4, "Lydgate *ex Voto*," identifies a strand of iconography drawn from a religious tradition in which a kneeling devotee presents a gift at a votive shrine. The "biographical" Lydgate, in robe and tonsure, appears in fifteen manuscript images, many depicting him on both knees before what we presume to be a patron. Drimmer astutely points out that the category of "author" has been mapped backward onto these images, some of which do not represent him at all, but instead focus on the objects of "devotion" (patron or sponsor). She argues that the images are not about him, but about the "social arrangements that generate literature, guarantee its value, and predicate its reception" (140). These "donation" images thus represent the vernacular author in a sanctifying submission to power.

Focused on single manuscripts, the two case studies of Part 3, "Histories," explore the later cultural consequences of the construction of indeterminate authorial identities, which facilitated the "exploitation" of their literary work by patrons with vested interests in advancing their own cultural agendas. In Chapter 5, "History in the Making: Lydgate's *Troy Book*," the manuscript in question is London, British Library, MS Royal 18 D.II, commissioned by William Herbert and Anne Devereux as a gift for the king. Though the royal gift was unconsummated, the manuscript remained in the Herbert family more than seventy years, where subsequent campaigns added illustrations that emphasized, in Drimmer's reading, the family's proximity to royal power. Drimmer adapts the term "stratigraphy" to mean the analysis of the "layers" of work done on individual manuscripts over time, in multiple phases. In this model, books do not speak to a missing past, but make a claim toward a future reading that can adapt, or "instrumentalize," the book. In Chapter 6, "History's Hall of Mirrors: Gower's *Confessio Amantis*," Drimmer reads New York, Morgan Library, MS M. 126 within the context of Edward IV's obsession with linking kingship to historical discourse. Connecting documents on the reorganization of the king's household (*Liber niger*) with images that depict the fashions of Edward's court, Drimmer demonstrates the way that illuminators selected narrative material from Gower's poem to focus on the values and dangers of kingship.

A short epilogue, "Chaucer's Missing History," provides a nice bit of symmetry in recasting the missing third author from Part 3. But it serves primarily to return us to the question of why Chaucer's *Canterbury Tales* attracted so little narrative illustration, and why Chaucer's work was so resistant to appropriation within the same Yorkist paradigm of history. The chapter concisely rearticulates the central premise of the book: namely, that focusing on the work of illuminators helps develop a more nuanced understanding of literary history.

As with any multidisciplinary study, readers from one field or the other will inevitably challenge singular claims, but no reader will doubt Drimmer's commitment to a fair, judicious treatment of all of the verbo-visual "matter" of the manuscripts that she engages. Middle English scholars will benefit greatly from looking at the images—some familiar, some less so—through Drimmer's eyes, especially when she homes in on the telling details overlooked by literary analysis. As is true of most scholarship in art history, the selection and presentation of images is the core of the argument, so readers will be grateful for the twenty-seven color plates and ninety-seven figures reproduced in the volume.

Her critical practice throughout the book is eclectic and pragmatic, with a strong intellectual apparatus built from major medieval art-historical figures of the last thirty years (Binski, Hamburger, Sandler, Smith) and enough literary theory to sustain an interesting conversation—a soupçon of Kristeva here, an amuse-bouche of Genette there. But Drimmer's training in visual traditions is matched by her commitment to engaging both the literature of late medieval England and its scholarship. Our disciplines need practitioners who assiduously strive not to theorize the primacy of either words or images. Drimmer is to be congratulated for bringing her discipline's insights and methods right into the core of late medieval literary production in a book that will generate ideas for scholars working in a wide range of fields.

ASHBY KINCH
University of Montana

ROBERT EPSTEIN. *Chaucer's Gifts: Exchange and Value in the "Canterbury Tales."* Cardiff: University of Wales Press, 2018. Pp. ix, 249. $140.00 cloth; $55.00 paper.

How much did you pay to read this review? How much time and labor did I spend writing it? Is it a commodity that *Studies in the Age of Chaucer* has put on the marketplace? Or is it an object offered freely for communal use? Is it, in other words, a gift?

Such questions continue to surface in battles between the guardians of copyright and proponents of open access to scholarly work. They have also captured the interest of Chaucerians, for whom the framework of economics and market exchange has offered a useful mode of analysis, as demonstrated by two recent articles, by Kenneth Chong and Matthew W. Irvin, in *SAC* 40 (2018 [217–55, 113–53 respectively]). Yet for Robert Epstein, this emphasis on commodities and markets has occluded other modes of exchange—namely, gifts. In his new *Chaucer's*

Gifts: Exchange and Value in the "Canterbury Tales," Epstein argues that "gifts are substantively different from commodities, and . . . gift exchange operates under its own logic that is distinct from that of commerce and the market" (8). In six efficient chapters, Epstein sketches the hermeneutics of the gift in order to challenge prevailing interpretations of Chaucer. In doing so, he offers up some strong readings of his own.

Epstein begins his argument in Chapter 1 with Chaucer's Plowman (perhaps the most giving of the pilgrims) and Franklin, and also with the theories of Marcel Mauss, whose landmark work *The Gift* set off an anthropological conversation about the social functions of gift exchange. On the one hand, the Plowman and Franklin participate in forms of exchange that feel market-based, through generous acts intended to accrue social capital. Yet, on the other hand, these social gains resist market computation, and their motivations are not explainable through economic self-interest alone. In the end, the character of the Plowman shows that "there are other ways of measuring value and other motivations for exchange than those of the marketplace" (42).

Epstein builds on this foundation in Chapter 2, when he takes up a much less gift-oriented tale, that of the Shipman. In this story, which most readers see as an example of sexual commerce, 100 francs circulate among the three protagonists, only stopping when the merchant's wife has spent them. The tale ends with her offering to compensate her husband for this expense by letting him "score" it on her "taille." I came to this chapter skeptical that a tale about accounting could also be about gifts. Yet as Epstein convincingly demonstrates, the story's initial exchange—the 100 francs the merchant gives to his friend, the monk—most resembles a gift, one given in an open-ended way without fees or interest. And while I am less convinced that the wife and her husband, who "wantownly" (*ShT*, VII.381) play after her loan "repayment," have an enjoyable sex life not reduced to economic terms (59), I have to concede that this moment defies simple accounting. This indeed proves Epstein's larger point: "To reduce all motivations in the tale to economic-minded competition is to obscure Chaucer's achievement and . . . intentions" (66).

In Chapter 3, Epstein pivots to Chaucer's fabliaux, specifically to the Miller's, Reeve's, and Merchant's tales. Here, he pushes back on the axiomatic association of the fabliau genre with market models of exchange. Thus, while *The Miller's Tale* might play with the idea of "quiting," or paying back, this insistence on one-for-one exchange is not by default a market model. Instead, "payback" is more easily understood as a gift, one "defined by a logic that sees the goal of exchange as the generation of social relations and the maintenance of obligations that ensure their continuation" (78). I lack the space to summarize the argument about each of these tales here. But Epstein's reading of *The Reeve's Tale* should give the general sense of his point. As he observes, this story opens with a quest for market equilibrium when two clerks vow to get a fair return for their college's grain. Yet it ends with superfluities not accountable to market logic. Chief among these is Malyne's return of the clerks' stolen flour, now in the form of a cake, which exceeds the compensation the clerks have already taken. This can only be a gift, and, as such, it disrupts the initial goal of a balanced account.

Chapter 4 is best framed by first examining Chapter 5, where Epstein dives deeper into clerical understandings of the marketplace. Using the friar in *The Summoner's Tale* and the Pardoner as his primary focus, he drills into the connections between salvation theology and the economics of the marketplace. These tales depart from a gift economy, and each story satirizes Church corruption. Yet, at the same time, the greedy friar from *The Summoner's Tale* and Chaucer's equally greedy Pardoner expose the ways that the marketplace itself fails to account for its own transactions. Loans accrue interest. Commodities appreciate in price. And in both of these cases, things take on more value without anything being exchanged. In the end, money itself (the goal for the characters in both these tales) has superfluities that the market cannot account for.

Chapter 4 punctuates this extended look at clerical greed. In it, Epstein considers gift giving through the framework of gender and a traffic in women. The chapter focuses primarily on Alisoun of Bath (with the Man of Law's Custance and the Second Nun's St. Cecilia brought in as complementary figures), and it falls into two distinct halves. In the first half, Epstein uses Annette Weiner's critique of Claude Lévi-Strauss to think through the ways that Chaucer complicates exogamous exchange, or what Lévi-Strauss would call a "traffic in women." Using Weiner's interest in the agential power of those traded, he considers Cecilia's self-guarded virginity and the Wife's own ability to sell herself as moments that disrupt male brokering of female bodies. Epstein ultimately finds Weiner's critique unsatisfactory, as it complicates but does not disrupt the core of Lévi-Strauss's claims about the tradability of women's bodies. More satisfying for Epstein (and for me) is Marilyn Strathern's reading of gender as produced *through* exchanges rather than serving as a precondition for them. And when such exchanges are gift exchanges, they become (according to Maussian logic) a means of domination. Applied to *The Wife of Bath's Tale*, this yields a stronger reading for Epstein. By transforming herself into a younger woman, the loathly lady gives herself as a gift to the rapist knight. But now he, as the recipient of the gift, is under obligation to reciprocate.

In the sixth and final chapter, Epstein returns to *The Franklin's Tale*. In doing so, he seeks to recover a tale from a mass of critics who refuse to see the characters' acts as anything more than self-interested market exchanges. As Epstein contends, the story tale invites us to ask a more nuanced question: how do characters who devote themselves to abstract ideals end up in contractual debt, the end of which is money? Whereas a free-market idealist might see this as a natural progression, Epstein (channeling David Graeber) sees this drift into debt as an unnatural byproduct of human development. This makes the story's closing cancellation of debts all that more significant. The culminating liberations from debt become a means for the characters "to envision a way out of ostensibly inescapable social bonds of debt and repayment" (195).

I enjoyed *Chaucer's Gifts* a lot. In a world filled with thousands of readings of the *Canterbury Tales*, Epstein says something new. My only real complaint is that Epstein sometimes overshadows his own readings of Chaucer with his engagement in other debates. Yes, a critic needs to map a landscape before charting their own course through it. Nevertheless, the long accounts of Bourdieu versus Derrida, descriptions of David Graeber's work on debt, and surveys of anthropological debates all felt at times a touch too long. If Epstein had cut these a bit, he could have engaged *even more* with other Chaucerians. In the moments he does this, he offers up smart arguments. Epstein's reading of *The Miller's Tale*, for instance, could have deepened if framed by Mark Miller's examination of this same story's investments in ethics as they connect to personal identity. And I would have loved to see him integrate Carolyn Dinshaw's classic "Eunuch Hermeneutics" into his discussion of the Pardoner.

My smaller quibble is with some details. When talking about *The Franklin's Tale*, for instance, Epstein writes that "it is significant that Aurelius shows [Dorigen] the Breton coastline apparently voided of rocks" (186). But this moment doesn't happen. Aurelius finds Dorigen in a temple; he tells her the coast is clear; and, strangely, she believes him. Luckily, Epstein's reading does not turn on this point. Nonetheless, he could have easily folded this bizarre detail into his analysis. Similarly, in his opening chapter, Epstein claims that the Second Estate is "represented by the Prioress, Second Nun, Monk, Friar, Clerk and Parson, and perhaps the Pardoner and the Summoner" (15). Yet missing from this list are the "preestes thre" who travel with the Prioress. Again, the detail is not crucial. But in a paragraph that offers percentage breakdowns of the pilgrims in each estate, it is good to get the numbers right.

These quibbles do not disrupt the strength of Epstein's larger claims. Gifts *do* come with perplexing features. And if we continue to read Chaucer through the lens of neoliberal self-interest, a lens that turns almost everything into a commodity, we will continue to be short-changed.

JENNY ADAMS
University of Massachusetts Amherst

SUSANNA FEIN AND DAVID RAYBIN, eds. *Chaucer: Visual Approaches*. University Park: Pennsylvania State University Press, 2016. Pp. xxiv, 302. $69.95 cloth; $34.95 paper.

Scholars of Middle English literature have reasons already to be grateful to Susanna Fein and David Raybin, and the splendid co-edited volume reviewed here adds yet another. Initiating collaborative projects, minding gaps in the scholarship of our field, fostering community: their contribution extends well beyond co-editing *Chaucer Review*, the journal whose fiftieth anniversary this handsome book celebrates. *Chaucer: Visual Approaches* offers a wealth of images, fresh ways to think about them, and fruitful exploration of their many implications for reading Chaucer.

The current digitally assisted renaissance in manuscript studies and recent advances, theoretical and practical, in the larger study of the material book have led to deeper and more ambitious investigations into premodern reading practices, an inquiry to which the essays in this volume contribute. Building on an indispensable foundation of earlier research into manuscript production and ownership, scholars have begun to ask more searching questions about what exactly late medieval readers *did* with their texts. How did they read? What imaginative associations did they make between words on a page and the contexts they brought to their reading, including their experience of images? How did aspects of page design condition their responses? Such questions call for the kinds of deeply researched, cross-disciplinary scholarship so generously on offer in this collection.

Part 1, "Ways of Seeing," begins with Ashby Kinch's "Intervisual Texts, Intertextual Images: Chaucer and the Luttrell Psalter." Using the example of two distinguished scholars, a literary critic and an art historian, who draw upon the Luttrell Psalter in studies of lasting value, Kinch argues that each one nevertheless falls short of a methodology in which image and text stand as aesthetic equals. Bringing the two together into a reciprocal relationship in which neither is reduced to "static cultural evidence," "free of mediating context," will require "new reading procedures," including attention to intervisuality, a counterpart of intertextuality, meant to encourage the reading of images with the same awareness of context, mediation, multiple meanings, and other sources of complexity we bring to reading texts such as Chaucer's (4, 12, 20). Kinch's is only one of many ambitious goals to emerge from this volume, and the full reciprocity for which he calls need not govern all visual approaches, but this opening essay sets a laudably high bar for cross-disciplinary work: the editors call it "bracing" (xvii).

Two essays in Part 1, Alexandra Cook's "Creative Memory and Visual Image in Chaucer's *House of Fame*" and Kathryn Vulić's "The Vernon Paternoster Diagram, Medieval Graphic Design, and the *Parson's Tale*," bring consideration of the visual to the project of mapping premodern reading practices. Both explore spatial models, one virtual and one material, for navigating, interpreting, and remembering texts. Cook's essay tracks Chaucer's thematization in *The House of Fame* of the artificial memory system taught by scholars such as John of Garland, showing how Chaucer's poem draws upon the imagined places of memory systems as a means of literary invention as well as a way of recalling the ancient past. Vulić seeks to fill in a lacuna in *The Parson's Tale*, the narrator's deflection of an exposition of the Paternoster to "maistres of theologie," by close-reading a wonderfully intricate diagram that explicates the prayer's contents and theological connections; her aim is to show "how images can facilitate the sort of devotional work the Parson's text advocates" (62). Between the two, Sarah Stanbury's "'*Quy la?*': The Counting-House, the *Shipman's Tale*, and Architectural Interiors" carries forward her groundbreaking work on materiality and domestic spaces in Chaucer, here focused on the counting-house as a relatively new interior space, a choice of setting that offers "a metacommentary on changing spatial and social practices of bourgeois life" (41). A final section reads Chaucer's counting-house against a rich array of contemporary paintings in which architectural cutaways serve to represent interior spaces; Chaucer's text and the selected images serve as equally astute witnesses to the implications of privacy in the development of "bourgeois ethics" (56).

The essays in Part 2, "Chaucerian Imagescapes," successfully model ways of reanimating "specific cultural realms of clustered imagery" that were vivid for Chaucer and his readers and "affected the ways experience was verbalized" but have often now become "much faded or forgotten" (xix). In "Standing under the Cross in the *Pardoner's* and *Shipman's Tales*," Susanna Fein shows how an image deeply familiar to all medieval readers, Christ's suffering on the cross, underlies in unexpected ways two scenes seemingly alien to it, thereby weaving "counter-meanings" into two Chaucerian tales. Laura Kendrick's "Disfigured Drunkenness in Chaucer, Deschamps, and Medieval Visual Culture" brings a fresh and varied collection of images to bear on comparisons of drunken men to apes found in the work of these two poets. Kendrick's close attention to the tone and moral valence implied both by her texts and by her images, ranging from the whimsical to the admonitory, extends to her visual materials the supple shades of meaning that characterize the works of her poets. Owing to its theoretical reach and relevance to medieval "Ways of Seeing," Jessica Brantley's "The *Franklin's Tale* and the Sister Arts" could also belong to Part 1. Beginning with the Franklin's profession of inability to use "colours" of "rethoryk," Brantley gives an admirably concise overview of the position of medieval theories of representation in the history of western art and uses that history to draw out some implications of the still underexplored recognition that "naturalism was not a particular goal of medieval aesthetics": "Far from aspiring to natural resemblance, medieval text-and-image combinations often work to emphasize the artificiality of each sign system and to articulate the distance that lies between them" (141, 143). By approaching the "sister arts" of painting and poetry together and acknowledging the shared constraints and mediations that operate in each, Brantley's essay offers another pathway toward reading text and image with equal nuance. Part 2's final essay, David Raybin's "Miracle Windows and the

Pilgrimage to Canterbury," introduces another significant way in which images in Chaucer studies can transcend the role of instrumental evidence used to support literary arguments. The strong likelihood is that Chaucer knew the brilliantly executed depictions of Thomas Becket's miracles in the stained-glass windows of Canterbury Cathedral—a group of lively narrative sequences that draw figures from all three estates into a larger story of sinning, penitence, healing, and pilgrimage—images so closely allied to the pilgrimage frame in the *Canterbury Tales* that, as Raybin persuasively argues, they rise to the level of a direct source, a role too long reserved for texts alone.

In Part 3, "Chaucer Illustrated," four essays amplify a significant argument that runs through the whole volume: "ways of seeing" actively influence "ways of reading." Joyce Coleman's "Translating Iconography: Gower, *Pearl*, Chaucer, and the *Rose*" explores "how iconography derived from *Roman de la Rose* exemplars was variously reconfigured" in three English manuscripts (177). By adapting this iconography to their own purposes, the producers of these manuscripts "'translated' a prestigious continental conception of authorship into Middle English" (193). Martha Rust's "'Qui bien aime a tarde oblie': Lemmata and Lists in the *Parliament of Fowls*" and Maidie Hilmo's "The Visual Semantics of Ellesmere: Gold, Artifice, and Audience" both use available knowledge about their respective manuscripts' historical readers to demonstrate how other visual features of the page work with text to produce enriched reading experiences, from the simple use of red underlining in manuscripts of *The Parliament* to the spectacular Ellesmere. A fitting end to this carefully crafted volume is Carolyn P. Collette's elegant essay "Drawing Out a Tale: Elisabeth Frink's *Etchings Illustrating Chaucer's 'Canterbury Tales*,'" in which Frink features as a creative and powerfully individual reader who both found and supplied in Chaucer instances of her own visual preoccupations—horses, nude figures, and physically dominant males—thereby "contributing her own imaginative dimension to the *Tales*" (263).

In their preface, the editors express their hope that "this book will deepen the ways that Chaucer's modern-day audience reads, teaches, and studies the poet," an aim this collection will surely fulfill (xv). Those who teach Chaucer's poetry will find new materials with which to introduce students not just to Chaucer's "world," but to medieval ways of seeing that world; scholars of Middle English will find in the book more original thought and more directions for future research than this skeletal account of its contents can capture.

NANCY MASON BRADBURY
Smith College

JAMIE C. FUMO, ed. *Chaucer's "Book of the Duchess": Contexts and Interpretations*. Chaucer Studies 45. Cambridge: D. S. Brewer, 2018. Pp. xi, 239. $99.00 cloth; $24.99 e-book.

This volume extends the spirit of Fumo's earlier book-length monograph, *Making Chaucer's "Book of the Duchess": Textuality and Reception*, by continuing to put pressure on the long-held scholarly view of *The Book of the Duchess* (*BD*) as naïve or under-developed juvenilia, instead attesting to the conceptual and poetic sophistication of Chaucer's first poem in English. In the introduction, Fumo lays out some of the book's main priorities, avowing the volume's commitment to interpretive multiplicity and openness. In addition to offering a range of perspectives from emerging scholars as well as established voices in Chaucer criticism, the essays highlight Chaucer's debt to continental medieval literature along with his English vernacular innovation. In this way, Fumo writes, *BD* "revels" in "paradoxes . . . not least of which is its status as both 'multilingual'—in the sense of playing across multiple linguistically coded registers—and for that, seminally 'English'" (2).

A book so committed to lingering in *BD*'s curiosities and contradictions might well resist definitive structure, as Fumo acknowledges in her introduction. The book's division into two sections is thus provisional and open to "multiple paths of dialogue" (3) among the essays. Part 1, "Books and Bodies," explores the interplay of textual and corporeal bodies in *BD*, including essays on codicological and paleographic questions and problems surrounding the material creation of the poem (Chapter 1), as well as the poem's treatment of the purpose of "fable" (Chapter 2), the "work of sleep" (Chapter 3), and the tensions between inarticulate feeling and voice (Chapter 4). While many of the first part's essays take up a comparative methodology, Part 2, "The Intertextual *Duchess*," takes such intertextuality as its conceptual focus. The essays in this part use the poem's complex web of allusions and afterlives to treat the subjects of literary history and poetic authority. In doing so, these essays touch suggestively on a host of provocative topics, including monuments and memorialization (Chapter 5); age, maturity, and character-formation (Chapter 6); ventriloquism, voice, and identity (Chapter 7); rhetorical *imitatio* and collaborative authorship (Chapter 8); and just what Chaucer was up to with his name lists of classical figures (Chapter 9).

Ardis Butterfield's response to the volume highlights several thematic overlaps connecting the chapters across each section and suggests that all of these threads may be understood in relation to the larger topic of memory, which, she argues, offered not only a technique but also an architecture that helped Chaucer to shape the poem (Chapter 10). In tracing the points of contact among the chapters in this volume, Butterfield identifies the problem and remedy of the narrator's cognitive and emotional "blankness," the poem's thematization and generation of intense emotions, and its emphasis on exploring psychosomatic networks and interplays (200–201). Yet there are numerous other threads that connect these essays, creating a vibrant conceptual fabric that elegantly attests to the sophistication and artistry of Chaucer's early poem. Here, I will tease out several interwoven threads from the volume's warp and woof, though other thematic fibers may also make themselves known.

A number of these essays are fundamentally concerned with *BD*'s metafictions, in particular the ways that the poem offers various forms of what Nicolette Zeeman has called "imaginative literary theory" (a concept cited in several of the essays). The nicely twinned second and third chapters examine how the poem's treatment of poetic and oneiric fiction challenges hard distinctions between idleness and work. In Chapter 2, B. S. W. Barootes shows how *BD* diverges from penitential discourse by distinguishing fables from songs, games, and other forms of entertainment and argues that Chaucer presents reading fables not as idleness, but as an important mode of action in the poem. Like Barootes, Rebecca Davis (Chapter 3) is interested in *BD*'s unusual configurations of work, particularly the ways that sleep is a form of psychosomatic labor and a metafictional trope. Because sleep is a liminal activity that crosses from the realm of the physical into the mental and back again, she argues, it is a productive place to think about the related mind–body phenomenon of writing poetry, at the core of which is "the problem of making manifest, or externalizing, a subjective, interior experience" (59).

Other chapters treat Chaucer's metafictions in relation to literary history and authorship. In Chapter 5, Jeff Espie finds in Ovid's Alcyone's imagined inscription on her own tomb a "potential but unfilled conclusion" (97) from which Chaucer draws an implied analogy between the actual physical monument for Blanche of Lancaster in St. Paul's Cathedral and the Black Knight's poetic monument to White. For Espie, this privileging of potentiality over conclusiveness figures literary history in terms of touch, placing authors adjacently, rather than in linear progression. Espie explores this dynamic in Spenser's *Daphnaïda*, ultimately arguing that Spenser's intertextuality offers an alternative model of literary history outside the patrilinear genealogy favored by other early modern authors. Philip Knox, in Chapter 7, is likewise interested in how Chaucer conceptualizes his place within literary history. Comparing Jean de Meun's inhabitation of the textual body of the dead Guillaume de Lorris with Chaucer's Morpheus reanimating and speaking through the dead body of Ceyx, Knox examines scenes that problematize voice and subjectivity through various figurative forms of ventriloquism. For Knox, the Black Knight's complaint "ruptures the surface of the narrative" and "stands outside it" even as it is presented as a part of that narrative (153). He suggests that this aperture offers an opening through which the historical John of Gaunt's mourning may enter the text in an "act of ventriloquism" through which Chaucer explores questions and problems around speaking for oneself and speaking for another (154).

Questions of voice and authorship inhere in Elizaveta Strakhov's essay in Chapter 8, which balances an interest in metafictionality with another related theme of this volume: the ways that *BD* explores the limits of language, especially in representing ideas and emotions. Strakhov argues that both Chaucer and Machaut dramatize the work of Morpheus (a key figure in many of the essays) to explore the rhetorical concept of *imitatio*. Machaut's treatment posits that exact replication of another poet's work is both possible and desirable because it secures patronage and promises collaborative authorship between poet and patron. Chaucer's idiosyncratic depiction of Morpheus as a "somnambulistic marionette" (170), in Strakhov's wonderful phrase, renounces this perspective, parodying the "the fantasy of perfect understanding between poet and patron" evident in Machaut (160). For Strakhov, Chaucer's *imitatio* "works best when it is self-consciously messy: that is, when it draws attention to its transmutation of sources" (167). This perspective, she notes, acknowledges the impossibility of pure or transparent transmission of meaning through language.

Several other chapters are also sensitive to this emphasis on the limits of language, and two in particular take an additional step to attend to the ways that *BD* probes the power of extra-semantic aspects of language—its poetic texture and sounds—as a means of expression more fitting to the affective fervor at the core of the poem. Marion Wells, in Chapter 4, draws from contemporary affect theory, which distinguishes between affect as a prearticulate feeling or "intensity" and emotion as a feeling that can "attempt to marshal partially conceptualized affective material into symbolic form" (75), tracing tensions in *BD* and its sources between "inarticulate bodily feeling" and "linguistic expressions of grief" (72). Ultimately, she proposes that the poem's poetic repetitions, resonances, and echoes gesture to the ways that the dream "opens up a space in which the body speaks" (82), giving voice to the affective pathways between the narrator and the Black Knight. Similarly, Ardis Butterfield shows how Chaucer repeatedly returns to images of the archive and connects these images with "chains of recollective verbal repetition" (210). In a lovely final gesture, Butterfield notes that one such mnemonic storehouse is a "sound archive" that amplifies an interplay of sound and silence through the course of the narrative, ultimately suggesting that it gives voice to memory and articulates "the sound of feeling" (212) in a way that is consistent with the poem's elegiac project.

This volume has made me aware of the ways that *BD* is, in a fundamental sense, a poem about voice. The perspectives at play in it reframe critical assessments of the youthful voice of a beloved poet and call attention to the other literary voices from Roman Antiquity (Ovid), thirteenth- and fourteenth-century France (Machaut, Jean de Meun) and early modern England (Spenser) that may be read in proximity with it. It is clear that Fumo's commitment to openness and multiplicity is also a commitment to polyvocality of perspectives on and in a poem rich with conceptual, affective, and poetic value. There is surely more work to be done in this vein. The time is right, for example, to attend to the influences of ancient Greek, Persian, and African authors whose medical theories of melancholy may offer us a fuller understanding of cross-cultural and cross-religious approaches to the mind–body questions at the center of the poem. This book can and should awaken a chorus of new voices on Chaucer's early poem and beyond.

ADIN E. LEARS
Virginia Commonwealth University

MATTHEW BOYD GOLDIE. *Scribes of Space: Place in Middle English Literature and Late Medieval Science*. Ithaca: Cornell University Press, 2019. Pp. xiv, 293. $55.00.

A surge of turn-of-the-century publications on the medieval geographical imagination has enriched scholarly understandings of the historical production of space and place. Matthew Boyd Goldie's *Scribes of Space* contributes to the field by arguing for a more concrete and empirical apprehension of spatial awareness than tends to be addressed in previous studies that incline towards the metaphorical or metaphysical. Presented as something of a corrective, Goldie's book is admirably restrained in this way, attending to local, proximate, human-scale geographies in which physical bodies are liable to move, touch, and jostle together. In energetic pursuit of quotidian spatial dimensions, available to ordinarily restricted earthbound observers, he carefully delimits a series of domains in which people could be expected to amble, survey their environs, draw up diagrams, and generally interact. For all that, *Scribes of Space* is an exceptionally spacious study of bounded areas precisely to the extent that it focuses, with acute particularism, on premodern mentalities and material conditions *in* place, yielding insights into several literary landscapes.

Scribes of Space presents four sets of paired chapters, each duo consisting of one more-or-less expository chapter on a scientific concept or controversy followed by another elaborating on its importance to vernacular literature. Goldie's main informants in the first instance range from Ptolemy and Aristotle to Hugh of St. Victor, Nicole Oresme, Thomas Bradwardine, and other Oxford Calculators. As for literary examples, Geoffrey Chaucer's writings are an abiding concern alongside several other familiar works in Middle English, i.e., Lydgate's *Siege of Thebes* (Chapter 2), *The Book of Margery Kempe* and *Mandeville's Travels* (Chapter 4), Robert Henryson's *Orpheus and Eurydice* (Chapter 6), and

The Testament of Cresseid (Chapter 8). This way of proceeding, intercalating compact entries in the history of science and technology with literary case studies, has its advantages: Goldie packs in detailed scientific tutorials for those who may not be familiar with specialist terminology and techniques (including chorography; measuring heights, depths, and breadths; and theories of impetus and propinquity), helpfully contextualizing the matters that follow in the literary-critical parts. A particular strength of *Scribes of Space*, however, lies in refusing to relegate nonliterary elements to "background material." Goldie shows how innovative and imaginative technical, pragmatic, and philosophical modes of expression often could be. Equally, he demonstrates that poetry conducts its own quasi-scientific investigations adjacent to—if not always directly influenced by—the latest theories of the schoolmen. "Middle English literature," Goldie contends, "explores philosophical ideas, but it also supplements the science with its own insights and developments" (151).

The initial two chapters are about what Goldie calls local or estral spaces, as figured in a fascinating series of administrative maps in which areas are "bounded, defined, and emplaced" (55). Here, edges are conspicuous in the depictions of walls, ditches, and roads, among other modest effects. Goldie argues for the primacy of everyday apprehensions of small-scale spaces, and finds support in drawings of Canterbury Cathedral's precincts and surviving maps of Cliffe, Sherwood Forest, Inclesmoor, and Thanet. None of this is very much like the esteemed *mappaemundi* or cosmological diagrams, and that is the point. Goldie's interest is rather in how localities express themselves to themselves, which, because they did not depend on fossilized conventions (and so are "less subject to repetition and a long list of authorities" [25]), disclose more useful, workaday senses of space. The scale and visual coherence of the local map depends, for example, on the veracity and utility of the things it depicts within a given locality. Goldie takes care to distinguish between homogeneous and heterogeneous projections of space, the latter finely evinced in maps that lack symmetry or consistent symbolism but that do convey practical information about how, say, lands or buildings function. But the contrast is subtle and shifting, and *Scribes of Space* is also at pains to show how the two cartographic modes often commingle. What comes through in the end is the assumption of workable or walkable "estral" spaces, ones in which the viewer is implicated and addressed as likely participant. The companion chapter on "local literature" turns to Chaucer's *Prioress's Tale* and then to a portrait of Chaucer's Canterbury pilgrims, namely the celebrated image accompanying Lydgate's *Siege of Thebes* in London, British Library, MS Royal 18 D.II. Assuming that some basic analogies hold among maps, stories, and pictures, *Scribes of Space* presents an extended and nuanced reading of the narrative and visual elements, arguing that the various kinds of representation reveal overlapping and sometimes conflicting spatializations (heterogeneous and homogeneous), situating readers at a crossroads in the history of spatial experience. For mapmakers, storytellers, and illuminators alike, the available resources for delimiting a place were manifold and not always consistent.

The next set of companion chapters explore mechanical and rhetorical underpinnings of commonplace ground-level perspectives, arguing that a "dominant mode of spatial hermeneutics may be called *horizonal*" (77). In contrast to the "overhead perspective" achieved by the likes of Macrobius, Dante, and Chaucer, and unlike the abstract geometrical lines generated by spherical astronomy, the horizonal is a more granular and object-oriented view. Drawing on works of practical geometry, including passages from Chaucer's *Treatise on the Astrolabe*, Goldie covers practical methods for the sighting of quotidian objects. Readers will be grateful for the pellucid explanation of how to calculate heights using the limb and shadow square, but the interesting point Goldie drives at is that observing subjects and objects are emplaced by means of intermediating devices such as astrolabes: a user's body becomes part of the equation. An associated chapter explores *The Book of Margery Kempe* and *Mandeville's Travels*, contending that both works abandon elevated views for the relatively embodied, local, or horizonal. Goldie acknowledges that Margery fails to record many local features of buildings and byways, leaving out details unnecessary to her spiritual journey (in fact she habitually raises places and people to the level of the exemplary and typical), something which sits in tension with any notion that her travels achieve views comparable to that of the above-mentioned instruments. In contrast, *Mandeville's Travels* does deal with astrolabes and describes the abstract hemispheric coordinates and circumnavigable routes of earth. Mandeville revels in the diversity of locales he moves through too, and favors a place-based perceptual experience. The modulation between concretion and abstraction, heterogeneous and homogeneous spatialization, is well evidenced in such cases and helps to suggest that spatial awareness is ordinarily relative to place.

The next half of the book concerns fascinating fourteenth-century developments in natural philosophy, starting with scholastic adaptations of Aristotelian physics. Two chapters explore the way natural place (*proprium locum*) was eclipsed by nonhierarchical conceptualizations of *impetus*, in which the force of a body in motion takes primacy ("now any place becomes as significant as any other" [125]). Oresme's novel graphs of motion show graduated intensities (e.g., acceleration), freeing up observers to consider moving objects apart from destinations alone. *Scribes of Space* brings the physical theory to bear on Chaucer's *House of Fame*, a dream vision in which the narrator "has impetus" without a clear objective. Chaucer may actually have been acquainted with aspects of the new mechanics, but Goldie's account of *The House of Fame* does not depend on direct influence. The idea of an unmotivated but forced narrator is illuminating no matter the wider (or narrower) philosophical context. Another set of paired chapters explore Oresme's notion of *propinquitas*, whereby proximity effects qualitative changes, producing novel and versatile configurations through the intension and remission of forms. Oresme has become something of a precursor to modern affect theory, given that, for him, friendship and hostility are among the phenomena that belong to the study of qualities and motions, but so are geometrical figures, animals, magnets, and so on. That spatial relations are—like physical impetus—somehow communicable helps contextualize what follows in a series of interpretations of Chaucer's *Legend of Good Women*, where volition is subordinate to the spatial arrangements and affectivity. But, again, there is no direct link between the theory and literary practice, as Goldie acknowledges. Other determinants such as popular romance motifs may influence the configurations of literary space (e.g., "Romance is a genre that obviously lends itself to the topic" [191]). If medieval theory and literary practice in these paired chapters are not quite as proximate as the structure of the book suggests, that is because the close readings stand on their merits. Not that the scientific matter in the lead-up chapters amounts to mere propaedeutics, but they can be appreciated apart from one another. An Afterword contains an exhilarating reading of *The Pardoner's Prologue and Tale*, presenting spaces of "ubiquity" and "uniquity." Everywhereness does not have any clear counterpart in contemporary natural philosophy, and that is no obstacle to a fine insight: places proliferate to such a point of extreme spatial

expansion that both medieval and modern notions of space are "contra-
dicted." Isn't the Pardoner a radical precisely for displacing space and
spatial theory?

Scribes of Space is a most welcome contribution to the study of medieval practices of space, articulating a cogent view of emplacement across
various media and modalities. It is also a substantial and rewarding
addition to the ongoing "scientific turn" in medieval literary studies
(exemplified by Kellie Robertson, Alexander Gabrovsky, and Julie
Orlemanski, among many others), expertly navigating medieval physics,
geography, practical geometry, and poetry. Anyone seeking scholarly
views on an eclectic range of evidence will benefit from the book.

J. ALLAN MITCHELL
University of Victoria

CARISSA M. HARRIS. *Obscene Pedagogies: Transgressive Talk and Sexual
Education in Late Medieval Britain*. Ithaca: Cornell University Press,
2018. Pp. xiii, 285. $42.95.

Obscene Pedagogies takes, as part of its subject, the timely question of
obscenity as a tool for teaching, reinforcing, and promoting rape culture
in England from the late fourteenth to early sixteenth centuries. Carissa
M. Harris roots her analysis in a black feminist framework that begins,
in the narrative tradition of critical race studies, with her own awareness
of race-based sexual violence drawn from family history and personal
experiences. Such an introduction serves as a necessary reminder of how,
in ways often dismissed in mainstream academic writing, personal experiences shape our work, and not only offer points of access, but also
represent moments when we take what we learn about the Middle Ages
and use it to see our present, refracted. Harris thus reminds us—
and any advanced undergraduates or graduates who come to this
monograph—how the culturally and temporally distant bears direct relevance today. This relevance is made explicit when Harris writes, "by
understanding how gender intersected with class, youth, and single
status to render certain bodies inordinately vulnerable to violence, we

can better understand how power operates and comprehend the urgent necessity of social change" (7).

The five chapters move from familiar to unfamiliar texts, from the *Canterbury Tales* through Scots flytings to pastourelles and lyric anthologies. These chapters also trace an arc that begins with male writers and characters using obscenity to teach rape culture and educate men about masculine embodiment, and then smoothly transitions to center women's uses of obscenity to articulate subjectivity, consent, peer education, and desire.

Chapter 1 lays the foundation for the volume by developing and discussing the concept of "felawe masculinity." "Felawe masculinity" emerges among homosocial communities of men who treat rape as jokes in ways that craft a pedagogy of sexual violence centered around sexual conquest and storytelling. "Felawe masculinity," in Harris's readings of the Miller's, Reeve's, and Cook's prologues and tales, affords men intimacy with each other through their promotion and enjoyment of rape culture. Harris intersperses her analysis of Chaucer's texts with references to the 2012 trial of Ched Evans, who—like Chaucer's Aleyn and Nicholas and Perkyn—added to his and other's enjoyment of sexual violence by recounting and rehearsing this violence in ways that render it humorous, justified, and normal. Harris concludes the chapter by discussing John's horrified response to Aleyn's plan to "swyve" Malyne in *The Reeve's Tale*, suggesting that John's refusal to play along offers a form of bystander intervention as an alternative perspective for readers to identify with, and describing how early readers of one manuscript of the *Canterbury Tales* censored obscenities and details of sexual assault. By attending both to the creation of "felawe masculinity," its teaching and uses of obscenity, and to moments of resistance, Harris concludes, we can more "fully understand the homosocial underpinnings of sexual education" (66) today and in the Middle Ages.

Chapter 2 explores another way men taught men through the use of obscenity. In the insult battles of Scots flytings, men urge their male peers to avoid women in order to save that energy for creative work. While Chaucer's characters perceive sexual conquest as a necessary aspect of "felawe masculinity," for flyters, "intercourse imperils one's masculinity and bodily sovereignty" (67). This discourse deploys misogynistic cultural traditions in order to represent women as domineering and infectious vectors of impotence, and uses obscenity to promote disgust with women; teach men about sex; and encourage them to, as

Harris puts it, "eschew sexual congress with women in favor of textual congress with other men" (79). Harris contextualizes the role of flytings historically in the court of James V to highlight the role of insult battles in men's instruction. In these ways, flytings furthered systemic misogyny by perpetuating gender inequities and portraying their misogynistic teachings as truths. Harris connects this use of flytings to the work of the Detroit hip-hop artist MC Angel Haze, demonstrating how misogyny can be challenged "to pave the way for more ethical sexual paradigms" (97). This pivot not only offers analysis of the transgressive potential of survivor speech, but also models how medieval and contemporary examples of sexual violence in literature can provoke fruitful conversation.

Chapter 3 directs us to the largely overlooked literary genre of pastourelles, and demonstrates both the workings of systemic misogyny and modes of resistance to its dominant narratives through the voices of women speakers who teach their audiences about rape and consent. In the English and Scots pastourelles discussed here, fictive women educate young women about "how to navigate life as embodied subjects in a world where assault is an ever-present possibility" (106). Harris stresses the diversity of narratives about women's experiences that pastourelles provide, for this diversity "allows readers to see rape not as following a single narrative . . . but rather as a power relationship taking a variety of forms" (109), interrelated through their emphasis on bodily autonomy and the refusal of consent. Such diversity serves as an educative function and a prevention strategy, confirming and challenging rape myths, even as the lyrics shed light on the history of antirape education and survival. Harris invites readers to move the discussion from book to classrooms, from the author's analyses to readers' own, accompanying the main text with an appendix that provides classroom-ready transcriptions, with vocabulary glosses, of the pastourelles discussed here and in the following chapters.

Chapter 4 expands the previous chapter's focus on pastourelles to examine their staging of women's voices engaged in same-sex peer education. They demonstrate, Harris argues, that this pedagogical practice has "the potential to engender changes in sexual culture that are as necessary today as they were in the Middle Ages" (151). A feature of these women's voices is their use of obscenity to center women's pleasure, a feature that, as Harris emphasizes, emerges concurrently with the rise of singlewomen as a legal and social category. Harris's playful prose directs readers' attention to feminine voices that use obscenity to celebrate their own desires and raise the possibility of women's sexual conquests, as when she describes one woman speaker's bragging about her ability to corner the market of virile men, thus refusing other women "their share of the penis pie" (155). This move anticipates the work of hip-hop artists such as Nicki Minaj by 500 years. In the erotics of singlewomen's songs, then, we witness the performance of women countering the abstinence taught in mother–daughter advice texts by laying claim to a bold sexuality. This discourse "enlightens and empowers," serving as an alternative to the curtailment of young women's erotic expression today as in the fifteenth and sixteenth centuries.

Chapter 5 develops the concept of "educative empathy" and shows how lyrics, particularly in their manuscript contexts, produce affective responses that can engender both education and change. Harris argues that, by empathizing with stories of rape survivors and victims of exploitation related in lyrics (especially when staged within the manuscript contexts of courtly lyrics and misogynistic works), scribes, transcribers, and performers, along with medieval and contemporary readers, can experience transformative learning. Harris focuses on Ashmole 176 and the Ritson manuscript, exploring how they outline a "pedagogical model grounded in wantonness, entailing both learning and unlearning about sexuality" (226). The voices of women's resistance contextualized in these manuscripts provoke empathy for their violation and disempowerment, while demanding acknowledgment of their individual subjectivities and intersectional disadvantages.

The conclusion draws neatly together these intertwining threads of contemporary concerns, modern experiences of sexual violence, and medieval modes of obscene pedagogy and misogyny through analysis of Donald Trump's "grab 'em by the pussy" boast. Harris observes that, "Now as in the Middle Ages, obscenity is used by some men to teach their peers how to deny another's sexual subjectivity and how to inflict violence on women and other men" (233). Drawing on the examples of women's voices of resistance discussed in the later chapters, Harris ends with a call to reconsider the possibility of obscenity: not to demean, but to elicit empathy for those who are marginalized and wounded.

This book marks a rare—but, one hopes, not for long—example of scholarship that employs skillful literary and cultural analysis to enlarge understanding of enduring social justice problems. That such scholarship emerges through engagement with the work of black feminists is not incidental, one of several elements in the book that indicate its potential as a model. Harris's work is valuable for her insights about discourses surrounding sexual violence in the late Middle Ages. It is equally valuable for how she teaches her audiences about the diversity of ways sexual violence can be perceived, deployed, taught, experienced, and resisted in the Middle Ages and in the present moment. Harris aims to educate and to create a space for change.

One of the accomplishments of this book is that Harris helps readers see men's use of obscenity to punish and women's use of it to empower, in the vein of not only Trump but also Cardi B today. While some of the most exciting points of the argument leave the reader wanting more, the possibilities that Harris develops in *Obscene Pedagogies* are rich, particularly when placed in conversation with #MeToo, Suzanne M. Edwards's *The Afterlives of Rape in Medieval English Literature*, Kate Manne's *Down Girl: The Logic of Misogyny*, and the work of other intersectional feminists. It is a book that should not be restricted to the shelves of medievalists.

HEATHER E. BLATT
Florida International University

SIMON HOROBIN AND ADITI NAFDE, eds. *Pursuing Middle English Manuscripts and Their Texts: Essays in Honour of Ralph Hanna.* Turnhout: Brepols, 2017. Pp. xxiv, 262. $98.00.

Born Californian, but raised Texan (attested by the accent and turns of phrase he has never relinquished), Ralph Hanna is probably best known as Professor of Palaeography at Oxford, his retirement from which post is the occasion of the volume under review. A worthy and entertaining tribute to Hanna's extraordinary and extraordinarily influential career is made by Vincent Gillespie as the volume opens; this is complemented by a list of Hanna's publications at the end of the volume (but, as Gillespie notes, Hanna is "probably the fastest critical gun in the west" [xii], so the list is already well out of date). Given the ubiquity and influence in Middle English studies of honoree and honorands alike, a review of each essay in this festschrift should, I think, entertain one main question, concerning the utility of the material. In Texas the question might be framed as, "Will these dogs hunt?" Without exception, the answer is affirmative, though perhaps on some occasions the prey was able to get away.

The first of twelve essays, Derek Pearsall's "The Tribulations of Scribes," holds a candle to Titivillus by offering a defense of the fallible scribe. Through Pearsall's relativizing approach, much maligned scribal "improvers" and reorganizers of defective or unfinished exemplars such as the *Canterbury Tales* become avatars of coherence for grateful readers and patrons. Cobblers, patchers, dramatizers, and simplifiers, such as those frequently adduced in the textual tradition of *Piers Plowman*, need also to be recognized as curators of collatable texts in nearly every case, while scribes belabored by supervisory (or authorial) micromanaging, such as some of those working on the *Confessio Amantis*, are redeemed as dedicated negotiators simultaneously of text space, decorative space, and that space conditioned by the presence of Latin.

Continuing with the theme of scribal practice, Linne Mooney's "A Scribe of Lydgate's *Troy Book* and London Book Production in the First Half of the Fifteenth Century" attempts to consolidate and amplify evidence for the output of the individual she calls (following the late A. I. Doyle) the "Selden scribe." Like Pinkhurst, he was one of a cadre of metropolitan copyists who appear to have specialized in certain authors. As yet identified only in highly illuminated manuscripts, he "seems . . . to have been considered *the* scribe to commission to prepare high-quality copies of the *Troy Book* in London in the first decades after Lydgate wrote it, and by patrons who could afford manuscripts of the highest quality" (20). As written, the essay makes it a little difficult to sort through what is actually new information, what is certain, and what is speculative; the nonidentification of the illustrative photographs with the sigils used in the discussion also slows things down, as does a lack of scale for each picture.

It may now be *verboten* to speak of value, of "great" or "classic" texts, and yet the usual suspects often reassert themselves through the sheer force of new insights they can yield. Thorlac Turville-Petre's "The Vocabulary of the Alliterative *Morte Arthure*" presents strong evidence that "the poem . . . reached a wider readership than any alliterative poem apart from *Piers Plowman* and possibly *Siege of Jerusalem*" (44). Well documented already, as Turville-Petre reports, is the wide regional (and temporal) range the poem had traversed as a source for other Middle English texts or as a copy to be owned—from Malory's Warwickshire—

London axis, through East Anglia and Lincolnshire, to Robert Thornton's Yorkshire, to the border country of the *Awntyrs off Arthure*, and into the Scotland of Wyntoun and Hary. The unique elements of the poem's vocabulary presented in the essay add to this sense of range, not just geographically, but in the recondite demands it appears to make on its readership (including in matters of law). The poem's unique "achievements" (61) can thus claim some of their genesis in regions and literary milieux extending well beyond the notional heartland of the Alliterative Revival.

Another important reassessment of a notional heartland—southwest Worcestershire, including the Malverns—is at stake in Simon Horobin's "Langland's Dialect Reconsidered." In 1985, M. L. Samuels recommended that the western dialect forms of MS X of *Piers Plowman* (San Marino, Huntington Library, HM 143, arguably the "best" C-text manuscript) be emulated in subsequent editions of all versions of the poem. For his reassessment, Horobin turns to two important dialectal and recensional witnesses to the B-archetype (Bx), MSS R and L (respectively, Oxford, Bodleian Library, MS Rawlinson Poet. 38, and MS Laud Misc. 581), now both accessible in searchable electronic transcriptions thanks to the *Piers Plowman Electronic Archive*. With the aid of the new and comprehensive datasets, Horobin is able to discern that R and L, although representing different textual groups, share common mixed dialectal features more often than they do exclusively western features. The evidence leads Horobin to suggest that Robert Adams could be on to something in having identified Langland with the priest William de Rokele, who may have started life in the west, but who is known to have lived in Essex, and who, as Adams has postulated, may have developed a mixed dialect even before adulthood, the result of the mobility of his higher social class. There is another possibility, also supported by Adams's research, that connects the Rokeles with the Buttes family of East Anglia. A further implication of Horobin's analysis, which will now need more thought, is the (contesting) authority of a demonstrably western manuscript such as X.

Further adjustment to Samuels's assertions about a linguistic profile is ventured in Anne Hudson's "Observations on the 'Wycliffite Orthography.'" In an article in 1963, and amplified implicitly in the 1986 *Linguistic Atlas of Late Mediaeval English* (*LALME*), Samuels advanced the case for a consistent use in Wycliffite writings of a standard literary language based especially on the central Midland dialects of Northamptonshire, Huntingdonshire, and Bedfordshire. A tendency in Wycliffite studies since then has been to treat the profile as a sectarian credential. Hudson, whose editorial experience with Wycliffite writings is unrivaled, questions both what makes the profile reflect a "standard" and by what means its geography has been discerned. Hudson returns to *LALME* to examine the basis of its manuscript localizations for the counties implicated in Samuels's profile, in particular Huntingtonshire, where most of the Wycliffite material, it turns out, has been allocated by the "fit" technique "in default of other firm evidence for the county" (92). The authority of the data for the other key counties is not much better, and Hudson, leading us toward a major change of paradigm, finds it reasonable to "abandon any attempt to localise to any exclusive geographical area the language/orthography in these Wycliffite manuscripts" (93).

Two studies examine compilation practices. Richard Beadle's "Cambridge University Library, MS Ll.1.18: A Southwell Miscellany" credits the assembly of the manuscript with someone connected to the household of the archbishops of York at Southwell, and working during the colorful tenures of William Booth (1452–64) and his successor, George Neville (1465–76). "Whatever his exact function was," says Beadle, "the compiler of Ll.1.18 seems to have thought it prudent to equip himself with a variety of texts that would act as a guide to fulfilling the expectations of a high-status household" (109). Beadle's study ends with enough new information to make the possibility of naming the compiler that much more likely. One of the two posthumously published essays in this volume, A. I. Doyle's "The Migration of a Fifteenth-Century Miscellany" works its manner of discovery in the opposite direction, starting with a name and moving toward the establishing of a living context. In various catalogues, a Cistercian "commonplace book," Oxford, Bodleian Library, MS Ashmole 750, is associated with John Kyllyng, a monk of Vale Royal in Cheshire. Doyle begins by taking issue with "commonplace" and finds instead "a selection of texts on a limited range of subjects, chiefly grammatical and pastoral, with later insertions and additions of related motivation."

In " 'I Saw a Dead Man Won the Field': The Genesis of *The Battle of Otterburn*," Richard Firth Green hypothesizes the existence of a lost *ur*-ballad from which the surviving poetic accounts of Otterburn descend, some of them late medieval/early modern, and some only recorded from oral recitation around the turn of the eighteenth century (James Hogg, a suspected fabricator, provides much of that record, but Green uncovers evidence to suggest that Hogg indeed had legitimate sources, including his uncle and mother). Having pieced together traces of evidence from a variety of sources, Green provides an outline of the narrative elements he believes the *ur*-ballad is likely to have contained (145–46) before returning to the earliest written versions to demonstrate how individual lines and discrepancies point to a better-integrated source that could have been the *ur*-ballad. Much of Green's reconstruction depends on a rehabilitation of Hogg, whose mother, as quoted on page 154, sounds, alas, suspiciously like an editor. If Green's essay aims to conjecture a whole pieced together from quite disparate parts, Alastair Minnis's "*The Prick of Conscience* and the Imagination of Paradise" makes a case for a state of irresolution in that most ubiquitous of Middle English poems. The first half of the essay takes up the question of how one imagines those aspects of heaven that cannot really be knowable either in this life or even through the resurrected body. Minnis then surveys one of the *Prick*'s known direct sources, *Les peines de purgatorie*, noting that the poet's "clear and straightforward" adaptation expands eightfold when he seeks to explain the seven specific joys of the soul in the *patria*, becoming in the process "less than adroit" (165). Minnis, perhaps over-innocent of mystical tradition, finds that the poem's "awkward transitions . . . are hardly satisfying," and yet "the enthusiasm with which the *Prick* poet presents the imaginations of his 'awen hede' is most appealing, the 'affeccyon' with which he regards them quite infectious" (173).

Andrew Galloway presents us with "Peter of Cornwall's Booktongue and the Invention of London Literature." Peter (1139–1221), an Augustinian canon at Holy Trinity Priory, Aldgate, and prior from 1197 until his death, did not coin a Latin equivalent of "booktongue": that is Galloway's nonce for oral sermons formalized by textual models. Nor did Peter actually invent or discover London literature. What he did do, according to Galloway, was organize and preface his "highly derivative" works (180) in an innovative manner, so as to have "*helped produce* a vibrant early *period* of 'London literature'" (178). The italics are mine: there is slippage of this sort throughout about the claims being made for influence as opposed to those made about derivation and/or experimentation. I do not see sufficient evidence for Peter's being a confirmed influencer in the textual practice of others (as opposed to being a namer of dedicatees, or an employer of teams of scribes, or personally envisioning a wide audience). Better is the account of the organizational and rhetorical techniques Peter adapted and experimented with, giving us a vignette of emerging attempts to improve access to salvific information.

In "The Prologues and Ends of *Piers Plowman* A," Anne Middleton takes on the perennial challenge of resolving the compositional priority of this version of the poem against the lateness of its surviving manuscripts. Middleton parses the "paratextual framing" that various A-manuscripts include at the boundary between Passūs VIII and IX, anticipating the beginning of the third (or "Dowel") vision of the poem. In an important epilogue, Middleton considers the ramifications of her findings for our understanding of the "versioning" of *Piers Plowman*:

> there can be no return to New-Critical accounts of the main surviving states of [the poem's] realization, both temporal and formal, as if these were products simply of the poet's taking further thought . . . His continued compositional efforts register his assessment of what users of his work had (and had not yet) understood of his heterogeneous enterprise. . . . The embodiments of the work made by A-redactors' paratextual supplementations . . . arose *mutatis mutandis* from similar motives . . . . Missing from the A-redactors' efforts, however, was the poet's formal boldness as well as his "skiles" in transmuting satiric anatomy into narrative hypothesis at Vision 3. (223)

Middleton's recent death is all the more to be mourned for the insights she could have contributed as scholarship begins to contend with what she has proposed.

In the final essay, Traugott Lawler proposes new punctuation or glosses for "Three Troublesome Lines in Chaucer's General Prologue." The piece has a my-way-or-the-highway approach that in each case risks suppressing "troublesomeness" that may well be authentic. Thus, while the first proposed change (*GP*, I.10: avoid parentheses, end the previous line with a comma, and gloss "So" as "To such an extent" or "So powerfully") eliminates Lawler's embarrassment over "fatuous" editorial statements about bird-lore, it fails to recognize the tendency of Chaucer's prior avatar-narrators to be fatuous themselves about bird-lore. Another "troublesome" example is the phrase "the space" at I.176; instead of the common glosses "meanwhile," "the course" (so *Riverside*), or "the custom," Lawler suggests "[in the] meantime" or "while he had the opportunity." This adds some humor of opportunism to the hipster-ecclesiast satire of the Monk, but *Riverside* is surely right to note the implied contrast with "streit," two lines above, and thence to suggest also Visser's gloss of "greater liberty"—giving space, as it were, to a Chaucer capable of verbal multivalence working beyond a single line. Another possibility is that Chaucer is contracting, for the sake of rhyme, a phrase he uses elsewhere, "space of lif," well attested in *MED*, with the sense in this context of "for [the span of his] life" (cf., in *Riverside*, *Bo*, V, pr. 6.22, 35, 36).

Perhaps the greatest gift Hanna has made to the field of medieval English studies is his modeling of ways to uncover and understand better not only the works of writers, but also the "narratives" told by their medieval scribes and readers, and then the postmedieval editors, critics, and *their* readers. Learned conjecture, assisted on occasion by rhetorical adventure, is often the trademark of—and focus of objections to—his work, but rarely is it uninteresting, uninformative, or uninspiring; that the book under review follows suit is perhaps the most enduring form of acknowledgment that can be made of the honoree's great gift.

STEPHEN H. A. SHEPHERD
Loyola Marymount University

ELEANOR JOHNSON. *Staging Contemplation: Participatory Theology in Middle English Prose, Verse, and Drama.* Chicago: University of Chicago Press, 2018. Pp. vii, 256. $90.00 cloth; $30.00 paper.

Eleanor Johnson's new study of Middle English contemplative literature (broadly understood) offers a series of exciting case studies in how formal literary effects can create spiritual benefits for readers. Her examples of what she calls "participatory" theology include some texts that one might have expected to find in a study of contemplative reading, such as *The Cloud of Unknowing* and Julian of Norwich's *Revelations*. But they also include texts one might more readily have expected to encounter under the banner of the active life: *Piers Plowman* (a famously *engagé* allegory), as well as such dramatic works as the N-Town *Mary Play*, *Wisdom*, and *Mankind*. In all of these contexts, Johnson is concerned to explore the ways in which contemplative experience is represented and indeed fostered by literary form—including poetic and prosodic patterning, lexical choices, and the explicitly fluent or disfluent deployment of Middle English as a vernacular. Emphasizing participation as the central concept in this theologico-literary vision, she connects the solitary contemplative with the world. She recognizes "a particular capacity in Middle English to initiate the work of divine contemplation" (47), and, even more particularly, she argues that spiritual participation is specially enabled by the forms of the medieval theater.

Other scholars have addressed the relation of contemplation and performance in late medieval literary cultures, but Johnson brings together a new and notably expansive set of examples through which to understand this relation better. As she puts it, "the homologies between plays and other contemplative writings go deeper than established thematic borrowings or citations, extending down to the fine detail of how literary and dramatic form and contemplative theology interpenetrate each other in the transmission of contemplative modes of knowing to a Middle English audience" (192). In a series of brilliant close readings, Johnson amply explores how structures of language and literature can be made to produce contemplative effects. Beginning with the Augustinian idea of participation as a foundation to knowing God, she describes the ways in which literature can create sensory experience, but as cognitive rather than affective—as she explains it, these words create sensations that make us think, rather than feel.

Johnson pushes hard on lexis in the *Cloud of Unknowing*, for example, in order to define the role of the sensory in the literature of spiritual contemplation. Characterizing human access to the divine through such words as *grope* and *blynde*, the *Cloud* emphasizes the role of bodily sensation, but also recognizes it as necessarily compromised. Repetitive monosyllabic prayers such as "love, love, love" or "God, God, God" allow readers to approach an understanding of God's time as "atomic," bringing them close to an experience of eternity, even though they remain time-bound. And Johnson shows how the *Cloud*'s generally atomic prose style is based on the special affordances of Middle English. (It is significant to this argument, for example, that the Latin words for love {*amor*} and God {*deus*} each contain two syllables.) The expression of contemplative temporalities is also central to the "three intersecting prose modalities" Johnson describes in Julian of Norwich, designed to help readers understand Jesus' temporality, his eternity, his perpetuity.

Julian's normative style is "temporal prose," in which she deploys many markers of time, from specific dates (May 8, 1373) to more general indications (today, yesterday, tomorrow). Her "ever ylike" prose emphasizes similitude through patterns of anaphora or repeating clauses such as those that famously repeat "it I am" or "alle shall be welle." Finally, Julian's "continual" prose describes experiences both sudden and lasting, including the homely images for which she is so well known: all of creation as a hazelnut, or drops of Christ's blood as fish scales.

Turning from the structures and rhythms of Middle English prose to alliterative poetry, *Staging Contemplation* makes *Piers Plowman* central to the case for expanding the concept of the contemplative into the world. Langland combines social and sensory modes of gaining knowledge, staging a reader's knowledge of self alongside knowledge of God: to use the language of the poem, Will seeks "kynde knowing" through "craft" in his "cors" (quoted at 78). Formally, the poem endorses these various modes of knowledge through a celebration of analogy and synthesis. Macaronic lines work to make English and Latin comparable, allowing Langland to demonstrate that there is no great or necessary separation between the things of heaven and the things of this world—indeed, the poem's verses represent "social engagement *as* contemplative participation" (76). With her reading of Langland, Johnson turns her attention from prose texts that draw readers into God's time, to poetic texts that value the eternal in human time—opening the way to considering those that were performed on late medieval stages.

Johnson argues that the poetic forms of Middle English drama represent a fulfillment of the participatory impulses seen in earlier contemplative texts. The *Mary Play* from N-Town, for example, uses acrostics, puns, and code-switching among languages to transform Latin and English into one another, linking the eternal and the time-bound. The way in which time is reversed in the movement from *Eva*'s fall toward the angel's redemptive "Ave," and, further, the way in which "Ave" is paired with its English analogue "heyl," provide linguistic commentary on the possibilities of vernacular salvation. The metatheatrical figure of Contemplacio serves to mediate among these temporalities, becoming an exemplar of incarnational power. Johnson also shows how the pageant of *Joseph's Doubt*, by staging a mistaken theology as an object of derision, offers comedy as a potent salvific device. *Wisdom* similarly exploits comedic effects in the play of likeness and unlikeness as indices of moral worth. Elaborate stage directions show that Anima and Wisdom, for example, are alike in clothes, speech, and moral heft. But Lucifer's disfluent English language offers a palpable contrast to them, as well as a temptation. Such formal qualities as rhyme schemes and line length track the changing affiliations between the powers of the soul and either God or Lucifer. *Wisdom* calls its audience into these transformations through participatory moments in which characters on stage comment on figures from unstaged life: a small boy who misbehaves, or "cosyn Jenet N" from the next town over. *Mankind* is the most surprising text to find in a study of Middle English contemplative writings, for the play's ribald and scatological humor is well known. Much of this humor is built on linguistic play between "English latyn" and Latinate English, variously attributed to decorous characters such as Mercy, or indecorous ones such as Mischief. The language calls attention to itself as humorous, but also, as Johnson shows, as a means toward showcasing both an audience's complicity in sin and its path toward redemption. Comedy creates alliances and ruptures in which the audience must recognize itself (even when "surprised by sin"). *Mankind* even dwells on the word "participation" itself, showing the importance of the concept—through comic drama, audiences participate in Middle English contemplative literature, as well as in God's wisdom and mercy.

Throughout *Staging Contemplation*, Johnson presents the kinds of exciting and detailed arguments with which one wants to engage. And, for all the persuasive power of the individual readings, the larger arguments of the book leave some room for discussion. For example, it is notable that in *Wisdom* and *Mankind* linguistic disfluency signals sin, whereas in the earlier texts it heightens attention to God. Perhaps it is worth explaining or exploring this contrast a bit further. It could be, for example, that this difference registers a distinction between more straightforwardly contemplative texts and dramatic adoption of tropes of contemplation. Moreover, slang strikes me not as disfluent, but as *super*fluent—showing not an attention-getting discomfort with language, but rather an attention-getting comfort with it. Also, if French slang heightens attention to Middle English, where does that leave the argument about the role of the vernacular? The complex trilingual environment of late medieval England might suggest, in other words, that it is not vernacularity but multilingualism that produces the contemplative effects Johnson describes. The range of effects possible in a multilingual environment seem to me quite distinct from the kinds of effects that Middle English can offer on its own (e.g., in Julian or in the *Cloud*), and much more interestingly, and deliberately, chosen. Finally, one might question the teleology implied by the argument—as Johnson traces a line from explicitly contemplative prose to boisterous plays arguing that drama is "ever more participatory" (14). For one thing, although the dates of the extant texts of medieval drama are very late, it is not clear that those dates reflect the only performances of those texts, nor the height of their popularity. In this study, *Piers Plowman* inaugurates the kind of social thinking seen in the plays, and yet it is contemporary with or even earlier than Julian's texts. Indeed, *Piers Plowman* is in every way the center of this study, and it even offers the final word: "the life of participatory contemplation and the life of active participation in the social world are and *should be* one life" (195). Although the drama plays a crucial role in staging contemplation, this conclusion as embodied in a Middle English alliterative poem is surely right, and Johnson's dazzling readings of Middle English literature of all sorts reveal the truth of it.

JESSICA BRANTLEY
Yale University

ROBERT J. MEYER-LEE AND CATHERINE SANOK, eds. *The Medieval Literary: Beyond Form*. Cambridge: D. S. Brewer, 2018. Pp. xii, 276. $99.00.

Ever since Kant, an object can only be judged beautiful insofar as it answers to no preconceived concept or interest, insofar as it embodies purposiveness but not a purpose. We might find the smooth surface of a marble statue agreeable to our senses, we might fancy it because it reminds us of a beloved pet, we might value its political message—but it would only be beautiful if, in addition to all these things, we also judged its form to be beautiful. As G. K. Chesterton quipped, the modern artist may use any symbols he wants as long as he doesn't mean anything by them. This modern beauty standard places medievalists in a difficult position. If we are to be competent moderns, we must talk about medieval aesthetic objects as purposeless. But we cannot truly represent those objects without talking about them as having a purpose, such as fostering individual and collective salvation or legitimating the ruling monarch. Indeed, medieval objects may have been considered beautiful insofar as they seemed likely to achieve such purposes. Clearly, it is incumbent upon us to develop ways of talking about medieval aesthetic forms neither as failed attempts to meet modern beauty standards nor as vehicles for transmitting religious or political doctrine.

Robert Meyer-Lee and Catherine Sanok's collection of essays valuably answers this call. They see their project as part of the recent return to formalist approaches within the broader field of literary studies, which in turn seeks to define and justify literary scholarship in the face of increasing institutional and public skepticism. They also make a special claim for the value of studying the deep past, where the inevitable anachronism of modern aesthetic categories becomes not a problem but, borrowing Caroline Levine's term, an "affordance" that encourages medievalists to interrogate both their own historical situatedness and that of their objects of study. Specifically, the postmedieval origin of the category of the literary encourages consideration of the ways it does and does not fit medieval texts. Did medieval readers and writers recognize texts we now think of as literary as belonging to a distinct category of discourse? If so, how did they define that category? What were its boundaries?

While all of the essays in the collection grapple with these fundamental questions, their approaches are otherwise wide-ranging, extending from a traditional concern with poetic form to an interest in the spatialized form of the manuscript page to explorations of the way aestheticized writing informs or is performed by its readers. This eclecticism represents both a strength and a weakness. Given the overall high quality of the essays, it gives readers a valuable sense of the range and dynamism of New Formalism within medieval studies. Cumulatively, the studies cultivate an attention to form and formal possibilities that will likely sharpen readers' close-reading skills across a variety of genres and media. This same intellectual range means, however, that the essays define "form" in so many divergent (and sometimes flatly contradictory) ways that the category risks being emptied of meaning. Relatively few of the essays engage with theoretical conversations about form, either modern or medieval, that would help to establish a common set of coordinates for the collection as a whole. One need not agree with Kant in order to find him helpful as a point of reference; indeed, for medievalists he is likely to be most helpful in revealing, by way of contrast, how medieval objects frustrate or challenge modern aesthetic expectations. The same can be said of medieval discussions of form. For medieval Neoplatonists, a crafted object is beautiful insofar as it participates in the transcendent form of Beauty, understood either as an aspect of God or as contained within the divine mind. In this paradigm, an object's form is located both beyond itself and beyond the material world. Even the most committed medieval Aristotelians followed the Neoplatonists in locating forms in the mind of God, but they also find them within empirical objects, where form functions as a masculine principle of order simultaneously yoked to and contrasted with feminine matter. Form, then, is immanent as well as transcendent. While these paradigms certainly do not represent the full range of medieval thinking about form, they do furnish useful reference points for discussing medieval aesthetic objects.

The perceptive opening essay by Claire Waters addresses Kant explicitly. She argues that although Marian miracle stories are often dismissed as instrumental, they are deeply invested in literary form, and indeed teach their readers to treat the most relentlessly repeated medieval formulae—the Ave Maria and the Paternoster—as aesthetic as well as spiritual objects. In Hoccleve's most famous Marian tale, the protagonist clothes the Virgin Mary in a beautiful garment by reciting the rosary with appreciation for its beauty, implying a Neoplatonic logic of participation. Waters's essay appears alongside contributions by Ingrid Nelson and Jessica Brantley that also focus on instrumental texts but, in contrast to Waters, treat form as immanent rather than transcendent. Both emphasize the materiality of the manuscript page. Nelson examines successive iterations of the Middle English lyric "Erthe toc of erthe" and surviving manuscripts of Walter de Bibbesworth's grammar, while Brantley argues for a greater appreciation of the continuity between literary and nonliterary writing in medieval books of hours. She focuses on hybrid manuscripts where the formulaic genre of the calendar is juxtaposed to, or even bleeds into, poetry elsewhere anthologized as literary, locating literariness in a writer's consciousness of form, often as contrasted with formula.

The middle section of the book includes essays by Kathryn Kerby-Fulton and Andrew Klein, Sarah Elliott Novacich, and Shannon Gayk, all concerned in some way with form as performance. Like Nelson and Brantley, Kerby-Fulton and Klein find the most authoritative expression of form in material books. Examining the *mise-en-page* of the bob in manuscripts of rhymed alliterative verse, they argue that its placement offers readers a choice of possible insertion points in their performance of the text. In doing so, they seek to overturn the implicitly Platonic logic of modern editions of these poems, in which the variety of manuscript formats point toward a single idealized form, in favor of an editorial practice more attuned to the immanence of form. Novacich, in contrast, uses the image of the celestial rose at the end of Dante's *Paradiso* to sketch an implicitly Neoplatonic model of form. She defines literary form as that which gathers around an often transcendent and always unrepresentable center, first in the *Paradiso* and then in *Sir Orfeo*. Gayk traces the jarring shifts in form and register in the Towneley *Shepherds' Plays* as they toggle between angelic performance and the shepherds' bumbling attempts at vernacular imitation. These contrasting performances-within-a-performance are reconciled in the shepherds' final litany, which recalls the vernacular genre of elevation prayers. Implicitly, then, the Incarnation fosters a degree of participation in the divine that was unattainable under the old dispensation.

The final section of *The Medieval Literary* considers the relationship between form and time. Anke Bernau examines *Patience*'s retelling of the story of Jonah, focusing on the way divine power is mediated by ambiguous verbal forms, first in the prophecy itself, then in its translation into English alliterative verse. Following Waters and Brantley, Bernau treats *Patience* as simultaneously beautiful and useful, tracking the ways it encourages readers to identify with the flawed and reluctant prophet. Seeta Chaganti's innovative essay uses dance reenactment and Robert Smithson's earthwork sculpture *Spiral Jetty* to explore the shifting lines of sight in the dancing scenes in Chaucer's *Franklin's Tale*. She sees these shifts as offering a respite from the ineluctable logic of cause and effect that otherwise dominates the tale's narration. Maura Nolan productively juxtaposes not only the medieval and the modern but also the concrete and the universal by reading Nicole Eisenman's 2007 *Portrait of a Guy Smoking* against the c. 1350 portrait of Jean le Bon and Chaucer's verbal portrait of Criseyde in the *Troilus*, arguing that each of these images points *both* to an individual *and* to one or more human types. As a result, categories such as personality and subjectivity—or even, as Harold Bloom once claimed, the human—come into being not at a specific historical moment but rather over and over again, through the dialectical opposition of type and individual. Finally, Emily Steiner returns to earlier contributors' concern with the immanent form of the manuscript book from a new angle, with a study of the early fourteenth-century book-collector Richard de Bury. She highlights the violence of his collecting, which wrested books from their traditional environments in an effort to produce literary history.

In exploring the ways medieval literary writing challenges our modern, primarily Kantian understanding of beauty, these collected essays promise to make us more sensitive readers of medieval aesthetic forms.

KATHARINE BREEN
Northwestern University

SHAWN NORMANDIN. *Chaucerian Ecopoetics: Deconstructing Anthropocentrism in the "Canterbury Tales."* New York: Palgrave Macmillan, 2018. Pp. x, 226. $84.99.

Chaucer is often the subject of ecocritical analysis in articles, essays, and book chapters, but rarely are whole monographs devoted solely to eco-readings of his works. Shawn Normandin's *Chaucerian Ecopoetics* is, then, a welcome new study affording sustained analyses of the *Canterbury Tales* over the course of six chapters, but doing so through the unexpected lens of deconstruction. Ecocriticism seeks to examine, in Glenn Love's words, the ways in which "the enveloping natural world is a part of the subject on the printed page before us," or at least how it "remains as a given, a part of the interpretive context." Green readings of medieval literature expose the anthropocentric focus of their objects of study and call into question simplified hierarchies of the living within an expanded, nonhuman frame of landscapes, flora, and fauna. Normandin takes seriously Jonathan Bate's argument that "ecocriticism should do more than provide ideology critiques" (18) and, like Bate, he turns to Paul de Man, who shows that language must mediate literary representations of nature and that this mediation perpetuates a gap between "the mind that distinguishes, negates, legislates, and the originary simplicity of the natural." The result of this approach is a series of vigorous and lively readings that unapologetically embrace Chaucer's anthropocentrism while, at the same time, illustrating the manner in which the poet's use of rhetoric and literary form "demystifies the vanity, paranoia, and bad faith attendant on the pretense that humans are ontologically superior to or radically different from other lifeforms" (6).

Chapter 1 introduces the book's methodology and quickly exchanges *anthropocentrism* for *anthropotropism*, a term typically used by theologians to describe narratives of God's turning to humanity. In their attacks on anthropocentrism, ecocritics unwittingly reaffirm humanity's singular ability to critique itself and to solve the very environmental crises for which it is responsible. An attention to anthropotropism, instead, befits Normandin's formalist approach, highlighting moments in the *Canterbury Tales* when the narrative shifts focus from nonhuman to exclusively human interests—such as when, in *The Pardoner's Tale*, the three rioters stop seeking Death (plague) and redirect their animosity at one another. But this anthropotropic lens also illustrates how Chaucer's perceived anthropocentrism "undercuts [the human's] conceptual coherence and compromises its aesthetic appeal" (10). Normandin's reading stems, in part, from de Man's own ecopoetics, which foregrounds not the interdependence and entanglement of all life but, rather, an "apartness" from ourselves and other forms of life that every living thing shares in the world (20). Chaucer's ecopoetics within the *Canterbury Tales*, with its "vivid mimesis and linguistic intricacy," constitutes ripe ground for analyzing "literature's divergent capacities for connection and withdrawal" (24).

Chapter 2 foregrounds *The Knight's Tale*'s literary language as a means for interaction *and* incongruence between nature and culture. The narrative's reconciliation of noble design and chaos never overcomes an implicit ecophobia evident in the extravagant destructions of the forest grove for Theseus's war-arena and Arcite's funeral pyre or, subtler, in the macabre imagery of Mars's temple. *The Knight's Tale*'s *ekphrasis* of the murals within this temple, including the frightening darkness of the Thracian forest, works ironically to emphasize and expose the constructed nature of these images, that they are "peynted" (*KnT*, I.1975). Ekphrasis, further, confounds the narrative's thrust through its very form—a diachronic series of sentences constituting the description of a synchronic image. Time is out of joint in *The Knight's Tale*, a fact illuminated also by the Knight's oft-cited *occupatio* (Normandin, instead, prefers *praeteritio*) in which he catalogues fourteenth-century English species of trees (I.2919–24), which affords narrative dissonance within the ancient Greek setting. This dissonance abounds in the tale's conclusion, in Theseus's proclamation of the First Mover's (Jupiter's) dominance despite our having just read how Saturn—the very form of chaos deified—governs the entirety of the narrative's climactic battle. And while the Knight's moral, "To maken vertu of necessitee" (I.3042), and the tale's structural chiasmus—from Ypolita's marriage to Creon's funeral, from Arcite's funeral to Emelye's marriage—jibe with Boethius's circular metaphysics, the many chaotic circles that emerge along the way, including Theseus's theater and the proliferation of "O"s in the duke's speech ("I rede that we make of sorwes two / O parfit joye, lastynge everemo" [I.3071–72]), undermine the story's overall Boethian logic.

Chapter 3 suggests that while *The Miller's Tale* betrays a biophilic impulse, its ultimate concern is metaphor. The Miller's fabliau, with its materialist ethic, illustrates the embeddedness of humans within nature. But the tale's naturalism is enabled only by its use of metaphor, which signals humanity's embeddedness, also, in language. Alisoun is *like* a caged animal, John is *like* Noah, and Nicholas's fart is *like* a biblical thunderclap. But metaphoric thinking in *The Miller's Tale* overwhelms its subjects; indeed, it equates to "dangerous knowledge" (88), a prying into the "privetee" of God and men, whether that is Nicholas's astrologic learning or Absolon's adulterous equation of Alisoun as his "sweete synamome" (*MilT*, I.3699). Ironically, the perils of such thinking in *The Miller's Tale* prove profoundly material for the human bodies burned and broken in its wake. Absolon's humiliation speaks most to the narrative's linguistic crux. We as readers have no idea which of Alisoun's "hole[s]" (I.3732) Absolon kisses, and this is no textual slippage. *The Miller's Tale* demands that we respect the limits of knowledge and, thus, the tale "imposes this respect on readers, who can only know what the tale lets them know" (92). But the Miller hedges. Theseus's failed circular logic and *The Knight's Tale* proliferation of "O"s reemerge in the ambiguous "nether ye" (*MilT*, I.3852) of the Miller's conclusion, reinvoking the very inquisitiveness the tale condemns. Human desire drives metaphoric thinking in *The Miller's Tale*, but in *The Reeve's Tale* nonhuman nature repeatedly preys upon the metaphorical tendencies of characters through its own "involuntary deceptiveness" (106). The black night, for example, pervades Symkyn's bedroom and enables the tale's climactic comedy of errors. As Normandin claims, "The contingencies of the material world always exceed the calculations of individual humans" (105). Language may be a vehicle through which humanity champions its Cartesian superiority to the nonhuman, but language also exposes humans to nature. The quitting game in Fragment I thus shows that the connection of humans with nature is in "the shared capacity of both human nature and the nonhuman world to produce false resemblances" (87).

In Chapter 4, Dorigen's ecophobic fear of "rokkes blakke" (*FranT*, V.859)—drives action in *The Franklin's Tale*, yet the story's primary concerns with marriage and promises revolve around the legitimacy of language. If the tale's emphasis on literalism aims to stabilize intention and meaning in language, then Normandin shows how "geological distress lapses into the pitfalls of performative utterance" (126). Ironically, as Dorigen and Aurelius seek human answers to nature's threat, the "inhumanity of language" itself is revealed (134). Dorigen's repeated responses to Aurelius's proposal, much like the Miller's metaphoric thinking, foreground the dangers of taking for granted language's play. The "iterability" of Dorigen's speech acts, to use Derrida's term, foregrounds language's disregard for human intention, undercutting the story's anthropocentric turn. Similarly, in Chapter 5, *The Physician's Tale* subordinates human concerns for justice to its own narrative survival. The tale begins by personifying Nature as the generative force of human excellence (Virginia). Yet the very terms of Virginia's allegorical perfection—her beauty and her virginity—provoke the shocking injustices that lead to her perplexing demise. As the Host declares, "Hire beautee was hire deth" (*PhyT*, VI.297). Virginia's allegorization, then, runs aground in the face of the tale's historiographic impulse—the slander orchestrated by the judge Apius, who is "knowen for *historial* thyng notable" (VI.156, my emphasis) and her father, the Roman *pater* who asserts his historical, legal right to filicide. Virginius undermines Virginia's martyrdom by precluding her confrontation with her persecutors; at the same time, he destroys the beautiful body Nature created in order to preserve her *natural* virginity. In other words, he "divides appearance from idea" (158). If Virginius aims to keep slander about his daughter at bay through her ritual killing, then the tale's great irony is that "[t]he story of her death is the only way to combat the slander" (169).

Memory confounds the aesthetics of *The Physician's Tale*, but Chapter 6 explains how *The Monk's Tale* ritualizes *ars memorie*. The Monk's serial tragedies do not willingly lend themselves to ecocritical reading, yet the episode of King Nabugodonosor (*MkT*, VII.2143–82) affords a path to understanding the tale's complicated juxtaposition of anthropocentrism and the "inhumanity of language." In his bovine turn, Nabugodonosor "eet hey as an oxe" (VII.2172), and so metaphorizes the chief ethical task of monastic reading: rumination, that is, "chewing," on words. To appreciate *The Monk's Tale*, which few critics have done, we must read like monks; at the same time, *ruminatio* does not lead necessarily to understanding. As Normandin explains, "In its linguistic acts (repetition of prayers, rumination on texts), monasticism struggles with the worldliness of the human languages it inherits" (193). The sheer number of figures volleyed about in the narrative and the abrupt shifts from one awful story to the next help the Monk "communicate tragic experience—misery undiluted by the comfort of understanding" (195).

With its deconstructive approach, *Chaucerian Ecopoetics* expands otherwise narrow ecocritical and object-oriented interpretations of medieval literature. If, in *The Franklin's Tale*, we desire a "lithic agency" from the ominous Breton rocks, we are reminded instead that rocks and humans share a "vulnerability to inscription" (142). Given the novel interpretive strategy of this book, we might expect Normandin to engage more directly and consistently with extant deconstructive readings of Chaucer. While he references the work of critics such as James Paxson, H. Marshall Leicester, and Peter Travis, a brief chapter of conclusion, which is curiously absent from this book, might have framed its arguments within Chaucerian deconstruction as a supplement to its ecocritical intervention. But this does not detract from a study whose rich analyses reward the attentive reader with compelling new perspectives on the *Canterbury Tales*. *Chaucerian Ecopoetics* is a significant work that unapologetically qualifies the sentimentality of ecocriticism's assaults on anthropocentric narratives—that is, the positive conclusion that both the human and nonhuman are entangled in an ecological web of interdependence—with de Manian scrutiny that demonstrates the ironic product of shared vulnerability: "apartness."

JOSEPH TAYLOR
University of Alabama in Huntsville

THOMAS A. PRENDERGAST AND JESSICA ROSENFELD, eds. *Chaucer and the Subversion of Form*. Cambridge: Cambridge University Press, 2018. Pp. ix, 224. $99.99.

At least since E. Talbot Donaldson's "Chaucer the Pilgrim," the image of Chaucer most familiar to scholars has been that of a poet whose task is "to build" from "incongruous and inharmonious parts" an "inseparable whole which is infinitely greater than its parts" (*Speaking of Chaucer*, 11–12). This Chaucer is a master of speech-modes, literary character, and narrative emplotment, and he uses every one of his formal tricks to produce a series of convincing verbal portraits of medieval life as it was lived. This collection of essays revisits Donaldson's New Critical approach to Chaucer, but turns the approach on its head. Where Donaldson and his many followers saw formal unity in the poet's works—or at least, in the Chaucer they knew and loved best—the essays in Rosenfeld and Prendergast's collection focus instead, as their editors put it, "on the failures of form: the resistance to poetic terminology, to formal consolation, to formal interpretation, beauty, and even to literariness itself" (9). For these writers, Chaucer is a poet not of mastery, but of subversion—a poet who sees form as a "site of challenge" (3), as an opportunity to defy, rather than fulfill, the reader's expectations of unity, congruency, and order. With this orientation, *Chaucer and the Subversion of Form* joins Robert Meyer-Lee and Catherine Sanok's recent *The Medieval Literary: Beyond Form* in pushing back against the focus on congruent and harmonious forms in earlier New Formalist criticism. Five years ago, formally minded medievalists looked for the outlines of a well-wrought urn in the literature they studied. In these essays, when they read for form, they look for the ordered chaos of a Rauschenberg combine—for a combination, as Prendergast and Rosenfeld put it, of "formal ambitiousness and inchoateness" that "situate the work in its specific cultural context and yet allow it to reach beyond" (6).

The chapters in this volume are divided into three groups of three. The first group, "The Failures of Form," reads Chaucer's forms against the literary techniques and philosophical ideas that these forms suggest but do not endorse. Jenni Nuttall's fine essay "Many a Lay and Many a Thing" argues that the poet's invocations of technical terms for poetry—including "lenvoy," "songe," "dytee," "ryme," "cadence," "compleynt," "lay," and "ballade"—are metacritical sites where he "pose[s] questions to himself and his readers" (22) about the activity and intentions of his verse. Ultimately, Nuttall suggests that Chaucer uses these terms not to identify the forms his poetry employs, but to signal just how much his forms differ from, and even resist, the norms of the poetry of his time. In "Chaucer's Aesthetic Resources," Jennifer Jahner explores the role that literary form has in trying, and invariably failing, to bridge the gap between the forms of things *an sich* and the embodiment of these forms in the particulars that we perceive. Focusing on Cambridge University Library, MS Ii.III.21—which joins a Latin copy of Boethius's *Consolation*, the *Boece*, and "The Former Age" and "Fortune" together—Jahner argues that, in contrast to Boethius and, later, Kant, Chaucer does not believe that, by grasping form, we can apprehend universal things. Instead, like Adorno, Chaucer demonstrates that our attempts to grasp form are invariably conditioned by history, and so any attempt to perceive form will be imperfect and full of "longing and uncertainty" (53). In the last essay of this cluster, Eleanor Johnson also argues that Chaucer rejects the idea that poetry is a window onto things as they really are. Her chapter, "Against Order," argues that literature, both medieval and modern, "challenge[s] the idea that linear causality is a stable hermeneutic" (61); moreover, criticism that "fetishiz[es] causality" (62) actually occludes the complex relationship that exists between people and events in literature. Johnson tests this thesis against three texts, Chaucer's *House of Fame*, Virginia Woolf's *To the Lighthouse*, and Lyn Hejinian's *My Life*—all of them dream visions that, in her account, advocate for a mode of associational knowing that allows feelings, experiential knowledge, and subject-position to inflect causal logic.

The second group of essays, "The Corporeality of Form," considers Chaucer's techniques for representing, and mediating, physical matter—here, the stuff of bodies, stars, and corpses. With "Diverging Forms," Jonathan Hsy brings the hermeneutic resources of contemporary disability studies to bear on *The Monk's Tale*, which, in Hsy's view, employs a stanzaic form that is sometimes "dysfunctional" (88), sometimes orderly. In this sense, the forms of *The Monk's Tale* respond to the stories of disability that the Monk tells: like his blinded, mad, and paralyzed subjects, these forms "test the perceived limits of human shape and potential" (87). Lisa Cooper's inventive essay "Figures for 'Gretter Knowing'" offers a literary reading of the *Treatise on the Astrolabe*. Organized according to Caroline Levine's four models of form, Cooper's chapter suggests that both the astrolabe and Chaucer's *Treatise* are tools for perceiving form in the world around us: networks of stars, rhythms of celestial movement, hierarchies of space, and—if only imperfectly—the whole cosmos of which we are a part. But our ability to perceive these forms depends, as Cooper stresses, on our position in relation to it—and so form itself is a relational thing, subject not merely to perspective (in both a literary and an astronomical sense) but to the matter that conditions its apprehension. Julie Orlemanski returns to the matter of the body in her excellent essay "The Heaviness of Prosopopoeial Form in Chaucer's *Book of the Duchess*." Here, Orlemanski explores the paradoxical idea that form, which is by definition distinct from matter, might itself possess a physical quality per se, such as "heaviness." Her test case is the Ceyx-and-Alcyone episode from *The Book of the Duchess*, where—in contrast to what one finds in Chaucer's sources—Morpheus speaks not as an impersonation of Ceyx, but from within Ceyx's reanimated corpse itself. For Orlemanski, Ceyx's corpse becomes an occasion to consider both the problem of literary ontology—the sorts of being, or non-being, that literary representations might have—and the concomitant problem of speaking for the dead. What sort of being, she asks, may Ceyx's corpse be said to possess while Morpheus speaks from within it, and, by extension, what sort of being do representations of the dead possess when a person, character, or poet tries to speak for them?

The third and final group of essays, "The Forms of Reception," asks how our understanding of Chaucer's poetry shifts when we focus on how it is, has been, and will be read. Thomas Prendergast starts the group off strongly with "Reading Badly," a persuasive account of *The Physician's Tale*. Here, Chaucer's Physician is presented as a bad reader, one who reads the figure of Virginia in a series of incompatible ways: sometimes spiritually (as a tropological exemplification of virtue), sometimes carnally (as a beautiful young woman who excites Apius's desire), and sometimes typologically (as an echo of Jephthah's daughter). None of these readings is fully satisfying, and so the tale as a whole is best understood as "a meditation" on the consequences of "bad reading" (154): the forms of beauty, when misread, can lead the reader into ethical error and even open up the author to accusations of error himself. Arthur Bahr's provocative essay "Birdsong, Love, and the House of Lancaster" asks whether knowing more about a manuscript circumscribes its aesthetic possibilities—or, as he puts it, whether "knowledge of a manuscript's patron or circumstances of production, for example, close[s] off and thus subvert[s] its potentialities as an aesthetic form" (165). His case study is Gower's Trentham manuscript, British Library, Add. MS 59495. We know a lot about Trentham: it contains Gower's hand, was composed at the tail-end of the poet's career, and was addressed (and likely presented) to Henry IV. But all of this knowledge does not suppress the open-ended literary possibilities suggested by the manuscript's forms—in particular, its use of bird imagery and Chaucerian echoes—

and so Trentham is far more than the "straightforward program of political praise" (173) that scholars have often taken it to be. Stephanie Trigg's concluding chapter, "Opening *The Canterbury Tales*," explores the many ways that Chaucer's *General Prologue* has "begun" the *Tales*, both in the past and in the present, and it also serves as a response to the volume as a whole. Trigg observes that, because of its historical, social, and pedagogical importance, the *Prologue* and the *Tales* must be understood in relation to their long editorial history. By attending to this tradition, we can better grasp how different critical impulses have produced the "Chaucer" that we teach in our classes: a historicist fidelity to manuscripts and context, on the one hand, and a formalist desire for a unified literary object, on the other.

As a whole, the essays in *Chaucer and the Subversion of Form* impress—and more important than that, they seem to want something else, something *new*, from Chaucer studies. But I did have two questions about the volume. The first concerns the editors' stated commitment to "a developing medievalist 'new formalism' that is both avowedly historicist and committed to rethinking the relationship between form and history" (3). In practice, this seems to mean relying upon philosophy and literary theory as the primary ancillary discourses for literary criticism, while also inflecting one's philosophical and theoretical tools with some historically minded skepticism. Such a reorientation of critical methods is very welcome. But one does wonder if all philosophy and theory is equally committed to an "avowedly historicist" practice, and what, in any event, the proper hermeneutic stakes—politically, epistemologically, aesthetically—for a medieval new formalism might be. The second question concerns the *via negativa* approach taken by most of the essays in this volume, which sometimes rely upon straw men or prosecute arguments with perhaps too much force. Certainly, Chaucer is sometimes a poet who embraces formal subversion—but on the other hand, what about his anger toward careless scribes in "Adam Scriveyn," or his anxiety about language change in *Troilus*? Certainly, not all literary discourse can be "flatten[ed]" into merely "historical discourse"—but if this is true, why is it any less "flattening" for medieval new formalists to do the opposite, by distinguishing "the particularity of *literary* form" from history (6–7)?

Such small quibbles aside, this collection will be warmly received by scholars working on Chaucer, medieval conceptions of form and the literary, and—perhaps especially—the intersection of medieval philosophy and literature. Medievalists interested in the state of New Formalist criticism at present will also want a copy of this handsome volume, as will those curious about how far a formally oriented medieval studies might take us in the future.

TAYLOR COWDERY
University of North Carolina—Chapel Hill

THOMAS A. PRENDERGAST AND STEPHANIE TRIGG. *Affective Medievalism: Love, Abjection and Discontent*. Manchester: Manchester University Press, 2019. Pp. viii, 154. $120.00.

When I took my two teenagers on their first trip to London many years ago, I had expected them to weep with amazement and appreciation. Instead, when I exclaimed, "Isn't this wonderful!," they yawned and mumbled something about it being like home, New Haven, but without the good pizza. Because their first experience of medieval architecture had been Yale University's dense collection of Gothic buildings, an amalgamation that can feel more medieval than modern London's scattered traces of the Middle Ages, America's university Gothic sufficed as a way for them to touch the medieval past. In their way, my teens were anticipating the arguments that Thomas Prendergast and Stephanie Trigg make more eloquently and thoughtfully in their latest collaboration, *Affective Medievalism: Love, Abjection and Discontent*.

It is not a novelty to argue that medieval studies and medievalism, which both look to the past through a glass darkly, make similar moves to bring the premodern past to the present—or return the present to the premodern past. Nor is it news that neither practice is able to reach absolute knowledge of the past (though "professional" medieval studies often pretends it can and faults "amateur" medievalism for failing to make a good-faith effort toward that perfect recuperation). In fact, a persistent habit of medieval studies (as David Matthews has shown) has been to relabel its outmoded and rejected formulations and practices as "medievalism." Prendergast and Trigg push these lines of thinking to make two intertwining arguments. First, medieval studies should admit to medievalism's proleptic priority and recognize the layers of medievalism that form the pretext to our understanding of the medieval past. Second, medievalism's responses to the Middle Ages frequently copy the ways medieval texts responded to their past. In this way, medievalism recovers medieval moves for interpreting or responding to the past, moves frequently shunned by postmedieval readers. The authors' two interlacing arguments ask us to stop seeing the intermediary layers of medievalism as the abject needing to be peeled away in order to reach the kernel of medieval authenticity. Instead, they argue, we should recognize the legitimacy of some of medievalism's tactics because medieval texts themselves repeatedly anticipate and model medievalism's *affective* practices. Building primarily and most explicitly on the conversations generated by Jeffrey Jerome Cohen, Carolyn Dinshaw, Aranye Fradenburg, Patricia Ingham, David Matthews, James Simpson, D. Vance Smith, Paul Strohm, David Wallace, and Nicholas Watson, *Affective Medievalism* works to reorient medieval studies' understanding of medievalism by relegitimizing affect as a mode for knowing the past. As they demonstrate, affect, the response rigorously shunned by professional medievalists, is a way of knowing common both to the medieval past and to medievalism.

In their project to legitimize affect in medieval studies, Prendergast and Trigg examine the dialectic between the medieval past and subsequent representations of that past. Their considerations weave a densely learned tapestry; however, for the purposes of this review, I will follow one strand: what the medieval texts have to tell us (and what medievalism seems already to know) about reading, interpreting, and loving the medieval past.

Prendergast and Trigg begin by considering the ways that postmedieval recreations of the Middle Ages have allowed us to think about the medieval past as a place and time isolated and absolutely prior to the present, a conceptualization that ignores how "temporal flexibility" was an essential aspect of medieval thought (32). Because Christian exegetics conceived an anagogical relationship between the past, the present, and the future, medieval Christians were adept at sensing the presence of other temporalities. Unlike some postmedieval readers who see this temporal flexibility as a "conceptual weakness," Prendergast and Trigg suggest it "consistently demonstrates an awareness . . . that temporalities are layers, over-lapping, and porous" (32). Most of all, this temporal flexibility, they argue, demonstrates that the Middle Ages did not view time as static and impervious to change. The authors see this temporal logic in three texts tying Christianity's universal salvific history to England's local political history: Gildas's *De excidio et conquestu Britanniae* (sixth century), *Sir Orfeo* (fourteenth century), and *Saint Erkenwald* (fourteenth century). All three hold different temporalities in creative tension with one another, imagining not merely how the present can impose meaning on the past but how the past can speak to the present. This flexibility sits in contrast to the "ontological stability and priority of the Middle Ages" frequently depicted in modern medievalisms, where the Middle Ages were a time and space that we postmedievals can try to understand, but that can never understand us. This fixed relationship is the enabling fiction of both traditional medieval studies and imaginative medievalism, as seen in early examples of "portal medievalism" (29) such as William Morris's *A Dream of John Ball* (1888) and *News from Nowhere* (1890), as well as Mark Twain's *A Connecticut Yankee in King Arthur's Court* (1889). Framed by the entry into (and out of) the medieval past, these fictions present time travel as a mode of understanding available only to moderns, a mode analogous to the medieval scholar's work. In both cases—medieval studies and medievalism—devotees ignore that "temporal flexibility" was an essential aspect of medieval thought.

To understand how medieval texts also prefigure medievalism's complex sense of abjection and wonder, Prendergast and Trigg's point of departure is the relic. Because medieval Christians recognized the difficulties behind venerating relics as metaphorical conduits conjoining the earthly and the heavenly, they often accompanied relics with narratives that foregrounded characters' doubt about a relic's authenticity in order to expel that doubt more forcefully. Together, these relics and their accompanying narratives replaced doubt with a sense of wonder that allowed venerated objects to break free from the need for epistemological certainty and to inhabit a space where "belief was required" in order to apprehend the object's wonder (59). Some of the earliest practitioners of negative medievalism, where the abject is conveniently tossed into the dustbin of the Middle Ages, were Protestant reformers who replicated the medieval tactic of tacking a narrative onto the relics. In contrast to medieval narratives, the reformers buttressed their claims that relics were a synecdoche "for the falsehoods of the past" (50) with narratives demonstrating the human agency behind relics and other objects of wonder. More recently, cinematic medievalism has replicated medieval Christianity's lure of the relic, providing narratives of loss and recovery that make the otherwise inscrutable item into an object of desire. Such medievalist recreations as Steven Spielberg's *Raiders of the Lost Ark* return us to a "more sceptical treatment of scepticism," thereby allowing us to focus on "the basis for belief underlying these objects" rather than forcing us to search for the human agency that creates the object's value through trickery or deception (66). In these ways, medievalism provides the modern (Christian) believer a model for connecting to medieval religious objects without the embarrassing label of *superstition*.

Having suggested how medieval medievalism models one approach for holding multiple temporalities in tension with one another, and then how cinematic medievalism encourages us to drop our skepticism when faced with wondrous objects (of the past), Prendergast and Trigg next sketch out the potential losses to medieval studies when it discards these two strategies in favor of maintaining a disciplinary space that rewards skepticism, patrols temporal boundaries, and admits no error. Suggesting we set aside our fear of making errors when we approach medieval objects and texts, the authors offer a more-than-commensurate reward: we can see the objects as connections to the sublime. The analogous models for embracing the abject are Christian mystics such as Catherine of Siena (who recognized the sublimity in the most abject objects) and Margery Kempe (who positions herself as the abject and forces the reader to take sides). Similarly, medievalism, with its overt embrace of the abjected Middle Ages, dwells on neither error nor averting error, seeking instead to make the medieval past live again. Medieval studies, the authors suggest, can look to both medieval figures and medievalism to see that scholars can bring life to their work by focusing less on recapturing medieval authenticity and more on reigniting our passions (91).

In order to find ways to revivify those passions, the authors seek a medieval model for medievalism's enthusiastic love for the Middle Ages. Though it might seem that medieval origins for this passion can be found in exegetical readings reducing medieval texts to a single interpretation based on *caritas*, those twentieth-century interpretations leave no space for acknowledging the emotions of either poet or reader—and, in refusing such acknowledgment, reject the long history of reading (in) the Middle Ages. They remind us that, despite our prejudices against affect as a means for engaging with the past, "medieval men and women certainly believed that [affect] gave *them* access to the past" (110). For a better analogy, the authors look again to medieval female mystics and their ardent desire for what otherwise seems unattainable. To achieve their desire, mystics tapped into a sense of memory that could be felt (and did not rely on their having been a historical witness). Seen from this perspective, medievalism's affective recreations seeking to return the reader (or viewer) to the medieval past cannot be rejected as amateurish; instead, they should be seen as granting the reader an inherently authentic, subjective presence. So, while some scholars warn against the dangers of too much sentiment and self-identification, medieval studies needs to acknowledge that affect is foundational to what we study, that it brings us closer to the Middle Ages, and that it already infiltrates our scholarship (whether we acknowledge it or not).

The book's argument ends with an immodest turn by considering what the Middle Ages and medievalism can teach the modern university. Building on Bill Readings's *The University in Ruins* and his advocacy of the medieval university with its community of scholars as a model worth recovering, the authors advocate that the humanities reclaim the medieval university's notion of faculty's disciplinary responsibility to imagine, design, and construct models for promoting intellectual inquiry and resisting external exigencies. Within this disciplinary model, medievalism becomes "an exemplary discourse" because it understands and promotes the lure of the historical or cultural object, the creation of narratives in the search for truth, and the turn to the past for understanding ourselves and the future (121). Meanwhile, while we wait for the rest of the university to catch on, medieval studies can look to the medieval past and to medievalism's postmedieval future for new forms of engagement that help us understand our past and imagine our future.

As the book's list of explicit interlocutors suggests, this effort to realign the relationship between medieval studies and medievalism comes primarily from non-European medievalists, whose first encounters with the pre-modern European past would have been through medievalism's simulacrum transported across space and time. In fact, the sense of the European Middle Ages as a spatial place in time has been intensified by its reception beyond the European land mass. These areas were not colonized by Europeans until after the end of the Middle Ages, or, perhaps more correctly, their colonization marks the end of the Middle Ages. For non-Europeans, our affection for (the study of) the Middle Ages was likely instigated and deeply mediated by some sort of medievalism, whether transplanted (such as manuscripts and other artifacts) or recreated (such as the university Gothic architecture that sufficed for my jaded teens). I suspect European medievalists can more easily ignore the degree to which medievalism has shaped their professional interests and academic passions.

A final note. In making an argument for "affective medievalism," Prendergast and Trigg acknowledge but do not dwell on one of the most troubling aspects of medievalism: its misuse by white supremacist and nationalist groups around the world who construct the Middle Ages as a place that understands the present, anticipates our problems, and provides viable solutions. As the authors admit, the ground has shifted significantly since they began working on this project, and current conditions require that the affective appeal of the medieval should be unharnessed only with caution. Our love for studying the medieval past should always be tempered, as they briefly warn, with the knowledge that the past's values do not always align with our own (6).

CANDACE BARRINGTON
Central Connecticut State University

MARY RASCHKO. *The Politics of Middle English Parables: Fiction, Theology, and Social Practice*. Manchester: Manchester University Press, 2018. Pp. 272. $120.00.

This study examines adaptations of Gospel parables in a broad range of Middle English texts. In a departure from standard ways of thinking about the relationship between literature and exegesis (e.g., deference to allegorical interpretation, and to the static authority of Latin textual tradition), the mode of reception envisioned here is a generative one. Not only did adaptation produce new scriptural narratives, it also led to the formation of what Raschko calls "parabolic fiction," which she singles out for its "socially and spiritually engaged" poetics (6). Variously evinced in poems, sermons, Gospel harmonies, and devotional treatises, parabolic fiction sought "to reconcile the divine word with the lived experience of late medieval culture" (5). Whereas previous claims for the significance of parables have tended to stress their ubiquity and their normative mediating functions, especially in sermons, this book instead attends to their structural and formal variability as narratives; such an approach is justified by the fact that parabolic fiction shares in the enigmatic, often fragmentary nature of its grounding biblical material, distinguishing such stories (so it is claimed) from related genres such as exemplary writing or psalmic adaptations, and soliciting a critical method sensitive to their provocative textual contingencies. Accordingly, each chapter unfolds dialectically, pairing a specific parable with key literary retellings, in long stretches delineating patterns of textual revision, with manuscript issues largely confined to the notes. Thoroughly researched and meticulously argued, *The Politics of Middle English Parables* succeeds in its ambitious effort to contextualize a uniquely paradoxical and suggestive body of late medieval religious writing.

Chapter 1 discusses the parable of the Laborers in the Vineyard (Mt 20:1–16), arguing that competing salvation theologies came into focus through its retelling in sermons and poetry. The long Wycliffite sermon cycle, Thomas Wimbledon's sermon *Redde rationem villicationis tue*, and John Mirk's *Festial* all reinforce the parable's liturgical associations by stressing "a reciprocal relationship between doing good works and receiving heavenly reward" (33). But if such adaptations upheld "a social structure in which labourers serve the material interests of more elite classes," the version of the vineyard parable we encounter in *Pearl*, Raschko argues in the last section of the chapter, challenges "the very foundation of a merit-based economy," instead emphasizing the abundance and sufficiency of God's grace (35, 46). Complicating literary-historical models that exalt the inert and self-enclosed aesthetics of alliterative poetry, this chapter shows how *Pearl* recasts parabolic material for audiences struggling to live virtuously in the world.

Chapter 2 continues the book's focus on paraliturgical contexts for spiritual instruction and lay theological inquiry. Here Raschko tracks adaptations of the Prodigal Son story (Lk 15:11–32) in sermons (the *Northern Homily Cycle* and edited selections from London, British Library, Royal MS 18 B.XXIII) and Middle English lives of Christ (the *Pepysian Gospel Harmony*, the *South English Ministry and Passion*, the *Mirour of Mans Saluacioun*), showing how it functioned in these texts as a highly adaptable catechetical script. Throughout the narrative's different versions, subtle but significant shifts in language, style, form, and storyline imaginatively restage the parable's confessional scene (a father who forgives his errant son) to accommodate variations in penitential belief and practice. The chapter concludes with an extended discussion of the (possibly Wycliffite) *Book to a Mother*. Here, Raschko joins other scholars—namely

Nicole Rice and Fiona Somerset—whose work has recently inspired critical reassessments of this fascinating but deeply ambiguous text. As she shows, *Book to a Mother* dramatically embodies the diversity surrounding late medieval Prodigal Son narratives, both translating the Gospel parable directly and then rewriting the story in commentary so as to make the episode "function more effectively as a guide to Christian living" (82). The extended scope in this analysis dedicated to use and instrumentality rather than ideological affiliation makes sense given how Raschko frames the transformative ethical effects of sermons and *vitae Christi*. Less clear—and it is a virtue of this study that it positions us to ask just such a question—is whether the same model for reading parabolic fiction can account for the devotional orientation of a collection as complex as *Book to a Mother*, which incorporates multiple genres of religious writing.

The next two chapters share a focus on parables with particular implications for the prosperous late medieval audiences who encountered them in textual collections as various as *Handlyng Synne*, Idley's *Instructions to His Son*, *Confessio Amantis*, *Piers Plowman*, *Þe Lyfe of Soule*, the *Pepysian Gospel Harmony*, the *South English Ministry and Passion*, and Gretham's *Mirror*. As in previous chapters, surveys of devotional and pastoral work are followed by more extensive treatment of a single key text. From this dialectical configuration Raschko concludes in Chapter 3 that the parable of the Rich Man (Dives) and Lazarus (Lk 16:19–31) was the site of considerable tension in terms of how Mannyng, Idley, and Gower accommodated themselves and their readers to the reality of material prosperity in the period, with Gower encouraging the wealthy "to look inward so that the reformation of each individual may rehabilitate the larger community"—pragmatic moral wisdom not too far removed from *pastoralia* and penitential collections such as those treated earlier in the chapter (130). The dialectical contrasts between poetry and *pastoralia* are more vivid in Chapter 4, not only because *Piers Plowman* forcefully intervenes in debates over spiritual improvement and perfection, but also because it reconceives salvific instruction altogether. If sermons and *vitae Christi* privilege exemplarity and imitation, Raschko maintains, *Piers Plowman* promotes charitable participation in the world; and it is in this respect that Langland's retelling of the Good Samaritan parable (Lk 10:25–37) in Passus XVII of the B-text takes on new ethical significance for his poetics.

An epilogue returns to *Piers Plowman*, in a reading of the pardon episode, but not before a final chapter offers yet another intricate assemblage of "parabolic fiction," this one more explicitly concerned with matters of exegesis and hermeneutics: the parables of the Wedding Feast and the Great Supper (Mt 22:1–14, Lk 14:15–24) as adapted in *Cleanness* and selections from the Wycliffite *Glossed Gospels*. Raschko's central claim in this chapter is that both *Cleanness* and the Wycliffite Gospel commentaries use these parables, which are fundamentally metaphorical in nature, to investigate questions of "scriptural polysemy" (181). Bringing these disparate materials together uncovers a rich seam of speculation on the interpretive difficulties and incitements of parabolic language. Although here and throughout much of the book Wycliffite biblical scholarship is an ancillary concern, largely abstracted from its governing textual and intellectual settings, the dearth of scholarship on the Gospel commentaries makes this chapter an especially welcome one. Scriptural "polysemy" also prepares us to appreciate Raschko's incisive epilogue on the pardon scene in *Piers*; by this point in the book, we can see why retold parables, or "parabolic fiction" properly so-called, might appeal to Langland, but Raschko makes a convincing case for approaching such stories as a late medieval genre in their own right, through which a wide array of Middle English authors navigated a complex religious world.

DAVID LAVINSKY
Yeshiva University

LINDSAY ANN REID. *Shakespeare's Ovid and the Spectre of the Medieval.* Studies in Renaissance Literature. Cambridge: D. S. Brewer, 2018. Pp. xiv, 270. $99.00.

Scholarly efforts to rethink the once sacrosanct period-divide between late medieval and early modern English culture have been under way for quite some time now, and the Studies in Renaissance Literature series has made several important contributions to these exertions. Lindsay Ann Reid's *Shakespeare's Ovid and the Spectre of the Medieval* is the latest—exhibiting the perspicacity, nuance, and scope that we have come to expect from the series.

The strength of this study is its dense and challenging close readings of ancient, medieval, and early modern texts. Reid selects "deliberately unexpected" (49) Shakespeare plays, by which she means texts that engage with Ovid, Chaucer, or Gower other than *Titus Andronicus, A Midsummer Night's Dream, Troilus and Cressida, Pericles,* and *The Two Noble Kinsmen.* Chapter 2 argues that the Ovidian influences on *The Taming of the Shrew* and *Cymbeline* flow through the medieval conduit of Chaucer's *Book of the Duchess.* In Chapter 3, Reid traces the affective experiences of the character Julia in *The Two Gentlemen of Verona* back to the classical tales of Ariadne, yet simultaneously demonstrates the importance of their decidedly un-Ovidian postclassical transformations for Shakespeare. Chapter 4's claim, that Shakespeare's use of the classical alba, or dawn-song, is inflected through Chaucer's *Troilus and Criseyde,* is convincingly presented, though I was never sure why the term "inverse alba" and not "nocturne" was used to describe moments such as Juliet's opening monologue in *Romeo and Juliet,* 3.2. Chapter 5 is, for me, the most fascinating and persuasive. Here, Reid makes the case that Gower's representation of Narcissus in the *Confessio Amantis* had a substantial influence on English literature for the following two centuries, including on Shakespeare's *Twelfth Night.* Uniquely, Gower styles a "heteronormative, cognitively erroneous Narcissus who falls in love with a female illusion" (172), and Shakespeare's comedy, with its multifaceted exploration of the fluidity of identity and gender performed by cross-dressed male actors, is a celebration of these "spectral medieval traditions" (198) par excellence.

Bookending these readings are two chapters featuring specific early modern material texts: the curious collection of Ovidian tales "penn'd after the ancient manner of writing in England" entitled *Chaucer's Ghoast* (1672), and Bodleian Library, MS Autogr. F.1, once widely believed to have been Shakespeare's personal copy of the *Metamorphoses.* Readers of *SAC* may be particularly interested in Chapter 1's survey of the curious amalgamations of Ovid, Chaucer, and Gower in *Chaucer's Ghoast,* and particularly the manner in which, as Reid shows, it recalls Speght's efforts to canonize Chaucer by conflating his epoch with classical Antiquity.

And yet, for all of the fascinating appeal of this quirky seventeenth-century text, I wish that Reid had chosen a different metaphor to describe the influence of Chaucer and Gower on Shakespeare than that of ghostly hauntings. The danger, as I see it, is that it risks perpetuating the view that the medieval is dead on arrival in Renaissance culture rather than vital and efficacious. It surrenders too much authority to the early modern poet. I hasten to state that Reid does not fall prey to this view; indeed, every chapter succeeds in showing that this is not the case. But, once she has borrowed the metaphor of the medieval specter from *Chaucer's Ghoast*, I do think that she misses an opportunity to engage with the influential work of a scholar who, in my opinion, does tend to value Shakespeare at the expense of his medieval antecedents. Shakespeare, according to Stephen Greenblatt, was haunted by the empty simulacra of medieval culture and liturgy from which his genius forged vigorous new dramatic forms, and a more direct confrontation with this still influential account would have been most welcome.

Despite Reid's explicit intention to eschew plays with obvious indebtedness to Ovid, Chaucer, or Gower, my own experience of reading *Shakesepeare's Ovid* was haunted nonetheless by the presence of the *Metamorphoses* in Act 4 of *Titus Andronicus*, and I wondered when a discussion of this seemingly direct and unmitigated contact between Shakespeare and the classical poet might appear. My expectations were not gratified until the book's afterword, and while I am open to Reid's view that this scene may be regarded "as *exceptional* rather than *emblematic* of Shakespeare's typical allusions to and engagements with 'Ovidian' mythological poetry" (208–9), I wish this point had been addressed sooner. Indeed, it might have aided the book's thesis to consider whether Shakespeare's parodic borrowing of the topoi of the alba in three successive scenes in Act 2 of *Titus* also bears a Chaucerian or Gowerian stamp. Aaron's opening speech in 2.1 compares Tamora's ascent to the throne as Saturninus's wife to the dawn "when the golden sun salutes the morn." As Rome's "imperial mistress," she is now peerless, or, in the words of Aaron's punning epic simile, she "overlooks the highest-peering hills." The crescive fortunes of this "new-made empress" embolden Aaron to "mount aloft" with her; having, in fact, "fettered [her] in amorous chains" that recall "Prometheus tied to Caucasus," he will now "mount her pitch" (2.1.5–20). The following scene opens amid the noise of hounds and horns as Titus bids his sons to "wake the Emperor and his lovely bride." Yet, despite the fragrant fields, the green woods, and the grey moon of dawn that his brief alba celebrates, he has passed a restless night of foreboding dreams, and the "dawning day" will not, in fact, bring "new comfort," but the destruction of his family (2.2.1–10). Finally, the "loathsome pit" in the third and most famous

scene is richly described with "classical" allusions that may also be mediated by postclassical texts and hermeneutic traditions such as those that
Reid so beautifully demonstrates in other chapters. I refer not simply to
the association of Bassianus and Pyramus, but once again to the parodic
use of the alba. Titus's sons state that the "drops of new-shed blood"
they find are "As fresh as morning dew distilled on flowers" (2.3.200–
201). This is a conspicuous metaphor to describe a place that, up to this
point, the play has persistently associated with the "dead time of night"
(2.3.99). The effect of all three parodic albas is to mock the supposedly
ascendant fortunes of the Andronici—to give the audience, in Reid's
words, a "dread of dawn" (119). But these scenes also represent modern
twists on this classical trope: Aaron anticipates sexual intimacy rather
than lamenting its loss; Titus, playing the role of the lark, fears the
morn, not the lovers Saturninus and Tamora; the dew-like blood of Bassianus portends Lavinia's rape and mutilation.

These perhaps idiosyncratic demurrals aside, Reid's work is an invaluable check to the still prevailing scholarly assumption that Shakespeare's
knowledge of Ovid and other classical authors was direct and straightforward. And it is to the credit of the Studies in Renaissance Literature
series, which has given us several wonderful studies of Renaissance
humanism, that it has published *Shakespeare's Ovid*. Accordingly, this
book would unquestionably help both undergraduate and graduate students complicate oversimplified and misguided accounts of Shakespeare's sources and influences—always at the expense of the Middle
Ages—which sadly remain all too prevalent.

KURT SCHREYER
University of Missouri–St. Louis

JAMES SIMPSON. *Permanent Revolution: The Reformation and the Illiberal
Roots of Liberalism*. Cambridge, Mass.: Belknap Press of Harvard
University Press, 2019. Pp. xv, 444. $35.00.

It is an oft-repeated axiom that the Protestant Reformation inaugurated
the modern liberal era in the West. In abbreviated form, the story,
derived largely from nineteenth-century "Whig" historiography, goes
something like this. When Martin Luther dared to assert that salvation

was effected by faith alone (*sola fide*), and that theology and ecclesiology were to be judged by the Bible alone (*sola scriptura*), he inspired a radical religious movement that would rapidly unfetter Europe from the repressive, fraudulent bondage of the medieval Church. By encouraging individual parishioners to read the Scriptures on their own, and by simultaneously suggesting that the devout—as members of a nonhierarchical priesthood of all believers—had a personal duty to evaluate every Christian creed and convention against biblical standards, Luther permitted, perhaps even facilitated, widespread dissent from established dogma. In conflict with the long-held authority of the papacy, the intellectual ground was thus prepared for the cultivation of modern liberalism, with its affirmation of individual rights (for example, the right to consent to governance) and its concomitant emphasis on individual responsibilities (for example, the responsibility to participate in the democratic process). James Simpson's new monograph, *Permanent Reformation: The Reformation and the Illiberal Roots of Liberalism*, challenges every major assumption behind this narrative.

In eighteen thought-provoking chapters (organized into seven parts), Simpson looks afresh at both the origins and the outcomes of the Protestant Reformation. His principal body of evidence comprises the literature of England, both polemical and imaginative, produced from the beginning of the sixteenth century to the end of the seventeenth century, or, roughly, from the reign of Henry VIII to that of Charles II. This substantial and varied literary archive, Simpson demonstrates, tells an unsettling tale. Though it is frequently avowed that modern liberalism descends in a direct line from the Reformation, an honest analysis of the literature of the time reveals that the genealogical relationship between liberalism and evangelicalism (Simpson's preferred term for Protestantism) might be better understood as a collateral one. Far from fostering liberal principles, Simpson stresses, the evangelical reasoning developed by Luther and his fellow reformers (Ulrich Zwingli, John Calvin, William Tyndale) advanced a stark authoritarianism in theology and politics—an authoritarianism that in one way or another shaped the work of writers as diverse as Edmund Spenser, William Shakespeare, John Milton, and John Bunyan. Moreover, to acknowledge the authoritarian tendencies of sixteenth-century Reformation theology is to recognize that the proto-liberalism that emerged in the closing decades of the seventeenth century (evident, for instance, in the political philosophy of John Locke) was formulated in complete antithesis to the dominant evangelical outlook. Modern liberalism, Simpson suggests, should not, therefore, be viewed as the anticipated, legitimate heir to the Reformation, but rather as Protestant Christianity's unexpected, and somewhat rebellious, younger sibling.

In addition to positing that evangelicalism and liberalism share an adjacent, sibling-like relationship (and thus an inevitable sibling-like rivalry), Simpson makes a second, larger, but more provisional, claim about the recursive structures of assertion and denial in all modern revolutionary contexts. Here, he borrows the phrase "permanent revolution" from Marxist theory (with an explicit nod to Leon Trotsky), using it as shorthand for his model of continuous reformation-in-refutation. Simpson proposes that it takes a minimum of 150 years for the fallout of any revolution to settle. With regard to the momentous upheaval of the Protestant Reformation, that period began, he submits, in the early sixteenth century, when Luther first endeavored to redesign Christian salvation, shunning the conciliatory customs of the Roman Church (such as the sacrament of penance) in favor of a soteriology based solely on divinely gifted faith. It ended a century-and-a-half later with the outright rejection by proto-Enlightenment thinkers of the many difficult social and psychological consequences of that Lutheran substitution. Herein lies the irony: precisely because evangelical discourse demanded that all tradition be subject to suspicion, it created the very conditions that would eventually limit its own reach. With this *particular* instance of repudiation-from-within in mind, Simpson applies his paradigm speculatively to modern revolutions *in general*: just as the extent of the Reformation was inexorably checked by the logic of evangelicalism, so, too, Simpson hypothesizes, will all revolutionary ideas inhibit their own progress in the end.

It should be noted that this study is not the first to confront the axiomatic "Whig" teleology about the long-term effects of the Reformation. Indeed, as Simpson himself points out, a very convincing attempt to counter this same teleology was made by Herbert Butterfield almost ninety years ago, in *The Whig Interpretation of History* (1931); additionally, as Simpson also points out, a number of eminent historians of early modern religion, including Karl Gunther, Peter Marshall, Ethan Shagan, and Alexandra Walsham, have revived Butterfield's critique of Protestant triumphalism in the past couple of decades. It should be noted, too, that *Permanent Revolution* does not represent Simpson's first effort to oppose the projection of liberalism onto Protestantism. Readers of this journal may already be familiar with the arguments of both *Burning to Read: English Fundamentalism and Its Reformation Opponents* (2010) and *Under the Hammer: Iconoclasm in the Anglo-American Tradition* (2011), in which two books Simpson highlights, respectively, the bleakest consequences of privileging fundamentalist (that is, literalist) habits of reading, and the grim dangers inherent in celebrating the destruction of images. Nonetheless, *Permanent Revolution* provides a useful reminder to the field of literary studies, where the nineteenth century's view of the Reformation seems to reappear at regular intervals. Recent scholarship on the arrival of Protestantism to Henrician England, for instance, still refers often to the many studies and editions of Tyndale published in the 1990s and early 2000s by the late David Daniell, who vigorously promoted the exultant narrative.

One disappointing omission in Simpson's otherwise wide-ranging study is any serious examination of literature by early modern women. Spenser, Shakespeare, Milton, and Bunyan all make steady appearances (Shakespeare and Milton, indeed, are cast as heroes, as they are shown to have found virtuoso ways to get around the strictures of the Reformation). William Tyndale, Henry Howard (the earl of Surrey), Sir Thomas Wyatt, Sir Thomas More, John Bale, Fulke Greville, Christopher Marlowe, Ben Jonson, John Donne, George Herbert, and John Locke are also all given significant parts to play. Yet Anne Askew, Anne Locke, and Mary Sidney are afforded only walk-on roles, while other talented women writers of the time—Katherine Parr, Aemelia Lanyer, Lady Mary Wroth, Katherine Philips, Margaret Cavendish, and Aphra Behn, to name just a few—are overlooked entirely. With respect to evangelicalism, the work of these women runs the gamut from fiercely loyal to passionately dissident. To subject it to close analysis, though, would likely disclose that female writers did not experience exactly the same Reformation as their male counterparts. It seems strangely emblematic of the evidence discussed in *Permanent Revolution* that the design for the dust jacket slices up a 1641 double portrait by Rembrandt van Rijn, retaining the painter's representation of the Mennonite preacher Cornelis Anslo (with his several books), but completely eliminating that of Anslo's wife and interlocutor, Aeltje Schouten.

That being said, the value of *Permanent Revolution* lies as much in its method of appraisal as in its selection of evidence. Simpson approaches the Reformation from the stand-point of a medievalist. Reading across the medieval/early modern divide, he is able to provide an innovative account of the interactions between enduring and emerging currents in sixteenth- and seventeenth-century literature. The result is a comprehensive, though pessimistic, theory of modernity, of what makes the modern world *modern*. If evangelicalism and liberalism are to be understood as metaphorical siblings, then the parent of both phenomena, uncovered by Simpson's analysis, is the advent under the Tudors of the single most important characteristic of modern governance, namely, the conception of the autonomous nation state. It was the centralization of power and culture, in the service of the sovereign nation, that birthed Protestantism and its many troubling traits—theological absolutism; the denial of free will; endless introspection and self-doubt; widespread paranoia and surveillance; an obsession with hypocrisy; pervasive iconoclasm and violence; anti-theatricality, witch-hunts, and the burning of heretics; and literalism leading to perpetual schism. And it was the same centralization that birthed liberalism, which counterbalances Protestantism by promoting democracy and the separation of powers, individual agency and free will, liberty of conscience, freedom of expression, equality of all persons before the law, toleration for minorities, and freedom of interpretation. The modern nation state will love and cherish both of its offspring, even as they contend with one another for attention and influence. This insight, finally, explains so many of the contradictory pressures one must negotiate while reading, teaching, or writing about early modern English literature. It may also explain a great deal beyond the paradoxes of literary history, including much of the political turmoil that has followed the Reformation on both sides of the Atlantic.

CLARE COSTLEY KING'OO
University of Connecticut, Storrs

EMMA MAGGIE SOLBERG. *Virgin Whore*. Ithaca: Cornell University Press, 2018. Pp. 294. $39.95.

Asking when the qualities of virginity—fragile, difficult to detect, and easily defiled—were transferred to the Virgin Mary, *Virgin Whore* confronts a medieval figuring of an earthy Mary who played the trickster, embarrassed her son, and seduced God with her sexual charisma. While recent decades have produced a body of influential work on the Virgin, this book's sustained analysis of Mary's role in the East Anglian N-Town manuscript pageants is a welcome addition. Drawing on diverse theological, artistic, historical, and literary sources, its focus on Mary in performance permits an important examination of the ways Mary became both the target of ridicule and vicious accusation and herself played the role of divine comedienne. The centering of early theater, so often on the margins of Marian studies, offers an exciting rethinking of how the Virgin's legendary lives were reimagined by lay communities.

The pageants dealing with Joseph's doubts about Mary are among the more scrutinized in early-drama criticism; however, Solberg's first chapter helpfully draws together a history of apocrypha, artwork, and theological texts in its focus on this episode in the N-Town manuscript. Solberg finds Joseph's question about Jesus' paternity amplified to farcical effect as the list of candidates grows. The history of Joseph's role as a legitimizing presence fortifying Mary's virginity and as threat to the virgin narrative is charted, covering the second-century Gospel of James, early Christian theologians, the physical diminishing of Joseph, and farce and fabliau tropes. Intriguingly, Solberg also briefly considers the racial stereotyping of Joseph's decrepitude and impotence as Jewish, set in opposition to Mary, "the young, beautiful, blossoming flower of Christianity" (27). While this is a small part of this chapter's argument rather than forming the book's core, it shows interesting intersections with the debates of Kathleen Biddick and Anthony Bale about gender in anti-Semitic art and literature. Solberg examines how sexual doubt is developed, including the pageant's exploitation of theological debates about how God impregnated Mary, and why, given the narrative's classical and Hebrew contexts, Joseph was justified in fearing that the angel Gabriel or God "jape[d]" with his wife. This introduces the monograph's recurring argument: that the more theologians, artwork, and plays attempted to fortify Mary's virginity, the more open it was to doubt, challenge, and testing.

Chapter 2 examines why the Gospels might have provoked this desire to produce supplemental "proofs" of Mary's virginity. This chapter includes a welcome discussion of early accusations against the Virgin, including the Hebrew New Testament parody *Toledot Yeshu*, as well as the history of the chastity trial from apocrypha to the N-Town's *Trial of Mary and Joseph* and the midwife's testing of Mary's virginity in the *Nativity*. Solberg identifies a long line of Marian skeptics and notes that, where historical chastity trials destroyed the subject being tested, Mary passes each trial, ready to be tested anew. Here, Solberg makes her original argument that the N-Town Mary takes these repetitive trials in a spirit of humor and play that "turns the trial by ordeal into a harmless game, violence into play, tragedy into comedy" (58). This reading of the trials as a "game" is secured firmly within the N-Town manuscript's East Anglian context, with its ecclesiastical trials, ritual humiliation of icons, and public suspicion of "white" marriages. The chapter ends by drawing an intriguing link between the cuckolded carpenter and his wife and Chaucer's *Miller's Tale*.

The third chapter complicates the *Ave/Eva* model, which constructs Mary as the typological opposite of Eve. It focuses on the cherry-tree episode in the N-Town pageant of the *Nativity*, arguing that Mary does not so much reverse Eve as demonstrate a surprising ability to mimic the pattern of Eve's actions yet get away with it: "God seems to reward Mary for re-enacting the scene of Eve's transgression" (84). This contrasts Joseph's desire to obey the law, whether it be the laws of religion or nature. The chapter analyzes the motif of Mary as the seducer and pacifier of the Old Testament God in relation to the allegory of the "mystic hunt of the unicorn" and N-Town's comparatively less-studied *Parliament of Heaven* pageant. Arguing that Mary is central to that pageant's allegorical dramatization of Peace and Mercy achieving preeminence over Justice and Truth, it finds that the latter become "shrewish" (92) while Mercy plays the role of the Virgin. This interpretation expands and complements the claims made by Miri Rubin that Mary is figured as triumphing over both Judaism and the God of the Old Testament. Again, the sexual undercurrent of these supersession narratives is never far away, and Solberg compares the *Parliament* to the conversation between Pluto and Proserpine in Chaucer's *Merchant's Tale* about how they should respond to May cuckolding January.

Chapter 4 charts the extension of Mary's holy history through several generations of ancestors. A welcome foregrounding of St. Anne as wife and mother identifies the emphasis that N-Town places on the mother's role in constructing her daughter's purity, while demonstrating Anne's importance as a more accessible model for wives and mothers than that provided by the Virgin. The chapter also examines the collapsing of distinctions between Jewish and Christian characters at the very point at which the *Marriage* pageant asserts the difference between the sexual values of virginity and procreation. Mary is then read against the "Bad Wives," Eve, Norea, and Gill. While Solberg's discussion of N-Town's

417

characterization of Noah's wife as virtuous is intriguing, given her rebellious contemporaries, the linking of this example to Gnostic heresies claiming Noah's wife acted as a champion of humanity might have benefited from comparison with, say, the Chester *Flood* pageant, where Noah's wife explicitly aims to bring her female community on board. Nicole Nolan Sidhu has also recently shown how the elements that make Noah's wife troublesome are character traits that made women valuable members of guild societies. However, the discussion of Mary's hindering Joseph in the *Flight into Egypt* offered an insightful comparison with Noah's wife, reminding us that, despite the N-Town's centering of Mary, it never allows its audiences to forget how difficult it must have been to be married to her. This point is further emphasized in a short discussion of Mak and Gill in the Towneley *Second Shepherds' Play*, which develops the motif of Mary as trickster and master of theatrical and theological illusion.

The fifth chapter develops this theme by examining the idea of Christianity as a "divine joke" (130) and the "scandalous foremothers" in Jesus' family tree. Conducting a close reading of the violent and sexual insults in *The Woman Taken in Adultery*, Solberg makes a case for Christianity's liberating, merciful promiscuity in the face of a judgment system again stereotyped as Jewish. In a striking parallel between the characterization of the Old Testament God as a jealous fabliau-cuckold and Jesus as the hero of an adulterous courtly-love romance narrative, she argues that the medieval Mary's intercession was imagined fundamentally to change the nature of God. Revealing Mary's role as a patroness of sinners whose birth canal provides an access to heaven, Solberg concludes by asking what happens to the balance of Justice and Mercy in the N-Town *Judgment Day*, in which Mary is notably absent.

The concluding chapter charts the changes in the reception of Mary and of biblical drama after the Reformation. This is contextualized through Mary's preeminence in accounts of iconoclastic attacks on images, her increasing figuring as a whore and an idol, and the Protestant attempt to reclaim Mary as a simple, chaste, obedient, yet not exceptional woman. Noting that Mary's plays were often the first to be cut as towns struggled to legitimize their pageants in increasingly hostile legislative environments, Solberg contributes to a growing body of literature discussing how "remnants" of medieval theater traditions were recycled and reappropriated for the London stage. The chapter examines the motifs of the Virgin pageants underpinning Shakespeare's portrayal of Joan of Arc in *1 Henry VI*. Here, Solberg notes how Joan's virginity and faith are gradually revealed as unstable signifiers, until Joan ends the play confirmed as a witch and a whore. Solberg claims that the sexual joke, once directed out from Mary to her accusers, now falls squarely on the shoulders of the alleged "virgin," Joan. While this argument is compelling, the study of only one Marian type on the post-Reformation stage (as opposed to Shakespeare's other "Virgin" types, such as Marina and Isabella) rather narrows the conclusion to a book that throughout emphasizes the multivalent, contradictory, and playful nature of the Virgin in performance.

Foregrounding Mary's role in early drama, *Virgin Whore* contributes not only to Marian studies but also to literary studies more widely by demonstrating early drama's use and transformation of tropes shared throughout the corpus of medieval literature. Providing a solid historical context for its arguments, this work will also be useful for scholars working on early performance, Jewish–Christian relations and anti-Semitism, Marian and Reformation theology, and medieval gender. Like the figure forming its subject matter, this is a visceral, courageous, and occasionally mischievous study.

DAISY BLACK
University of Wolverhampton

ARVIND THOMAS. *"Piers Plowman" and the Reinvention of Church Law in the Late Middle Ages*. Toronto: University of Toronto Press, 2019. Pp. xiv, 267. $75.00.

Arvind Thomas opens his important study of canon law in *Piers Plowman* with the story of a "cleric and canon" named Walter de Brugge, whose will, dating from 1396, includes not only "a book called *Pers Plewman*" (5), but also several canonist volumes. Much has been made of Langland's "textual community," and Thomas argues that Langland would also have written for men such as Walter. Langland shows extensive knowledge of the key maxims and ideas found in canon-law explanations of the stages of confession (contrition, confession, absolution, and satisfaction). In addition, Thomas believes that *Piers Plowman* actively engages with such issues as defining usury, establishing evidence of contrition, and enforcing restitution. Whereas others have suggested that Langland despaired of achieving institutional change, Thomas suggests that Langland never relinquishes his "vision of clerical reform" (9).

In recent years, the study of law and literature has become increasingly theoretical, and for Thomas the intersection between the disciplines is a two-way street. He argues that we should "reconceptualize poetry as productive of, not just derivative from, the discourse of canon law" (10–11). Langland may have felt inspired to share his reformist agenda because during the Middle Ages canon law was not a closed body of rules. Although the *Corpus iuris canonici* was largely complete by Chaucer's time, the tradition remained alive through the dynamic manner of applying the norms to individual cases. A poet might equally "shape" the law by both *finding* established rules and *founding* new ideas. In this way, the law might be imaginatively reinvented, a process that Thomas meticulously documents over the course of five well-researched chapters that immerse us in Langland's legal context.

Chapter 1 tackles the performative aspects of contrition. Characters such as Mede and Sleuthe treat repentance "as a theatrical performance" (32), and while Langland's critique is usually read as anticlerical satire, Thomas points out that canon law did place much emphasis on ascertaining outward proof of inner remorse. Canonists constructed a semiotic system to describe the way confession acted as sign of contrition, contrition acted as referent of confession and sign of purgation (forgiveness), and purgation acted as referent of contrition. In addition, contrition might be demonstrated through tears and by avoiding laughter. These signs helped the confessor recognize true shame (*verecundia*), which, as Langland points out in Passus XX, is to be distinguished from the kind of shame (*pudor*) that prevents one from going to confession in the first place. By contrast, Mede is presumptuous enough to appropriate clerical authority and invert the language of confession. For instance, in C III.59–63 she defends lechery on the basis that "sclaundre" (which should bring shame) can be ignored, that mercy (think of *misericordia*) might be granted, and that any harm may be "amended." By reminding us of the correct terminology, "the poem finds fault not with the procedures of canon law but with those entrusted with their implementation" (61). According to Thomas, the C-version (especially Passus III) does most to demonstrate this discrepancy.

Passus III of the C-text also expands on the subject of usury, and although the term is less visible than in B (though see C III.113), the definition becomes more expansive. For Langland, usury includes *pre manibus* (advance) payments, commercial practices such as forestalling, and a range of sins associated with simony. A review of the legal literature shows that canonists gradually introduced qualifications that would allow making a profit or charging interest in cases where the lender could claim doubt (*dubium*) about the future market value. Since Conscience condemns *pre manibus* payments on the basis that the worker does not know if he will live long enough to do the work, it seems that Langland is less flexible than his sources. On the other hand, Langland elaborates a more positive, spiritual model of usury when he describes the feudal gift-giving that follows the logic of the parable of the Talents, where the gift can be recalled if it is misused. Whereas sinful usury deals with fungible items such as bread or wine that can be consumed—thus making it impossible to distinguish between ownership and possession—spiritual usury fairly charges interest (love, loyalty, good works) and establishes a "relacioun rect" between the laborer and his master. This is a rich and complex chapter, and although I had some questions (e.g., are Mede's gifts of golden cups and rings truly consumable items?), Thomas ably records the canonist lines of thought that crisscross the generally secular focus of Passus III.

In Chapter 3, Thomas focuses on Passus VI and the question of restitution (an aspect of making satisfaction). In the C-text, Repentaunce turns a rule (*regula*) into a law (*ius*) by insisting that without proper restitution even the pope cannot absolve a usurer (C VI.253–57). As the language becomes less pastoral and more juridical, Langland ignores various canonist glosses that point out that sometimes restitution may be impossible (for instance, if the penitent is insolvent) or undesired (if the prior owner obtained the goods illegally). Langland also insists that clerics who retain the goods will be guilty until restitution is made. Thomas here perhaps makes too much of the fact that some canonists say little about the priest's obligation to return a stolen item (one would think this would be implied), but he insightfully demonstrates that when it comes to restitution, C presents "a vision of the rigour of the rule" (145). This attempt to curtail the plenary power of the pope (156) fits well with Langland's skepticism about bought pardons generally. Even at the end of the poem, Piers receives the power to absolve all sins except the sin of debt (B XIX, C XXI).

When, in Chapter 4, Thomas tackles another maxim—"Nullum

malum inpunitum . . . nullum bonum irremunderatum" (no evil unpun-
ished . . . no good unrewarded)—we might expect a similar focus on
the *rigor iuris*. After all, Reason tells the king in Passus IV that he will
have no pity ("reuthe") on Mede. It comes as somewhat of a surprise,
then, that Thomas instead draws our attention to the way Langland
requires confessors to interpret the maxim with charity and love. Equity
is of course highly valued in canon law, and Thomas reviews the many
uses of the maxim in Langland's possible sources. Yet, when the clerks
gather to construe the maxim "kyndeliche" (a word usually translated
as "correctly" or "properly"), I am not entirely convinced that the adverb
clearly "takes on the sense of an equitable mode of reading a norm"
(203). In both B and C, the context suggests that the clerks are up to
no good, and it is in fact the king who is asked to do the real work of
turning the law into a laborer: "Lat thy confessour, syre king, construe
this in Englische / And if ye worche it in werke Y wedde bothe myn
handes / That lawe shal ben a laborer" (C IV.142–4). Given that the
king ("ye") is the main actor, it may be slightly misleading to claim that
"Reason's call to confessors to 'werchen' the quotation into 'werk'
denotes satisfaction . . . not only as agricultural labour exemplifying the
hard penances to be undertaken by the penitent but also as a hermeneutic labour exemplifying the canonical principles of interpretation to be
followed by the confessor" (196). For this reader, the metaphorical equation of satisfaction with labor remains more in the background, and the
maxim is not shifted "from the domain of generalized secular law to that
of the canon law of penance." Instead, Thomas's detailed exploration of
canonist usage of the maxim suggests that the movement may well be
in the opposite direction.

The final chapter is likely the most challenging, as Thomas reads the
description of the pardon in the B- and C-versions of Passus XIV as a
series of oppositions. In B, the "patente" directly symbolizes Christ's
body, and the focus is on an oral and personal covenant made visible
through a material and feudal analogy. In C, the "chartre" reminds us
of a written document and the language becomes more distant and
deferred. The mode has shifted from symbolism to verbal allegory, and
the language is less Christological and more institutional. Although the
juxtaposition seems at times too neat—for instance, in B the patent's
parchment is made of such allegorical personifications as Patience and
Poverty—Thomas's main point is an excellent one: the C-version does
not entirely give up on the penitential process. If anything, Thomas

reminds us of the complexity of the poem, the way its call for radical reform and its desire for restoration can co-exist in ways that produce sudden shifts and unexpected results. Indeed, this is an ambitious and rewarding book that reveals Langland's sustained and profound commitment to reinventing canonist thought.

CONRAD VAN DIJK
Concordia University of Edmonton

MARION TURNER. *Chaucer: A European Life.* Princeton: Princeton University Press, 2019. Pp. xvii, 624. $39.95.

In the first volume of this journal, John H. Fisher, co-founder of the New Chaucer Society, reviewed two new lives of Chaucer, John Gardner's *The Life and Times of Chaucer* (1977) and Derek Brewer's *Chaucer and His World* (1978). He began with a cautionary paragraph, noting the absence of biographical materials for persons living before 1600 and the frustrations inherent in the Crow-Olson *Chaucer Life Records* (1966), which contains "the sorts of details preserved by bureaucracy" (170). Each biographer of Chaucer has faced a Chaucer who—despite the many documents granting him places to live, safe-passages in foreign lands, pitchers of wine, positions in the customs office, or suits of clothes—remains a mysterious and elusive absence in his works, even alongside the textual persona we know as Geffrey. That persona is but one more baffle, perhaps Chaucer's greatest baffle, between him and his audience.

Lives of Chaucer necessarily are also accounts of his world, a world that seems increasingly strange as we move further into the twenty-first century and away from the religious and social structures that underpinned the realities Chaucer lived in, accommodated, and critiqued. In *Chaucer's London* (1968), D.W. Robertson, Jr. sought an entry into Chaucer's life by describing London's streets, customs, and history. In *The Life of Geoffrey Chaucer: A Critical Biography* (1992), Derek Pearsall employed the *Chaucer Life Records* as a structure for his analysis of Chaucer's writings in relation to his life experience—as *valettus* and esquire, as Royal Esquire and Customs Officer, and as participant in or observer of the tumultuous reign of Richard II: as a public figure, that is, whose private self can only be a matter of speculation. More recently, Paul Strohm, in *Chaucer's Tale: 1386 and the Road to Canterbury* (2014), has used a single year as an entry into the dynamics of Chaucer's professional and social existence.

Marion Turner carves out a space for another biography by locating the facts of Chaucer's professional and writing life within the context of English and European history and material culture. Building on the work catalyzed by Jocelyn Wogan-Browne and Ardis Butterfield that insists upon fourteenth-century England's multilingual and multicultural reality, Turner reads the documentary "details" as evidence for a Chaucer who was a citizen of the many worlds he inhabited in court and city, and a willing and capable citizen of England abroad, in Italy, France, and Spain. She deepens our understanding of what it meant for Chaucer to spend his early life in London and much of his young manhood in service in the households of Elizabeth, countess of Ulster; her husband, Lionel, earl of Ulster; and, sometime in the early-to-mid 1360s, Edward III. Turner's descriptions of the demands of court life, at once fluid, incessantly mobile, and rigorous; of the difficulties of travel abroad as a diplomatic messenger during the Hundred Years War; and of the sensory effects of northern Spain, France, or Italy on a Londoner underline this period as a real education for a gifted and observant young man.

Turner's reading of Chaucer as shaped by his European experiences is particularly important in Part 1 of the book. Here, she focuses upon the first thirty years (1342–74) of Chaucer's life—child, schoolboy, member of three great households, royal messenger, and soldier—as a period of great mobility that shaped his sensibilities; exposed him to new influences; and stamped him with the political acuities, social perceptions, and professional capacities that allowed him to live, work, and write in a time of great challenges. As Turner notes in her Introduction, she has chosen to think about Chaucer's life as categorized by the spaces in which Chaucer lived and the material culture that characterized them. She therefore offers a reader key details about London houses, merchant life, the mobility and variety of the noble household, and the realities of overseas travel. Her approach locates Chaucer within the comforts and discomforts of a working commoner who lived within circles of privilege and power. This first section is particularly strong in its attention to the historical background of the Hundred Years War and Chaucer's role in the noble households in which he served. Turner's work on Chaucer's trip to Spain in 1366 and to Genoa and Florence in 1372–73 weaves both his life and his poetry into the issues of trade and war central to the commissions on which he served.

Though the European cast of Chaucer's life is less apparent after the 1370s, Turner's emphasis upon the nature of the spaces in which Chaucer lived and moved deepens her account in Part 2 of the civic culture of London. Here, she draws upon her earlier strong work on London's volatile political culture during the 1380s in order to underline Chaucer's ability to navigate times dangerous for those too close to royal power. In Part 3, in suggesting the degree to which Chaucer forged and depended upon his networks in Kent, she offers a fresh analysis of Chaucer's life during and after the Merciless Parliament of 1388, including his appointment as a forester for North Petherton in the 1390s.

This last period of Chaucer's life, with his associations south of the Thames and his professional commitments, was also a period of great creativity for him. It is during the 1390s that he wrote many of the *Canterbury Tales* and possibly began to shape the book by linking some of them together into what we now refer to as fragments. The decade, of course, is also a period of political tension, as Richard II announced his majority and began to move upon those who had crossed him in the Merciless Parliament. In his last year, Chaucer moved back into the center of political life, leasing an apartment in the gardens of Westminster Abbey. In her account of these years and her description of the precincts of the abbey and the many types of interests it served, Turner underscores the ways in which Chaucer made spaces for himself in the precincts of London and then reinhabited a world composed of the political, commercial, and spiritual impulses and institutions that had preoccupied him for his entire life.

The subject of Chaucer and women threads its way through the book, but is perhaps most apparent in Chapter 8, entitled "Cage," which Turner parses metaphorically as a prison cell, referencing Chaucer's translation of Boethius, and also as an enclosure like a womb or a nunnery. Here, Turner raises the subject of Chaucer's daughter, the Elizabeth Chaucer noted in *Chaucer Life Records* (545) as professed at St. Helen's in London in 1377, whose move to Barking Abbey was paid for by John of Gaunt in 1381. At Barking, Elizabeth joined Margaret Swynford, Katherine Swynford's daughter. As Turner points out, we know nothing else about Elizabeth; probably, she and Margaret were born in the mid-to-late 1360s and were raised together in the household of Gaunt, where Philippa Chaucer served Gaunt's second wife Constance. Katherine, Philippa's sister, was, of course, Gaunt's longtime mistress and eventually his third wife. Turner raises the 1380 case of Cecily Champaigne in this chapter, discussing both Champaigne's accusation against Chaucer of *raptus* and the documents recording his payment and her release of the charges against him (*Chaucer Life Records*, 343–47). Turner brings together several incidents—including the death of Chaucer's mother in 1381—that in the *Life Records* are spread out.

Although I would not say that "Chaucer was losing women in droves" (210) at this time, the chapter considers some important facts frequently passed over by biographers, and also suggests the limits of our knowledge of those facts and their meanings. Turner emphasizes the importance of the medieval convent as an "essential part of the social fabric, not places of removal and separation" (206). She also reminds us that an Elizabeth Chaucer did exist and that John of Gaunt paid for her expenses and gifts the whopping sum of £51 8s. 2d. The information in the chapter poses some necessary questions about Chaucer's familial and professional relationships. A scrutiny of Gaunt's registers shows just how far his gifting arm reached and how often it traveled. Thus affinities are made, and Gaunt understood the terms of his own world. Chaucer would not have wished to disentangle himself nor his wife from such an affinity, but he also created for himself modes of speaking about power. Although I am skeptical of a tendency to see Chaucer in relation to our expectations about relationships—the assumption that Chaucer's marriage to Philippa was an unhappy one or that he had trouble with women or that John of Gaunt controlled him—Turner raises some important talking points about the nature of medieval marriages at various social levels and about the nature of patronage. These are issues pertinent to inquiries into the nature of power and the relationships power engenders or that exist within systems of power.

Despite my occasional quibbles (including at the sometimes mysterious chapter titles, such as "Cage," "Milky Way," "Tower," or "Garden," which make the book hard to use), I welcome *Chaucer: A European Life* into the Chaucer library. Turner has created a narrative from the documentary details, from her analysis of contemporary political and social circumstances, from her reading of Chaucer's works, and from the exigencies of the medieval material world. She is particularly attentive to primary documents, calendars, letter-books, and parliament rolls, and judiciously handles her coverage of prior and current scholarly work on

Chaucer. She includes a gallery of plates—of objects, works of art, and photographs of places—that admirably captures the world she describes. She has given us new ways of thinking about Chaucer, grounded her biography in sound scholarship, and offered much to discuss. The Chaucer whom Turner describes retains his mystery and his allure: he is smart and capable, a good manager, a shrewd reader of documents and political climates, a man whose instincts allowed him not simply to survive but to write despite and within rough times. This is a strong biography, well suited to the needs and interests of our own Chaucerian moment.

LYNN STALEY
Colgate University

MATTHEW X. VERNON. *The Black Middle Ages: Race and the Construction of the Middle Ages*. New York: Palgrave Macmillan, 2018. Pp. xiii, 266. $89.00 cloth; $69.99 e-book.

Those of us who take a critical stance toward medieval studies as a field and the ways that it perpetuates white supremacy and expels people of color from its ranks are often asked, especially by scholars from other areas, why we are trying to save medieval studies. Why not move on to other fields of study that are more inclusive? Although the answers vary among medievalists, my answer has always been that medieval literature and culture do not belong to white academia, nor do they belong to white supremacists. Perhaps this is why I found Matthew X. Vernon's *The Black Middle Ages: Race and the Construction of the Middle Ages* to be one of the most important books on medievalism and the Middle Ages to date. Vernon's insightful archival work, the strength of his arguments, and the nuance he brings to discussions of the Middle Ages are but a few of the reasons his book is a must-read in medieval studies, nineteenth- and twentieth-century medievalisms, and African-American studies.

Vernon carefully integrates materials from both African-American and medieval studies, demonstrating that nineteenth- and twentieth-century African-Americans used the Middle Ages to reject their erasure from America's founding origin myths, in which the nation was often presented as Anglo-Saxon in history and identity. *The Black Middle Ages* is divided into six chapters, and many of these chapters begin by deconstructing the ways that white writers and academics use the Middle Ages to equate the concept of the nation with a concept of whiteness. The chapters' substantive analysis, however, centers on the African-American writers and academics who create counter-narratives to this imagined white nationhood (shaped from a constructed white mythical past) by including African-Americans in national narratives of progress. It is difficult to do justice to the richness of the materials that Vernon brings to each chapter, and the plethora of African-American voices that he brings into the conversation. I can only say that if you can stop reading this review and simply read his *The Black Middle Ages*, then you should do so right now.

The opening introductory chapter, "Reading out of Time—Genealogy, African-American Literature, and the Middle Ages," outlines the ways that political and literary figures of the eighteenth and nineteenth centuries—including Thomas Jefferson, John H. Van Eyrie, and Walt Whitman—drew on and helped create a fantasy of the English Middle Ages as racially pure (and white). These white intellectuals imagined the Middle Ages as a framework through which to construct a narrative of national progress, a narrative that simultaneously erased the voices of those who threatened its logic. At every turn, however, African-Americans challenged these medieval myths by exposing them as false, creating a counter-narrative of the Middle Ages that laid bare the fantasy of whiteness in arguments about citizenship and American belonging (18). W. E. B. Du Bois offers a case in point, with his *Darkwater: Voices from within the Veil* (1920) clearly demonstrating how the United States and Europe used the Middle Ages to create ideologies that justified colonization and imagined a community of whiteness extending far back into the past (20).

Chapter 2, "Medieval Self-Fashioning: The Middle Ages in African-American Scholarship and Curricula," shows how African-American intellectuals used the Middle Ages to renegotiate terms of belonging by rejecting the notion of the Anglo-Saxon period as an era of racial purity, instead describing a multicultural medieval England that supported the possibility of racial mixing as a means to reach political power. Vernon shows that African-American and abolitionist writers such as Frederick Douglass; Lydia Maria Child, author of the short story "The Black Saxons" (*The Liberator*, 1841); and William Day, who wrote the poem "The

Black Saxons: A Tale of America" (1850), had a substantial interest in the Norman Conquest. Likening African-Americans to Anglo-Saxons who resisted the conquering Normans, these writers resisted, too, the dominant interpretation of the Anglo-Saxons as racially pure and white. This kind of revisionary work also appeared in other print venues, such as the *Anglo-African Magazine* (1859–62), which compared the Anglo-Saxons to the inhabitants of Africa and argued, in Vernon's words, that "the African-American voice would be as integral to the shape of the nation as its medieval past" (62). So, too, the *African Methodist Episcopal Church Review* used medievalism to articulate the complex political struggles of African Americans (e.g., Cordelia Ray's "Dante," 1885), and to connect feudalism to African-American slavery (e.g., Edward L. Blackshear, "The Negro as Passive Factor in American History," 1901). The chapter ends by pointing out how African-American intellectuals such as William Braithwaite used the survival of the English language after the Norman invasion to articulate possibilities for writing under conditions of oppression: its status as a vernacular language, open to the incorporation of new voices, made it the appropriate medium through which to compare the oppression of the Anglo-Saxons and the oppression of African-Americans.

Chapter 3, "Failed Knights and Broken Narratives: Mark Twain and Charles Chestnutt's Black Romance," questions the opposition between blackness and racial myth-making. The chapter analyzes how Mark Twain's *A Connecticut Yankee in King Arthur's Court* (1889) and Charles Chesnutt's *The House behind the Cedars* (1900) used the destabilizing nature of medieval romance to evoke and critique the mythologies at the heart of Walter Scott's *Ivanhoe* (1820). While Twain punctures *Ivanoe*'s version of romance by borrowing from the collapsing Arthurian realm of Malory's *Le Morte Darthur* (1485), Chesnutt breaks with the mythopoetic power of *Ivanhoe* by refusing to position blackness as a form of temporal and genealogical deviation. Chesnutt creates a mixed-race African-American heroine, Rowena Warwick (Rena for short), who rejects her position as the love interest of Tryon—the racist, white protagonist who cannot stop himself from loving her—and Wain, the black man interested in her. She flees from both men, which results in her death. Rena's death destabilizes the myth of an Anglo-Saxon American future and testifies, Vernon argues, to "the impossible logic of post-Reconstruction racial ideologies; she bodies forth as an attestation of a wholly different historical trajectory to that of Anglo-Saxon progress" (150).

Chapter 4, "History, Genealogy, and Gerald of Wales: Medieval Theories of Ethnicity and Their Afterlives," takes the themes of the previous chapters—racial myth-making; scientific, historical, and ethnographic knowledge production; and the ways that writers and intellectuals break away from these narratives of progress—to demonstrate that such concerns are also present in medieval texts. By using a postcolonial lens and black theory, especially Frantz Fanon's idea of the "colonized intellectual," Vernon outlines how Gerald of Wales acted as a "colonized intellectual" by undertaking a project that "fails to realize he is using techniques and a language borrowed from the occupier" (Fanon, cited by Vernon, 171). He theorizes that Gerald of Wales's *The History and Topography of Ireland* (c. 1188) was "produced in response to the problems of colonial imagination that put into contest Welsh and Irish alterity from Anglo-Norman elites" (168). Gerald of Wales created an intellectual account of Ireland that supported colonization of the island and placed Gerald as an agent of the medieval English nation. In the process, he used the same language that supported expansion into Wales. Nevertheless, his account of Ireland creates ambivalence within the text insofar as it shows the dangers of colonization. Gerald acts as both colonizer and colonized, which helps explain why Gerald's account "would create an intellectual template for imagining the Irish that would be repeated for hundreds of years, through ages and countries he could not possibly have envisioned" (198).

The last two chapters move Vernon's study to the late twentieth and early twenty-first centuries. Chapter 5, "Other Families: Dryden's Theory of Congeniality in Dante, Chaucer, and Naylor," demonstrates how Gloria Naylor uses a black female vernacular and medievalism to reject dominant narrative modes in order "to make the larger political argument about the existence of a pluralistic, polyvocal community" (215). Naylor delves into questions about the place of African-American literature, and especially the deep and justified fears that African-American literature would be confined through its racialization as a "minority literature" (213). Both *Linden Hills* (1985) and *Bailey's Café* (1992) demonstrate Naylor's use of John Dryden's theory of congeniality, a mode of translation that understands the potential of reframing an early text for a new audience in order to achieve new critical perspectives. In these novels, Naylor deploys Dante and Chaucer respectively through a rich interpretation of the vernacular to theorize a space for African-American literature that "evades race as confine" (213). Both texts leave the reader with a sense of incompleteness at the same time that they articulate how medieval canonical voices such as Chaucer and Dante can be galvanized to incorporate new voices, new modes of writing, and new critical perspectives.

Chapter 6, "Coda," returns to romance through the movie *Django Unchained*, directed by Quentin Tarantino. Vernon argues that unlike *Pulp Fiction*, which uses the phrase "get medieval" in ways that demonstrate a misunderstanding of what getting medieval means, *Django Unchained* does, in fact, get medieval. The film juxtaposes white-dominant narratives of the United States—in which the medieval past appears as romance and myth, specifically the myths of Siegfried and Brunhilda, the Wild West, and the romantic antebellum south—with African-American characters. The centering of African-Americans in these imagined white spaces disrupts racial myth-making in similar ways to the work of the African-American writers discussed above. Vernon finishes his book by stating that "*Django* fully comprehends the potency of cultural spolia, fragments from the Middle Ages and the nineteenth century, juxtaposed to create a fantastic lie or a riotous truth. It has gotten medieval" (261). This ending shines with the same decorum and brilliance that the rest of the book demonstrates—for, in my opinion, what is left unspoken but beautifully implied is that it took white artists and intellectuals until the twenty-first century to arrive at the same conclusions that African-American artists and scholars had come to in the long nineteenth century. While white America has assumed that they have been getting medieval, it is African-American intellectuals who understood the power of race in the construction of the Middle Ages. By recovering the ways that African-Americans use the Middle Ages and the ways that Africana Studies can transform the analysis of the Middle Ages, the book creates an "anti-genealogy," showing how African-American writers fashioned a Middle Ages that fundamentally revised the national and racial suppositions of white writers and scholars. In the process, Vernon recovers an important part of American history, helps to redirect studies of medievalism and the Middle Ages, and opens up our field to new realms of inquiry.

NAHIR I. OTAÑO GRACIA
University of New Mexico

LAWRENCE WARNER. *Chaucer's Scribes: London Textual Production, 1384–1432.* Cambridge: Cambridge University Press, 2018. Pp. xvi, 222. $105.00 cloth; $84.00 e-book.

Just as he did with his previous two books—*The Lost History of "Piers Plowman"* (2011) and *The Myth of "Piers Plowman"* (2014)—Lawrence Warner dismantles in *Chaucer's Scribes* some widely accepted ideas in the study of late Middle English literature. Never one to shy away from scholarly disagreement, Warner once again urges readers to reconsider the "mythologies" of our field. As the title provocatively suggests in its echoing of Linne Mooney's explosive 2006 *Speculum* article "Chaucer's Scribe," he is responding to the claims about Adam Pinkhurst and the scribes of the London Guildhall made by Mooney, Simon Horobin, and Estelle Stubbs over the last decade-and-a-half. Drawing upon paleographical, linguistic, historical, philological, and editorial material, Warner's critique of this corpus highlights hitherto overlooked logical and evidentiary problems with the existing arguments. His refutation of a single central location (the Guildhall) for much Middle English literary copying, run by a small group of copyists who knew Chaucer, compels scholars to consider "a more diffuse history" of scribal activity in medieval London (4). However, while Warner launches an impressively detailed challenge to the conclusions drawn by Mooney, Stubbs, and Horobin, he also acknowledges the importance of their work and invites "continual testing" of not only their claims but his as well (11).

Warner begins with the best known of "Chaucer's Scribes," Adam Pinkhurst. Chapter 1, "Adam," focuses largely on the "discovery" of Adam Pinkhurst's connection to Chaucer, the emotional power of this connection for medieval scholars, and the role of Chaucer's famous short poem "Adam Scriveyn" in the identification. In her 2008 article "Reading Chaucer's Words to Adam," Alexandra Gillespie raised important questions about the evidence for Pinkhurst's identity as the Adam of the poem, and Warner extends that skepticism, arguing that Mooney's conclusions about the poetic Adam's identity and Pinkhurst as the Hengwrt/Ellesmere (Hg/El) scribe are based on a tautology rather than material evidence: "the discovery that Adam Pynkhurst was the scribe of Hengwrt and Ellesmere shows that we ought to read 'Adam Scriveyne' as a reliable historical document; the reliable historicity of 'Adam Scriveyne' shows that we ought to identify Pynkhurst as the scribe of these *Canterbury Tales* manuscripts" (14). Throughout the book, Warner highlights similar moments in which an argument's logic becomes circular, such as the identification of John Marchaunt as Scribe D in Harley 7334 (101), the position of Richard Frampton as a Guildhall clerk (106–7), and the attribution of a 1390 deed to Marchaunt (99–100). His careful focus on what the evidence offers leads Warner to explore not only the historical and material evidence linking "Adam Scriveyne" to Adam Pinkhurst and Chaucer, but the metrical evidence as well, which he suggests casts doubt on Chaucerian authorship. The poem can only work as evidence for Pinkhurst being close to Chaucer if indeed Chaucer wrote the poem and if Pinkhurst was the copyist of Hg and El. But, as noted above, Warner points out how these separate claims are being used to reinforce one another rather than being tested on their own strength.

Chapter 2, "The Pynkhurst Canon," moves from challenging the central, exciting moment of identifying Adam Scriveyn with Adam Pinkhurst to evaluating the texts now attributed to him. The key premise of this chapter is Warner's dismantling of two widely accepted ideas: that Adam Pinkhurst was Scribe B of the Trinity Gower, and that Pinkhurst/Scribe B copied Hg/El as well as Trinity, B.15.17 (W), a *Piers Plowman* manuscript. His conclusion is that Scribe B is not Pinkhurst and therefore that Pinkhurst did not copy Hg/El or any of Chaucer's other texts, but that he *did* copy the Trinity *Piers*. Central to this chapter is Warner's contention that the attribution of Hg and El to Pinkhurst is due not to careful comparison of these manuscripts' hands to Pinkhurst's own confirmation, but to "supposed 'signatures' or 'marks' in the form of decorative features" (which he challenges) and to the "sheer force of rhetoric" in which Pinkhurst is revealed "unmistakeably" to be the Hg/El scribe—in other words, a shaping of evidence to fit the theory of scribal attribution (32). Using Mooney and Stubbs's own focus on decorative features, Warner ultimately concludes that the Pinkhurst corpus comprises just four items—including W, but not Hg/El—rather than the eighteen listed by Mooney et al. Chapter 3, "Pynkhurst's London English and the Dilemma of Copy-Text," extends Warner's argument about Pinkhurst's identification by exploring its implications for the viability of Samuels's Type III London English is a linguistic category. If a single scribe (and possibly his apprentices) was not responsible for so many Middle English texts, then the existence of a Type III London English is indeed tenable. The arguments here were compelling, although I found this chapter's transitions from Type III English, to an analysis of the Mercers' petition, to the process involved in choosing W as a copy-text for the Athlone *Piers Plowman*, to be somewhat confusing to track.

Chapters 4 and 5, "Looking for the Scribe of Huntington Library Hm 114" and "The Guildhall Clerks," move the reader from Pinkhurst to Mooney and Stubbs's other scribal attributions. Mooney and Stubbs's 2013 book *Scribes and the City* identified and discussed the scribes/clerks Richard Osbarn, John Marchaunt, Thomas Hoccleve, Richard Frampton, and John Carpenter, and Warner evaluates and sometimes challenges their conclusions. A central feature of his argument in these chapters is that the London Guildhall was not the hub of literary activity that Mooney and Stubbs have suggested, but that literary and civic copying took place in a wide range of locations around London. Warner launches this part of his argument by first contending that Richard Osbarn was *not* the Hm 114 scribe and that the Hm 114 scribe's primary location was not the Guildhall. One of the strengths of this chapter is Warner's provision of a greatly expanded corpus of this scribe's writings—about sixty texts, many of which are governmental or civic in nature, and some of which are literary. These all demonstrate, Warner indicates, that "the clerk identified as the Hm 114 scribe recorded the decisions, activities, and traditions not just of the Guildhall, but of London and beyond" (91). Warner concludes this chapter by highlighting some of the interesting anecdotes recorded by this scribe—the "voices, stories, and narratives of medieval London" (94)—and speculates about possible connections between his civic copying and his interest in copying tales such as the *Troilus* and *Piers*. In Chapter 5, Warner moves on to the other Guildhall clerks, first arguing that there is no clear, consistent evidence supporting Mooney and Stubbs's assertions that (a) Scribe D of the Trinity Gower is John Marchaunt of the Guildhall and (b) Adam Pinkhurst must have worked with him at some point. He does accept Mooney and Stubbs's three new attributions to the scribe Richard Frampton, although he is not convinced that Frampton was a Guildhall clerk, and is partially convinced of their new attributions to John Carpenter, one of which he considers a "great triumph" (108) for *Scribes and the City*. The chapter concludes by reiterating his challenge to the claim that the Guildhall was a central literary repository and instead suggests that literary activity in London was more widespread and diffuse.

Chapter 6, the book's final body-chapter, focuses on the central role of Thomas Hoccleve in London's literary and civic landscape. Taking the features of the six manuscripts now accepted as Hoccleve's, as well as the editorial stemma of the *Regiment of Princes* and metrical errors in the Royal *Regiment* manuscript, Warner challenges Mooney's landmark argument that BL, MS Royal 17 D.XVIII is a holograph copy of the *Regiment*. He argues that Mooney et al. have essentially forced the evidence for Hoccleve's work as a copyist to fit their vision of the London Guildhall as a central literary hub, rather than considering the evidence on its own terms. His argument also indicates that this forced interpretation of evidence applies to the contention that Hoccleve and Chaucer knew one another well. Warner suggests that the scholarly investment in, for example, attributing Hengwrt's hands C, D, and E to Hoccleve (who is Hand F) allows us to see Hoccleve as having a key editorial role in that manuscript, as opposed to being "tangential" in its production (129). He highlights the paleographical problems with these attributions and instead accepts A. I. Doyle and M. B. Parkes's original conclusions. Indeed, throughout the book, Warner often returns to and confirms Doyle and Parkes's original observations about scribal hands.

Warner's concluding chapter is titled "Where Is Adam Pynkhurst?," which may well be how readers feel at the end of this journey through the intricacies of scribal hands, medieval documents, linguistics, and poetic metrics. One realizes that it is easier to accept the end-point of an argument without evaluating its details—particularly if that endpoint is as emotionally energizing and exciting as the Pinkhurst and other scribal identifications have been. However, Warner's book reveals what a trap this can be. Even if readers do not accept all of Warner's arguments and attributions—I myself questioned a few of them—there is no doubt that he engages with evidence on its own terms rather than fitting it into an existing framework. One of his greatest strengths is how he encourages other scholars to evaluate his interpretation of the evidence, just as he evaluated that of Mooney, Stubbs, and Horobin. Paleographical analysis in particular is more of an art than a science and requires other forms of evidence to support it. Warner urges medieval scholars "with only a passing acquaintance with paleography" (140) not to leave all paleographical conclusions to the "experts" but instead to delve into the evidence themselves. Indeed, the separation of paleography from the rest of medieval studies is a problem that Warner returns to throughout his conclusion. His insistence that "scrutiny makes for a much healthier state of affairs" (141) in our field is absolutely correct, and he is aware that this principle applies to his own work as well.

While he presents a dizzying array of evidence in this book, he also provides for readers images of or links to the manuscripts he is discussing, and is very clear about the arguments to which he is responding (he often quotes directly rather than summarizing). Warner's detail-oriented and carefully developed analysis of the evidence for scribal culture in medieval London is a healthy challenge to our field and an encouragement to all of us who do not consider ourselves "paleographers" to get down and dirty with manuscripts—digitized or not—and draw our own conclusions about the evidence we find.

NOELLE PHILLIPS
Douglas College

MICHAEL J. WARREN. *Birds in Medieval English Poetry: Metaphors, Realities, Transformations.* Cambridge: D. S. Brewer, 2018. Pp. 269. $99.00.

Birds have fascinated medievalists since before the "animal turn"—witness Beryl Rowland's *Birds with Human Souls* (1978)—and monographs on the subject have proliferated since scholars such as Jeffrey Jerome Cohen, Gillian Rudd, and Dorothy Yamamoto invited us to engage with nature. Michael J. Warren's *Birds in Medieval English Poetry* is a welcome addition to such scholarship. Warren is familiar with theoretical work by Gilles Deleuze and Félix Guattari, Jacques Derrida, and Claude Lévi-Strauss, and well-versed in ornithology, but his argument relies on careful and nuanced close readings of five early English poems. Warren maintains that birds in these poems cannot be read as purely metaphorical, and so scholars must attend to how they reveal real birds in ways that "hint at diverse, interpenetrating orientations" where "natural and cultural histories overlap, reciprocate and interweave" (5). After an introduction, Warren focuses each chapter around a central poetic work: (1) *The Seafarer*, (2) the Exeter Book Riddles, (3) *The Owl and the Nightingale*, (4) Chaucer's *Parliament of Fowls*, and (5) the "Tale of Tereus" in Gower's *Confessio Amantis*.

Reveling in contact between human and avian, between bodies and thought, and between science and art, *Birds in Medieval English Poetry* attends to both allegorical figuration and natural philosophy to argue that because birds resist categorization with their penchant for transformation via flight, migration, molting, singing, and oviparous reproduction, they are "crucial to the potentialities, effects and limitations" of human imagination and experience (18). As Warren explains near the end of the Chaucer chapter, "If animal imagery has long been understood as casting the nonhuman in human terms in order to explore human matters, sometimes we catch something of the animal terms, too, reversing our attempts to superimpose so that some of what we intend for the human tenor . . . rubs off on the feathered vehicle" (175). In essence, Warren enacts the Nightingale's reminder that fables are never completely fictional (line 128 in *The Owl and the Nightingale*), taking medieval ornithology seriously while also giving due diligence to medieval secular and religious concerns and to modern scholarly debates.

Chapter 1 begins with Bede's story of the sparrow from the *Historia ecclesiastica* to establish a connection between bird and soul in biblical and Anglo-Saxon allegory that is relevant for understanding *The Seafarer*: "As in the famous sparrow analogy, we encounter the same fluctuations between hall-life and the daunting outside world, the mind that weighs up the two in opposition, and birds that are associated with both these worlds" (28). This foundation allows Warren to read the poem as a unified whole, whereby "a curious avian materiality" inhabits both the naming of seabirds in the ocean setting at the beginning of the poem and the figure of the lone-flier that marks the turn from seascape to *contemptus mundi* (29). Attending to bird habits and habitations, Warren reads both passages as simultaneously "factual and figurative," so that the obscurity of the afterlife inheres in the acknowledgment that birds cannot replace human companions in the first passage (63). Literal and figurative modes converge to reveal that the deprivation and loneliness of embodied physical journeying prepare the speaker for a posthumous unknown.

Building on observations about avian foreignness, Chapter 2 argues that "in being both nameable and anonymous [birds] suit riddles' tendencies to obfuscate and disambiguate concurrently" (66). When combined with the lack of solutions in the Exeter manuscript, the swan (Riddle 7), the barnacle goose (Riddle 24), the jay (Riddle 8), the elusive Riddle 57, and especially the fingers and quill of Riddle 51, for Warren, "encourage willingness to admit uncertainties, to recognize but not circumscribe the web of sprawling, inclusive contiguities between animate and inanimate individuals" (84). Birds, like riddles, then, inspire wonder and irresolution.

The Owl and the Nightingale, subject of Chapter 3, depicts a famously unresolved debate, and Warren offers new insight into how the poem intertwines "the natural and the cultural" to "determine the birds' identities" (133). Focusing particularly on the Owl, the chapter shows that the poem distorts the bird's identity by adapting contradictory exegetical interpretations and conflating different owl species from the bestiary tradition. Attuned to the humor in the poem—as in the observation that the Owl's defense of her messy nest turns the Book of Nature model "entirely on its head" (124)—Warren also reads the poem's abusive differentiations in the context of anti-Semitic strigine imagery in Norwich Cathedral to remind us that indiscriminate hatred such as that exhibited by the two birds can have violent social consequences.

The chapter on Chaucer's *Parliament of Fowls* again takes comedy seriously, concentrating on line 499. Warren rightly sees the goose, cuckoo, and duck cries—"Kek kek! kokkow! quek quek!"—as destabilizing human allegory by foregrounding both linguistic barriers and the possibility of "biotranslation" (150). The interruption of animal voices in a poem where bird utterances are otherwise seamlessly represented in Middle English confronts us with the narrator, who either attempts to translate the base noise of these lower orders, or whose dreamscape ability to understand birds suddenly fails, or who accurately reports overheard bird calls amidst other bird voices that he can understand. The moment is silly but suggests that "humans are not the only subjective beings capable of meaning" (167). Warren highlights the numerous translations at work in the poem, from Italian and French to Middle English, from birdsong to human song, and from oral to written to show that "it is possible for allegory to liberate rather than constrain, to be something other than a form that simply converts into humanized symbolic meaning and demands a singular reading" (175).

Chapter 5 is the most contained: it makes no claims about the unity or form of Gower's *Confessio Amantis*, concentrating on the single "Tale of Tereus." Through source study and careful analysis of Gower's language, Warren maintains that the metamorphosis of the three main characters highlights both an individual body's vulnerability to fragmentation and a disquieting multiplicity of bodies in rape and cannibalism. The reading acknowledges interspecies consonances and incompatibility: the nightingale, swallow, and lapwing continue to think as Philomela, Procne, and Tereus, but now have voices and forms that foreground birdlore and explain the origin of whole species. Despite this tight focus, the chapter also connects the tale to Gower's *Vox clamantis* and Chaucer's *Troilus and Criseyde*, among other works.

The book's breadth, transgressing boundaries between Old and Middle English studies, will make it useful to experts in those areas as well as to teachers of early literature surveys, but that breadth is also its weakness. Chapters 1 and 2 demonstrate the value of studying birds in the Exeter Book more fully. Warren does discuss *The Wanderer* as a counterpoint to *The Seafarer*, and *The Phoenix* appears in both chapters, but attention to the whole manuscript would no doubt please scholars of Old English. I was so engaged in Chapter 3's exploration of the conflicting meanings and behaviors of owls in the bestiary tradition that I wished there had been more time to examine the tradition of nightingales in Latin and vernacular lyrics. Additionally, more could be said about human–animal communication in Chaucer's work (especially the *Canterbury Tales*) and about hybridity in Gower's. Nonetheless, it is not a bad thing for a book to leave readers wanting more when the readings are this perspicacious. Ultimately, *Birds in Middle English Poetry* contributes significantly to ecocritical, literary, and medieval studies. It shows that asking new questions of familiar texts reveals exciting insights into how medieval people understood their natural environment and how allegory operates. It invites us to remember the dynamic importance of birds in the Anthropocene and concludes with a generous glossary of bird names that will facilitate further study.

WENDY MATLOCK
Kansas State Unversity

MARJORIE CURRY WOODS. *Weeping for Dido: The Classics in the Medieval Classroom*. Princeton: Princeton University Press, 2019. Pp. xxi, 176. $39.95.

Despite all we know about the schoolbooks of medieval classrooms, we know very little about how particular texts were taught. Thanks to Marjorie Curry Woods's magisterial monograph, *Classroom Commentaries: Teaching the "Poetria nova" across Medieval and Renaissance Europe* (2010), we know that Geoffrey of Vinsauf was a standard author for poetical and rhetorical instruction from the thirteenth to the fifteenth century throughout much of Europe. And while Woods and other scholars of medieval pedagogy, such as Martin Camargo and Irina Dumitrescu, have compellingly recaptured scenes of teaching through analyses of manuscript commentaries, interlinear glosses, and literary descriptions of classroom practices, actual instructional methods are often elusive and seemingly impossible to identify. As a means to this end, *Weeping for Dido: The Classics in the Medieval Classroom* illustrates Woods's continuing commitment to define what she calls the "relentlessly practical" (3) nature of medieval pedagogy, focused specifically on the texts of the Virgilian tradition. Woods reveals that these Latin works, which range from the *Aeneid* to the *Ilias latina* to the *Achilleid*, were not merely read for the purposes of expanding vocabulary or developing writing skills— they were performed collaboratively to teach adolescent boys what it means to feel a whole range of emotions, especially the sorrow of women.

Weeping for Dido is based on the E. H. Gombrich Lectures that Woods gave at the Warburg Institute in 2014, which is especially appropriate for a book designed to be read aloud (see below). In "A Short Introduction," Woods explains how her graduate-school encounter with Augustine's famous confession that he wept for Dido led her to examine Virgil's place in the medieval classroom, along with two lesser-known companion texts, Statius's unfinished *Bildungsroman* known as the *Achilleid* and a redaction of Homer's *Iliad* known as the *Ilias latina*. Woods devotes the first two chapters to these texts, working with more than 140 manuscripts from the twelfth to the fifteenth century that were produced or annotated in Germany, Italy, England, and France. In both of these chapters, Woods reveals how schoolboys were prompted to perform the voices of women, ranging from Dido to Andromache, even assuming the role of the cross-dressing Achilles, who pretends to be a girl to avoid going to war in the *Achilleid*. The third and final chapter explicitly addresses the pedagogical tradition of boys reciting and embodying the emotional speeches of women. Woods frames what follows the introduction with the following claim: "[W]hile women were overwhelmingly absent from this schoolboy classical world except in texts, their emotions permeated and sometimes dominated the classroom experience" (10–11).

Chapter 1, "Memory, Emotion, and the Death of a Queen," focuses on the teaching of the *Aeneid*, specifically what boys learned from the suffering and suicide of Dido. Woods begins with Augustine's *Confessions* and his account of memorizing the travels of Aeneas, which forced him to empathize with the "pitiful" abandonment and death of Dido. With Augustine as the pedagogical prototype, Woods turns to the medieval manuscripts of the *Aeneid*, some of which reflect a rhetorical program of annotation based in the teaching of letter-writing manuals and Cicero's *De inventione*. Other copies of the *Aeneid*, such as the famous *Carmina Burana* manuscript (Munich, Bayerische Staatsbibliothek, MS Clm 4660), demonstrate through illustration and interlinear glossing that "immersion and luxuriating in the pain of literary characters allowed schoolboys to experience varieties of emotion not encouraged or even tolerated outside the classroom" (22). As Woods points out, classroom manuscripts of the *Aeneid* also highlight the death and suffering of characters such as Dido and Creusa as a mnemonic strategy that helped students internalize, sing, or even contextualize their speeches. In one remarkable set of glosses on Dido's lament in Book IV in Staatsbibliothek zu Berlin, MS Ham. 678, Aeneas's cruelty and Dido's humiliation are accentuated through interlinear annotations that repetitively name the lovers and offer stage directions for classroom performance (45–46). Through close analysis of the textual apparatus in these manuscripts, Woods reveals the pedagogical complexity of Virgilian *pathos*.

Turning to curricular prequels of the *Aeneid*, Chapter 2, "Troy Books for Boys," examines the roles of the *Achilleid* and the *Ilias latina* within elementary-level Latin education. Woods begins with the *Achilleid*, a coming-of-age narrative for Achilles, who disguises himself as a woman to avoid going to war against Troy. While this may be "delicious gender-bending material" (49), Woods suggests that "the *Achilleid* may have reassured male students that temporary identification with and performance of female emotions and actions could be just that: temporary" (52–53). Once again, Woods demonstrates how characters' speeches are parsed for a variety of rhetorical purposes, especially the identification of Ciceronian *partes orationis* and *attributa personarum*. These latter "attributes of characters," used by lawyers in their presentation of defendants in court, became a set of classroom guidelines for characterizing, for example, Achilles' *habitus*, which refers both to his wearing of women's clothes (i.e., their habit) and to his acquisition of a particular kind of training (i.e., acting like a woman). This cross-dressing becomes a way for Achilles to become intimate with women such as Deidamia, whom he eventually rapes. While annotations on this horrifying scene reflect both laughter and disgust, Woods is quick to point out that Achilles assumes the *habitus* of a woman "to act out his masculine feelings of aggression, not to experience women's emotions" (86). On the other hand, the *Ilias latina*, or "Latin Homer," which served as a curricular sequel to the *Achilleid*, provided no such uncertainty about masculine identities. As opposed to the *Achilleid*'s focus on adolescent development, the *Ilias latina* was a "Boys' Own *Iliad*" (87), in which the Ciceronian attributes focused on the name and nature of each character, subdividing each into categories of (im)mortality, sex, nationality, birthplace, family, and age. In addition to this rhetorical analysis, schoolboys were invited to experience and express the losses of war, including the death of a loved one, such as Hector of Troy. Together, these classical schoolbooks offered students opportunities to affirm an uncomplicated definition of masculinity, improve their oratorical skills, and develop their emotional intelligence.

In the third and final chapter, "Boys Performing Women (and Men)," Woods attends to specific performance cues in manuscripts that contain these classroom texts. Building upon previous studies of rhetorical delivery that reveal how often boys were expected to perform women's roles, Woods carefully demonstrates how glossators marked speeches with terms that explicitly instruct readers how to speak particular lines in the text. For example, Dido's lament about her abandonment by Aeneas in Book IV of the *Aeneid* is glossed with reference to the *Rhetorica*'s pathetic tone, which requires a restrained and deep voice, a sad countenance, and violent gesticulation. Woods proceeds to demonstrate how these same schoolboys would have already become accustomed in their earlier education to performing disturbing scenes of rape, such as those found in the *Achilleid* and the *Pamphilus*, which were accompanied with glosses that suggest that students "identified as easily with the victims as with the perpetrators of sexual violence" (126). Implying that "reading against the grain" was an accepted or even encouraged practice, Woods ends the chapter with the claim that women's speeches hold a "central and consistent" place within "the history of Western pedagogy" (145), an argument that is perhaps the most compelling and important of the book.

For a relatively short monograph, *Weeping for Dido* exceeds the sum of its parts, offering both a provocative argument about the role of emotional instruction in medieval classrooms and an innovative presentation of evidence. I want to emphasize this latter feature because the claims about specific teaching practices in each chapter depend upon extensive paleographical work that Woods makes accessible to a wide variety of audiences. Rather than merely reproduce photographs of select pages of annotated manuscripts or transcribe relevant glosses, Woods juxtaposes images of folios with Latin transcriptions and English translations that replicate the spatial relationships between particular lines of poetry and their glosses, demonstrating visually how particular texts would have been performed, often with sidebars and elaborations that clarify the grammar or context of a line, offer an emotional reaction to a particular phrase, and/or suggest a spoken tone or emphasis for specific words. When Woods analyzes the language of her transcriptions to reveal a particular teaching moment, she distinguishes the annotations from the text with bolding and brackets, encouraging the reader to read the text aloud and speak the glosses in a separate tone of voice. By prompting her audience to perform her text, Woods practices what she preaches, a unique feature of a scholarly book that would undoubtedly impress Geoffrey of Vinsauf, whose *Poetria nova* teaches the writing of poetry through verse. The result is a book that is more than a stunning work of scholarship—it is an immersive experience that transports the reader across space and time into the sounds and fury of women in the medieval classroom.

ALEX MUELLER
University of Massachusetts Boston

Books Received

Barrington, Candace, and Sebastian Sobecki, eds. *The Cambridge Companion to English Law and Literature*. Cambridge: Cambridge University Press, 2019. Pp. xiii, 220. $24.99 paper.

Bertolet, Craig E., and Robert Epstein. *Money, Commerce, and Economics in Late Medieval English Literature*. New York: Palgrave Macmillan, 2018. Pp. x, 185. $99.99 cloth; $79.99 e-book.

Boffey, Julia, and Christiania Whitehead, eds. *Middle English Lyrics: New Readings of Short Poems*. Cambridge: D. S. Brewer, 2018. Pp. xvii, 310. $99.00.

Burger, Glenn D., and Holly A. Crocker, eds. *Medieval Affect, Feeling, and Emotion*. Cambridge: Cambridge University Press, 2019. Pp. x, 249. $99.99.

Putter, Ad, and Judith Jefferson, eds. *The Transmission of Medieval Romance: Metres, Manuscripts and Early Prints*. Cambridge: D. S. Brewer, 2018. Pp. xiv, 241. $99.00.

Sobecki, Sebastian, and John Scattergood, eds. *A Critical Companion to John Skelton*. Cambridge: D. S. Brewer, 2018. Pp. vii, 233. $99.00.

Sullivan, Karen. *The Danger of Romance: Truth, Fantasy, and Arthurian Fictions*. Chicago: University of Chicago Press, 2018. Pp. 299. $35.00 paper.

Warren, Nancy Bradley. *Chaucer and Religious Controversies in the Medieval and Early Modern Eras*. Notre Dame: University of Notre Dame Press. Pp. xiii, 213. $100.00 cloth; $45.00 paper.

An Annotated Chaucer Bibliography, 2017

Compiled and edited by Stephanie Amsel

Regular contributors:

Mark Allen, *University of Texas at San Antonio*
Stephanie Amsel, *Southern Methodist University* (Texas)
Brother Anthony (Sonjae An), *Sogang University* (South Korea)
Tim Arner, *Grinnell College* (Iowa)
Debra Best, *California State University at Dominguez Hills*
Thomas H. Blake, *Austin College* (Texas)
Agnès Blandeau, *Université de Nantes* (France)
Matthew Brumit, *University of Mary* (North Dakota)
Margaret Connolly, *University of St. Andrews* (Scotland)
Stefania D'Agata D'Ottavi, *Università per Stranieri di Siena* (Italy)
Geoffrey B. Elliott, *Independent Scholar* (Texas)
Thomas J. Farrell, *Stetson University* (Florida)
Jamie C. Fumo, *Florida State University*
James B. Harr III, *Wake Technical Community College* (North Carolina)
Douglas W. Hayes, *Lakehead University*
Ana Sáez Hidalgo, *Universidad de Valladolid* (Spain)
Andrew James Johnston, *Freie Universität Berlin* (Germany)
Yoshinobu Kudo, *Keio University* (Japan)
Wim Lindeboom, *Independent Scholar* (Netherlands)
Warren S. Moore III, *Newberry College* (South Carolina)
Daniel M. Murtaugh, *Florida Atlantic University*
Thomas J. Napierkowski, *University of Colorado at Colorado Springs*
Teresa P. Reed, *Jacksonville State University* (Alabama)
Will Rogers, *University of Louisiana at Monroe*
Christopher Roman, *Kent State University* (Ohio)
Martha Rust, *New York University*
Thomas R. Schneider, *California Baptist University*
David Sprunger, *Concordia College* (Minnesota)
Anne Thornton, *Abbot Public Library* (Marblehead, Massachusetts)
Winthrop Wetherbee, *Cornell University* (New York)
Elaine Whitaker, *Georgia College & State University*
Susan Yager, *Iowa State University*

Ad hoc contributions were made by Roger Dahood, University of Arizona. The bibliographer acknowledges with gratitude the invaluable contribution and support from Mark Allen, Professor Emeritus, University of Texas at San Antonio.

This bibliography continues the bibliographies published since 1975 in previous volumes of *Studies in the Age of Chaucer*. Bibliographic information up to 1975 can be found in Eleanor P. Hammond, *Chaucer: A Bibliographic Manual* (1908; reprint, New York: Peter Smith, 1933); D. D. Griffith, *Bibliography of Chaucer, 1908–1953* (Seattle: University of Washington Press, 1955); William R. Crawford, *Bibliography of Chaucer, 1954–63* (Seattle: University of Washington Press, 1967); and Lorrayne Y. Baird, *Bibliography of Chaucer, 1964–1973* (Boston, Mass.: G. K. Hall, 1977). See also Lorrayne Y. Baird-Lange and Hildegard Schnuttgen, *Bibliography of Chaucer, 1974–1985* (Hamden, Conn.: Shoe String Press, 1988); Bege K. Bowers and Mark Allen, eds., *Annotated Chaucer Bibliography, 1986–1996* (Notre Dame: University of Notre Dame Press, 2002); and Mark Allen and Stephanie Amsel, eds., *Annotated Chaucer Bibliography, 1997–2010* (Manchester: Manchester University Press, 2015).

Additions and corrections to this bibliography should be sent to Stephanie Amsel, Department of English, Southern Methodist University, 108C Clements Hall, PO Box 750435, Dallas, Texas 75275-0435. An electronic version of this bibliography (1975–2016) is available via The New Chaucer Society Web page at http://artsci.wustl.edu/~chaucer/, or directly at http://uchaucer.utsa.edu. Authors are urged to send annotations for articles, reviews, and books that have been or might be overlooked to Stephanie Amsel, samsel@smu.edu.

Classifications

Abbreviations of Chaucer's Works

ABC	*An ABC*
Adam	*Adam Scriveyn*
Anel	*Anelida and Arcite*
Astr	*A Treatise on the Astrolabe*
Bal Compl	*A Balade of Complaint*
BD	*The Book of the Duchess*
Bo	*Boece*
Buk	*The Envoy to Bukton*
CkT, CkP	*The Cook's Tale, The Cook's Prologue*
ClT, ClP, Cl–MerL	*The Clerk's Tale, The Clerk's Prologue, Clerk–Merchant Link*
Compl d'Am	*Complaynt d'Amours*
CT	*The Canterbury Tales*
CYT, CYP	*The Canon's Yeoman's Tale, The Canon's Yeoman's Prologue*
Equat	*The Equatorie of the Planetis*
For	*Fortune*
Form Age	*The Former Age*
FranT, FranP	*The Franklin's Tale, The Franklin's Prologue*
FrT, FrP, Fr–SumL	*The Friar's Tale, The Friar's Prologue, Friar–Summoner Link*
Gent	*Gentilesse*
GP	*The General Prologue*
HF	*The House of Fame*
KnT, Kn–MilL	*The Knight's Tale, Knight–Miller Link*
Lady	*A Complaint to His Lady*
LGW, LGWP	*The Legend of Good Women, The Legend of Good Women Prologue*
ManT, ManP	*The Manciple's Tale, The Manciple's Prologue*
Mars	*The Complaint of Mars*
Mel, Mel–MkL	*The Tale of Melibee, Melibee–Monk Link*
MercB	*Merciles Beaute*

MerT, MerE–SqH	The Merchant's Tale, Merchant Endlink–Squire Headlink
MilT, MilP, Mil–RvL	The Miller's Tale, The Miller's Prologue, Miller–Reeve Link
MkT, MkP, Mk–NPL	The Monk's Tale, The Monk's Prologue, Monk–Nun's Priest Link
MLT, MLH, MLP, MLE	The Man of Law's Tale, Man of Law Headlink, The Man of Law's Prologue, Man of Law Endlink
NPT, NPP, NPE	The Nun's Priest's Tale, The Nun's Priest's Prologue, Nun's Priest's Endlink
PardT, PardP	The Pardoner's Tale, The Pardoner's Prologue
ParsT, ParsP	The Parson's Tale, The Parson's Prologue
PF	The Parliament of Fowls
PhyT, Phy–PardL	The Physician's Tale, Physician–Pardoner Link
Pity	The Complaint unto Pity
Prov	Proverbs
PrT, PrP, Pr–ThL	The Prioress's Tale, The Prioress's Prologue, Prioress–Thopas Link
Purse	The Complaint of Chaucer to His Purse
Ret	Chaucer's Retraction {Retractation}
Rom	The Romaunt of the Rose
Ros	To Rosemounde
RvT, RvP, Rv–CkL	The Reeve's Tale, The Reeve's Prologue, Reeve–Cook Link
Scog	The Envoy to Scogan
ShT, Sh–PrL	The Shipman's Tale, Shipman–Prioress Link
SNT, SNP, SN–CYL	The Second Nun's Tale, The Second Nun's Prologue, Second Nun–Canon's Yeoman Link
SqT, SqH, Sq–FranL	The Squire's Tale, Squire Headlink, Squire–Franklin Link
Sted	Lak of Stedfastnesse
SumT, SumP	The Summoner's Tale, The Summoner's Prologue
TC	Troilus and Criseyde

Th, Th–MelL	*The Tale of Sir Thopas, Sir Thopas–Melibee Link*
Truth	*Truth*
Ven	*The Complaint of Venus*
WBT, WBP, WB–FrL	*The Wife of Bath's Tale, The Wife of Bath's Prologue, Wife of Bath–Friar Link*
Wom Nob	*Womanly Noblesse*
Wom Unc	*Against Women Unconstant*

Periodical Abbreviations

Anglia	Anglia: Zeitschrift für Englische Philologie
Anglistik	Anglistik: Mitteilungen des Verbandes deutscher Anglisten
ANQ	ANQ: A Quarterly Journal of Short Articles, Notes, and Reviews
Archiv	Archiv für das Studium der Neueren Sprachen und Literaturen
Arthuriana	Arthuriana
Atlantis	Atlantis: Revista de la Asociacion Española de Estudios Anglo-Norteamericanos
AUMLA	AUMLA: Journal of the Australasian Universities Language and Literature Association
BAM	Bulletin des Anglicistes Médiévistes
BJRL	Bulletin of the John Rylands University Library of Manchester
BSCS	Bulletin of the Society for Chaucer Studies
C&L	Christianity and Literature
CarmP	Carmina Philosophiae: Journal of the International Boethius Society
CE	College English
ChauR	Chaucer Review
CL	Comparative Literature (Eugene, Ore.)
Clio	CLIO: A Journal of Literature, History, and the Philosophy of History
CLS	Comparative Literature Studies
CML	Classical and Modern Literature: A Quarterly (Columbia, Mo.)
CollL	College Literature
Comitatus	Comitatus: A Journal of Medieval and Renaissance Studies
CRCL	Canadian Review of Comparative Literature/Revue Canadienne de Littérature Comparée
DAI	Dissertation Abstracts International
EA	Etudes Anglaises: Grand-Bretagne, Etats-Unis
EHR	English Historical Review

EIC	*Essays in Criticism: A Quarterly Journal of Literary Criticism*
EJ	*English Journal*
ELH	*ELH: English Literary History*
ELN	*English Language Notes*
ELR	*English Literary Renaissance*
EMS	*English Manuscript Studies, 1100–1700*
EMSt	*Essays in Medieval Studies*
Enarratio	*Enarratio: Publications of the Modern Language Association of America*
English	*English: The Journal of the English Association*
Envoi	*Envoi: A Review Journal of Medieval Literature*
ES	*English Studies*
Exemplaria	*Exemplaria: A Journal of Theory in Medieval and Renaissance Studies*
Expl	*Explicator*
FCS	*Fifteenth-Century Studies*
Florilegium	*Florilegium: Carleton University Papers on Late Antiquity and the Middle Ages*
Genre	*Genre: Forms of Discourse and Culture*
H-Albion	*H-Albion: The H-Net Discussion Network for British and Irish History, H-Net Reviews in the Humanities and Social Sciences* http://www.h-net.org/reviews/home.php
HLQ	*Huntington Library Quarterly: Studies in English and American History and Literature* (San Marino, Calif.)
Hortulus	*Hortulus: The Online Graduate Journal of Medieval Studies* http://www.hortulus.net/
IJES	*International Journal of English Studies*
JAIS	*Journal of Anglo-Italian Studies*
JBSt	*Journal of British Studies*
JEBS	*Journal of the Early Book Society*
JEGP	*Journal of English and Germanic Philology*
JELL	*Journal of English Language and Literature* (Korea)
JEngL	*Journal of English Linguistics*
JGN	*John Gower Newsletter*
JMEMSt	*Journal of Medieval and Early Modern Studies*
JML	*Journal of Modern Literature*
JNT	*Journal of Narrative Theory*

456

L&LC	*Literary and Linguistic Computing: Journal of the Association for Literary and Linguistic Computing*
L&P	*Literature and Psychology*
L&T	*Literature and Theology: An International Journal of Religion, Theory, and Culture*
Lang&Lit	*Language and Literature: Journal of the Poetics and Linguistics Association*
Lang&S	*Language and Style: An International Journal*
LeedsSE	*Leeds Studies in English*
Library	*The Library: The Transactions of the Bibliographical Society*
LitComp	*Literature Compass* http://www.literaturecompass.com/
MA	*Le Moyen Age: Revue d'Histoire et de Philologie* (Brussels, Belgium)
MÆ	*Medium Ævum*
M&H	*Medievalia et Humanistica: Studies in Medieval and Renaissance Culture*
Manuscript	*Manuscript Studies*
ManuscriptaM	*anuscripta: A Journal for Manuscript Research*
Marginalia	*Marginalia: The Journal of the Medieval Reading Group at the University of Cambridge* http://www.marginalia.co.uk/journal/
Mediaevalia	*Mediaevalia: An Interdisciplinary Journal of Medieval Studies Worldwide*
MedievalF	*Medieval Forum* http://www.sfsu.edu/~medieval/index.html
MedPers	*Medieval Perspectives*
MES	*Medieval and Early Modern English Studies*
MFF	*Medieval Feminist Forum*
Mirabilia	*Mirabilia: Electronic Journal of Antiquity and Middle Ages*
MLQ	*Modern Language Quarterly: A Journal of Literary History*
MP	*Modern Philology: A Journal Devoted to Research in Medieval and Modern Literature*
N&Q	*Notes and Queries*
Neophil	*Neophilologus* (Dordrecht, Netherlands)
NM	*Neuphilologische Mitteilungen: Bulletin of the Modern Language Society*

NML	New Medieval Literatures
NMS	Nottingham Medieval Studies
NYRB	The New York Times Review of Books
Parergon	Parergon: Bulletin of the Australian and New Zealand Association for Medieval and Early Modern Studies
PBA	Proceedings of the British Academy
PBSA	Papers of the Bibliographical Society of America
PLL	Papers on Language and Literature: A Journal for Scholars and Critics of Language and Literature
PoeticaT	Poetica: An International Journal of Linguistic Literary Studies
Postmedieval	Postmedieval: A Journal of Medieval Cultural Studies
PQ	Philological Quarterly
Quidditas	Quidditas: Journal of the Rocky Mountain Medieval and Renaissance Association
RCEI	Revista Canaria de Estudios Ingleses
RenQ	Renaissance Quarterly
RES	Review of English Studies
RMSt	Reading Medieval Studies
SCJ	Sixteenth Century Journal
SAC	Studies in the Age of Chaucer
SAP	Studia Anglica Posnaniensia: An International Review of English
SAQ	South Atlantic Quarterly
SB	Studies in Bibliography: Papers of the Bibliographical Society of the University of Virginia
SCJ	The Sixteenth-Century Journal: Journal of Early Modern Studies (Kirksville, Mo.)
SEL	SEL: Studies in English Literature, 1500–1900
SELIM	SELIM: Journal of the Spanish Society for Medieval English Language and Literature
ShakS	Shakespeare Studies
SIcon	Studies in Iconography
SiM	Studies in Medievalism
SIMELL	Studies in Medieval English Language and Literature
SMART	Studies in Medieval and Renaissance Teaching
SN	Studia Neophilologica: A Journal of Germanic and Romance Languages and Literatures
SoAR	South Atlantic Review

SP	*Studies in Philology*
Speculum	*Speculum: A Journal of Medieval Studies*
SSt	*Spenser Studies: A Renaissance Poetry Annual*
TCBS	*Transactions of the Cambridge Bibliographical Society*
Text	*Text: Transactions of the Society for Textual Scholarship*
TextC	*Textual Cultures: Texts, Contexts, Interpretation*
TLS	*Times Literary Supplement* (London, England)
TMR	*The Medieval Review* https://scholarworks.iu.edu/journals/index.php/tmr
Tr&Lit	*Translation and Literature*
TSLL	*Texas Studies in Literature and Language*
UTQ	*University of Toronto Quarterly: A Canadian Journal of the Humanities*
Viator	*Viator: Medieval and Renaissance Studies*
WS	*Women's Studies: An Interdisciplinary Journal*
YES	*Yearbook of English Studies*
YLS	*The Yearbook of Langland Studies*
YWES	*Year's Work in English Studies*

Bibliographical Citations and Annotations

Bibliographies, Reports, and Reference

1. Amsel, Stephanie. "An Annotated Chaucer Bibliography, 2015." *SAC* 39 (2017): 393–460. Continuation of *SAC* annual annotated bibliography (since 1975); based on contributions from an international bibliographic team, independent research, and *MLA Bibliography* listings. 237 items, plus listing of reviews for 33 books. Includes an author index.

2. Barr, Jessica, and Katharine W. Jager. "Later Medieval: Chaucer." *YWES* 92 (2013): 264–306. A discursive bibliography of Chaucer studies for 2011, divided into four subcategories: general, *CT*, *TC*, and other works.

3. Jones, Natalie, and Ben Parsons. "Chaucer." *YWES* 95 (2016): 309–32. A discursive bibliography of Chaucer studies for 2014, divided into five subcategories: general, *CT*, *TC*, other works, and reputation and reception.

4. Parsons, Ben, with contributions from Louise Sylvester and Roberta Magnani. "Later Medieval: Chaucer." *YWES* 93 (2014): 257–76. A discursive bibliography of Chaucer studies for 2012, divided into five subcategories: general, *CT*, *TC*, other works, and reputation and reception.

5. Parsons, Ben, and Natalie Jones. "Chaucer." *YWES* 94 (2015): 237–62. A discursive bibliography of Chaucer studies for 2013, divided into five subcategories: general, *CT*, *TC*, other works, and reputation and reception.

6. ———. "Chaucer." *YWES* 96 (2017): 285–311. A discursive bibliography of Chaucer studies for 2015, divided into five subcategories: general, *CT*, *TC*, other works, and reputation and reception.

Recordings and Film

7. Armstrong, Dorsey. *The Black Death: The World's Most Devastating Plague, 19: Literary Responses to the Black Death*. The Great Courses. San Francisco: Kanopy Streaming, 2016. Streaming video; 30 min. Also available as part of a 4-disc set of CDs (Chantilly, VA: The Teaching

Company). Includes commentary on *Piers Plowman*; Boccaccio's *Decameron*; and the impact of the plague on Chaucer's life, *CT* (especially *PardT*), and *BD*, claiming that Chaucer "could not have been Chaucer" if not for the plague.

8. Barwell, Graham, and Christopher Moore. "World of Chaucer: Adaptation, Pedagogy, and Interdisciplinarity." In Jenna Ng, ed. *Understanding Machinima: Essays on Filmmaking in Virtual Worlds* (New York: Bloomsbury, 2013), pp. 207–26. Explores the goals and accomplishments of an interdisciplinary (English studies and communication) pedagogical experiment in adapting portions of *CT* to the online game *World of Warcraft*, commenting on the processes of animation, mediation, and machinimation involved in students learning to "retell stories through a digital medium not initially designed for that purpose."

9. di Carpegna Falconieri, Tommaso, and Lila Yawn. "Forging 'Medieval' Identities: Fortini's Calendimaggio and Pasolini's *Trilogy of Life*." In Bettina Bildhauer and Chris Jones, eds. *The Middle Ages in the Modern World: Twenty-First Century Perspectives* (*SAC* 41 [2019], no. 122), pp. 186–215. Briefly invokes Chaucer, noting Pasolini's 1971 film, *The Canterbury Tales*, and its adaptation of Chaucer's work to highlight increasing cultural degradation as works are transmitted.

10. Kelly, Kathleen Coyne. "The BBC *Canterbury Tales* (2003)." In Gail Ashton, ed. *Medieval Afterlives in Contemporary Culture* (*SAC* 39 [2017], no. 93), pp. 134–43. Comments on each of the BBC television versions of Chaucer's narratives (*MilT*, *WBP*, *KnT*, *PardT*, *ShT*, and *MLT*), exploring how adaptation, updating, and remediation duplicate or change aspects of Chaucer's aesthetics and morality.

11. Peverley, Sarah. "Staging Chaucer: Mike Poulton and the Royal Shakespeare Company's *Chaucer's 'The Canterbury Tales*.'" In Gail Ashton, ed. *Medieval Afterlives in Contemporary Culture* (*SAC* 39 [2017], no. 93), pp. 48–57. Describes the dramatic adaptations of selections from *CT* presented by the Royal Shakespeare Company in November 2005, exploring how the adaptations and their staging at times modify and at times convey the "key elements" of Chaucer's work, particularly his vitality, "human compassion," generic variety, and concern with the "transience" of earthly existence.

12. Wells, Paul. "Jonathan Myerson's *The Canterbury Tales*: The Screenwriting Sovereignty of Animation." *Journal of Screenwriting* 7 (2016): 65–81. Uses the concepts and terminology of animation studies

(e.g., "metamorphosis, condensation, anthropomorphism, choreography, fabrication, performance, sound, etc.") to gauge how and to what extent Jonathan Myerson in his *The Canterbury Tales* (1998) is able to "reveal and exemplify" the "wit, themes and outlook" of Chaucer's *CT*.

See also nos. 149, 197, 240, 336.

Chaucer's Life

13. Kaijima, Takashi. "The Age of Chaucer." *Bulletin of Hijiyama University* 24 (2017): 27–35. A short introduction to Chaucer's England, his contemporaries, his life, and his literary careers. In Japanese with English abstract.

14. Lightsey, Scott. "Biography of Geoffrey Chaucer." In James M. Dean, ed. *Geoffrey Chaucer* (*SAC* 41 [2019], no. 128), pp. 21–33. Includes biography of Chaucer's life, including his service and work within royal courts, his family, and history of his writings.

15. ————. "Chaucer's International Presence." In James M. Dean, ed. *Geoffrey Chaucer* (*SAC* 41 [2019], no. 128), pp. 171–85. Contends that Chaucer's "international presence," due to his European travels connected to his position and service within the court, "instilled in him a European sensibility distinctly at odds with his modern image as the avatar of Englishness."

See also nos. 7, 55, 121, 145, 154, 157, 169, 177, 201, 229, 281.

Facsimiles, Editions, and Translations

16. Kennedy, Caroline, ed., and Jon J. Muth, illus. *Poems to Learn by Heart*. New York: Disney-Hyperion, 2013. 191 pp; color illus. Anthologizes poetry for a juvenile audience, arranged topically. Includes the first eighteen lines of *GP* in Middle English (pp. 168–69) in a section entitled "Extra Credit."

17. Wilcockson, Colin. "Illustrating Chaucer's *Canterbury Tales*: Eric Gill's Woodcuts for the Golden Cockerel Press." *Anglistik* 25, no. 1 (2014): 29–43. Discusses the "relationship of engravings to narrative" in Eric Gill's woodcuts for the Cockerel Press four-volume edition of *CT* (1929–31), focusing on its frontispieces and "late or climactic moments

in the tales," with b&w illustrations. Comments on the sexual explicitness in book illustration, comparing Gill's works with those by Edward Burne-Jones, Aubrey Beardsley, and others.

See also nos. 8, 11, 19, 65, 74, 98, 105, 110, 156, 240, 253, 266, 313, 336.

Manuscripts and Textual Studies

18. Cannon, Christopher. " 'Wyth her owen handys': What Women's Literacy Can Teach Us about Langland and Chaucer." *Essays in Criticism* 66 (2016): 277–300. Sketches "the mode of literacy" that "occupies a borderland just beyond the precincts of surviving evidence," exploring "the role of dictation" rather than "a sequence of errors in copying that stands between" versions of such texts as *TC* and *Piers Plowman*. Includes comments on Adam Pinkhurst's role as Chaucer's scribe; the frontispiece to *TC* in Cambridge, Corpus Christi College, MS 61; and the irregularity of final -*e* in Chaucerian manuscripts.

19. Cook, Megan L. "Joseph Holland and the Idea of the Chaucerian Book." *Manuscript* 1, no. 2 (2017): 165–88. Describes Joseph Holland's "thoroughgoing renovation" of the Chaucer manuscript he owned in the sixteenth century (now Cambridge University Library, MS Gg.IV.27), detailing how he imitated the corpus and presentation found in Thomas Speght's 1598 edition of Chaucer's works, and exemplifying how transmission can affect "the way medieval books are read and preserved"—even though "[m]ost traces of Holland's involvement have been removed" in later restoration of Gg.IV.27.

20. Farrell, Thomas J. "Secretary *a* in Ellesmere's Latin Quotations." *ChauR* 52, no. 4 (2017): 396–425. Traces the use of the minuscule *a* in the Latin quotations of the Ellesmere manuscript to support the argument that these annotations derive from the ways Chaucer imagines the form of *CT*.

21. Horobin, Simon. "The Nature of Material Evidence." In Tim William Machan, ed. *Imagining Medieval English: Language Structures and Theories, 500–1500* (*SAC* 41 [2019], no. 144), pp. 147–65. Considers how manuscript evidence informs our understanding of Middle English, addressing the value of autograph manuscripts and personal letters, the process of standardization, and the importance of sociolinguistics. Includes analysis of the habits of Chaucer scribes Geoffrey Spirleng and

Adam Pinkhurst and maintains that, generally, when "copying Chaucer, scribes tended to preserve older London forms associated with Chaucer's own usage."

22. Horobin, Simon, and Aditi Nafde, eds. *Pursuing Middle English Manuscripts and Their Texts: Essays in Honour of Ralph Hanna*. Turnhout: Brepols, 2017. xxiv, 262 pp. Collection of essays on the production, reception, and editing of medieval English manuscripts. For an essay on Chaucer, see no. 175.

23. Johnston, Michael, and Michael Van Dussen, eds. *The Medieval Manuscript Book: Cultural Approaches*. Cambridge: Cambridge University Press, 2015. xii, 302 pp. Focuses on aspects of the cultural situations of the medieval book. Examines elements of bibliography, social context, linguistics, archeology, and conservation within a broader view of the theory and praxis of manuscript study. For an essay related to Chaucer, see no. 28.

24. Kraebel, A. B. "Chaucer's Bible: Late Medieval Biblicism and Compilational Form." *JMEMSt* 47, no. 3 (2017): 437–60. Focuses on how manuscript compilations, especially biblical materials, are evoked in *CT*. Argues that a strictly historical approach to this material is inadequate and examines how an author can use the material form of books for specific literary purposes.

25. Ma, Ruen-Chuan. "Codex Theory: Codicology and the Aesthetics of Reading in Late Medieval England." *DAI* A79.01 (2017): n.p. Examines the treatment of books as physical objects in the works of Chaucer, Gower, and Hoccleve, suggesting that this treatment may create a way of perceiving the text on the part of the reader.

26. Phillips, Noelle. "Compilational Reading: Richard Osbarn and Huntington Library MS HM 114." *YLS* 28 (2014): 65–104. Explores the "compositional choices" made in the compilation of the texts included in San Marino, Huntington Library, MS HM 114, and maintains that *TC* (among others) was copied early and incorporated into this larger collection in response to a purchaser's request.

27. Stinson, Timothy L. "(In)completeness in Middle English Literature: The Case of the *Cook's Tale* and the *Tale of Gamelyn*." *Manuscript* 1, no. 1 (2017): 115–34. Considers literary completeness, its relations to philosophies of perfection, and "the ways in which incompleteness is a special characteristic of Middle English literature," particularly in manuscript studies. Surveys kinds of incompleteness in *CT*, and focuses on

scribal responses to the fragmentary *CkT*, suggesting that digital editions can "equip readers to explore the constant elaboration, the polyvalent properties and voices of manuscript texts."

28. Taylor, Andrew. "Vernacular Authorship and the Control of Manuscript Production." In Michael Johnston and Michael Van Dussen, eds. *The Medieval Manuscript Book: Cultural Approaches* (*SAC* 41 [2019], no. 23), pp. 199–214. Explores the "various degrees of control" exerted by medieval vernacular poets over the production of their manuscripts, maintaining that evidence from the Hengwrt and Ellesmere manuscripts indicates Chaucer "was clearly not moving expeditiously toward a complete, finished, and definitive version of his work."

29. Thaisen, Jacob. "Initial Position in the Middle English Verse Line." *ES* 95 (2014): 500–513. Establishes that scribes are less likely than otherwise to introduce their own spellings of words that occur in initial position in verse lines, exploring why in psycholinguistic terms, and suggesting several implications for manuscript study. The discussion is based on data derived from ten manuscripts of *CT*.

30. Wakelin, Daniel. "Not Diane: The Risk of Error in Chaucerian Classicism." *Exemplaria* 29 (2017): 331–48. Explores the mistakes of scribes in copying and comprehending details regarding classical characters and classical allusions in poetry, and how poets' phrasing implies awareness of those risks and seeks to mitigate them. These problems in transmission reveal how classicism, which later became a monumental tradition, was a risky interaction in some of its earliest phases. These problems also suggest the risks of writing for scribal transmission in general.

31. Williams, Tara. "The Ellesmere Dragon." *Word & Image* 30 (2014): 444–54. Discusses the two marginal dragons found in the Ellesmere manuscript of *CT*, arguing that, like dragons in bestiaries and iconography, they "symbolize the marvelous," but they also "prompt readers to attend to the marvelous aspects of Chaucer's poem." Includes 4 color illus.

See also nos. 89, 131, 164, 175, 184, 235, 247–48, 268, 276, 309, 322, 329, 333.

Sources, Analogues, and Literary Relations

32. Barker, Justin. "Matter and Form in Medieval English Literature." *DAI* A78.12 (2017): n.p. Argues that Aristotelian theories of

matter, form, and substance interact with medieval poetics, particularly in such works as *ManT*, *SqT*, *Sir Gawain and the Green Knight*, and those of Hoccleve and Metham.

33. Biggs, Frederick M. *Chaucer's 'Decameron' and the Origin of the 'Canterbury Tales.'* Cambridge: D. S. Brewer, 2017. 275 pp. Addresses connections between Boccaccio's *Decameron* and *CT*, with particular focus on *ShT*, *MilT*, and *WBT*. Presents a "hermeneutic argument" that explores areas including "alchemy, domestic spaces, economic history, folklore, Irish/English politics, manuscripts, and misogyny" in works of Boccaccio and Chaucer.

34. Burke, Kevin J. "Chaucer's Philosopher: Boethian Contexts for Reading Chaucer's Poetry." In James M. Dean, ed. *Geoffrey Chaucer* (*SAC* 41 [2019], no. 128), pp. 53–67. Examines influence of Boethius on Dante, Boccaccio, and Chaucer. Focuses on how understanding *The Consolation of Philosophy* enhances the "philosophical reflection" and reception of *TC* for readers.

35. Cole, Andrew. "John Gower Copies Geoffrey Chaucer." *ChauR* 52, no. 1 (2017): 46–65. Examines the ways in which Gower and Chaucer use their source material differently. Gower uses Ovid to emphasize morality while Chaucer uses Ovid to explore both the courtly and the romantic.

36. Cooper, Helen. "The Ends of Storytelling." In Russell A. Peck and R. F. Yeager, eds. *John Gower: Others and The Self* (*SAC* 41 [2019], no. 50), pp. 91–107. Finds "ideas of mortality, the end of life, and the end of storytelling . . . closely linked" in Gower's *Confessio Amantis*. Argues that the work leads the narrator, the poet, and the audience to a conclusion in which all "can share in his hope of joy on the other side of the apocalypse, the end of the world, the end of story." Reflects how this shared understanding and vision are presented in *CT*, especially in *GP*, *KnT*, *ParsT*, and *Ret*.

37. Driscoll, William D. "By the Will of the King: Majestic and Political Rhetoric in Ricardian Poetry." *DAI* A78.09 (2017): n.p. Examines *CT* and Gower's *Confessio Amantis* as part of an imaginative reaction to the political circumstances following the Second Barons' War, arriving at a new role in "speaking to and for" the Henrician community.

38. Federico, Sylvia. *The Classicist Writings of Thomas Walsingham: 'Worldly Cares' at St. Albans Abbey in the Fourteenth Century*. Woodbridge: York Medieval Press, 2016. viii, 207 pp.; 7 b&w illus. Studies the works of Thomas Walsingham for their importance in the field of late

fourteenth-century English "public classical literature," helping to define this field by focusing on nuances in Walsingham's treatments of political events in classicized terms, imagery, and allusions, compared with treatments by contemporaneous writers, especially Chaucer. Includes discussion of Chaucer's Monk and his tale as an ironic commentary on Walsingham, revisions of previously published discussions of *MLT* and *TC* in relation to Walsingham's writing, explorations of the political vocabularies of Anglo-Latin and vernacular writings of the time, and a description of differences between "classisizing" literature and humanism.

39. Franke, William. "'Enditynges of worldly vanitees': Truth and Poetry in Chaucer as Compared with Dante." In *Secular Scriptures: Modern Theological Poetics in the Wake of Dante* (Columbus: Ohio State University Press, 2016), pp. 43–69. Addresses the "bifurcation of philosophy and theology intervening between Dante and Chaucer," arguing that Chaucer "never demonstrated any confidence that poetry could in any way represent the reality of the divine." Assesses the "empiricism" of *LGW*, *HF*, *TC*, and *CT* and maintains that, for Chaucer, "the one and only positive, yet critical purpose" of poetry is "the disillusioning function."

40. Gilbert, Dorothy, ed. *Marie de France: Poetry, New Translations, Backgrounds and Contexts, Criticism*. Norton Critical Editions. New York: Norton, 2015. xv, 407 pp. Includes *Th* and a selection from *MerT* in the section called "Backgrounds and Context."

41. Gruenler, Curtis A. *"Piers Plowman" and the Poetics of Enigma: Riddles, Rhetoric, and Theology*. Notre Dame: University of Notre Dame Press, 2017. xii, 586 pp. Approaches Chaucer's works briefly through contrast with *Piers Plowman*, which is the key text in a tradition of literature defined by "a distinctive poetics of enigma." Observes that Chaucer explores horizontally across the earthly world of humanity and society, as opposed to the "vertical," spiritual trajectory of *Piers Plowman*. Considers this change to be exemplary of what would happen to enigma if the sacred and the secular were increasingly separated.

42. Hardaway, Reid. "Ovid's Wand: The Brush of History and the Mirror of Ekphrasis." *DAI* A79.03 (2017): n.p. Addresses Chaucer's works as part of a larger examination of the influence of Ovid's *Metamorphoses*, particularly his employment of ekphrasis—the use of poetry to portray other types of art.

43. Havely, Nick. *Dante's British Public: Readers and Texts from the*

Fourteenth Century to the Present. Oxford: Oxford University Press, 2014. xviii, 355 pp.; b&w illus. Assesses the general or "public" familiarity with Dante and his works in British culture, acknowledging his impact on poets such as Chaucer, Milton, and T. S. Eliot, but exploring instead a more pervasive presence. Includes references to Chaucer's familiarity with Dante's works, to the knowledge of Dante among clerics in "the time of Chaucer," and to how Dante's and Chaucer's canonicity developed in Tudor England. Also comments on possible connections between Chaucer and Adam Easton, an English Benedictine who "possibly anticipated Chaucer as the first English writer to refer to Dante by name."

44. Lawler, Traugott, and Ralph Hanna III, eds., using materials collected by Karl Young and Robert A. Pratt. *Jankyn's Book of Wikked Wyves*, Vol. 2, *Seven Commentaries on Walter Map's "Dissuasio Valerii."* Chaucer Library. Athens: University of Georgia Press, 2014. xii, 605 pp. Edits the seven known commentaries on Walter Map's "Letter of Valerius to His Friend Ruffinus, Dissuading Him from Marrying," with Latin–English facing pages and scholarly apparatus. The Introduction (pp. 1–14) clarifies the importance of the material as a source for *WBT* and for Chaucer's Friar, placing it in the tradition of fraternal and pro-celibacy commentaries. Volume 1 was published in 1997; see *SAC* 22 (2000), no. 54.

45. Machulak, Erica R. " 'Is he a clerk, or noon?' Arabic Sources, Vernacular Aristotelianism, and Authorial Responses to the Evolving Social and Intellectual Context of Later Middle English Literature." *DAI* A80.06 (2017): n.p. Suggests that authors including Chaucer, Langland, Hoccleve, and Johannes de Caritate employed Aristotelian and pseudo-Aristotelian sources (many derived from Arabic sources) in the course of exploring types of literary and cultural authority.

46. Matthews, David. "Autobiographical Selves in the Poetry of Chaucer, Gower, Hoccleve, and Lydgate." In Adam Smyth, ed. *A History of English Autobiography* (Cambridge: Cambridge University Press, 2016), pp. 27–40. Surveys the "presentation of self" in late medieval English literature, gauging the relative degree of "truth value" and describing how authors "entwine life-writing into their larger projects." Uses *Ret* and Chaucer's ironic "playful portrayal of himself" elsewhere as touchstones for discussion of self-portrayals by writers such as the Harley lyricist and Adam Davy, as well as Gower, Hoccleve, and Lydgate.

47. McConnell, Matthew Clinton. "Women's Gathering: The

Auchinleck Manuscript and Women's Reading in 14th Century London." *DAI* A78.06 (2017): n.p. Sets MS Advocates 19.2.1 (Auchinleck) and the works of Chaucer in conversation, suggesting that both works demonstrate concern about the agency of women, since they are tied to the culture of women readers of the romance.

48. Minnis, Alastair. "Aggressive Chaucer: Of Dolls, Drink and Dante." *Medieval Translator/Traduire au Moyen Age* 16 (2016): 357–76. Maintains that, despite the critical tradition of Chaucer's self-effacing persona, there are significant assertions of his own poetic authority in *ThP* and *HF*, and perhaps even challenges to Dante. Explores details of diction and imagery ("popet," "elvyssh," drinking one's own drink, etc.) to argue that, at times, "Chaucer's claims to poetic authority are aggressive" or "passive-aggressive."

49. _____. "Other Worlds: Chaucer's Classicism." In Rita Copeland, ed. *The Oxford History of Classical Reception in English Literature*, Vol. 1, *(800–1558) (SAC* 41 [2019], no. 126), pp. 413–34. Aligns Chaucer's depictions of classical culture and his attitudes toward pagan belief, arguing that his "remarkable degree of cultural relativism" and his "reluctance to resort to simplistic forms of Christian triumphalism" are "delimited" only by his rejection of polytheism. His respect for ancient moral philosophy is evident in *KnT* and *PhyT*; for classical science, in *SqT*, *FranT*, and *CYT*. *SqT* also reflects Chaucer's interests in "Orientalism."

50. Peck, Russell A., and R. F. Yeager, eds. *John Gower: Others and the Self*. Publications of the John Gower Society. Cambridge: D. S. Brewer, 2017. viii, 381 pp. Collects sixteen essays from the Third International Congress of the John Gower Society and divides into three groups: Part 1, "Knowing the Self and Others"; Part 2, "The Essence of Strangers"; Part 3, "Social Ethics, Ethical Poetics." The collection contains numerous references to Chaucer and his works, some illustrating common threads between Gower and Chaucer, others pointing to differences between the two poets. For essays pertaining to Chaucer, see nos. 36, 53, 56.

51. Rabil, Albert Jr. "Geoffrey Chaucer, the Wife of Bath (ca. 1395) and Christine de Pizan, from *Legend of the God of Love* (1399) to *City of Ladies* (1405): A New Kind of Encounter between Male and Female." In Karen Nelson, ed. *Attending to Early Modern Women* (Newark: University of Delaware Press, 2013), pp. 189–206. Suggests that Chaucer and Pizan may have created "female voices to speak in opposition to male

misogyny" at about the same time because they shared similar educations and the same "cultural and intellectual universe," most evident in their familiarity with Ovid, the *Roman de la Rose*, and Boethius's *Consolation of Philosophy*. Describes the antimisogynist elements of *WBPT* and Pizan's works.

52. Ruether-Wu, Marybeth. "Revel, Reiving, and Outlawry: Regulating the Body Politic in Late Medieval Popular Literature." *DAI* A79.02 (2017): n.p. Discusses Chaucer and Langland in this study of outlawry, suggesting that the sovereign ban may be interpreted as a Galenic purgation of imbalance in the body politic.

53. Scanlon, Larry. "Gower, Lydgate, and Incest." In Russell A. Peck and R. F. Yeager, eds. *John Gower: Others and the Self* (*SAC* 41 [2019], no. 50), pp. 156–82. Argues that "alone of the three 'fathers of English poesy [Chaucer, Gower, and Lydgate],' Gower openly grapples with an acute awareness of the cultural centrality of a concept that extends from a betrayal of love's intimacy to social, political, and even poetic, dysfunction." Concludes that "Gower's exploration of incest posed a problem that Chaucer felt impelled to address, and that Lydgate felt impelled to try to solve." In exploring the divergences between Gower and Chaucer, regards Gower's examination of incest as "fuller and more searching," and Chaucer's treatment—as addressed in *MLH*, *MLT*, and *CIT*—as falling on the side of "dominant repression."

54. Shonk, Timothy A. "'For I hadde red of Affrycan byforn': Cicero's *Somnium Scipionis* and Chaucer's Early Dream Visions." In Nancy van Deusen, ed. *Cicero Refused to Die: Ciceronian Influence through the Centuries* (*SAC* 41 [2019], no. 129), pp. 85–121. Argues that Cicero's *Somnium Scipionis* "had a much greater impact" on *BD*, *PF*, and especially *HF* than is usually acknowledged, showing that Cicero's themes and imagery permeate Chaucer's works and dominate his literary imagination for "some ten years." Also comments on the relative chronology of the three Chaucerian works.

55. Sobecki, Sebastian. "'And gret wel Chaucer whan ye mete': Chaucer's Earliest Readers, Addressees and Audiences." *Critical Survey* 29, no. 3 (2017): 7–14. Explores what we know about Chaucer's earliest audiences, and how his work was used and discussed in his lifetime. Considers use of manuscripts by Hoccleve and Chaucer's named addressees, Bukton, Scogan, and de la Vache. Lists contemporary references to Chaucer in the poetry of Gower, Deschamps, Clanvowe, and Usk.

56. Taylor, Karla. "Reading Faces in Gower and Chaucer." In Russell A. Peck and R. F. Yeager, eds. *John Gower: Others and the Self* (*SAC* 41 [2019], no. 50), pp. 73–90. Argues that *ClT*, using "distinctively Gowerian terms" such as "corage" and "visage," is Chaucer's response to Gower's perceived challenge at the conclusion of the *Confessio Amantis* for Chaucer "to drop his well-known political reticence and take a personal stand on the sorry state of English political affairs in the last decade of the fourteenth century." Perceives *ClT* as turning the table on Gower by pointing to Genius's advice in Book VII of the *Confessio* for a king to "shape his face so as to control what it expresses to others" as "inconsistent with Gower's commitment to plainness and transparency, both ethical and referential" in the education of a king.

See also nos. 25, 57, 73, 82, 86, 90, 92, 95, 103–4, 122, 126, 135, 138, 140, 152, 165, 178–79, 185, 187–88, 195, 198, 200, 206, 213, 215, 217, 219–23, 230, 246, 251–52, 255, 260, 262, 280, 282, 284, 292, 294–96, 299, 303, 310, 314, 321, 323, 326, 328, 334.

Chaucer's Influence and Later Allusion

57. Armstrong, Guyda. *The English Boccaccio: A History in Books*. Toronto: Toronto University Press, 2013. xv, 464 pp.; 25 b&w figs. Describes the translation and reception history of Boccaccio's work in English "from the fifteenth century to the twentieth," including discussion of the role of Chaucer and of Chaucer studies as impetus for nineteenth-century interest, popular and professional, in Boccaccio as a source for Chaucer.

58. Barr, Helen. " 'Wrinkled Deep in Time': Emily and Arcite in *A Midsummer Night's Dream*." *Shakespeare Survey* (2013): 12–25. Argues that Shakespeare's *A Midsummer Night's Dream* alludes to *KnT* (particularly figures of Emelye and Arcite) in ways that "perforate the boundaries" of the chronology of Shakespeare's borrowings the from the tale in *Dream* and in *The Two Noble Kinsmen*. Though absent in *Dream*, the characters and their plots are present in images and allusive details that raise vexing questions about temporality and source relations.

59. Bellamy, Dodie. "Cunt Chaucer." In *Cunt Norton* (Los Angeles: Les Figues Press, 2013), pp. 8–9. An erotic prose poem that combines a pastiche of Chaucerian quotations, faux Middle English, and a narrative of sexual activity that alludes recurrently to *NPT*.

60. Bernstein, Charles. "Brush Up Your Chaucer (from Kiss Me, Tommy!)." In *Recalculating* (Chicago: University of Chicago Press, 2013), pp. 46–48. Parodies Cole Porter's lyrics for "Brush Up Your Shakespeare," using Chaucerian topics and emphases; purportedly composed for a conference of the New Chaucer Society.

61. Boldrini, Lucia. " 'Among Schoolchildren': Joyce's 'Night Lesson' and Chaucer's *Treatise on the Astrolabe*." In Gerald Gillespie and Haun Saussey, eds. *Intersections, Interferences, Interdisciplines: Literature with Other Arts* (Brussels: P. I. E. Peter Lang, 2014), pp. 35–46. Describes the "Night Lesson" chapter of James Joyce's *Finnegans Wake* and argues that it shares a number of features with *Astr*.

62. Bukowska, Joanna. "Between Geoffrey Chaucer's *Canterbury Tales* and Peter Ackroyd's *Clerkenwell Tales*: A Dialogue of the Contemporary Novel and Medieval Literary Conventions." In Jacek Fabiszak, Ewa Urbaniak-Rybicka, and Bartosz Wolskieds, eds. *Crossroads in Literature and Culture*, Second Language Learning and Teaching (New York: Springer, 2013), pp. 19–40. Examines intertextual relations between *CT* and Ackroyd's *Clerkenwell Tales*, acknowledging the dependencies of the latter, but emphasizing its postmodernist techniques and themes.

63. Cook, Megan L. "Nostalgic Temporalities in *Greenes Vision*." *Parergon* 33, no. 2 (2016): 39–56. Describes how Chaucer and John Gower appear as two poets/storytellers in *Greenes Vision* (1592), offering "authorization and legitimization" to Robert Greene's work "within a specifically English tradition," colored by "ambivalent nostalgia for an idealised literary past." Comments on Greene's possible knowledge of *Ret*, on his possible familiarity with portraits of Chaucer and Gower, and on *The Cobbler of Canterbury* as a "burlesque" of *CT*.

64. Coppola, Manuela. "A Tale of Two Wives: The Transnational Poetry of Patience Agbabi and Jean 'Binta' Breeze." *Journal of Postcolonial Writing* 52 (2016): 305–18. Uses postcolonial theory to argue that Agbabi and Breeze "interrogate the borders of British poetry and its 'modernity,' " by capitalizing on the "subversive elements already present" in *WBPT*, "from the subtle irony and the crafty use of the 'vernacular' to the foregrounding of female empowerment." The two "contemporary revisions of the canon mirror an intertextual, transnational practice that was already widely present in the Middle Ages."

65. Crawford, Hannah. " 'Bride-habited, but maiden-hearted': Language and Gender in *The Two Noble Kinsmen*." In Gordon McMullan, Lena Cowen Orlin, and Virginia Mason Vaughan, eds. *Women Making*

Shakespeare: Text, Reception and Performance (New York: Bloomsbury, 2014), pp. 25–34. Shows that the list of hard-words included in Thomas Speght's 1602 edition of Chaucer's *Werkes* influenced the linguistic inventiveness of Shakespeare and Fletcher's *Two Noble Kinsmen*.

66. de Feria, Lina *Los aires de Antinoo*. Madrid: Eolas Ediciones, 2016. 64 pp. Includes a thirteen-line poem entitled "Chaucer" (p. 15).

67. Delahoyde, Michael. "Lyric Poetry from Chaucer to Shakespeare." *Brief Chronicles: The Interdisciplinary Journal of Authorship Studies* 5 (2014): 69–100. Tallies a number of specific "[i]nfluences, echoes, or borrowings from Chaucer in English poetic tradition as it developed between Henry Howard, earl of Surrey, and Shakespeare, mentioning familiar instances and adding ones previously unnoticed. Remarks that Chaucer "may be the single most important influence" on Shakespeare's works, and identifies a particularly large number of echoes in the Elizabethan collection *A Hundreth Sundrie Flowres*.

68. Evans, Robert C. "Chaucer, John Donne, and 'The Flea': A 'Robertsonian' Perspective." In James M. Dean, ed. *Geoffrey Chaucer* (*SAC* 41 [2019], no. 128), pp. 144–58. Proposes viewing Donne's poem "The Flea" from the theoretical perspective of D. W. Robertson, and argues that "if we read Donne's poem as Robertson reads Chaucer, a different kind of Donne emerges" than previously shown by scholars.

69. ———. "Chaucer, Nash, and 'The Choice of Valentines.'" In James M. Dean, ed. *Geoffrey Chaucer* (*SAC* 41 [2019], no. 128), pp. 201–15. Presents overlap between Chaucer's writings and the writings of Thomas Nashe, particularly the late sixteenth-century poem "The Choice of Valentines," which is "considered to be the most pornographic piece of writing to survive" Shakespeare's time. Argues that Nashe's poem is connected to Chaucer in that "both writers often taught traditional Christian messages by using highly ironic methods."

70. Hadbawnik, David. "The Chaucer-Function: Spenser's Language Lessons in *The Shepheardes Calender*." *Upstart: A Journal of English Renaissance Studies* (2014): n.p. Web. March 3, 2019. Argues that Spenser emulates Chaucer in "furthering the project of language formation in English." Attending to Chaucer's model in *CT* (and to Richard Mulcaster's precepts), Spenser uses interactive speakers who have various dialects and lexicons to generate neologisms, and he thereby attains "the reputation for language-formation in English that had built up around Chaucer over the previous two centuries."

71. Haverty, Charles. "Whan that Aprill." In *Excommunicados: Stories*

([Iowa City]: University of Iowa Press, 2015), pp. 136–53. Alludes to the opening of *GP* in its title, and includes a character who recites Chaucer and is interested in Chaucerian apocrypha.

72. Holton, Amanda. "Chaucer's Presence in *Songes and Sonettes.*" In Stephen Hamrick, ed. *Tottel's Songes and Sonettes in Context* (Burlington: Ashgate, 2013), pp. 87–110. Surveys Chaucer's influence on *Tottel's Miscellany*, commenting on various allusions and the inclusion of *Truth* in the collection (although "deliberately anonymized"), and exploring more thoroughly how he is "strongly resisted," i.e., how aspects of his work are suppressed, "both actively and passively," particularly his "variety of voice" and "his interest in female speech" and "female complaint." Includes comments on *Ros*, *Anel*, *LGW*, *TC*, and *SqT*, identifying how, where, and to what extent they are echoed—or not—in the *Miscellany*.

73. Jones, Chris. "Digital *Mouvance*: Once and Future Medieval Poetry Remediated in the Modern World." In Bettina Bildhauer and Chris Jones, eds. *The Middle Ages in the Modern World: Twenty-First Century Perspectives* (*SAC* 41 [2019], no. 122), pp. 168–85. Attends to histories of reinterpretation and translation of medieval poetry of Chaucer and of *Sir Gawain and the Green Knight*. Focuses on the return to medievalism by British poets of the twenty-first century, including Seamus Heaney. *Sir Gawain and the Green Knight*'s appearance on Twitter is also noted.

74. Kelen, Sarah A. "New Poet, Old Words: Glossing the *Shepheardes Calender.*" In Heidi Brayman Hackel, Jesse M. Lander, and Zachary Lesser, eds. *The Book in History, the Book as History: New Intersections of the Material Text: Essays in Honor of David Scott Kastan* (New Haven: Beinecke Rare Book and Manuscript Library, Yale University, 2016), pp. 235–55. Compares and contrasts Immeritô's and E. K.'s attitudes toward language and archaism in Edmund Spenser's *Shepheardes Calender*, with particular attention to how the "overly generous glossing" of the text presumes a "reader's familiarity with medieval verse, particularly that of Chaucer." Comments on Thomas Speght's approach to "hard words" in his 1598 edition of Chaucer's works, and includes illustrations.

75. Knight, Rhonda. "Writing like a Fan: Fan Fiction and Medievalism in Paul C. Doherty's Canterbury Mysteries." *Mediaevalia* 36–37 (2015–16): 291–314. Describes Paul C. Doherty's seven murder mysteries based on *CT*, exploring them as deeply allusive appropriations rather than adaptations, and theorizing how Chaucer-adept readers of

this fan fiction can achieve Lacanian *jouissance* as well as pleasure. Comments on elements of fan fiction in Chaucer's own writing, and describes *CT* as a "template" for all multi-genre narratives that involve "a group of strangers, travel, and storytelling."

76. Knight, Stephen. "Medieval Comic Relief: Cannibal Cow, Duck's Deck and Carry on Joan of Arc." *Postmedieval* 5 (2014): 154–68. Treats three examples of eighteenth-century comic medievalism as the "male adolescence of the Enlightenment": Henry Fielding's presentation of Arthurian material as "farcically lascivious discourse" in *Tom Thumb*, the "pre-modern prurience" of Voltaire's *La Pucelle d'Orléans*, and Alexander Pope's sexualized adaptations of *WBP* and *MerT*.

77. Langdell, Sebastian. " 'What shal I calle thee? What is thy name?' Thomas Hoccleve and the Making of 'Chaucer.' " *NML* 16 (2016): 250–76. Investigates the "moral version of Chaucer that emerges" in Hoccleve's *Regiment of Princes*, arguing that it is a kind of poetic authority produced "in the face of an increasingly militant and repressive English Church," and that, unlike other early versions of Chaucer, it reflects a growing international trend in Christianizing poetic predecessors.

78. Lees-Jeffries, Hester. "What's Hecuba to Him? Absence, Silence and Lament in *Troilus and Criseyde* and *Troilus and Cressida*." In Andrew James Johnston, Russell West-Pavlov, and Elisabeth Kempf, eds. *Love, History and Emotion in Chaucer and Shakespeare: "Troilus and Criseyde" and "Troilus and Cressida"* (*SAC* 41 [2019], no. 315), pp. 61–75. Assesses Hecuba as a "potent absent presence" in Shakespeare's *Troilus and Cressida*, and comments on the possible influence of *LGW* and *TC* on Shakespeare's *Rape of Lucrece* as well as his Trojan play. Includes attention to Dido and Penelope.

79. Lerer, Seth. *Tradition: A Feeling for the Literary Past*. The Literary Agenda. Oxford: Oxford University Press, 2016. xiii, 135 pp. Investigates the role of "tradition in the literary imagination" and the value of literature, particularly the "value of close and nuanced reading for our understanding of both past and present." Includes discussion of George Orwell's engagement with Chaucer in *1984* and comments on orality and literacy in *CT*, especially *MilP*. Also assesses the "problem of attention" in *CT*, i.e., its consideration of audience attention in the making of meaning.

80. Lipton, Emma. "Law, Chaucer, and Representation in Lydgate's 'Disguising at Hertford.' " *JEGP* 113 (2014): 342–64. Demonstrates

that Lydgate's "Disguising" the wives' use of Chaucerian "performative and legalistic speech acts" is set in evocative conflict with the "theatricality of monarchical justice," arguing that Lydgate learned from Chaucer's *WBPT* how "requital works as dramatic principle" and how performative speech contests authority.

81. Lovesey, Peter. *The Stone Wife: A Peter Diamond Investigation*. New York: Soho Crime; London: Sphere, 2014. 358 pp. A detective mystery in which a stone-tablet illustration of the Wife of Bath provokes the killing of a Chaucer professor during an auction. The story includes a putative portrait of Chaucer and surmises about his life.

82. McCarthy, Conor. "Time, Place, Language, and Translation: Ciaran Carson's *The Inferno* and *The Táin*." In Bettina Bildhauer and Chris Jones, eds. *The Middle Ages in the Modern World: Twenty-First Century Perspectives* (*SAC* 41 [2019], no. 122), pp. 239–53. Uses Chaucer and the *Pearl*-poet as metonyms for the tasks of translating and updating medieval works for later readers. Evokes both works in these translations, if at times obliquely.

83. Normandin, Shawn. "Sylvia Plath Rhymes with the Wife of Bath." *Expl* 71, no. 1 (2013): 56–59. Suggests that *WBP*, III.707–10 inspired lines 1–3 of Sylvia Plath's poem "Daddy."

84. Perry, Thomas. *The Book of the Lion*. New York: Mysterious Bookshop, 2014. Bibliomysteries. eBook; also printed in limited numbers. Short story that involves a Chaucer scholar, a manuscript of Chaucer's *Book of the Leoun* (*Ret*, X.1087), and an extortion scheme.

85. Randall, Jackie. *Emelin*. Rouse Hill, NSW: Schillings, 2016. 174 pp. Item not seen; WorldCat information indicates this is a children's novel, set in the Middle Ages, about a gifted girl who flees her home in order to protect a Chaucer manuscript.

86. Reid, Lindsay Ann. "Bibliofictions: Ovidian Heroines and the Tudor Book." *DAI* A74.08 (2014): n.p. Assesses how "mythological heroines from Ovid's *Heroides* and *Metamorphoses* were catalogued, conflated, reconceived, and recontextualized in vernacular literature," particularly as they reflect his "interest in textual revision and his thematization of the physicality and malleability of art in its physical environments." Includes recurrent attention to Chaucer as he helped to convey Ovidian concerns into Tudor England.

87. Renarde, Giselle. *The Price of a Good Cup of Coffee: A Lesbian Romance Short*. [Los Gatos, Calif.]: Smashwords, [2015]. eBook. The woman that infatuates the narrator is a barista whom she calls "Chaucer

girl," so named because she was first seen holding a copy of *The Complete Works of Geoffrey Chaucer*.

88. Robertson, Elizabeth. "Chaucer's and Wordsworth's Vivid Daisies." In Bettina Bildhauer and Chris Jones, eds. *The Middle Ages in the Modern World: Twenty-First Century Perspectives* (*SAC* 41 [2019], no. 122), pp. 219–38. Examines Chaucer's impact on medievalisms of early and later Romantic English poets. Portrays Chaucer's influence on Wordsworth, not only in deliberately medievalist work, but throughout his corpus, focusing on daisies and their presentations in text as the means to make the connections.

89. Rogers, Janine. "A Compaignye of Sondry Folk: Mereology, Medieval Poetics and Contemporary Evolutionary Narrative in Richard Dawkins' *The Ancestor's Tale*." *Interdisciplinary Science Reviews* 39, no. 1 (2014): 47–61. Argues that in *The Ancestor's Tale* Richard Dawkins "uses Chaucer's poetics to address interpretative problems with evolution," particularly the "anthropocentric" notion that "humanity is the 'result' of evolution." Dawkins's uses of the frame story, the pilgrimage allegory, and the manuscript stemmata of *CT* reveal a concern with unity in diversity that he shares with Chaucer. Dawkins treats fossils as relics and the evolutionary record as an analogue to manuscript transmission, bridging the science/literature divide and, in Chaucerian fashion, "disrupting established orders."

90. Simpson, James. "'The Formless Ruin of Oblivion': Shakespeare's *Troilus and Cressida* and Literary Defacement." In Andrew James Johnston, Russell West-Pavlov, and Elisabeth Kempf, eds. *Love, History and Emotion in Chaucer and Shakespeare: "Troilus and Criseyde" and "Troilus and Cressida"* (*SAC* 41 [2019], no. 315), pp. 189–206. Treats the literary tradition of Troy as a war in which different versions of the story struggle to claim validity. Focuses on how Shakespeare seeks to "deface and disable the entire tradition," rendering it "unfit for any but the lowest human habitation" by adapting elements that derive from the "ephemera" of Dares and Dictys and by "breaking down the protected spaces" of *TC*.

91. Smallwood, Philip. "Great Anna's Chaucer: Pope's *January and May* and the Logic of Settlement." In Cedric D. Reverand II, ed. *Queen Anne and the Arts* (Lewisburg: Bucknell University Press, 2015), pp. 99–117. Explores Alexander Pope's "transformation" of *MerT* in his *January and May*, focusing on his "reading of Chaucer," and his poem's "consonance with the time of Queen Anne." Also comments more generally

on Pope's reception and uses of Chaucer's narratives, including instances where he can be seen to be "out-Chaucering Chaucer."

92. Sokolov, D. A. *Renaissance Texts, Medieval Subjectivities*. Pittsburgh: Duquesne University Press, 2017. ix, 350 pp. Argues that the Petrarchism commonly held to have begun in English with Wyatt and Surrey is, instead, an alteration of a tradition already prevalent among English writers such as Chaucer, Gower, Hoccleve, and Lydgate. In particular, claims that Langland's ideas of physical and artistic reward directly influence Wyatt's sonnets and Spenser's *Amoretti*; Chaucer's *BD* undergirds Henry Howard and Philip Sidney's *Astrophil and Stella*; Lydgate's *Temple of Glas* and *Complaynte of a Louers Lyfe* become points of departure for Samuel Daniel's *Delia* and Michael Drayton's *Idea*; and Hoccleve's "La male regle" and Henryson's *Testament of Cresseid* position pathological affect to emerge in Shakespeare's sonnets. Additionally, Chaucer's early engagement with Petrarchan constructions frustrates the usual assertion that the Renaissance is a break-point with the past.

93. Suzuki, Masayuki. "Pilgrims Collected and Classified: Reading William Blake's *Chaucer's Canterbury Pilgrims*." *English Department Journal* (Miyagi Gakuin Women's University) 45 (2017): 27–54. Analyzes William Blake's *Chaucer's Canterbury Pilgrims* by paying special attention to its ordering of the pilgrims, and investigates Blake's understanding of Chaucer and his intention in his classification of the pilgrims. In Japanese.

94. Tarquini, Mindy. *Hindsight: A Novel*. Tempe: Spark Press, 2016. 319 pp. First-person fiction featuring Eugenia Panisporchi, who teaches Chaucer, and who remembers all of her past lives, which connect with her present one. Includes trans-temporal recollections of when she met "Mr. Chaucer" and encountered models for several of his Canterbury pilgrims and their characters.

95. Wainwright, Michael. "The Logical Basis of Oxford's *Troilus and Cressida*." *Brief Chronicles: The Interdisciplinary Journal of Authorship Studies* 5 (2014): 139–70. Argues that *Troilus and Cressida* combines the concern with Boethian logic and necessity found in *TC* with Ramist thinking, indicating that Edward de Vere, earl of Oxford, was the author of the play. The combination prompts a game-theory analysis of how "necessary but unsportsmanlike" solutions resolve dilemmas in the play.

96. Walker, Lewis. "The Wife of Bath and *All's Well that Ends Well*." *Renaissance Papers* n.v. (2015): 51–68. Argues that details and attitudes

depicted in *WBPT* and in the description of the Wife in *GP* influenced various aspects of Shakespeare's *All's Well that Ends Well*.

97. Warren, Nancy Bradley. "Chivalric Men and Good(?) Women: Chaucer, Gender, and John Bossewell's *Workes of Armorie*." *ChauR* 52, no. 1 (2017): 143–61. Looks at how Bossewell's *Workes of Armorie* uses *LGW*, *WBT*, and *BD* in exploration of the construction of masculine identity.

98. Zarins, Kim. *Sometimes We Tell the Truth*. New York: Simon Pulse, 2016. 437 pp. A young-adult novel, modeled on *CT*, in which senior high school students on a bus trip from Canterbury, Connecticut to Washington, D.C. share stories about their awakening sexuality. Characters' names (including the primary narrator, Jeff Chaucer) and their tales are modernized adaptations from *CT*.

See also nos. 10–11, 105, 126, 158, 172, 174, 183, 197, 240, 260, 288, 311–12, 315, 317, 324–25, 327–29, 332, 334.

Style and Versification

99. Li, Xingzhong. "'Of harmes two, the lesse is for to chese': An Integrated OT-Maxent Approach to Syntactic Inversion in Chaucer's Verse." In Don Chapman, Colette Moore, and Miranda Wilcox, eds. *Studies in the History of the English Language VII: Generalizing vs. Particularizing Methodologies in Historical Linguistic Analysis* (Berlin: De Gruyter Mouton, 2016), pp. 107–30. Seeks to "account for constraints governing Chaucer's syntactic inversions with a purpose to uncover Chaucer's underlying metrical principles," employing a combination of "optimality theory" and "Maxent Grammars" and analyzing "every tenth line" of the pentameter verse in the Riverside edition of Chaucer's works.

100. Lockhart, Jessica Jane. "Everyday Wonders and Enigmatic Structures: Riddles from Symphosius to Chaucer." *DAI* A79.07 (2017): n.p. Examines the use of riddling and the structure of riddles as a means of representing "the wondrous in the everyday." Specifically considers Chaucer's use of this in *BD* and *PF*. Additionally suggests the *Secretum philosophorum* as an intertext in *HF*.

101. Nakayasu, Minako. "Chaucer's Historical Present: A Discourse-Pragmatic Perspective." In Liliana Sikorska and Marcin Krygier, eds. *Evur Happie & Glorious, Ffor I Hafe at Will Grete Riches* (New York: Peter

Lang, 2013), pp. 41–60. Clarifies the nature and functions of the historical present tense in English, and examines Chaucer's "discourse-pragmatic" uses of it in *KnT*, particularly alternations of "present and past tenses in discourse" where the narrator "dynamically synchronises the story with the here and now of the hearers with the aid of the present tense, while employing the past tense to signify a segment of discourse."

102. Putter, Ad. "In Appreciation of Metrical Abnormality: Headless Lines and Initial Inversion in Chaucer." *Critical Survey* 29, no. 3 (2017): 65–85. Observes that in Chaucer's short-line verse, headless lines are much more common than initial inversion, whereas in his iambic pentameter the exact opposite occurs. Argues that Chaucer and his predecessors used such metrical licence "very deliberately, not only for emphasis and rhetorical effect but also to clarify narrative and syntactical organization." Notes in particular its appearance "in the context of non-indicative moods, lists and catalogues, direct speeches and changes of addressee, transition between narrative sections, and enjambement."

103. Trigg, Stephanie. "Chaucer's Silent Discourse." The Biennial Chaucer Lecture. The New Chaucer Society Twentieth International Congress, July 11–14, 2016, Queen Mary University of London, Mile End. *SAC* 39 (2017): 33–56. Studies the "speaking face" depicted in Chaucer's works (*TC*, *Buk*, *BD*, and *ClT*), discussing the trope as a subset of facial expression in the history of emotions. The first writer in English to do so, Chaucer has his characters and narrators translate facial discourse into speech and thereby show us "how we can make emotional and cognitive connections with each other." Comments on the history of the trope in Boccaccio and Machaut, and explores the dialects and registers of silent speaking.

104. Werthmüller, Gyöngyi. "Final -*e* in Gower's English Poetry, in Comparison with Chaucer's." *South Atlantic Review* 79, nos. 3–4 (2015): 6–19. Tabulates evidence of the greater regularity of stress in Gower's verse than in Chaucer's, particularly in nouns and adjectives that feature the apocope of final unstressed -*e*. Attributes this regularity to the influence of Gower having written French verse, and calls for more thorough exploration of this and related phenomena.

See also nos. 18, 114–16, 139, 174, 178, 180, 265, 333.

Language and Word Studies

105. Chance, Jane. "*Apartheid* in Tolkien: Chaucer and *The Lord of the Rings*, Books 1–3 (1925–1943)." In *Tolkien, Self and Other: "This Queer Creature"* (New York: Palgrave Macmillan, 2016), pp. 133–76. Considers the roles of apartheid and linguistic queerness in the class-based characterizations of various hobbits in Tolkien's *The Lord of the Rings*, suggesting that Tolkien's scholarly study of Chaucer's literary dialects and his glossary for the never-published "Clarendon Chaucer" reflect similar concerns with race- and class-based linguistic features.

106. Cooper, Helen. "Unhap, Misadventure, Infortune: Chaucer's Vocabulary of Mischance." *Critical Survey* 29, no. 3 (2017): 15–26. Considers Chaucer's extensive and subtle use of "the full vocabulary of *chance* and *mischance*." Shows how his use of privatives and negative prefixes with these words "inflect[s] his larger concerns with Fortune (usually personified as an agent) and the mutability of the world."

107. Fruoco, Jonathan. "Chaucer as a Sociolinguist: Understanding the Role of Language in Chaucer's Internationalism." In James M. Dean, ed. *Geoffrey Chaucer* (*SAC* 41 [2019], no. 128), pp. 216–30. Traces the history of English from earlier times to Chaucer's age to reveal Chaucer's facility with language, focusing on his powerful and special words. Refers to J. R. R. Tolkien's 1934 lecture to the Philological Society, and claims that Chaucer was not only a gifted poet but also a remarkable philologist, aligned with linguists of the nineteenth and twentieth centuries.

108. Green, Clarence. "Introducing the *Corpus of the Canon of Western Literature*: A Corpus for Culturomics and Stylistics." *Lang&Lit* 26, no. 4 (2017): 282–99. Introduces a *Corpus of the Canon of Western Literature* (*CCWL*) based on Harold Bloom's *The Western Canon* and utilizes corpus stylistics to "operationalize" the argued coherence of the western canon. Using *CT* as an example, illustrates how tagging was less accurate with texts written before 1800. Also reveals that *TC* was found to have one of the shortest mean word lengths and narrowest vocabulary ranges in the poetry analyzed in the *CCWL*, while *CT* had one of the longest mean sentence lengths.

109. Hanna, N[atalie]. "Gender and Social Status in Chaucer's Language." *DAI* C75.01 (2016): n.p. Examines "the semantics and pragmatics of nouns that denote gender and social status in Chaucer's

literature, e.g., "knyght," "lady," "leche," "wyf'," focusing on *MerT*, *FranT*, *ABC*, and *TC*, but addressing most of Chaucer's works.

110. Karpova, Olga M., and Olga M. Melentyeva. "Chaucer & Shakespeare Glossaries: Do Modern Users Still Need Them Today?" In Faina I. Kartashkova and Olga M. Karpova, eds. *Multi-Disciplinary Lexicography: Traditions and Challenges of the XXIst Century* (Newcastle upon Tyne: Cambridge Scholars, 2013), pp. 73–95. Surveys the hard-word tradition of lexicography in Chaucer and Shakespeare studies, particularly in editions of their works, and suggests that new works are still needed to serve twenty-first-century users.

111. Melentyeva, Olga A. "Old Words in Chaucer Dictionaries as the Linguistic Heritage of Great Britain." In O. M. Karpova and F. I. Kartashkova, eds. *Life beyond Dictionaries* (Newcastle upon Tyne: Cambridge Scholars, 2015), pp. 76–90. Surveys the tradition of English "old word" and "hard word" dictionary- and glossary-making, locating Chaucerian compilations (e.g., Greaves, Speght, Urry, etc.) at the beginning of the tradition and tracing developments in practice into the twentieth century. Calls for a more comprehensive reference work that documents and exemplifies the history of linguistic and encyclopedic information pertaining to difficult words in Chaucer's lexicon.

112. Nakayasu, Minako. "Spatial-Temporal Systems in *A Treatise on the Astrolabe*. In Juan Camilo Conde Silvestre and Javier Calle Martín, eds. *Approaches to Middle English: Variation, Contact and Change* (*SAC* 41 [2019], no. 124), pp. 243–59. Conducts a "systematic analysis of the synchronic spatio-temporal systems" in *Astr*, taking "deixis into consideration," defining terms, and analyzing the interactions of "pronouns, demonstratives, adverbs, tense forms, and modals," along with temporal markers such as *now* and *forseide*, and describing the dynamics of variation between "proximal and distal perspectives."

113. Ohno, Hideshi. "Emotional Expression in Chaucer: With Special Reference to *Herte*." *Hiroshima Studies in English Language and Literature* 61 (2017): 69–84. Focuses on words and phrases collocating with *herte*, *minde*, and *soule* in *CT* and *TC* and analyzes how Chaucer "exerts his influence on the reader's/audience's emotion" through the use of these words.

114. Wawrzyniak, Agnieszka. "Metaphors, Metonymies and Their Coreferentiality in the Conceptualization of Love and Heart in Chaucer's *Canterbury Tales*." In Michael Bilynsky, ed. *Studies in Middle English: Words, Forms, Senses and Texts* (*SAC* 41 [2019], no. 123), pp. 311–28.

Analyzes the metaphors, metonymies, and "metaphors based on metonymies" used in descriptions of love and of heart in *TC*, exploring the cultural dependence and/or universality of the figures, particularly differences between medieval and modern usage.

115. Werthmüller, Gyöngyi. "Final -*e* in Gower's and Chaucer's Monosyllabic Premodifying Adjectives: A Grammatical/Metrical Analysis." In Juan Camilo Conde Silvestre and Javier Calle Martín, eds. *Approaches to Middle English: Variation, Contact and Change* (*SAC* 41 [2019], no. 124), pp. 179–97. Considers several factors (apocope, compounding, etymology, and metrical environment) in the presence or absence of final -*e* in Gower's and Chaucer's monosyllabic adjectives, clarifying Gower's relative regularity by identifying the paucity of exceptions to his usual practice.

116. Yager, Susan. "Chaucer's Language." In James M. Dean, ed. *Geoffrey Chaucer* (*SAC* 41 [2019], no. 128), pp. 99–112. Outlines the basics of Middle English orthography and pronunciation, and Chaucer's vocabulary and literary models for students. Claims that learning to read Middle English, and understanding concepts of manuscript, edition, and translation, enhance understanding of critical conversations about Chaucer. Focuses on analyzing *Ros* and the Clerk's portrait in *GP* to provide strategies for reading difficult passages, including examining syntactical patterns and reading aloud, and to reveal that Chaucer's iambics can convey a variety of emotions.

117. _____. "Reading Lessons: Chaucer and the Comfort of Uncertainty." In James M. Dean, ed. *Geoffrey Chaucer* (*SAC* 41 [2019], no. 128), pp. 68–79. Argues how humor and multiple points of view make Chaucer's work essential reading in the "polemical atmosphere" of the present time. Contends that readers must pay careful attention when interpreting Chaucer's frequent ambiguities, reversals, and moments of stasis; yet, final judgments concerning, e.g., Chaucer's use of *ascaunces*, "as if," are often impossible. Emphasizes how a looseness in description, characterization, and connections between tales and tellers fosters an atmosphere of toleration for contemporary readers of Chaucer's works. Focuses on *CT*, *WBT*, *BD*, *PF*, and *TC*.

See also nos. 21, 48, 56, 65, 70, 74, 99, 104, 175, 184, 192–93, 197, 207, 218, 256–57, 263, 277, 279, 314.

Background and General Criticism

118. Adams, Jenny, and Nancy Mason Bradbury, eds. *Medieval Women and Their Objects*. Ann Arbor: University of Michigan Press, 2017. x, 294 pp. Collection of essays that represents multifaceted views of gender and material culture in late medieval France and England. For seven essays related to Chaucer see nos. 203, 226, 243, 250, 259, 271, 298.

119. Allen, Valerie, and Ruth Evans, eds. *Roadworks: Medieval Britain, Medieval Roads*. Manchester Medieval Literature and Culture. Manchester: Manchester University Press, 2016. xiv, 367 pp.; illus. & maps. Twelve essays by various authors and an introduction by the editors explore the material and symbolic status of roads in medieval history and literature. The volume includes a bibliography and index. For three essays that pertain to Chaucer, see nos. 164, 168, 316.

120. Armstrong, Dorsey, Ann W. Astell, and Howell Chickering, eds. *Magistra doctissima: Essays in Honor of Bonnie Wheeler*. Kalamazoo: Medieval Institute Publications, Western Michigan University, 2013. vii, 273 pp. Contains nineteen essays by various authors, with an introduction by the editors, on literary and historical topics, Arthuriana, and women in the Middle Ages. For three essays that pertain to Chaucer, see nos. 184, 201, 207.

121. Augustyn, Adam. *Authors of the Medieval and Renaissance Eras, 1100 to 1660*. New York: Britannica Educational Publishing. in association with Rosen Educational Services, 2014. xv, 358 pp.; color illus. Describes the lives and accomplishments of some 100 international writers. The section on Chaucer (pp. 84–92) summarizes his life and career as a public servant, integrating discussion of his major works in chronological order and emphasizing *CT*, ranking it "one of the greatest poetic works in English." Includes a color reproduction of the Chaucer portrait from the Ellesmere manuscript.

122. Bildhauer, Bettina, and Chris Jones, eds. *The Middle Ages in the Modern World: Twenty-First Century Perspectives*. Oxford: Oxford University Press, 2017. ix, 346 pp. Collection of essays addressing medieval and medievalism themes and how they continue to impact contemporary perspectives. The introduction includes a history of medievalism from the fourteenth to the twenty-first centuries, and remarks how

Chaucer's works satirize heroic romance. For other essays pertaining to Chaucer, see nos. 9, 73, 82, 88.

123. Bilynsky, Michael, ed. *Studies in Middle English: Words, Forms, Senses and Texts*. SIMELL, no. 44. New York: Peter Lang, 2014. 367 pp. Collection of essays reflecting contemporary topics in linguistic and literary research on the Middle Ages. For three essays that pertain to Chaucer, see nos. 114, 265, 279.

124. Conde Silvestre, Juan Camilo, and Javier Calle Martín, eds. *Approaches to Middle English: Variation, Contact and Change*. SIMELL, no. 47. New York: Peter Lang, 2015. 259 pp. Includes papers from the eighth International Conference on Middle English, University of Murcia, Spain, 2013. For two essays that pertain to Chaucer, see nos. 112, 115.

125. Cooper, Helen. "*The Chaucer Review:* Then and Now." *ChauR* 52, no. 2 (2017): 169–72. Traces the changes and continuities of fifty years of *ChauR*.

126. Copeland, Rita, ed. *The Oxford History of Classical Reception in English Literature*, Vol. 1, *800–1558*. Oxford: Oxford University Press, 2016. xi, 758 pp. Includes twenty-eight sections by various authors (four by Copeland) who address the impact of the classics on medieval and early modern English culture: education, mythology, historiography, moral philosophy, humanism, translations, individual authors, and more. References to Chaucer and most of his works recur throughout, with attention to his "engagement" with classical writers such as Boethius, Lucan, Ovid and "Ovidianism," Statius, and Virgil, as well as his depictions of Troy, Greece, and Rome, and discussion of his influence on later English classicism. The volume offers primary and secondary bibliographies as well as a comprehensive index. For an essay that pertains to Chaucer and classicism, see no. 49.

127. Dean, James M. "Chaucer's Reality Fiction." In *Geoffrey Chaucer* (*SAC* 41 [2019], no. 128), pp. 128–43. Focuses on Chaucer's storytelling style, which combines fiction, invention of literary characters that bring in "details and personalities from 'life,' " and metafictive narrative elements.

128. _____, ed. *Geoffrey Chaucer*. Critical Insights Series. Ipswich, Mass.: Salem Press, 2017. xiv, 255 pp. Collection of essays that explores various literary aspects of Chaucer's oeuvre, with particular focus on the "international motif" and "transnational" themes found in many works. Essays address critical contexts and readings to help understand Chaucer

and medieval literature. Includes bibliography and chronology of Chaucer's life and writings. For essays related to Chaucer, see nos. 14–15, 34, 68–69, 107, 116–17, 127, 145, 163, 166, 170, 251, 270.

129. Deusen, Nancy van, ed. *Cicero Refused to Die: Ciceronian Influence through the Centuries*. Boston, Mass.: Brill, 2013. viii, 214 pp. Ten essays by various authors and an introduction by the editor that consider the influence of Cicero on western language and literature from late Antiquity to the early modern era. For two essays that pertain to Chaucer, see nos. 54 and 303.

130. Downes, Stephanie, and Rebecca F. McNamara. "The History of Emotions and Middle English Literature." *LitComp* 13, no. 6 (2016): 444–56. Surveys "current critical trends" in the history of emotions and in Middle English literature, considering modern and postmodern criticism of *TC* ("a poem of emotional extremes") and *Sir Orfeo*, and suggesting future directions for the study of emotions through medieval literature.

131. Evans, Gareth Lloyd. "An Unwitting Return to the Medieval: Postmodern Literary Experiments and Middle English Textuality." *Neophil* 100 (2016): 335–44. Argues that "postmodern literary experiments tend to enact, and embody, an unwitting return to medieval modes of textuality," observing how *PF*, *CT* as a whole, individual tales, and the multiplicity of variant manuscripts "actively resist a sense of closure or unitary perspectives." Compares several postmodern examples.

132. Fedewa, Kate. "Composing the Classroom: Imagining the Medieval English Grammar School." *DAI* A74.11 (2014): n.p. Explores the "means and purposes" of Latin literary education in late medieval England, examining the "subject position" imagined for school children in pedagogical materials. Also comments on how Chaucer and Langland evoke a "grammatical nostalgia" that influences their views of the world outside the classroom.

133. Fradenburg, L. O. Aranye. "Life's Reach: Territory, Display, Ekphrasis." In *Staying Alive: A Survival Manual for the Liberal Arts* (Brooklyn, N.Y.: Punctum, 2013), pp. 223–61. Contemplates and appreciates the "indisputable fact of our common aliveness," exploring various topics for evidence of cognitive and aesthetic similarities: biosemiotics, real estate advertising, human natal development, communal grooming, and the temporal yearnings of Virgilian ekphrasis and its reflexes in *BD* and *HF*.

134. Fruoco, Jonathan. *Geoffrey Chaucer: Polyphonie et modernité*. Paris:

Michel Houdiard Editeur, 2015. 262 pp. Item not seen. WorldCat records indicate that this is a version of the author's 2014 doctoral dissertation.

135. Galloway, Andrew. "Imagining the Literary in Medieval England." In Tim William Machan, ed. *Imagining Medieval English: Language Structures and Theories, 500–1500* (*SAC* 41 [2019], no. 144), pp. 210–37. Contemplates the category of "the literary" in medieval English texts, surveying prior attempts to define or describe the category and indicating their utility. Comments on a range of Chaucerian topics, including the "cunningly self-authorizing discursive form" of Chaucer's dream visions; the goals of the original Chaucer Society; Chaucer's translation of Petrarch's sonnet as Troilus's "song"; and the possibility that, for Chaucer, "the idea of 'the literary" is the "problem and desire of possessing something earthly that is wholly valuable in itself, rather than merely referentially meaningful."

136. Graham, April Michelle Anderson. " 'Penelopëes Trouthe': Female Faithfulness in Late Medieval English Literature." *DAI* A79.08 (2017): n.p. Using the figure of Penelope as representative of the Faithful Woman, examines use of the figure in numerous late medieval works, including *Anel*, *BD*, *FranT*, and *MLT*.

137. Harbin, Andrea. R., and Tamara O'Callaghan. "Hyperprint Texts and the Teaching of Early Literature." *SMART* 21, no. 2 (2014): 111–26. Exemplifies and considers the utilities of "hyperprint" texts for teaching medieval literature, offering an extended example of the first twenty-five lines of *MilT*, augmented by five "fiducial markers" (QR-coded) that enable a reader/user, without leaving the primary text, to link (via a smartphone or similar device) to subsidiary illustrative or pedagogical material such as audio, video, and internet sites.

138. Hines, Jessica N. "In Search of Pity: Chaucerian Poetics and the Suffering of Others. *DAI* A78.09 (2017): n.p. Considers how Chaucer (in *ClT*, *LGW*, and *ParsT*) develops the concept of pity from other European sources, and privileges the concept in English literary discourse.

139. Hsy, Jonathan. "Disability." In David Hillman and Ulrika Maude, eds. *The Cambridge Companion to the Body in Literature* (Cambridge: Cambridge University Press, 2015), pp. 24–40. Explores how disability studies have expanded to include consideration of relations between "embodiment and literary form," focusing on representations of deafness in the fifteenth-century Castilian *Arboleda de los enfermos* (*Grove of the Infirm*) of Teresa de Castagena, but including discussion of

John Gower's autobiographical concern with blindness, Chaucer's depictions of bodily affliction in *MkT* (emphasizing stylistic concerns), Margery Kempe's "chronic illness or mental disability," and William Shakespeare's treatment of physical deformation in *Richard III*.

140. Johnson, Eleanor. "Critical Poetics: A Meditation on Alternative Critical Vernaculars." *Postmedieval* 6, no. 4 (2015): 361–74. Describes several ways of addressing modern "experimental poems *as* criticism," and suggests that, adumbrating such metapoetic practice, the juxtaposition of *Th* and *Mel* "constitutes a wondering literary-theoretical response to Boethius' *Consolation*" in which poetry (*Th*) "engages the senses" while prose (*Mel*) "engages the reason."

141. Kern-Stähler, Annette, Beatrix Busse, and Wietse de Boer, eds. *The Five Senses in Medieval and Early Modern England*. Boston, Mass.: Brill, 2016. xiii, 298 pp. Collection of essays presenting perspectives on interrelationships between sense perception and secular and Christian cultures in England from the Middle Ages to the Early Modern period. For essay on Chaucer, see no. 305.

142. Knudson, Karen R. "The Power of the Medieval Solomon-Magus and Solomon-Auctor Revealed through *The Canterbury Tales*, *Sir Gawain and the Green Knight*, and *The Tale of the Sankgreal*." *DAI* A78.03 (2016): n.p. Includes discussion of Chaucer's "two brief glimpses" of Solomon as a figure of wisdom in *CT*, and more extended discussion of Solomon as author in *Mel*, *WBP*, *MerT*, and *ParsT*.

143. Lavezzo, Kathy. "Critical Thriving: Chaucer, the *Nun's Priest's Tale*, and the MLA." In Eileen A. Joy, ed. *Still Thriving: On the Importance of Aranye Fradenburg* (Brooklyn, N.Y.: Punctum, 2013), pp. 25–31. Considers the value of retaining the Chaucer Division of the Modern Language Association, maintaining its importance as long as "attention to [Chaucer's] corpus continues to unhinge, transform, and trouble received ideas about being in the world." Comments on the "slippery multiplicity" of *NPT* as a reason that Chaucer criticism can and should thrive.

144. Machan, Tim William, ed. *Imagining Medieval English: Language Structures and Theories, 500–1500*. Cambridge Studies in Medieval Literature, no. 95. Cambridge: Cambridge University Press, 2016. xiii, 320 pp.; illus. Thirteen essays by various authors consider new and traditional conceptualizations of medieval English language and literature. For two essays that pertain to Chaucer, see nos. 21 and 135.

145. McKinley, Kathryn. "Transnational Chaucer." In James M.

Dean, ed. *Geoffrey Chaucer* (*SAC* 41 [2019], no. 128), pp. 113–27. Considers the "international" aspects of Chaucer's works and Chaucer's "European nature as a writer." Emphasizes the importance of Chaucer's "ability to draw upon international vernaculars . . . and retain elements of his own culture" in his works, by focusing primarily on *HF*. Also, discusses Chaucer's life, family, and travels.

146. Moseley, C. W. R. D. "Introduction." *Critical Survey* 29, no. 3 (2017): 1–6. Emphasizes the way in which Chaucer's poems engage in dialogue with his audience, changing the way we can engage with "the fundamental questions of knowledge, understanding, beauty, and pleasure."

147. Nakley, Susan. *Living in the Future: Sovereignty and Internationalism in the "Canterbury Tales."* Ann Arbor: University of Michigan Press, 2017. ix, 270 pp. Examines the views that accept Chaucer's nationalism as a given and those that focus on his international or European identity and vision. Draws on concepts of sovereignty and domesticity appearing "primarily in romantic and household contexts," and finds the interdependence between nationalism and internationalism evident in *CT*, in which "England emerges as a community grounded in the ethical demands of inclusivity." Claims "that *CT* must be included in serious discussions concerning sovereignty and internationalism in both English literature and late medieval political thought."

148. Novacich, Sarah Elliott. *Shaping the Archive in Late Medieval England: History, Poetry and Performance.* Cambridge: Cambridge University Press, 2017. xi, 214 pp. Explores how "poetic form, staging logistics, and the status of performance" contribute to our understanding of how medieval thinkers imagined the "ethics and pleasures of the archive." Discussion of *HF*, *MLT*, *MilT*, and *Rom*.

149. Pugh, Tison. "Teaching Chaucer through Convergence Culture: The New Media Middle Ages as Cross-Cultural Encounter." In Karina F. Attar and Lynn Shutters, eds. *Teaching Medieval and Early Modern Cross-Cultural Encounters* (New York: Palgrave Macmillan, 2014), pp. 215–28. Comments on the advantages of using new media to help students gain appreciation and expertise in studying Chaucer; includes descriptions of undergraduate classroom activities that use cinema, Chaucer blogs, YouTube videos of rap versions of Chaucer's poetry, and performance adaptations of selections from *LGW*.

150. Ramírez-Arlandi, Juan. "La literatura inglesa medieval en Sudamérica: Jorge Elliott y *The Canterbury Tales*." In Salvador Peña and

Juan Jesús Zaro, eds. *De Homero a Pavese: Hacia un canon iberoamericano de clásicos universales* (Kassel: Reichenberger, 2017), pp. 39–64. Analyzes the translation techniques used in the Spanish version of *MilT* and *RvT* made between 1949 and 1956 by Chilean scholar, theater director and translator Jorge Elliott García. Claims that the purpose of this verse translation was to increase the readership of *CT* by offering a more poetic rendering, aiming at providing an effect equivalent to that of the original.

151. Robertson, Kellie. *Nature Speaks: Medieval Literature and Aristotelian Philosophy*. Philadelphia: University of Pennsylvania Press, 2017. x, 443 pp.; illus. Discusses how Aristotelian natural philosophy—physics—was debated in the Middle Ages, and its influence on the aesthetic practice of Latin and vernacular writers, including Chaucer, Jean de Meun, Guillaume de Deguileville, and Lydgate. Argues that these debates focus on the authority of nature in the context of a Christian world, and that "the controversial reception of this science fundamentally changed the kinds of poetic accounts of the world."

152. Sisk, Jennifer. "Chaucer and Hagiographic Authority." In Eva von Contzen and Anke Bernau, eds. *Sanctity as Literature in Late Medieval Britain* (Manchester: Manchester University Press, 2015), pp. 116–33. Explores how Chaucer addresses the sacred authority of hagiography, posing it in tension with the poet's own authority in *LGWP*, and examining authority and authorization in the "pseudo-hagiographies" of *CT* (*MLT*, *ClT*, and *PhyT*) where Chaucer recontextualizes the conventions of saints' lives in secular settings and experiments with several "alternative methods of textual authorisation." Observes that "confessional performances follow immediately upon tales that strive for hagiographic authority."

153. Smith, Sheri. "Answers to Prayer in Chaucer." *DAI* C75.01 (2016): n.p. Examines answers to prayer in *BD*, *HF*, *KnT*, *FranT*, "hagiographic tales" (*SNT*, *PrT*, *MLT*, and *ClT*), and *TC*, arguing that Chaucer engages significant "theological and philosophical issues."

154. Sutherland, John. *A Little History of Literature*. New Haven: Yale University Press, 2013. vii, 275 pp.; b&w illus. Surveys the history of literature "from the Epic of Gilgamesh to Harry Potter," including a chapter called "English Tales: Chaucer" (pp. 26–32) that summarizes Chaucer's life, *TC*, and *CT*, characterizing both poems as "supremely great" and "momentously innovative," and emphasizing Chaucer's use of English and his social variety.

155. Thomas, Alfred. "Chaucerovy Čechy." ["Chaucer's Bohemia"]. *Bohemica litteraria* 19, no. 1 (2016): 7–28. Describes the erudition of Anne of Bohemia, reads *CT* "alongside contemporaneous works in Czech, German, and Latin" (languages familiar to Anne), and maintains that Anne was Chaucer's "imagined reader" who "shaped the way he wrote and what he chose to write." In Czech, with an abstract in English.

156. Tucker, Shawn. *Virtues and Vices in the Arts: A Sourcebook*. Oakville: David Brown; Eugene, Ore.: Cascade; Cambridge: Lutterworth, 2015. ix, 288 pp.; b&w illus. Surveys representations of the virtues and vices in western art and literature from Plato and Aristotle to C. S. Lewis and Paul Cadmus, offering excerpts and brief discussions of individual works. The section on medieval representations, "The Medieval Apex," includes a selection from *ParsT* (X.846955, "Luxuria") in J. U. Nicolson's 1934 modern translation, and characterizes *ParsT* as an "excellent example" of a "pastoral sermon," a genre that is "meant to train people in the principles of penance, contrition, confession, and satisfaction or absolution."

157. Turner, Marion. "Chaucer." *Oxford Handbooks Online: Scholarly Research Reviews*. Free access available at http://www.oxfordhandbooks .com/view/10.1093/oxfordhb/9780199935338.001.0001/oxfordhb-97 80199935338-e-58?rskey = ycbEz7&result = 1. 2015 (accessed February 23, 2019). Surveys "current critical trends" in Chaucer studies, focusing on "twenty-first-century interest in interconnectedness, intersubjectivity, and cultural networks." Then discusses "Chaucer's own understanding of the construction of the self in relation to others and to the spaces in which he lived and worked," concluding with an "analysis of the mental structures depicted" in *BD* and *HF* as they reflect Chaucer's "understanding that private spaces can be problematic for imaginative and personal development."

158. Wallace, David. *Geoffrey Chaucer: A New Introduction*. Oxford: Oxford University Press, 2017. ix, 172 pp. Focuses on Chaucer's "global renaissance" and the importance of Chaucer's range of writing, which combines poetry, science, tragedy, and astrology to influence writers from Shakespeare to Sylvia Plath.

159. Yamanaka, Margaret. "On Reading Jerry Ellis' Travel Diaries: A Comparison of *Walking the Trail* and *Walking to Canterbury*." *Bulletin of Gifu Women's University* 47 (2017): 11–18. Compares two travel diaries by Jerry Ellis (1974–). Includes a detailed description of *Walking to*

Canterbury—A Modern Journey through Chaucer's Medieval England, which contains references to *NPT*, *SumT*, *WBT*, and *ParsT*.

The Canterbury Tales—General

160. Baker, Alison A. "Opposing Forces: Understanding Gods in Medieval and Early Modern Literature." *SMART* 23, no. 1 (2016): 351–61. Proposes a "mnemonic device" for six of the Roman classical gods (Apollo, Diana, Venus, Mars, Minerva, and Bacchus) "that can be used to teach and understand" them in *CT* and in Spenser's *Faerie Queene*.

161. Breckenridge, Sarah Dee. "Space, Economics, and the Poetic Imagination in England's Literary Landscapes, 1125–1590." *DAI* A75.04 (2014): n.p. Examines a series of English literary texts in which "the portrayal of landscape does both elegiac and political work." Includes *CT*, which "represents a new sphere of civic and economic movement within established space."

162. Canton, James, ed. *The Literature Book*. New York: DK, 2016. 352 pp. In a chapter called "Renaissance to Enlightenment, 1300–1800," includes a section (pp. 68–71) entitled "Turn over the Leef and Chese Another Tale: *The Canterbury Tales* (c. 1387–1400), Geoffrey Chaucer" that describes *CT*, its innovations, and social variety, with several side-bar topics and illustrations in color and b&w.

163. Dean, James M. "On Geoffrey Chaucer." In *Geoffrey Chaucer* (*SAC* 41 [2019], no. 128), pp. 3–20. Provides overview of Chaucer as storyteller and narrator in *CT*, *BD*, *HF*, and *TC*.

164. Evans, Ruth. "Getting There: Wayfinding in the Middle Ages." In Valerie Allen and Ruth Evans, eds. *Roadworks: Medieval Britain, Medieval Roads* (*SAC* 41 [2019], no. 119), pp. 127–56. Uses the methodologies of urban studies and space studies to investigate the "cultural and cognitive aspects of medieval wayfinding," and comments on *CT* and the illustrations of the Ellesmere manuscript as evidence of how medieval travelers used and understood their roads.

165. Khoshbakht, Maryam, Moussa Ahmadian, and Shahrukh Hekmat. "A Comparative Study of Chaucer's *The Canterbury Tales* & Attar's *The Conference of the Birds*." *International Journal of Applied Linguistics & English Literature* 2, no. 1 (2013): 90–97. Compares *CT* with Farid al-Din Attar's *The Conference of the Birds*, observing similarities in the shared motif of spiritual journey and techniques of narration and characterization. Differences between the religious backgrounds of the two poets, however, are evident in their thematic emphases.

166. Ladd, Roger A. "Selling Satire: Gower, Chaucer, and the End of the Estates." In James M. Dean, ed. *Geoffrey Chaucer* (*SAC* 41 [2019], no. 128), pp. 81–96. Examines how Chaucer and Gower handled the genre of "estates satire," and speculates how "their social critique moves away from an estates satire framework." Addresses mercantile practice in *MerT*, *MLT*, and *WBT*, and claims that Chaucer, like Gower, "is able to include substantial critique of economic practices in the actions" of characters in *CT*.

167. Lawton, David. *Voice in Later Medieval English Literature: Public Interiorities*. Oxford: Oxford University Press, 2017. xi, 243 pp. Approaches late medieval vernacular culture in terms of "voice," and suggests that "voice" is the subject of *CT*. Argues that Chaucer "frames" his work "between the praise of voice and the censure of it prevalent in pastoral rhetoric and represented by the Parson."

168. Legassie, Shayne Aaron. "The Pilgrimage Road in Late Medieval English Literature." In Valerie Allen and Ruth Evans, eds. *Roadworks: Medieval Britain, Medieval Roads* (*SAC* 41 [2019], no. 119), pp. 199–219. Examines the "artistic and ideological purposes" of the notion of a pilgrimage road in the "imaginary of the Middle Ages," focusing on late medieval England and commenting on the attention (or lack of attention) to the road in *CT* and the Ellesmere illustrations, particularly where they evince "metaliterary" concerns.

169. Picard, Liza. *Chaucer's People: Everyday Lives in Medieval England*. London: Weidenfeld & Nicolson, 2017. xx, 341 pp. Frames and analyzes the pilgrims of *CT* in terms of the social contexts surrounding their professions in Chaucer's lifetime and the antecedent few decades, interestingly moving directly against perceived social ordering to do so. Begins with the rural pilgrims before moving to the more urban, then the religious, then the military. Pilgrims' encapsulations of aspects of later medieval English life, both observed and contemporaneously figured, are used to reaffirm Chaucer's understanding of the breadth of the societies in which he lived.

170. Sadlek, Gregory M. "Harry Bailey's Labor and Time Consciousness on Chaucer's Canterbury Pilgrimage." In James M. Dean, ed. *Geoffrey Chaucer* (*SAC* 41 [2019], no. 128), pp. 37–52. Explores how *CT* reflects Chaucer's "orientation toward life that celebrates *bisynesse* [business/busyness] and abhors wasteful idleness." Focuses on the importance of the Host and Chaucer's "marking of the time" in *CT*.

171. Sharma, Manish. "Hylomorphic Recursion and Non-Decisional

Poetics in the *Canterbury Tales.*" *ChauR* 52, no. 3 (2017): 253–73. Argues that Chaucer is indecisive in *CT* when it comes to his relation to nominalism and realism, maintaining a grey area between the two through love.

172. Wong, Hui-wai. "Nobody Listens to the Story in *The Time Machine?* Re-Examining Benjamin's Nostalgia for Storytelling from Lacan's Theory of Transference." *Sun Yat-Sen Journal of Humanities* 36 (2014): 115–42. Discusses the narrative frame of H. G. Wells's *The Time Machine* as part of the "story-within-story narrative model" epitomized by *CT*, describing features of Chaucer's frame-narrative and arguing that Wells's presentation is unique in that the embedded audience disbelieves the narrator, who must recurrently insist on their attention and belief.

See also nos. 7–8, 11–12, 20, 26, 28, 30, 32, 35–37, 62, 75, 79, 89, 93–94, 98, 108, 113, 131, 142, 149–50, 154–55, 247.

CT—The General Prologue

173. Doğan, Sadenur. "The Three Estates Model: Represented and Satirised in Chaucer's *General Prologue* to *The Canterbury Tales.*" *Tarih kültür ve sanat araştırmaları dergisi/Journal of History, Culture, and Art Research* 2, no. 2 (2013): 49–56. Describes how in *GP* the descriptions of the Knight, the Parson, and the Plowman reflect the ideals of their respective social estates, and how the descriptions of the Monk, the Reeve, and the Wife of Bath exemplify Chaucer's uses of estates satire for the rest of his pilgrims.

174. Kowalik, Barbara. "*Eros* and Pilgrimage in Chaucer's and Shakespeare's Poetry." *Text Matters: A Journal of Literature, Theory and Culture* 3 (2013): 27–43. Discusses "erotic desire and the motif of going on pilgrimage" in the opening of *GP* and in Shakespeare's Sonnets, reading Chaucer's lines 1–18 closely as a kind of sonnet and observing numerological patterns that reinforce a transition from erotic desire to religious devotion. Shakespeare, in contrast, uses religious pilgrimage to evoke motion toward his beloved.

175. Lawler, Traugott. "Three Troublesome Lines in Chaucer's General Prologue: 11 (So priketh hem Nature), 176 (The space), 739 (Crist spak himself ful brode)." In Simon Horobin and Aditi Nafde, eds. *Pursuing Middle English Manuscripts and Their Texts: Essays in Honour of Ralph*

Hanna (*SAC* 41 [2019], no. 22), pp. 225–39. Claims that line 11 is not parenthetical and that "so" is an adverb of degree, in "They sleep all night with their eyes open, nature pricks them so in their hearts." In line 176, "the space" means "in the meantime," and not the object of "held." As for line 736, ample evidence from the Gospels, the non-canonical sayings, and some Psalms makes clear how much latitude Jesus allowed himself in his speech—and Chaucer's own similar latitude, *sermo humilis* in imitation of Christ, marks his art as Christian.

176. Matsuda, Takami. "Palmer and *corpus mysticum* in the *Canterbury Tales*." *SIMELL* 32 (2017): 1–15. Points out that a reference to a palmer in *GP* recalls both the pilgrimage for one's own penance and the vicarious pilgrimage. Argues that the idea of mutual help among all the Christian members (*corpus mysticum*) underlies that the system of pardon and vicarious pilgrimage are burlesqued in *PardPT* and *SumT*. Suggests that the idea of *corpus mysticum* also "provides a narrative and thematic framework" of *CT*.

177. Sobecki, Sebastian. "A Southwark Tale: Gower, the 1381 Poll Tax, and Chaucer's *The Canterbury Tales*." *Speculum* 92, no. 3 (2017): 630–60. Argues that Chaucer spent much of the 1380s and 1390s in Southwark as a recipient of a sort of patronage from William Wykeham, chancellor of England, alongside others such as Gower and John Cobham. Asserts that *GP* is based on the format of the 1381 Southwark Poll Tax's "check-roll or counter roll" format, which contrasts other claims that *GP* is based on estates satire.

See also nos. 16, 35, 71, 96, 116–17.

CT—The Knight and His Tale

178. Cervone, Cristina Maria. "(Im)materiality and Chaucer's Temple of Mars." *ELN* 53, no. 2 (2015): 103–17. Explores "inversions of the material and the immaterial" in the description of the temple of Mars in *KnT*, describing how the narrator of the description is both "subjectless and immaterial," and investigating "how we think about what we imagine we know." Differing from its source in Boccaccio, Chaucer's version is rife with synaesthesia, nested ekphrases, "unanchored physical details," and near-allegorical devices that evoke questions about the nature of thought, interpretation, and human agency.

179. Cross, Cameron. "'If Death Is Just, What Is Injustice?' Illicit

Rage in *Rostam and Sohrab* and *The Knight's Tale.*" *Iranian Studies: Journal of the International Society for Iranian Studies* 48 (2015): 395–422. Uses *KnT* as a "comparand" in understanding the tension between "outrage and reason" in the tale of Rostam and Sohrab in Fardowsi's medieval Persian frame-tale narrative *Shahnameh* (*Book of Kings*). Like Fardowsi's, Chaucer's tale struggles and ultimately fails to console rationally the human despair and rage that result from disorder in the cosmos. Includes discussion of narrative frames and Boethian concerns.

180. Johnston, Andrew James. "Ekphrasis in the *Knight's Tale.*" In R. Howard Bloch, Alison Calhoun, Jacqueline Cerquiglini-Toulet, Joachim Küpper, and Jeanette Patterson, eds. *Rethinking the New Medievalism* (Baltimore: Johns Hopkins University Press, 2014), pp. 181–97. Explores how in *KnT* ekphrasis (here the "verbal depiction of fictional images rather than of real ones") serves "a specific politics of representation" in which "the verbal and the visual" and "the classical and the medieval" are locked in "ineluctable conflict." Comments on the temples in *KnT* (especially that of Mars), their relation to the theater, the descriptions of Emetreus and Lygurge, subjectivity, self-reflexivity, voyeurism, "poetic narcissism," the paradoxical aims of chivalry, and "Lollard iconophobia."

181. ———. "Medieval Ekphrasis: Chaucer's *Knight's Tale.*" In Gabriele Rippl, ed. *Handbook of Intermediality: Literature—Image—Sound—Music* (Berlin: De Gruyter, 2015), pp. 50–64. Sketches "medieval approaches to vision, to the relations between text and image and to ekphrasis" before assessing *KnT* as Chaucer's critique of "attempts to essentialise and keep separate different media and genres, especially the verbal and the visual." Focuses on the temples, Emily's ablutions, and the tournament battle.

182. Lee, Dong Choon. "Double-Sidedness of Architecture and Space in Chaucer's *Knight's Tale* and *Troilus and Criseyde.*" *MES* 25, no. 1 (2017): 49–66. Analyzes the architectural constructions, especially walls, in *KnT* and *TC*. Claims that the "effect of a wall in Chaucerian narratives is the double-sidedness," because walls can invite and discourage connections between inside and outside spaces.

183. Rogerson, Margaret. "Reading Chaucer 'in Parts': The *Knight's Tale* and *The Two Noble Kinsmen.*" In Jan Shaw, Philippa Kelly, and L. E. Semler, eds. *Storytelling: Critical and Creative Approaches* (New York: Palgrave Macmillan, 2013), pp. 167–80. Observes how *KnT* signals transitions, scene changes, gestures, and even costuming, perhaps inspiring

Shakespeare and Fletcher to create *The Two Noble Kinsmen* by dividing the Chaucer poem into written "parts" for actors before assembling their entire play.

184. Stallcup, Stephen. "*Lectio difficilior* and All That: Another Look at Arcite's Injury." In Dorsey Armstrong, Ann W. Astell, and Howell Chickering, eds. *Magistra doctissima: Essays in Honor of Bonnie Wheeler* (*SAC* 41 [2019], no. 120), pp. 43–58. Explores the textual and lexical ambiguities of the scene of Arcite's mortal fall in *KnT* (I.2684–91), discussing "furie" (forty manuscripts read some form of *fire*), "pighte," and "pomel" (neither of which is lexically certain). Suggests that emending "heed" to "stede" at line 2689 resolves the ambiguities of the latter two.

185. Tasioulas, Jacqueline. " 'Dying of Imagination' in the First Fragment of the *Canterbury Tales*." *MÆ* 82, no. 2 (2013): 213–35. Explores "the role of the imagination" in *KnT*, with attention also to *MilT* and *RvT*, focusing on the "cerebral process" in the "amorous desire" of the characters, especially Arcite, whose lovers' malady results from his "lack of imaginative control." Summarizes medieval notions of psychology and imagination, discusses adaptations of Boccaccio and Boethius in *KnT*, and analyzes the recurrent concern with seeing, imagining, desiring, and willing in the first three narratives of *CT*.

186. Wadiak, Walter. *Savage Economy: The Returns of Middle English Romance*. Notre Dame: University of Notre Dame Press, 2016. xiv, 196 pp. Traces the evolution of the to the start of the sixteenth century, and its repositioning from an aristocratic genre to one that was embraced by the common audience. Claims this move marks a shift from violence in its early stages to one of "gift-giving" as the romance evolved to its form by the year 1500. Although well-known contemporary examples of romance are considered, the study focuses on *KnT* and *Sir Gawain*. References *CYT*, *FranT*, *MilT*, *ShT*, *SqT*, *Th*, and *WBT*.

187. Yu, Wesley Chihyung. "Arcite's Consolation: Boethian Argumentation and the Phenomenology of Drunkenness." *Exemplaria* 28 (2016): 1–20. Explores how the figure of a drunken man, originating in Boethius's *Consolation of Philosophy* and *De topicis differentiis*, and used by Chaucer in Arcite's complaint in *KnT*, I.1260–67, "blurs the line between universal and particular" and thereby challenges the categories of traditional argumentation. The figure serves as the "syntactical locus

of a dynamic exchange between two authoritative axes of knowledge-making [metaphysics and sensory] that strives to situate temporal conditions." Also comments on the names written in ice in *HF*.

See also nos. 10, 35, 49, 58, 101, 153, 213.

CT—The Miller and His Tale

188. Heffernan, Carol F. "Laughter in Horace's Ode I. 9 and Chaucer's *Miller's Tale*." *Neophil* 97 (2013): 191–97. Suggests the "possible influence" of Horace's Ode I.9 on Alisoun's laugh in the dark in *MilT*, observing similarities in erotic setting, imagery, and opposition between youth and age.

189. Pekşenyakar, Azime. "'I shall thee quyte': Fabliau Women's Spatial Resistance in the *Miller's Tale* and the *Reeve's Tale*." *Interactions: Ege Journal of British and American Studies / Ege Ingiliz ve Amerikan incelemeleri dergisi* 25, nos. 1–2 (2016): 149–59. Explores spaces, places, and gendered power relations in *MilT* and *RvT*, arguing that Alisoun, Malyne, and Symkyn's wife all use trickery to evade spatial oppression and achieve pleasure.

190. Smilie, Ethan K., and Kipton D. Smilie. "Re-Imagining the Class Clown: Chaucer's Clowning Clerics." *Interdisciplinary Humanities* 31, no. 3 (2014): 32–52. Surveys Marxist scholarship concerning "class clowns" in American school rooms, classroom management of them, and their vocational potential. Then discusses Nicholas of *MilT* and John and Aleyn of *RvT* as students "who 'work the system' for the sake of leisure and to show off"—class clowns whose pranks "perpetrated class divisions" rather than producing actual change.

See also nos. 10, 32, 79, 137, 148, 185–86.

CT—The Reeve and His Tale

191. Bertolet, Craig E. "Dressing Symkyn's Wife: Chaucer's *Reeve's Tale* and Bad Taste." *ChauR* 52, no. 4 (2017): 456–75. Analyzes the ways in which Chaucer uses the word 'sight' in order to examine concepts of taste and tastelessness in *RvT*.

192. Johnson, Travis William. "Affective Communities: Masculinity

and the Discourse of Emotion in Middle English Literature." *DAI* A75.01 (2014): n.p. Investigates the lexicons of emotion and "codes of masculinity" in a range of late medieval English literary texts, including *RvT*.

193. Okamoto, Hiroki. "'Curious fact': Fading of Northernisms in *The Reeve's Tale*." *BSCS* 5 (2017): 3–21. Reconsiders the role of the clerks' northern dialect in *RvT* as well as the Reeve's Norfolk dialect, paying particular attention to the fading of the former within the tale.

See also nos. 185, 189–90.

CT—The Cook and His Tale

194. Purdon, Liam O. "'And of that drynke the Cook was wonder fayn': A Reconsideration of Hogge of Ware's Drunkenness." *ChauR* 5, no. 2 (2017): 202–16. Proposes that the Cook is suffering from illness, which challenges the traditional interpretation of the Cook as a drunkard.

See also no. 26.

CT—The Man of Law and His Tale

195. Birns, Nicholas. "Chaucer, Gower, and Barbarian History: 'The Man of Law's Tale' and the Prologue to Gower's *Confessio Amantis*." In *Barbarian Memory: The Legacy of Early Medieval History in Early Modern Literature* (New York: Palgrave Macmillan, 2013), pp. 44–59. Assesses the uses of late Antique historiography in *MLT* and in Gower's Prologue to his *Confessio Amantis*, comparing Gower's depiction of the late Roman empire and that of Otto of Freising's *Chronica*, and arguing that the ultimate source of *MLT* is Paul the Dean's *Historia Langobardorum*, particularly evident in Chaucer's feminizing of the name "Hermengilde" and in the "twin-pronged conversion motif" of Custance's failure to convert the sultan and success in converting Alla.

196. Erwin, Bonnie J. "Why We Can't Stop Fighting about Chaucer's Man of Law." *Enarratio* 20 (2016): 41–66. Argues that *MLT* and *MLE* are "fundamentally concerned with the transmission of affect." The tale "dramatizes how affect operates as a physical force that realigns individual and collective identities," while the narrator's style, combined

with pilgrims' responses to the tale in *MLE*, "models how affects can leap between narrative worlds and between communities." Through the tale and responses, Chaucer tests "possibilities for how readers might be moved," provoking modern critical "disputes."

197. Hsy, Jonathan. "Translation Failure: The TARDIS, Cross-Temporal Language Contact, and Medieval Travel Narrative." In Jason Barr and Camille D. G. Mustachio, eds. *The Language of Doctor Who: From Shakespeare to Alien Tongues* (Lanham: Rowman & Littlefield, 2014), pp. 109–23. Explores three examples of literary representation of cultural contact across language boundaries: an episode from the *Doctor Who* television series, *MLT*, and the BBC adaptation of *MLT*, identifying parallels among cross-linguistic contact, cross-temporal contact, and cross-ethnic contact in these works for the ways that they "limn the malleable and shifting contours of Englishness." Considers Chaucer's Custance as a "woman who traverses and perpetually adapts to an array of shifting cultural settings."

198. Lim, Hyanyang K. "Counterfeit Correspondences: Documentary Manipulations and Textual Consciousness in Gloucester's *Confession* and *The Man of Law's Tale*." *MES* 25, no. 1 (2017): 67–97. Explores Chaucer's reservations about the reliability of written documents by examining Donegild's counterfeit letters in *MLT* and Thomas Woodstock, duke of Gloucester's *Confession*, written in 1397. Examines problems of written documents implicated in both narratives, such as "documentary manipulations, fears of inception, and suspicions of forgery."

199. Quinn, William A. "String Theory and 'The Man of Law's Tale': Where Is Constancy?" *Critical Survey* 29, no. 3 (2017): 48–64. The Ptolemaic universe of *MLT* should have a still center, but neither this tale nor the *Tales* as a whole seems to reflect "a single interpretive order." Thematic and tonal threads pull in different directions, as if the tale harbored an anticipation of today's highly speculative "string theory," which "admits the possibility of a multiverse in which numerous concurrent realities (of reader-responses) can coexist."

200. Staley, Lynn. "Fictions of the Island: Girdling the Sea." *Postmedieval* 7 (2016): 539–50. Contrasts Custance of *MLT* with her source in Trevet's *Cronicles*, exploring the depictions of the sea in the two poems as well, arguing that women and water are tamed by "providential control" in Chaucer, especially when seen in light of Alatiel of Boccaccio's

Decameron and of the "desire to domesticate the sea" in Lydgate's "Mumming for the Mercers of London."

See also nos. 10, 38, 148, 152–53, 166, 201, 269.

CT—The Wife of Bath and Her Tale

201. Cohen, Jeffrey Jerome. "British Chaucer." In Dorsey Armstrong, Ann W. Astell, and Howell Chickering, eds. *Magistra doctissima: Essays in Honor of Bonnie Wheeler* (*SAC* 41 [2019], no. 120), pp. 25–33. Interrogates Chaucer's diminishment or elimination of Scottish, Irish, and especially Welsh aspects of his narrative materials in *WBT*, *FranT*, and *MLT*, arguing that he associated the Celtic fairy world with death, as it is also associated in *Sir Orfeo*. Also comments on Chaucer's possible contacts with Celtic people and urges postcolonial awareness in study of the past.

202. Edwards, Suzanne M. *The Afterlives of Rape in Medieval English Literature*. The New Middle Ages. New York: Palgrave Macmillan, 2016. xvii, 183 pp. Investigates the "discourses of [rape] survival" in medieval literature and its historical contexts, addressing the aftereffects of rape as they are depicted in saints' lives, anchoritic literature, accounts of raped wives (particularly Lucretia in Gower and Heurodis in *Sir Orfeo*), and *WBT*. Argues that, in light of the 1382 Statute of Rape, *WBT* "diagnoses how masculine distinction and privilege underwrite their own impossibility" and how the presentation of desire in *WBPT* warns "against overvaluing gender difference as an interpretive scheme."

203. Fein, Susanna. "The 'Thyng Wommen Loven Moost': The Wife of Bath's Fabliau Answer." In Jenny Adams and Nancy Mason Bradbury, eds. *Medieval Women and Their Objects* (*SAC* 41 [2019], no. 118), pp. 15–38. Argues that the power of *WBT*, though it is commonly regarded as a *lai*, comes from an underlying subversion by the use of fabliau, which makes the tale a "hybrid story." The "question of what women most want" has surprising affinities with the extravagantly obscene fabliaux *Les quatre souhaiz de saint Martin* and *Les trois dames qui troverent un vit*—not only in Alisoun's fabliau-like asides about friars and Midas's wife, but even in its narrative core.

204. Inskeep, Kathryn. "Embodying Loathliness: The Loathly Lady in Medieval and Postfeminist (Con)texts." *DAI* A74.12 (2014): n.p.

Studies the "role of stigma in determining the social value of a lone woman of loathly proportions or perceptions," discussing a range of texts, medieval to postmodern, including two chapters on *WBPT* that assess the loathly lady as the "alter ego" of the Wife of Bath.

205. Noji, Kaoru. *Eloquence of Chaucer's Women: The Wife of Bath, Criseyde, and Prudence.* Tokyo: Hon-no-Shiro, 2017. xiv, 230 pp. Examines eloquence of the Wife of Bath, Criseyde, and Prudence. Focuses on Chaucer's intention in creating these female characters.

206. Perfetti, Lisa. "Feminist Humor without Women: The Challenge of Reading (in) the Middle Ages." In Peter Dickinson, Anne Higgins, Paul St. Pierre, Diana Solomon, and Sean Zwagerman, eds. *Women and Comedy: History, Theory, Practice* (Lanham: Fairleigh Dickinson University Press, 2013), pp. 41–53. Asks to what extent *CT* and Boccaccio's *Decameron* advocate "women's equality," exploring female laughter in these works, and focusing on Boccaccio's Pampinea and on the Wife of Bath as a "comic performer who has an intent to play."

207. Stock, Lorraine Kochanske. "Just How Loathly Is the 'Wyf'? Deconstructing Chaucer's 'Hag' in *The Wife of Bath's Tale*." In Dorsey Armstrong, Ann W. Astell, and Howell Chickering, eds. *Magistra doctissima: Essays in Honor of Bonnie Wheeler* (SAC 41 [2019], no. 120), pp. 34–42. Objects to the labeling of the loathly "wyf" in *WBT* as a "hag," arguing that the latter term is inappropriate and tendentious, especially because the tale lacks a description of ugliness found in its analogues.

208. Strouse, A. W. "Literary Theories of Circumcision." *DAI* A78.09 (2017): n.p. Uses *WBT* as a case study in the development of circumcision's use as a metaphor for situations ranging from shifting of intellectual ground to the process of reading itself.

209. Sylvester, Ruth. "Shifting Traditions: Chaucer's Narrative Accomplishment in *The Wife of Bath's Tale* Considered in the Context of the Shift from Oral Tradition to Literate Print Tradition." *ETC: A Review of General Semantics* 71, no. 3 (2014): 248–57. Summarizes differences between oral and literate communication, describes *CT* as a product of a transitional "manuscript culture," and discusses how *WBP* lends verisimilitude to the speaking voice of *WBT*, an example of Chaucer's virtuosity in a "time of cultural shift."

See also nos. 10, 32, 51, 64, 76, 80–81, 96–97, 117, 159, 166, 186, 214, 217, 220.

CT—The Friar and His Tale

210. Matsuda, Takami. "The Ravishment of Body and Soul in the *Friar's Tale* and the *Summoner's Tale*." *Spicilegium* 1 (2017): n.p. Web publication. Examines *FrT* and *SumT* in the "context of the late medieval vision of the afterlife," and argues that the "two tales tell how one is constantly in the dangerous liminal situation between damnation and salvation, between being physically ravished to hell by the devil and being carried to heaven by angels in mystical ravishment."

211. Saltzman, Benjamin A. "The Friar, the Summoner, and Their Techniques of Erasure." *ChauR* 52, no. 4 (2017): 363–95. Looks at how both erasure and the anxiety that erasure produces in material culture are revealed in *FrT* and *SumT*.

CT—The Summoner and His Tale

212. Hardwick, Paul. "Chaucer's Friar John and the Place of the Cat." *ChauR* 52, no. 2 (2017): 237–52. Portrays the symbolic and naturalistic use of the cat and applies these concepts to *SumT* and its critique of the mendicant orders.

213. Nava, Gabriela. "Ventosidades, culos y otros elementos del realismo grotesco en el relato breve (el *Decamerón*, los *Cuentos de Canterbury*, las *Cent nouvelles nouvelles*)." *Mediaevalia* 45 (2013): 62–73. Analyzes the grotesque Bahktinian realism of inversions and bodily functions in medieval narratives; includes comments on the "prayer-belch" and farting in *SumT* and on ass-kissing and farting in *MilT*, compared and contrasted with analogous materials.

214. Tambling, Jeremy. *Histories of the Devil: From Marlowe to Mann and the Manichees*. New York: Palgrave Macmillan, 2016. xvii, 308 pp.; 2 b&w illus. In a chapter entitled "Medieval and Early Modern Devils: Names and Images" (pp. 45–74), assesses the devil-dressed-in-green of *FrT* and its associations with the fairies in *WBT*; also comments on the characters in *PardT* and *CYT* "who are already devils," whose souls have "gone before their bodies died."

See also nos. 159, 176, 210, 238.

CT—The Clerk and His Tale

215. Bullón-Fernández, María. "Poverty, Property, and the Self in the Late Middle Ages: The Case of Chaucer's Griselda." *Mediaevalia* 35

(2014): 193–226. Argues that Chaucer raises questions in *ClT* about relations between poverty and the nature of the self, gauging the extent to which Griselda's agency, selflessness, and lack of "things" are factors in Walter's "inhuman" treatment of her, and asking whether her "lack of property is a part of the reason she is so readily turned into an allegorical virtue" by Petrarch and others.

216. Narinsky, Anna. "Anti-Dualism and Social Mind in Chaucer's *Clerk's Tale*." *Partial Answers: Journal of Literature and the History of Ideas* 14, no. 2 (2016): 187–216. Treats "the operations and qualities of fictional minds" in *ClT*, "as well as the narrative means through which they are conveyed," examining Griselda, Walter, and the "group consciousness" of the Saluzzan people in light of "modern cognitive sciences," and arguing that Chaucer rejects the mind–body dualism of the "internalist" view of cognition in favor of one that emphasizes the "intermental" interdependence of mind and social environment.

217. Normandin, Shawn. "'Non Intellegant': The Enigmas of the *Clerk's Tale*." *TSLL* 58 (2016): 235–55. Reads *ClT* closely as a "fundamentally enigmatic parable" that, as part of the "glossing group" of the *CT*, focuses on interpretation and hermeneutic resistance. Chaucer alternately abbreviates and amplifies his Petrarchan source "so that interpretive authority . . . will lie dormant and enigma will thrive." Simultaneously, the Clerk seeks subtly to mandate clerkly glossing in a "passive-aggressive" response to the Wife of Bath, emphasizing Griselda's inability and/or unwillingness to interpret words and events.

See also nos. 53, 56, 103, 138, 152–53, 218.

CT—The Merchant and His Tale

218. Hanna, Natalie. "'To take a wyf': Marriage, Status, and Moral Conduct in 'The Merchant's Tale.'" *Historical Reflections/Réflexions historiques* 42, no. 1 (2016): 61–74. Tabulates and analyzes the "gender-based" nouns used of the marital couple in *MerT*, compared with uses elsewhere in *CT*, focusing on uses of "wyf" and "housbonde" (61 versus 4 uses in *MerT*), and on the locution of "taking" a wife. Such usages connect January of *MerT* with Walter of *ClT*, and while neither tale challenges stereotypical roles overtly, *MerT* raises "profound social concerns" through its "terming" of marital status.

219. Kendrick, Laura. "Medieval Vernacular Versions of Ancient

Comedy: Geoffrey Chaucer, Eustache Deschamps, Vitalis of Blois and Plautus' *Amphitryon*." In S. Douglas Olson, ed. *Ancient Comedy and Reception: Essays in Honor of Jeffrey Henderson* (Berlin: De Gruyter, 2014), pp. 377–96. Investigates the performative nature of Deschamps's "relatively faithful French translation," *Geta et Amphitrion*, and proposes an occasion when it might have been performed. Contrasts Deschamps's treatment of Plautus's Latin original with those of other writers, including Chaucer, who "assimilated and mixed motifs from Latin comedies without acknowledgment" in *CT*. Exemplifies Chaucer's practice of combining motifs by discussing the pear-tree scene of *MerT*.

220. Turner, Joseph. "Rhetoric and Performing Anger: Proserpina's Gift and Chaucer's *Merchant's Tale*." *Rhetorica* 34 (2016): 427–54. Argues that Proserpina's angry response to Pluto in *MerT* (IV.2264–70) "highlights the historical relationship between Chaucer's depiction of women's speech, medieval grammatical [classroom] instruction, and theories of delivery" that derive from Geoffrey of Vinsauf's *Poetria nova*. Considers the role of angry speech in "leveling the playing field between men and women" in *MerT* and in *WBP*, and calls for revived interest in studying literature in relation to rhetoric.

221. Wicher, Andrzej. "Geoffrey Chaucer's *The Merchant's Tale*, Giovanni Boccaccio's *The Tale of the Enchanted Pear-Tree*, and *Sir Orfeo* Viewed as Eroticized Versions of the Folktales about Supernatural Wives." *Text Matters: A Journal of Literature, Theory and Culture* 3 (2013): 42–57. Discusses *MerT*; Boccaccio's *Decameron*, VII.9; and *Sir Orfeo* as "slightly different" varieties of the enchanted-tree motif, emphasizing their structural similarities, their uses of enchantment, and the relative happiness of their endings.

See also nos. 40, 76, 91, 166, 241, 330.

CT—The Squire and His Tale

222. Crane, Susan. "A Cautionary Elephant." *ShakS* 41 (2014): 29–39. Argues that two of Chaucer's emphases in *SqT* modify source material from Boethius's *Consolation of Philosophy* and thereby undo the "binary divide between humankind and animal kinds." The "falcon's species vacillation" and Canace's "cross-species kindness" show "that medieval thought about animals is neither uniform nor stable."

See also nos. 31, 49, 72, 186.

CT—The Franklin and His Tale

223. Bonazzi, Nicola. "Da Dianora a Marietta: Metamorfosi di un'illusione cortese." *Heliotropia: Forum for Boccaccio Research and Interpretation* 11 (2014): 181–97. Traces the development of the relations between illusion and courtliness from Boccaccio to James Lasdun's story in the *The Siege*, including a discussion of *FranT* that focuses on the "demande d'amour" that concludes the tale.

224. Christopher, Joe R. "C. S. Lewis's Problem with 'The Franklin's Tale': An Essay Written in the Seventieth Anniversary Year of *The Allegory of Love*." In Salwa Khoddam, Mark R. Hall, and Jason Fisher, eds. *C. S. Lewis and the Inklings: Reflections on Faith, Imagination, and Modern Technology* (Newcastle upon Tyne: Cambridge Scholars, 2015), pp. 121–32. Explores why C. S. Lewis chose not to discuss *FranT* in his *Allegory of Love*, arguing that Lewis made the decision because he wanted to attribute the "final defeat of courtly love by the romantic conception of marriage" to Edmund Spenser in his *Faerie Queene*. However, *FranT* was a "transmutation" of courtly love into marriage 200 years before Spenser wrote.

225. Coats, Kaitlin. "'Artes that been curious': Questions of Magic and Morality in Chaucer's 'The Franklin's Tale.'" *Sigma Tau Delta Review* 11 (2014): 90–99. Considers the ambivalent role of magic in *FranT*, arguing that vacillation "between belief and skepticism, truth and illusion, nature and sorcery" help Chaucer to create "a divide between perception and reality" and undermine the "purported moral system" of the tale.

226. Johnson, Eleanor. "Objects of the Law: The Cases of Dorigen and Virginia." In Jenny Adams and Nancy Mason Bradbury, eds. *Medieval Women and Their Objects* (*SAC* 41 [2019], no. 118), pp. 201–28. Discusses Chaucer's thematic thread of accessibility of legal rights to women in *FranT* and *PhyT*. Dorigen, in *FranT*, and Virginia, in *PhyT*, are women trapped as objects of medieval law, or as properties whose control or outright ownership is the subject of dispute between men. Focuses on the contractual restrictions placed on women and the patriarchal lens through which women are objectified.

227. Lesler, Rachel. "*Trouthe* or Illusion: Masculine Honor vs. Feminine Honor in the 'Franklin's Tale.'" *Sigma Tau Delta Review* 13 (2016): 40–47. Explores the alignment of *trouthe* and freedom in *FranT*, particularly as they relate to gendered honor, arguing that Dorigen's efforts to honor her marital *trouthe* limit her freedom.

228. McGraw, Matthew Theismann, "The Supernatural and the Limits of Materiality in Medieval Histories, Travelogues, and Romances from William of Malmesbury to Geoffrey Chaucer." *DAI* A75.05 (2014): n.p. Includes discussion of *FranT* as one among several examples of late medieval English romances that explore "noble identity and chivalric values" and use magic to place these values in starker relief than can be accomplished realistically.

229. Olson, David W. *Celestial Sleuth: Using Astronomy to Solve Mysteries in Art, History and Literature*. New York: Springer, 2013. xvii, 355 pp.; color and b&w illus. Includes discussion of *FranT* (pp. 282–93), tabulating historical astronomical data and arguing that Chaucer "used the configuration of the Sun and Moon in December 1340 as the inspiration for the time of year [late December] and for the central plot device [high tide]" of the tale. Suggests that the date may have caught his eye because it was his birth year.

230. Sweeney, Michelle. "Lady as Temptress and Reformer in Medieval Romance." *EMSt* 30 (2015): 165–78. Examines how "knights are reformed" and some are "even saved by the women who tempt them" in several medieval romances, including Chrétien's *Knight of the Cart*; Marie de France's *Lanval*; *Sir Gawain and the Green Knight*; and *FranT*, where Dorigen is "the temptress and the protector, all rolled into one complicated package."

231. Turner, Joseph. "Speaking 'Amys' in the *Franklin's Tale:* Rhetoric, Truth, and the *Poetria nova*." *ChauR* 52, no. 2 (2017): 217–36. Focuses on the concept of manipulation in language and magic in *FranT*.

See also nos. 49, 153, 186, 201.

CT—The Physician and His Tale

232. Ponce, Timothy. " 'To hange upon a tree': A Didactic Catharsis of Crucifixion through Moral Subversion in Chaucer's 'Physician's Tale.' " *Sigma Tau Delta Review* 13 (2016): 25–31. Traces the Jewish and Christian understandings of crucifixion, arguing that the image underlies the "didactic nature" of *PhyT* where "repeated images of injustice" are "placed in dialogue with the symbolism of the cross," reminding the reader of "divine grace."

233. Schiff, Randy P. "The Physician and the Forester: Virginia,

Venison, and the Biopolitics of Vital Property." In Randy P. Schiff and Joseph Taylor, eds. *The Politics of Ecology: Land, Life, and Law in Medieval Britain* (Columbus: Ohio State University Press, 2016), pp. 82–103. Argues that the narrator's comments on poachers and governesses in *PhyT* are not digressive, but part of a broader "biopolitical" concern that "clearly condemns the parental absolutism that leads to Virginius's murder of his daughter" and aptly cultivates "a politics of life" as an alternative to the traditional "thanatopolitical status quo" of legalistic authority.

234. Seal, Samantha Katz. "Reading like a Jew: Chaucer's *Physician's Tale* and the Letter of the Law." *ChauR* 52, no. 3 (2017): 298–317. Reads *PhyT* as a conflict between Jewish literal hermeneutics and a more metaphorical Christian reading of faith.

235. Spearing, A. C. "What Is a Narrator? Narrator Theory and Medieval Narratives." *Digital Philology* 4, no. 1 (2015): 59–105. Questions the "narrator theory of narration," critiquing the "concept of the internal, potentially unreliable narrator"; examining "the history of the term *narrator*"; studying "the theories of narration implied by scribal annotations in some medieval manuscripts" (including manuscripts of *TC*); and challenging narrator-based (or "dramatic") readings of *PhyT*, suggesting that the tale should be read as "one of Chaucer's several thought-experiments in the exploration of pagan worlds."

See also nos. 49, 152, 226, 269, 327.

CT—The Pardoner and His Tale

236. da Costa, Alex. "The Pardoner's Passing and How It Matters: Gender, Relics and Speech Acts." *Critical Survey* 29, no. 3 (2017): 27–47. Reconsiders the possibility that the Pardoner is a woman passing as a man in *PardT*, which raises anxieties about the relation of outward appearance and inner substance. These parallel anxieties about the authenticity of relics and the validity of religious speech acts, including those involved with the transubstantiation of the elements of the Eucharist.

237. Lampert-Weissig, Lisa. "Chaucer's Pardoner and the Jews." *Exemplaria* 28 (2016): 337–60. Treats the Old Man of *PardT* as a figure of the Wandering Jew, exploring relations between the figure and the transtemporal materiality of relics, and linking it with "other explicit

and implicit references to Jews" in the depiction of the Pardoner (especially his hare-like glaring eyes) and his tale. Includes attention to oath-taking and the Host's threat to the Pardoner.

238. Linkinen, Tom. *Same-Sex Sexuality in Later Medieval English Culture*. Crossing Boundaries: Turku Medieval and Early Modern Studies. Amsterdam: Amsterdam University Press, 2015. 334 pp.; illus. Includes a chapter, "Sharing Laughter" (pp. 205–32), that identifies examples from late medieval art and literature where laughter constitutes "moral censorship" of same-sex desire or actions, then focuses on the Pardoner; his relation with the Summoner in *GP*; and the grotesquery, mockery, and laughter generated by his offer of his relics at the end of *PardT*.

239. Smith, D. Vance. "Death and Texts: Finitude before Form." *Minnesota Review* 80 (2013): 131–44. Argues that in *PardT* "allegory and form straddle the boundaries of finitude in order to raise the question of how finitude is constituted," thereby sharing or anticipating several concerns and questions raised by object-oriented, materialist philosophy. Paradoxically concerned with death and the mundane transcendence of relics, *PardPT* explores the boundaries and continuities between sign and signified, finitude and infinity, and singularity and form.

See also nos. 7, 10, 176, 214.

CT—The Shipman and His Tale

240. Dove, Jonathan, composer. *An Old Way to Pay New Debts: Opera in One Act (Un vecchio modo di pagare I nuovi debiti)*. London: Edition Peters, 2015. Opera score; 99 pp. Item not seen. WorldCat records indicate that this facsimile of Dove's musical score includes a libretto by Alasdair Middleton based on *ShT*, and Italian singing translation by Adam Pollock. Also published as the third part of Dove's trilogy: *Racconti di speranza e desiderio (Tales of Hope and Desire)*.

241. Pekşen, Azime. "'Fantasye and curious bisynesse': *The Merchant's Tale* and *The Shipman's Tale*." In Mehmet Ali Çelikel and Baysar Taniyan, eds. *English Studies: New Perspectives* (Newcastle upon Tyne: Cambridge Scholars, 2015), pp. 36–45. Analyzes how May in *MerT* and the wife in *ShT* "evade the oppressions" of marriage and "subvert their

subjugation through negotiating and challenging the mercantile narration." Each female protagonist "generates her own meanings and pleasure."

See also nos. 10, 186.

CT—The Prioress and Her Tale

242. Blurton, Heather, and Hannah Johnson, eds. *The Critics and the Prioress: Antisemitism, Criticism, and Chaucer's "Prioress's Tale."* Ann Arbor: University of Michigan Press, 2017. 218 pp. Explores the anti-Semitism of *PrT*, producing "a discussion animated by the ways in which antisemitism has emerged as the problematic that organizes scholarly response," and resists dismissing or excusing prejudice and hate in *PrT*. Tracks history of *PrT* criticism, its sources and the potentially problematic methodology of traditional source studies, the history of antifeminism linked to anti-Semitism in criticism of *PrT*, and the reception of *PrT* in the fifteenth century. Combines a detailed history and analysis of criticism to "help scholars break free of some old patterns and seek out fresh modes of engagement" regarding the understanding and teaching of *PrT*.

243. Chickering, Howell. "The Object of Miraculous Song in 'The Prioress's Tale.'" In Jenny Adams and Nancy Mason Bradbury, eds. *Medieval Women and Their Objects* (*SAC* 41 [2019], no. 118), pp. 56–68. Focuses on materiality and objects in *PrT*, specifically the corpse, the antiphon, and the "greyn," and their "transcendence of the miraculous object." Claims that these objects illustrate Carolyn Bynum's notion of material objects involved in miraculous change. Concludes with a look at the "greyn" and the tale itself, both of which are purposefully inserted into a mouth (the clergeon's/the Prioress's), and considers connections between the object and the oral.

244. Dahood, Roger. "Boy Crucifixion, Sainthood, and the Puzzling Case of Harold of Gloucester." In Susan Powell, ed. *Saints and Cults in Medieval England: Proceedings of the 2015 Harlaxton Symposium*, Harlaxton Medieval Studies, 27 (Donington: Shaun Tyas, 2017), pp. 140–55. Claims that the clergeon in *PrT* invokes Hugh of Lincoln, one of a number of Christian boys purportedly crucified by Jews in mockery of Christ's Passion. Addresses why the victims in such stories are boys, not adults as Jesus was when he was crucified, and argues that peculiarities

in Harold of Gloucester's story suggest that the boy victim arises primarily from Christian interpretation of Exodus 12:3–9, the Passover narrative.

245. Murton, Megan. "The *Prioress's Prologue*: Dante, Liturgy, and Ineffability." *ChauR* 52, no. 3 (2017): 318–40. Argues that the use of Dante's *Paradiso*, LIII in the initial presentation of faith in *PrT* reflects Chaucer's sophisticated engagement with the ways humans try to articulate transcendent truth.

246. Warren, Nancy Bradley. "Sacraments, Gender, and Authority in the *Prioress's Prologue and Tale* and *Pearl*." *C&L* 66, no. 3 (2017): 386–403. Contends that although *Pearl* and *PrPT* treat the Eucharist as orthodox, they nonetheless evoke religious debates concerning Lollardy and, relatedly, continental female mysticism. Argues that both the works feminize sacramental work, preach in ways that particularly parallel the life of St. Birgitta of Sweden and female Lollard instructors, and champion vernacular Scripture.

See also nos. 153, 294, 309.

CT—The Tale of Sir Thopas

247. Hamada, Satomi. "Describing the Link between Orality and Literacy: Chaucer's *Tale of Sir Thopas* in the Transitional Period." *SIMELL* 32 (2017): 17–35. Places *CT* in the transitional period from oral to literal culture, and argues that the change of vocabulary from "herken" in *Th*'s initial sections to "listen" in its third fitt indicates different functions of these sections in Chaucer's parody of metrical romance. Analyzes what the visual divisions of the text made in manuscripts tell us about the structure of *Th*.

248. Raybin, David. "*Sir Thopas*: A Story for Young Children." *SAC* 39 (2017): 225–48. Contends that *Th* is an entertaining, nonpedagogical story written for children, the earliest example in English literature. Explores how details of the tale might appeal to a young audience and posits that its manuscript layout was "calculated to appeal" to youth. Labels Part VII of *CT* the "Children's Group," in which Chaucer explores how an adult "might choose to speak to children."

See also nos. 40, 48, 140, 186, 249.

CT—The Tale of Melibee

249. Graßnick, Ulrike. "'This litel tretys': Chaucer's Mirror for Princes *The Tale of Melibee*." In Simon Rosenberg and Sandra Simon, eds. *Material Moments in Book Cultures: Essays in Honour of Gabriele Müller-Oberhäuser* (New York: Peter Lang, 2014), pp. 3–15. Argues that as a mirror for princes *Mel* offers an "implicit critical view of Richard II," especially when read in the context of *CT*, which elsewhere provides a "complex analysis of advisers, advice, and the handling of counsel." Comments on the advice given in *NPT* as well as in *Mel*, and the contrast between literary parody in *Th* and "serious pragmatic literature" in *Mel*.

See also nos. 140, 205, 269, 305.

CT—The Monk and His Tale

250. Bradbury, Nancy Mason. "Zenobia's Objects." In Jenny Adams and Nancy Mason Bradbury, eds. *Medieval Women and Their Objects* (*SAC* 41 [2019], no. 118), pp. 39–55. Considers the exchange of objects in the Zenobia/Cenobia story in *MkT* not as a punitive measure for pushing back on gender constructs or a validation of the Monk's blatant misogyny, but rather as a moment of empowerment.

251. Dean, James M. "The Mortal Spectacle: History in *The Monk's Tale*." In *Geoffrey Chaucer* (*SAC* 41 [2019], no. 128), pp. 186–200. Discusses how Chaucer's storytelling narrative structure of *MkT* reflects the Italian genre of "*casus* tragedy," learned from Dante and Boccaccio.

252. Houlik-Ritchey, Emily. "Reading the Neighbor in Geoffrey Chaucer and Pere López de Ayala." *Exemplaria* 28 (2016): 118–36. Treats as "neighboring texts" Chaucer's account of Pedro I of Castile and León (*MkT*, VII.2375–90) and that of Pere López de Ayala in *Cronica del rey don Pedro*, theorizing the notion of "neighbor"; exploring the inclusions, omissions, and enigmas of the two texts; clarifying the political conditions underlying these depictions; and investigating the ethical dimensions of them as ambiguous historicizations.

253. Lapham, Lewis H., ed. "c. 1390: England. Rain Check." *Lapham's Quarterly* 9, no. 3 (2016): 28–29. Provides Nevill Coghill's modern translation of *MkT*, VII.2727–66 (Croesus), included among a variety of literary samples and commentaries on the theme of luck.

254. Stone, Russell. "Chaucer's Alexander the Great and the 'Monk's Tale': Reconsidering the Fourteenth-Century Reception of a Pagan's Tragedy." *M&H* 42 (2017): 23–42. Observes that Chaucer's treatment of Alexander in *MkT* is largely consistent with how Alexander is depicted in fourteenth-century romances and monastic allusions. Suggests that Chaucer declines to condemn Alexander as an unworthy pagan, despite being familiar with these traditions.

See also nos. 38, 139.

CT—The Nun's Priest and His Tale

255. Baker, D. P. "A Bradwardinian Benediction: The Ending of the Nun's Priest's Tale Revisited." *MÆ* 82, no. 2 (2013): 236–43. Maintains that the referent for "my lord" at the end of *NPT* (VII.3445) is Thomas Bradwardine, and identifies parallels between the ending and Bradwardine's *De causa Dei*.

256. D'Agata D'Ottavi, Stefania. "Chauntecleer's *Small Latin* and the Meaning of *Confusio* in the *Nun's Priest's Tale*." *Medieval Translator/ Traduire au Moyen Age* 16 (2016): 345–55. Argues that when Chauntecleer "purposely mistranslates" the proverb about women being man's "confusio" (*NPT*, VII.3163–65), he puns on "the two possible connotations of the word . . . and mischievously discard[s] the negative one."

257. Sauer, Michelle M. "Queer Pedagogy, Medieval Literature, and Chaucer." *SMART* 23, no. 2 (2016): 17–26. Urges clarification and deployment of queer pedagogy in teaching medieval literature, citing examples of its utilities in a classroom discussion of production and reproduction in *NPT*, nuances of "deviance" in Middle English, and the tangibility of bodies in medieval understanding.

258. Stuhr, Tracy Jill. "Re-Sounding Natures: Voicing the Non-Human in Medieval English Poetry." *DAI* 77.03 (2015): n.p. Examines "how the non-human (the natural, not the other-worldly) world and its creatures were voiced in several late medieval English texts," including *NPT* and *ManT*.

See also nos. 59, 143, 159, 249.

CT—The Second Nun and Her Tale

259. Benson, C. David. "Statues, Bodies, and Souls: St. Cecilia and Some Medieval Attitudes toward Ancient Rome." In Jenny Adams and

Nancy Mason Bradbury, eds. *Medieval Women and Their Objects* (*SAC* 41 [2019], no. 118), pp. 267–87. Discusses *SNT* as Chaucer's only hagiographical work to evaluate the medieval perception of art. Contrasts the medieval devotion to earthly relics in relation to St. Cecilia's desire to shed the physical and enter the spiritual, while paralleling her life with artistic representations of her cult.

260. Howard, H. Wendall. "Who's Cecilia? What Is She?" *Logos: A Journal of Catholic Thought and Culture* 18, no. 3 (2015): 15–32. Considers the historicity of St. Cecilia, her association with music, and various accounts of her life and legend, including the *Passio Caeciliae*, *SNT*, an opera by Licinio Refice and Emidio Mucci, John Dryden's "A Song for St. Cecilia's Day," Thomas Connolly's *Mourning into Joy*, Raphael's *The Ecstasy of St. Cecilia with Sts. Paul, John the Evangelist, Augustine, and Mary Magdalene*, and other depictions of her as the "patron saint of music."

261. Klassen, Norm. "Mary's Swollen Womb: What It Looks Like to Overcome Tyranny in the Second Nun's Prologue and Tale." *Renascence* 68, no. 2 (2016): 77–92. Explores the contrast between the Marian womb imagery of *SNP* (VIII.43–49) and the deflated bladder of Almachius's power in *SNT* (VIII.437–41), finding in the contrast "a vision of the Church that attests freedom and obedience, as well as Chaucer's embracing the task of the Christian artist who would imitate a creator who generates dependence without control."

262. Long, Mary Beth. " 'O sweete and wel beloved spouse deere': A Pastoral Reading of Cecilia's Post-Nuptial Persuasion in *The Second Nun's Tale*." *SAC* 39 (2017): 159–89. Considers the shift in "social and rhetorical roles" of Cecilia in *SNT*—from sweet wife to ardent polemical martyr—and argues that both are consistent with views of female speech in pastoral literature, particularly confessional manuals and hagiography. These "speaking behaviors" are "wholly congruent" with the Second Nun as Benedictine nun and teller of *SNT*.

See also nos. 153, 305.

CT—The Canon's Yeoman and His Tale

263. Bennett, Alastair. "Covetousness, 'Unkyndenesse,' and the 'Blered' Eye in *Piers Plowman* and 'The Canon's Yeoman's Tale.'" *YLS* 28 (2014): 29–64. Shows that the "blered" eye image in *CYT* (VIII.730)

and *Piers Plowman* indicates covetousness, associated with "unkynde" or unnatural separation from community and knowledge.

See also nos. 49, 186.

CT—The Manciple and His Tale

264. Matsuda, Takami. "Lie and Fable in Chaucer's *Manciple's Tale*." *Geibun-Kenkyu* 113, no. 2 (2017): 29–39. Argues that both the structure and the content of *ManT* explore the relativity of truth and lie. Regarding the structure, the dependence on literature of practical wisdom raises a doubt as to the tale's authority as an exemplum. As for the content, *ManT* is "no longer about the delayed discovery of truth as in *Othello*," and instead focuses on Phoebus's "confused state of mind," in which "truth is whatever he wishes to believe."

See also no. 31.

CT—The Parson and His Tale

265. Yoshikawa, Fumiko. "The Mapping of Rhetorical Strategies Related to Persuasion in Middle English Religious Prose." In Michael Bilynsky, ed. *Studies in Middle English: Words, Forms, Senses and Texts* (*SAC* 41 [2019], no. 123), pp. 343–60. Studies the generic variety, rhetorical features, and persuasive power of four works of medieval English literature, including *ParsT*, tabulating the relative incidence of rhetorical questions, appeals to authority or logic, poetic devices, vocatives, humor, personal pronouns, etc.

See also nos. 35, 138, 156, 159, 167, 305, 335.

CT—Chaucer's Retraction

266. Cook, Megan L. "'Here taketh the makere of this book his leve': The *Retraction* and Chaucer's Works in Tudor England." *SP* 113 (2016): 32–54. Analyzes the absence of *Ret* from editions of *CT* published between 1532 and 1721, along with the publication of *Adam* in 1561, arguing that the combination affected views on textual accuracy and authorial control in Chaucer reception.

267. Ott, Ashley Rose. "Unreadability and Erasure in Medieval English Texts and Incunabula, c. 1350–1500." *DAI* A79.07 (2017): n.p. Considers *Ret* in the context of texts rendered physically inscrutable, forbidden, or recanted as literary/rhetorical strategies.

See also nos. 35, 46, 63.

Anelida and Arcite

See nos. 72, 136.

A Treatise on the Astrolabe

268. Chism, Christine. "Transmitting the Astrolabe: Chaucer, Islamic Astronomy, and the Astrolabic Text." In Faith Wallis and Robert Wisnovsky, eds. *Medieval Textual Cultures: Agents of Transmission, Translation and Transformation* (Berlin: De Gruyter, 2016), pp. 85–120. Describes the variety of cultural uses to which the astrolabe was put historically, and argues that the "complex back-histories of multicultural compilation," the "multifocal transmission," and the "imaginative pedagogy" of *Astr* assert a "reluctance ever to fasten upon just one authoritative end," and thereby reflect the open-endedness of the instrument and of scientific development more generally, helping to explain the large number of manuscripts of Chaucer's treatise.

269. Taylor, Jamie K. "'A suffisant Astrolabie': Childish Desire, Fatherly Affection, and English Devotion in *The Treatise on the Astrolabe*." *SAC* 39 (2017): 249–74. Explores the "ideological work" of children in Chaucer's literature, commenting on Sophie in *Mel*, Virginia in *PhyT*, Maurice in *MLT*, and Lewis in *Astr*. Treats the latter as a metonym for vernacular readers and for the potential of technological learning (also found in the brass steed of *SqT*) through which Chaucer projects an image of "Englishness" that "coalesces around paternal love and technological learning" and depends in part upon the sufficiency of Oxford to emulate or replace Rome in a national imaginary.

270. Tobienne, Francis, Jr. "Charting Chaucer: Travel, Mechanical Magic, and Controlling the Narrative." In James M. Dean, ed. *Geoffrey Chaucer* (*SAC* 41 [2019], no. 128), pp. 159–70. Concerns Chaucer's authorship of *Astr*, and "what that instrument contributes to Chaucer's idea of travel."

See also nos. 61, 112.

Boece

See nos. 305, 307.

The Book of the Duchess

271. Adams, Jenny. "Transgender and the Chess Queen in Chaucer's *Book of the Duchess*." In Jenny Adams and Nancy Mason Bradbury, eds. *Medieval Women and Their Objects* (*SAC* 41 [2019], no. 118), pp. 248–66. Considers *BD* and the metaphor of chess, particularly the way in which the rules of the game are remediated in the action of the poem. Looks at gender-crossing in relation to *BD*, but transcends previous arguments focusing on the chess allegory. Considers the game's "polychronic meanings" as a model for other medieval chess scenes. Claims that the queen's return as the male pawn links reanimation with gender fluidity, as does her alternate title as *fers*.

272. Dalton, Emily. "Improper Translations: Naming and Vernacular Poetics in Medieval England." *DAI* A79.03 (2017): n.p. Considers names in *BD* as part of a larger examination of nomenclature's role in defining Englishness within the context of other linguistic traditions.

273. Fumo, Jamie C. "The 'alderbeste yifte': Objects and the Poetics of Munificence in Chaucer's *The Book of the Duchess*." *Exemplaria* 28 (2016): 277–96. Adapts the "gift theory" of Jacques Derrida; considers the historical context of the marriage of John of Gaunt and Blanche of Lancaster; and focuses on the scene of White's ring-giving (as reported by the Black Knight), considering the poem itself as a gift. Argues that *BD* portrays White as the "exalted (but silent and absent) gift-giver" in *BD* and that the poem "transmutes into fiction" the "performance of gifts" of the historical marriage.

274. Liendo, Elizabeth. "'In hir bed al naked': Nakedness and Male Grief in Chaucer's *Book of the Duchess*." *PQ* 96, no. 4 (2017): 405–24. Seeks to understand *BD* as an exploration of (male) grief beyond its presumed historical occasion and to relate the subject and structure of the poem by explicating the recurring references to literal and metaphorical nakedness—especially that of Alcyone and the Man in Black.

275. Meyer, Shannon Rae. "From Tower to Bower: Constructions of Gender, Class, and Architecture in Middle English Literature." *DAI* A76.07 (2015): n.p. Considers "the trope of the female body entowered" in selected romances and lyrics, *BD*, and the Paston letters.

See also nos. 7, 54, 97, 100, 103, 117, 133, 153, 157, 163, 327, 331.

The Equatorie of the Planetis

276. Rand, Kari Anne. "The Authorship of 'The Equatorie of the Planetis' Revisited." *SN* 87 (2015): 15–35. Presents new evidence that "shows that the author [of *Equat*] was not Chaucer," connecting the unique manuscript of the treatise (Cambridge, Peterhouse, MS 75.I) with the work and life of John Westwyk, a monk of Tynemouth. Includes paleographical discussion, seven figures in color, and commentary on the "radix Chaucer" note in the Peterhouse manuscript.

The House of Fame

277. Binski, Paul. *Gothic Wonder: Art, Artifice and the Decorated Style, 1290–1350*. New Haven: Yale University Press, 2013. ix, 454 pp.; b&w and color illus. Describes and illustrates the "visual arts as a whole" in late medieval England. The index records some twenty references to Chaucer, including a section on *HF* (pp. 345–48) that shows that "the two largest passages of writing about architecture at the end of the [fourteenth] century are found in *HF* and that its lexicon mediate[s] between verbal and visual craft."

278. Cartlidge, Neil. "Ripples on the Water? The Acoustics of Geoffrey Chaucer's *House of Fame* and the Influence of Robert Holcot." *SAC* 39 (2017): 57–97. Discredits the idea that the Eagle's disquisition on sound in *HF* is conventional Aristotelianism, mediated by Robert Grosseteste or Walter Burley, arguing that the details of the multiplying ripples and the combination of science and myth were influenced instead by Robert Holcot's commentary on the Book of Wisdom. Describes Holcot's career among the Oxford Calculators (Mertonians) and explains Holcot's influence on *HF* and elsewhere in Chaucer.

279. Green, Eugene. "Finding Pragmatic Common Ground between Chaucer's Dreamer and Eagle in *The House of Fame*." In Michael Bilynsky, ed. *Studies in Middle English: Words, Forms, Senses and Texts* (*SAC* 41 [2019], no. 123), pp. 165–83. Explores the pragmatic linguistic devices Chaucer uses to establish a common ground of communication and "create convincing exchanges" between the Dreamer and the Eagle in *HF*, identifying and analyzing various concerns: "back-channel," lexicon, "turn-taking," "polarizing," and more.

280. Guastella, Gianni. *Word of Mouth: "Fama" and Its Personifications in Art and Literature from Ancient Rome to the Middle Ages*. Oxford: Oxford

University Press, 2016. xiv, 440 pp.; b&w illus. Includes a chapter entitled "Chaucer, *House of Fame*" (pp. 355–83) that describes *HF* and characterizes Chaucer's treatment of literary reputation as unusual in lacking the "moralistic slant" of his predecessors, opting instead for a "disillusioned (and often clearly amused)" perspective that the "world of stories (and literature) is governed by chance."

281. Lightsey, Scott. "Chaucer's Return from Lombardy, the Shrine of St. Leonard at Hythe, and the 'corseynt Leonard' in the *House of Fame*. Lines 112–18." *ChauR* 52, no. 2 (2017): 188–201. Explores the significance of Chaucer's travels through Kent. Claims that *HF* resonates with the cult and Church of St. Leonard in Kent.

282. Mertens Fleury, Katharina. *Zeigen und Bezeichnen: Zugänge zu allegorischem Erzählen im Mittelalter*. Philologie der Kultur. Würzburg: Königshausen & Neumann, 2014. 414 pp.; b&w figs. Studies the uses of allegory in western literature—classical, continental, and English, from Prudentius to George Herbert—with emphasis on growth and variety in the tradition, signals to allegory in the texts, and embedded uses of allegory as well as wholly allegorical narratives. Includes discussion of allegorical aspects of *HF* and its relations with earlier allegorical traditions.

283. Schneider, Thomas R. "Motion in Late Medieval English Literature: Impulse, Randomization, and Acceleration." *DAI* A75.05 (2014): n.p. Studies physical motion, readerly motion, and other motions related to texts in late medieval English literature, including a chapter on Chaucer's "engagement with motion as a concept in natural philosophy" in *HF* and *PF*, connecting it with the physics of William of Ockham.

284. Sung, Wei-ko. "Petrarch and Chaucer on Fame." *EurAmerica: A Journal of European and American Studies* 46, no. 1 (2016): 1–44. Surveys "the idea literary fame" in classical and medieval traditions (Homer, Hesiod, Virgil, Statius, and Dante); analyzes Petrarch's notion more extensively; and examines *HF* to show that though Chaucer, "like Petrarch, was intimately familiar with the fickleness and absurdity of worldly fame, he betrays a longing for a posthumous literary fame." Includes an abstract in Chinese.

See also nos. 37, 48, 54, 100, 133, 145, 148, 153, 157, 163, 187, 291, 309, 323, 332.

The Legend of Good Women

285. Burger, Glenn. "'Pite renneth soone in gentil herte': Ugly Feelings and Gendered Conduct in Chaucer's *Legend of Good Women*" *ChauR* 52, no. 1 (2017): 66–84. Connects *LGW* with the *Livre du Chevalier de la Tour Landry* and the *Menagier de Paris*. Suggests that the domestic sphere of *Livre du Chevalier de la Tour Landry* and the *Menagier de Paris* offers a place for productive, satisfying love; however, love that is illegible and destructive is revealed in *LGW*.

286. Collette, Carolyn. "Chaucer's Poetics and Purposes in the *Legend of Good Women*." *ChauR* 52, no. 1 (2017): 12–28. Investigates Chaucer's multiple registers of speech in order to explore social harmony and discord in *LGW* as it pertains to women's desires.

287. Cook, Megan L. "Author, Text, and Paratext in Early Modern Editions of the *Legend of Good Women*." *ChauR* 52, no. 1 (2017): 124–42. Claims that *LGW* may have been viewed in the fifteenth and sixteenth centuries as a response to *TC* and as an allegory for how Chaucer may have interacted with patrons.

288. Dinshaw, Carolyn. "Afterword: Re-Reading; or, When You Were Mine." *ChauR* 52, no. 1 (2017): 162–66. Provides an afterword to the special issue on *LGW*, focusing on the theme of love's loss, and presents an argument that Prince's song "When You Were Mine" provides a foil for the women of *LGW*.

289. Dumitrescu, Irina. "Beautiful Suffering and the Culpable Narrator in Chaucer's *Legend of Good Women*." *ChauR* 52, no. 1 (2017): 106–23. Explores the role of the narrator in *LGW* as being culpable in his deception by telling idealized stories of women who suffer and die.

290. Harlan-Haughey, Sarah. "The Circle, the Maze, and the Echo: Sublunary Recurrence and Performance in Chaucer's *Legend of Ariadne*." *ChauR* 52, no. 3 (2017): 341–60. Examines the ways in which *LGW*'s *Legend of Ariadne* reflects Chaucer's concerns over the cyclical and repeating tragedies of history.

291. Keller, Wolfram R. "Geoffrey Chaucer's Mind Games: Household Management and Literary Aesthetics in the Prologue to the *Legend of Good Women*." In Thomas Honegger and Dirk Vanderbeke, eds. *From Peterborough to Faëry: The Poetics and Mechanics of Secondary Worlds; Essays in Honour of Dr. Allan G. Turner's 65th Birthday* (Zürich: Walking Tree, 2014), pp. 1–24. Describes the medieval understanding of "faculty

psychology"—the three cells or ventricles where imagination, logic, and memory reside—and argues that *HF* "takes the audience" through the three ventricles, while exploring the creative potential of the persistent "imaginational disharmony." *LGWP* depicts the "poet's journey through his own noisy mental apparatus," problematizing imaginational disharmony and compelling his audience to explore the efforts and pleasure of interpretation.

292. Lee, Jenny Veronica. "*Confessio Auctoris*: Confessional Poetics and Authority in the Literature of Late Medieval England, 1350–1450." *DAI* A74.02 (2013): n.p. Investigates how Chaucer, Gower, Langland, Usk, and Hoccleve use confessional discourse to challenge Latinity and "authorize their own literary productions." Includes discussion of the "self-abasing literary self-portrayals as penitents" found in Chaucer's *LGW* and Gower's *Confessio Amantis*.

293. McCormick, Betsy, Leah Schwebel, and Lynn Shutters. "Introduction: Looking Forward, Looking Back on the *Legend of Good Women*." *ChauR* 52, no. 1 (2017): 3–11. Explores why *LGW* unsettles readers and outlines this special issue of *ChauR*.

294. Rushton, Cory. "Philomela Accuses." In *Disability and Medieval Law* (Newcastle upon Tyne: Cambridge Scholars, 2013), pp. 157–73. Investigates several motifs in the *LGW* account of Philomela: victimhood, "inappropriate sovereignty," muteness, orality and legal witnessing, "tapestry-as-prosthesis," rape as a property crime, and lack of legal remedy, arguing that Chaucer's tale evinces "interest in women's control over their own bodily integrity" simultaneously acknowledging that this interest is "ultimately unproductive when . . . not matched with action." Includes comments on *PrT* and on Ovid's and Gower's versions of the story of Philomela.

295. Schiff, Randy P. "On Firm Carthaginian Ground: Ethnic Boundary Fluidity and Chaucer's Dido." *Postmedieval* 6, no. 1 (2015): 23–35. Argues that in the Dido account of *LGW* Chaucer "channels" deep-seated cultural "anxiety about Phoenicians as he asserts his place in a Roman-centered Western tradition." By "removing the story of Dido's diasporic leadership, and misidentifying her realm as a generalized Libya," Chaucer sides with Roman expansionism, and by presenting "Dido as a pitiful lover who ignominiously dethrones herself for Aeneas," he "aestheticizes Rome's reduction of Carthaginian dynamism into a desert."

296. Schwebel, Leah. "Livy and Augustine as Negative Models in the

Legend of Lucrece." *ChauR* 52, no. 1 (2017): 29–45. Argues that Chaucer employs Livy's and Augustine's stories of Lucretia as a way to hold up feminine virtue, rather than repeating their negative attributes exhibited in the source material.

297. Shutters, Lynn. "The Thought and Feel of Virtuous Wifehood: Recovering Emotion in the *Legend of Good Women.*" *ChauR* 52, no. 1 (2017): 85–105. Discusses how *LGW* represents marital affection as contentious and unstable.

298. Staley, Lynn. "Anne of Bohemia and the Objects of Ricardian Kingship." In Jenny Adams and Nancy Mason Bradbury, eds. *Medieval Women and Their Objects* (*SAC* 41 [2019], no. 118), pp. 97–122. Examines works that focus on Queen Anne by Clanvowe, Maidstone, and Chaucer (*LGW* and *PF*). Claims that these works function "chronologically, thematically, and politically" as a means to articulate the female power and agency of Anne, giving her a mediated voice.

299. Trivellini, Samanta. "The Myth of Philomela from Margaret Atwood to . . . Chaucer: Contexts and Theoretical Perspectives." *Interférences littéraires/Literaire interferenties* 17 (2015): 85–99. Available at http://www.interferenceslitteraires.be. Considers four frame-tale versions of the Philomela story—Margaret Atwood's "Nightingale" in *The Tent* (2006), George Pettie's in *A Petite Pallace of Pettie His Pleasure* (1576), Chaucer's in *LGW*, and Gower's in *Confessio Amantis*—focusing on interactions among narrative point of view, frame structure, and metapoetics. Suggests that Chaucer's version may be seen as "a self-aware game with his readership, and . . . as Chaucer's ironic commentary on moralizing conceptions of literature." Includes an abstract in English and in French.

See also nos. 37, 72, 78, 97, 138, 149, 152, 321.

The Parliament of Fowls

300. Bayiltmiş Öğütcü, Oya. " 'The Pleasure of the Text': The *Parliament of Fowls* as the Site of Bliss for Chaucer and His Readers." *Mirabilia* 18, no. 1 (2014): 235–46. Using concepts derived from Roland Barthes, argues that *PF* is both a "text of pleasure with its reflection of courtly culture" and a "text of bliss with its unconcluded conclusion."

301. Crane, Susan. " 'The lytel erthe that here is': Environmental Thought in Chaucer's *Parliament of Fowls.*" The Presidential Address.

The New Chaucer Society. Twentieth International Congress, July 11–14, 2016. Queen Mary University of London, Mile End. *SAC* 39 (2017): 3–29. Argues that *PF* offers an "innovative model of species uncertainty" that aligns with posthumanist rejection of human specialness. The poem evokes and challenges the dualism of Scipio's dream, offering alternatives in the animism of the tree catalogue and the totemism of the avian hierarchy. None of the three ontologies stands authoritatively and their uncertainties are reinforced by the multisensory details of *PF*, the performability of the poem's ending, and the antirationalism of the dream vision.

302. Judkins, Ryan R. " 'There came a hart in at the chamber door': Medieval Deer as Pets." *Enarratio* 18 (2013): 23–48. Surveys historical and literary evidence that deer were kept as pets in the Middle Ages, including discussion of deer parks and Nature's garden in *PF*, which "Chaucer's audience would almost certainly have understood as a deer park."

303. Koff, Leonard Michael. "Dreaming the Dream of Scipio." In Nancy van Deusen, ed. *Cicero Refused to Die: Ciceronian Influence through the Centuries* (*SAC* 41 [2019], no. 129) , pp. 65–83. Explores how Chaucer's adaptations in *PF* of Macrobius's Neoplatonic commentary on Cicero's *Dream of Scipio* anticipate "the humanist recovery of Ciceronian ideals," particularly the "ideal of marriage and mating as civic duty" and the "possibility of a monarchical continuity that counsels adjudication between personal prerogatives and the social duties of love."

304. Moseley, C. W. R. D. " 'Tu numeris elementa ligas': The Consolation of Nature's Numbers in *Parlement of Foulys*." *Critical Survey* 29, no. 3 (2017): 86–113. Contends that Chaucer is "expecting, indeed exploiting, the gap between the reception of a poem when it is heard socially and its afterlife as a text," when it is a different thing. Argues "that a poem's form is itself a way of communicating ideas."

305. Newhauser, Richard G. "The Multisensoriality of Place and the Chaucerian Multisensual." In Annette Kern-Stähler, Beatrix Busse, and Wietse de Boer, eds. *The Five Senses in Medieval and Early Modern England* (*SAC* 41 [2019], no. 141), pp. 199–218. Explores the "full sensory expression" in Chaucer's "construction of space," emphasizing the interconnectedness of the five senses in medieval understanding and their ethical dimensions that require proper training to engage volition correctly. Includes observations about these concerns in *ParsT*, *Mel*, *Bo*,

SNT, and *PF*, where the interconnectedness of the senses is an ideal achievable in heavenly places, and dismantled in hellish ones.

306. Obenauf, Richard. "Censorship and Intolerance in Medieval England." *DAI* A77.01 (2015): n.p. Considers *PF* and other works in a discussion of how "the roots of formal print censorship in England are to be found in earlier forms of intolerance."

307. Wuest, Charles. "Chaucer's Enigmatic Thing in *The Parliament of Fowls*." *SP* 113 (2016): 485–500. Argues that the enigmatic "thing" thrice referred to in *PF* is a "structuring device" but also a "reflection on the process of translation, specifically Chaucer's translation of Boethius's *Consolation of Philosophy*." *PF* depicts "translation as an activity inherently unstable and yet also productive."

See also nos. 54, 100, 117, 131, 283, 298, 331.

The Romaunt of the Rose

308. Flannery, Mary C. "Personification and Embodied Emotional Practice in Middle English Literature." *LitComp* 13, no. 6 (2016): 351–61. Includes discussion of Sorrow in *Rom*, treating the poem as one that maps "an imaginative space in which to represent (and perhaps also elicit) emotion, one that interweaves emotional with embodied, sensory experience," and one that may "reflect the author's vision of how emotions work, particularly in relation to one another."

See also nos. 100, 148.

Troilus and Criseyde

309. Boenig, Robert. "Chaucer and the Art of Not Eating a Book." In Dorsey Armstrong, Alexander L. Kaufman, and Shaun F. D. Hughes, eds. *Telling Tales and Crafting Books: Essays in Honor of Thomas H. Ohlgren* (Kalamazoo: Medieval Institute, 2016), pp. 323–44. 2 b&w illus. Contrasts the unequivocal hermeneutics of "eating a book"—i.e., internalizing the text of the Bible and its "one true meaning"—as depicted in the illustration of the *Cloisters Apocalypse* (Metropolitan Museum of Art, Cloisters Collection, MS 68.174) with the nondirective authorial stance depicted in Chaucer addressing the court audience in the *TC* manuscript, Cambridge, Corpus Christi College, MS 61. Identifies a number

of instances of such nondirective strategies in Chaucer's poetry and comments on his uses of the Apocalypse in *PrT* and *HF*.

310. Boyar, Jenny. "Lyric Form and the Charge of Forgetfulness in Medieval and Early Modern Poetry." *DAI* A78.01 (2016): n.p. Traces "the creative potentials of technologies of memory in the rise of English lyric poetry," focusing on Chaucer and Thomas Wyatt, and including assessment of how "innovations of lyric form are introduced" in *TC* "at moments in which memory is most compromised" and when Chaucer is "most unhinged" from his sources.

311. Drakakis, John. "The Presence of *Troilus and Cressida*: Shakespeare's Refurbishment of Chaucer's *Troilus and Criseyde*." In Andrew James Johnston, Russell West-Pavlov, and Elisabeth Kempf, eds. *Love, History and Emotion in Chaucer and Shakespeare: "Troilus and Criseyde" and "Troilus and Cressida"* (*SAC* 41 [2019], no. 315), pp. 109–24. Contrasts the presentations of interiority in *TC* and Shakespeare's *Troilus and Cressida* as a basis for analyzing Shakespeare's vacating his play of chivalric principles.

312. Flannery, Mary C. "'Sum men Sayis . . .': Literary Gossip and Malicious Intent in Robert Henryson's *Testament of Cresseid*." *Forum for Modern Language Studies* 50, no. 2 (2014): 168–81. Explores Chaucer's idea of "gossip" in *TC* (and elsewhere), especially as it relates to literature and Criseyde's reputation, examining more extensively Henryson's emphasis on malice rather than idle speech and its relationship with "literary notoriety" in *Testament of Cresseid*.

313. Glaser, Joseph, trans., and Christine Chism, intro. *"Troilus and Criseyde" in Modern Verse*. Indianapolis: Hackett, 2014. xxxviii, 256 pp. Translates *TC* into modern English rhyme royal stanzas, with footnotes and occasional marginal glosses. The introduction (by Christine Chism, pp. vi–xxx) addresses the social contexts of the poem; anachronisms; Chaucer's audience; the frontispiece from Cambridge, Corpus Christi College, MS 61 (included in color as a cover); sources; and the presentation of Criseyde. Glaser's translator's preface (pp. xxxi–xxxviii) considers style and verse.

314. Johnston, Andrew James. "Gendered Books: Reading, Space and Intimacy in Chaucer's *Troilus and Criseyde*." In Johnston, Russell West-Pavlov, and Elisabeth Kempf, eds. *Love, History and Emotion in Chaucer and Shakespeare: "Troilus and Criseyde" and "Troilus and Cressida"* (*SAC* 41 [2019], no. 315), pp. 171–88. Investigates two crucial scenes of reading in *TC*—Criseyde's reading with her attendants in Book II

and Pandarus's voyeuristic reading of a romance in the consummation scene—finding in their contrasts two opposed models of reading: one that "privileges hermeneutic activity" and the other that prefers "affective immersion." Setting ("paved parlour" versus bedchamber), the meanings of "romaunce," and the poem's "intense familiarity" with the story of Thebes complicate the gendered opposition of reading habits.

315. Johnston, Andrew James, Russell West-Pavlov, and Elisabeth Kempf, eds. *Love, History and Emotion in Chaucer and Shakespeare: "Troilus and Criseyde" and "Troilus and Cressida."* Manchester Medieval Literature and Culture. Manchester: Manchester University Press, 2016. viii, 208 pp. Includes twelve essays by various authors and an introduction by the editors on affect, periodization, queer history, and Chaucer's and Shakespeare's versions of the story of Troilus and Criseyde/Cressida. For nine essays that pertain to Chaucer, see nos. 78, 90, 311, 314, 317–18, 325, 327–28.

316. Jones, Sarah Rees. "The Word on the Street: Chaucer and the Regulation of Nuisance in Post-Plague London." In Valerie Allen and Ruth Evans, eds. *Roadworks: Medieval Britain, Medieval Roads* (SAC 41 [2019], no. 119), pp. 97–126. Explores the "design and regulation of real streets" in late medieval Britain, and "streets as symbolic of capital" in contemporaneous literature, art, and architecture. Includes comments on windows and doors in *TC*.

317. Keller, Wolfram R. "Arrogant Authorial Performances: Criseyde to Cressida." In Andrew James Johnston, Russell West-Pavlov, and Elisabeth Kempf, eds. *Love, History and Emotion in Chaucer and Shakespeare: "Troilus and Criseyde" and "Troilus and Cressida"* (SAC 41 [2019], no. 315), pp. 141–56. Argues that in *TC* Criseyde is the "embodiment of literary invention," enacting a "poetological" claim to fame, both humble and arrogant. Through his Cressida, Shakespeare presents a similar "counter-authorship," one that reflects the playwright's engagement with the sixteenth-century "Poets' War."

318. Mahler, Andreas. "'Potent Raisings': Performing Passion in Chaucer and Shakespeare." In Andrew James Johnston, Russell West-Pavlov, and Elisabeth Kempf, eds. *Love, History and Emotion in Chaucer and Shakespeare: "Troilus and Criseyde" and "Troilus and Cressida"* (SAC 41 [2019], no. 315), pp. 32–45. Maintains that Chaucer in *TC* and Shakespeare in *Troilus and Cressida* present love as detached from history or topicality, depicting it through irresolvable plural discourses—Platonic, Petrarchan, courtly love-sickness, and more—and thereby

"performing it aesthetically, without any particular truth value but its own."

319. McMillan, Samuel F. "Medieval Authorship at Reason's End: The *Roman de la Rose*'s Legacy of Misrule." *DAI* A80.05 (2016): n.p. Argues that the *Roman de la Rose* "initiates a literary tradition that understands reason to be in tension with and even antithetical to imaginative writing," examining in this light works by Chaucer (*TC*), Gower, Lydgate, and Hoccleve, exploring in them a "writerly art based in misrule."

320. Meecham-Jones, Simon. "'He in salte teres dreynte': Understanding Troilus's Tears." In Stephanie Downes, Andrew Lynch, and Katrina O'Loughlin, eds. *Emotions and War: Medieval to Romantic Literature* (Basingstoke: Palgrave Macmillan, 2015), pp. 77–97. Considers the concept of "manhod" (III.428) in *TC* in relation to critical discussions of Troilus's masculinity, reading Troilus's emotions in light of late medieval literary and social conventions and arguing that Chaucer's experiment in emotion is neither conventional nor condemnatory: "Troilus attempts to fashion a wholly original performance of masculinity in his loving of Criseyde."

321. Nelson, Ingrid. *Lyric Tactics*. Philadelphia: University of Pennsylvania Press, 2017. 214 pp. Asserts that Chaucer's inset lyrics in *TC* and *LGW* have a "tactical" quality that gives them flexibility and contingency. In *TC*, Antigone's song, using both English practices and French and Italian sources, demonstrates "a tension between negotiation and [Petrarchan] absolutism" that reflects the narrative's concern with "individual and communal desires." In *LGW*, especially Prologue F, lyrics are integrated with exemplary narrative, giving lyric an ethical role and "suspending [exempla's] "drive toward closure."

322. Pérez-Fernández, Tamara. "The Margins of the Scribe: Analysis of the Marginal Annotations in the Manuscripts of Chaucer's *Troilus and Criseyde*." Ph.D. Dissertation. Universidad de Valladolid, 2017, n.p. Examines marginal annotations in the surviving manuscripts of *TC* with the purpose of exploring both the reception of the poem and the role of the scribes in its textual transmission. The marginalia are analyzed not only from a textual, thematic, linguistic, and paleographical point of view, but also from the perspective of the copyists and their preferences when reading and annotating Chaucer's text, which contributes to understanding the profiles of these scribes.

323. Raby, Michael. "Sleep and the Transformation of Sense in Late

Medieval Literature." *SAC* 39 (2017): 191–224. Explores the permeable boundary between waking and sleep, sensation and dream, in Dante's *Commedia*, *TC*, and Machaut's *Fontaine amoureuse*, each sleep-scene drawing on Ovidian tales of transformation. Comments on Chaucer's adaptation in *HF* of Dante's golden eagle, and examines Pandarus's awakening in *TC* to the sound of a swallow/Procne, suggesting that the indeterminate nature of the waking reenacts Philomela's silence.

324. Rude, Sarah B. "'I se and undirstonde': Vision, Reason, and Tragedy in Late Middle English Literature." *DAI* A79.01 (2017): n.p. Examines the medieval conception of sight (both as sense and as ingress of the seen to the soul) in *TC* and Malory.

325. Strohm, Paul. "The Space of Desire in Chaucer's and Shakespeare's Troy." In Andrew James Johnston, Russell West-Pavlov, and Elisabeth Kempf, eds. *Love, History and Emotion in Chaucer and Shakespeare: "Troilus and Criseyde" and "Troilus and Cressida"* (*SAC* 41 [2019], no. 315), pp. 46–60. Identifies parallel concerns with privacy and erotic tension in *TC* and Shakespeare's *Troilus and Cressida*, both of which pose the closed space of the bedchamber against the pressures of crowdedness in Troy/London, gossip, and public observation. Suggests that the "invention and execution" of Shakespeare's depiction depend upon the "restricted environment" of Chaucer's poem.

326. Sung, Wei-ko. "Troy in the *Troilus and Criseyde*." *Tamkang Review* 45, no. 2 (2015): 25–45. Describes the "role Troy played in medieval literary imagination" as a foundation myth, and explores how the "destinies of some of the major figures" in *TC* are "inextricably" interwoven with that of Troy. Includes an abstract in English and in Chinese.

327. Trigg, Stephanie. "'Language in her eye': The Expressive Face of Criseyde/Cressida." In Andrew James Johnston, Russell West-Pavlov, and Elisabeth Kempf, eds. *Love, History and Emotion in Chaucer and Shakespeare: "Troilus and Criseyde" and "Troilus and Cressida"* (*SAC* 41 [2019], no. 315), pp. 94–108. Analyzes Criseyde's "speaking face" in *TC*, along with similar depictions of suggestive facial beauty in *BD*, *PhyT*, and Shakespeare's *Troilus and Cressida*. Attends most closely to Criseyde's "ascaunce" look in *TC*, I.288–94.

328. Wallace, David. "Changing Emotions in *Troilus*: The Crucial Year." In Andrew James Johnston, Russell West-Pavlov, and Elisabeth Kempf, eds. *Love, History and Emotion in Chaucer and Shakespeare: "Troilus and Criseyde" and "Troilus and Cressida"* (*SAC* 41 [2019], no. 315), pp.

157–70. Comments on Chaucer's expansion in *TC* of the emotional range of Boccaccio's *Il filostrato* and focuses on Shakespeare's expansion and narrowing of Chaucer's poem in *Troilus and Cressida*: Shakespeare develops a "generic range" in the play that is as expansive as Part I of *CT* but, influenced by Robert Henryson's *Testament of Cresseid*, he undercuts Chaucer's depiction of love in *TC*, presenting its effects as diseased.

329. Wingfield, Emily. "Chaucer's *Troilus and Criseyde* and Robert Henryson's *Testament of Cresseid*." In *The Trojan Legend in Medieval Scottish Literature* (Cambridge: D. S. Brewer, 2014), pp. 121–49. Examines Criseyde in *TC* and Cresseid in Henryson's *Testament* as "emblems and symbols of the Trojan textual tradition," exploring how the themes of reading, writing, and Criseyde-as-text are "physically embodied" in Oxford, Bodleian Library, MS Arch. Selden B.24, and how Henryson's poem "makes readers far more conscious of the process of reading and interpretation" than does Chaucer's.

330. Zimmerman, Erin Royden. "Making Myth Matter: Interrogating Narrative and Reconstructing Metanarrative in Classical Myth Adaptation." *DAI* A74.11 (2014): n.p. Includes comments on Cassandra, Persephone, and Philomela as victims of "acquaintance rape" in Chaucer's works (*TC*, *MerT*, and *LGW*), treating his and other versions (classical, medieval, and modern) as adaptations of myths that create "metanarratives that shame rape survivors and demean the violence of the rape act." Offers alternative ways of adapting these stories.

See also nos. 18, 28, 33, 37, 38, 72, 78, 90, 95, 103, 108, 113, 114, 117, 130, 135, 153–54, 163, 182, 205.

Lyrics and Short Poems

331. Gorst, Emma Kate Charters. "Middle English Lyrics: Lyric Manuscripts 1200–1400 and Chaucer's Lyric." *DAI* A 77.06 (2016): n.p. Investigates two "networks of meaning" within which to view late medieval English lyrics: the relationships among lyrics in manuscript collections (using "network mapping software") and the relationships between embedded lyrics and "narrative events" in *CT*, *PF*, and *BD*.

332. Haley, Gabriel Michael. "Niche Poetics: Institutional Solitude and the Lyric in Late Medieval England." *DAI* A73.12 (2013): n.p. Argues that the monastic ideal of "contemplative solitude" was an innovative resource in English literature between Richard Rolle and Robert

Henryson. Maintains that Chaucer deployed it comically in *HF* and that, along with notions of Chaucer's exceptionality, it helped to shape the reception of Chaucer's lyrics.

An ABC

Adam Scriveyn

333. Weiskott, Eric. "Adam Scriveyn and Chaucer's Metrical Practice." *MÆ* 86 (2017): 147–51. Exemplifies how metrical phonology ("the linguistic forms that fill out metre") supports A. S. G. Edwards's claim (in "Chaucer and 'Adam Scriveyn,'" *MÆ* 81 [2002]) that Chaucer may not have written "Chaucers Wordes unto Adam, his Owne Scriveyn." In line 3, "longe" and "lokkes" scan as monosyllables, but Chaucer's use of these and similar words is disyllabic elsewhere, and such disyllabic usage was for Chaucer "virtually non-negotiable." Metrical evidence suggests fifteenth-century authorship, and the rime royal stanza suggests the era's "nascent cult of Chaucer."

The Complaint of Chaucer to His Purse

334. Bennett, Kristen Abbott. "At the Crossroads: Intersections of Classical and Vernacular English Protest Literature in *Pierce Penilesse*." *Upstart: A Journal of English Renaissance Studies*, August 10, 2015: n.p. Includes discussion of the influence of Chaucer's *Purse* and Thomas Hoccleve's *La male regle* on Thomas Nashe's *Pierce Penilesse*, examining the elements of comedy and "moral uncertainty" in Chaucer's poem and its "accretion of polygeneric expectations," as well as its echoes of Ovid and impact on Hoccleve and Nashe. Available at https://upstart.sites.clemson.edu/Essays/protest/bennett_crossroads.xhtml.

Envoy to Bukton

See nos. 55, 103.

Envoy to Scogan

See no. 55.

Former Age

335. Hole, Jennifer. "Wealth and Lordship in Late Medieval Literature." In *Economic Ethics in Late Medieval England, 1300–1500* (Cham:

Palgrave Macmillan, 2016), pp. 99–125. Surveys literary depictions of economic ideals and economic abuses among the aristocracy in *ParsT*; *Form Age*; *Wynnere and Wastoure*; *Piers Plowman*; and works by Gower, Hoccleve, and Lydgate, focusing on the "portrayal of lords and rulers, both as offenders and as ethical role models," and concluding that the writers were generally "conservative commentators on economic ethics," reflecting Church teachings and nostalgia for an idealized, precommercial past.

To Rosemounde

336. Muhly, Nico, composer. "The Map of the World." For high voice and piano. London: St. Rose Music/Chester Music, 2015. Musical score; 4 pp. (c. 3 minutes 30 seconds). Includes lyrics from a portion of *Ros* (lines 1–7, 15), translated by Forrest Hainline.

To Truth

See nos. 55, 72, 116.

Chaucerian Apocrypha

See nos. 26, 71, 84.

Book Reviews

337. Adams, Jenny, and Nancy Mason, eds. *Medieval Women and Their Objects* (*SAC* 41 [2019], no. 118). Rev. Maija Birenbaum, *SAC* 39 (2017): 297–301.

338. Arner, Lynn. *Chaucer, Gower, and the Vernacular Rising: Poetry and the Problem of the Populace after 1381* (*SAC* 37 [2015], no. 155). Rev. Leah Klement, *Speculum* 92, no. 1 (2017): 209–10.

339. Beaumont, Matthew. *Nightwalking: A Nocturnal History of London, Chaucer to Dickens.* (*SAC* 39 [2017], no. 96). Rev. Aya Yatsugi, *Japan Branch Bulletin, Dickens Fellowship* 40 (2017): 29–33; in Japanese.

340. Blurton, Heather, and Hannah Johnson, eds. *The Critics and the Prioress: Antisemitism, Criticism, and Chaucer's "Prioress's Tale"* (*SAC* 41 [2019], no. 242). Rev. Samantha Katz Seal, *SAC* 39 (2017): 304–8.

341. Calabrese, Michael. *An Introduction to "Piers Plowman"* (*SAC* 40 [2018], no. 67). Rev. Lawrence Warner, *TMR* 17.04.05. n.p.

342. Cannon, Christopher. *From Literacy to Literature: English 1300–400* (*SAC* 40 [2018], no. 136). Rev. Michael Calabrese, *SAC* 39 (2017): 316–20; Timothy Miller, *TMR* 17.07.11, n.p.

343. Cervone, Cristina Maria, and D. Vance Smith, eds. *Readings in Medieval Textuality: Essays in Honour of A. C. Spearing* (*SAC* 40 [2018], no. 138). Rev. Eric Weiskott, *TMR* 17.10.18, n.p.

344. Collette, Carolyn P. *Rethinking Chaucer's "Legend of Good Women"* (*SAC* 38 [2016], no. 209). Rev. Keiko Hamaguchi, *SIMELL* 32 (2017): 93–109; in Japanese.

345. Copeland, Rita, ed. *The Oxford History of Classical Reception in English Literature*, Vol. 1, *800–1558* (*SAC* 41 [2019], no. 126). Rev. Victoria Moul, *Renaissance Quarterly* 70, no. 4. (2017): 1651–52.

346. D'Arcens, Louise. *Comic Medievalism: Laughing at the Middle Ages* (*SAC* 38 [2016], no. 42). Rev. Jenna Mead, *SAC* 39 (2017): 320–25.

347. Farmer, Sharon, ed. *Approaches to Poverty in Medieval Europe: Complexities, Contradictions, Transformations, c. 1100–1500* (*SAC* 40 [2018], no. 144). Rev. Charlotte Stanford, *TMR* 17.04.10, n.p.

348. Fein, Susanna and David Raybin, eds. *Chaucer: Visual Approaches* (*SAC* 40 [2018], no. 145). Rev. Hisashi Sugito, *Bulletin of the Society for Chaucer Studies* 5 (2017): 35–37; in Japanese.

349. Forni, Kathleen. *Chaucer's Afterlife: Adaptations in Recent Popular Culture* (*SAC* 37 [2015], no. 38). Rev. Satomi Hamada, *SIMELL* 32 (2017): 143–52; in Japanese.

350. Fumo, Jamie C. *Making Chaucer's "Book of the Duchess": Textuality and Reception* (*SAC* 39 [2017], no. 197). Rev. Dianne Williams, *SAC* 39 (2017): 336–39.

351. Ginsberg, Warren. *Tellers, Tales, and Translation in Chaucer's "Canterbury Tales"* (*SAC* 39 [2017], no. 34). Rev. Karla Taylor, *Speculum* 93, no. 4 (2017): 1189–91.

352. Gray, Douglas. *Simple Forms: Essays on Medieval English Popular Literature* (*SAC* 40 [2018], no. 148). Rev. Richard Firth Green, *TMR* 17.04.08, n.p.

353. Green, Richard Firth. *Elf Queens and Holy Friars: Fairy Beliefs and the Medieval Church* (*SAC* 40 [2018], no. 93). Rev. Cathy Hume, *TMR* 17.04.15, n.p.

354. Johnston, Andrew James, Ethan Knapp, and Margitta Rouse,

eds. *The Art of Vision: Ekphrasis in Medieval Literature and Culture* (*SAC* 39 [2017], no. 109). Rev. Fabio Camilletti, *RenQ* 70, no. 1 (2017): 370–71.

355. Johnston, Michael, and Michael Van Dussen, eds. *The Medieval Manuscript Book: Cultural Approaches* (*SAC* 41 [2019], no. 23). Rev. Benjamin C. Tilghman, *Manuscript* 2 (2017): 239–42.

356. Kelly, Kathleen Coyne, and Tison Pugh, eds. *Chaucer on Screen: Absence, Presence, and Adapting the "Canterbury Tales"* (*SAC* 40 [2018], no. 17). Rev. Geoffrey W. Gust, *SAC* 39 (2017): 339–43.

357. Kerby-Fulton, Kathryn, John J. Thompson, and Sarah Baechle, eds. *New Directions in Medieval Manuscript Studies and Reading Practice: Essays in Honor of Derek Pearsall* (*SAC* 39 [2017]. no. 28). Rev. Elon Lang, *SAC* 39 (2017): 343–47.

358. Kern-Stähler, Annette, Beatrix Busse, and Wietse de Boer, eds. *The Five Senses in Medieval and Early Modern England* (*SAC* 41 [2019], no. 141). Rev. Simon Smith, *RenQ* 70, no. 3 (2017): 1127–28.

359. King, Andrew, and Matthew Woodcock, eds. *Medieval into Renaissance: Essays for Helen Cooper* (*SAC* 40 [2018], no. 98). Rev. Joseph D. Parry, *RenQ* 70, no. 2 (2017): 801–2.

360. Lavezzo, Kathy. *The Accommodated Jew: English Antisemitism from Bede to Milton* (*SAC* 40 [2018], no. 156). Rev. Mo Pareles, *SAC* 39 (2017): 351–54.

361. McKinley, Kathryn. *Chaucer's "House of Fame" and Its Boccaccian Intertexts: Image, Vision, and the Vernacular* (*SAC* 40 [2018], no. 289). Rev. Karla Taylor, *TMR* 17.11.09, n.p.

362. McKinstry, Jamie. *Middle English Romance and the Craft of Memory* (*SAC* 40 [2018], no. 161). Rev. Christine Kozikowski, *TMR* 10.10.14, n.p.

363. Nelson, Ingrid. *Lyric Tactics: Poetry, Genre, and Practice in Later Medieval England* (*SAC* 41 [2019], no. 321). Rev. Dan Birkholz, *TMR* 17.20.28; n.p.; Helen Cushman, *SAC* 39 (2017): 367–70.

364. Novacich, Sarah Elliott. *Shaping the Archive in Late Medieval England: History, Poetry and Performance* (*SAC* 41 [2019], no. 148). Rev. Amanda Walling, *SAC* 39 (2017): 370–74.

365. Nowlin, Steele. *Chaucer, Gower, and the Affect of Invention* (*SAC* 40 [2018], no. 165). Rev. Jeffrey G. Stoyanoff, *SAC* 39 (2017): 374–78.

366. Quinn, William A. *Olde Clerkis Speche: Chaucer's "Troilus and Criseyde" and the Implications of Authorial Recital* (*SAC* 37 [2015], no. 169). Rev. Timothy D. Arner, *Speculum* 92, no. 1 (2017): 295–97.

367. Prendergast, Thomas A. *Poetical Dust: Poets' Corner and the Making of Britain* (*SAC* 40 [2018], no. 27). Rev. Alessandra Petrina, *TMR* 17.06.16, n.p.

368. Rigby, Stephen H., and Alastair J. Minnis, eds. *Historians on Chaucer: The "General Prologue" to the "Canterbury Tales"* (*SAC* 38 [2016], no. 188). Rev. Matthew Giancarlo, *RenQ*, 70, no. 1 (2017): 395–96.

369. Robertson, Kellie. *Nature Speaks: Medieval Literature and Aristotelian Philosophy* (*SAC* 41 [2019], no. 151). Rev. Taylor Cowdery, *SAC* 39 (2017): 378–82.

370. Rouse, Richard H., and Mary A. Rouse. *Bound Fast with Letters: Medieval Writers, Readers, and Texts* (Notre Dame: University of Notre Dame Press, 2013). Rev. Julie Orlemanski, *MP* 113 (2016): 167–69.

371. Scala, Elizabeth. *Desire in the "Canterbury Tales"* (*SAC* 39 [2017], no. 130). Rev. Brenda Deen Schildgen, *RenQ* 70, no. 1 (2017): 396–98.

372. Sidhu, Nicole Nolan. *Indecent Exposure: Gender, Politics, and Obscene Comedy in Middle English Literature* (*SAC* 40 [2018], no. 173). Rev. Roberta Magnani, *SAC* 39 (2017): 383–86.

373. Spearing, A. C. *Medieval Autographies: The "I" of the Text* (*SAC* 36 [2014], no. 113). Rev. Yoshinobu Kudo, *SIMELL* 32 (2017): 127–41.

374. Thomas, Alfred. *Reading Women in Late Medieval Europe: Anne of Bohemia and Chaucer's Female Audience* (*SAC* 39 [2017], no. 122). Rev. Joyce Coleman, *Speculum* 92, no. 2 (2017): 590–91.

375. Travis, Peter W., and Frank Grady, eds. *Approaches to Teaching Chaucer's "Canterbury Tales"* (*SAC* 38 [2016], no. 109). Rev. Daniel T. Kline, *Speculum* 92, no. 4 (2017): 1260–61.

376. Wallace, David. *Geoffrey Chaucer: A New Introduction* (*SAC* 41 [2019], no. 158). Rev. Megan E. Murton, *SAC* 39 (2017): 387–90.

Author Index–Bibliography

540

Index

Page numbers of illustrations are indicated in the index by *italics*.